VINCENT VAN GOGH

Bouquet of Fritillaria.
Louvre, Paris.

ART
Through the Ages

AN INTRODUCTION TO ITS
HISTORY & SIGNIFICANCE

BY HELEN GARDNER, M.A.

PROFESSOR OF THE HISTORY OF ART

IN THE SCHOOL OF THE ART

INSTITUTE OF CHICAGO

Revised Edition

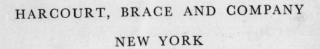

HARCOURT, BRACE AND COMPANY

NEW YORK

W11
G17a.3

PREFACE

This book is limited to the story of visual arts — architecture, painting, sculpture, and some minor arts. It shows their development from the remote days of the glacial age in Europe through the successive civilizations of the Near East, Europe, America, and the Orient, to the present time. Although the presentation is admittedly designed to meet the needs of introductory art courses in colleges and normal schools, it is hoped that the book will also be useful to the general reader and traveler.

This new edition of *Art Through the Ages* differs from the original edition published in 1926 in several ways. Readers will already be aware of one important improvement; they will have realized that the format has been enlarged and new plates made for the entire book. This larger format, together with the use of a "finished" paper, not only permits an increase in the number of illustrations by one-third, but also permits them to be printed *along with* the text matter. These changes have not only improved the book as an example of the bookmaker's art but have greatly facilitated the ease of reference to the illustrations.

In content, the most important improvements consist of additions of new material: (1) The chapters covering Sumerian, Egyptian, Persian, Aboriginal American, and Primitive art have been expanded to take into account the discoveries of recent archaeological research. (2) The chapter on art in the United States has been re-written and enlarged. (3) An entirely new chapter on modern art has been added. (4) Etruscan art has been given more space. (5) Russian medieval art has been included. (6) A brief chapter is now devoted to the Baroque. (7) The bibliographies have been brought up to date. (8) New maps and a pronouncing index have been added.

In content there is one additional modification of the original edition. Greater emphasis has been put on the character and evolution of visual art forms and upon the importance of materials and technical processes. To this end, a brief introduction has been added to summarize the visual elements of art expression.

The organization of material, essentially the same as in the original edition, is based upon years of experience in teaching the history of art in the School of the Art Institute of Chicago. It is a chronological organization in which each era is studied as a unit of culture and analyzed for the more important geographic, social, economic, political, and religious conditions which determine the kind and character of art produced. Following this background of civilization material there is a discussion and analysis of a few examples of those visual arts in which the era found its chief expression. A concluding statement summarizes the significant points of the art expression of the era.

This organization of material is based upon the theory that a work of art is, on the one hand, a social document, an expression of varying life conditions. It is, on the other hand, an individual visual form. Therefore, in addition to an understanding of the cultural background, an understanding of art implies first, a study of the character of the form and content and, second, *why* such a form and content came into being. When creating forms artists must use certain *materials* such as wood, stone, pigment, and metals. They must handle certain *elements* such as shape, color, line, texture, volume. And they work according to certain *principles* such as rhythm, proportion, emphasis, harmony. As materials, elements, and principles are fundamental and universal, some knowledge of them is indispensable to an understanding of art.

In regard to the classification outlined above, a word of caution and explanation is necessary. Works of art cannot be classified dogmatically. They are too closely interrelated. For example, a statue or a relief may be so integral a part of a building that its form can be understood only as a part of the design of the building. A painting frequently decorates a wall or a page of a manuscript and much of its composition and color is determined by this function. A stained-glass window plays a part in the whole interior ensemble and is not merely an example of the minor arts.

There is still another reason why classification should not be too dogmatic. Until the last two hundred years, artists were craftsmen and frequently one man pursued several crafts equally well. Phidias was painter as well as sculptor; Leonardo was engineer, musician, painter, and sculptor; Piero della Francesca was a mathematician; in fact, in the Renaissance it was the rule and not the exception that a man could, for example, build a palace, carve a statue, paint a ceiling, and design and execute a piece of jewelry. Individualism and specialization are modern. Yet the older ideal of the versatile craftsman working in a variety of mediums is being revived by many artists today.

Until recent times the distinction between "major" arts and "minor" arts did not exist. By the term "minor" arts, we designate metal works, books and manuscripts, textiles, ceramics, furnishings, carvings — all that world of smaller objects, "minor" only in size, through which creative ability has found abundant expression and for which there seems to be no adequately inclusive term.

With these qualifications, the method here followed enables the student to develop a breadth of capacity for appreciation, lays for him a broad foundation for specialized work in art, and increases his ability to correlate the arts. Equipped thus, he will be able to read Homer in the light of Aegean Art; to realize the inextricable unity of all the arts in the thirteenth century or the eighteenth century in France; to experience the ceaseless movement of a Dürer etching in a Bach fugue; to see Romanticism equally in Wordsworth, Wagner, and Delacroix; to understand the affinity of poetry and landscape painting in China; and see the modern concentration upon problems of abstract form equally in Gertrude Stein, Pablo Picasso, and Igor Stravinsky.

In order to cover so vast a field in one volume, unsparing elimination has been necessary, and only significant movements considered. The objective has been to focus attention upon the works of art as art and to omit biographical and anecdotal matter, not because such material has no legitimate place, but because it is secondary and can be found easily in almost any library. Controversial questions of attribution and influences have been omitted as belonging properly to specialized books. The space thus gained has been used for analysis of the few works discussed, in the conviction that thorough study of a few works is more helpful than the recital of names and dates.

An indispensable part of the study of art is the illustration. Few works, therefore, are discussed for which there is no illustration for reference. The bibliographies have been compiled with a well-equipped but not specialized art library in mind. Hence, rare and costly books have usually been omitted, and among the works in foreign languages only a few have been included which are particularly desirable for their illustrations.

The writing of so comprehensive a book as well as the assembling and sifting of so large a mass of details make necessary the advice and coöperation of many individuals. Such coöperation has been given cordially and generously on the part of individuals, museums, and publishers. For criticism on the manuscript of the first edition the author was indebted to Professors T. G. Allen, J. H. Breasted, W. E. Clark, Edith Rickert, Walter Sargent, E. H. Wilkins, of the University of Chicago; to Professor Grant Showerman of the University of Wisconsin; and to Mr. R. B. Harshe and Mr. C. F. Kelley of the Art Institute of Chicago; for criticism of the second edition, to Miss Kathleen Blackshear of The Art Institute of Chicago, Mr. J. C. Boudreau of Pratt Institute, Professor B. M. Donaldson of the University of Michigan, and Professor F. J. Roos, Jr. of Ohio University.

The difficult task of securing illustrations was lightened appreciably by the generous assistance of individuals, libraries, museums, and publishers, acknowledgment of which is made with each cut. Especial help on the illustrations as well as in details of research was generously given by Miss Etheldred Abbot, Librarian, and her assistants of the Ryerson and Burnham Libraries of the Art Institute, and by Miss Margaret L. Jackson and her assistants of the Photograph Department.

For the analytical drawings of paintings and sculpture the author is indebted to Miss Kathleen Blackshear; for other drawings and maps, to Marjorie H. Batchelder, Electra P. Cryer, Elizabeth Fisher, and Leroy Lodin. For bibliographical research, to Helen Mitchell; for proof and index, to Marion F. Williams and Hazel C. MacAdam; for pronunciation, to Helen Mitchell and Eugene V. Prostov.

By no means the least source of genuine appreciation, especially in the light of so difficult a problem as that presented by the scheme of illustration, has been the unfailing patience and generous coöperation of the publishers.

April 30, 1936   H. G.

INTRODUCTION

The Visual Elements of Art Expression

Any approach to a study of art immediately reveals an inherent paradox. On the one hand the essential nature of art in the abstract is mysterious, intangible, indefinable. On the other hand works of art are actual, tangible, concrete objectifications which are apprehended through the senses. We see paintings, we see and hear literature, we hear music, we feel the surfaces of a piece of carving or pottery, and the texture of a piece of satin or velvet. These concrete objectifications differ widely in kind and character just as the patterns of mind and spirit and modes of visualization differ widely among the many peoples of the world. No one pattern of art expression is valid alone as a basis of study of the nature of art, or as a sole criterion for the development of judgment. Only by acquiring a knowledge of definite, concrete material on a broadly inclusive base, free from prejudice, is one in a position to discern the nature of that mysterious, intangible something which is the essence of art.

The acquisition of this knowledge consists in no small degree in the training of the senses: the ear for musical and literary expression; the eye and the touch for visual and tactile. Such sensory training is a prerequisite for the understanding of the forms with which the artist is working, for the understanding of their origin and character, and of the reasons for their evolution — which is the History of Art.

Peoples have objectified their concepts and emotions in differing forms: in music, in drama and the dance, in literature, pottery, painting, textiles, carvings, buildings — to mention some of the more important. Most peoples have developed a variety of forms for self-expression, among which are a basic unity and interdependence; and while every work of art is an individual entity, it is so integrated in its milieu that it is best understood, both as to its form and to its content, in its relationship to the other expressions of that milieu. For example, the music, literature, costumes, painting, and the furnishings of eighteenth-century France are all varying manifestations of the one pattern of French aristocratic life. In like manner one notes the unity of all the arts in Baroque Italy; and that of the American Indian of the southwest. The lack of unity and coherence, and the predominance

of experimentation in contemporary life are reflected in similar manifestations in all the contemporary arts. Some peoples appear to have
found a characteristic expression of the highest esthetic quality in the
so-called "minor arts"; the Chinese, for example, in their porcelains;
the Persians in their illustrated books, carpets, and pottery; the American Indians in their weavings and pottery. These works of art frequently possess both superlative abstract form and profound meaning,
deeply rooted in human experience, however symbolic the character
of the expression. Chinese bronzes are an excellent example of this
unity.

Thus to understand art and the history of art presupposes some grasp
of its formal elements, an assumption of the scientific attitude of the
concert annotator when he analyzes a composition for its combinations
of tones into themes and themes into the whole composition. The
student of literature takes the same scientific attitude when he scru-
tinizes the character of words and the modes by which they are combined into sentences and paragraphs. Thus in the visual arts one
fundamental of understanding lies in a grasp of visual elements. The
material itself and the visible evidences of the processes by which it is
shaped are inescapable factors. Mass, volume, planes or surfaces,
space, line, light and dark, color, texture — these are visual elements
of construction by means of which the artist builds a composition, the
ultimate basis of which is "geometry, the elemental bones of all visible
esthetics" (Donald Culross Peattie).

As an indispensable prerequisite for any historical study, a brief
summary of these elements in a few of the visual arts and some fundamental principles of their use is here appended as a review for those
who have already acquired a knowledge of them and as a guide for
those to whom they are unfamiliar.

ARCHITECTURE

Architecture is an art in which the artist constructs a hollow volume
or group of volumes out of such materials as stone, brick, wood, concrete, steel, aluminum, and other metals, glass, tile to serve a definite
function. From a ground plan, determined by site and function, rise
walls and roof to bound and organize an interior space. As these
defining walls and roof also serve as exterior surfaces of the hollow
volume, the exterior must bear a close relationship to the interior.
Function determines the form that this hollow volume takes: a fine
building *looks* its purpose. Similarly the material determines its constructional or engineering principle. Practically all engineering reduces to the following systems: lintel, arch, or steel construction.

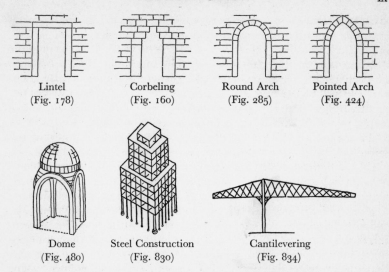

Lintel
(Fig. 178)

Corbeling
(Fig. 160)

Round Arch
(Fig. 285)

Pointed Arch
(Fig. 424)

Dome
(Fig. 480)

Steel Construction
(Fig. 830)

Cantilevering
(Fig. 834)

Hand in hand with mechanical engineering goes what we may call esthetic engineering. Every fine building is on the one hand a volume or group of volumes so constructed that it serves its function and is stable. On the other hand it is a geometric volume — cube, cylinder, pyramid, sphere — or group of volumes, so composed that the shapes, proportions, color and texture, play of light and shade, and all relationships are pleasing and every detail is subordinate to the basic abstract organization.

Geometric Solids and Buildings Based upon Them.   A, cube;
B, pyramid; C, cylinder; D, sphere.

Finally every building has a topographical and cultural setting which determines the kind and character of the structure.

SCULPTURE

Sculpture is also an art of organizing mass or volume; of composing volumes, planes, light and dark areas, textures, and in some materials, contours, into an abstract unity, whatever the subject matter. Thus sculpture approximates architecture in that it deals with a similar formal problem. It is also intimately allied to the latter art in that it is frequently an inseparable part of the building and functions as one element in the total esthetic engineering. In form, sculpture may exist in three dimensions, as sculpture in the round; or it may be attached to a background from which it projects, as relief; or it may be sunk into the ground, as intaglio. The materials of the sculptor are various stones, wood, horn and ivory, clay, and many metals. Each has its own hardness, texture, color, capacities and limitations, and therefore they are not interchangeable. In fact, the effectiveness of a fine piece of sculpture lies to a large extent in the relation between the artist's conception of the subject matter and the kind of material he has used for its objectification. The use of stone, wood, and ivory entails carving; that is, cutting away from the original piece of material until what is left is the figure or figures. This cutting may result in a figure whose planes are largely parallel to the original block of stone, which is quarried in generally rectangular blocks; or in one in which the masses and planes seem to move in conformity to the surface of a cylinder, frequently found in carvings in wood and horn and probably conditioned by the cylindrical nature of the material; or it may result in one in which the masses and surfaces move backward and forward or spiral throughout the entire space.

Relief in a Few Main Planes (Fig. 207)	Four-sided Organization (Fig. 41)	Cylindrical Organization (Fig. 706)	Spiraling Organization (Fig. 510)	Bronze Design (Fig. 210)

Working in clay is the opposite of carving in that it consists of a building-up process in the most plastic of the sculptor's materials. Clay is amenable to rapidity of execution and thus highly suitable for a spontaneous or fleeting expression which can be made permanent by firing, glazing, or casting in metal. The use of metal, except on a small scale, presupposes a building-up process involving the use of clay or wax and the pouring of molten metal in the casting (see p. 137). Thus the plasticity of the temporary basic medium and the fluidity and ultimate toughness of the permanent material result in a quality quite in opposition to carving in hard, friable, weighty stone, and enable the sculptor to create light, free, open designs. The rigidity, color, and reflective character of many metals and the frequent use of the chisel or graver in the finishing suggest emphasis upon edges and upon line.

PAINTING

Painting is the art of organizing a flat surface by means of pigment and thus is theoretically a two-dimensional art. Like sculpture it has been largely functional until modern times. It has served as mural decoration, for example, or book illustration, or as a panel such as an altarpiece for a specific location. These functions have determined in no small degree the subject matter and the form. The painter composes with line, light and dark, color, and texture. Some painters visualize and objectify the world, their raw material, in terms of line and flat or relatively flat color areas with well-defined edges; others, as spots of color with blurred edges and gradual transitions from light to dark. Some painters retain the two-dimensional character of the surface; others create an illusion of depth. It may be shallow depth with movement largely lateral as in relief, and with the receding planes parallel to the planes of the original surface. Or it may be deep space with planes receding at an angle to the original surface, with movement backward and forward, often complex and interlocking.

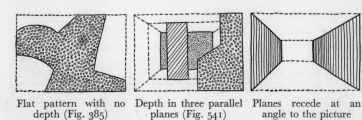

Flat pattern with no depth (Fig. 385)

Depth in three parallel planes (Fig. 541)

Planes recede at an angle to the picture plane (Fig. 565)

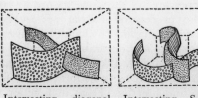

Intersecting diagonal planes (Fig. 559)

Intersecting S-Curve planes (Fig. 564)

There are various ways of placing pigment on a surface permanently. The more important are: fresco; tempera and tempera-oil; oil (with underpainting or direct); water color (transparent, opaque, or Chinese ink). Each technique, with its individual brush stroke, texture, and quality of color produces a result peculiar to itself alone. Fresco is singularly adaptable to mural decoration partly because, being limited to special colors, it presents a tonality without the violent contrasts that might appear to break the wall; and partly because the pigment becomes chemically incorporated with the surface and thus becomes a part of its very texture. Tempera, a painstaking technique, has a smooth hard surface with depth and luminosity of color, and a linear decorative quality. The various oils make possible a freer expression, richer color, atmospheric effects, greater solidity, and more complex spatial organization. Direct oil is peculiarly adaptable, like clay with the sculptor, for spontaneous expression. This is true also with transparent water color, perhaps the lightest, most evanescent of mediums. Whichever technique the painter employs, he visualizes his subject as an organization of lines, shapes, volumes, light and dark colors. He builds a picture out of these formal, visual elements — again esthetic engineering. In the language of these elements the painter speaks the content of the picture. As in literature, it is not only *what* is said but the *manner* of saying it, a composite of formal structure and content, that constitutes art.

POTTERY (CERAMICS)

Pottery, except for tiles, is like sculpture in the round in that it is an art of three dimensions; and it is close to sculpture in clay in that it consists of a building-up process in the same plastic material. In fact many fine pieces defy classification as between sculpture and pottery. According to the character of the material and the manner of firing, pottery consists of earthenware (which has a relatively coarse base, is fired at low heat, and must be glazed to be impervious), porcelain (made of an especial, fine clay mixed with a fusible, hardening ingredient like feldspar, is fired at high temperature, and is glassy and impervious), and stoneware (of the same nature as porcelain but of coarser texture). The process of making pottery is fourfold: the preparation of the clay, the shaping (by hand, by coiling, on the wheel, or by molding), the glazing and decorating (by relief, incising, polishing, or painting), and the firing. Like a fine building, a fine piece of pottery possesses a basic geometry in its form and a visible as well as actual unity of form and function. From its function as a container and from the method of its making, ceramic form is basically spherical, cylindrical, or egg-shaped. Such additions as handles, covers, or spouts, to be successful, relate to this basic unit of shape.

Basic Shapes and Relationship of Parts in Ceramic Form. (Fig. 232)

Thus a master potter shows a command over the shape and proportions of the object as a whole and of part as related to part: of the neck to the body, for example, and of the lip to the body and to the base. He knows that in fabrics strong in color, such as those of a one-hue glaze, the contour is an important visual element in stressing relationships and in indicating the rhythmic movement of masses and surfaces. So also color and texture, uniform or in contrasting areas; and decoration (painted, relief, or incised), which in its suitability of scale maintains the relationships of mass, and in its character stresses the continuity and movement of rounding surfaces — these too are visual elements that determine the visual effectiveness of any ceramic product.

METALWORK

Metalwork consists of a very large group of objects made of gold, silver, copper, bronze, brass, pewter, iron or steel, aluminum, chromium — to mention the more important metals. All metals share, each in varying degrees, hardness, tenacity, and thus durability; elasticity for manipulation; opaque and reflecting surfaces. They also share, in varying degrees, capacities upon which depend their use as materials for the artist: capacities for fusibility, ductility, and malleability. Being fusible, a metal can be molded, small pieces cast solid, larger pieces cast hollow by the cire perdue or by modern mechanical processes. Being ductile, it can be drawn into wires or threads. Being malleable, it can be beaten or hammered into sheets, at times of incredible thinness, gold for example. These sheets can be beaten into shape over molds; or can be cut into flat patterns and shaped; or can be perforated into patterns. Malleability and ductility provide the artist with a very plastic material in a heated state, iron especially, which he can hammer, weld, turn and twist into innumerable shapes, and thus provide a light, open design, such as a gate or grille, which affords visibility and at the same time protection because of its strength. For ornamentation, chasing or engraving is perhaps the simplest method; repoussé is also common. Repoussé consists of beating a sheet of metal into a mold of resistant material, so as not to break the metal, and thus leave a pattern in relief on one side and in intaglio on the other. Another decorative process is damascening, that is, inlaying in a metal base shapes or figures of other metals of different color and texture; another is plating, covering one metal wholly or in part with another metal; still another is enameling, cloisonné (p. 232) or champlevé (p. 330) for the purpose of introducing a wider range of hue and texture. Metalwork, because of the nature of the medium, is adaptable both for the irregular hand-wrought shapes and also for the meticulously precise shapes made by the machine. In both, the visual evidence of the manner of working the raw material is a part of the pleasure derived — the strokes of the hammer in wrought silver, the slight irregularities of the tractable iron, and the machinelike precision of the steel implement. With its rigid form and hard, precise edges, whether handwrought or machine made, metalwork stands in direct opposition to ceramic objects made of the most pliant of mediums and shaped, even on the wheel, by the slightest pressure of hands or fingers, and finished with smooth, rounding, frequently irregular edges even in the thinnest porcelain and with a flow of glaze over the body. As in ceramics, texture is an important visual element in all metalwork and frequently a maximum of effect is due to an opposition of a smooth highly reflective surface to one worked in repoussé or chased. In addition, strong contrasts of light and dark, because of this reflective quality, and emphatic lines and edges are visual elements used by the artist for the expression of proportion and relationships of parts, and of that vitality and rhythmic movement of repeated and contrasted shapes, surfaces, and contours which is basic in any fine example of metalwork.

TEXTILES

Textiles are fabrics made by weaving. The process of weaving requires a loom and two sets of threads: a warp, strung on the loom, and a weft (woof) which, by interlacing through the warp constructs a surface. Thus a textile is two-dimensional; it is a surface constructed and organized in one process. The elements at the disposal of the weaver for making this surface visually pleasing are texture (the tactile element is highly important), color, and a linear pattern that carries a rhythmic movement over the surface. The raw materials are fibers (animal, vegetable, synthetic), of varying character and quality, spun into threads of different fineness and strength. Most textiles are functional and function determines what threads shall be used, and how.

One kind of fiber and process of weaving will be used when a textile, like a blanket or carpet, is to provide warmth or is to have hard usage, to be walked on, for example. Another kind of fiber and another process of weaving will be used to make a light, delicate textile for coolness, or for hanging in soft folds. Although every textile is made by the fundamentally simple interlacing of threads at right angles, there is a great variety of weaves dependent upon the manner of inserting the weft (plain cloth, tapestry, twill and satin, damask) and upon the use of additional wefts as in brocaded and pile fabrics. A high quality textile, whether a heavy carpet or a silk or a sheer muslin frankly exhibits the way in which the fibers interlace and the resultant geometry of its design.[1]

BIBLIOGRAPHY

Barnes, A. C., *The Art in Painting*, Harcourt, Brace, 2nd rev. ed., 1928

Casson, Stanley, *The Technique of Early Greek Sculpture*, Oxford, 1933

Le Corbusier, Charles (Jeanneret, C. E.), *Towards a New Architecture*, Payson and Clark, 1927

Cox, G. J., *Pottery*, Macmillan, 1926

Doerner, Max, *The Materials of the Artist* (tr. Eugen Neuhaus), Harcourt, Brace, 1934

Franklin, Christine (Ladd), *Colour and Colour Theories*, Harcourt, Brace, 1929

Gardner, Helen, *Understanding the Arts*, Harcourt, Brace, 1932

Gill, Eric, *Sculpture*, Ditchling, Sussex, 1925

Guillaume, Paul, and Munro, Thomas, *Primitive Negro Sculpture*, Harcourt, Brace, 1926

Hamlin, T. F., *The Enjoyment of Architecture*, Scribner, 1921

Hildebrand, Adolph, *The Problem of Form in Painting and Sculpture* (tr. Meyer and Ogden), Stechert, 1907

Hooper, Luther, *Hand-Loom Weaving*, Pitman, 1920

Laurie, A. P., *Materials of the Painter's Craft*, Lippincott, 1911

—— *New Light on Old Masters*, Macmillan, 1935

—— *The Painter's Methods and Materials*, Lippincott, 1926

Munro, Thomas, *Scientific Method in Aesthetics*, Norton, 1928

Pearson, Ralph, *Experiencing Pictures*, Harcourt, Brace, 1932

—— *How to Look at Modern Pictures*, Tudor, 1925

Pope, Arthur, *An Introduction to the Language of Drawing and Painting*, Harvard University Press, 1929–1931, 2 vols.

Read, Herbert, *Art and Industry*, Harcourt, Brace, 1935

Reath, N. A., *The Weaves of Hand-Loom Fabrics*, Philadelphia, The Pennsylvania Museum, 1927

Richter, G. M. A., *The Craft of Athenian Pottery*, Yale University Press, 1923

Rindge, A. M., *Sculpture*, Harcourt, Brace, 1929

Sargent, Walter, *The Enjoyment and Use of Color*, Scribner, 1923

Wilson, H., *Silverwork and Jewelry*, Pitman, 2nd rev. ed., 1931

Wölfflin, Heinrich, *Principles of Art History* (tr. Hottinger), Holt, 1932

Youtz, P. N., *Sounding Stones of Architecture*, Norton, 1929

[1] In addition to the arts included it is suggested that the same kind of analysis of elements be applied to garden architecture; to woodwork as found in furnishings and carvings; to the graphic arts (etching, engraving, lithograph, woodcuts); to glass, and to the arts of the book.

CONTENTS

B. Architecture
C. Sculpture
D. Painting
E. The Minor and Industrial Arts
F. Summary

APPENDIX

LIST OF COLOR PLATES

MAPS

Part One

PREHISTORIC ART IN EUROPE

CHAPTER I

Paleolithic Art from Earliest Times
(to about 20,000 B.C.)

A. HISTORICAL BACKGROUND AND THE MINOR ARTS

When in the long development of human life did art first appear, and why? What was its character? Was it childishly crude, or was it in any way comparable to those accomplishments which the world has looked upon as its greatest? Did it reveal any grasp of those fundamentals which underlie all great art expression?

Until recently the life story of man was thought to have been brief, perhaps a few thousand years at most. The researches of the past half-century, however, have shown that, instead of these few thousand years, vastly remote ages — a million years or more — and an amazingly slow evolution of civilization lie behind man of today. This growth we can read only in human remains and in extant objects made by man until we reach the invention of writing, only four or five thousand years ago. From that point we are guided by the written document as well.

In 1879 a Spaniard who was interested in the problem of the antiquity of man was exploring in a cave on his estate at Altamira in northern Spain, searching for further examples of flint and carved bone; already he had found such relics in this cavern. With him was his little daughter. Since the cave was dark, he was working by the light of a lamp, while the child was scrambling over the rough rocks. Suddenly she called out, "Bulls! Bulls!" pointing to the ceiling, so low that he could touch it with his hand. To satisfy the child, he lifted his lamp and there saw on the uneven surface numbers of bison and other animals naturalistically painted in bright colors. When the discovery was published and the painting declared to be the work of men who lived ages ago, people shook their heads. And, for a time, the skeptics had their way. "Impossible," they said. "The work is

too good and the color too fresh; some erratic person of recent years
has done this for some unknown purpose." Slowly, however, the belief began to grow among a few that all these things were revealing
ages of far greater antiquity than man had ever dreamed of. Slowly
skepticism broke down, and further great discoveries have yielded
enough evidence for us to catch a glimpse of man and his activities
in this remote age.[1]

When, then, in this long evolution of human activities did art first
appear? And under what phase of art expression?

Europe at the time of earliest man [2] offered a physical environment greatly different from that today. Already three glacial epochs
had passed, and the warm moist climate of the third interglacial
age provided man a comfortable habitation. We see him, a hairy,
rugged, strong-jawed man, without clothing, possessing a small
stone hand ax and fire, living a life of self-defense against the wild
elephant, the hippopotamus, the wolf, and the rhinoceros.[3] His predecessors during long millenniums had made two vital discoveries: the
control of fire and the use of stone for tools. The former man had
first observed, perhaps, as lightning cleft a tree and started flames in
the dry leaves or as red-hot lava burst from the crater of a volcano;
the latter he gradually adopted to replace his wooden implement so

---

[1] By "prehistory" is meant human history before the invention of writing. It
includes the Stone Age and in some localities the Bronze and Iron ages, for the discovery or introduction of metal and the invention of writing vary widely in different
localities. The following table outlines the main epochs:

A. Eolithic (Dawn of the Stone Age) 1,000,000–500,000 B.C.
    Java and Peking men

B. Paleolithic (Old Stone Age) 500,000–20,000 B.C.	*Warm, third inter-glacial*
1. Chellean (Chelles, a town near Paris) Piltdown and Heidelberg men	
2. Mousterian (Le Moustier, a site in the Dordogne Valley) Neandertal man	*Cold, fourth glacial*
3. Aurignacian (Aurignac, a small village in the French Pyrenees) Cro-Magnon man (a small cave in the Dordogne Valley)	
4. Solutrean (Solutré, a site in east-central France)	
5. Magdalenian (La Madeleine, near Les Eyzies in the Dordogne)	
C. Mesolithic (Middle or Transitional Stone Age) 20,000–12,000 B.C.	*Temperate of today*
D. Neolithic (New or Late Stone Age) 12,000–3000 B.C.	
E. Bronze 3000–1000 B.C.	
F. Iron 1000 B.C.–A.D.	

[2] For the earliest human remains, see G. G. MacCurdy, *The Coming of Man*, University Society, 1932, Chaps. V–VI.
[3] Eight vivid life-sized dioramas of prehistoric men and their environment have
recently been installed in the Field Museum. For reproductions and descriptions see
the pamphlet *Prehistoric Man* by Henry Field, Field Museum of Natural History,
Chicago, 1933. See also H. F. Osborn, *Men of the Old Stone Age*, 3d ed., Scribner, 1924,
for reconstructions of both human and animal types.

that he could protect himself better, obtain his food more easily, and combat animals larger than hare and rabbit. The early stone implements, such as the scraper and the hand ax, or fist hatchet (FIG. 2), which evolved after ages of experiment in chipping stone, seem purely utilitarian. They are not hafted, but are grasped by the hand for clubbing or for crude cutting. Gradually there appears in these tools something more than a capacity for better striking and a sharper cutting edge — a feeling for proportion and symmetry. Here may we not recognize that of

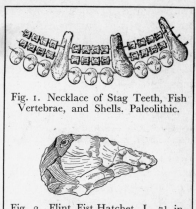

Fig. 1. Necklace of Stag Teeth, Fish Vertebrae, and Shells. Paleolithic.

Fig. 2. Flint Fist Hatchet. L. 7½ in. British Museum, London.

two flints which cut equally well one is more pleasing than the other because of a quality in the form that has nothing to do with the utility of the tool yet unmistakably enhances the object to the eye. Such a feeling for form, for a balance between the *what* and the *how*, we recognize as a fundamental art impulse.

This sensitivity to form reveals itself increasingly in the late Chellean and the Mousterian ages, the ages of the Neandertal hunter. The climate was becoming cool as the fourth glacial age approached. The animals migrated or adapted themselves to the changing conditions. Now the mammoth and the woolly rhinoceros, the reindeer and the arctic fox, became abundant. Man sought shelter in overhanging cliffs, and while contending with the beasts for cave shelters discovered that fire at the mouth of his cavern protected him not only from marauding animals but from the damp cold as well. The increasing variety and quality of his implements — axes, knives, scrapers, points — aided him not only in procuring and preparing food but also in skinning and dressing pelts for clothing for himself and, with the appearance of family life, for his family.

In addition to his growing sensitiveness to the form of his tools is a response to the quality of his material, evidence for which Dr. MacCurdy finds in tools made from rock crystal and topaz.[1] Color has made its appeal, and our hunter appears to have decked his body and his skin clothing with ornament. Even in the face of an energy-consuming climate, then, latent impulses that are fundamental in the arts were finding expression.

[1] See MacCurdy, *op. cit.*, p. 108 and Frontispiece.

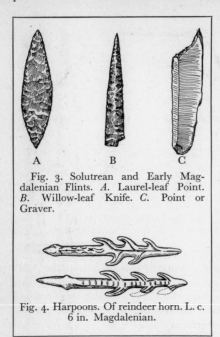

Fig. 3. Solutrean and Early Magdalenian Flints. *A*. Laurel-leaf Point. *B*. Willow-leaf Knife. *C*. Point or Graver.

Fig. 4. Harpoons. Of reindeer horn. L. c. 6 in. Magdalenian.

In the meantime a great migration, probably from Asia, brought a new race, the Cro-Magnon,[1] up the Danube, or along the northern coast of Africa into the habitable parts of Europe, for Africa and Europe were still land-connected. While the glaciers were relatively small in extent, the climate was extremely cold, though dry and not so taxing as the damp cold of the Mousterian times. Game was abundant and extraordinarily varied — mammoth, reindeer, bison and wild cattle, horse, ibex, bear and rabbit, ducks, geese, and ptarmigan. The newcomers were hunters, and lived, like their predecessors, under shelving rocks and at the entrances to caves. They clothed themselves with skins, which they had learned to sew together with bone needles. To the comfort thus secured they added the note of embellishment, as we infer from a necklace (FIG. 1) made by some hunter who had a decided feeling for the relationship of the parts. With ameliorated climatic conditions and a better physical and mental endowment than Neandertal man, Cro-Magnon man made rapid and marked advances culturally and particularly in the arts — reaching in the Magdalenian culture a climax of prehistoric art.

The old tools carried on, but far in advance of the Mousterian in the quality of form and in precision and beauty of cutting. In the thin, sharp laurel-leaf points and willow-leaf knives of the Solutreans (FIG. 3), most skillful of the Cro-Magnon stoneworkers, we find a refinement in the shape and proportion and in the character of the curve, and a rhythmic movement over the surface made by the flakings. A new process in stoneworking, pressure against the flint with a small piece of bone, enabled the craftsman to produce a tool that was as effective for use as it was pleasing to the eye. New materials derive from the

[1] The cultures known as Aurignacian, Solutrean, and Magdalenian belong to the larger unit known as Cro-Magnon, whose people stand in marked contrast to Neandertal man but close to the modern human type.

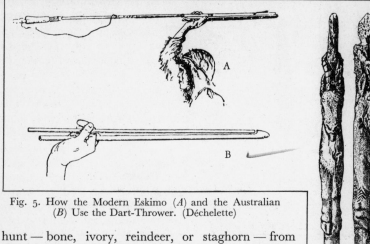

Fig. 5. How the Modern Eskimo (*A*) and the Australian (*B*) Use the Dart-Thrower. (Déchelette)

hunt — bone, ivory, reindeer, or staghorn — from which, with his sharp stone points, he not only fashioned bone javelin points, needles, harpoons (FIG. 4), arrow-straighteners, batons, and dart-throwers or throw sticks (FIG. 5) but decorated them, sometimes with lines and conventional pattern, sometimes with the animal form (FIG. 6). Around a reindeer horn an ibex has been carved in such a way that the figure is not "applied" to the surface but is an integral part of a cylindrical object and in no way interferes with the javelin resting firmly against the crotch. Note, for example, how the horns snugly encircling the stick em-

Fig. 6. Dart-Thrower. Of reindeer horn. L. 10½ in. (Piette)

phasize this cylindrical shape. To feel such a relationship between the cylindrical core and the animal form requires no mean intelligence and sensitivity. Likewise the baton in FIG. 7 reveals a highly imaginative quality in the relationship between the piece of horn and the head of a fox, while the cross markings not only enable the hand to hold the baton more securely but furnish a rhythmic movement over the surface.

On stone, ivory, and horn, on both flat and curving surfaces[1] the hunter-artist engraved many figures —some, linear or geometric ornament; a great many, animals. In the *Bison with Turned Head* (FIG. 9) one is impressed partly by its striking

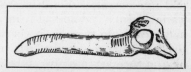

Fig. 7. Baton with Fox's Head. Of staghorn. L. c. 14 in. Magdalenian.

vitality and partly by the formal beauty expressed by the simplest

[1] Many of these engraved pieces are fragments and thus their purpose is unknown.

Fig. 8. Grazing Reindeer. Engraved around a piece of reindeer antler. L. 5 in. (Heim)

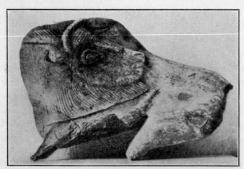

Fig. 9. Bison with Turned Head. Carved in rein-deer horn. From the rock shelter La Madeleine, Dordogne. Magdalenian. As the figure is broken its function is uncertain.

means. The head is so turned that it is entirely framed by the massive bulk of the body, and its pattern involves a vivid play of curve and counter-curve and a surface con-trast obtained by the use of incised lines as a deco-rative convention to indi-cate the mane. FIG. 14 shows an infuriated mam-moth charging forward. There is a largeness, a strikingly direct statement of a few essentials expressed by a line so sure that it is convincing, and so economical that it incorporates all details without specifically stating them. The animal is in profile, with only two legs showing; and there is no shading, no background. The whole figure is sensi-tively adjusted to the space which it fills. In the *Grazing Reindeer* (FIG. 8) a momentary pose is expressed with great naturalism. This keen-visioned hunter had observed the action of every part of the animal as it bent its head to browse, and with phenomenal memory he transferred the vision, with a sharp flint point, to the piece of horn. If the scratches beneath the reindeer are intended to suggest landscape, it is a unique

Fig. 10. Herd of Reindeer. Engraved on the wing bone of an eagle. L. 8 in. (Capitan and Breuil)

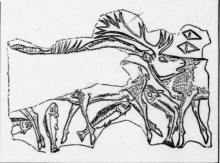

Fig. 11. Deer and Salmon. Engraved on reindeer horn. L. 5½ in. Magdalenian.

example of such representation. In the *Deer and Salmon* (FIG. 11) we have what is rare: a conscious grouping of several figures. The movements of each animal and the forward movement of the group are portrayed with a few essential lines. Even the backward turn of one head, which may represent the animal calling to the herd, helps the artist to integrate the head and antlers with the other figures without overlapping — which seems definitely to have been avoided, as one notes in the placing of the salmon. These fish may symbolize a stream, and the two lozenges above the stag may be the engraver's signature. In the *Herd of Reindeer* (FIG. 10) a visual impression is expressed forcibly by emphasizing, through distortion and repetition, the most characteristic feature, the antlers.

B. PAINTING

So far the manifestations of the art impulse in early man appear in his tools, weapons, and small personal belongings. To see his more monumental expression in painting and sculpture we shall penetrate several caverns of France and Spain, subterranean water channels varying in length from a few hundred to some four thousand feet and now choked, at places almost impassably,[1] by deposits, stalactites, and stalagmites. Far into these caverns, far beyond the sheltering entrance

[1] For an interesting account of a recent discovery of sculpture and also a vivid picture of the perilous undertakings incident to the exploration of subterranean caves, see Norbert Casteret, "Discovering the Oldest Statues in the World," *National Geographic Magazine*, August, 1924, p. 123.

Fig. 12. Woolly Rhinoceros. Drawing at Font-de-Gaume. L. c. 25 in. Aurignacian.

Fig. 13. Bison. Incised and drawn on a cave wall. Aurignacian. (After a drawing by Breuil)

Fig. 14. Charging Mammoth. Engraved on a piece of ivory tusk. (De Mortillet)

where the Cro-Magnon hunter lived, the hunter-artist, in utter quiet and darkness, with the help of artificial light engraved and painted on the walls many pictures, chiefly of animals.[1] For light he used a tiny stone lamp, filled with marrow or fat and supplied with a wick, perhaps of moss. For drawing he used chunks of red and yellow ochre, and for painting he ground these same ochres into powder and mixed them with some medium, perhaps animal fat. With a large flat bone for a palette, with brushes which he could make from reeds or bristles, and with scrapers for smoothing the wall and sharp flint points for engraving, his tools were complete. FIG. 13 shows a chalk drawing of a *Bison* which shares with the *Charging Mammoth* a quality of simple complete statement based upon a keen vision of the peculiar characteristics of the specific animal, the essentials of which are expressed by a bold continuous line. The horns are in front view, perhaps because the memory picture triumphed over the visual illusion, or perhaps because of the formal relationship thus made possible between the horns and the hump — that same feeling for shapes and their interrelations which we have been noting in the flints, dart-throwers, and engravings.

In the *Woolly Rhinoceros* (FIG. 12) is the same visual grasp of the

[1] For a picture of the Cro-Magnon artist at work see Charles Knight's reconstruction in Osborn, *op. cit.*, PL. VII.

animal form, equally convincing and monumental. Here the contour is broken and more varied, and is accented at points as if to suggest the mass of the figure, while short lines indicate hair and serve as rudimentary shading.

The *Reindeer* of FIG. 15 has been completely painted and modeled naturalistically in light and dark. It was first incised on the wall which had been somewhat smoothed by the scraper and outlined in paint; then the details were added, and the figure modeled in various tones. It seems natural, almost realistic. Yet note the character of the line of the back, the beauty of line as line — in the horns, for example. Through the painted figure, as through the chalk drawings, there

Fig. 15. Reindeer. The cave of Font-de-Gaume, France. C. 15,000 B.C. (Cartaillac and Breuil)

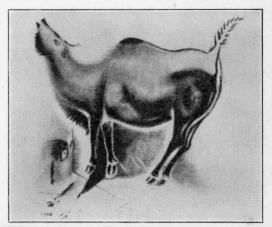

Fig. 16. Bellowing Bison. Cave of Altamira, Spain. C. 15,000 B.C.

runs an inexplicable something, whether the figure is at rest or in movement, a life rhythm (for lack of a more precise term), which makes it not a stuffed animal but a vitally living creature. In the *Bellowing Bison* (FIG. 16) for instance, how the painting makes one realize that single measured movement which controls every part of the body! Noteworthy also here is a rudimentary attempt, in the hind legs, at three-dimensional drawing.

There is a great variety in these primeval paintings, variety both of kind and of pose — mammoth, bison, reindeer, horse, boar, wolf;

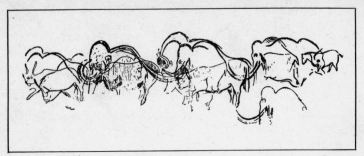

Fig. 17. Procession of Mammoth and Other Animals. L. c. 14 ft.
Cave of Font-de-Gaume, France. (Capitan and Breuil)

standing, walking, browsing, running, crouching. The majority are
isolated figures, often superimposed, inexplicably, one on another,
and with no relationship to each other or to the wall space, such as
was evident in the engravings and carvings. A notable exception is
the *Procession of Mammoth* of FIG. 17. Each painting reflects the keen
observation of the hunter-artist, and especially an extraordinary
memory for instantaneous poses, whose accuracy has been proved
and hardly surpassed by the motion-picture camera of today. Yet
this observation was of the selective type. It saw and recorded only
those essential aspects which interpret the appearance and character
of the animal, its grace or awkwardness, its cunning or dignity.

But why were these paintings hidden in dark caverns in the heart
of the mountain? And why do they represent almost entirely the game
animals? Some scholars explain them as expression only, an outlet
of the art impulse for its own sake in terms of the artist's own environment as a hunter. Others, with more probability and by analogy with
practices of primitive peoples of today, see in them a magic purpose.
These obscure isolated caverns may have been sacred places, and
the bison painted on the wall may have been intended to bring success
in the hunt, as the ibex carved on the dart-thrower may have been
believed to make the arm more sure and powerful in bringing down
the game. At the same time, admitting the magic purpose, has not
the art impulse found its outlet? For is there not combined in these
paintings the same dual attainment of effective function and satisfying form that we noted even in the early flints?

In southeastern Spain Paleolithic paintings of an entirely different,
and not yet entirely explicable, nature have been discovered. They
are but a few inches in dimension and consist of a whole group of
figures, both human and animal: hunting, fighting, and dancing
scenes expressed with great vigor and an exaggeration of movement

Fig. 18. Hunters. H. c. 4 in. Caves of Eastern Spain. (Obermaier and Wernert)

in distinct contrast to the imposing dignity and serenity of the paintings at which we have been looking. They give evidence of an entirely opposite point of view toward form, for now it is not the visual perception of the object that the hand records, but a mental concept of it,[1] with no regard for rational proportions or appearance. These painters put together, quite unnaturalistically, symbols for the different parts of the body, which convey the artist's idea with great conviction; for example, the dynamic movement in FIG. 18.

C. SCULPTURE

The animal carvings on the throw sticks (FIGS. 6, 7) foreshadow the capacity of the Paleolithic artist as a true sculptor, fully realized in the Cap-Blanc *Frieze of Animals*, the general effect of which is what the Abbé Breuil calls an unforgettable impression of amazement. A life-sized horse carved in relief ten or twelve inches high displays the same largeness of vision as the paintings. Grandly simple masses say everything that is necessary for purposes of representation and still remain related masses in stone of impressive monumentality. On a smaller scale, the same is true of the *Clay Bison* modeled on the floor of the cavern of Tuc d'Audoubert.

D. SUMMARY

Finally, as the ice melted in the increasing warmth, the reindeer migrated north, the mammoth and the woolly rhinoceros disappeared, and the hunter-artists vanished. Why and where? These are still unanswered questions, but the hunter-artists left behind them in their tools and weapons, personal belongings, paintings, and sculpture an art expression that shows an ability to infuse the objects of everyday

[1] See R. E. Fry, *Vision and Design*, Coward-McCann, 1924, "The Art of the Bushmen," for a discussion of these two contrasting attitudes.

Fig. 19. Scandinavian Daggers. Of stone flaked by pressure. L. 11½ in. Neolithic (After Müller).

life with the fundamentals of form. In the paintings and carvings of figures they proved themselves able to grasp essentials as they present themselves to the eye, and to express them with an economical and forceful naturalism. At the same time they revealed a feeling for line and shape and their inter-relations as something desirable in themselves.

"From the standpoint of priority of antiquity then, the artist has special reason to be proud. He follows a calling that had its worthy devotees ages before any other method of leaving imperishable records of human thought was known. Man was artist before he was maker of even hieroglyphs; he tamed his imagination and his hand to produce at will objects of beauty long ages before he tamed the first wild beast or made the humble plant world do his bidding. The farmer, whose calling we are apt to think of as representing the life primeval, is a mere upstart in comparison with one who practices the fine arts." [1]

CHAPTER II

Mesolithic and Neolithic Art
(about 20,000–2000 B.C.)

A. HISTORICAL BACKGROUND AND THE MINOR ARTS

The Paleolithic Age gave way, perhaps because of climatic and cultural changes, to a transition period known as the Mesolithic. Europe became geographically, climatically, and biologically the Europe of today. Man still roamed as a hunter but seemed entirely devoid of the art impulse that manifested itself so vigorously in the Paleolithic Age. His tools were crude. The only art objects to warrant attention in a brief survey are the painted pebbles of the Azilians,

[1] G. G. MacCurdy, *Human Origins*, Appleton, 1926, 2 vols., Vol. I, p. 246.

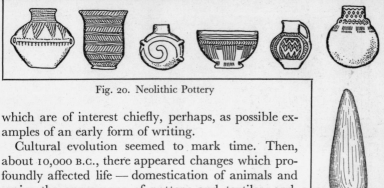

Fig. 20. Neolithic Pottery

which are of interest chiefly, perhaps, as possible examples of an early form of writing.

Cultural evolution seemed to mark time. Then, about 10,000 B.C., there appeared changes which profoundly affected life — domestication of animals and grain; the appearance of pottery and textiles, and, late in the period, metal. With the cultivation of grain and the appearance of the farmer, permanent homes and village life replaced the nomad and his cave-dwelling; and abodes developed into the comfortable homes of the Swiss lake villages.

Fig. 21. Polished Stone Implement. Originally mounted in a handle. L. 8¾ in. British Museum, London.

New industries required new tools, which continued to be made chiefly of stone. Some of these, fashioned by the old method of chipping and flaking by pressure, attained a climax of stonecutting in their beauty of shape and proportions, in the precision and rhythm of their flaking (FIG. 19). But a new method of tool-making, that of grinding and polishing, appeared, by means of which man could obtain a smooth surface and a fine cutting edge, and by attaching a wooden handle supply himself with a tool comparable to those of modern times (FIG. 21).

Some of the demands made by permanent, more secure, and better equipped homes were met by pottery and textiles. The idea of clay fashioned into a shape and hardened by fire may have been suggested by the attempt to make a basket impervious to fire and to protect it by smearing clay on it before placing it over the flames. Neolithic pottery was made by hand, for the potter's wheel was apparently unknown. It was simple and rugged, sometimes pleasing in shape and proportion, with decoration — concentric lines, spirals, zigzags, dots, chevrons, the basic universal motifs — well adapted to the shape and often strengthening the structural lines and surfaces (FIG. 20). Only a few pieces of textiles have survived, but many items such as spinning whorls, loom weights, and bundles of fibers are evidence of the weaving of cloth and of baskets. These latter articles, together with tools and implements, not only supplied the home but constituted objects of trade; for commerce had arisen, and with the interchange of goods

Fig. 22. Dolmen. Normandy.

came interchange of ideas, more definite social groupings, and a great acceleration in man's development in comparison with the long aeons of time consumed in his early advances.

B. BUILDING

With the growth of communities, social organization, and trade and industry, monumental stone structures appear. *Dolmens* (*dol*, table, and *men*, stone), tombs or monuments to the dead, consisted of several stones set on end with a covering slab, hence the name (FIG. 22). Single megaliths, *menhirs* (*men*, stone, *hir*, on end), at times seventy feet high, were set up on end individually, or were arranged in long rows, as at Carnac in Brittany. Their purpose, though not clear, may have had to do with a cult of the dead or the worship of the sun. Sometimes they were arranged in a circle known as a *cromlech*, the most imposing of which is *Stonehenge* (FIG. 23).[1] This circle consists of an outer ring of huge monoliths capped with lintels roughly cut just as they came from the quarry and laid without mortar. Inside this is a line of smaller stones; then a broken ring of five pairs of huge monoliths, each with its lintel; and again an inner broken circle of smaller stones, inside of which is a large slab that may have served as an altar. In the arrangement there is a feeling for order and symmetry, and a rhythm that is varied by alternating the large and small concentric circles. Such a structure is not properly speaking architecture. But it is the nearest approach to it that we find in western Europe until Roman times.

[1] For recent studies and excavations of *Stonehenge*, based upon air photography, see "Stonehenge" article, Encyclopædia Britannica, 14th ed.

C. SUMMARY

On the whole, in comparison with the art expression of the Paleolithic hunter that of Neolithic man is crude. His contribution to human welfare lay in other directions. It was a widespread culture, and somewhere in its area and at some time in its course man made one

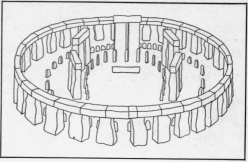

Fig. 23. Stonehenge, Restored. Salisbury Plain, England. D. c. 100 ft.

of his greatest discoveries — metal. But as he had "lived in at least a fair degree of contentment on this earth for a million years, more or less," as Dr. MacCurdy reminds us, he went on using his time-tried stone tools for a considerable length of time. Gradually the material with the greater capacity made its way forward, now here, now there. And at roughly the same time another great invention, writing, provided him with a cultural tool for rapid advancement. And with that invention we have entered the historical era.

BIBLIOGRAPHY

Avebury, John Lubbock, Lord, *Prehistoric Times*, 7th ed., Holt, 1914
Boyle, M. E., *In Search of Our Ancestors*, Little, Brown, 1928
Breasted, J. H., *Ancient Times*, 2d ed. rev., Ginn, 1935
Brown, G. B., *The Art of the Cave Dweller*, R. V. Coleman, 1928
Burkitt, M. C., *Our Early Ancestors*, Macmillan, 1927
Childe, V. G., *The Dawn of European Civilization*, Knopf, 1925
——— *The Most Ancient East*, Knopf, 1929
Kühn, Helmut, *Kunst und Kultur der Vorzeit Europas*, Berlin, 1929
——— *Die Malerei der Eiszeit*, Munich, 1922
MacCurdy, G. G., *The Coming of Man*, University Society, 1932
——— *Human Origins*, Appleton, 1926, 2 vols.
Munro, Robert, *The Lake Dwellings of Europe*, London, 1890
——— *Paleolithic Man and Terramara Settlements in Europe*, Macmillan, 1912
Osborn, H. F., *Men of the Old Stone Age*, 3d ed., Scribner, 1924
Parkyn, E. A., *An Introduction to the Study of Prehistoric Art*, Longmans, 1915
Peake, H. J. E., and Fleure, H. J., *Hunters and Artists*, Yale University Press, 1927 (The Corridors of Time, Vol. II)
Piette, Edouard, *L'art pendant l'âge du renne*, Paris, 1907
Sawtell, R. O., and Treat, Ida, *Primitive Hearths in the Pyrenees*, Appleton, 1927
Smith, G. E., *The Search for Man's Ancestors*, Warne, 1931

Sollas, W. J., *Ancient Hunters and Their Modern Representatives*, 3d ed. rev., Macmillan, 1924
Spearing, H. G., *The Childhood of Art; or, The Ascent of Man*, rev. ed., Holt, 1930
Swindler, M. H., *Ancient Painting*, Yale University Press, 1929
Wells, H. G., *The Outline of History*, rev. ed., Garden City Publishing Co., 1931

See also the General Bibliography, pp. 749-751.

Part Two

ART OF THE ANCIENT NEAR EAST

CHAPTER III

Egyptian Art

1. EARLY EGYPT AND THE OLD KINGDOM
(about 4500–2475 B.C.) [1]

A. HISTORICAL BACKGROUND

From the top of the Great Pyramid we look out over the undulating floor of a vast desert plateau through which cuts a narrow valley of luxuriant green, of fields and palms fringing a winding river. Above blazes a glorious sun in a cloudless sky. This is Egypt (FIGS. 24, 25, 26).

Of this environment several facts persistently confronted the Egyptian: the brilliant sun, the Nile River, and the great geographical contrasts of his land — the barrenness and stern majesty of illimitable deserts; the rich fertility and delights of the valley with its trees, grains, flowers, birds: all gifts of the Sun and the River. And so insistently did these facts of environment impress themselves on his mind that they early became dominating forces in his attempt to account for his inexplicable world. Evil and beneficent spirits animated all things. In the daily spectacle of the sun he envisaged a mighty god Re (Ra), or Amon-Re, sailing across the sky each day in his bark, and back to the east by night along a river of the nether world. In the annual rise of the Nile he saw the resurrection of Osiris, who after a tragic earthly life and death became god of the dead. And just as Osiris entered upon a new existence in another world and just as nature with the rise of the Nile burst into new life, so to every Egyptian lay open the opportunity for a similar experience of revived life after

[1] There is considerable difference of opinion among scholars on the question of Egyptian chronology and of the spelling of Egyptian names. In Chapter III of this book, the chronology is that of J. H. Breasted; the spelling follows that of the Oriental Institute of the University of Chicago.

Fig. 24. Egypt.

death. This hope constituted one of the most powerful influences in Egyptian civilization and Egyptian art.

While Paleolithic man of western Europe was coping with the rigors of a glacial age his relative in North Africa was enjoying a more leisurely life in a land of abundant rain and luxuriant vegetation. Then, with a change of climate in northern Africa which brought about desert conditions, Stone Age man and the animals gathered about the oases or migrated to the abundant waters of the Nile Valley. Along the river he built his hamlets, tamed the animals, and began to plant grain. Before 3000 B.C. he had evolved a system of picture writing, invented a calendar, worked out a system of irrigation, and had discovered metal, perhaps accidentally as the molten drops of copper separated from the rock in his campfire in Sinai. Tiny states began to emerge along the river, and slowly coalesced into two kingdoms, Upper and Lower Egypt, which were finally united about 3400 B.C. by a king called Menes. At the head of the political and social system we see a supreme pharaoh, who probably owned all the land; a group of nobles suppressed, receiving their appointments from him; the mass of the people (with possible exceptions) slaves. The chief economic basis was agriculture, though the industries of the potter, the stonecutter, and the goldsmith were highly developed, and commerce was carried on with the Beduins of Sinai, and with the Aegean lands. The government became highly efficient and thoroughly organized, with different administrative departments. Toward the end of the period, however, a change can be discerned. As the nobles gained in power, the strength of the pharaoh weakened, while the official class became hereditary, laying the foundation of a feudal state.

Fig. 25. Egypt at Low Nile. At the top of the steep bank is the cultivated area, with palm trees; in the background rise the cliffs of the desert plateau. (Author)

The Egyptian noble we see living in a villa set in a garden with trees and pools of water, all surrounded by a high wall. His working life was spent for the most part in the out-of-doors (FIG. 46), where he found many of his pleasures, too. For we see him in his reed boat, accompanied by his family, hunting fowl in the papyrus swamp; out on the desert after game; or watching the work in the fields (FIG. 27). In the upper rows the harvesters are cutting the grain, leaving a high stubble just as they do in Egypt today; below, men with staves are driving the donkeys back and forth over the threshing-floor, tying the grain in great bags and loading it on the donkeys' backs or tossing

Fig. 26. Pyramids of Gizeh. IV Dynasty (2900–2750 B.C.).

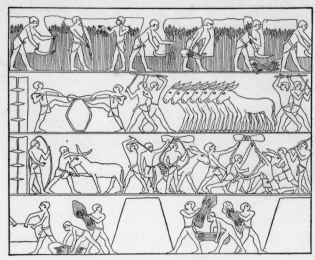

Fig. 27. Work in the Fields: Reaping, Threshing, and Stacking. From the mastaba of Ti, Saqquara.

the bundles into the granaries. Stock-raising played a large part in the life of the Egyptian. In driving the cattle to pasture, frequent canals must be crossed (FIG. 28), and the cowboy with a kindly heart carries on his back the young calf that is anxiously looking back toward the cow.

The Egyptian loved this out-of-doors, lived in it, observed keenly all the plants, animals, and birds that he found there, and then painted or carved them on his walls and shaped his useful things of everyday life after them. His house was equipped with well-designed furniture and utensils of wood, ivory, glazed pottery, metal, and many kinds and colors of stone; his costume was of linen with abundant jewelry — all of which required the services of many craftsmen working in many materials.

Materials for all the arts were at hand or readily obtained: limestone and sandstone from the Nile cliffs and granite from the great dikes at the cataracts; alabaster and the hard diorite, porphyry and breccias, valuable for their color, texture, and striation, from the near-by deserts; abundant gold from Nubia; copper from Sinai. A little silver, lapis lazuli, carnelian, turquoise, and other semiprecious stones were at hand; colors from the earth and from metals; gums and honey for use as binding vehicles. Wood was scarce.

A vivid picture of Egyptian life comes from the tombs, for, as we have said, the provision for life hereafter was one of the chief con-

Fig. 28. Herd of Cattle Fording a Canal. From the mastaba of Ti, Saqquara.

cerns of existence in this world. The Egyptian believed that there was a force called the *ka* which was the counterpart of the body. It came into being with the body, continued through life with it, was in all features like it, though invisible, and at death accompanied it into the next world. As the *ka* and the body were coexistent, the body must be carefully preserved through mummification, and the *ka*, through offerings of all kinds. Thus to secure for the spirit land, which was but a reflection of this world, both necessities and luxuries, it was necessary to paint or carve all these scenes upon the tomb walls or to place small models in the burial chambers each of which, with the proper incantation, would function normally in the hereafter.

B. ARCHITECTURE

Recall for a moment the Egyptian landscape: stern, vast, of generally horizontal lines in the valley floor, and in the strata and crests of the cliffs. No gently curving hills or jagged picturesque mountains relieve the monotony. A contrastingly luxuriant valley, a thread of an oasis, twists through the rocky desert plateau. Recalling also the social organization, the religious domination, and the available materials, what forms and purposes would one expect their architecture to embody? Apart from the palaces and houses, temporary and flimsy though comfortable enough in the warm climate, it is not surprising to find as the dominant architectural expression massive, enduring tombs and temples of stone.

In the Old Kingdom, the desire to create a permanent safe abiding-place for the dead led to the erection of tombs, of which the pyramids,[1] or royal tombs, are the climax. A distant view of the *Pyramids of*

---

[1] The pyramid field extends for about 50 miles on the western bank of the Nile south from the Delta, in the vicinity of the Old Kingdom capital, Memphis (FIG. 24); for Lower Egypt was the center of civilization in the Old Kingdom.

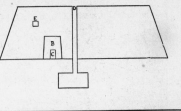

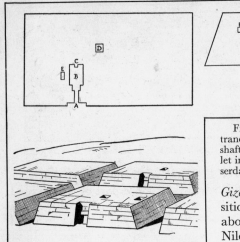

Fig. 29. Typical Mastaba. *A*, entrance; *B*, chapel; *C*, false door; *D*, shaft down which the sarcophagus was let into the burial chamber below; *E*, serdab for the statue. L. 40–50 ft.

Fig. 30. Group of Mastabas. *Mastaba* is an Arabic word meaning a bench or terrace.

Gizeh (FIG. 26) reveals their position on the desert plateau safe above the highest level of the Nile. They rise with unbroken line and surface from the plateau base to an apex, comprising a form of great simplicity and dignity. Contrast for a moment the façade of a Gothic cathedral (Fig. 438) with its multiplicity of vertical lines, each pointed arch, statue, pinnacle, buttress, and tower contributing to the soaring quality and to the broken light and shade; notice how different is the feeling of unrest and exaltation there experienced from the quiet repose that comes from the unity of the unbroken line and surface of the pyramid.

Such a structure, simple geometric form though it is, was not conceived in a moment but was the result of a long evolution. The furthest back we can trace the Egyptian, he buried his dead in a pit over which he heaped up the sand, holding it in place with stones and twigs. By slow process this pit and sand heap grew; the actual chamber below the ground became rectangular and was faced with wood, brick, and finally stone. At the same time the mound above was covered with brick or stone, which followed in a general way the lines of the sand heap and thus attained a shape that looks like a low truncated pyramid, called a *mastaba* (FIG. 30). Finally, some king ambitious to erect a still mightier tomb began to pile mastaba upon mastaba, forming a step pyramid; and then, by filling in the steps, attained the pure pyramidal form.[1]

At first the mastaba was simple (FIG. 29), built of solid material except for the small chapel that served as a reception room of the

[1] For a graphic illustration of this development, see J. H. Breasted, *Ancient Times*, new ed., Ginn, 1935, p. 74.

Fig. 31. Pyramids of Khufu and Khafre, Restored. Gizeh. (Hoelscher)

ka, where the family and priests gathered to place the offerings before the false door facing the east, through which the *ka* came from the spirit land of the west. A tiny secret chamber known as the *serdab*, or cellar, was built in the heart of the structure to contain a statue of the deceased that could represent him in the spirit world, should anything happen to the actual body. This chapel became quite complex, as time went on, with additional rooms and corridors which were covered with reliefs that vividly picture the everyday life of the Egyptian, for the benefit, as we have said, of the *ka*.

The largest of the *Pyramids of Gizeh* is that of *Khufu* or Cheops (Figs. 26, 31). With the exception of the galleries and burial chamber (Fig. 33) it is solid masonry of limestone which was roughly cut in the quarries in the eastern Nile cliffs directly across the river and floated over at high Nile to the base of the plateau where the tomb was to be built. There the masons finished cutting the stones and marked them with red ink to indicate the place of each in the structure. Then they were laid course upon course by great gangs of slaves who dragged them by sheer human labor up the temporary ramps.[1] The angles left by the decreasing courses were filled with casing stones of a pearly-white limestone, cut with such nicety that the eye can scarcely detect the joinings. Thus the pyramid presented a perfectly smooth surface from foundation to tip.[2]

Nicety of engineering is seen as well in the fact that without modern surveying instruments and machinery, but with only a knotted rope

---

[1] An unfinished pyramid in the foreground of Fig. 31 shows these ramps.
[2] A few of these casing stones can still be seen at the base. The ragged condition of the pyramid is due to the depredations of the Moslem builders of Cairo.

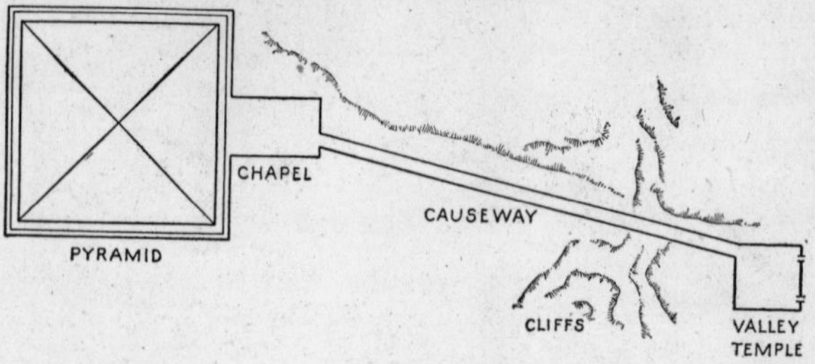

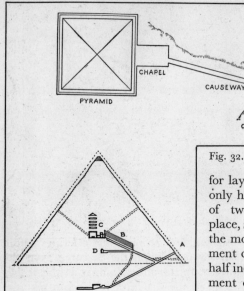

Fig. 32. Plan of a Pyramid Complex.

Fig. 33. Section of the Pyramid of Khufu.
A. Entrance. *B*. Grand Gallery. *C*. King's
Chamber. *D*. Queen's Chamber.

for laying out the huge base and only human labor to drag stones of two-and-one-half tons into place, so accurate is the work that the most delicate modern instrument can detect only about one-half inch of error in the measurement of one side. Yet it is not alone huge size, successful mechanical engineering, and skill in stonecutting that constitute the art of such a structure, but its formal engineering as well — the proportions, and the simple dignity of the form, so consistent with its function and so adapted to its geographical setting.[1]

On the east side of the Great Pyramid are three small pyramids belonging to members of the royal family, while clustered about are rows of mastabas of the great nobles who, having been associated with the pharaoh in life, wished to continue in this place of honor even in the tomb. The pyramid of the pharaoh, however, is the dominating structure of the whole cemetery (FIG. 31), just as he himself had been the dominating power of Egyptian life.

The middle pyramid of the triple group at Gizeh, the *Pyramid of Khafre*, is somewhat smaller than that of Khufu, indicating a waning, economic as well as political, in the power of the pharaoh. This pyramid is very important for our purpose, however, because from the

[1] The massiveness, solidity, and weight of the *Pyramid of Khufu* is better realized when one recalls some dimensions (in round numbers): base, 775 ft., covering 13 acres; height, 450 ft. (originally 480 ft.); the flat space now on the top, 30 ft. square. According to Petrie the structure contains about 2,300,000 blocks of stone, each of which averages in weight 2½ tons. These stones are chiefly limestone except about the burial chambers, where very finely cut granite is used.

remains surrounding it
we can study all the additional structures, which,
together with the pyra-
mid itself, comprise the
pyramid complex. To
do this let us look first
at the mastaba-shaped
structure in the right foreground of FIG. 31. This
building is near the town
in the valley, at the base
of the plateau on which
the pyramid stands. In
order to provide for the
spirit of the dead, offerings must be placed at the
tomb frequently. The hot
climb up over the sandy
hill led to the erection of
a covered causeway from
the valley up to the little

Fig. 34. Valley-Temple of the Pyramid of Khafre,
Restored. c. 2850 B.C. (Hoelscher)

chapel adjoining the eastern side of the pyramid. For as the spirit
land lay in the west, the spirit must come toward the east to receive
the offerings. Hence tombs were built on the western bank, and the
chapel was on the eastern side of the pyramid. The beginning of
the causeway presupposed some kind of entrance or vestibule. To
provide that is the function of the building in the valley.

Looking at the ground plan (FIG. 32), we see that a pyramid complex consists of (a) the pyramid itself, within or below which was
the burial chamber; (b) the chapel adjoining the pyramid on the
eastern side, where the offerings were made and ceremonies performed, and where were kept in store chambers the linen, grain, honey,
oil, and other offerings of food and drink and the rich ceremonial vessels (FIG. 54) for use in the daily rites; (c) the covered causeway leading over the cliffs; and (d) the valley-temple, or vestibule of the
causeway, down in the valley.

Let us look more closely at the valley-temple (FIG. 34). It is built
on the lintel system, that is, the upright supports are bridged over with
horizontal beams, or lintels. Here the supports and lintels are huge
red-granite monoliths, finely proportioned, skillfully cut and polished,
and entirely devoid of decoration. Alabaster slabs cover the floor,
while seated statues are ranged alongside, the only embellishment.

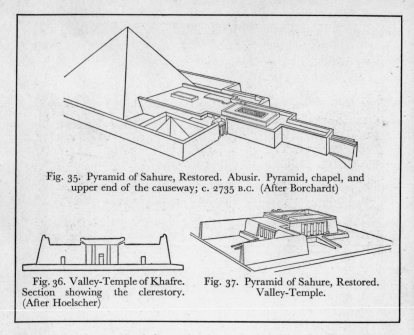

Fig. 35. Pyramid of Sahure, Restored. Abusir. Pyramid, chapel, and
upper end of the causeway; c. 2735 B.C. (After Borchardt)

Fig. 36. Valley-Temple of Khafre.   Fig. 37. Pyramid of Sahure, Restored.
Section showing the clerestory.   Valley-Temple.
(After Hoelscher)

This interior, protected from the hot sun by the great blocks, must
have been cool and dim. It is lighted by a few rays filtering in from
above, slantwise. This is because the pillars of the central aisle are
higher than the side walls, and the roof over the central part is therefore at a higher level than over the sides. In the vertical space left between these two levels are slits in the stone, through which the light
comes, forming an embryonic clerestory (FIG. 36), a structural feature
that became so characteristic of early Christian churches. With its
plain, simple dignity, it is a remarkably impressive room, harmonizing
with the simple massive tomb to which it led.

Leaving Gizeh and traveling up the river to Abusir, let us look at
the chapel and valley-temple of the *Pyramid of Sahure* (FIGS. 35, 37, 38),
built about a hundred years after that of Khafre and much smaller in
size. Here we see something not found at Gizeh — columns, in place
of rectangular pillars, and wall paintings. From the natural forms of
his environment the Egyptian found in the palm tree, with its tall
trunk and spreading leaves, an inspiration for the design of his columns. The elegance of this design, in no way hampering the column's
function of support, together with the bright colors on the walls lends
an air of splendor which contrasts sharply with the austere simplicity
of the *Valley-Temple of Khafre*.

Fig. 38. Pyramid of Sahure, Restored. Abusir. Colonnaded hall of
the chapel. c. 2735 B.C. (Borchardt)

C. SCULPTURE

As architecture in early Egypt was employed largely to protect
the dead, so sculpture was bound up with the desire either to perpetuate or to serve the dead. Should the body, though carefully mum-
mified, by any chance perish, then a statue as near like the original
as possible might represent the body in the world to come. Hence
we are not surprised to find portraiture early developed.[1] In the
statue of *Ranofer* (FIG. 39), a statue in the round,[2] we see a figure
facing directly forward with the left foot advanced and arms held
close to the side.[3] He wears a linen kilt and a large wig, the characteristic costume of the day. The wig, by simplifying the contour,
adds to the compactness of the figure, which is massive and rather

[1] As with the pyramids, a long evolution in carving for which we have incomplete
evidence must be presupposed for the high accomplishment of the Old Kingdom
sculpture.

[2] *In the round* and *relief* are technical terms applied to sculpture. The first means
that the statue is fully modeled in three dimensions so that it is possible to walk around
it; *relief* means that the figures are but partly modeled, projecting beyond the background to which they are attached, sometimes very little (known as *low relief* or *bas-
relief*) and sometimes so far that they are nearly in the round but still attached (known
as *high relief*). There is no sharp line of demarcation between bas-relief and high relief,
and both are frequently combined in the same work.

[3] This figure illustrates the "law of frontality," by which is meant that the figure
is facing directly to the front with no turning to right or left and that a central axis
cuts it into two equal parts, though the two parts may not be posed identically. Such
a pose is not confined to Egypt. For materials and methods of working, see M. A.
Murray, *Egyptian Sculpture*, Scribner, 1930.

Fig. 40. Statue of a Lady, Probably a Princess. H. c. 10 in. IV Dynasty (2900–2750 B.C.). Metropolitan Museum, New York. (*Journal of Egyptian Archaeology*)

Fig. 39. Ranofer. V Dynasty (2750–2625 B.C.). Cairo Museum.

angular. The individual traits of the man are submerged in the generalized features; the firmly placed, erect head and the whole bearing denote a man of the noble classes.

The *Princess* (FIG. 40), though fragmentary, and though it may have been a seated figure, shows the same rigid frontal pose as that of *Ranofer*. She wears a tightly fitting linen garment with two straps over the shoulders; a broad collar-necklace; and the usual wig, beneath which appears the natural hair, smoothly parted over the forehead. In this statue a vivacious note is added by the use of rock crystal for the eyes and of color, which not only covers the entire surface but adds details, such as brows and necklace, not carved in the stone. The flesh is a yellowish tone because the Egyptian woman led a more secluded life than the man, whose skin, tanned by his out-of-door life, is usually painted a dark reddish color. The lips are red, the necklace red and blue, the hair and brows black. Thus while the color is partly naturalistic it is, even more, decorative, for it is laid on flat and strongly differentiates the parts of the figure.

In *Khafre* (FIG. 41) we see the pharaoh seated in the same frontal position as *Ranofer* and the *Princess*. On his throne is the intertwined lotus and papyrus, symbol of united Egypt; about his head are the protecting wings of the hawk, symbol of his semidivine station. His linen headdress covers his forehead smoothly and falls in plaited folds over the breast; the false ceremonial beard is partly broken off. He wears the simple kilt of the Old Kingdom. While the characterization, like that of Ranofer, is generalized, its imperturbable calm and monumentality convey an impression of what was more significant than the individual traits — the enduring power of the pharaoh, the

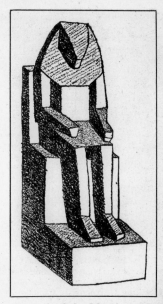

Fig. 41. Khafre. Life size, IV Dynasty (2900–2750 B.C.). Cairo Museum. (Metropolitan Museum). The analysis illustrates the relation of the main planes of the figure to the planes of the original block of stone.

abstract idea of sovereignty. This impression arises from the character of the form, which in turn is partly determined by its material. The figure is carved from diorite, a stone so hard that it will turn a steel tool; consequently the character of the material has to a large extent determined the summary character of the carving. The large planes are cut generally parallel to the planes of the block of stone, and there is no movement from side to side. Furthermore the figure, the bird, and the throne compose, with a feeling of inevitability, into a unity whose largeness and architectural quality enable the statue to take its place with perfect harmony in the severely simple hall for which it was carved (FIG. 34).[1] These three statues, although grandly dignified generalized types, are vividly characterized and vitally alive.

When we turn to the statues of the lower classes, the type gives way to the individual, as in the *Sheikh el-Beled* (FIG. 42).[2] The *Sheikh* is

[1] For a more detailed analysis see Helen Gardner, *Understanding the Arts*, Harcourt, Brace, 1932, pp. 151 ff. For another Old Kingdom royal portrait, finely preserved, see the *Mycerinus and his Queen*, standing figures, in the Boston Museum of Fine Arts.

[2] When the natives who were helping in the excavations caught a glimpse of this statue, so impressed were they by its resemblance to their own village chief that immediately they called out "Sheikh el-Beled!" which means "Chief of the Village," a name it has borne ever since.

Fig. 42. Sheikh el-Beled. Of wood. IV Dynasty (2900–2750 B.C.). Cairo Museum. (Oriental Institute, University of Chicago)

Fig. 43. Seated Scribe. H. c. 2 ft. Of limestone, painted. V Dynasty (2750–2625 B.C.). Louvre, Paris. (Giraudon)

a self-satisfied, likable fellow, perhaps a middle-class overseer. Although the statue is still frontal, the uplifted arm breaks its rigidity. Here the sculptor was working in wood and made the arms of separate pieces; hence he could use a freer pose. Originally the wood was covered with linen glued on to furnish a surface for painting.

In the *Seated Scribe* (FIG. 43) we see a keen alert servant with a spare face, square jaw, and thin lips — a shrewd man with a sense of humor. He sits cross-legged, Eastern fashion, with his pen in his hand (as is indicated by the position of the fingers) ready to take down what his master will dictate. The statue is carved from limestone and painted dark red. The legs, back, and arms are blocked out in large masses only; the breast, shoulders, and head alone are individualized. Yet the expression of momentary expectancy — an abstract idea — which fills the entire figure has been caught and transformed into the enduring permanency of stone in a manner that is large and truly sculptural.

As we turn to the reliefs we find that the figures are carved so low that they approach painting more closely than sculpture. Among examples of early work is the *Palette of King Narmer* (FIG. 44), which was dedicated in the temple by this king, in commemoration of some victory. It is carved on both sides; on one, Narmer stands clutching his fallen enemy by the hair and with lifted mace is about to smite

Fig. 44. Palette of King Narmer. Slate. H. c. 20 in. Cairo Museum.

him; below, two running figures represent the fleeing army. The
other side is divided into four zones, the upper one of which bears
the name of the king in the center, balanced on each side by the head
of the goddess Hathor; in the second the king, large of stature as be-
fits his station, followed by a sandal-bearer and preceded by his prime
minister and four standard-bearers, is looking at his enemies, whose
bodies, with their decapitated heads carefully placed between their
legs, lie on the ground before him in two rows. The next zone is
occupied by two curious animals whose long necks intertwine to form
a circular depression, their angry lion heads kept apart by two men
who pull vigorously on ropes attached to their necks. In the lowest
zone is a bull, symbolic of the king, battering down the walls of the
enemy's town and trampling his foes underfoot. In this early relief
we can discern several characteristics of Egyptian work. The first is
the conventional way in which the human figure is drawn — the head
and legs in profile, the torso and the eye in front view; in other words,
mental concepts of the different parts of the figure without reference
to purely visual impressions. The second is the lack of perspective.
For example, the artist wished to show two rows of bodies lying on
the ground; unable to do this, he placed one body above another
— the usual way of expressing distance in Egyptian drawing. The
third is sensitiveness to design in the adaptation of the figures to the
space. The two animals with intertwined necks balance each other

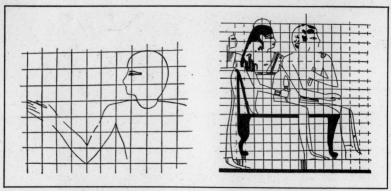

Fig. 45. Proportion Squares on Tomb Walls. (*Journal of Egyptian Archaeology*)

even to their tails, which curl up over their backs to form an almost complete circle, repeating the motif of the central circle, which is again repeated in the horns of the Hathor heads above, a repetition which strengthens the unity of design. The two little figures pulling so vigorously on the ropes well fill the space remaining on each side of the animals. Furthermore, the figures were carved by a man who was very sure-handed in the use of his chisel. The firm unfaltering lines that express essentials only are discernible in all the figures of the palette.

The great mass of Egyptian reliefs decorated the tomb chapels, the walls of which were covered with scenes from everyday life — the production of grain; the raising of cattle; the making of boats, jewelry, vases; hunting on the desert or in the papyrus swamp; and this all for the utilitarian purpose, as we have said, of providing the dead with the necessities and the pleasures of life. The scenes are arranged in horizontal zones (FIG. 27) and the figures are drawn mostly in profile with very little grouping that necessitates overlapping, except in the case of the animals, where depth is shown by repeating the silhouette. Though the figures are drawn with the conventions that we observed in studying the *Palette of Narmer*, still they are filled with vigor and movement, while the animals show great naturalism based upon a careful observation of the animal form and also the animal characteristics — the calm placidity of the oxen and the pathetic gloom of the donkeys. A frank acceptance of two points of view is again seen in the oxen, where the front view of the horns is placed upon a profile view of the head. All the figures are painted in bright flat colors that are partly naturalistic but largely regardful of a color harmony that creates a wall decoration apart from the subject interest.

How the artist went about his work we have learned from some

Fig. 46. Ti Hunting in the Papyrus Marsh. From the mastaba of Ti,
Saqquara. V Dynasty (2750–2625 B.C.). (Steindorff)

of the tombs where the walls have been left unfinished. He planned
his decoration with the help of guide lines to proportion both the
spaces and the figures (FIG. 45); then he sketched the latter in, made
an incision along the lines of the preliminary sketch with a chisel,
and cut away the background, leaving his design in relief. If the stone
was too uneven to offer a good foundation for painting, he covered
it with a thin coating of fine plaster. His pigment he mixed with some
binding medium, probably a gum, and applied it to the dry stone
or plaster with brushes made of reeds, in flat, even tones, using no
light and shade. Whatever modeling was done, was done by the contour line made in the preliminary sketch and by the chisel.

The never-failing sense of design that characterizes Egyptian art
reveals itself in the relief of *Ti Hunting in the Papyrus Marsh* (FIG. 46).
Ti, large of stature as usual, is in his reed boat; from the river, filled
with hippopotamuses and fish, rise the stems of papyrus plants, conventionalized to form a background for the figures. As the straight

Fig. 47. Geese of Meidum. So called because the panel was found in a tomb

lines approach the top of the panel, however, some of them bend under the weight of the weasel that is stealing up to the nest of young birds, whose parents fly anxiously about. The scene among the flowers and buds above balances that on the river below; yet both are connected and emphasized by the background of the vertical stems.

Fig. 48. Panel of Hesire. Wood. H. c. 4 ft. c. 2800 B.C. Cairo Museum.

A tomb relief that embodies the same characteristics in another medium is the panel of *Hesire*, carved in wood (FIG. 48). Though a single figure is represented, it is not placed in the center of the panel; yet the balance is maintained by the staff, and the writing utensils which Hesire holds in his left hand; the horizontals of the feet, baton, girdle, and shoulders happily balance the otherwise insistent verticals. Look more closely at the figure itself. To appreciate its high quality we must frankly accept the conventional way in which different parts of the body are drawn from different points of view. This was not because the Egyptian could not execute a profile, as we shall see, but simply because this conventional method of drawing the figure, established early in Egypt, held a more powerful grip upon the artist than did a naturalistic rendering. Possibly actual rather than visual truth appealed more strongly. For example, the artist knew that a man had two arms although in a profile he could

chapel near Meidum. IV Dynasty (2900–2750 B.C.). Cairo Museum.

see but one; and his instinct bade him indicate the fact rather than record the visual image. In the case of *Hesire*, the feeling of distortion is not disconcerting, so skillfully has the artist united the parts and so compelling, decoratively, is the entire panel. In this relief, we feel the proud bearing of a noble and also the strength of a man of determination. Note the individualized face, with its high cheekbones and firm mouth; the careful modeling about the neck, shoulders, and knees; and the firmness and strength of the carving.

D. PAINTING

In the Old Kingdom [1] painting as distinct from colored stone carving is seldom found, the best-known example being the *Geese of Meidum* (FIG. 47). On a panel are two pairs of waddling ducks and geese feeding; small clumps of herbage are scantily suggested. The artist who painted this panel had observed ducks and geese closely enough to be familiar with the clumsy gait and the "grave self-sufficiency" of the ducks, with the curves of the neck of the goose as it bends for food and with the characteristic markings of the plumage. The significant aspects alone he has reproduced in his painting, using essential lines only and flat tones, with no light and shade and no perspective. Furthermore, he has arranged his birds in such a way that they form a composition balanced but free from monotony because of the variety in the plumage. The result is a work of superbly decorative design.

E. MINOR ARTS

The dignity and vitality of Old Kingdom building, carving, and painting repeats itself in the minor creations of the various craftsmen — the stonecutter and the goldsmith, for example. The stonecutter

[1] See note 1, p. 27. For interesting prehistoric paintings on pottery and walls, see Jean Capart, *Primitive Art in Egypt*, London, 1905, and V. G. Childe, *The Most Ancient East*, Knopf, 1929.

Fig. 49. Drilling Stone Vases. One worker remarks, "This is a beautiful vase that I am making"; the other replies, "Indeed it is."

Fig. 50. Ripple-Flaked Knife. L. c. 10 in. Brussels Museum. (Brussels Museum)

Fig. 51. Bowl, Engraved with the Name of Menes. Porphyry. D. 8 in. c. 3400 B.C. Oriental Institute, University of Chicago. (Oriental Institute)

had inherited a tradition dating far back into prehistoric times (FIG. 50); and with the invention, before 3000 B.C., of the stone-pointed drill with a shaft, fly wheel, and crank for turning (FIG. 49) and, somewhat after 3000 B.C., of the tubular drill of metal, he was enabled to produce vessels of astonishing quality for various household purposes — for the table, for storage, and for the toilet. Such hard stones as porphyry, diorite, and hematite were used, as is seen in FIG. 51, where the variegated color of the stone adds a decorative quality. A bowl like this was first shaped from the block of stone, then the inside was drilled out. If it had a wide mouth, it might be put on a wheel and ground while revolving like a bowl being shaped on a potter's wheel. Among the softer stones alabaster was widely used, not only for its attractive ivory color but also because its veining could be utilized as a decorative element, and the stone could be worked to a transparent thinness. The vessels are generally simple and rugged in shape, and vary in size from a tiny jar for unguent to great storage jars, bowls, and plates a foot in diameter. Ornament is rarely found, for the craftsman depended for his effects upon shape and proportions; and upon the material for its own intrinsic weight, color, and texture. It is an indication of the craftsman's sensitivity that we find a small unguent jar made from delicate alabaster and a large storage jar from heavy porphyry.

The goldsmith, with an abundant supply of material, had developed many ways of working it. He could cast, chase, solder, ham-

Fig. 52. Bracelet. Gold, turquoise, and amethyst. c. 3400 B.C. Cairo Museum.

Fig. 53. Head of a Hawk. Gold. H. 4 in. Cairo Museum. (Fechheimer)

mer, plait. In the bracelet of FIG. 52, for example, the cast-gold rosette, derived from the lotus flower, is joined to groups of turquoise and gold beads and large balls of amethyst, a motif repeated, except for the rosette, in the second group of beads, and the two are connected by a twisted band of hair and of gold wire that is wrought to the same diameter as the hair. Not only the technical skill — the soldering can scarcely be detected with a magnifying glass — but a sobriety of taste and design are as manifest here as in the *Pyramids* or the statue of *Khafre*. So also a hawk's head (FIG. 53), originally attached to a bronze body by rivets still left just below the neck. Here the goldsmith has hammered the metal into shape, probably over a mold, soldered the parts together, and inserted eyes cut from red jasper. Like the painter of the *Geese of Meidum* (FIG. 47), he had observed his bird form well, and with an amazing economy of modeling has given expression to the essential form and character of the hawk.

To take one more example, a ceremonial vase from one of the pyramids at Abusir (FIG. 54) shows the combined craft of the goldsmith and the lapidary. In making this vase the artist first cut out a wooden core, which he covered with gold, and then inlaid the metal with blue lapis lazuli. The design on the neck and the band just below the shoulder, derived from the iridescent peacock plumage, unifies the composition and also emphasizes the hieroglyphs that are arranged so decoratively on the shoulder of the vase. The elegance of the shape the artist has enhanced by making his design follow the structural lines, at the same time obtaining a balance of vertical and horizontal line by a zonal arrangement.

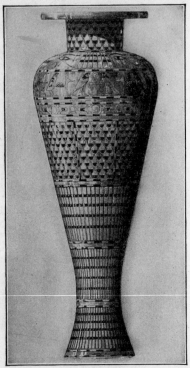

Fig. 54. Ceremonial Vase, Restored.
Of gold and lapis lazuli. H. c. 2 ft.
c. 2750 B.C. (Stoedtner)

F. SUMMARY

By the beginning of the Old Kingdom those conventions had been
established which controlled, with
but one important break, at the
time of the Empire, the long course
of Egyptian art. The builders of
the Old Kingdom were primarily
tomb-builders, and their stone tombs
are still massive, static, and enduring, thoroughly in harmony with
their site and function. Into them
fitted the imposing portrait sculpture that was required by religious
belief, conventional in form and
conception, tending to the abstract,
filled with living reality. The paintings and painted reliefs were based
upon conventions, mental rather
than visual concepts of the world,
keen observer and lover though the
Egyptian was of his own immediate
environment; they were finely chiseled, gaily decorative, and teeming
with eager life. The minor arts provide additional evidence of sensitivity to material and of effective
design through the use of conventional forms. Each, whether minor
or major, is a directly forceful expression of great decorative beauty,
of dignity and sobriety, and of extraordinary craftsmanship.

(For Bibliography see p. 71.)

2. THE MIDDLE KINGDOM AND EMPIRE (2160–1090 B.C.)

A. HISTORICAL BACKGROUND

The tendency toward weakening the power of the pharaoh to the
advantage of the nobles had plunged the country into a period of
struggle and disorder. Out of this eventually arose a feudal state, at
the head of which still stood the pharaoh; but he maintained his power
by balancing the nobles one against another. Economically it was a
period of great prosperity. Agriculture was developed by building canals

and reclaiming the land; commerce was carried on not only in the south but also with Asia and the Aegean islands. And now Egypt became a military power. Athirst for conquests, it extended its boundaries not only far south into Nubia but east to the Euphrates. So on the monuments

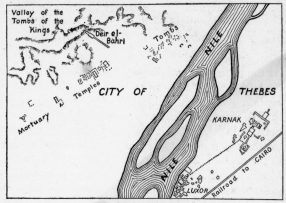

Fig. 55. Map of Thebes, showing the most important temples and tombs. The dwellings have disappeared.

we see military subjects: weapons, chariots, and the horse, which, coming with the pre-Indo-Europeans from the grasslands of central Asia, finally reached the Nile Valley about 1700 B.C. The wealth that came from the booty taken in these wars made possible the development of the capital city, Thebes, into a great metropolis with magnificent palaces, tombs, and temples ranged along both banks of the river (FIGS. 24, 55).

A considerable advance had been made in thought and religion. The Egyptian could now look back over his own history for centuries. The fresh and vital faith of the Pyramid Age, in the light of the futility of man's greatest efforts, changed to pessimism, which is reflected in the portraits of the age (FIG. 78) and also in the literature.

"I have heard the words of Imhotep and Harzozef,
 Whose utterances are of much reputation;
 Yet how are the places thereof?
 Their walls are in ruin,
 Their places are no more, —
 As if they had never been.
 None cometh from thence,
 That he might tell us of their state;
 That he might restore our hearts,
 Until we too depart to the place,
 Whither they have gone.
 Encourage thy heart to forget it,
 And let the heart dwell upon that which is profitable for thee.
 Follow thy desire while thou livest,

.   .   .   .

Celebrate the glad day!
Rest not therein!
For lo, none taketh his goods with him,
Yea, no man returneth again, that is gone thither." [1]

At the same time we discern a new note in reference to the future life; for to the earlier faith in the possibility of a hereafter was added a conception of a day of judgment when the final weighing of the deeds of this life would condition the next. Hence, on the tombs we find inscriptions of this kind: "I gave bread to the hungry, water to the thirsty, clothing to the naked, and a ferryboat to the boatless." "I was father to the orphan, husband to the widow, and a shelter to the shelterless." Magic formulae were written on papyrus and buried with the dead to assist him on the judgment day as he stood before Osiris for the weighing of his deeds. This practice, however, led to great corruption on the part of the priests, from whom it was possible to purchase formulae by which evil deeds would not testify against a man.

It was an age also of the development of folk tales, when stories of adventures and of animals took shape, forming the basis of the tales of Sinbad the Sailor, and Brer Fox and Brer Rabbit.

This broadening horizon of thought and the growth of the idea of world-empire fired the imagination of a young king (1375–1358 B.C.), who, applying the principle of political power to the realm of religion, conceived the idea of one god and creator, whom he called Aton, an old name of the sun god Re. He then broke both politically and religiously with the powerful though corrupt priesthood at Thebes, took for himself the name Ikhnaton, which means "spirit of Aton," and set up a new capitol at a place that he called Akhetaton (now known as Amarna) meaning "Horizon of Aton." Something of the spirit of the new faith we feel in the hymns that Ikhnaton wrote:

The Splendor of Aton

"Thy dawning is beautiful in the horizon of heaven,
    O living Aton, Beginning of life!
When thou risest in the eastern horizon of heaven,
    Thou fillest every land with thy beauty;
    For thou art beautiful, great, glittering, high over the earth;
    Thy rays, they encompass the lands, even all thou hast made.

.   .   .   .

How manifold are all thy works!
    They are hidden from before us,
    O thou sole god, whose powers no other possesseth.

[1] J. H. Breasted, *A History of Egypt from the Earliest Times to the Persian Conquest*, Scribner, 1924, p. 206.

Thou didst create the earth according to thy desire,
While thou wast alone:
Men, all cattle large and small,
All that are upon the earth,
That fly with their wings,
The countries of Syria and Nubia,
The land of Egypt.
Thou settest every man in his place,
Thou suppliest their necessities." [1]

Egypt by this time, however, was too crystallized by the traditions of thousands of years, too enthralled by its nobles, military leaders, and particularly by the powerful priesthood of Amon, to accept an idea so contrary to tradition. Ikhnaton, by nature not a practical man of affairs, became absorbed entirely in the religion of Aton. The result was that, through upheavals at home and invasions from without, the empire dwindled while its ruler pursued his monotheistic ideals. At his death the power at Thebes was restored and the empire partly reorganized by Seti I (1313–1292 B.C.) and Ramses II, the Great (1292–1225 B.C.), but it was never firmly reëstablished. Egyptian history continues long after this time, but in art, after the time of Ramses the Great there is little that we have not already seen in the periods we have studied.

Life in "Hundred-gated Thebes" and at Amarna, too, was luxurious and magnificent. The enormous wealth of the pharaoh enabled him to erect a palace with decorations that reproduced for him the outdoor world in which he delighted. On the floors and walls, which were painted or decorated in glazed tiles, were represented ducks swimming in the water and the animal life of the marshes (FIG. 89); across the deep-blue background of the ceiling flew flocks of birds, and butterflies. The furniture was superbly designed and skillfully constructed (Figs. 91, 92). Magnificent gold and silver vessels, blue faïence lotus cups, glass vases of various colors, rich jewelry (FIGS. 93–103) — all these tell of a magnificence quite in contrast to the sterner dignity of the Pyramid Age.

B. ARCHITECTURE

As the Old Kingdom was preëminently the period of the pyramid-builder, so the Middle Kingdom and Empire were that of the temple-builder. This was not because burial no longer demanded the elaborate

[1] Breasted, *op. cit.*, pp. 371 ff., where a complete translation is given, in a parallel arrangement with one of the Hebrew Psalms, which it approximates to an amazing degree.

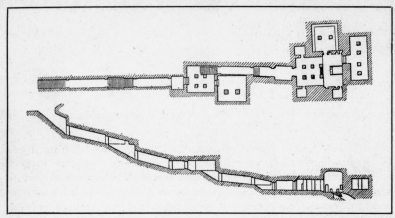

Fig. 56. Tomb of Seti I. Section and plan. Thebes, Valley of the Tombs
of the Kings. XIX Dynasty (1350–1205 B.C.). (Benoit)

care shown earlier. An even more scrupulous attention was given to
the protection of the body, but in a different way. Robberies and
neglect had shown the futility of the pyramid for perfect preservation;
and while pyramids continued to be built by the earlier pharaohs of
the period, they were small, and made of brick. Today they are little
more than mounds, though their substructures have yielded rich finds
of jewelry and other mortuary equipment.

The nobles no longer sought a locality for burial near that of the
king, but hollowed out their tombs and chapels in the cliffs bordering
the Nile. The pharaohs themselves, perhaps following the example of
their retainers, chose for their burial site a wild, desolate valley west
of the cliffs at Thebes now known as the Valley of the Tombs of the
Kings (FIG. 55), where deep in the rocky hills they carved burial
chambers which were reached by long corridors sometimes extending
five hundred feet into the hillside (FIG. 56).[1] The entrances were carefully concealed; and because of the impracticability of making offerings
at the actual tombs, the mortuary temples, which correspond to the
chapel abutting the eastern side of the pyramid, were separated from
the tombs and built on the eastern side of the cliffs along the bank of
the river; but in each case the temple was on the axis of the tomb and
hence in the same relative position as the pyramid chapel. Furthermore, these temples were dedicated to the gods, and each provided the
king who built it with a place for worshiping his patron god during
his lifetime, and then served as his mortuary chapel after death. Hence

[1] The *Tomb of Tutenkhamon*, discovered in the valley in 1922, is a rock-cut tomb of
this type.

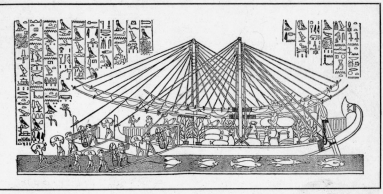

Fig. 57. Deir el-Bahri. Relief showing the loading of the ships in Punt. An inscription reads: "The loading of the ships very heavily with marvels of the country of Punt; all goodly fragrant woods of God's-Land, heaps of myrrh-resin, with fresh myrrh trees, with ebony and pure ivory, with green gold of Emu, with cinnamon wood, khesyt wood, with ihmut-incense, sonter-incense, eye-cosmetic, with apes, monkeys, dogs, and with skins of the southern panther, with natives and their children. Never was brought the like of this for any king who has been since the beginning." Breasted, *Ancient Records of Egypt*, II, 265. (Egypt Exploration Society)

they became elaborate and sumptuous, befitting both the kings and the gods of a mighty empire.

The noblest of these royal mortuary temples, though untypical in some ways, is *Deir el-Bahri*,[1] the temple of Queen Hatshepsut (Fig. 58). The site that the Queen selected for her temple was a sloping bay in the western cliffs (Fig. 55), above which towered the rocks weathered into columnar shapes, the vertical lines of which contrast happily with the long horizontals of the plateau edge, while the rough surfaces afford deep shadows and a more broken mass of light and shade than is usual in Egypt. Mindful of these conditions, Hatshepsut and her architect Senmut built the temple in a series of colonnaded terraces connected by ramps and rising to the very cliffs in which were cut the sanctuary and shrines. Notice in the distant view how effectively the long horizontals and verticals of the colonnades and their rhythm of light and dark repeat the pattern of the cliffs above — an intentional relationship between the architectural design and its natural setting.

In reconstructing this temple as it was in Hatshepsut's day, we must picture these terraces not as the barren places they now are, but as luxuriant gardens, filled with frankincense trees and strange, rare plants brought here from the faraway land of Punt. The Queen tells

---

[1] *Deir el-Bahri*, meaning "The North Monastery," is the modern Arab name of the locality, from a monastery, now destroyed, that was built on the site.

Fig. 58. Temple of Queen Hatshepsut. Deir el-Bahri.
XVIII Dynasty (1580–1350 B.C.)

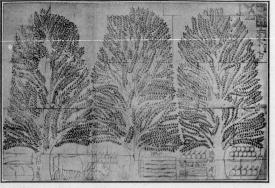

Fig. 59. Deir el-Bahri. Frankincense trees. (Naville)

us in the inscriptions and reliefs on the walls of the temple how she sent an expedition of ships to this country (FIG. 57) at the command of Amon-Re, to obtain the plants:

"I will cause you to know that which is commanded to me, I have hearkened to my father . . . commanding me to establish for him a Punt in his house, to plant the trees of God's-Land beside his temple, in his garden, according as he commanded. It was done . . . I have made for him a Punt in his garden, just as he commanded me, for Thebes. It is large for him, he walks about in it." [1]

Consistency and a reserved taste both in the general plan and in every part give this temple a striking unity and quiet dignity. In the colonnades, for example, the pillars are either simply rectangular or chamfered off into sixteen sides rather than of the more elaborate lotus or papyrus form, and are sensitively proportioned and spaced. The great amount of sculpture that adorned the temple is very definitely an integral part of the entire design. The statues in the round,[2]

[1] J. H. Breasted, *Ancient Records of Egypt*, University of Chicago Press, 1906–07, 5 vols., Vol. II, p. 295.

[2] Many of these statues have been found in a badly broken condition by the Egyptian Expedition of the Metropolitan Museum of Art and are being reconstructed in that museum. See "The Egyptian Expedition 1930–1931," Metropolitan Museum

perhaps two hundred in number — sphinxes guarding the approach, statues of the Queen flanking the doorways and the pillars or kneeling along the procession path — are purely architectural in their simple masses, as are the painted low reliefs (FIGS. 59, 60) which cover all the walls. The bright color and the gardens, however, add a vivacious note. "It was a gorgeous way up which the procession of Amon passed. . . . In its brilliancy under the Egyptian skies the long vista must have been a magnificent reiteration of a claim to almost superhuman power." [1]

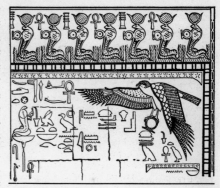

Fig. 60. Deir el-Bahri. Polychrome decoration showing the hawk of lower Egypt that hovers protectingly about the pharaoh. The motif of the border is the *uræus* combined with the sundisk. The figures are painted in bright colors, chiefly red and blue, with a little green and yellow. (Naville)

The typical Egyptian temple to the gods we shall illustrate by a small temple at *Edfu* (FIGS. 61, 62, 63), because of its clear plan and its excellent state of preservation. To one approaching, the dominating feature is the great façade, or pylon, which is simple, massive, with sloping walls and generally unbroken lines. The broad surface too is unbroken, except for the doorway with its overshadowing cornice, the four grooves to hold the great flagstaffs, and the low reliefs. A round molding finishes both the top and the sides. Passing through the doorway, we enter an open court surrounded on three sides by a colonnade. Beyond rises a roofed hall, the hypostyle hall, where the cool dimness contrasting with the bright sunshine of the open court, together with the rhythm of the massive shafts, inspires a feeling of solemnity. Still farther beyond lies the sanctuary, low, dark, mysterious, and secluded. A girdle wall, beginning at the pylon, surrounds the structure. This temple at *Edfu* shows us then the general arrangement of a typical pylon temple (FIG. 64), which always includes a pylon, an open colonnaded court, a hypostyle hall, a sanctuary, which is sometimes surrounded by smaller chambers for the storage of the temple treasures and for the use of the priests, and a girdle wall.

of Art, *Bulletin*, March, 1932, Sec. II; "The Egyptian Expedition 1928–1929," *Ibid.*, November, 1929, Sec. II; and the *Bulletin* for April, 1932.
   [1] "The Egyptian Expedition 1930–1931," Metropolitan Museum of Art, *Bulletin*, March, 1932, Sec. II, p. 14.

Fig. 61. Temple of Horus. Edfu. View from the side, showing the pylon and open court. (Gaddis and Seif)

Fig. 62. Temple of Horus. Edfu. View from the top of the pylon, showing part of the open court, the hypostyle hall, sanctuary, and girdle wall. (Gaddis and Seif)

This plan quite definitely evolved from ritualistic requirements. Egyptian religious practices were not congregational, as were the Greek, the Buddhist, or the Christian. Only the pharaoh and the priest could enter or view the sanctuary; a chosen few were admitted to the hypostyle hall; the masses, only into the open court; the girdle wall shut off the entire site from the outside world. The passage, which became progressively mysterious, from the large sunlit court to the small secret unseen sanctuary, naturally inspired a feeling of solemnity and awe.

From this essential plan, once evolved, the conservative Egyptian did not deviate for hundreds of years, even after the Greeks and the Romans brought other ideas into the Nile Valley.

It is not surprising to find that the Egyptian temple, like the pyramid, is simple and massive, when we recall again the geographic conditions of the country — that narrow strip of luxuriant river valley, bordered on both sides by vast sterile deserts; a landscape of predominantly horizontal lines; and over all a continuously clear sky and overwhelming sunshine. Protection from the heat demanded thick walls with few apertures, and covered colonnades. So the temple in its outline presents a sternly simple mass of horizontal and vertical lines with great unbroken surfaces of wall space. But as we walk around the building and see its ornamentation and reconstruct in our own minds those parts of its decoration which are now lost, we realize that in addition to the simple mass and unbroken line there is a wealth of decorative detail which not only affords a contrast but also enhances through its richness. Low reliefs painted in bright colors [1] cover the long reaches of wall space both inside and outside, producing a vibrant surface, without, however, destroying the feeling of solidity in the wall. The approach is along a broad avenue bordered on both sides by statues of recumbent rams with metal disks between their horns. In front of the massive pylon stand two obelisks (FIG. 64) nearly a hundred feet high, covered with hieroglyphs, their glittering metal tips catching and reflecting the sunshine. On each side of the doorway stands a colossal statue of the pharaoh, harmonizing in its simple massiveness with the massive pylon; in the grooves rest the huge wooden staffs that carry the flags floating above the cornice. The great door of cedar of Lebanon is inlaid with shining metal, while surrounding and framing the whole structure are the rich green masses of palms and the brilliant sky. A magnificent and awe-inspiring sight.

The two most famous temples of the Empire are *Luxor* and *Karnak* (FIG. 66). If we look at these closely, we shall see that they are merely complex arrangements of the simple plan of *Edfu;* for it became the custom for each succeeding pharaoh to add to

[1] This color has almost disappeared. Certain walls of the *Temple of Seti I* at Abydos retain enough to give an excellent idea of the extraordinary effectiveness of the Egyptian type of mural decoration.

Fig. 63. Temple of Horus. Edfu. View from the back of the temple toward the pylon.

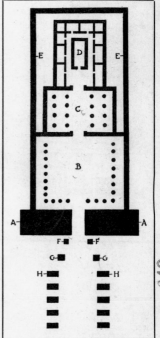

Fig. 64. Plan of a Typical Pylon Temple. *A*, pylon; *B*, court; *C*, hypostyle hall; *D*, sanctuary; *E*, girdle wall; *F*, colossal statues of the pharaoh; *G*, obelisks; *H*, avenue of recumbent animals.

his glory by build-ing an additional hypostyle hall or pylon for what was already a com-plete temple. One fact only needs to be mentioned that *Edfu* does not il-lustrate. In the hypostyle hall of *Karnak* (FIG. 65) the central rows of columns are higher than the side rows, which means that the roof over the cen-ter is higher than that on the sides. The wall space connecting these two levels is filled with perforated stone windows. Here is a fully developed clere-story, the begin-nings of which we saw in the valley-temple of the *Pyr-amid of Khafre* (FIGS. 34, 36).

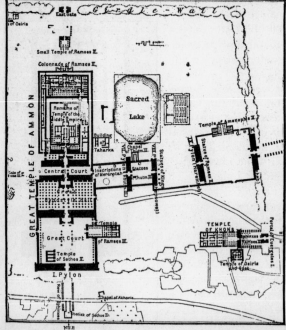

Fig. 66. Temple of Amon. Karnak. In process of building, for c. 2000 years, to the I cent. B.C. Ramses I, Seti I, and Ramses II, all of the XIX Dynasty (1350–1205 B.C.), built the great hypostyle hall. (Baedeker)

The decorative motifs that the Egyptian used in the embellish-ment of his temples were taken chiefly from the lotus, the papyrus, and the palm. The palm we saw used in the colonnade of the *Pyra-*

Fig. 67. Temple of Amon. Karnak. Central aisle of the hypostyle hall. The columns are 66 ft. high, and the capitals 22 ft. wide at the top. XIX Dynasty (1350–1205 B.C.). (Gaddis and Seif)

mid of Sahure (FIG. 38). The lotus was very popular with the Egyptians. We see children gathering it in the streams while the elders enjoy the perfume, weave it into garlands, or mass bunches of it over the water jars, to keep the water fresh. Two varieties chiefly were used as decorative motifs, the blue and the white. The craftsmen used its form to shape their cups and to fashion their cosmetic boxes; they carved it from ivory, wove it into their textiles, and molded it for glazed wall tiles. So, too, the builders employed it to decorate their columns (FIG. 68) — not with the highest success, however, as is shown especially in the lotus flower capital, where the spreading petals militate against the feeling of solidity and stability that should characterize a member whose function is to support. More successful is the cluster of buds.

The papyrus plant (FIG. 69), now extinct in Egypt but in early days plentiful, produced a flower whose feathery petals formed a bell-shaped mass. The columns forming the central row of the hypostyle hall of *Luxor* (FIG. 70) have capitals the shape of which has been suggested by the papyrus flower, while the columns of the colonnade in the background are based on a cluster of papyrus buds. The stems of this cluster are tied tightly below the buds, whose swelling contours form the capital. Were it not for this broad band to hold the stems

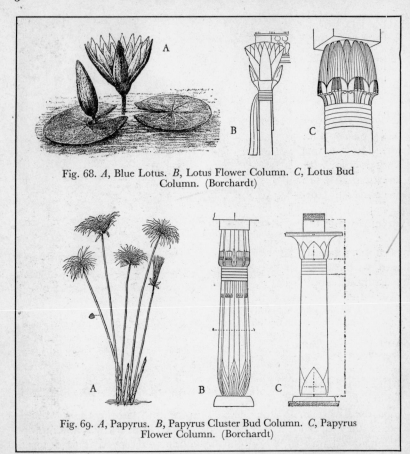

Fig. 68. *A*, Blue Lotus. *B*, Lotus Flower Column. *C*, Lotus Bud Column. (Borchardt)

Fig. 69. *A*, Papyrus. *B*, Papyrus Cluster Bud Column. *C*, Papyrus Flower Column. (Borchardt)

firmly together, the shaft would give one a feeling of insecurity by seeming incapable of performing its function of support. The shafts of both the flower and the bud type contract at the base, as does the stem of the plant; for the Egyptian, when conventionalizing his plant forms, closely observed nature. In design, proportions, and work-manship, these colonnades at *Luxor* are among the noblest to be found in the pylon temples.

The more apparent does this become when we turn to the hypostyle hall of *Karnak* (FIG. 67). Here, according to the usual convention, the columns of the central aisle are of the papyrus flower type; those of the side aisles, of the papyrus bud. But compare the latter with the bud type at *Luxor*. At *Karnak*, only the general contour of the

Fig. 70. Temple of Amon. Luxor. Right: central colonnade of an unfinished hypostyle hall; center and left: double colonnaded court. XVIII Dynasty (1580–1350 B.C.). (Gaddis and Seif)

cluster has been retained, producing a heavy, ungainly shaft. It is as if the architects, in haste to complete this mighty hall, were depending upon bulk and barbaric splendor to create an effect. And, indeed, they were partly successful in their attempt, for notwithstanding the shabby workmanship a certain overwhelming impressiveness results from the mere number and size of these mighty shafts.[1]

[1] It is interesting to note that the Egyptian did not use cement in these gigantic structures, but depended upon the huge weight of the stones to hold them in place. For his technical methods of lifting these stones to such heights, see Somers Clarke and Reginald Engelbach, *Ancient Egyptian Masonry*, Oxford Press, 1930.

Fig. 71. Temple of Amon. Luxor. Pylon, with statues of the pharaoh, both standing and seated, and one obelisk; the companion obelisk now stands in Paris. XIX Dynasty (1350–1205 B.C.). (Gaddis and Seif)

Fig. 72. Rock-Cut Temple of Ramses II. Abu Simbel. Seated statues of
Ramses 66 ft. high. (Oriental Institute of the University of Chicago)

Equally impressive and architecturally fitting is the colossal sculpture
used at the entrance and in various parts of the temple — masses of
stone as simply geometric as the pylon itself but at the same time portraits, impersonal to be sure, of the pharaoh (FIGS. 71, 72).

The domestic architecture of the Empire,[1] though but scantily preserved because of the perishable materials of which most of it was
constructed, appears to have presented to the eye as simple geometric
masses and unbroken lines as the temples (FIG. 73). Because the windows were few and small, a central hall rising above the other rooms
afforded a clerestory for lighting; and the flat roof was utilized for an
open loggia, or for a garden when the houses were packed closely together in the crowded city. In a royal palace such as that at *Medinet
Habu* there was every comfort and luxury, including a private bath
with each room, as well as a grandly impressive audience hall (FIG. 74)
reminiscent of the temple hypostyle hall. In this audience hall an important note is the roof, which is vaulted rather than made of lintels as
in the temple hall.[2]

[1] For domestic architecture see "The Town House in Ancient Egypt" by N. de G.
Davies, *Metropolitan Museum Studies*, Vol. I, Pt. II, 1928–29; Henri Frankfort on private
houses in Amarna, *Journal of Egyptian Archaeology*, November, 1922, pp. 144–49; and the
Medinet Habu publications of the Oriental Institute of the University of Chicago relating
to the palace of Ramses III (reports available; folios with color plates in preparation).
[2] The Egyptian understood the arch, but used it chiefly in substructures.

Fig. 73. Reconstructed Town Houses at Amarna. The conical objects in front of the houses are corncribs with steps for filling from the top. (*Journal of Egyptian Archaeology*)

Fig. 74. Reconstructed Audience Hall in the Palace of Ramses III at Medinet Habu, Thebes. XX Dynasty (1198–1167 B.C.). (Oriental Institute of the University of Chicago)

C. SCULPTURE

Besides colossal architectural sculpture in the round at the entrances, reliefs covered the temple walls; on the inside with representations of a religious nature, such as the king making offerings to the god; on the outside with records of the pharaoh's wars and hunts. In the tombs were scenes relating to the life of the dead. In the *Funeral Procession* (FIG. 75), for example, the figures are arranged as usual in zones. But the grouping is becoming a little more complex, with more overlapping of the figures. In the lower zone at the right are the two sons of the deceased, following the bier. Their figures are superb expressions of abandonment to grief, in marked contrast to the elegant formality of the nobles behind them. Such an expression of emotion in itself shows a great change in Egyptian art. Furthermore, the freedom with which the body is made to express the emotion, and the surprisingly good drawing here seen, the greater ease and

Fig. 75. Funeral Procession of a High Priest. Upper zone: garden scene, servants setting up the funeral booth; lower zone: funeral procession. XVIII Dynasty (1580–1350 B.C.). Staatliche Museum, Berlin. (Staatliche Museum)

Fig. 76. Osiris and Goddesses. XIX Dynasty (1350–1205 B.C.). Temple of Seti, Abydos. (Kodak)

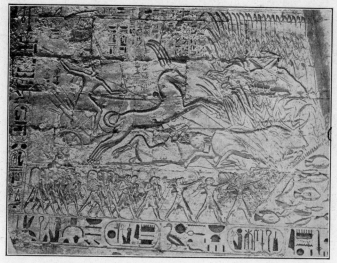

Fig. 77. Wild Bull Hunt. On the pylon of the Temple of Ramses III at
Medinet Habu, Thebes. XX Dynasty (1198–1167 B.C.)

facility of line, in contrast to the angularity of the Old Kingdom
reliefs, are indications that the sculptors were turning to nature rather
than following implicitly the traditional methods of representation.
Note here that the ground is not cut away, leaving the figures in relief, but that a deep groove is chiseled along the contours, giving the
effect of a heavy line. Notice also the more elaborate costume of the
Empire period.

The naturalistic tendency seen in such a relief received powerful
impetus from Ikhnaton's revolution. The new faith with its conception of a sole creator of all life turned men's attention to nature and
lifted art expression above mere traditional convention. But reaction
in art as well as in religion set in after the failure of the revolution.
The priests of Amon had triumphed. Not only did they attempt to
eradicate the heresy by destroying the works of art created by the
Amarna artists, and by removing from them all references to the hated
Aton, but they enshackled the artists with their dogmatic conceptions
even more securely than before. For it was the priests who controlled
both the subject and the method of representation. Still, even with
these restrictions, a brief period of high attainment was reached by
the Egyptians before their art was strangled by crystallizing conventions, as we see in the *Wild Bull Hunt* (FIG. 77), in which the king
is spearing bulls in the swamps along the river (indicated by fish in
the corner). Above a base of spearmen and archers moving with

Fig. 78. Amenemhet III. Obsidian. H. c. 5 in. XII Dynasty (2000–1788 B.C.). MacGregor coll., Tamworth. (*Journal of Egyptian Archaeology*)

Fig. 79. Ikhnaton. Painted sandstone. H. c. 8 in. 1375–1358 B.C. Staatliche Museum, Berlin. (Grantz)

vigorous rhythmic swing, the zonal arangement gives way to the large panel of the pharaoh in his chariot and three animals carved with bold vigor, the chariot group in terms of the old convention, the animals with extraordinary visual reality; and all tied together in a compositional unity.

The wall decorations in the *Temple of Seti I* at Abydos (FIG. 76), on the other hand, illustrate the crystallized convention. The figures are highly conventional in form, but the carving is very sure, with graceful sweep of contour and softly rounded relief which casts delicate shadows. With no interior modeling and no feeling for structure (note that both hands are the right), the figure has become a highly stylized convention, affected, stilted, entirely lacking in the vivacity of the Old Kingdom reliefs. Yet the entire wall space, with the sensitively related panels, the beauty of the carving, and the color laid on flat in large areas, stands as a superb piece of mural decoration.

The portraits reveal a naturalizing tendency; the individual, with his idiosyncracies and emotions, is emerging from the Old Kingdom generalizations and abstractions. In *Amenemhet III* (FIG. 78) we see not only the warrior and the ruler, but the individual man who lived and thought intensely. In the strong mouth, the drooping lines about the nose and eyes, and the shadowing brows, we discern a man who, though still powerful, has lost faith. "In all his energetic effigies is cast a shadow as of one who had lived to see the extinction of some great hope, or the dawn of some great threat." The head is carved

Fig. 80. General Harmhab. Represented as a contemplative scribe. Of gray granite, 3 ft. 10 in. high. XVIII Dynasty (1580–1350 B.C.). Metropolitan Museum, New York. (Metropolitan Museum)

Fig. 81. Selkit. A guardian goddess from the tomb of Tutenkhamon. Wood overlaid with gold. Height 2 ft. Cairo Museum. (Howard Carter)

in obsidian (note its reflective quality), a stone so obdurate that it must have put to the test the most accomplished skill in cutting, grinding, and polishing; yet so large and powerful is the characterization that the diminutive size becomes colossal in its impressiveness.

In the head of *Ikhnaton* (FIG. 79) we do not feel primarily the ruler or even the official class to which this man belongs. What is significant is the thoroughly human characterization of that remarkable young king; emphasizing, in the pose of the head, the long neck, the drooping mouth and lids, and in the almost effeminate delicacy, the essential elements of his character, which was first of all that of the dreamer and idealist.

For the expression of individual charm, the head of *Nofretete* (Color Plate I, opposite p. 40), wife of Ikhnaton, stands preëminent. In the long slender neck, the sensitive mouth, and the delicate modeling, one feels an aristocratic, queenly bearing combined with a simple, unaffected grace. A use of color that is more conventional than naturalistic differentiates and relates the parts; and places emphasis upon the recurrent themes of cylindrical masses and curves.

When we compare these three heads with those of *Khafre*, *Ranofer*, and the *Princess*, we observe a striking difference. We miss the vivacity, the alertness, and the serene grandeur of the earlier work, in which

Fig. 82. Wrestlers. Beni Hasan.
(Egypt Exploration Society)

Fig. 83. Wall Decoration of a Tomb. Beni Hasan. Detail of right side showing the noble harpooning fish. (Egypt Exploration Society)

individuality, though present, is subordinated to the abstract idea of sovereignty or nobility. In its place we find that the chief aim of the artist has been to express the significant characteristics of the individual, his emotions and his inner life.

The revolutionary character of the Amarna school is strikingly illustrated by the titulary goddesses from the *Tomb of Tutenkhamon* (FIG. 81), in which the turn of the head is a hint, rare in Egyptian sculpture, of a truly three-dimensional quality.[1] But the hint never became articulate. In the *Harmhab* (FIG. 80) is an adherence to the traditional pose, yet with differences, as in the affectation, verging on effeminacy, in the boyish features (a style affected as an Ikhnaton influence), and in the stooped shoulders which produce a meditative air. In fact there is a hint of elegant artificiality in the *Harmhab* that is entirely absent from the straightforward, alert, square-shouldered Old Kingdom *Scribe* (FIG. 43). But in the *Harmhab* is beautiful stonecutting. An organization of rounded masses is tied to a rectangular base. (Note the repetition of the base in the lower part of the figure.) On its surfaces are chiseled, delicately and firmly, various conventional devices for hair, linen, and flesh which follow and accent the movement of the surfaces,

[1] Though all statues in the round actually possess depth, by no means do all of them give a visual impression of unity in space. Most Egyptian statues are distinctly four-sided, like four reliefs carved on the four sides of the block of stone. On this see Adolf Hildebrand, *The Problem of Form in Painting and Sculpture*, Stechert, 1932.

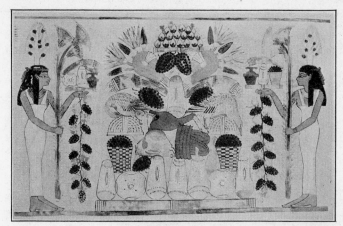

Fig. 84. Group of Offerings. From the tomb of Nakht (Fig. 85). (Metropolitan Museum)

as well as represent with thorough consistency a wig, an XVIIIth Dynasty linen costume, and folds of flesh.

D. PAINTING

Although painting had been practiced in Egypt from prehistoric times, in the Old Kingdom it functioned more as an accessory to relief than as an independent art. In the Middle Kingdom and the Empire, however, the painters began to omit the relief and to paint directly on the wall, partly because the walls of the tombs excavated in the cliffs were too coarse and rough for carving and partly because of the greater ease

Fig. 85. Tomb of Nakht. Thebes. XVIII Dynasty (1580–1350 B.C.). (Metropolitan Museum)

and freedom of the brush over the chisel. The rough walls were covered with stucco and plaster, on which the figures were drawn in firm

Fig. 86. Painted Decoration of a Tomb Ceiling.

outline with the help of squaring for proportioning (Fig. 45), and the inclosed space was filled in with flat color. This was not true fresco, for the pigments were mixed with some binding medium such as gum and applied to a dry surface. It was an art of tomb and palace decoration; in the tomb it served a magic purpose, also, as in the Old Kingdom. There were many stock subjects, such as hunting and banquet scenes. In Fig. 83, for instance, the noble is out in the papyrus marsh in his reed boat, harpooning fish. His figure is expressed in the conventional way, as was proper for one of his station. In the river scene below, however, there is a freedom of action that reveals the capacity of a conventional figure to express all kinds of movement. This is also evident in the *Wrestlers* (Fig. 82), though here and there one discerns an attempt on the part of the painter to break with convention and approximate visual appearance. Yet after all, this attempt changes but little the general pattern of the figure whose varied repetition creates so stirring and so decorative a wall surface.

Fig. 85 gives us a glimpse into a tomb [1] whose decorative scheme is based on a system of a dado, four zones, and a border, with a zigzag ceiling pattern which copies the ceiling decoration of an Egyptian house (see also Fig. 86). The zonal arrangement is ordered into a symmetrical balance about the false door which was provided for the spirit to enter in order to receive the offerings presented by the kneeling figures and heaped up in the lower zone (Fig. 84). Like that of the human

[1] For fine color reproductions of this tomb, see N. de G. Davies, *The Tomb of Nakht at Thebes*, Metropolitan Museum of Art, 1917.

Fig. 87. Banquet Scene.
From the tomb of Nakht,
Thebes. XVIII Dynasty
(1580–1350 B.C.).

Fig. 88. Fowling Scene.
From a Theban tomb.
XVIII Dynasty (1580–
1350 B.C.). British Mu-
seum, London. (British
Museum)

figure, the drawing of the objects is not based upon visual perception
from a consistent point of view but upon traditional conventions. Of
these objects — loaves of bread, onions, grapes, fowl, quarters of meat,
lotus, papyrus — some are seen in profile, some in front view, some
from above; but are all combined into a pattern of subtly varied symmetry and great esthetic power through the repetition with variation
of shape, motif, color, value, texture. Here a perfectly intelligible expression of symbolic meaning that penetrated deeply into contemporary life is combined with a powerful esthetic expression, quite abstract
in character. On the side walls the formality is broken by the large

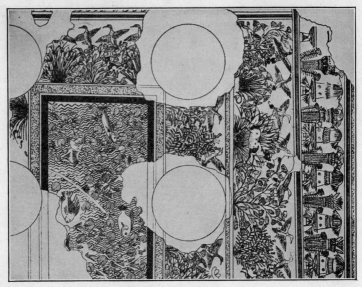

Fig. 89. Painted Floor Decoration. Detail. From the palace of Ikhnaton. Amarna. (Petrie)

figures of the noble and his wife and by the vivacious scenes of agriculture and stock-raising. On the opposite wall (not seen in the illustration) is a *Banquet Scene* (FIG. 87), where six guests are seated upon mats near a blind harper. They wear long, thin garments, wigs held by fillets, and on the crown of the head a conical object containing perfumed unguent; they have wreathed lotus flowers about their heads or hold the flowers in their hands; all wear elaborate collar-necklaces and large disk earrings, one of which a little serving-maid is adjusting. There is greater freedom of pose and variety of movement here than in Old Kingdom work, and a suavely flowing line that has a beauty of its own. The figures overlap and are related compositionally, line, shape, and color repeating, varying, and contrasting. This is also true in a *Fowling Scene* (FIG. 88) in which the noble is standing in his boat and with his boomerang is driving the birds from the papyrus swamp. In his right hand he holds three birds that he has caught, while his hunting cat, on a papyrus stem just in front of him, has caught two more in her claws and is holding the wings of a third with her teeth. His two companions, perhaps his wife and little daughter, are enjoying the lotus that they have gathered. While the water and the figures are represented by the usual conventions, the cat, fish, and birds show a trend toward a naturalism based upon visual perception.

Fig. 90. Papyrus Marsh. From the Northern Palace at
Amarna. Age of Ikhnaton. The niches may have been resting-
places for birds. (Metropolitan Museum)

This tendency to naturalism received great impetus, as did sculpture, from Ikhnaton. In his own palace at Amarna, for example, the
floor decoration of one room represented a pool of water surrounded
by the appropriate zones of life and vegetation (Fig. 89). In the center
is the pool, with birds, fish, and aquatic plants; bordering this is the
marshland with birds flying about; beyond, the meadow land with
tall grasses through which calves are running. All the forms, both
plant and animal, are painted with a new freedom. An illusion of
nature, however, does not dominate; for the Egyptian's never failing
sense of design has grouped the scenes into an orderly arrangement by
inclosing them with firm lines and a conventional outer border, so
that representation and decoration are happily blended.

A quite remarkable instance of the Egyptian's attempt to combine
visual perception with traditional convention is found in the wall
decoration of a small room in the *Northern Palace* at Amarna. The room
appears to open on a *Papyrus Marsh* with birds (FIG. 90). In place of
the traditional zonal organization the wall area, above a half conventional, half naturalistic border of marsh flora, is filled with a representation continuous around the four walls. One feels that the painter
was reaching out spontaneously into a new field of visual exploration
but was still too deeply imbedded in his traditional forms to abandon
them.

Fig. 91. Cedar-Wood Chair. Decorated in embossed gold, claws of ivory. Cairo Museum. (Howard Carter)

Fig. 92. Royal Armchair. Wood overlaid with gold and inlaid with polychrome faïence, glass and stone. Cairo Museum. (Howard Carter)

E. MINOR ARTS

Magnificent furniture has survived in the tombs. Some of it apparently had been used in the palace before it served as mortuary equipment. Of the chairs from the *Tomb of Tutenkhamon*,[1] a simple one (FIG. 91) illustrates particularly well the functional, structural, and esthetic excellence of the design. It is made of cedar wood with carvings and ornaments of gold which combine into a design of architectural quality inscriptions and symbols — the sun disk, the uraeus, royal birds with the two crowns, the figure of millions of years, the life sign, the names of the pharaoh. A second (FIG. 92) is a royal armchair, which displays the ostentatious magnificence of the times. Its wooden frame is sheathed in gold; the front legs terminate in gold lions' heads, symbols of the powers of the pharaoh; and the arms are made of serpents in gold and faïence, whose heads, as they join the back, terminate in the double crown of Upper and Lower Egypt. The back panel shows a domestic scene in which the Queen is placing some ointment from a jar in her hand upon the collar-neck-

[1] The discovery of this tomb in 1922, one of the most startling archaeological discoveries of modern times, revealed for the first time the almost unbelievable magnificence of royal burial equipment in the Empire. For the history of the discovery, and illustrations and descriptions of the equipment, see Howard Carter and A. C. Mace, *The Tomb of Tut-ankh-amen*, London, 1927–33, Vols. I–III.

Fig. 93. "Perfume Spoon." Wood. Louvre, Paris. (Giraudon)

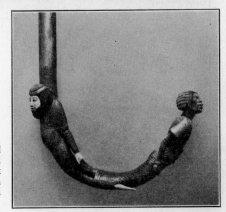

Fig. 94. Handle of a Ceremonial Walking-Stick. The two interlocked figures, of ivory and ebony, represent Asiatic and African captives. From the Tomb of Tutenkhamon. (Howard Carter)

lace of the King; while through a break in the upper border the Sun sends forth rays terminating in hands — the symbol of Aton — to envelop the two. The young wife here represented was the daughter of Ikhnaton; and early in their reign Tutenkhamon and his Queen appear to have remained loyal to Aton [1] only to be brought back to the traditional worship of Amon by the political power of the priesthood. The figures of the elaborately dressed pair and the details of the background are worked out in silver, colored glass, and faïence in the gold. The effect is a brilliant picture, a magnificent tour de force, but at the expense of that satisfaction felt when ornament functions both in material and in design as one element in a unified whole.

In addition to furniture there was a demand for great quantities of smaller articles for household equipment and personal use which employed many craftsmen working in various materials — stone, wood, ivory, glazed terra cotta, glass, metal, semiprecious stones. The stoneworker brought the Old Kingdom traditions of his craft to a point of technical virtuosity, as is seen in the elegant alabaster vases from Tutenkhamon's tomb. The design incorporates elaborate seminaturalistic handles, though it is all cut from one piece of stone, and the body of the vase is worked to a translucent thinness. Wood was particularly

[1] Evidence of this is seen in the early form of the king's name, Tutenkhaton.

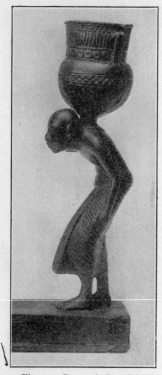

Fig. 95. Cosmetic Jar. Wood,
8¾ in. high. XVIII Dynasty
(1580–1350 B.C.). Liverpool Museum. (Liverpool Museum)

Fig. 96. Necklace with Pectoral.
XII Dynasty (2000–1788 B.C.).
Metropolitan Museum, New York.
(Metropolitan Museum)

Fig. 97. Pectoral of Senusert II (detail of Fig. 96).
Gold, inlaid and engraved. W. 3¼ in. at the base.

Fig. 98. Wine Jug. Of silver with engraving; handle and rim of gold. H. 7 in. XIX Dynasty (1350–1205 B.C.). Cairo Museum. (Metropolitan Museum)

Fig. 99. Glass Vase. Dark blue, with dragged pattern in light blue, yellow, and white. H. 3¼ in. Metropolitan Museum, New York. (Metropolitan Museum)

desirable for carving small toilet articles such as the cosmetic receptacles of a cosmetic-loving people. In this material especially, with its capacities for design freer than in stone, one sees how the Egyptian relied for his designs upon the human, plant, and animal life with which he was familiar. The *"Perfume Spoon"* of FIG. 93 combines into a functional and esthetic unity a duck and a girl swimming. The duck forms the receptacle, with the opening between the wings, and the girl, the handle, both forms being united by the girl's arms and by the repetition of the heads. In another carving (FIG. 95), which represents a slave bending beneath the weight of the jar, one delights in the contrasting polished and carved surfaces. In a walking-stick of Tutenkhamon (FIG. 94) two captives of the pharaoh, with bodies carved and sheathed in gold, are unified with the curve of the handle and serve to provide the hand a firm hold.

Glazing had been known by the Egyptian from prehistoric times and early had been used to cover tiles for wall decoration. It had then been applied to various objects, but in the Empire period it reached a climax of technical development and also of the variety of its uses — beads, pendants, scarabs, amulets, vases, figurines, and architectural decorations. The blue color, particularly deep and pure, the craftsmen obtained from copper by a long process that required great skill in the preparation of the material and patience in tending the furnaces during the long, even roasting, for no mechanical devices were known to regulate the heat. A typical household utensil of this glazed

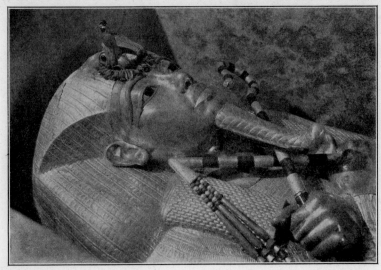

Fig. 100. Effigy of Tutenkhamon upon the First Coffin. Gold over wood inlaid with glass, faïence, and lapis lazuli. Cairo Museum. (Howard Carter)

ware is a *Lotus Cup* (FIG. 101) of particularly elegant shape that is derived from the half-open flower.

Glass was not the common, inexpensive medium among the Egyptians that it is at present, for the blowpipe was not invented until about the first century B.C. Therefore it was necessary to mold the hot glass over a copper and paste core that could later be removed — a slow, laborious process. Such a vase as that illustrated in FIG. 99 was made in this way. It is deep blue in color. For decoration, threads of light blue, yellow, and white glass were wound about the still hot neck and body and dragged back and forth by a hooked instrument, forming the zigzag that is known as the "dragged pattern." In a *Hippopotamus* (FIG. 103), an essentially clay form of bulky rounding masses is covered with a rich blue glaze with drawings of different parts of the lotus plant, which not only signify the natural habitat of the animal but in their shapes follow and emphasize the surfaces of the mass.

Metal-workers and lapidaries were in demand because of the great amount of gold used in the furniture and the many small articles, and particularly because of the importance of jewelry in the Egyptian costume — crowns, collar-necklaces, necklaces with pendants, armlets, bracelets, ornaments and clasps for all parts of the clothing — easily perceived in the sculpture and paintings. The lavish use of this metal became particularly evident at the discovery of the Tutenkhamon

Fig. 101. Lotus Cup. Of blue faïence.

Fig. 102. Jewel Casket, Reconstructed. Ebony, inlaid with ivory, gold, blue glaze, and carnelian. L. 17½ in. XII Dynasty (2000–1788 B.C.). Metropolitan Museum, New York. (Metropolitan Museum)

tomb, especially in the concentric gold coffins (FIG. 100), magnificent examples of the goldsmith's craft, as are the diadem found on the head of the King, and the collar-necklaces. The latter are elaborate examples of a popular form of jewelry. The chain and pectoral, or pendant, was also popular. The chain in FIG. 96 consists of drop beads arranged in pairs in a fourfold unit of blue-green feldspar, lapis lazuli, carnelian, and

Fig. 103. Hippopotamus. Of faïence. L. about 8 in. XII Dynasty (2000–1788 B.C.). Metropolitan Museum, New York. (Metropolitan Museum)

gold with a gold clasp ingeniously designed with a dovetail groove and a tongue. The pectoral (FIG. 97) is an open-work gold plate engraved on the underside and inlaid on the upper side with turquoise, lapis lazuli, and carnelian. In the center a kneeling figure of a man is holding palm branches on which rests the royal cartouche, flanked on each side by a royal falcon, while the intermediate space is filled with the uraeus and the sun disk, from which is suspended the sign of life. The birds are united skillfully to the central design by the uraeus, the life sign, and the claws braced against the palm branches; and all parts are held together by the firm base. The blues of the lapis and turquoise are well balanced, and the whole design is unified by the careful distribution of the red carnelian.

The wide use of jewelry brought demand for jewelry containers. An example of great beauty and refined taste (FIG. 102) was found in the same tomb as the necklace of FIG. 96. Its beauty lies partly in the color harmony — ebony, ivory, gold, blue faïence, and carnelian — but largely in the quiet richness of a design based upon carefully proportioned panels that follow the structural lines of the casket. The narrow panels are decorated alternately with gold ornaments and strips of blue faïence crowned with a square of red carnelian, and their decorative effect is heightened by the quiet, unadorned ivory rectangle above. The curve of the base harmonizes with the hollow cornice and with the curved lid, in which are inlaid Hathor heads of gold, blue faïence, and carnelian.

The silver supply was far less abundant than the gold, and hence silver vessels were much rarer. A *Wine Jug* (FIG. 98) illustrates its use and also an imaginative power in forming the handle in the shape of a gazelle, which, with hind legs resting upon the body of the jug and forelegs pressed against the neck, is eagerly stretching up to sniff the wine.

F. SUMMARY

The Middle Kingdom and the Empire were ages of great productivity and accomplishment in all the arts. Wealth fostered magnificence and display on a colossal scale. The temple-builders erected for their gods mortuary temples and dwellings that were grandly simple, though gigantic; solid and enduring masses of stone, decorated with sculpture which, whether as colossal statue or low painted relief, was supremely architectural — an impressive manifestation of a form determined by ritualistic requirements, the material at hand, and the local setting.

The sculptors and painters had inherited the traditional conventions that had been established in the formative period and had reached a climax in the Old Kingdom. But we miss the vivacity, the freshness, and the sincerity that come from the struggle through which any people passes in an archaic age when ideas and conventions are forming. The wider outlook upon life that characterized the Empire period, and particularly the influence of Ikhnaton's religious revolution, led the artists along a path that a few had already begun to discover for themselves — the path of nature. For a brief time visual perception rather than mental concept or memory picture became the basis of form; freedom and ease and the beauty of the freely curving line supplanted angularity and stiffness, and inspired the artists with new creative power. But the Egyptians were not yet ready for so radical a change. By nature conservative, they soon fell back upon the conventions, now beautiful empty forms, artificial rather than vital, that crystallized their art. A strangely uniform art for many centuries was the art of the Egyptians. But though they could never break from their shackles, they always remained superbly skillful in line, whether of the brush or of the chisel, and always superbly decorative.

In the minor arts "use and beauty are still undivided." Everywhere one discerns great technical skill and fertility of imagination, combined with an innate sense of design that admirably adapted the forms of nature to a utilitarian or a decorative end.

BIBLIOGRAPHY

Baedeker, Karl, *Egypt and the Sûdân: Handbook for Travellers*, Leipzig, 1929
Baikie, James, *The Life of the Ancient East*, Macmillan, 1923
Bell, Edward, *The Architecture of Ancient Egypt*, Harcourt, Brace, 1915
Breasted, J. H., *Ancient Times*, 2d ed. rev., Ginn, 1935
—— —— *The Dawn of Conscience*, Scribner, 1933
—— —— *Development of Religion and Thought in Ancient Egypt*, Scribner, 1912
—— —— *A History of Egypt from the Earliest Times to the Persian Conquest*, 2d ed., Scribner, 1924
Capart, Jean, *Egyptian Art*, tr. by W. R. Dawson, Stokes, 1923
—— —— *Lectures on Egyptian Art*, University of North Carolina Press, 1928
—— —— *Primitive Art in Egypt*, tr. by A. S. Griffith, London, 1905
Childe, V. G., *The Most Ancient East*, Knopf, 1929
Clarke, Somers, and Engelbach, Reginald, *Ancient Egyptian Masonry*, Oxford Press, 1930
Cossio, M. B., and Pijoan, José, *Summa artis*, Madrid, 1931–34, Vols. I–VI, Vol. III
Davies, N. de G., *The Tomb of Nakht at Thebes*, Metropolitan Museum of Art, New York, 1917
Fechheimer, Hedwig, *Die Plastik der Aegypter*, Berlin, 1923
—— —— *Kleinplastik der Aegypter*, Berlin, 1921
Frankfort, Henri, ed., *The Mural Painting of El-'Amarneh*, London, 1929
Laurie, A. P., *The Materials of the Painter's Craft in Europe and Egypt*, Lippincott, 1911
Lythgoe, A. M., *The Treasure of Lahun*, Metropolitan Museum of Art, *Bulletin*, December, 1919, Sec. II
Maspero, Sir G. C. C., *Art in Egypt*, Scribner, 1912
—— —— *Manual of Egyptian Archaeology*, tr. by A. S. Johns, Putnam, 1914
—— —— *Popular Stories of Ancient Egypt*, tr. by Mrs. C. H. W. Johns, Putnam, 1915
Murray, M. A., *Egyptian Sculpture*, Scribner, 1930
Petrie, Sir W. M. F., *Arts and Crafts of Ancient Egypt*, McClurg, 1910
—— —— *Decorative Patterns of the Ancient World*, London, 1931
—— —— *Social Life in Ancient Egypt*, Houghton Mifflin, 1923
Ross, Sir E. D., ed., *The Art of Egypt through the Ages*, Studio, 1931
Schäfer, Heinrich, and Andrae, Walter, *Die Kunst des alten Orients*, Berlin, 1925
Swindler, M. H., *Ancient Painting*, Yale University Press, 1929
Weigall, A. E. P. B., *The Life and Times of Akhnaton, Pharaoh of Egypt*, rev. ed., Putnam, 1923
Worringer, Wilhelm, *Egyptian Art*, tr. by Bernard Rackham, Putnam, 1928

See also the General Bibliography, pp. 749–751.

CHAPTER IV

Art in the Tigris-Euphrates Valley and Persia

1. SUMERIAN ART (about 4000–1925 B.C.)

As we leave the Nile Valley, with an impression of the Egyptian civilization made vivid by the wonderful state of preservation of the monuments, and travel eastward into Asia to the Valley of the Two Rivers (FIG. 104), in which arose another civilization, roughly contemporary with the Egyptian, we look in vain for tombs and temples, or palaces. "Standing on the summit of this mound one can distinguish along the eastern skyline the dark tasselled fringe of the palm-gardens on the river's bank, but to north and west and south as far as the eye can see stretches a waste of unprofitable sand. To the south-west the flat line of the horizon is broken by a gray upstand-ing pinnacle, the ruins of the staged tower of the sacred city of Eridu . . . and to the north-west a shadow thrown by the low sun may tell the whereabouts of the low mound of al 'Ubaid; but otherwise nothing relieves the monotony of the vast plain over which the shim-mering heat-waves dance and the mirage spreads its mockery of placid waters. It seems incredible that such a wilderness should ever have been habitable for man, and yet the weathered hillocks at one's feet cover the temples and houses of a very great city." [1]

Why this condition of complete ruin? Of the two rivers that form this valley, the western, the Euphrates, is quiet and majestic, with few tributaries, and is almost unnavigable because of the cataracts in the north and the sandbars in the south. The eastern river, the Tigris, rising in the mountains to the north and east, and augmented by large tributaries, is more rapid, and forms the highway of commerce for the valley. Today we see the modern Mesopotamian transport-ing his cargo on this river in the same kind of round tub-shaped boat that his predecessors used thousands of years ago. Both rivers, flooded during the season of heavy rains, bring down vast quantities of rich alluvium, as does the Nile in Egypt, forming an amazingly productive soil. But these floods prove equally destructive when un-controlled; they not only change the courses of the rivers but soon reduce buildings made of nonresisting material, such as the Baby-lonians used, to heaps which the sands blowing in from the desert convert into rather natural-looking mounds.

[1] C. L. Woolley, *Ur of the Chaldees*, Scribner, 1930, p. 13.

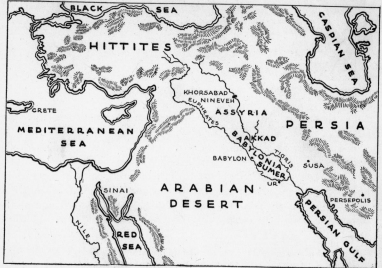

Fig. 104. The Ancient Near East.

The valley divides naturally into two parts, the lower, generally called Babylonia,[1] being flat river bottoms, extraordinarily fertile; and the upper, Assyria, along the higher reaches of the Tigris, more barren, reaching up into the plateau country. Taken as a whole, this valley, in contrast to Egypt with its secure isolation, its peaceful and strangely uniform civilization, is exposed on the west to the Arabian Desert and on east, north, and northwest to highland plateaus, and is thus open ground for peaceful wanderers and warring invaders. The story, then, of the valley is one of conflicting groups, racially differentiated; of infiltration, conquest, absorption. Out of this shifting complexity arose four outstanding cultures: the Sumerian (with Semite elements), the Assyrian, the Chaldean, and the Achaemenian Persian.[2]

A. HISTORICAL BACKGROUND

Our earliest glimpses of the peoples of the Valley of the Two Rivers take us into the Neolithic Age, perhaps into the same cultural stratum that we find in Egypt.[3] In that age certain people, we know not who,

[1] Strictly speaking, "Babylonia" is not applicable until Babylon became the capital under Hammurabi about 2100 B.C.

[2] Probably also the Hittite (at their climax about 1500 B.C.), at present obscure though emerging through the work of archaeological expeditions in Anatolia and through the recent partial decipherment of the Hittite writing.

[3] Statements and dates in the history of this valley and its surrounding highlands

Fig. 105. Temple of the Mother Goddess, Ninkhursag. Near Ur. Reconstruction of one entrance. Late IV millennium B.C. (Joint Expedition of the British Museum and the University Museum, University of Pennsylvania.)

discovered metal and a system of writing, at a time probably roughly contemporary with the same discoveries in the Nile Valley, that is, between 5000 and 3000 B.C.[1] At the dawn of historical times we find in the lower Tigris-Euphrates Valley the Sumerians, clean-shaven men with aquiline noses, carrying the shield, who may have migrated into the valley from the eastern plateaus. They were an agricultural people, and eventually built strong walled towns such as Ur and Lagash. Then in from the western deserts drifted Semite nomads, the Akkadians, bearded men equipped with the bow and arrow, who turned from grazing to agriculture, absorbed much of the Sumerian culture, and built their own cities farther north — Kish, Akkad, Babylon. Though the Sumerian culture, in general, prevailed, the ruling power swung back and forth between the two peoples, the Semites producing two of the mightiest kings, Sargon (active 2750 B.C.) and Hammurabi (2123–2081 B.C.), under whom Babylon became the capital of the first Babylonian Empire.

This lower part of the Valley of the Two Rivers was a rich agricultural land owing to control of the floods by irrigation, though trading was a major activity of the community. Religious beliefs and practices

must be set down tentatively because of the very recent discoveries, which partly verify and partly make more problematical earlier statements. Important expeditions are at work on various sites: in the Hittite country of Anatolia, around Nineveh, at Ur, Kish, Persepolis — to mention a few.

[1] The last part of the Stone Age, when copper was beginning to be used, is now spoken of as the Aëneolithic.

Fig. 106. Animal Frieze from the Temple of Ninkhursag. (Joint Expedition of the British Museum and the University Museum, University of Pennsylvania.)

centered about great nature gods: Anu, god of the sky; Enlil, creator and ruler of the earth and "lord of the storm," who sent both beneficent and destructive floods; Ea, lord of the depths and as lord of waters, a healing, benevolent god; Nannar or Sin, the moon god; Shamash, the sun god; and Ishtar (Venus), goddess of love and fertility. In contrast to the Egyptian, the Sumerian took too gloomy a view of a future world, "the place whence none return," to give burial elaborate attention. Though personal burial equipment, especially of royalty, was sumptuous, the tomb and its decoration provide neither monumental architecture nor an intimate picture of life. It was the present life that mattered, the palace for its enjoyment and the temple to propitiate the gods for material prosperity. The god was an earthly ruler and a great landowner; Nannar, for example, was king of Ur and as such had a court with a huge organization covering every activity from that of the high priest and minister of war to that of the director of donkey transport. Thus the temple and its adjuncts were a huge mundane establishment, and the priesthood became an important factor in the business life of the country, renting out land, bartering in wool, cattle, herds, fruits, perfumes, and the products of the craftsmen, especially the goldsmiths.

B. ARCHITECTURE AND SCULPTURE

Poverty in building materials faced the Sumerian. His rich agricultural valley provided him with little wood and no stone — only the mud of the river bottoms. Brick, then, both baked and unbaked, must supply his need except for a small amount of imported stone. So when building on a large scale with this small material, too small to span

Fig. 107. Copper Relief from the Temple of Ninkhursag. British Museum, London. (British Museum.)

any considerable distance, as could the stone lintels of the Egyptian, the Sumerian was compelled to adapt the arch as his basic structural principle.[1]

Our earliest glimpse reveals the *Temple of Ninkhursag*, the Mother Goddess (FIG. 105), in the suburbs of Ur, a small temple but important because in its gay colorfulness and decorative schemes we see early use of practices which constantly recur in the history of the valley. It stood in the corner of a spacious platform and was built of brick with wood lintels, sheathed in copper. Stone steps with wood paneling led up to an entrance whose doorway was guarded by copper lions with inlaid eyes, white shell teeth, and red stone tongues, to ward off malevolent spirits. At each side of this door of palm wood, two columns covered with triangular inlays of black and red stone and mother-of-pearl supported the lintel, on which rested a large copper panel with high relief (FIG. 107). Along the platform edge were copper statues of cows and bulls, and up on the walls was a frieze of animals in copper and friezes of animals, birds, and men carved in limestone and shell set in black shale (FIG. 106). Against the whitewashed brick this decorative scheme of color and shining copper must have created an impression of gaiety and splendor. The platform, the guardian figures, the friezes with long rows of figures, decorative and at the same time strongly narrative, the vivid color — all these we shall meet constantly in Babylonia, Assyria, and Persia.

Perhaps the most characteristic structure of the Valley of the Two Rivers is the *ziggurat*, a tower of several stories, probably the dominating feature of every Sumerian town of any consequence. The *Ziggurat at Ur*, recently excavated, will serve as a type illustration. It belongs to the *Temple of Nannar*, the moon god, god and king of Ur. The temple occupies one side of the Sacred Area and about it are

[1] A true arch consists of wedge-shaped blocks, usually of brick or stone, called *voussoirs*, fitted together to roof over the space between two supports. The central voussoir, at the crown of the arch, is called the *keystone* because when this block is put into place, usually last, the arch is firmly set.

Fig. 108. Ziggurat at Ur. Reconstructed. H. 92 ft. 2300–2180 B.C. (Joint Expedition of the British Museum, and the University Museum, University of Pennsylvania.)

grouped, rather irregularly, temples of Ningal, the moon goddess, and of minor related deities, and various secular structures belonging to the court of the god.[1] A large court, on a terrace ten feet above the Sacred Area level, surrounded by storerooms and chambers, leads to a large upper terrace with the small shrine and the massive four-storied ziggurat. Platforms and terraces, so characteristic of buildings in this valley, are easily explained as protection from recurring floods. Not so evident is the origin of the ziggurat. If the Sumerians migrated from the hill country, the tower with an altar on its summit may well be the "Mountain of God," or the "High Places" where they were wont to worship, created artificially in their new homes on the plains.

The *Ziggurat at Ur* (FIG. 108), set in a spacious terrace, consists of four stages, decreasing in size and height upward, the lowest, fifty feet in height, forming a massive base. This stage is broken on one side by a triple stairway of one hundred steps each branch of which converges upon an entrance leading directly up to the shrine, thus centering interest upon the focal point, both architectural and religious, and also providing a fine setting for the elaborate pageantry connected with the ceremonial rites. The structure is a solid mass consisting of a core of earth and crude brick with a thick facing of baked brick laid in bitumen, with pitch-dipped reed mats laid between every few courses.[2] The walls have a decided batter (an inward slope) and all the surfaces and lines are slightly curved, giving the mass compactness and relieving it of the illusion of sag found in long unbroken lines.[3]

[1] For an air view see Frontispiece to C. J. Gadd, *History and Monuments of Ur*, Dutton, 1929, and the *National Geographic Magazine*, August, 1928.

[2] The mound made by the ruin of this ziggurat is known locally as Al Mughair, "Mound of Pitch."

[3] See remarks on the *Parthenon* (p. 134), in which these variations from regularity were first scientifically studied.

Fig. 109. Stele of Naramsin. C. 2550 B.C. Louvre, Paris. (Mansell)

Fig. 110. Gudea. Diorite. H. 3½ ft. C. 2450 B.C. Louvre, Paris.

The stages were differentiated not only in size and proportion but also in color, which seems to have been used symbolically. Above the white court rose the black lower stage suggesting the underworld; a red middle story, the earth; and the blue shrine with gilded dome, the heavens and the sun.[1] Added to these large, strongly contrasted areas of color was the greenery of the trees and gardens, which seem to have been planted on all the terraces.[2] Thus a ziggurat must have been a colorful and imposing "Mountain of God."

With a few exceptions, the sculpture consists of reliefs which served a decorative and narrative purpose in the building or reliefs on a monument such as the *Stele of Urnammu*, one zone of which (FIG. 113) shows a group of figures crisply cut in fairly high relief and simply organized into a balanced group. The scene represents King Ur-nammu pouring a libation into a vase containing date-palm leaves, before Ningal on the left and Nannar on the right. The god holds

[1] The color is very problematical. That color was used is not questioned. But the actual hues found may have been ancient restoration, and the symbolism is uncertain. The statements above follow Mr. Woolley's suggestions.

[2] Such are the famous Hanging Gardens of Babylon; and the Tower of Babel at Babylon was a ziggurat similar to that at Ur, only on a larger scale.

Fig. 111. Statue of a Queen Who Reigned at Susa c. 1500 B.C. Bronze. Louvre, Paris.

Fig. 112. Ningal. White marble, eyes of lapis lazuli and shell. H. c. 4 in. c. 4000 B.C. University Museum, Philadelphia. (Joint Expedition of the British Museum and the University Museum, University of Pennsylvania.)

Fig. 113. Stele of Urnammu. 2300 B.C. University Museum, Philadelphia. (Joint Expedition of the British Museum and the University Museum, University of Pennsylvania.)

a pickax, a measuring rod, and a builder's line, symbolizing his order to the king to build him a temple; in the fragmentary zone below the king is seen with the builder's tools on his shoulder, carrying out the divine orders. The figures are clothed in the heavy woolen garments characteristic of the costume of the valley. While there are seen some of the conventions noted in Egypt, as in the shoulders, there is an extraordinary vitality in these figures, vigor and largeness in the modeling, and technical excellence in the stonecutting. The fact that the objects and figures both seated and standing just fill the space adds to the decorative effect. This zonal arrangement gives way in the *Stele of Naramsin* (FIG. 109) to a centering of all movement upon the isolated figure of the King, who is leading his army through a wooded mountainous country against an enemy now conquered and

Fig. 114. Seal of King Sargon I. 2750 B.C. Red jasper. H. 1½ in. Coll. de Clercq, Paris.

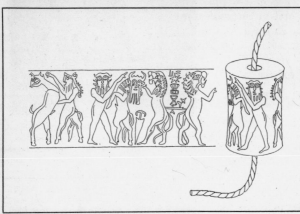

Fig. 115. A cylinder seal, with cord attachment, and the impression made when it is rolled over soft clay. H. c. 1 inch.

imploring mercy. Though the carving is not so well preserved as in *Urnammu's* stele, one feels the dramatic fervor of the scene and the fine vitality in the expression of the individual figures. Here is an art whose accomplishment presupposes a long development, an earlier stage of which is seen in the much more archaic *Reliefs of Urnina* and the *Vulture Stele* of the Louvre.

Sculpture in the round, which is comparatively rare — probably because of the lack of stone — is best illustrated by the statues from Tello (Lagash). FIG. 110, carved from diorite which must have been imported from a considerable distance and at great expense, represents *Gudea*, priest-king of Lagash. He is seated in frontal position with hands tightly clasped in the attitude of devotion. He wears a woolen cap, the fleece kilt of the priest-king, here covered with inscriptions, and a long woolen mantle which falls away from the right shoulder, leaving the arm exposed. Notwithstanding the squat proportions,[1] there is a massiveness and a close knitting of the parts which at every turn re-

[1] Possibly determined by the proportions of the block of stone. Compare with the other figures from Tello, especially the so-called *Architect* (Louvre).

minds us of the block of hard stone. The patterning of the eyebrows and that of the cap harmonize with the pre-cise cutting of the eyes, mouth, and hands; the modeling of the face and arm is very sensitive, neither wholly stone nor wholly flesh but a very subtle balance between; and throughout the figure runs an energetic vitality. Here, then, is a capacity to infuse stone with a living quality and at the same time to perpetuate the intrinsic qualities of the stone. This capacity is seen again in the head of *Ningal* (FIG. 112), in which the sculptor reacts to a softer stone, marble, with peculiar sensitiv-ity, and infuses it with a gentler ani-mation. FIG. 111, a bronze portrait of a queen, is a geometrically simple shape with a monumental dignity and a deco-rative treatment of detail highly suit-able to the medium.

Fig. 116. Vase from Lagash. Silver with bronze base. H. c. 14 in. c. 2850 B.C. An inscription around the neck records the name of the king who placed this vase in the temple as a votive offering. Louvre, Paris.

C. MINOR ARTS

The fine quality of carving seen in the sculpture repeats itself, in minia-ture size, in the cylinder seals. The seal consisted of a cylindrical piece of stone, usually about an inch and a half high, pierced for the attachment of a cord (FIG. 115). Seals were made of various colored stones, both hard and soft, such as hematite, obsidian, agate, carnelian and jasper, lapis lazuli, and alabaster. They were deco-rated with a design in intaglio, so that when the seal was rolled over the soft clay a raised impression was made, as in the use of sealing wax today. With this impression the Sumerian sealed, signed, and identi-fied his letters and documents, which were written on clay tablets. On a *Seal of King Sargon* (FIG. 114) on each side of the central group is a mythological figure, perhaps Gilgamesh, one knee bent upon the ground, holding a vase from which issue two streams of water; in the center, back to back, are two bulls that lift up their heads to drink and with their horns hold ingeniously the inscription containing the name of Sargon; below is the conventional wavelike representation of a stream. The scene refers to water as the gift of the gods. In this

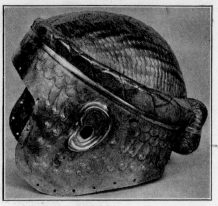

Fig. 117. Gold Cup. 3500–3200 B.C. University Museum, Philadelphia. (Joint Expedition of the British Museum and the University Museum, University of Pennsylvania.)

Fig. 118. Gold Helmet. Life size. 3500–3200 B.C. Baghdad Museum. (Joint Expedition of the British Museum and the University Museum, University of Pennsylvania.)

seal we perceive the organization of the figures into a carefully related, balanced group tied firmly together by the wave lines of the river, with pleasing contrasts of texture in the smooth and rough areas. The modeling, particularly in the bulls, shows a powerful naturalism and at the same time no hesitation on the part of the engraver to use conventional forms in the horns, hair, and water. Upon recalling the very small curved surface upon which the design is engraved, in intaglio, we realize the extraordinary skill in carving, every line of which, strong and unfaltering, was graved by hand, not by the drill which, imported later, brought deterioration in the quality of seal-cutting.

This amazing technical skill is apparent in the products of the metalworkers and other craftsmen as well. Thanks to sumptuous royal burial equipment, although it involves the ghastly spectacle of human sacrifice, we glimpse the gorgeousness of personal adornment, the richness and at times impeccable taste in furniture, implements, and utensils. Among the metals copper seems to have been especially prized, and the craftsmen reveal an understanding of various processes of working it. They cast small figures in it; they beat it into thin plates for sheathing beams and columns not only to protect the underlying material but also to secure its color and texture for decorative purposes; they hammered sheets of it over molds, thus obtaining relief — a process known as *repoussé* — and engraved on it details and decorative patterns. To make sculpture in the round they built up a wooden core, covered it with bitumen, in which the modeling was done, and then hammered over it thin plates of copper. The *Temple of Ninkhursag* illustrates all these uses. Of especial quality is the great relief over the doorway (FIG. 107), consisting of a lion-headed eagle with outspread wings clutching the backs of two stags. The heads of the animals are in the round, perhaps cast. The vitality so characteristic of Sumerian art is present, expressed by naturalistic forms in the animals and conventional form in the eagle. The subject is popular in Sumerian art, though of uncertain meaning, and is found in carvings, on the seals, and on a silver vase (FIG. 116), where it is engraved with variations four times about the body. On the shoulder of the vase, above this decorative band, is a row of half-crouching heifers, similar to the frieze on Ninkhursag's temple. On the vase the engraving is done with extraordinary firmness and calligraphic beauty.

Fig. 119. Harp, Reconstructed. Bull's head of gold and lapis lazuli. 3500–3200 B.C. University Museum, Philadelphia. (Joint Expedition of the British Museum and the University Museum, University of Pennsylvania.)

While the Sumerians were affluent in their use of silver, with gold they were lavish, almost barbarically so, if we are to judge from the equipment of the *Royal Tombs* at Ur. Here is a *Cup* (FIG. 117) of masterly proportions and strong contour, its surface hammered into flutings which emphasize both the surface direction and the contour, while a delicately engraved herringbone pattern and double zigzag finish both the lip and the base. In a gold helmet (FIG. 118) are found repoussé and engraving of a quality hardly to be surpassed either in technical excellence or in design. The hair is treated conventionally, making a beautifully varied pattern of wave lines, spiraling, and sharply angular braiding which covers the entire surface.

The combination of gold with other materials is illustrated in a

Fig. 120. Standard. Detail. 3500–3200 B.C. Baghdad Museum. (Joint Expedition of the British Museum and the University Museum, University of Pennsylvania.)

harp (FIG. 119) of wood inlaid with a geometric pattern of shell, lapis lazuli, and red stone. The sounding-box terminates in a bull's head of gold whose eyes, beard, and horn tips are of lapis, giving a dashingly bold effect. The sloping end of the box is filled with four zones containing figures, of engraved shell set in a dark ground, which represent animals playing human rôles: a hound, with dagger in his belt, and a lion are carrying food and drink; an ass plays the harp (note the bull's-head terminal) for a dancing bear. The meaning of these representations is not clear. But whether the scenes are parodies or represent religious ceremonies of a magic character, the narrative element is predominant, and the figures reveal the same vivid perception of the animal form and characteristics that we have seen elsewhere in Sumerian art. Again, on the sides of a *Standard*, in the form of a triangular box on a pole, is the recurrent motive of narration and processional arranged in zones. The figures, of engraved shell, are inlaid in lapis lazuli, with an occasional dash of red. Here is vividly pictured *Peace and War* (FIG. 120), in which are seen the king and his chariot, his attendants, army, and captives, all forecasting the great series of narrative reliefs in Assyria and Persia.

D. SUMMARY

The Sumerian-Semite age, culminating in the first Babylonian Empire,[1] was a heroic age that is summed up in the Babylonian Gil-

---

[1] There is a great dearth of works of art from Babylon of the first Empire, the *Stele of Hammurabi* (Louvre) being the chief monument.

Fig. 121. Temple at Ashur. Restored. 1125–1100 B.C. (Andrae)

gamesh epic. The people were farmers and traders, interested in the
here and now, worshiping great nature gods who dwelt in their cities
as god-kings. With only one plentiful material — brick — they built
gay, colorful palaces and temples, with the monumentally grand ziggurat towering over all. Their vigor and vitality reveals itself not in
abstractions, but in a robust naturalism in their sculpture; in barbaric sumptuousness in their vessels and utensils; and in their technical skill in handling many materials. A vitality permeates all their
products, expressed now realistically, now conventionally, but always
based upon a vivid realistic perception of their immediate world.

2. ASSYRIAN ART (about 1000–612 B.C.)

A. HISTORICAL BACKGROUND

Turning to the upper Tigris-Euphrates Valley (FIG. 104) we find
the Semite settlements of Ashur dominated by the kings of Sumer and
Akkad and harassed by the tribes of the surrounding highlands, especially by the Kassites, a pre-Indo-European people from the northeastern plateaus who were drifting into the valley, bringing with them
the horse (about 2000 B.C.); and by the Hittites of Anatolia, who in-
vaded the valley about 1925 B.C. This latter people, but little known
until recent times, comprised a loosely united federation of moun-

Fig. 122. Palace of Sargon II. Restored. Dur-Sharrukin (Khorsabad).
722–705 B.C. (Place)

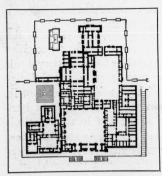

Fig. 123. Palace of Sargon.
Khorsabad. (Place)

taineers who worshiped the great Mother Goddess. At their capitol Hatti (the modern Boghaz Keui), at Carchemish, Tell Halaf, and other sites they built massive fortress-palaces with bold architectural sculpture at the entrances.[1] We see gigantic ponderous basalt statues of deities standing on the backs of animals; the Great Mother, seated on a pedestal adorned with monsters, as elemental as the rock itself; reliefs of ceremonial processions and hunting scenes filled with movement; and over the surfaces of some of the figures, though entirely subservient to the dominating planes, plays a wealth of decorative detail.[2]

At the hands of these invaders the Babylonian Empire of Hammurabi declined and fell. But the people of Ashur, toughened by the buffetings, gradually pushed outward to subdue, incorporate, and organize into a powerful empire, centered at Nineveh, not only western Asia to the Mediterranean Sea but Babylonia and Egypt as well. Very quickly this empire flowered (885–612 B.C.), and with equal rapidity

[1] See the Frontispiece to Max, Freiherr von Oppenheim, *Der Tell Halaf*, Leipzig, 1931, for a reconstruction of the palace entrance.
[2] There seems to be a definite and important influence of Hittite art upon the Assyrian, in its vitality, its uses of architectural sculpture, its composition and subject matter, the details of which are still to be worked out.

it fell, in its own turn, to new invaders, the Semitic Chaldeans from the western desert and the Iranian Medo-Persians from the northeastern plateaus.

Fig. 124. Palace of Sargon. Façade (detail of Fig. 123). (Place)

The Assyrian state was essentially military, and though controlled by inhuman force was organized efficiently. Its ferocity is reflected in the purely Assyrian sun god from whom it took its name, Ashur, a savage, aloof deity rather than a royal city-dweller like the great nature gods of Sumeria. There is a tingling energy about the Assyrian, an animal ferocity and cruelty whether he is fighting or hunting. Even his Oriental luxuriousness and indolence are grim, as we see in a festive scene

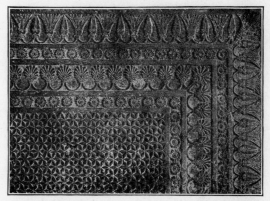

Fig. 125. Paving Slab from the Palace at Nineveh. Alabaster. c. 700 B.C. British Museum, London. (Mansell)

(FIG. 128) in which the king, reclining at ease attended by servants and musicians, sips his wine while he watches the head of his vanquished enemy hanging from a tree with vultures flying about. Vivid pictures of all Assyrian life are found in the great series of reliefs that decorated the gigantic palaces and served to display and exalt constantly the might of the king.

Sumerian forms are basic in Assyria but are adapted to meet the demands of a different type of civilization. This is clear in the buildings and their sculptural decorations.

Fig. 126. A Guardian of the Gate. From the palace of Ashurnasirpal II. Metropolitan Museum, New York. (Metropolitan Museum)

Fig. 127. A Winged Being and the King's Arms-Bearer. From the palace of Ashurnasirpal II, Nimrud (Kalhu). IX cent. B.C. Metropolitan Museum, New York. (Metropolitan Museum)

Fig. 128. King Ashurbanipal and His Queen. 668–626 B.C. British
Museum, London. (Mansell)

Fig. 129. A Median Bringing
Horses to King Sargon II (722–
705 B.C.). Metropolitan Museum, New York. (Metropolitan
Museum)

Fig. 130. Dying Lioness. From
palace at Nineveh. 668–626 B.C.
British Museum, London. (Mansell)

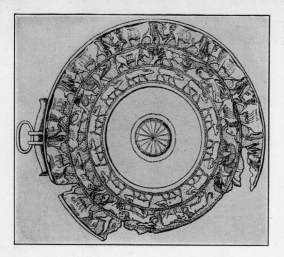

Fig. 131. Bronze Bowl. VIII cent. B.C. British Museum, London.

B. ARCHITECTURE AND SCULPTURE

As for materials, stone, though near at hand, was not easily procured and hence was limited in its constructional use to foundations and substructures but was lavishly employed for reliefs; brick served for the superstructure. The temples follow the Sumerian type seen at Ur, with platform, open courts, and dominating ziggurat (FIG. 121). The palace is more characteristically Assyrian — the here and now on a grand scale. Sargon's palace at Dur-Sharrukin (Khorsabad) will serve as the representative type (FIGS. 122, 123, 124). It is a vast rambling structure of stone and brick, covering about twenty-five acres of ground, palace and temple combined. There are two entrances to the platform, one by a ramp for vehicles, the other by a monumental double stairway leading directly to the main entrance. The plan shows a great many small rooms grouped about two open courts: one, reached by the main entrance, a center for the affairs of state and the royal living-quarters; the other, toward the rear, for the domestic service. At the left is the temple, at the back of which rises the ziggurat. The palace façade (FIG. 124) shows a massive crenelated wall broken by huge rectangular towers flanking an arched doorway, about which stand, like guardian sentinels, colossal winged bulls with human heads. Around the arch and on the towers are friezes of brilliantly colored glazed tiles — the whole effect sumptuous and grandly impressive. Dazzling brilliance seems to have been an objective, to judge from the words of an Assyrian king: "The splendid temple, a brilliant and magnificent dwelling . . . I made its in-

Fig. 132. Ishtar Gate. Restored. Babylon. 606–539 B.C. (Koldewey)

terior brilliant like the dome of the heavens; decorated its walls, like the splendour of the rising stars, and made it grand with resplendent brilliancy." [1]

The colossal bulls, or lions, at the entrance (FIG. 126) serve both to ward off enemies, visible and invisible, and to provide an impressive and fitting architectural decoration. They are partly in the round and partly in high relief, and naïvely combine the front view at rest with the side view in movement, contriving the latter by the addition of a fifth leg. The gigantic size, the bold vigorous carving, the fine sweep of wings, and the patterning of the surface by the conventional treatment of details — all these contribute to their impressiveness and architectural fitness.

On the interior these palaces were paved with stone slabs (FIG. 125) carved with lotus motifs, an influence from Egypt, and with the more characteristically Mesopotamian rosette and palmette. The brick walls were sheathed below with limestone and alabaster reliefs, miles, literally, of ceremonial, military, and hunting scenes, arranged in zones. Above were brightly colored paintings. The reliefs of Ashurnasirpal (FIG. 127) contain large firmly planted figures which just fill the space, single figures endlessly repeated, often without defined relationships, though at times they are balanced about a tree of life. The thickset figures with carefully curled hair and beard are sheathed in

[1] Inscription of Tiglath-Pileser I (1100 B.C.) quoted in P. S. P. Handcock, *Mesopotamian Archaeology*, Putnam, 1912, p. 142.

Fig. 133. Lion of Procession Street. Restored. Glazed tile. Babylon.
L. 7 ft. 606–539 B.C. (Stoedtner)

heavy fringed robes and bedecked with jewelry. They stand in profile,
though both shoulders are seen and the eye is front view; they are
cut clearly and firmly in parallel planes, with little modeling except
where the limbs are exposed, and there the exaggerated muscles form
a vigorous pattern. Details are engraved rather than modeled and
inscriptions cut across both background and figure. There is something clear, definite, and majestic about these quiet colossal figures.

In the age of Sargon II and Sennacherib the relief is higher (FIG. 128),
more rounding with a tendency toward naturalism. (Contrast the
servant's hand with those in FIG. 127.) The figures overlap, are composed into a unit, become pictorial with landscape setting and movement, and reveal a greater interest in narration than in decoration.
There is more modeling, especially in the horses' heads, and a beautifully varied patterning of the surface through differing conventions
used for the mane, trappings, servant's hair, and cloak.

In Ashurbanipal's palace are many banquet (FIG. 128) and hunting scenes, and though the wall as a whole suggests episodes rather
than decorations, there are found here some magnificent expressions
of animal life. Hunting was one of the chief pastimes of the Assyrian.
On horseback, in chariot, and with hunting dogs, he sought the wild
asses on the plateau and above all the lion. In one scene the muscular
hunting dogs are straining at the leash in their eagerness to dash across
the plateau after the wild asses. In another, the King, mounted, is
spearing one lion while another wounded fiercely attacks a riderless
horse. Or again, the *Dying Lioness* (FIG. 130) pierced with arrows that

Fig. 134. View of Persepolis. Left, Grand Stairway, Entrance, and Gate of Xerxes; center, two Royal Audience Halls; right, palaces of Darius, Xerxes, and Artaxerxes. VI–IV cents. B.C. (Oriental Institute, University of Chicago)

have paralyzed her hind legs, drags herself along the ground still fighting — magnificently grim expressions chiseled clearly and forcefully.

C. MINOR ARTS

Among the craftsmen of Nineveh, the metalworker shows skill in handling and designing his material, if we are to judge from a shallow bronze bowl decorated in repoussé with concentric rows of animals about a central rosette (FIG. 131). One notes here a pleasing gradation in scale in the three borders. The innermost contains gazelles moving to the right; the middle, various animals with the direction of movement uncertain; the outer, bulls moving toward the left. The figures are naturalistically conceived, with conventional details such as manes and wings. The effect is highly decorative, in no small measure reminiscent of the animal frieze on the *Temple of Ninkhursag* at Ur (FIGS. 105, 106).

D. SUMMARY

In Assyria we find an architecture of worldly magnificence, huge palaces of innumerable rooms around open courts. They are built of stone and brick with flashing surfaces of brilliantly colored tile, and colossal, grandly impressive sculpture at the doorways. On the interior walls are seen an endless succession of reliefs picturing incidents of war,

Fig. 135. Stairway to the Royal Audience Hall. Persepolis. (Oriental Institute, University of Chicago)

Fig. 136. Subjects Bringing Gifts of Animals, Spears, and Vessels to the King. Detail from the Stairway to the Royal Audience Hall, Persepolis. (Oriental Institute, University of Chicago)

the hunt, and a luxurious life, a grandiloquent repetition of scenes to satisfy the vanity of the monarch. It is an art as forceful as its creators were energetic. Here are not the static elegance, the abstractions, the sensitivity to relationships, found in Egyptian art, but a brusk power in expressing everyday events, many of them violent, lived and perceived intensely; and often in a form that is architecturally fitting.

3. CHALDEAN OR SECOND BABYLONIAN ART (612–539 B.C.)

A. HISTORICAL BACKGROUND

At the fall of Nineveh, two kingdoms were established, the Chaldean in the south, and the Medo-Persian on the eastern plateaus. Nebuchadnezzar, the Chaldean, built Babylon anew so that it surpassed Nineveh in the splendor of its palaces, temples, and Hanging Gardens. This is the Babylon of which the Greek traveler Herodotus wrote, and the

Fig. 137. Capital from the Palace of Artaxerxes at Susa. H. of column c. 67 ft. Louvre, Paris. (Oriental Institute, University of Chicago)

Fig. 138. Frieze of Archers. Glazed tile. From the palace of Darius at Susa. H. c. 5 ft. Louvre, Paris. (Alinari)

city of the Hebrew captivity. Commerce and business flourished. The science of astronomy made advances. The Chaldeans divided the circle into 360 degrees, laid out the signs of the zodiac, and knew at least five planets. But the power and magnificence of Chaldean Babylon was short-lived, for in 539 B.C. it opened its gates to Cyrus, the Persian.

B. ARCHITECTURE

Until recently nothing but a mound marked the traditional site of Babylon. Among the buildings since excavated the *Ishtar Gate* (FIG. 132) illustrates best the chief contribution of the Chaldean builder — ceramic architectural decoration. The general design of the gate, which is double, conforms to the types we have found in Sumeria and Assyria. Glazed tile we found in the shrine on the summit of the ziggurat at Ur. At Khorsabad its use had been extended widely, but the surface of the bricks, even when figure work was used, was flat. The Chaldean builders added relief. On the *Ishtar Gate*, for example, rose, forty feet above the pavement, tier after tier of animals in relief in brilliant enameled tile. From the *Ishtar Gate* to the *Temple of Marduk* led the Procession Street, along which processions passed on festal days. The walls bordering this street were decorated with sixty huge

Fig. 139. Armlet. Gold. H. 5 in.
C. 400 B.C. British Museum, London.
(Dalton)

lions (sacred to Ishtar) molded in relief and glazed in white and yellow or yellow and red against a ground of turquoise or dark blue, with the usual rosette motif in the border (FIG. 133). Though snarling and ferocious, these lions, because of the conventional treatment of muscle and mane and the fine long sweep of back and tail, are peculiarly decorative. Near the *Ishtar Gate* rose the huge *Palace of Nebuchadnezzar* with its terraced gardens, and at no great distance the great ziggurat of the *Temple of Marduk* (the "Tower of Babel") also with its Hanging Gardens. Indeed this main gateway of Chaldean Babylon, and the adjacent palaces and temples with their brilliant gleaming surfaces flashing in the sunshine in the midst of rich tropical gardens, must have impressed one with their gorgeous magnificence.[1]

4. ACHAEMENIAN PERSIAN ART (539–331 B.C.)

A. HISTORICAL BACKGROUND

The end of the Assyrian power and the establishment of the Chaldean had been brought about by the combined efforts of the Semitic Chaldeans and the Medo-Persians, Iranian (a branch of the Indo-European) peoples who had migrated from the northern grasslands and gradually built up an empire on the mountainous plateaus east of the Tigris-Euphrates Valley.[2] The Medo-Persians appear to have brought with them a conception of religion formulated by their great prophet Zoroaster (Zarathustra), which recognized the conflict of Good (Ahuramazda, Ormazd) and Evil (Ahriman), the ethical value of right con-

---

[1] The process of making enameled reliefs is not known. The enamels used by the Chaldeans are opaque and hard, and indicate great ability on the part of the craftsmen to keep the colors from flowing into each other. Probably each brick was molded and enameled separately according to its place in the design. See Koldewey and Andrae on this (bibliography at end of chapter).

[2] We know almost nothing of the peoples of this plateau before the Persian flowering in the sixth and fifth centuries B.C. From the time of the Stone Age village of about 4000 B.C., with its remarkable painted pottery, recently discovered by the Oriental Institute of the University of Chicago, to the time of the Achaemenidae there is almost a complete gap, which it is expected the expeditions now in the field will help to fill.

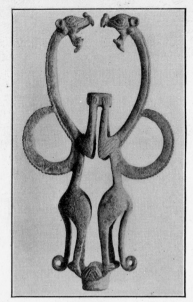

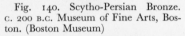

Fig. 140. Scytho-Persian Bronze. c. 200 B.C. Museum of Fine Arts, Boston. (Boston Museum)

Fig. 141. Silver Vase Handle. In the form of a winged ibex. Achaemenid Persian. H. c. 10 in. Berlin.

duct, and the final triumph of Good. About 550 B.C. Cyrus, a Persian vassal of the Median Empire, threw off the yoke and with his powerful archers and daring horsemen swept over western Asia, swiftly conquering from the Persian Gulf to the Mediterranean Sea. Before his armies Babylon fell in 539 B.C. Still further conquest added Egypt to the empire, which was thoroughly organized and enjoyed a remarkable period of prosperity under Darius. It was a humane, intelligent rule, though no rights of citizenship were extended to the people. The king's word was the one law. While these earlier emperors were rulers with a conscience and a feeling of responsibility for their rule, their followers became luxurious Oriental despots. Decline set in, and the decadent state fell before the armies of Alexander the Great in 331 B.C.

B. ARCHITECTURE AND SCULPTURE

The present chief source of our knowledge of Achaemenian building is Persepolis [1] (FIG. 104), apparently a royal suburb of the Persian

[1] Persepolis is now being excavated and restored by the Oriental Institute of the University of Chicago. See *Asia*, September–October, 1933; *National Geographic Magazine*, October, 1933; and the publications of the Oriental Institute relating to this project.

capital, built chiefly by Darius and Xerxes. Upon a huge platform stood a group of palaces and audience halls (FIG. 134) approached by a great double stairway, with an entrance flanked by colossal human-headed bulls. Stone was plentiful in this mountainous country. Hence the platform, the great monumental stairways with their thousands of feet of carvings, the gateways, and the columns of the great audience halls were of stone, though brick was used in walls, and wooden lintels for roofing. The most noticeable thing, not found in the architecture of the valley and sharply differentiating Persepolis from Khorsabad, is the use of the column on a grand scale. The audience hall (*apadana*) is a characteristic building, a vast hall filled with columns to hold the roof, built on a terrace and approached, as was the entire Persepolis group, by a broad monumental stairway (FIG. 135). In the hall the king held audience, surrounded by his bodyguard and court, receiving both local subjects and representatives from the vast empire, who are pictured in the reliefs on the stairway (FIGS. 135, 136). The total impression is one of magnificent, stately ceremonial. The slender fluted columns are peculiarly Achaemenian, illustrating the Iranian love of the animal figure, in whole or in part, as a decorative motif, which is seen in the capitals composed of the foreparts of two bulls placed back to back above a group of volutes (FIG. 137). The wooden lintels were covered with brilliant color and gold, and the walls sheathed with enameled tiles, the effect of which is best realized in the *Frieze of Archers* from Susa (FIG. 138), in which is represented in a quietly rhythmic procession the famous bodyguard of the king. These archers, dressed in elaborately embroidered robes and armed with spears, bows, and large quivers, are molded and glazed; the flat bricks of the background are decorated with characteristically Mesopotamian motifs such as the palmette.

How many of these forms the Persian possessed before the building of Persepolis we do not now know. He seems to have appropriated motifs and forms from the various peoples with whom his conquests brought him in contact: from Babylonia and Assyria, from Ionia and Egypt. Yet so thoroughly adapted are these forms that the *Hall of One Hundred Columns* of Xerxes, for example, is an entirely different entity from the *Hypostyle Hall* at Karnak.

Sculptured friezes play an important part at Persepolis for both decorative and narrative purposes. The spacious double stairways which formed so impressive an approach to the audience halls were decorated with friezes and panels in low relief, separated by moldings and finished with crenelations. FIG. 136 shows a detail of the great procession of royal guards and representatives of various parts of the empire bringing tribute and gifts to the king. The evenly spaced single

Fig. 142. Sarmatian Belt-Clasp.
Hermitage, Leningrad.

Fig. 143. Sarmatian Ornament.
Hermitage, Leningrad.

figures, broken into groups by the conventional trees and varied by the occasional use of animal forms, have the decorative quality of the Sumerian (Fig. 105) and the early Assyrian (Fig. 127). The accomplished cutting of the stone, both in the suavely rounding surfaces and in the crisply chiseled conventional details, is in itself an element of beauty. About all these sculptures, apart from the decorative and narrative elements, there is a serenity, a something apart from reality, quite distinct in feeling from the dynamic naturalism of the Assyrian, which may be, as M. Grousset has suggested, a reflection of the "abstract spiritualism" of the Iranian faith.

C. MINOR ARTS

The Iranians, like other members of this group of civilizations, were skilled metalworkers; they excelled in gold, to judge from an armlet (Fig. 139) whose decoration consists of two winged monsters, the bodies and hind legs of which are indicated in relief while the wings, breasts, and necks are covered with cloisons (see p. 96) once filled with colored stones cut to fit the depressions. This is an early and interesting use of the cloison that was to play so important a part in Byzantine decoration (Fig. 340). The animal forms are highly conventionalized, so that their simplified outline forms a bold, vigorous design peculiarly fitted to the medium. It was not the purpose of the artist here to use the charmingly naturalistic expression of the animal form that we found on the Egyptian jug (Fig. 98), but by a severe simplification to utilize the decorative pattern that the form suggested. In some of the Luristan bronzes [1] also we find this vivid grasp of the essentials of an object expressed by means of conventions that are extraordinarily decorative (Fig. 140). Others display a vivid naturalism of the kind seen in the *Winged Ibex* handle (Fig. 141).

[1] A great number of small objects made of several kinds of bronze have been excavated recently in the mountains of Luristan, a province of western Persia south of Kermanshah. Though they include objects of personal adornment such as long pins, weapons, and ceremonial objects, a great number are from harnesses and chariots. Scholars differ widely as to their dates.

At this point it may be well at least to mention the highly important metalwork of the nomadic peoples of northern Eurasia (Russia, Siberia, Turkestan, Mongolia, China), which shows an affinity with the Sumerian and the Persian and may have a common origin with them.[1] Over this vast area extended after Neolithic times a unified culture of nomadic peoples whose great vitality found expression in a style of equal vitality and of extraordinary artistic excellence. It was an art confined to the making and embellishing of objects of everyday life among nomadic hunters, and its chief subject was the animal. The medium was sometimes bronze, bone, or wood, but largely gold, which local mines provided in abundance. In this art we find processions of animals, two interlocked fighting animals (FIG. 142), objects terminating in animals' heads. At times color was added by the use of enamels or cut stones. While occasionally naturalism appears, especially when these peoples came in contact with the Greeks and the Romans, the forms are chiefly conventional ones adapted to the exigencies of space-filling and are superbly decorative (FIG. 143).

D. SUMMARY

Achaemenian art was a kingly art, vital and of great splendor — splendor of scale, of materials, and particularly of color. Its most important buildings were built to house a thoroughly human, though absolute, monarch in befitting magnificence. Spacious stone stairways with elaborate carvings and forests of decorative stone columns combined to give this regal impression. Though its forms are outwardly serene, they are vital. Their essentials are grasped with directness and expressed, whether by convention or naturalistically, with peculiarly decorative fitness.

BIBLIOGRAPHY

Andrae, Walter, *Coloured Ceramics from Ashur, and Earlier Ancient Assyrian Wall Paintings*, London, 1925
Baikie, James, *The Glamour of Near East Excavation*, Lippincott, 1928
———— *The Life of the Ancient East*, Macmillan, 1923
Breasted, J. H., *Ancient Times*, 2d ed. rev., Ginn, 1935
Childe, V. G., *The Most Ancient East*, Knopf, 1929
Cossio, M. B., and Pijoan, José, *Summa artis*, Madrid, 1931–34, Vols. I–VI, Vol. II
Gadd, C. J., *History and Monuments of Ur*, Dutton, 1929
Garstang, John, *The Hittite Empire*, Long & Smith, 1929

[1] This art — its origin and its relationship with Sumerian, Persian, Greek, Far Eastern, and west-European art — has recently been the subject of much scholarly research and the term *Urasian animal art* is now being applied to it. See Rostovtsev (p. 101).

Grousset, René, *The Civilizations of the East*, tr. by C. A. Phillips, Knopf, 1931
Hall, H. R. H., *The Ancient History of the Near East*, 8th ed. rev., Macmillan, 1932
—— —— *Babylonian and Assyrian Sculpture in the British Museum*, Paris, 1928
Handcock, P. S. P., *Mesopotamian Archaeology*, Putnam, 1912
Harcourt-Smith, Simon, *Babylonian Art*, Stokes, 1928
Jastrow, Morris, *The Civilization of Babylonia and Assyria*, Lippincott, 1915
Koldewey, Robert, *Excavations at Babylon*, Macmillan, 1914
Olmstead, A. T. E., *History of Assyria*, Scribner, 1923
Oppenheim, Max, Freiherr von, *Der Tell Halaf*, Leipzig, 1931
Pottier, Edmond, *L'art hittite*, Paris, 1926, Pts. I–II
Rostovtsev, M. I., *The Animal Style in South Russia and China*, Princeton University Press, 1929
Sarre, F. P. C., *Die Kunst des alten Persien*, Berlin, 1922
Schäfer, Heinrich, and Andrae, Walter, *Die Kunst des alten Orients*, Berlin, 1925
Schneider, Hermann, *History of World Civilization*, Harcourt, Brace, 1931, 2 vols.
Woolley, C. L., *Dead Towns and Living Men*, rev. ed., Oxford Press, 1929
—— —— *The Development of Sumerian Art*, Scribner, 1935
—— —— *The Sumerians*, Oxford Press, 1928
—— —— *Ur of the Chaldees*, Scribner, 1930

See also the General Bibliography pp. 749-751.

CHAPTER V

Aegean Art

(about 3000–1100 B.C.)

A. HISTORICAL BACKGROUND

When Aegeus was king of Athens, Minos the great sea king of Crete, having conquered the Athenians in a war to avenge the treacherous murder of his son, levied upon Athens a tribute of seven youths and seven maidens to be sent every nine years to feed the great Minotaur that he kept in a vast, intricate building known as the Labyrinth. Two of these human levies had already been paid and the time was approaching for sending a third, when Aegeus' son Theseus asked to be chosen as one of the seven youths in the hope that he might kill the monster and so free his country from this horrible tribute. The sail of the tribute ship was black in recognition of her gruesome mission. As Theseus lifted anchor, he agreed with his father that if his attempt was successful he would carry a white sail on the return trip. When he arrived in Crete and appeared before the king, his beauty and the fate awaiting him so aroused the fair-haired Ariadne, daughter of Minos, that she assisted Theseus to enter the Labyrinth carrying a sword with which he killed the monster; he then retraced his steps by means of a thread that she had given him. With Ariadne and his com-

Fig. 144. A Prince or Priest-King.
Painted relief, restored. From Palace at Knossos. c. 1500 B.C. (Evans,
The Palace of Minos, Macmillan)

Fig. 145. Head of a Young Girl.
Fresco from Knossos. H. c. 9 in. c.
1500 B.C. Candia Museum. (Metropolitan Museum)

panions he fled from the island. But, in the joy of his return, he forgot to hoist the white sail; and old King Aegeus, standing on the cliffs and peering out over the sea to catch the first glimpse of the returning boat, on seeing the black sail cast himself into the sea, which, after him, was called the Aegean. And Theseus became king of Athens.

So reads the old Greek legend. Up to the year 1900, however, no remains had been found to substantiate the story. Already Heinrich Schliemann had proved that the Homeric tales of Troy were based on historical fact. Schliemann, as a child, had been told the story of the Trojan War and of the great walls that protected the ancient city; and in spite of opposition he strongly maintained his belief that those walls must still be standing. He had acquired a small amount of education, but in the little grocery store in which he sold herring and butter, sugar and candles, from five in the morning until eleven at night, he had not a moment for study. However, he kept warm in his heart the love of learning, and his dream of one day finding the walls of Troy. One evening there entered the little shop a man who, dissatisfied with his lot, had given himself up to drink, "which, however, had not made him forget his Homer; for on the evening that he entered the shop he recited to us about a hundred lines of the poet,

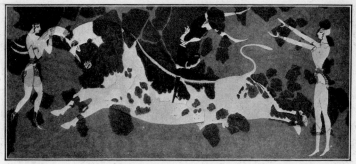

Fig. 146. Toreador Scene. Fresco. c. 1500 b.c. Candia Museum.
(Metropolitan Museum, New York)

observing the rhythmic cadence of the verses. Although I did not understand a syllable, the melodious sound of the words made a deep impression upon me, and I wept bitter tears over my unhappy fate. Three times over did I get him to repeat to me those divine verses, rewarding his trouble with three glasses of whiskey, which I bought with the few pence that made up my whole fortune. From that moment I never ceased to pray God that by His grace I might yet have the happiness of learning Greek." [1] Now the desire burned more fiercely than ever; but not until middle life, when he finally amassed a fortune, was he free to follow his dream. He then went to the locality which his knowledge of the Iliad led him to believe was the site of Troy, and there found nine cities built one on the remains of another. There were ancient walls and signs of a great conflagration, and Schliemann proclaimed that he had found the actual city. Subsequent excavations proved that the site was correct, but that he had erred in deciding that the second instead of the sixth was Homer's Troy. He continued his excavating at Mycenae, whence sailed the proud chieftains to avenge the capture of Helen, and his success was even more startling. Massive fortress-palaces, elaborate tombs, great quantities of gold jewelry and ornaments, cups and inlaid weapons — all revealed a pre-Hellenic civilization of high culture and wide extent that is now called Mycenaean.

But Mycenae, after all, did not prove to have been its center. Sir Arthur Evans had long considered Crete a potentially fertile field for investigation. Under Turkish rule, excavation was impossible; but when in 1898 Crete was free from the Turkish régime the opportunity came, and about 1900 work began. In a short time, Evans' faith was rewarded far beyond his expectations. His spade did not dig very

[1] Schliemann, *Ilios, the City and Country of the Trojans*, Harper, 1881, p. 7.

Fig. 147. Fragment of a Seal Showing the Transportation of a Horse (with the design completed by dotted lines). The large size of the horse, which is drawn over the ship rather than in it, may indicate the importance of the event. For probably it represents the importation of the thoroughbred horse from the Near East to Crete. (*British School Annual*)

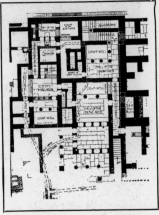

Fig. 148. Palace of Minos. Knossos. Plan of the domestic quarter, with dotted lines to indicate the drainage system. (*British School Annual*)

deep before it had uncovered the palaces of the old kings. Sea kings they were. No fortified walls protected their palaces, for the broad reaches of water around their island served in the place of walls. Their ships plied to the three continents to which their island was gateway (FIGS. 104, 174). Of these sea kings, whose power extended over the islands of the Aegean and over parts of the mainland, the greatest was Minos. His *Palace at Knossos* (FIG. 149) was a large, rambling structure, in parts several stories high, built about open courts, with broad stairways, colonnaded halls, bathrooms, a drainage system, finely paved floors, oil-tinted parchment windows, and gaily decorated walls. Perhaps the very throne upon which the king sat we see in the so-called throne room. Long corridors led to magazines where, in huge jars, were stored wine, oil, grain, and honey. Everything spoke of comfort and luxury. Pottery cups of eggshell thinness, decorated both in naturalistic and in conventional designs, producing a rich harmonious effect; gold cups with reliefs of animal life (FIG. 172); finely designed gold ornaments, decorated with relief and engraving (FIG. 171); a gaming-board glittering with gold and silver, ivory, and blue enamel — all these tell of wealth and splendor.

It was a proud people who ruled the sea from these luxurious palaces. Here is a *Prince* (FIG. 144) or perhaps a *Priest-King*, consciously proud, alertly alive, a lithe athletic figure, with long curly hair topped with peacock plumes, clad in a simple loincloth fastened by a heavy belt

Fig. 149. Palace of Minos. Knossos. Colonnaded hall, restored.
c. 1500 B.C. (Evans)

about his attenuated waist. Here is a *Young Girl* (Fig. 145) jaunty
and piquant with her gay beribboned dress, loose curls, and individualized features. Here is a group of ladies (Fig. 151), with flounced
skirts, low-cut laced bodices, flying locks — eagerly gossiping. The
great crowd seems to be present at some festival, probably religious
because a shrine is evident; or possibly bull-grappling. Fig. 146 illustrates this popular sport. Here a youth is vaulting over the back
of a charging bull toward the outstretched arms of a girl acrobat at
the right, while another girl, at the left, grasping the horns of the bull
is about to leap after her companion. Here we may see some of the
captive youths sent into the bull ring to please the Cretan lords.[1]

So this picture of Cretan life substantiates the old Greek legend.
The intricate maze of rooms in the palace and the frequent vivid
pictures of scenes in bull rings furnish a background for the Theseus

[1] The earlier interpretation of such a scene, very frequent in Cretan art, as a sort
of gladiatorial fight has generally been modified in the direction of seeing in it merely
a popular sport for the display of dramatic movement and agility — a "toreador" or
"cowboy" affair. While it "may represent one of the sports in which the Cretans
delighted, its origin was in all probability a rite in honor of the bull god. Perhaps
captives were dedicated to this sport. . . . But there may have been trained toreadors
who engaged in the sport for its excitement. This scene would then become merely
a film from a Minoan circus." — M. H. Swindler, *Ancient Painting*, Yale University
Press, 1929, p. 84.

Fig. 150. Cupbearer.
Fresco from Knossos.
H. c. 5 ft. c. 1500 B.C.
Candia Museum. (Met-
ropolitan Museum)

legend. Furthermore, the broad paved courts well may be "the dancing-ground that Daedalus wrought at Knossos for fair-haired Ariadne," while the gold cups and inlaid swords bear witness to "every form of lovely craftsmanship, resting on all things, as he [Homer] says, like the shining of the sun." [1]

Who were the people who developed this civilization,[2] the first on the northern side of the Mediterranean Sea? We do not know their origin. In Neolithic times they were there. Early they had bronze and a system of writing, not yet deciphered. The climate of Crete is mild and sunny, but though the winter rains make production easy in the fertile places, it is not primarily an agricultural land. Its location in the Mediterranean makes it the gateway to three continents. Thus the Cretans became a seafaring people, traders and colonizers (FIG. 147), bartering their own wares, notably their pottery and metalwork, around the Aegean, in Asia, and in Egypt, where their pottery seems to have been popular judging from the number of representations of it in Egyptian tomb paintings. Apparently they were not a united people but a group of city-states, Knossos, Phaestus, Gournia, and others. Their religion consisted of nature worship, with rites performed not in great temples but sometimes before little shrines in the palaces though chiefly in caves, gorges, and groves. "Spiritual devotion in such surroundings," Mr. Forsdyke suggests, "must have led . . . to an intimate and emotional understanding of life and beauty in all the works of nature." [3]

At the time of its climax, under King Minos, the Cretan civilization had spread to the islands and the mainland, to Mycenae, Tiryns, and Troy, where, however, conditions were somewhat different from those on the island. Warlike Achaean Greek nomads were beginning to filter in, which necessitated fortifications. As they became more

[1] W. H. Pater, *Greek Studies*, Macmillan, 1895, "The Heroic Age of Greek Art."
[2] Several names are used for this civilization, "Aegean" being the most inclusive. It is frequently called "Minoan," after its most famous king and most brilliant age, though strictly speaking, the term is anachronistic if used before 1500 B.C. At present there seems to be a tendency to apply "Cretan" or "Minoan" to that aspect of the civilization which definitely belongs to the island of Crete; "Helladic" to that of the mainland; and "Cycladic" to that of the islands.
[3] E. J. Forsdyke, *Minoan Art*, Oxford Press, 1931, p. 29.

Fig. 151. Temple Fresco. Restored. From a small sanctuary in the Palace at Knossos. C. 1600 B.C.

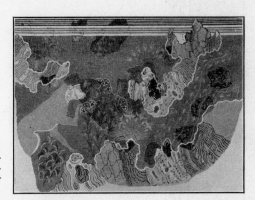

Fig. 152. Blue Monkey. Fresco from a town house. C. 1600 B.C. (Metropolitan Museum, New York)

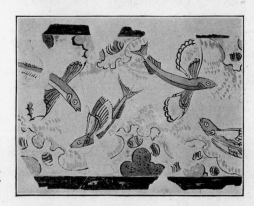

Fig. 153. Flying Fish. Fresco. Candia Museum. (Metropolitan Museum, New York)

107

Fig. 154. Citadel at Tiryns. Restored.
(Luckenbach)

Fig. 155. Citadel at Tiryns. Corbeled gallery.
(Perrot and Chipiez)

numerous and more powerful, there was a restless shifting about, with frequent conflicts between the barbarian invaders and the inhabitants. Such a conflict we see in the Homeric tale of the siege of Troy. Finally, the last great wave of invaders, known as the Doric Greeks, swept across to Crete, burned the *Palace at Knossos*, and by 1100 B.C. had taken possession of the Aegean world. The Cretan culture, already giving evidence of decay, continued for some time and made definite and valuable contributions to the second civilization to arise, in historical times, in Europe, the Hellenic.[1]

B. ARCHITECTURE AND PAINTING

The demands for building were simple and limited. There was no demand in Crete for tombs, temples, halls of justice, not even for fortresses. Only a palace for the king and his retainers, large, comfortable, gay, with ample staircases and courtyards for pageants and shows. Such is the *Palace at Knossos* (FIG. 148), which consists of a large number of rooms grouped about a central court: living-rooms of all

[1] The history of Crete falls into three divisions: Early Minoan (about 3500 to 2200 B.C.), Middle Minoan (2200–1600 B.C.), and Late Minoan (1600–1100 B.C.). In the early part of the Late Minoan occurred the reign of King Minos (about 1500). The Homeric Age, so called because it is described in the Homeric poems, which were written much later, includes the period of the great migrations and conflicts from about 1350 to 1100 B.C.

kinds, with bathrooms, audience halls, chapels,
workshops, and huge magazines. At several
points fine broad stairways led to upper stories;
for the palace was built on a hillside and in
some places was several stories high. In the
colonnaded hall (FIG. 149) we see one of these
stairways. The foundation and the lower parts
of the building were built of huge, finely cut
blocks of stone, but the columns were of wood.
Each column has a small circular base, carries
a cushionlike capital with a square block to
support the lintel, and tapers toward the base,
a curious fact, not yet satisfactorily explained,
but characteristic of Aegean column construction (FIGS. 151, 160). Both columns and walls
were painted brightly.

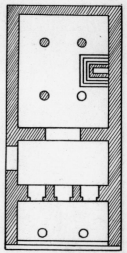

Fig. 156. Plan of a
Megaron.

Painting, in other words, was mural decoration, the chief decorative element of the palaces, and its subject matter was Cretan life:
bullfights, processionals and ceremonials, many
scenes from nature, birds, animals, flowers, fish and sea life. The *Cupbearer* (FIG. 150), a detail from a procession, is holding a gold-mounted
silver vase. He has long curly hair, wears an elaborately embroidered
loincloth with a silver-mounted girdle, silver ornaments on his arms,
neck, and ankles, and on his wrist an agate seal. The pinched waist, the
reason for which we do not know, is characteristic of both the men and
the women of Crete. The effect of the procession must have been highly
decorative, as the dark [1] figures moved rhythmically against the flat,
vivid blue background. Although, as in Egyptian painting, the flat
tones serve the purpose of decoration, still the youth standing so erect,
with shoulders thrown far back, is not cold, formal, and conventional,
but full of life and keenly conscious of the pride of his race and the nobility of the ceremony that he is performing.

The *Toreador Scene* (FIG. 146) shows how well these painters could
represent a dramatic moment, fill it with spirit, with instantaneous
poses, and still, as it were, keep it on the wall. Here the remarkable
vivacity and decorative quality are both made effective by the long
sweeping curves in the body of the bull combined with the S-curves
in the horns and tail and in the vaulting youth, and by the vivid patterning of the surface.

In one of the *Temple Frescoes* [2] (FIG. 151) crowds are massed about

---

[1] As in Egypt, male figures are painted red and female yellow.
[2] Also called *Miniature Frescoes* because of the small scale, which was necessitated

Fig. 157. Fragment of a Tomb Ceiling. Carved green schist. Orchomenos. (*Journal Hellenic Studies*) Compare, for decorative motifs, Figs. 86 and 125.

a shrine as if attending some ceremonial or show.. Over large washes of red, indicating men, heads are outlined in black with white collars and white eyes, producing a very convincing impression of a crowd. In contrast to the crowd represented by this "shorthand" method are groups of ladies, on each side of the shrine, with the entire figure painted in detail. Their elaborate dresses (they perhaps are ladies of the court) are painted in bright colors, and the effect of their spirited conversation is heightened by augmenting gestures.

In the nature scenes one finds not only understanding but a profound love of nature and a high degree of imagination in representing it. In the *Blue Monkey* (FIG. 152) a monkey is treading, through papyrus flowers, over fantastically veined rocks from which grow clumps of crocuses and trailing vines. The essentials of each form are set down spontaneously and imaginatively in large flat areas of strong color, quite disregardful of nature's hues: the monkey is blue, the crocuses are red with blue or yellow leaves, the rocks are of every color of the Cretan's palette, the ground is red. Everything, even the rocks, is alive with its own inherent, impelling reality, yet in its visual form on the wall achieves a new imaginative entity. In the *Flying Fish Fresco* (FIG. 153) the impression is of an easy swinging movement and countermovement combined with a short quick movement in the rocks and edges of the fins, like surging waves which break in light crests: an impression of blues, yellows, browns, definitely and happily distributed over a flat surface. Something of the spontaneity of the

by the size of the room, about 6 by 15 feet; a dado fills the lower part of the wall with the frescoes above on the eye level.

Fig. 158. Frieze. Of alabaster with blue glass inlay. Tiryns.

painting is due to the use of true fresco technique, which demands a sure, quick brush stroke and gives little opportunity for repainting.[1]

As we leave these charmingly gay places on the island and pass over to the mainland we perceive a difference. At *Tiryns* (FIG. 154) on the hilltop is a massive fortress-palace with walls twenty or more feet thick, built of unhewn or roughly dressed stone, called Cyclopean walls by the later Greeks. Through them at places run galleries (FIG. 155) made of great stones in horizontal layers, roofed over by making each course project over the one below until the opening is closed, thus forming a corbeled arch.[2] Here the projecting blocks are roughly beveled. Though resembling Knossos on a smaller scale, *Tiryns* contains in its *megaron*, or hall of state, the nucleus of the establishment, an element not found in Crete. The megaron is a rectangular room with a hearth in the center around which are four columns to support the roof; at the entrance is a vestibule and porch (FIG. 156). Here are reflected a colder climate and another race, from the north.

There is a sternness about these fortress-palaces, relieved, however, by frescoes similar to the Cretan, carvings (FIGS. 157, 158), and, at Mycenae at least, by monumental architectural sculpture. At this fortress-palace the stone in the walls about the entrance is more finely cut than elsewhere in the structure. The door itself is formed of two great pillars capped with a huge lintel, above which the layers of stone are not solid, but by forming a corbeled arch leave a triangular opening to relieve the weight on the lintel. This space is filled with

[1] True fresco means painting in watercolor upon wet plaster with which the pigment becomes chemically incorporated and therefore cannot be altered or removed. It is to be distinguished from the painting upon a dry stone or stucco wall as in the Egyptian paintings.
[2] To be distinguished from the true arch, made of voussoirs.

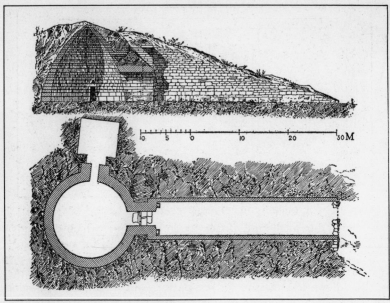

Fig. 159. Tomb Called the "Treasury of Atreus." Mycenae. (Perrot and Chipiez)

Fig. 160. Lion Gate. Mycenae. Probably late Minoan.

a slab on which are carved in high relief the two lions from which the gate is named (Fig. 160). The lions stand in a balanced position on either side of a shaft, on the base of which they rest their forepaws. Holes near the top indicate that the heads, now lost, were made of separate pieces of stone or metal. Groups similar to this are seen on Cretan seals and probably constitute a heraldic device. The lions are carved with breadth and vigor, and the whole design admirably fills the triangular space in which it is placed, harmonizing in dignity, strength, and scale with the massive stones that form the walls and the gate. In its visual as well as functional effectiveness it seems to partake of the spirit of the warring Agamemnon and Menelaus.

Fig. 161. Head of a Bull. Painted plaster relief. L. 26 in. Candia Museum. (Metropolitan Museum, New York)

Another type of building found on the mainland was the so-called beehive tomb. When first discovered, it was thought these structures were storehouses for treasure; hence the most important is known as the *Treasury of Atreus* (FIG. 159). Probably for the sake of protection, it was built into the hill and approached by a long passage cut through the side. Its beehive shape is

Fig. 162. Snake Goddess. Gold and ivory. H. 6½ in. c. 1500 B.C. Museum of Fine Arts, Boston. (Boston Museum)

formed by corbeling courses of stone laid on a circular base. The small rectangular chamber at the side is hewn from the rock. Frequent holes in the interior seem to indicate that decorations, such as bronze rosettes, were affixed. In the monumental entrance we find the same combination of lintel and corbeled-arch construction as in the *Lion Gate*. Among the motifs of decoration, we see on the column the chevron; on the bands above, the spiral, rosette, and palmette. The columns here, as at Knossos, taper toward the base.

C. SCULPTURE

Sculpture in the round, judging from the small amount extant, seems not to have interested the Aegean peoples. Perhaps the chief examples are the figurines of ivory, usually combined with gold, best illustrated by the *Snake Goddess* (FIG. 162). On her head is an elaborate coronet, the holes in which indicate gold attachments, probably ornaments and the usual curls. The flounces of her skirt are banded with gold and her outstretched hands hold two gold snakes that coil about her arms. Like the *Cupbearer*, she stands proudly erect with shoulders thrown back, firmly grasping the snakes, a forceful figure based upon a strong

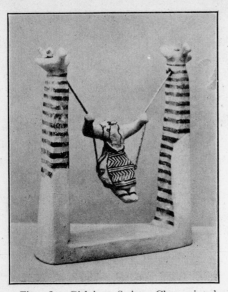

Fig. 163. Girl in a Swing. Clay painted. H. 5½ in. c. 1600 B.C. Metropolitan Museum, New York. (Metropolitan Museum)

curve in the back and the vigorous diagonals in the arms.[1] The head is not conceived as an oval mass upon which the features are engraved, but as an organic structure of which they are an integral part. Mention should be made of the clay figurines of Cretan ladies, simply and sketchily molded and gaily glazed, which show such an intelligent feeling for material; and of the *Girl in a Swing* (FIG. 163), in which one discerns a peculiar sensitivity for clay as the medium for a summary momentary expression.

Sculpture in relief appears frequently, in stone, clay, and various metals. The *Head of a Bull* (FIG. 161), probably a fragment from a bullfighting scene, gives one a vital impression of an enraged animal; while a small steatite vase, the *Harvester Vase* (FIG. 165), furnishes an equally vital impression of a riotous crowd and one perfectly in unison with a curving surface of stone. A crowd of harvesters singing and shouting follow a figure with a shaven head carrying a sistrum. Their forward movement and lusty exuberance are expressed with a direct forcefulness. At the same time the pitchforks, carved in low relief, hug the surface tightly and even the figures, though in higher relief, are an integral part of the surface.

The same kind of miniature carving in intaglio that we observed in the cylinder seals of Babylonia (FIGS. 114, 115) we find in the Cretan seals, which however are not the cylinder type but are settings in rings and bracelets with the design cut on the bezel. A variety of hard stones of various colors were used and a variety of subject matter, often, apparently, with heraldic significance. The animal subjects are especially noteworthy for their vivacious life and beauty of composition and carving.

[1] A possible companion figure, the *Divine Boy*, recently discovered, has many parallel characteristics, and may indicate that both figures belonged to a shrine group. For this see Sir A. J. Evans, *The Palace of Minos*, Macmillan, 1921–30, Vols. I–III, Vol. III, pp. 436 ff.

D. MINOR ARTS

Among the craftsmen of Crete the potter was of special consequence, since his wares were important articles of commerce. In the early *Kamares Ware* [1] (Fig. 166) we find a robust shape with a lustrous black ground on which is a quasi-geometric pattern of creamy white interspersed with yellow and red, forming a brilliant and harmonious piece of decoration. The tendency of the potters, as time went on, was away from geometric and conventional design toward the nat-

Fig. 164. Octopus Vase. H. c. 8 in. 1600–1500 B.C. Candia Museum. (Metropolitan Museum, New York)

uralistic, with decorative motifs taken from their own immediate world of nature. Sea life, for example, furnished the decorative scheme of a filler [2] (Fig. 167); dolphins and the fish net covering the body, sprays of seaweed covering the shoulder, neck, and rim. Note that the dark glaze is used for the figures against the clay ground; and that each motif is conventionalized to just the decorative unit that harmonizes with the proportions of the filler and the curvature of its surface. This is particularly true of the *Octopus Vase* (Fig. 164), in which the tentacles reaching out over the curving surfaces make one particularly aware of the volume of the vase. From the land, crocuses, iris, lilies, reeds, and grasses present to the artist's seeing eye patterns which have all the reality of nature and at the same time are an organic part of the wall of a jar. "Tall grasses fence the slim body of a tapered cup which in turn refines their elegance." [3]

Among the large jars called *Palace Style* because many have been found at Knossos and appear to belong to the period of its most splendid development, that represented in Fig. 168 has an interesting design of skillfully interlaced birds combined with concentric bands and spirals, painted with a bold sweep of line. Areas of light and dark are broken here and there by a patterning of dots and wave lines, every part moving in unison with the curving surface. In Fig. 169 the double-ax motive plays through the design — in the shape of the

[1] So called from the cave on Mt. Ida where a large number of examples have been found.

[2] So named because, as it is pierced at the bottom, its purpose was probably that of filling one vessel from another, like a modern funnel.

[3] Forsdyke, *op. cit.*, p. 17.

Fig. 165. Harvester Vase. Black steatite. H. c. 4 in. The lower part of the vase is lost. c. 1500 B.C. Candia Museum. (*Monumenti antichi*)

handles, in the space between the handles, and between the horns of the ox, on the rim, and on the foot. It probably has some religious significance, and the vase may have been used for ceremonial purposes. Notice the naturalistic sprays of olive in the midst of an otherwise conventional design.

Another craftsman of great importance was the metalworker, as we see in a bronze basin (FIG. 170). The rim is hammered out into a pattern of conventionalized lilies that spring diagonally from a beading and terminate in flamelike waving lines, the exuberance of which contrasts delightfully with the formal conventional treatment of the lilies. The same pattern decorates the finely tapering handle, to which a feeling of strength is added by the large raised beads in the center.

In the work of the goldsmith some of the jewelry of gold leaf exhibits the charming naturalism so characteristic of Minoan work. In other examples, in those from Mycenae in particular, geometric design is predominant, especially the spiral, which is used with great variety and forcefulness of line; and also such conventionalized forms as the butterfly (FIG. 173). The climax of the work of the goldsmith is found in the *Vaphio Cups* [1] (FIG. 172), which are of a teacup shape, each made of two plates of gold, one of which was worked in repoussé to decorate

[1] So called because they were found in a grave at Vaphio in Laconia.

Fig. 166. Kamares Vase. From Knossos. H. c. 9 in.
2000–1800 B.C. Candia Museum.

the outside, the other left plain to make a
smooth finish on the inside. They were then
fastened together and the handles riveted
on; some of the details were engraved. On
one cup is a bull-hunting scene filled with
the greatest movement. In the center is a

Fig. 167. Dolphin Filler.
1600–1500 B.C. (Seager)

bull caught in the meshes of a net, a second furiously charging, im-
pales with his horns a hunter whose companion falls to one side, while
a third bull dashes madly from the fracas. On the other cup is a
quiet scene, possibly representing bull-hunting by means of a decoy
cow. At the right a peaceful bull has been attracted and moves toward the cow; at the left the same bull, captured and hobbled by the
trapper, is bellowing in anger. The three scenes are well united by the
trees and the trapper, and the whole design admirably composed to
fit the space. In both cups there is an astonishing feeling for and interpretation of animal life, but at the same time, as in the paintings,
an adaptation to the material and to the space. The bull caught in
the net, for example, may be impossible from the point of view of nature but is quite "correct" as forming a part of a vigorous pattern of
sweeping curves. The relief is just high enough to give a rich play of
light and shade, to which the sheen of the gold brings additional
splendor.

Another type of metalwork is seen in a dagger blade (FIG. 171).
The figures are inlaid on a bronze base, with different kinds and

Fig. 168. Palace Style Vase. H. c. 30 in.
1500–1350 B.C. National Museum, Athens.
(Metropolitan Museum)

Fig. 169. Palace Style Vase. 1600
1500 B.C. (Seager)

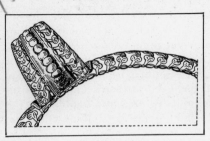

Fig. 170. Handle and Rim of a
Bronze Basin.

colors of metal, such as gold, silver, and some black material. On one side is a lion hunt. Five men with spears, shields, and arrows are attacking the lions, two of whom are fleeing, while a third, wounded, turns to attack. The bodies of the fleeing animals, elongated as if to accentuate their rapid movement, fit marvelously into the tapering shape. This process of metalworking is known as damascening.[1] On the metal base, usually bronze, the design is outlined with a sharp instrument and the parts to be inlaid are cut out, leaving a depression with a slight undercutting on the edges. Into this depression pieces of different colored metal, cut to fit, are sunk and pressed firmly into

[1] From Damascus, not because the craft originated in that city but because the metalworkers living there became famous for their product. See color reproductions of several daggers in Evans, *op. cit.*, Vol. III, Pl. XX.

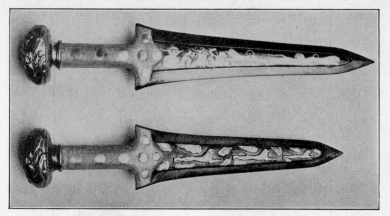

Fig. 171. Dagger Blades from Mycenae. Bronze, inlaid with gold, electrum, and some black substance. 1600–1500 B.C. Restored reproductions in the Metropolitan Museum, New York. (Metropolitan Museum)

Repoussé

Fig. 172. Vaphio Cups. Gold H. 3½ in. 1600–1500 B.C.
National Museum, Athens.

Fig. 173. Gold Disks from Mycenae. Purpose unknown.
D. 2½in. 1600–1500 B.C.

the undercut edges. The surface is then smoothed and polished. Details are sometimes engraved.

E. SUMMARY

In Aegean art, notably in that of Crete, we find nothing imposing or mysterious, no gorgeous panoply of a royal court, but a style directly expressive of a democratic people intimate with nature. It is a refreshing, sprightly art, imaginative and naturalistic rather than abstract. Its restlessness and movement reflect an exuberance of body and mind. The adventures of the Cretans on the sea were equaled by the love of pleasure at home to which their palaces bear witness. These palaces with their equipment and articles of personal adornment constitute practically the entire Cretan art expression, except for similar articles made for trading. They were equipped comfortably, even luxuriously, and their walls were gay with frescoes which picture life on land and on sea, and decorate as well. The unceasing variety in Aegean pottery and paintings (contrast the unceasing repetitions in Egypt and Assyria), the vivacity and oddity of their color relations, reflect the eagerness, restlessness, and adventuresomeness of the Cretan sea kings; and the magnificence of their metalwork is witness that the descriptions in Homer of the shield of Achilles and the house of Alcinoüs were based not upon imagination, but upon the actual appearance of the civilization which they reflect.

BIBLIOGRAPHY

Baikie, James, *The Sea-Kings of Crete*, Macmillan, 1920
Bell, Edward, *Prehellenic Architecture in the Aegean*, London, 1926
Bossert, H. T., *Altkreta*, Berlin, 1923
Breasted, J. H., *Ancient Times*, 2d ed. rev., Ginn, 1935
Burrows, R. M., *The Discoveries in Crete*, Dutton, 1907
Buschor, Ernst, *Greek Vase-Painting*, Dutton, 1922
Evans, Sir A. J., *The Palace of Minos*, Macmillan, 1921–30, Vols. I–III
Forsdyke, E. J., *Minoan Art*, Oxford Press, 1931
Fowler, H. N., and Wheeler, J. R., *Handbook of Greek Archaeology*, American Book Co.,
    1909
Glasgow, George, *The Minoans*, London, 1923
Hall, H. R. H., *Aegean Archaeology*, Putnam, 1914
—— —— *The Ancient History of the Near East*, 8th ed. rev., Macmillan, 1932
—— —— *The Civilization of Greece in the Bronze Age*, London, 1928
Hawes, C. H. and H. A. B., *Crete, the Forerunner of Greece*, Harper, 1911
Mackenzie, D. A., *Myths of Crete and Pre-Hellenic Europe*, London, 1917
Mosso, Angelo, *The Palaces of Crete and Their Builders*, Putnam, 1907
Pater, W. H., *Greek Studies*, Macmillan, 1928 (first published 1895)
Pendlebury, J. D. S., *A Handbook to the Palace of Minos at Knossos*, Macmillan, 1933
Rodenwaldt, G. M. K., *Die Kunst der Antike*, Berlin, 1927
Schuchhardt, Karl, *Schliemann's Excavations*, tr. by Eugènie Sellers, Macmillan, 1891
Sheppard, J. T., *The Pattern of the Iliad*, London, 1922
Swindler, M. H., *Ancient Painting*, Yale University Press, 1929
Tsountas, Chrestos, and Manatt, J. I., *The Mycenaean Age*, Houghton Mifflin, 1897

See also the General Bibliography, pp. 749–751.

Part Three

CLASSICAL ART

CHAPTER VI

Greek Art

1. GEOMETRIC, ARCHAIC, AND FIFTH–CENTURY ART
(about 1100–400 B.C.)

A. HISTORICAL BACKGROUND

In marked contrast to Egypt, a land monotonous with the long horizontals of alluvial plain between desert plateaus and under invariable sunshine, Greece [1] is a country of diversified geography and climate (FIG. 174). The deeply indented bays of its rugged coast line make the country half land and half sea; mountain ridges divide it into many small units. The semitropical climate, with its varying conditions of rain and sunshine, is free from extremes of heat and cold. The unusually crystalline atmosphere is softened by a haze. Both sky and sea are brilliant in color. Little wonder is it that the Greeks, who were by nature sensitive to beauty and gifted with imagination, in their joy in nature should people the mountains, woods, streams, the sky, and the sea with divinities; that they should picture Zeus, the king of this realm of gods, as reigning from their loftiest peak, Olympus; the Muses, as dwelling in the deep, cool groves on the long slopes of Parnassus and Cithaeron; and Apollo, the god of wisdom, as speaking from the awe-inspiring clefts of Delphi. These geographic and climatic conditions probably had something to do with the eager individualistic strain in the race.

Who were the Greeks? They appear to be the product of a racial intermingling, with at least three components: the Mediterranean race, the Cretan culture, the Indo-European invaders. About 2000 B.C. these latter nomads began drifting in and mingling with the native inhabitants. About 1500 B.C. the Dorians, cruder, more militant Indo-

---

[1] In using the word "Greek" one needs to remember that the Greeks called themselves "Hellenes" and their country "Hellas."

Fig. 174. Crete and Greece.

European invaders, began to penetrate the Aegean lands. To this period belongs the siege of Troy, which is typical of the numerous conflicts between the Aegean strongholds such as Troy or Mycenae and the invaders. Those of the conquered peoples who had the means fled; the remainder mingled with the conquerors. Slowly they amalgamated, the invaders, with no system of writing, taking over certain elements of the gifted Cretan civilization. It was the Indo-European, however, whose religion, language, and fresh energizing power triumphed.

Early the enterprising Hellenes became a trading and colonizing people, and thus not only enlarged the geographic and cultural boundaries of Hellas but made contacts with the older civilizations — Egypt, Babylonia-Assyria, Phoenicia — from which they acquired

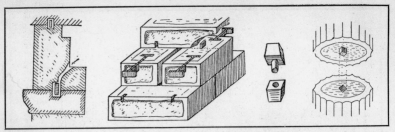

Fig. 175. Cramps and Dowels. Iron or bronze cramps hold the stones of the same course; iron dowels, packed with lead poured in through channels left for that purpose, hold the stones of different courses.

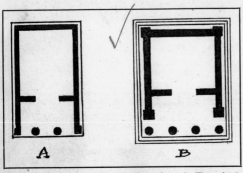

Fig. 176. Plans of Greek Temples. *A.* Temple *in antis*, so called because the portico is formed by the projecting side walls, *antae*, and two columns set between them. An example is the *Treasury of the Athenians* at Delphi. *B. Prostyle* temple, so called because the columns stand in front of the cella and extend the width of it. Sometimes an additional colonnade is placed at the back of the temple and it is then called *amphiprostyle*. An example is the *Temple of Nike Apteros* (*Wingless Victory*) on the Acropolis at Athens.

ideas, motifs, conventions, processes. Tribal organizations evolved into city-states, each an individual unit, ruled first by kings, then by nobles, then by tyrants or benevolent despots; and finally came the extraordinary experiment of complete democracy. To govern was not an accomplishment of the Greeks.

In religion, nature worship evolved into nature personification. The gods assumed human form, of grandeur and nobility though not free from human frailty. Man, in other words, became "the measure of all things"; to create the perfect individual became an ideal. Hence the interest in athletics and the characteristic Olympic games, athletic, literary, and musical contests celebrated every four years in honor of Zeus.

Athens, in many ways, stands as the symbol of Greek culture, though one must not forget the contributions in science, philosophy, and the arts, of Asia Minor and Magna Graecia. Should one visit Athens at the time of its brief flowering after the Persian wars, what would he see? An enterprising business city of about a hundred thousand people situated on a fertile plain about a lone hill, some four or five miles inland from a bustling harbor. In appearance the city was

Fig. 177. The Acropolis. Athens. This rocky hill stands about 500 feet above the plain. In the background are the slopes of Mt. Hymettus.

Fig. 178. Parthenon. Athens. Of Pentelic marble. 447–432 B.C.

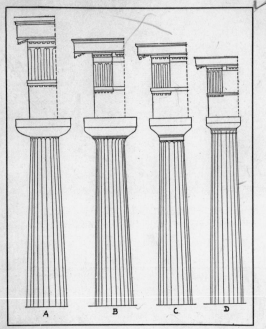

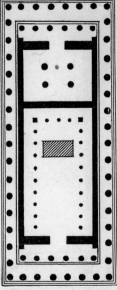

Fig. 179. The Evolution of Proportion in the Doric Order. *D* is the Parthenon, which appears to have attained the subtlest relationship of parts.

Fig. 180. Parthenon Plan. Athens. A peripteral temple based upon the plan of Fig. 176 *B*, but with an additional room for the treasure.

rather mean, an unplanned mass of small sun-dried brick houses along winding lanelike streets with no sidewalks and no drainage system. The chief open place was the agora, or market place, with its plane trees for shade; it was surrounded by public offices and covered colonnades called stoas. Though the market always served its primary purpose as a central place for the sale of vegetables, cheese, honey, and flowers, its actual use was much wider; for here the citizens congregated to lounge in the cool of the stoa, to discuss the latest political development or a new philosophical idea. Outside the walls were olive groves, and the gymnasiums where the men went daily, primarily for the bodily exercise that played so large a part in the education and daily life of the Athenian, but also, again, for discussion. And above both the olive groves and the roof tops towered the Acropolis, or higher city, formerly the fortress but in this age crowned with temples rising in bright colors against an intensely blue sky.

Since an important part of the conduct of business, at times even the entire responsibility, was assumed by slaves, the Athenian had a

Fig. 181. Two Drums, showing the cuttings left in the center for the bronze or wooden pivot which held the stones in place, correctly centered, and about which they were ground to secure a perfect joining. (Penrose)

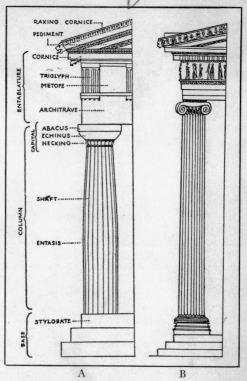

FIG. 182. A. The Doric Order. B. The Ionic Order.

great deal of leisure to spend in the open and to devote largely to the commonwealth — the world's first important experiment in democracy. This democracy manifested itself in the great religious festivals such as the Panathenaic procession, in which all the citizens, men and women, old and young, were represented; or at the dramatic performances of Aeschylus and Sophocles, where the audience of citizens approved with silence or applause, or condemned with a shower of figs and olives. The comedies of Aristophanes were enjoyed to the utmost when they satirized the great figures of the day with a daring that would be tolerated in no city not truly democratic. Quality was demanded in these plays by an audience that was composed of a people of all classes who were not art critics or theorizing esthetes but who as an everyday matter of fact knew good drama from bad. "But they knew," says Mr. Livingstone, "that it was better themselves to enact the drama of life than to see it on the stage. They were more interested in life than in art."

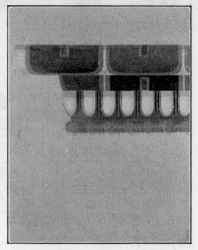

Fig. 183. Parthenon. Entablature. The parts were differentiated and united by means of color.

Fig. 184. Hawk's-Beak Molding from the Parthenon. Painted in red, blue, and gold. (After Penrose)

B. ARCHITECTURE AND SCULPTURE

With no use for the home except as an unpretentious place in which to eat and sleep, with no monarch to house royally, with religious rites performed in the open, what reason did the Greek have to build? Far earlier than we can trace the practice by monuments, the Greek carved statues of his gods, statues that were very sacred. To carve the statue and to protect it, then, was a motivation for both sculpture and architecture. Not mere protection, however, but beautiful protection, with additional sculpture partly for embellishment, partly to tell something of the deity symbolized within, and partly as votive offerings. In addition to those purely religious in purpose, statues were erected to commemorate important events, and particularly the victors at the great national games. It is, after all, a very simple and limited range of purpose, but the very key to Greek art.

Materials in abundance were at hand. Plenty of timber, and mountains, literally, of marble: Hymettus, just east of Athens, with its bluish-white stone; Pentelicus, north of the city, with its glittering white stone peculiarly adapted for carving. The islands of the Aegean, Paros in particular, supplied varying quantities and qualities. The ivory and the metals, especially bronze, of which great quantities were used, it was necessary to import. In building, cement was not

Fig. 185. Erechtheum. Athens. c. 420–409 B.C. (Clarence Kennedy)

used; the stones were held firmly by a series of cramps and dowels (FIG. 175).

There is a great gap between Aegean
art and the emergence of the truly Greek
expression about 600 B.C. Cretan culture
was already in decadence when the barbarous Dorians by their migration arrested
all cultural growth until they had assimilated the vastly superior civilization with
which they had come in contact, and had
evolved along individual lines. Probably
very early they carved statues and built
wooden structures to protect them, which by 600 B.C. they had translated into less perishable stone.[1] The temple discloses, in its plan,
a close affinity with the Mycenaean megaron (FIG. 156), and even
in its most elaborate form retains the utmost simplicity: a single room
with one door and no windows, and a portico, with two columns,
made by extending the walls (FIG. 176 A), or with a colonnade across
the entire front sometimes repeated across the back (FIG. 176 B); or any
of these plans entirely surrounded by a colonnade and hence called
peripteral (FIG. 180).[2]

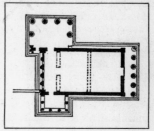

Fig. 186. The Erechtheum.
The temple probably contained
more than one shrine.

[1] The wood-construction origin of the Greek stone temple, though a controversial
point, seems to explain many details: the triglyphs as ends of the beams; the metopes
as the wall space between the beams, early decorated with terra cotta; the blocks on
the underside of the cornice as the ends of the roof rafters.

[2] Examples of the *templum in antis* (FIG. 176 A) are the *Athenian* and *Siphnian Treasuries*
at Delphi; of the *amphiprostyle* (FIG. 176 B), the *Temple of Athena Nike* (*Nike Apteros*),
Athens; of the *peripteral* the *Parthenon* at Athens (FIG. 180; single colonnade), and
the *Temple of the Olympian Zeus* at Athens (FIG. 250; double colonnade).

Fig. 187. Eastern Porch of the Erechtheum. The Parthenon in the background. (Clarence Kennedy)

Fig. 188. The Upper Part of a Column from the Eastern Porch of the Erechtheum. British Museum, London.

In elevation the temples classify as Doric or Ionic order, which may be described as racial styles, the Doric developing chiefly on the Greek mainland and in the west, the Ionic in Asia Minor. Chronologically the two orders evolved in parallel and reached their most refined expression at Athens in the *Parthenon* and the *Erechtheum*, respectively.

In the earliest Doric temples [1] the style is already formed and one might expect an adventurous people to develop a new style. Not so the Greek. His adventurousness was of an intellectual kind; and while all the elements of the style were present in definite relationship early, there remained the refining of these relationships in every detail, until the imaginative sensitiveness of the artist could go no farther, a process which covered about two centuries (FIG. 179). In this conservative attitude of the Greek lies the key to an understanding of his art as well as an explanation of its extraordinary limitations.

The finest example of the Doric order is the *Parthenon* [2] (FIG. 178).

[1] The *Heraeum* at Olympia (about 620 B.C.); the *Basilica* (540 B.C.), and the *Temple of Demeter* (520 B.C.) at Paestum in Italy; the *Temple of Apollo* at Corinth (540 B.C.).
[2] The *Parthenon* was the temple of Athena Parthenos, meaning "Athena the Maiden," who was the patron goddess of Athens. Its ruined condition is due to the fact that at the time of the war between the Turks and the Venetians in 1687, the building was used as a powder magazine and exploded when hit by a well-aimed shot. A large part of the remaining sculpture was obtained by Lord Elgin, with the permission of the Turkish Government, in 1801–03, and became the property of the British

Fig. 189. Fragment of a Cornice from the Siphnian Treasury. Delphi. Delphi Museum. (Clarence Kennedy)

Fig. 190. Carving from the Erechtheum, with Honeysuckle, Bead and Reel, Egg and Dart, and Leaf and Dart Motifs. Acropolis Museum, Athens. (Alinari)

It stands on the crest of the Acropolis, simple and strong, its rectangular shape harmonizing perfectly with the contours of the hill, and its broken light and shade playing into the varying tones of the mountain landscape (FIG. 177). The general impression is one of repose; of a very sensitive balance between the supporting members and the weight to be supported, between the vertical line and the horizontal line, both largely unbroken. Everything contributes to calm. Contrast for a moment the restless movement of a Gothic cathedral (FIGS. 437–40) and the serene movement of the Parthenon becomes even more apparent.

The plan of the temple (FIG. 180) shows a double cella, one room

Museum in 1816. Very recently the fallen columns and lintels have been set back into place.

Fig. 191. Statuette of a Horse. Bronze. H. c. 7 in. VIII cent. B.C. Metropolitan Museum, New York. (Metropolitan Museum)

serving to house the cult statue, the other as the treasury. The elevation (Fig. 182 A) serves for a study of the Doric order.[1] From the stylobate, the upper member of the triple base, the columns rise directly without individual bases, like trees from the ground. The shaft diminishes in diameter as it rises and its contour is a very subtle curve, barely perceptible and known as the *entasis*. The grooves, or flutings, of the shafts with their soft shadows and repeated vertical lines both strengthen the rhythm and emphasize the feeling of support in the shaft, and finally individualize the columns by contrasting them with the plain wall of the cella against which they are seen. The shafts are not monoliths but consist of separate drums bonded together by dowels of wood and metal (Fig. 181) with such nicety that the joinings were originally scarcely visible.

The capital consists of three parts — the necking, the echinus, and the abacus. The purpose of a capital is to form the transition from the shaft to the lintel; that is, from the vertical supporting member to the horizontal entablature. A successful capital will not make this transition too abruptly. In the Doric capital we get our first suggestion of the horizontal in the necking; yet the vertical flutings, instead of ending at this point, play up into the capital to the point at which we feel more insistently the horizontal, that is, at the row of concentric ridges that separate the necking and the echinus. The simple vigorous curve of the echinus then carries the line up to the square abacus; not directly, however, for it turns inward as it meets the block, thus avoiding abruptness. The beautiful strength of this curve, rising so vigorously and then turning inward so gracefully, was not worked out by the Greek in a short time but only after a long series of experiments

[1] The order is the unit of style, and includes base, column, and entablature, their details, proportions, and decoration.

dealing with the angle and the proportions. In the rectangular abacus we are carried easily into the horizontal architrave. Thus by a carefully thought out design based upon skillful interplay of direction, we pass gradually from vertical to horizontal, from supporting elements to supported.

The entablature (FIG. 183) consists of architrave, frieze, and gable, or pediment. The architrave is severely plain and the frieze is composed of alternating triglyphs and metopes.[1] If the wood-construction theory of the origin of the Doric temple is valid, out of a discarded function [2] the Greek has made an esthetic necessity. For the triglyphs repeat the verticals of columns in a more rapid tempo. The architrave and the frieze are both separated by a simple stringcourse, and united by the molding with beadlike ornaments beneath each triglyph. The deeply projecting cornice finishes the design and protects the frieze from the rain. Unity of design between the frieze and the cornice is obtained by undercutting the cornice to correspond

Fig. 192. "Apollo" Piombino. Bronze. Early V cent. B.C. Louvre, Paris.

with the triglyphs and metopes, and by the use of color. A second cornice, known as the raking cornice, finishes the pediment.

Another important element of unity in the design is the color. To paint stone buildings was the usual practice of the Greeks. The color was not applied uniformly to the whole building but was concentrated upon the upper part. Red and blue predominated, with touches of green, yellow, black, and gilding (FIG. 184). The triglyphs with the decoration both above and below were blue; the stringcourses and metopes, and the undercuttings of the cornice, red. The unpainted parts may have been rubbed with wax. By the use of color the builder could bring out more clearly the relationship of the parts, could soften the glitter of the stone, and give a background for the sculptural decorations.

We have spoken of the curve or entasis found in the column. This

[1] *Triglyph:* rectangular stone with three groovings (two whole and two half); *metope:* the space between (the triglyphs).
[2] According to the wood-construction theory the triglyphs and metopes originated in the beam ends and the spaces between; and the undercuttings of the cornice, in the ends of the roof rafters.

Fig. 193. Seated Man. From the Sa-
cred Way of the Temple of Apollo near
Miletus. 550–530 B.C. British Museum,
London. (British Museum)

Fig. 194. Hera of
Samos. Marble. H. 6 ft.
c. 550 B.C. Louvre, Paris.
(Giraudon)

variation from the straight line is characteristic of all parts of the building. The stylobate has a slight upward curve (a rise of three and three-
fifths inches for a length of two hundred and twenty-eight feet); the
columns incline inward, and are placed not at equal intervals, but
closer together toward the corners, lending a feeling of stability at
those points. In fact there is not a straight line in the building. While
the purpose of the Greek in avoiding straight lines and complete
regularity was undoubtedly to correct optical illusions, it also seems
probable "that the builders of the Parthenon (whether by intelligent
imitation or by intuitive artistic taste) had applied to architecture
the same secret of beauty which governs natural forms — the tempering
of geometric accuracy by minute deviations in the interest of irregularity." [1]

The sculptural decoration in the metopes and pediments performs
the function of enriching an otherwise austere design by adding irregularly broken masses of light and shade and curved broken lines in
just proportion.[2] It is not abstract decoration, however. Its subject

[1] Rhys Carpenter, *The Esthetic Basis of Greek Art*, Longmans, 1921, p. 195.
[2] For sketches to illustrate this see Gardner, *Understanding the Arts*, p. 40.

Fig. 195. Statue of the "Apollo" type. H. 6 ft. 4 in. c. 600 B.C. Metropolitan Museum, New York. (Metropolitan Museum)

Fig. 196. Head of the Statue of the "Apollo" type (Fig. 195). Metropolitan Museum, New York. (Metropolitan Museum)

matter relates to Athena, related deities and heroes, and thus infuses the unity of form with a unity of meaning.[1]

In the Ionic *Erechtheum* [2] (FIGS. 185–88, 182 B) we note, by comparison with the *Parthenon*, more slender proportions, greater elegance and grace, richer embellishment. In detail, the columns have individual bases, one member of which is delicately carved; on the necking is a honeysuckle band; the echinus is decorated with bead and reel, egg and dart, and the double guilloche (FIG. 188). Perhaps the most conspicuous part of the Ionic capital is the double scroll or volute inserted between the narrow echinus and the abacus. The architrave is divided into three horizontal faces and the frieze was originally covered by a continuous band of low relief, in place of the Doric triglyphs and metopes. The stringcourses and cornices, doorway, and wall bands are delicately carved with dentils, egg and dart, bead and reel, honeysuckle, and braid patterns (FIGS. 189, 190).

[1] For a very sensitive analysis of the *Parthenon* from the point of view of a modernist architect and of its close relation to modernism in building see C. E. Le Corbusier, *Towards a New Architecture*, Harcourt, Brace, 1927.

[2] The *Erechtheum*, so named after Erechtheus, to whom it was dedicated in part, conforms in plan (FIG. 186) to FIG. 176 B but has several unusual features, which may have been due partly to the irregular character of the ground on which the temple stands and partly to the number of shrines that it contained. For it was said to mark the site of the contest between Poseidon and Athena for possession of Athens, and to shelter within its area the mark made by the trident and the salt spring of the former and the olive tree of the latter, as well as other sacred relics.

Fig. 197. Figure Found on the Acropolis. Marble, painted. H. c. 4 ft. Early
V cent. B.C. Probably a votive figure. Acropolis Museum, Athens.
(Alinari)

Fig. 198. Figure Found
on the Acropolis. Mar-
ble, painted. Acropolis
Museum, Athens. Early
V cent. B.C.

This ornament, though rich, is confined to certain places and is strictly
subordinated to the design of the whole. The Greek marble was particularly adaptable to the carving of moldings which show not only
beauty of chisel work but of profile, and reveal a sensitive and intelligent choice of the particular decorative motif that is adapted to
a concave, convex, or angular type of molding.[1] The value of these
moldings to the Greek may be judged from the fact that he paid,
according to the building inscriptions of the *Erechtheum*, the same price
for carving one foot of egg and dart as for one human figure.

Architectural decoration, both in relief and in the round, was the
purpose of much of Hellenic sculpture, though many independent
statues were made for cult, votive, and commemorative purposes.
Much of it was carved from the same material as the building and
was painted, not naturalistically but conventionally, to harmonize
with a polychrome structure. If this use of color appears strange,
one needs only to recall the tradition of color in architecture and
sculpture in the eastern Mediterranean and western Asiatic countries
— Egypt, Babylonia, Assyria, Persia, Asia Minor, Crete.

As for technical processes,[2] the sculptor carved the stone directly and

[1] See T. F. Hamlin, *The Enjoyment of Architecture*, Duffield, 1916, Chap. V.
[2] For technical processes and tools see Stanley Casson, *The Technique of Early Greek
Sculpture*, Oxford Press, 1933; G. M. A. Richter, *The Sculpture and Sculptors of the Greeks*,

Fig. 199. Horses from a Frieze on the Treasury of the Siphnians, Delphi. c. 525 B.C. (Clarence Kennedy)

Fig. 200. Mortuary relief. c. middle VI cent. B.C. Berlin.

used clay only when his conception required the use of clay as a medium. Bronze was popular, worked by solid casting, by hammering over a wooden core, or by cire-perdue casting.[1]

One more preliminary point remains to be mentioned, the cycle. Although the cycle in civilization is a complex and moot problem, one easily discerns in the figure sculpture of a given culture, when enough evidence is available, a certain general course of development consisting of an early struggle, a mastery, and a decline. Such a cycle is so clear in the evidence afforded by Greek sculpture [2] that we shall consider its evolution and the factors affecting it.

Geometric and archaic sculpture is the expression of a vigorously growing people. The artist in his struggle for expression uses simple forms tending to the geometric, with each part a conventional device, a symbol created by mind and memory [3] rather than a naturalistic rendering based directly upon visual experience. These parts are com-

---

Yale University Press, 1930; and Rhys Carpenter, *The Sculpture of the Nike Temple Parapet,* Harvard University Press, 1929.

[1] In the *cire-perdue* (wax lost) process of casting, a core of clay or some crude material was shaped roughly into the form of the finished work. Over this a coating of wax was laid in which the sculptor did his finished modeling. The wax was then covered by a coat of fine pipe clay, the consistency of cream, laid on with a brush very carefully so as to reproduce, when hard, every minute detail of the wax. Successive coats were added and then layers of coarser material until a thick, firm shell was formed. Vent holes were made and the whole mass heated so that the wax was melted and drawn away, leaving in its place a thin space between the core and the pipe-clay mold. Into this the molten bronze was poured. When the metal had hardened, the shell was broken away, the core dug out, and the surface polished, and sometimes details were added by chasing.

[2] Clearly and concisely stated by Rhys Carpenter, *The Esthetic Basis of Greek Art,* Longmans 1921, pp. 113 ff.

[3] For this explanation see Emanuel Loewy, *The Rendering of Nature in Early Greek Art,* London, 1907.

Fig. 201. Figures from
a Frieze on the Treasury
of the Siphnians, Delphi.
C. 525 B.C.

bined architecturally, that is, are built into a perfectly articulated
entity, as in the *Bronze Horse* (FIG. 191; compare FIG. 211), to which
the abstract conventions constantly repeated lend a decorative quality
and in which there is never lost a recognition of the material nor a
fine craftsmanship in its handling.

These qualities we recognize in the *Hera of Samos* (FIG. 194).[1] The
Hera is basically a cylinder. The goddess stands in frontal pose, feet
together, the right arm held tightly to the side, the left bent to the
breast, probably holding some attribute. The figure is very compact,
with fine strong contour, particularly as it sweeps out to join the
figure to the base. There is an indication of the simple planes of the
figure in the upper part. Linear conventions carved on the stone indicate linen in the long undergarment and wool in the mantle; and
the two are united by a strong curve that repeats the contour curve.
The simple quiet harmony of all parts, the long unbroken lines and
quiet surfaces, imbue the *Hera* with a reposeful majesty. This feeling
permeates the seated figures from a temple near Miletus (FIG. 193).
An impression of power derives from the sheer massiveness and weight
of the stone; and dignity from the simple four-sided organization, as
in the *Khafre* (FIG. 41). Conventional devices, breaking up the surfaces, not only represent different kinds of cloth but set up movement
over the surfaces and create pattern.

  [1] One should at least mention among the earliest expressions in the Greek cycle
the polychrome wood statues which have inevitably disappeared and the early stone
statues such as the *Artemis* found at Delos (Athens, National Museum) in which is a
timid approach to a rectangular block of stone and an overshadowing of the representation by the material.

Fig. 202. Ar-
cher. From the
Temple   at
Aegina (Fig.
203). (Clarence
Kennedy)

One is vaguely reminded of Egyptian statues by one of the so-called *Apollo* figures in the pose with left foot advanced, in the broad square shoulders, and in the four-sided organization (FIG. 195). Here is a solid figure constructed of a few broad planes definitely related to the four-sided block of stone. On these planes anatomical details are indicated by shallow groovings or ridges, not obvious, but clearly enough seen to show that each is related to the other in a pattern. The boldly conceived device for the hair [1] falling in the back in an angular mass (repeated in the angular fingers), with the half angular, half curved knot of the fillet, furnishes a decorative note which complements the patternings of the torso and limbs. Notice how the conventional ear (FIG. 196), in line a continuation of the line of the jaw and in grooving a repetition of the eyelid, is the unifying element of the hair and the face. Almost any archaic head shows protruding eyes; abrupt transitions between the planes of the face giving the impression of prominent cheekbones; mouth with upturned corners; [2] and stylized hair. All the conventions of this statue are cut firmly, and with their repeating lines and motifs create a formal pattern of great esthetic power.[3]

In the bronze *Piombino* (FIG. 192) greater freedom of pose and modeling is due partly to the material and partly to a more naturalistic rendering of schematic devices. The protruding eyes are taking

[1] This is to be distinguished from the Egyptian wig. Greek men wore the hair long until in the fifth century B.C.

[2] Causing the "archaic smile," which appears to result from the difficulty in making the transition between the lips and the cheeks.

[3] For archaic heads of other civilizations see FIGS. 688, 785–787.

Fig. 203. Temple at Aegina, Eastern Pediment. Incident from the Trojan War. Conjectural restoration by Furtwängler. c. 500 B.C. Glyptothek, Munich.

their natural place within the eye socket; the "archaic smile" is disappearing; the hair hints at the thickness of its mass, and the drapery at actual deep folds. All this one sees in the female figures, probably votive, found on the Acropolis at Athens (FIGS. 197, 198). They all stand in the same frontal position, left foot advanced, right hand holding up the mantle, the left arm bent at the elbow and extended as if holding something. The ladies here represented wear linen chitons indicated by ripple marks and woolen mantles that fall in broad conventional folds from the right shoulder. The marble is undercut along the edge of the folds, giving a feeling of depth, and is painted to represent the decorative border and the all-over pattern of the goods. The elaborately dressed hair falls down behind in conventional waves, and a few locks, separating, fall over the breast. Notwithstanding the vigorous, half-abstract, decorative beauty in these statues, one feels, possibly, an over-elaboration and a lack of that perfect unity of all details found in the *Apollo*.

The early reliefs have the same stylistic character as sculpture in the round, and in addition solve the problem peculiar to relief: the suggestion of actual depth in the really very shallow depth imposed by the material. Early the Greek attacked this problem, as we see in a *Mortuary Relief* (FIG. 200) in which the sculptor is attempting to carry the eye clearly into space by a series of shallow parallel planes. The bungling almost inevitable in an early courageous attempt has disappeared in the friezes of the *Siphnian Treasury* at Delphi (FIG. 199), where the eager horses give a sense of vivid reality of life, a sense of the figure in space, and decorative beauty. All this is true likewise of the *Seated Goddesses* on the same building (FIG. 201).

We have already caught a glimpse of the path of evolution which the cycle is taking. Beginning with simple, almost geometric basic forms, with conventional devices for details, all of which are brought into a harmonious unit possessing decorative beauty in its formal qualities alone, the sculptor begins to temper these forms by observing

Fig. 204. Temple of Zeus. Olympia. Western Pediment, Battle of
Centaurs and Lapiths, restored by Treu. c. 460 B.C.

nature and making his statue represent a little more of what the eye
actually sees. The pedimental figures of the *Temple of Aegina* (FIG. 203)
illustrate this change. The scene probably represents some episode
from the Trojan War. Athena, with aegis and spear, stands in the
center, yet has no immediate connection with the fighting groups,
which are arranged in a balanced position on either side. In each
group a warrior with helmet, shield, and drawn sword attacks his
falling opponent, to whose help a friend rushes with outstretched arms.
Behind him an archer, with bent knee, takes aim at the warrior,
while a fallen wounded soldier occupies the corner. The most noticeable thing in the group is the freedom of movement and variety of pose.
The figures are modeled with a vigor and an understanding of the
human physique that reflect a careful observation of nature. The
Archer (FIG. 202), for example, is complicated in pose in comparison
with the statues that we have studied; but the form is so compact
and so simple in outline as to be almost geometrical. It is the contrasting direction of line seen in the vertical of the back, the horizontal
of the arm, and the diagonal of the firmly braced leg that gives one
so strong an impression of the powerful draw upon the bow and, at
the same time, a feeling of the perfect equilibrium of the whole figure.
Many of the conventions are still present; the angular conventions
in the cuirass, for example, strike a harmonious note in the total
angularity of the figure.

The use of figures in the round to decorate the pediment of the
temple posed the Greek a problem with which he struggled from the
earliest temples of which we have evidence to the *Parthenon*. A gable
is a difficult space to fill without being too obvious in treating the
central axis and the narrow corners. On the old *Temple of Athena* at
Athens the *Three-bodied Monster* (Acropolis Museum), with coiling tail
and bold conventional coloring, in its simple directness must have
been peculiarly decorative. At *Aegina*, while any judgment is hazardous
because of the uncertainty in the arrangement of the fragmentary

Fig. 205. Apollo. From the Western Pediment of the Temple of Zeus, Olympia.

Fig. 206. Figure from the Eastern Pediment of the Temple of Zeus, Olympia.

figures, the sculptor's eager yearning toward naturalism in each figure
seems to have overbalanced its architectural fitness and we are far
too conscious of the fact that the kneeling and reclining figures are
posed as they are because of exigencies of space.

As we turn to the pediment of the *Temple of Zeus* at Olympia, where
again the remains are very fragmentary, we find a battle scene between the Centaurs and the Lapiths (FIG. 204) in which the drunken
Centaurs are attempting to carry off the Lapith women. In the center
stands Apollo, calmly majestic as if witnessing the scene but not of it;
on each side are the combatants, in balanced groupings of twos and
threes with reclining figures in the corners. Each group is a unit, so
skillfully connected with the next that a movement seems to rise and
flow rhythmically from the corners to Apollo in the center. In comparison with the pediment of *Aegina* the design is more complicated,
and the unity among the figures and their relation to the space are
more subtle. *Apollo* (FIG. 205) stands austerely erect, the outstretched
arm and turn of the head balancing the vertical of the body, and
producing an effect that is architecturally fitting and monumental.
There is simple modeling without detail in both the figure and the
drapery, which is arranged in broad folds that enhance the majestic
effect. The figure has great vitality and at the same time poise and
restraint, so that both the conception and the expression harmonize

Fig. 207. Three-sided Relief. Sometimes called "Ludovisi Throne." Subject unknown. Marble. H. 40 in. C. 480 B.C. Terme (National) Museum, Rome. (Alinari)

in their forceful directness. In a detail from the eastern pediment (FIG. 206) the clear definite relationships of parts are evident. This sculpture of Olympia, simple, direct, and of monumental breadth in its half-abstract forms, in its acceptance of the material (for its effect is neither entirely of stone nor entirely of flesh but of a perfect balance between the two), and in its lingering archaic conventions half-naturalized but still of formal beauty — this sculpture constitutes for many beholders the Greek climax.[1]

This balance between the ideal of thought form (conventions, symbols) and the ideal of seen form (visual appearance), which manifests itself in a restrained naturalism and in a feeling for material, we see again in the so-called *Ludovisi Throne* (FIG. 207), neither the purpose nor the subject of which is definitely known. As decorative design we have a composition of single curves and S-curves about the central head, with stabilizing verticals in the folds of drapery. The beautiful texture of the stone, the feeling of order and logic in the inseparable unity of stone and figure, the skilled, sensitive cutting of the varied conventions for hair and textiles, conventions which are quite under the control of the firm organization yet lend to it a living quality through their unobtrusive variations — these attributes are outstanding, and in view of them who would cavil at gropings and inaccuracies from the point of view of naturalism?

[1] This late archaic art from about 480 to 450 B.C. is usually known as the transitional age. It is well to recall that this is the generation following the Persian Wars.

Fig. 208. Charioteer of Delphi. Bronze. H. 6 ft. Part of a chariot group. Delphi Museum.

As an example of the bronze work of the late archaic age, the *Charioteer of Delphi* (FIGS. 208, 209) will serve. The dark color with reflections and sharp contours, the crisp edges of the details necessitated by the dark color of the material, are characteristic of work in bronze. The statue belonged to a group with chariot and horses, and was probably erected to commemorate a victory at the races. It represents a youthful aristocrat who stands firmly on both feet, holding the reins in his outstretched hand — for he himself, apparently, had driven his chariot in the races. He is dressed in the customary garment of a driver, which is girdled high and held in at the shoulders and back to keep it from flapping. The hair is confined by a band tied behind. The eyes, which are made of glass paste and shaded by lashes of hair-like strips of bronze (a curiously inconsistent detail, an example of virtuosity in attempted naturalism but fortunately inconspicuous), and the slightly parted lips add vivacity to the face. We feel the austerity of archaic work in the figure, especially in the lower part, where the folds of the dress have almost the architectural quality of a fluted column; in the sharp lines of the brow; and in the conventional way in which the hair is worked above the band. But we notice also the naturalistic curls below the band; the masterly modeling in the hand and in the feet, the toes of which are clutching the ground; the slight twist of the torso that gives one the feeling of an organic structure beneath the dress. The statue is a portrait, yet there are but few individualistic traits about it. Broad generalization characterizes it so far as representation is concerned. Like the sculptures at Olympia, monumental conception combines with directness and dignity of expression. The form reveals the naturalistic tendencies of the day, largely in details. But the formal beauty of archaic conventions, repeated and varied rhythmically, still controls the manner of expression.

Another bronze of this age, the *Discobolus* (Discus-thrower) of

Myron [1] (Fig. 210), contrasts with
the *Charioteer* in its movement, unusual for the fifth century b.c. Here
an instantaneous pose has been
caught between the backward and
the forward thrust of the arm in
hurling the quoit, and out of it, by
means of formal qualities, has been
made an abstract expression of concentrated force. For although the
human figure has been used to convey the idea, one is primarily aware
of the great sweep of an arc beginning with the quoit, moving along
the right arm, the curve of the
shoulders, down the left arm, taken
up in the right leg, and so strongly
felt that its very momentum easily
carries the eye over the space back
to the quoit. Cutting across and finally uniting with this arc is a great
S-curve, and a stabilizing vertical,
the axis, from shoulder to weight-
holding leg. The face, contrary to

Fig. 209. Charioteer of Delphi
(Fig. 208), Head.

what we should expect at such an intense moment, is impassive and
broadly generalized. Such a free, noncompact pose, suitable for bronze,
again shows the artist's complete understanding of the capacities of his
material. This sensitivity to bronze was seen in the geometric horse
(Fig. 191), impossible to have been done in stone, and again in a fifth-
century horse (Fig. 211) which shows the same feeling for material and
also, by comparison, the same trend toward naturalism in the animal
as in the human figure. This new naturalism, however, is used with
great discretion, and the impression of energetic spirit results largely
from the use of archaic conventions, moderately tempered.

A statue that brings us to the end of the transitional age is the *Athena
Lemnia* of Phidias [2] (Figs. 212, 213), which stood on the Acropolis at
the left side of the road that leads from the great gateway to the *Par-*

---

[1] The original of this statue is lost. A considerable number of copies exist, from
which Fig. 210 is constructed. For the question of copies in Greek sculpture see
Richter, *op. cit.*

[2] While it cannot be proved conclusively that this statue is a copy of the original
bronze by Phidias, it is generally thought to be so. The body is now in Dresden, the
head in Bologna — a fact easily explained, since Greek statues were often made of
several pieces of marble, a finer quality being used for the head.

Fig. 210. Myron. Discobolus. Reconstructed copy of the bronze original. Terme (National) Museum, Rome.

thenon. She stands erect, though with more freedom of pose than the *Charioteer*. She wears the woolen Doric chiton, which falls in rich folds, somewhat severe, and over this the aegis. The head is turned to the right and slightly lowered. Contrary to the usual representations, she does not wear her helmet, but carries it in her hand. Thus Phidias has emphasized her more gracious aspect — "the thoughtful Athena with the delicate cheeks," according to a Latin writer. One here discerns a sculptor governed by what his eye sees, yet by no means absolutely. The figure is an organic structure with capacity for movement; the drapery, undercut to suggest depth, begins to look like cloth and falls in more casual folds; the mass of hair has volume, though the details are conventionally treated; the features, though generalized and broadly carved, take their natural places as part of the structure of the head.

By some, as we have said, the sculpture of the late archaic age is considered the climax of the Greek cycle; by others, the *Parthenon* sculpture. It is a moot point whether the sculpture of the *Parthenon*, even in parts, is the work of Phidias. His most famous statues, the *Athena* of the *Parthenon* and the *Zeus* of the temple at *Olympia*, were made of gold and ivory, and hence have long since disappeared, and our knowledge of his art can best be gained through the sculptural decorations of the *Parthenon*, which we know were made under his supervision, and which may be, in parts, actually by his hand.

The sculptural decorations of the *Parthenon* are found at three points: the pediments, the metopes, and an additional continuous frieze [1] which runs around the top of the cella wall and thus inside the colonnade. The purpose of this sculpture, as we have already noted, is to round out an otherwise incomplete design. The metopes provide movement by compositions of two struggling interlocking figures in high relief — Centaurs and Lapiths, gods and giants, Greeks and Amazons. In FIG. 216 a Lapith is sinking to the ground, his arm still in the straps

---

[1] Not to be confused with the regular Doric frieze of triglyphs and metopes. This continuous frieze, an Ionic feature, is unusual.

of his shield, while the victorious Centaur is about to crash down upon him the jar that he holds behind his head. The two figures are ingeniously interlocked into a compact group not only by the pose of the figures, the arrangement of the limbs, but also by the skillful placing of the disks of the shield and jar. Therefore the group, although it represents a struggle, is contained within a very simple outline that traces on the flat background a pattern adapted with great mastery to the square shape of the metope.

Fig. 211. Statuette of a Horse. Bronze. H. c. 14 in. c. 470 B.C. Metropolitan Museum, New York (Metropolitan Museum)

The subject of the eastern pediment (FIG. 215), the ancient writers tell us, was the birth of Athena, who sprang full-armed from the head of Zeus. Again, the remains are fragmentary, but from a drawing made by a Frenchman traveling in Athens in 1674 we can get a glimpse of part of the composition. In the left corner, the sun god Helios in his chariot is rising out of the sea. Only the head, shoulders, and arms of Helios and the heads of the horses are shown. The horses approach a seated male figure turned toward them, who may personify Mt. Olympus, though usually identified as Dionysus. Closely connected are two seated figures, probably Demeter and Persephone, approached by a standing figure. The center is entirely gone. On the right are three seated female figures closely grouped, one turned toward the center. In the corner projecting over the cornice is seen the head of one of the horses of Selene, the moon goddess, who is sinking into the west as Helios rises in the east. In the *Three Fates* (FIG. 214) there is a quiet majesty, a highly generalized form with all the elements of the human structure expressed in their essential aspects only, and a balance between the material and the subject matter. The single figure at the left is in the frontal position, is foursided, and quite one with the block of marble, although there is considerable movement in the limbs and head. The drapery, though by comparison with the archaic it is quite naturalistic, upon close observation proves to create a definite undulating pattern. So, notwithstanding the advance of naturalism, we find sculpture that still recognizes the integrity of the material and which is monumental in its breadth and serene majesty.

The frieze along the top of the cella wall, in very low relief, is seen

Fig. 213. Athena Lemnia (Fig. 212), Head.

Fig. 212. Phidias (?).
Athena Lemnia. (See
note 2, p. 145)

in half-light against a colored ground between
the columns, enriching the plain wall and bringing movement into a static composition. It represents the Panathenaic procession that took place
every four years when the citizens of Athens
gathered in the market place and carried to the
Parthenon the peplos or robe for the statue of Athena. On the western
side of the building the procession is forming — youths are lacing
their sandals, holding their horses or mounting, guided by marshals
who stand at intervals, and particularly at the corners to slow down
the movement and guide the horsemen at the turn. On the two long
sides the procession moves in parallel lines, a cavalcade of spirited youths, chariots, elders, jar-carriers, and animals for sacrifice. The
movement becomes slower and more solemn as it nears the eastern side,
when after turning the corner it approaches the seated divinities, who
appear to be guests of Athena at her great festival.[1] The cavalcade
of mounted youths (FIG. 217) is filled with rhythmic movement and
spirited action. The backward glance of some of the youths gives a balance to the general forward movement of the procession; and the infinite variety in the poses of the youths and the horses frees it from
any feeling of monotony. There is a flat background with no distance

[1] A convenient and inexpensive reproduction of the entire frieze, which is necessary
for a realization of the unity of composition and the rhythmic flow of line, is published
by the University Prints, Newton, Massachusetts.

Fig. 214. Parthenon, Eastern Pediment: Three Female Figures, called the "Three Fates." British Museum, London. (British Museum)

and no unnecessary details. We have, in fact, all the essential elements of a procession of spirited youths expressed with a naturalism tempered by decorative fitness. Notice how the figures just fill the space; how the heads, whether the figures are standing or mounted, are on a level; [1] how the flanks of the horses form a central band of largely unbroken surface, and their legs beat a rapid rhythm in the lower third of the panel. Originally details and accents were stressed by color and even bronze reins added — a disconcertingly realistic detail. In the slab representing the jar-carriers (FIG. 218) the insistent motif of a youth carrying a jar upon his right shoulder is repeated, making a design of decorative quality, ease, and grace of rhythm that is readily felt but only understood when one observes the subtle variations that occur in the pose of the head, the arms, and the hands, and in the arrangement of the drapery.

A contemporary of Phidias was Polyclitus, whose well-known interest in working out an ideal set of proportions for the human figure [2] is illuminating because it enables us to coördinate the interests of sculptor and of builder and to realize that they are identical, namely, the refinement of proportions. Something of the Polyclitan style we see in a bronze statuette of a *Maiden* with turbanlike headdress (FIG. 220). The weight rests on the right foot; the left is slightly raised, so that the figure is thrown into an easy pose. It is simply constructed, with suavely flowing planes causing high lights on the reflecting surfaces to set up a quiet rhythm — a design well suited to the bronze medium.

[1] This particular practice of distorting natural proportions for decorative purpose is known as *isocephaly* (heads equal, or on a level). It is a practice by no means limited to Greece but is universal.

[2] Illustrated in his *Doryphorus*, the statue of an athlete called the *Canon*. It exists only in hard dry Roman copies found in the museum at Naples and elsewhere.

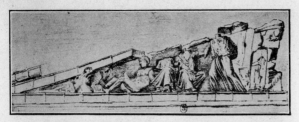

Fig. 215. Parthenon, Eastern Pediment: Birth of Athena. c. 438 B.C. Drawing by Jacques Carrey, 1674 A.D. Bibliothèque Nationale, Paris.

The style of Phidias and of Polyclitus dominated Greek sculpture during the late fifth century B.C. when the Greek's objective became, more definitely, natural appearance. A fragment from the balustrade of the *Temple of Athena Nike* (FIG. 219) has a little flavor, perhaps, of virtuosity in the extraordinary skill shown in revealing the figure beneath the drapery, and in the slight turning-away from a perfect balance between stone and cloth to a slight overbalance on the side of an illusion of cloth. At the same time there is a masterly expression of movement, quite abstract, in the folds which hang between the arm and the leg, a rhythmic flow of concentric curves, to secure which seems to have been the reason for the uplifted leg — an excellent example of the use of pose or gesture to obtain an effect of lyric charm.

C. MINOR ARTS

Among the elements of the Aegean culture that the Greek appears to have taken over and expanded was the pottery trade. In the course of time, as increasing exports created a demand for containers for such articles as oil and honey in addition to requirements of general household use, the potters' quarters at Athens, known as the Ceramicus [1] was no inconsiderable part of the city. Esthetically pottery serves as a criterion of the Greek style, especially of those early centuries whose buildings and sculpture are lost and of fifth-century painting which has disappeared.

[1] Situated both inside and outside the Dipylon Gate. The name is derived from the Greek word for "potter," whence our "ceramics."

Fig. 216. Parthe-
non, Metope: Cen-
taur and Lapith.
British Museum,
London. (Mansell)

While the Mycenaean was fashioning his stately *Palace Style* jars
(FIGS. 168, 169), a new kind of pottery was appearing, of simple, if
not crude, rugged shape with geometric decoration, and occasional
abstract natural forms. In comparison with the Cretan the decorative
scheme and its relation to the shape seem to have been intellectually
considered rather than spontaneously felt. FIG. 221 will serve as an
illustration, in which the distribution of the motifs relative to each
other, to the shape, and to the handles shows the same feelings for
relationship that we saw in our analysis of the Doric order. This
Geometric pottery, made from about 1100 to 800 B.C., culminated in the
Dipylon ware,[1] of which a large funerary amphora (FIGS. 221, 222) is
an example. Its vigorous shape and small handles, none too sensitively
proportioned, are decorated in a rich brown glaze on light clay, with
bands containing geometric motifs and human figures, the latter oc-
curing with extreme rarity in Aegean pottery. Here at the outset we
see the Greek concentrating upon his chief concern, man. The subject
is a funeral procession. Though the drawing is primitive and the figures
are symbolical, the decorative quality is far more effective than in
later, more naturalistic drawing (FIG. 238). As one stands by these
huge Dipylon jars he feels something of the majesty of the *Hera of*

[1] So called because these vases have been found in great numbers in the cemetery
near the Dipylon Gate of Athens.

Fig. 217. Parthenon Frieze, North-
were painted on or made of metal
Marble. H. 40 in. British Museum,

Fig. 218. Parthenon Frieze. Northern Side: Jar-Carriers, Acropolis
Museum, Athens. (Mansell)

Samos (FIG. 194), whose prototypes were probably being carved in
wood when the Dipylon period was at its height.

Considering the extent of pottery-making, the number of shapes which
the Greek used is surprisingly small. Having worked out a few, each
according to its functional requirements, he devoted himself to refining the proportions, contours, placement of the handles, and decoration. Here again is the same interest in refinements within narrow
limitations that we saw was a dominant interest in architecture and
sculpture. Of these shapes those most frequently found are: the *amphora*, the general storage jar (FIG. 222); the *hydria*, the water jar
(FIG. 225); the *crater*, the bowl for mixing wine (FIG. 226); the *cylix*,
the drinking-cup (FIG. 227); the *oinochoë*, the wine pitcher (FIG. 228);
and the *lecythos*, the oil flask (FIG. 229). In determining the uses of
these vases [1] we are guided by the paintings on the vases themselves;
for in these paintings the Greeks have given us an amazing revelation
of their everyday life (FIG. 230). The shapes vary in different periods

[1] The common, though misleading, term generally used in speaking of Greek
pottery. One needs to remember that these "vases" were largely the pots and pans
of everyday life and the containers used by the trader, though some were used for
religious and funereal purposes.

ern Side: Cavalcade of Youths. Accessories, such as the bridles and reins, and affixed by rivets, the holes for which are seen in the horses' heads. London. (Mansell)

and locations. Those here illustrated are taken from the best period, chiefly the fifth century B.C.

As the Greek expanded his trade and colonization, we see evidences in his pottery of closer contact with the older civilizations of the Near East. Rows of animals (FIG. 231), winged beasts, and rosettes recall Assyria (FIG. 131); the lotus, Egypt. With the passing of the seventh century B.C., the Orientalizing age, the Greek draws in upon his chief concern — himself and his immediate interests, secular and religious. The animal friezes and geometric motifs, often so decorative and suitable as motifs on a curving surface, disappear before the frankly humanistic attitude. Probably no other people have used the human figure so preponderantly in ceramic decoration as did the Greeks. Therefore it is profitable to look into their use of it for their purpose. Out of the great mass of existent Greek pottery we shall select a few characteristic pieces.

The *François Vase* (FIG. 233) [1] is a crater with volute handles, of extraordinary vigor both in its shape and in its proportion, and decorated with concentric bands filled with human and animal figures. These are painted in black-figured technique, that is, in a black glaze with touches of white or purple on the natural reddish clay, which is left as a background. On the foot, in the battle of the cranes and pigmies, is animated movement and decorative patterning; the rays above happily suggest the spreading movement of the surface of the crater, but this is halted abruptly by the horizontal bands, in some of which one feels the preponderance of the narrative interest over the decorative. Here are pictured various mythological scenes, the Calydonian hunt, the funeral games of Patroclus, the procession of the gods to the wedding of Peleus and Thetis.

[1] Named after the man who found it in a grave in Italy.

Fig. 219. Nike Fixing Her Sandal. From the Temple of Athena Nike. 421–415 B.C. Acropolis Museum, Athens.

Fig. 220. School of Polyclitus. Maiden. Bronze. H. 10 in. Late V cent. B.C. Antiquarium, Munich. (Clarence Kennedy)

Soon the white and purple colors give way to the black glaze alone on the reddish clay. The zonal arrangement disappears and in its place a few larger figures furnish the decoration, sometimes grouped in a reserved panel, as in an amphora of Exekias [1] (FIG. 232). This is a strong compact shape in which the handles not only harmonize with the curve as an integral part of the design, but are attached in such a way that they appear to fulfill their function of supporting the weight. The surface is painted solid black, except for the band with rays just above the base, the decorated panel on the body, and the handles. In the large panel we see Ajax and Achilles seated on stools, bending intently over their game of draughts. Ajax, on the right, as the inscription tells us, calls out "Three"; Achilles, on the left, "Four." It is a close game. All the elements make for a design that is balanced, yet subtly varied: one hero is helmeted, the other not; slight differences occur in the position of the limbs and spears and the decoration of the shields. There is much greater naturalism than formerly in the pose

[1] The name of the maker or decorator or the shop from which the vase came is frequently painted on it. None of these names is mentioned in Greek literature; they seem to have belonged to men of humble social position.

and proportion of the figures, and greater freedom in drawing. The skill and sure-handedness seen in the profusion and delicacy of the incised lines of the hair, and in the very elaborate cloaks, are a delight in themselves. One recognizes a kinship, stylistically but without infringement of medium, between this work and archaic sculpture in the formal and decorative beauty of the figures and of the schematic devices used for details. A cylix of Exekias (FIG. 234), with a representation of Dionysus sailing over the sea carrying his gifts to mankind, is even more decorative in its adaptation of the figures to the circular shape.

As we turn to FIGS. 235, 236 we notice that we are looking at a vase of different technique, for here the figures and decorative patterns are the reddish color of the clay; the details and background, black.

Fig. 221. Geometric Amphora, Dipylon Style. Colossal size. VIII cent. B.C. National Museum, Athens.

This is known as the red-figured ware, which was decorated in the following manner: after the vase was shaped the painter with a blunt tool incised his design in the clay; he then painted a broad band around the outside of the outline thus marked off, and frequently a thin raised black line, then painted in the details, and finally filled in the background with black glaze. The advantage of this style over the black-figured ware was that the line made by a brush or a pen allowed much more freedom in drawing than the incised line. The school of painting that was rapidly developing at this time in Athens was probably a primary influence on the style of pottery decoration. And the popularity of the cylix at this time may be due to the fact that its broad flattish surfaces offered a large enough area for groups of figures. Yet, paradoxically, the potter was concentrating, as were the builders and carvers, upon the niceties of form — proportion, thinness of walls,

Fig. 222. The *Amphora* (meaning to carry on both sides, referring to the two handles) was a vessel for storing provisions — wine, corn, oil, honey. It had an opening large enough to admit a ladle, and usually a cover to protect the contents. Vase painting showing two men with amphorae, probably filled with wine for the large bowl between them.

Fig. 223. Details from a Dipylon Jar.

Fig. 224. Geometric Vase. H. 4 in. Between 900 and 660 B.C. Ashmolean Museum, Oxford.

Fig. 225. The *Hydria* (from the Greek word for "water") was the water jar, used chiefly to bring water from the spring. It has three handles, two for lifting and one for carrying. Vase painting showing two youths filling their hydriae at a fountain.

Fig. 226. The *Crater* (from the Greek verb "to mix") was the bowl for mixing the wine and water, the usual beverage of the Greek; hence it had a wide mouth. Vase painting showing the youths filling their cylixes from a crater.

Fig. 227. The *Cylix* (from the Greek root "to roll," referring to the vases being turned on the wheel) was the chief form of the drinking cup. Vase painting showing a banquet scene; the man at the right is drinking from a cylix; the one on the left is holding his out to be filled; cylixes and oinochoë hang on the wall.

Fig. 228. The *Oinochoë* (from the Greek verb "to pour out wine") was the wine jug. The lip is pinched into a trefoil shape, which facilitates pouring. Vase painting showing a youth pouring wine from a slender, high-handled oinochoë into a cylix.

character of profile, integration of handle with body. Nor did he enlarge his very limited color scheme. Yet one feels creeping into the craft a conflict between ceramics (the art of clay shapes and suitable decoration) and painting, between clinging to the limitations of the medium and vying with the painter.

In the cylix of Euphronios (FIG. 235) are represented scenes from one of the labors of Heracles, the cattle of Geryon; on one side the fight over the cattle, on the other side the animals being driven away by four youths. Though the narrative element is lively, the effect is still primarily decorative. In the herd of cattle the flat silhouettes of the bodies are shaped to the space as if they inevitably belonged there; and in the central disk the figures of the youth and the horse form a compact pattern that seems to partake of the rotary motion of the circle and at the same time to restrain that movement by the severely angular lines of the cloak. The elaborate folds of the garments are conventionally treated, as in the *Acropolis* statues (FIGS. 197, 198), and are drawn with fine firm lines that have a decorative quality of their own and indicate a technical ability of first rank.

From the point of view of drawing the human figure, as a problem isolated from ceramics, it is interesting to note a gradual progression toward visual appearance, a problem which occupied the Greek from the time of the Dipylon ware and which can be summarized in one detail, the eye (FIG. 237). In proportion as he neared his objective he seemed to lose his feeling for ceramic decoration, even though he kept the figure flat, drew and modeled with line alone, and included no details of background except a few hints in abstract form. The *Sunrise Crater* (FIG. 238) will serve to illustrate how one misses the fine decorative quality of the black-figured and early red-figured ware.

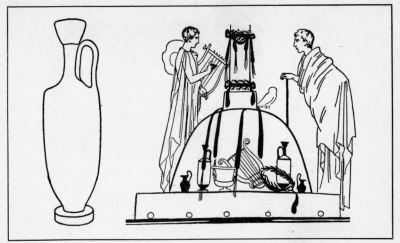

Fig. 229. The *Lecythos* (oil flask) has a long narrow neck adapted to pouring the oil slowly. It was used chiefly in funeral rites. Vase painting showing two men at a tomb; on the plinth are lecythi, oinochoë, a crater, a lyre, and a wreath.

One realizes that literary content and what one may call the painter's province have triumphed over ceramic requirements.

The metalworker was important, and his wares reflect the general style of his day. Bronze was always a favorite medium with the Greeks, who used it widely, not only for sculpture but also for various kinds of utensils — pots and pans, dishes for the table, sacrificial vessels, tools, weapons. An example is a shallow bowl (FIG. 239) with flaring rim quite devoid of ornamentation except for the handle, which is elaborately decorated on both sides. At the point of attachment we see an animated boxing scene, the lithe bodies of the athletes so grouped that while they vigorously pursue their sport, yet as a group they do not interfere with the decorative purpose. Below this section is a smooth place left for the thumb when holding the handle — an indication of the fundamental feeling for utility; this is finished by a palmette which with its projecting lines terminates in a giant, whose snaky legs intertwine to form an open ring for hanging up the dish. Another bronze utensil is a sturdy pitcher with a long lip (FIG. 240) which not only balances the handle but facilitates pouring. The decoration is confined to the handle and lip and is quite subordinate to the structural surfaces. Both the bowl and the pitcher illustrate the Greek practice of concentrating ornament at important points for the sake of accent, or for specific design reasons. Their decoration is controlled by the same purpose and the same logic as is the sculpture on the *Parthenon*.

Fig. 230. Scene in a School. From a cylix painted by Duris. On the left the Athenian boy is taking a lesson on the lyre; in the center he is reciting before a master who is following with his scroll; at the right sits the boy's slave, who accompanies him to school; on the wall hang cylixes and lyres. (*Archäologische Zeitung*)

Fig. 231. Rhodian Oinochoë.
(Morin Jean)

Another important kind of metal object was the mirror, a disk of highly polished bronze with a protective cover on which the decoration was concentrated. In Fig. 241 this decoration consists of a head, repoussé work of such high relief that the metal is very thin; details, such as the brows, lashes, and finer hairs, are delicately incised, as are the simple concentric circles forming the border. The generalized type of the head and the treatment of the hair, partly naturalistic but highly decorative, relate the mirror to the fifth-century style.

Evidence of the same evolution of style in the minor arts as in sculpture and painting is particularly clear in the coins and gems. Strange though it may seem, the finest Greek coins were struck not at Athens nor even anywhere in continental Greece, but in Magna Graecia, particularly at Syracuse in Sicily. In the *Demarateion* [1] (Fig. 243), on the obverse is a four-horse chariot, with a Victory flying above; in the segment below, a running lion, and about the edge, a row of dots;

[1] These coins are named after Demarate, wife of the tyrant Gelon. According to one story, after their defeat at Himera, the Carthaginians obtained very favorable terms from Gelon through the influence of Demarate, to whom they gave a large amount of silver from which these coins were struck.

Fig. 232. Amphora, Painted by Exekias: Ajax and Achilles Playing Draughts. Black-figured. 550–525 B.C. Vatican, Rome. (Furtwängler-Reichhold)

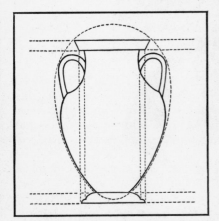

An analysis of Fig. 232 reveals a basic egg shape and a subtle relationship of part to part. The jar probably had a cover which contributed to the shape and proportions.

Fig. 233. François Vase. H. c. 2 ft. First half VI cent. B.C. Archaeological Museum, Florence. (Furtwängler-Reichhold)

Fig. 234. Cylix, Painted by Exekias: Dionysus Sailing over the Sea. Black-figured. D. 14½ in. 550–525 B.C. Munich. (Furtwängler-Reichhold)

Fig. 235. Cylix,
Painted by Euphro-
nios: Cattle of Ger-
yon. Red-figured. D.
17 in. c. 500 B.C. Mu-
nich. (Furtwängler-
Reichhold)

Fig. 236. Theseus
Cylix. Painted by
Euphronios. Early
V cent. B.C. Louvre,
Paris.

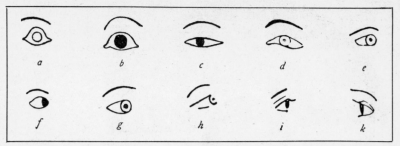

Fig. 237. Evolution of the Drawing of the Eye. In the earliest work the eye is represented front view, almost circular in form and the pupil as a circle or disk (*a* and *b*); the outline next becomes elliptical (*c* and *d*); then the lids begin to separate at the inner corner and the pupil to be pushed inward, though still circular (*e*, *f*, and *g*); finally the lids open up, the pupil becomes elliptical, the upper lid is properly shaped and the correct profile is attained (*i* and *k*). (British Museum, London)

Fig. 238. Crater: Sunrise Scene. Red-figured. H. 12⅜ in. C. 400 B.C. British Museum, London. Note the compactness of the shape and the relation of the handles to the body. (Furtwängler-Reichhold)

on the reverse a profile head, perhaps of the nymph Arethusa, in a faint circle, is surrounded by four dolphins with a Greek inscription which reads in translation "of the Syracusans." It will be noticed that the coin is thicker and less even in shape than modern coins, and that the metal runs up around the edge on one side of the reverse. This is because Greek coins were struck by hand on an anvil that held the die,[1] without a circular frame to keep the metal from running over the edge. The relief, too, is higher; for the Greek was not hampered by the modern necessity of "stacking." What we observe first, as in the pottery, is the feeling for the adaptation of the figures to the space. Though the object is small, there is a quiet orderliness and a feeling of amplitude. The circle of the disk is repeated by the dolphins and inner ring until the eye inevitably reaches the head in the center. The design is clear and effective, particularly when it is compared with that of the later coins decorated with the same type (FIG. 244) in

[1] Of course the skill of the engraver lay in the cutting of the die in intaglio, of which the finished coin is an impression.

Fig. 239. Shallow Bowl. Bronze. L. 17½ in. with the handle. Detail of handle. Metropolitan Museum, New York. (Metropolitan Museum)

Fig. 240. Jug. Bronze. H. 12 in. Metropolitan Museum, New York. (Metropolitan Museum)

which the naturalistic tendency has entailed decorative loss. Here the relief is higher, casting considerable shadow; the hair is arranged naturalistically, with ringlets escaping here and there as if to soften the contours; the dolphins are subordinate because of the larger size of the head; a circle of dots incloses the design. On the reverse is the victorious four-horse chariot, seen three-quarters view, dashing forward under the lash of the driver toward whom a Victory is flying with the crown; in the segment below is a suit of armor, the prize of the race.[1] A coin from Agrigentum (FIG. 245) is notable, among coins of many countries which have used the eagle as a coin type, for the grouping of two eagles with contrasting movement and for the adaptation of the group to the space.

Another activity of the engraver lay in the carving of gems that were mounted in rings and used as seals. FIG. 246 shows Eros carrying off a struggling girl. The two figures are skillfully grouped, and with the boldly cut wings fill the oval space with a quiet balance despite the animated movement. Perhaps an inheritance from the Cretan was the love of the animal and bird forms and their frequent use on the seals (FIG. 247). In the *Flying Heron* (FIG. 242) we see first a sympathetic

[1] This coin type is indicative of the popularity of chariot-racing in Syracuse.

Fig. 241. Bronze Mirror Cover. D. 7⅝ in. Late V cent. Metropolitan Museum, New York. (Metropolitan Museum)

Fig. 242. Gem. Engraved by Dexamenos with a flying heron. Bluish chalcedony. L. 2 in. 450–440 B.C. Hermitage, Leningrad.

observation of nature. In the erect head, the legs thrust back, and the position of the wings, we get a superb rendering of a bird in flight. There is firmness in the sweeping curves of the wings and a marvelous delicacy in the lines indicating the soft plumage. A sim-

Fig. 243. Silver Coin of Syracuse, Called the *Demarateion*. C. 479 B.C. British Museum, London.

ple line near the edge frames the design. A sympathetic study of bird life, design, and masterful technical ability combine in this gem. Like the coins, the gems are relief sculpture in miniature. In carving them the craftsman probably used a metal drill with powdered emery and oil, so that the process required not only keen eyesight but a very sensitively trained touch, and a patience that considered neither time nor money.

D. SUMMARY

Early the Greek imposed upon himself, perhaps unconsciously, types and narrow limitations within which he was to concentrate upon niceties of relationship down to the smallest degree — an art of discipline. The small size and simple plan of the temple, refined upon in

Fig. 244. Syracusan "Medallion." Signed by Euaenetus. Late V cent. B.C. British Museum, London.

Fig. 245. Coin of Agrigentum. V cent. B.C. Munich.

Fig. 246. Gem: Eros Carrying a Struggling Girl. Carnelian. L. ¾ in. Early V cent. Metropolitan Museum, New York. (Metropolitan Museum)

the proportion of every part to every part; the limited range of subject matter and pose in his sculpture; the abandonment of the gay polychrome pottery for the severer black and red-figured wares — these illustrate his attitude. The archaic age, after assimilating outside influences, produced a truly Greek style in the robust temples; and in the highly vital sculpture which possessed a clearly felt balance between the artist's conception and the material through which it was objectified; and which possessed a decorative beauty through the use of simplified masses and conventional detail.

This dynamic archaic art evolved, in the fifth century, into an art of subtler refinements, into a discreet naturalism of great breadth. An analysis of its apparent simplicity reveals the fact that it is based not upon a failure to understand form with all its details, but upon that balance between mind and eye, acquired through centuries of endeavor, which could select what was essential and permanent and omit the irrelevant. Such selective power, which reveals an innate sense of balance and proportion, enabled the architect, for example, to restrain his ornament, realizing that the unity and harmony of the whole design was his primary purpose and that details of sculpture, carvings, or color must be made to serve and enhance that harmony, and not to intrude as if ornament were an end in itself. In carving or drawing the human figure, the same qualities enabled the artist to represent a broadly generalized impersonal aspect of man. In his coins, pottery, and other household utensils is the same vitality and decorative beauty within the capacities and limitations of the material; the same preponderant interest in niceties and refinements of shape and contour; and the same reposefulness as in the temple or the statue. In all these art forms the dominant, if limited, concern of the Greek is apparent — man as the measure of all things.

(For Bibliography see p. 179.)

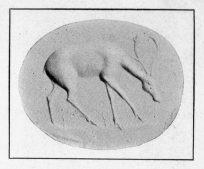

Fig. 247. Gem: Stag. V cent. B.C. Museum of Fine Arts, Boston (Boston Museum)

2. FOURTH–CENTURY AND HELLENISTIC ART
(400 B.C. to the first century B.C.)

A. HISTORICAL BACKGROUND

The disastrous Peloponnesian War left Greece drained of its strength and reduced Athens politically to a secondary place. Sparta and then Thebes took the leadership, both unsuccessfully, until Philip of Macedon, shrewdly playing upon mutual jealousies, brought the country to subjection and a semblance of unity. The work of his son Alexander was to spread Hellenic culture, by his conquests, over large areas of the East. Athens was no longer the center of this civilization, but only a provincial city-state in comparison with the magnificent cosmopolitan metropolises of Asia Minor and Egypt — Ephesus, Rhodes, Pergamon, Alexandria (FIG. 174).

Another result of the Peloponnesian War was to turn the Greek from his ideal of the state to that of the individual. "Know thyself," Socrates had taught as he went about daily among the people in the streets, the agora, and the gymnasium and by questioning endeavored to help them to gain "wisdom" empirically, to weigh and judge out of their own experience rather than to consult an oracle. The serene idealism of the fifth century that was born of a simple robust faith and had produced the *Parthenon* and Sophocles gave way to the unrest of skepticism, to realism, and to the intellectual independence of Plato and Aristotle. The spirit of eager inquiry, inherited from the earlier Ionian philosophers and mathematicians, attained a truly scientific mentality in such thinkers as Aristotle and Archimedes, and made valuable contributions to science, measuring with fair accuracy the circumference and the diameter of the earth, long since known to be spherical, and discovering many facts about astronomy, geometry, the natural sciences, and medicine.

Fig. 248. Corinthian Capital from Epidaurus.

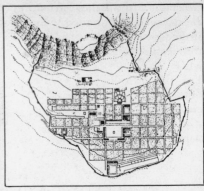

Fig. 249. Plan of Priene.

While Greece had been passing through the cycle of growth, flowering, and decay, Rome, in the Italian peninsula, had been slowly developing. Gradually it had conquered Italy, Sicily, and Carthage, and then, partly through circumstance and partly through desire for expansion, it came eastward, defeated the Macedonian power, and made Greece a Roman province. While this was a political victory, it was not a cultural one. Hellenic ideas continued to dominate both in the East and in the West, though deeply modified by the taste of the victors; and under new conditions even furnished many of the fundamentals of medieval culture.

B. ARCHITECTURE

The result of the Peloponnesian War was a cessation of building in the countries immediately affected. But in Asia Minor there was great activity, and the Ionic temple reached a climax of grandeur, if not of refinement, in the *Temple of Artemis (Diana)* at Ephesus, a peripteral temple with a double colonnade and elaborately sculptured bases for many of the columns [1] — an illustration of the emphasis upon ornament for its own sake at the expense of the clarity, unity, and proportion in the fifth-century temples.

The more varied, complex, and cosmopolitan culture, especially of the Hellenistic age, created a demand for a greater variety of buildings — choragic and sepulchral monuments (*Monument of Lysicrates* and *Mausoleum of Halicarnassus*), sumptuous open-air altars (*Pergamon*),

---

[1] For a restoration of this temple see W. J. Anderson and R. P. Spiers, *The Architecture of Ancient Greece*, Scribner, 1927, PL. L.

theaters (at *Epidaurus*, of *Dionysus* at Athens), civic structures (stoas), and even the towns and cities as a whole (*Priene* and *Ephesus*). For the conception of town-planning in the modern sense had been heretofore largely lacking. Athens, Delphi, Olympia, were groups of buildings set down hit or miss, while *Priene* (FIG. 249) was laid out on a plan definitely related to the topography of the site and to the activities of the community.

The Doric order practically disappeared with the ascendancy of the Ionic and its variant, the Corinthian. It is chiefly the capital (FIG. 248) that differentiates the latter two, with its bell-shaped core decorated with two rows of conventionalized acanthus leaves from which rise volutes, the longer ones reaching out to support the corners of the abacus, the shorter uniting with a floral ornament to decorate the core, the whole design effecting success-

Fig. 250. Temple of the Olympian Zeus. Athens. Begun 174 B.C.

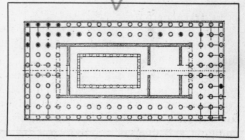

Fig. 251. Plan of the Temple of the Olympian Zeus. The solid circles indicate the extant standing columns.

fully the transition from the circular column to the rectangular abacus. The Corinthian order was a favorite with the Romans and appears in the Greco-Roman buildings erected after the Romans appeared in the East, such as the *Temple of the Olympian Zeus* (FIGS. 250, 251), which, though built by Greeks on the plan of the *Parthenon* except for the double colonnade, in scale at least and hence in grandiose impressiveness represents quite a different age and a different ideal from that of the *Parthenon* on the Acropolis near by.

Fig. 252. Praxiteles. Hermes
(Fig. 253), head.

Fig. 253. Praxiteles. Hermes with the Infant Dionysus. Marble. H. 7 ft. c. 350 B.C.
Olympia. (Clarence Kennedy)

C. SCULPTURE

Changing ideals made themselves manifest in sculpture, though its function remained much the same as in the sixth and fifth centuries. Skepticism as to the old faith, the enhancement of the individual, the reliance upon reason — changes such as these predestined that the generalization and the impersonality of the fifth century should give way to something individual and personal, to an expression of personal emotions and idiosyncrasies. In the *Hermes* of Praxiteles (FIG. 253), for example, one is inclined to feel a definite personal charm more insistently than he feels marble. The god is represented standing, resting his weight on the left arm, a pose that gives an easy curve to the body. On this arm he holds the infant Dionysus, who reaches for the bunch of grapes that the god probably was holding in his right hand. There is a languid ease and grace throughout the figure. Hermes is looking not at the child, but off into space, with a dreamy expression in his eyes and a half-smile playing about his mouth; the whole figure, particularly the head (FIG. 252), is deep in the mood of reverie. The modeling is exquisite. Soft shadows follow the planes as they flow imperceptibly one into another. With the utmost delicacy the marble is

Fig. 254. Aphrodite. Found at
Cyrene in Northern Africa. Marble.
c. 100 B.C. after IV cent. type.
Terme (National) Museum, Rome.

Fig. 255. Demeter. From the temple
of Demeter at Cnidus. Marble. c. 350
B.C. British Museum, London. (Clarence
Kennedy)

finished, so that over the features a fleeting expression seems to be
gliding, and the delicacy is enhanced by the contrastingly rough way
in which the hair is indicated, and by the deep folds of the realistic
drapery, whose broken masses by contrast stress the flowing surfaces of
the figure. Aphrodites were popular, particularly an *Aphrodite*, now
lost, made by Praxiteles for the Cnidians. Something of the quality of
these we may see in the *Aphrodite of Cyrene* (FIG. 254) and in a *Head from
Chios* (Boston Museum) in which the features seem veiled, so imperceptibly do the planes merge. Such effects as these can be obtained only
by brilliant technical skill in stone-carving.

The work of Scopas, judged from a few rather battered heads, shows
intensity of feeling, especially by means of the upturned head and the
deep-set eyes shadowed by heavy brows. These fourth-century sculptors, however, did not entirely abandon the traditions of the fifth
century, as we see in the *Demeter of Cnidus* (FIG. 255), in which the
generalized majesty of Phidias is combined with the individual human-

Fig. 256. Frieze of the Mausoleum of Halicarnassus. c. 350 B.C.
British Museum, London. (Mansell)

ness of Scopas and Praxiteles. The goddess is heavily draped in her
cloak, one corner of which is drawn up over the back of the head,
throwing into relief the quietly tragic face. But compare the drapery
of the Demeter with that of the single *Fate* (FIG. 214). In the former,
the casualness of the folds of actual cloth, copying the accidents of
natural appearance, has taken the place of a carefully considered
design based upon natural appearance and upon its suitability for
stone. Therein lies one difference between the fourth and the fifth
centuries: the illusion of natural appearance is contesting the va-
lidity of the stone. This is again illustrated in one of the friezes on
the *Mausoleum* (FIG. 256) depicting a fight between a Greek and an
Amazon. The figures are thin and lithe, somewhat strained in pose;
their faces have the same expression of human passion as their bodies;
and the restless drapery intensifies the impetuosity that sweeps through
the group — all at the expense of those precise formal relationships
which made for the decorative beauty of fifth-century friezes.

An important sculptor of the generation following Praxiteles and
Scopas was Lysippus, court sculptor of Alexander the Great. No work
of his is known to be extant, but two important innovations of this time
may possibly be credited to him. One was the change in taste, noticeable in all the arts, in the matter of proportions. The new canon of
taste required a more slender supple figure, which may, indeed, have
been influenced by the second innovation, foreshadowed to be sure
in earlier work — the realization of the figure in space, truly three-
dimensional carving (FIG. 258). Volume always exists in a statue in
the round but by no means is there always a visual grasp of space.
The earliest figures were in a stiff, frontal position, with the planes

Fig. 257. Frieze from the Altar of Zeus at Pergamon. c. 175 B.C.
Pergamon Museum, Berlin.

closely related to the four sides of the stone block, and seen better
from one or two positions. Even when the figure was loosened up,
especially in the limbs, and then was thrown into a curve, it was still
more or less four-sided and seen satisfactorily only from some one
point of view. In this respect the *Apollo* (FIG. 195) and the *Hermes*
(FIG. 253) are more closely related than the *Hermes* and the *Apoxyomenos* (FIG. 258), in which the statue is still limited by the ideal space
determined by the block of stone, but within it the planes swing backward and forward and from any point of view the eye is carried easily
and inevitably through this space.[1]

Such a movement of planes is found in the *Nike of Samothrace* (FIG. 259),
as is clearly seen if the statue is compared with the *Nike of Paeonius*,
or the *Nike* on the east pediment of the *Parthenon*. The turn in the
torso not only guides into depth but produces a feeling of movement
that is strongly supplemented by the clinging wind-swept drapery,
whose restless curves and minute folds are so complicated that they
almost become a tour de force. As it is, the sculptor just saved himself
by bringing their main lines into harmony with the planes of the figure.

The tendency toward restlessness and the expression of intense feeling
reached a climax in the *Altar at Pergamon*, on the frieze of which is
represented the battle between the gods and the giants (FIG. 257).
Athena, moving rapidly toward the right, clutches one of the winged
giants by the hair, forcing him to the ground; on the right Earth,
mother of the giants, a half-length figure, looks appealingly to Athena;

[1] Comparisons for three-dimensional quality can be made intelligently only by
seeing the figures from several points of view. Series to illustrate this evolution can
be found in Richter, *op. cit.*

Fig. 258. Lysippus (?). Copy of the
Apoxyomenos. Marble. Late IV cent.
B.C. Vatican, Rome.

Fig. 259. Nike of Samothrace.
To commemorate a naval victory
in 306 B.C. Louvre, Paris.

above her, Victory approaches to crown the goddess. Force is there,
powerfully displayed. The artist obtained it by using violent contrasts,
such as those in the lines of direction in the bodies of Athena and the
giant; by extravagant modeling; and by the agonized expression of the
faces. He has filled his space, even introducing half-length figures to do
so, but at the price of disorder, a disorder held firmly within the frieze,
however, by the bordering moldings. The extravagantly rich base reflects the baroque taste of Hellenistic culture just as the austere Olympian and Phidian sculptures reflect that of the fifth century. If one
wishes violent disordered movement with realistic details he finds it
at *Pergamon;* if he wishes quiet ordered movement with conventional
details clearly related, he finds it on the *Siphnian Treasury,* at *Olympia,*
and on the *Parthenon.* It is a matter of taste.

Realism reached a climax in such statues as the *Aphrodite of Syracuse*
(Fig. 260), in which the feeling for stone as stone has quite surrendered
to the ambition of making stone look like soft warm flesh. It again
reveals itself in the modeling of the *Pergamon* figures and the *Laocoön*
(Vatican) in which intensity of emotion and of movement is seen not

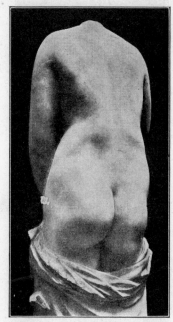

Fig. 260. Aphrodite of Syracuse. Hellenistic. Marble. Museum of Syracuse.

Fig. 261. Old Market Woman. Marble. II cent. B.C. Metropolitan Museum, New York. (Metropolitan Museum)

only in the modeling but in the faces and in the writing serpents, which however tie the three figures into a compact group; and in the Hellenistic pictorial reliefs such as the *Peasant Going to Market* (Vienna). The subject matter became more varied and included genre (FIG. 261) now trivial or frivolous, now charming, now repulsive — frequently of high technical excellence, but hardly of significance.

In the midst of unconvincing, insignificant expressions, however brilliant they may be technically, one usually finds archaistic tendencies. For in an age of decline as the seeds of a new era are being sown, the most sensitive artists are likely to turn for stimulation to more robust works of art, to primitive and archaic art. This probably explains the simple dignity and calm of the *Aphrodite (Venus) of Melos* (Louvre), which seems to share the fifth-century largeness of expression yet without its vitality. Other examples actually copy the earlier forms, especially the conventions for the drapery and the hair.

One group in the field of late sculpture stands alone, the *Tanagra Figurines*, perhaps the most charming examples of Greek genre. Thousands

Fig. 263. Lady with a Fan. Tanagra Figurine. Terra cotta, painted. H. 8 in. Museum of Fine Arts, Boston. (Boston Museum)

Fig. 262. Vase Painting. British Museum, London. (Gardner, *The Principles of Greek Art*. Macmillan)

have been found, chiefly in graves, and their purpose is unknown. They represent all kinds of everyday scenes, trivial in subject but dainty in execution and bright in color. The robes are usually rose or blue, the hair a reddish brown, the shoes red; and the fans or other accessories have touches of gilding. In all of them there is a natural grace and charm; and the little lady in Fig. 263 wrapped in her cloak, with her jaunty hat and fan, is even coquettish. These figurines frequently reveal a spontaneous momentary pose suitable for expression in clay, and in them we see true clay technique. To be sure, great quantities of these figurines were made in molds, a single subject often being constructed out of several parts, so that by changing the head or the arms a considerable amount of variety could be obtained.

D. PAINTING

That schools of painting existed, and paralleled sculpture in an evolution from geometric and conventional to naturalistic and realistic, we know from literary evidence, from reflections in pottery decoration, and from Roman copies. But the actual paintings are entirely gone, the mural paintings in the stoas and other public buildings as well as the panel pictures. As shadowy to us as ghosts are these famous painters so far as our visual knowledge of their work is concerned. There was Polygnotus, contemporary of Phidias, who was a painter as well as a sculptor. Polygnotus attempted, by placing figures one

Fig. 264. Battle Scene between Alexander and Darius. Mosaic. From the floor of the House of the Faun, Pompeii. L. 17 ft. C. 100 B.C. Naples Museum.

above another, to suggest depth; he used a very limited range of color and appears to have created, with others, as grandly monumental a style in painting as the sculptors attained in the temple at *Olympia* and in the *Parthenon*. Then there was Apollodorus the "Shadow-Maker" (fifth century), who seems to have experimented with the use of shadow to make his figures appear round, in conformity with the general naturalistic trend of the day. Zeuxis and Parrhasius (fifth and fourth centuries), Apelles and Protogenes (of the time of Alexander the Great), are characters in famous stories which stress technical skill and realism. A basis for actual knowledge or judgment of their painting is entirely lacking.

While the Greek painters experimented in perspective, light and shade, and color, line seems to have been their preëminent means of expression, used both to model and express volume and also calligraphically (FIG. 262). In the *Alexander Mosaic* (FIG. 264), which is probably a Roman copy based on a Greek painting, we perhaps catch a glimpse of a Greek composition on a large scale, though allowance should be made for the mosaic technique. The scene represents some battle, usually thought to be that of the Issus. The center of interest is the horseman in the foreground who has been pierced by the spear of Alexander and is falling from his wounded steed. Darius is fleeing in his chariot, but he looks back at the wounded man with anguish in his face and arm outstretched as if in helpless appeal. Another horseman in the foreground has dismounted, and while attempting to hold his horse looks toward his wounded companion as if to offer his mount. Here, then, is a well-defined center of interest toward which all the main lines of the composition lead. The vigor in the

Fig. 265. Gold Necklace. IV cent. B.C. Metropolitan Museum, New York. (Metropolitan Museum)

charge of the Greeks, the consternation of the routed Persians, the real anguish in the face of Darius, are expressed with directness. There is bold and fairly correct foreshortening, notably in the horses in the foreground. The background is flat, with no indication of landscape except a gnarled tree. The upper third of the panel is perfectly flat and unadorned except for the highly decorative tree and the spears, and offers an interesting contrast to the vigor and movement of the lower part; while the insistent diagonals are opposed to the largely curvilinear composition of the figures.

E. MINOR ARTS

In the fifth century the ceramic industry was already declining, for unknown reasons, and by the fourth century had almost disappeared. But the work of the goldsmith was much in demand not only about the Aegean but among the Scythians and Sarmatians of southern Russia.[1] From the earliest days jewelry — necklaces, earrings, pins, bracelets, rings — was important in the costume of Greek women, though not of the men as it was in Egypt, Assyria, and Crete; and the art of the goldsmith may have been an inheritance from the Aegeans. Before the Hellenistic age gold was used chiefly for its own sake, for its color and texture, and for the shimmer of surface which resulted from the various processes of working it — casting, repoussé, engraving, soldering, granulation, filigree — with variations of color through a sparing use of enamel. In a necklace, for example (FIG. 265), the goldsmith has plaited five strands for the band from which hang small pendants attached by tiny starlike florets, which probably once were filled with enamel. Each petal of these is edged with a hairlike wire soldered to its edge; the plaited band terminates in palmette ornaments daintily executed in filigree work, to which are affixed the filigree rosettes that form the clasp. The main design is kept simple and dignified; but subordinate to this and enhancing it, is a wealth of exquisitely wrought detail that adds a note of delicacy. In the Hellenistic age the quality of craftsmanship declined and the introduction of semi-precious stones added a more obvious richness.

[1] See p. 100. Note particularly the mutual interactions of racial art traditions, the Iranian tending toward conventional treatment, the Greek toward naturalistic.

F. SUMMARY

In the fourth century we see Phidian austerity giving way to ease and grace, divine majesty and serenity to human sentiment, and tempered naturalism to an illusion of natural appearance. More detailed modeling; an emphasis upon delicate surface treatment; a naturalistic tendency in the use of color; and the conquest in sculpture of space, that is, the attainment of truly three-dimensional figures — all these characteristics are a logical evolution of the naturalistic trend. These characteristics of the trend developed in the Hellenistic age into theatrical emotionalism and realism, and triviality in the face of poverty of ideas. A truly magnificent technical skill busied itself, like a virtuoso, in surface treatment for its own sake, in making stone look like soft flesh quite disregardful of the natural capacities and limitations of the material. Ornament became riotous, an end in itself, and thus broke down the complete unity which characterized the more disciplined work of earlier centuries. The archaistic tendency that now appeared was only one more mask of a decadent age. But Hellenistic art was cosmopolitan, and in reaching Eastward was mingling again with forces there, the result of which was to be the flowering, several centuries hence, of Byzantine culture.

BIBLIOGRAPHY

Alexander, Christine, *Jewelry, the Art of the Goldsmith in Classical Times*, Metropolitan Museum of Art, New York, 1928
Anderson, W. J., and Spiers, R. P., *The Architecture of Ancient Greece*, the first part of *The Architecture of Greece and Rome*, rev. by W. B. Dinsmoor, Scribner, 1927
Beazley, J. D., *Attic Black-Figure*, Oxford Press, 1928
—— and Ashmole, Bernard, *Greek Sculpture and Painting to the End of the Hellenistic Period*, Macmillan, 1932
Bell, Edward, *Hellenic Architecture*, Harcourt, Brace, 1920
Borovka, G. I., *Scythian Art*, tr. by V. G. Childe, Stokes, 1928
British Museum, *A Guide to the Principal Coins of the Greeks from about 700 B.C. to A.D. 270*, British Museum, London, 1932
Buschor, Ernst, *Greek Vase-Painting*, tr. by G. C. Richards, Dutton, 1922
Carpenter, Rhys, *The Esthetic Basis of Greek Art*, Longmans, 1921
—— —— *The Humanistic Value of Archaeology*, Harvard University Press, 1933
—— —— *The Sculpture of the Nike Temple Parapet*, Harvard University Press, 1929
Casson, Stanley, *The Technique of Early Greek Sculpture*, Oxford Press, 1933
Collignon, Maxime, ed., *Le Parthénon*, Paris, 1912
Cossio, M. B., and Pijoan, José, *Summa artis*, Madrid, 1931–34, Vols. I–VI, Vol. IV
Dickinson, G. L., *The Greek View of Life*, 7th ed., Doubleday Page, 1925
Fowler, H. N., Wheeler, J. R., and Stevens, G. P., *A Handbook of Greek Archaeology*, American Book Co., 1909
Gardiner, E. N., *Olympia: Its History and Remains*, London, Oxford Press, 1925
Gardner, E. A., *Ancient Athens*, new ed., Macmillan, 1907

Gardner, E. A., *The Art of Greece*, Studio, 1925
—— —— *Greece and the Aegean*, McBride, 1934
—— —— *A Handbook of Greek Sculpture*, 2d ed., Macmillan, 1915
—— —— *Six Greek Sculptors*, Scribner, 1910
Gardner, Percy, *The Principles of Greek Art*, Macmillan, 1914
—— —— and Bloomfield, Sir R. T., *Greek Art and Architecture*, Oxford Press, 1922
Goodyear, W. H., *Greek Refinements, Studies in Temperamental Architecture*, Yale University Press, 1912
Hambidge, Jay, *The Parthenon and Other Greek Temples; Their Dynamic Symmetry*, Yale University Press, 1924
Johansen, Peter, *Phidias and the Parthenon Sculptures*, tr. by Ingeborg Andersen, Copenhagen, 1925
Lamb, Winifred, *Greek and Roman Bronzes*, Dial Press, 1929
Laurie, A. P., *Greek and Roman Methods of Painting*, Macmillan, 1910
Lawrence, A. W., *Classical Sculpture*, Peter Smith, 1929
—— —— *Later Greek Sculpture*, Harcourt, Brace, 1927
Livingstone, R. W., *The Greek Genius and Its Meaning to Us*, 2d ed., Oxford Press, 1915
—— —— ed., *The Legacy of Greece*, Oxford Press, 1921
Loewy, Emanuel, *Polygnot, ein Buch von griechischer Malerei*, Vienna, 1929
—— —— *The Rendering of Nature in Early Greek Art*, tr. by John Fothergill, London, 1907
Marquand, Allan, *Greek Architecture*, Macmillan, 1909
Minns, E. H., *Scythians and Greeks*, Putnam, 1914
Pater, W. H., *Greek Studies*, Macmillan, 1928 (first pub. 1895)
Paton, J. M., ed., *The Erechtheum*, restored by G. P. Stevens, text by L. D. Caskey and others, Harvard University Press, 1927
Pfuhl, Ernst, *Masterpieces of Greek Drawing and Painting*, tr. by J. D. Beazley, Macmillan, 1926
Pottier, Edmond, *Douris and the Painters of Greek Vases*, tr. by Bettina Kahnweiler, 2d ed., Dutton, 1917
Poulsen, Frederik, *Delphi*, tr. by G. C. Richards, Bonnier, 1922
Pryce, F. N., *Catalogue of Sculpture in the Department of Greek and Roman Antiquities*, British Museum, London, 1928–31, Pts. I–II
Richter, G. M. A., *Ancient Furniture, a History of Greek, Etruscan and Roman Furniture*, Oxford Press, 1926
—— —— *Animals in Greek Sculpture*, Oxford Press, 1930
—— —— *Handbook of the Classical Collection*, Metropolitan Museum of Art, New York, 1930
—— —— *The Sculpture and Sculptors of the Greeks*, Yale University Press, 1930
—— —— *The Craft of Athenian Pottery*, Yale University Press, 1923
Ridder, A. H. P. de, and Deonna, Waldemar, *Art in Greece*, tr. by V. C. C. Collum, Knopf, 1927
Robertson, D. S., *A Handbook of Greek and Roman Architecture*, Macmillan, 1929
—— —— and Hege, Walter, *Die Akropolis*, Berlin, 1930
Rodenwaldt, G. M. K., *Die Kunst der Antike*, Berlin, 1927
Roes, Anna, *Greek Geometric Art, Its Symbolism and Its Origin*, Oxford Press, 1933
Rostovtsev, M. I., *The Animal Style in South Russia and China*, Princeton University Press, 1929
—— —— *Iranians and Greeks in South Russia*, Oxford Press, 1922
—— —— *Out of the Past of Greece and Rome*, Yale University Press, 1932
Smith, A. H., *The Sculptures of the Parthenon*, British Museum, London, 1910
Solon, L. V., *Polychromy*, Architectural Record, 1924

Swindler, M. H., *Ancient Painting*, Yale University Press, 1929
Walston, Sir Charles, *Essays on the Art of Pheidias*, Century, 1885
Walters, H. B., *The Art of the Greeks*, 2d ed. rev., Macmillan, 1922
—— —— *Catalogue of the Engraved Gems and Cameos, Greek, Etruscan, and Roman*, British Museum, London, 1926
—— —— *History of Ancient Pottery, Greek, Roman, and Etruscan*, Scribner, 1905, 2 vols.
Warren, H. L., *The Foundations of Classic Architecture*, Macmillan, 1919
Zimmern, A. E., *The Greek Commonwealth*, 5th ed. rev., Oxford Press, 1931

See also the General Bibliography, pp. 749–751.

CHAPTER VII

Etruscan and Roman Art
(about 1000 B.C. to 500 A.D.)

A. HISTORICAL BACKGROUND

Although the early histories of Greece and Italy run nearly parallel, chronologically, the former reached a climax in the fifth and fourth centuries B.C., a period during which the latter was still slowly developing. The story of early Rome is a story of struggle for existence, particularly against the Etruscans, who came to Italy probably from Asia Minor and were closely allied culturally to the Greeks. In the sixth century B.C. they were in control of all Italy from their heavily fortified cities — Corneto, Cervetri, Veii, Perugia, Orvieto, Praeneste, and other sites in what is now Tuscany. They were farmers, traders on sea as well as on land, cruel warriors and pirates. At home they lived luxuriously in gaily decorated houses, feasted and danced unrestrainedly. They were adept in working metal and clay. They constructed their fortifications, city gates, bridges, aqueducts, and sewers of heavy stone masonry on the arch principle; small buildings they made of wood gaily painted or faced with colored terra-cotta tiles. Their temple was based upon the Greek prostyle plan (FIG. 176 B), rested on a high base with a flight of steps, and was probably made of brick with wooden columns and a heavy wooden superstructure brightly painted.[1] With an emphasis upon a future life not unlike that of the Egyptian, they paid much attention to burial, so that the tombs, which were built or carved in the hillside, and which imitated the

---

[1] There is no even fairly well preserved Etruscan temple extant. For a reconstruction see W. J. Anderson and R. P. Spiers, *The Architecture of Ancient Rome*, rev. by Thomas Ashby, Scribner, 1927, PL. VIII; or S. F. Kimball and G. H. Edgell, *A History of Architecture*, Harper, 1918, FIG. 37.

Fig. 266. Apollo of Veii.
Terra cotta painted. c. 500
B.C. Villa Papa Giulio,
Rome. (Anderson)

interior of Etruscan houses, furnish us in their
wall paintings a picture of Etruscan life. And
the sarcophagi, with their recumbent figures,
supply some of the best examples of sculpture.

The Etruscans showed a peculiar preference
for clay — a local material excellent both as
to quality and quantity. For architectural decoration they made terra-cotta tiles which are
highly decorative in their pattern and gay colors, notably so the masklike roof tiles. Likewise their sculpture in the round, the *Apollo
of Veii* (FIG. 266), for example, is clay rather
than stone, though one feels the archaic Greek
stone prototype. But in the awkward vigor of
the stride, in the boldly conceived form, and in
the striking, conventional use of color there is
the crude vigor of the Etruscan. In the recumbent figures of the sarcophagi is a similar eager
vitality. Even if the later clumsy cinerary urns
show lack of sensitiveness, the early life-sized
mortuary figures, such as the examples in the
British Museum, the Louvre, and in Rome
(FIG. 268), reveal a definite relationship between the figures and the sarcophagus. With
the flowing surfaces painted in conventional
color, with the patternlike archaic features
and expressive hands, they are direct and convincing both in form
and in the expression of an inner vitality and significance.

Another favorite medium was bronze. In the head of the so-called
Orator (FIG. 267) is a forceful personality, realistically portrayed; in
the *Chimera* (FIG. 269), a more conventional treatment, very vital and
decorative; in both, a fine technical command of the material. Bronze
was used also for many smaller objects, cinerary urns, toilet boxes, and
mirrors which were engraved with mythological and genre scenes
imitative of the Greek products, which were imported in great quantity by the wealthy Etruscans. One feels in them a provincial Greek
art with a stamp of verve and boldness and with an unusual decorative beauty — qualities that are repeated in Etruscan jewelry.

These qualities impress one looking at an Etruscan tomb (FIG. 270)
fashioned after an actual Etruscan room with sloping roof; both the
roof and the walls are gaily painted, the roof chiefly with conventional,
geometric designs, the walls with scenes of funeral banquets, dancing,
athletic contests, hunting. These paintings, thoroughly decorative, are

usually in fresco, though at times painted directly on the stone. The bright color is used conventionally in flat tones within outlines, with no regard for the hues of nature, for one horse may have a red and a yellow leg or a blue coat and a red mane. In this *Tomb of the Leopards* (so called from the two hunting leopards in the gable) is a banquet scene perhaps too conventionally imitative to be interesting except for the truly decorative quality of the lines and the lights and darks that fill the wall area. On the side wall, however, are dancing figures filled with action and rhythmic movement that make charming decorative motifs. In like manner the *Flute-Player* (FIG. 272) of the *Tomb of the Triclinium* expresses the feeling of joyous movement, of the rhythm of inner vitality translated into objective form by simple direct conventions. In the *Hunting*

Fig. 267. Orator. Bronze. IV or III cent. B.C. Archaeological Museum, Florence.

and Fishing Tomb (FIG. 271) is an extraordinary expression of true landscape, a fresh spontaneous expression based upon a visual grasp of nature quite akin to that of Cretan painting, though the means of expression are as conventional as in the *Blue Monkey* (FIG. 152).

What the art of Rome would have been had Roman civilization remained within the boundaries of Italy it is futile to ask. In its early days Rome employed Etruscan builders and ceramic workers; and later it did not forget the high temple platform nor, eventually, Etruscan realistic portraiture. But the fact is that its conquest of Etruria was followed by the subjugation of the entire peninsula; and thence, with an imperial policy well defined, Rome was forced to enlarge its boundaries until they included the entire Mediterranean basin and most of western Europe. Early Rome came in contact with Greece and conceded an indebtedness. "Conquered Greece led the conqueror captive," said Horace, a poet of the Augustan age. Shiploads of Greek marbles and bronzes were brought to Rome by generals and provincial governors to adorn their palaces, and when the supply was exhausted, copies were made or Greek artists were employed to create new ones.

Fig. 268. Sarcophagus from Cervetri. Terra cotta, painted. VI–V cent. B.C. Villa Papa Giulio, Rome (Anderson).

Because of their contacts with Magna Graecia, the Romans had not been unaware of Greek art. But only in the late republican and Augustan ages came the terrific impact of Hellenism. Art became to a large extent mere copying of Greek works. Finally assimilation took place and imperial Rome emerged as a product of Etruscan, Roman, and Greek elements, though possibly still strongly enough Greek for its art to be called a continuation of the Hellenic tradition working according to Roman tastes and ideals. In portrait sculpture and in architecture especially, however, Rome made definite, individual contributions.

In the main, the energy of Rome was utilized in conquest and administration and its conquests opened the way for the spread of its civilization. Roman cities sprang up especially in what is now Spain, France, and England, each a center for the propagation of Roman government, language, and customs, and closely connected with Rome by magnificently built roads. Both by force of circumstance and by temperament the Roman was warlike, practical, fond of pleasure. His life, in comparison with the simplicity of the Athenian, was complex, for the demands of life were much greater. Rome about 200 A.D. was the magnificent capital of the greatest empire the world had yet known, an empire that was efficiently organized, with fifty thousand miles of magnificent highways on land and on sea safe for travel and for commerce. The city itself (FIG. 273), of more than a million people, was not only cosmopolitan but magnificent. The scale, power, and complexity of the Empire called for impressive scale in the structure and appearance of its capital. And while the practical demands arising from the administration of a great empire required the building of roads, bridges, sewers, and aqueducts, the imperial ideal called for public buildings that would express on an adequate scale the dignity, power, and diversified interests of the state. To build practically and grandly required skill in engineering. Thus arose Rome's contribution to architecture, though its chief gift to world-civilization lay in the field of law and organization.

Fig. 269. Chimaera. Bronze, restored. V cent. B.C. Archaeological Museum, Florence.

With the wealth that came with conquest, there crept in pleasure-loving ideals, luxuriousness, and decay. In time the great Roman Empire became a hollow shell, and the frontiers gave way on all sides. By 500 A.D. Rome itself had fallen before the northern tribes that had been harassing its boundaries ever since Julius Caesar had driven them back in the first century B.C.

B. ARCHITECTURE

In Greek architecture we discerned a concentration upon the temple. In Rome, on the contrary, as the capital of a complex world-empire, practical as well as esthetic needs led to the erection of many kinds of buildings, secular as well as religious, and frequently on a scale hitherto untried. Ample material was at hand — abundant wood, stone (marble, travertine, tufa), good clays for brick, lava and pozzolana (sandy earth) for concrete. Those materials not at hand could be imported easily by the Roman fleets — rare colored marbles, nearly fifty varieties of which were used for their color and texture. But ample as this material was, the quantity and scale of Roman building precluded extensive use of solid stone masonry and of the lintel system. Brick and concrete covered with stucco or faced with stone or marble veneer supplanted solid stone construction, with the arch rather than the lintel system as the structural principle.

The chief engineering problem involved in Roman architecture was how to inclose and roof over a vast space, to give it proper illumination and still keep the space open and free of the columns that would be necessary were a flat roof used, as in the hypostyle halls of Egypt (FIG. 65). Given the problem of roofing over a rectangular room by the simplest arch system, the result will be a barrel vault (FIG. 274), which is, in essence, a succession of arches joined together, resting directly upon the side walls, which must be thick enough to support the weight. This vault can be made of stone or brick masonry, or of

Fig. 270. Tomb of the Leopards. Corneto. V cent. B.C.

concrete by building up a temporary wooden framework known as centering, the exact size and shape of the finished vault, to hold the mass until it is set. The vaulting that we see in Fig. 274 B and C and Fig. 284 has been made by cutting the barrel vault at right angles at regular intervals by other barrel vaults, securing what is known as the cross or groin vault, because the line of intersection is called the groin. A barrel vault over so large an area not only would have been heavy in appearance but would have allowed no space for windows. Hence the advantage of the groin vault is not only that it is lighter in appearance because of its broken surface but also that it admits of clerestory windows. The use of the groin vault secures another advantage. In the barrel vault the thrust, that is, the downward and outward forces exerted by the vault, is felt along the entire length of the wall; in the groin vault, only at the points at which the groins converge. Hence it is at these points only that heavy buttressing is needed and the interior is thus kept free of load-carrying walls. Proper support is secured by heavy walls built at right angles, which are pierced by arches and thus form side aisles to the main hall (Fig. 282).

Of the public-service structures — roads, bridges, aqueducts, sewers — the Romans, like the Etruscans, build solidly and well. Their stone bridges combine utilitarian requirements and fine sweep of line. The aqueducts, which still swing across the Campagna to bring the mountain water to Rome or span streams in several tiers as in the *Pont*

Fig. 271. Hunting and Fishing Fresco. Corneto. VI cent. B.C.

du Gard (FIG. 275), have a stark beauty of adequate function united
to the rhythmic movement of well-spaced arches.

Of religious buildings the *Temple of Fortuna Virilis* (Rome) and the
Maison Carrée (FIG. 276) illustrate one type of temple derived obviously
from the Greek peripteral style, but differing in the high base
with projecting moldings and a flight of steps extending across the
front. Its cella is larger than the Greek and becomes incorporated
with the colonnade part way along the sides and across the back
(FIG. 277).[1]

The circular temple was popular. Sometimes it was peripteral, as
one sees in the temple near the Tiber in Rome and in that at Tivoli.
Of all circular temples the most imposing is the *Pantheon* (FIG. 279),
which consists of a circular wall with but one opening, the doorway.
On this wall rests a dome, low and rather inconspicuous on the exterior;
at the entrance is a colonnaded portico of Greek design. As one steps
within (FIG. 280) he is surprised. For the dull unpromising exterior
gives little hint of the wonderful spaciousness and light within. This
impression results from a very simple space-design carried out on a
large scale — a dome set on a circular wall and lighted by an aperture
in the crown. Thus it seems to have been the purpose of the builder
to make his dome impressive from the interior. The walls are covered
with rich marble facing; the dome is deeply coffered and was originally
decorated with bronze rosettes. Domes had been constructed before
this but never on such a scale. The Roman's ideal of great scale made
him daring, while his practical nature and engineering skill kept him
within the bounds of structural possibilities. The walls, twenty feet
thick, are made of brick and concrete and are solid except for the
niches about which are imbedded in the masonry relieving arches of
brick that extend the entire thickness of the wall and carry the thrust

[1] A column thus incorporated with the wall is known as an *engaged column*.

Fig. 272. Flute-Player. Tomb of the Triclinium, Corneto. Early V cent. B.C.

of the dome to the solid masonry.[1] The dome is constructed of horizontal layers of brick laid in thick cement, the load of which is carried by a series of ribs converging on the crown. Between these ribs are the typical Roman coffers, which both diminish the weight and ornament the dome.

Civic buildings were important in an imperial capital and together with important temples were grouped about the forums. The *Roman Forum* was originally the market place where the peasants brought their produce for sale; booths and shops ran along the sides. But early, religious and civic activities began to encroach; the shops were crowded out to the side streets and the *Forum* became primarily the center of the city's civic life. In the open space were commemorative statues of emperors and generals, and the great platform from which public speeches were made; entirely surrounding it and crowning the surrounding hills were imposing buildings. The *Imperial Forums* built by various emperors from Augustus on, reach a culmination in the *Forum of Trajan* (FIG. 278), where all the units of the vast group are definitely related to each other and to a unified design instead of being merely set down wherever there was space and the topography permitted, as in the old *Roman Forum*. It is perhaps illuminating to recall that the *Forum of Trajan* was designed by an architect from the East, Apollodorus of Damascus. Hills were leveled to make space for this enormous forum, which in plan strikingly resembles, as scholars have pointed out, the Egyptian temple. Through a monumental archway one passed into an open court with colonnades on three sides and great circular wings with shops; thence into the basilica with its many columns and beyond into the temple of the deified emperor.

Since every forum was a center for trade and administration, an important civic building was the basilica, a covered hall used for various purposes, particularly for a law court. The *Basilica Julia* (FIG. 281) was an oblong structure with a semicircular tribunal, or apse, at one end, where the judge sat, and was divided by rows of

[1] For illustration see Anderson and Spiers, *op. cit.*, p. 78, FIG. 19.

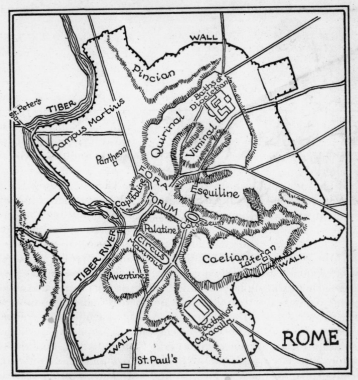

Fig. 273. Rome. A map to indicate the general location of important
classical and medieval sites.

columns or piers into a central and side aisles; the roof of the central
aisle was higher than that of the side aisles, thus forming a clerestory.
Looking at the exterior, we notice that the structural principle is not
the lintel system of the *Maison Carrée* (FIG. 276) but the arcade, that
is, a series of arches. Between the arches, however, are engaged
columns that support an entablature running the entire length of the
building. In this arrangement we find one of the most characteristic
features of Roman architecture, a combination of the arch and lintel
systems. Structurally it is the arch that is the vital part of the construction; the column and entablature serve only as decoration. In
this, an early basilica, the evenly spaced arcades support a wooden roof.
In a late example, the *Basilica of Maxentius* (FIG. 282), fully developed
vaulting is used, barrel over the aisles and groin over the nave, thus
enabling the builder to make use of isolated supports and huge arches
so overpowering even in the ruins today.

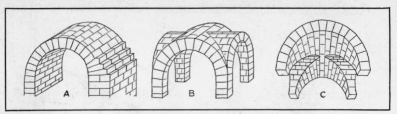

Fig. 274. *A*. Barrel Vault. *B*. Groin Vault seen from above. *C*. Groin
Vault seen from below.

The places of amusement, the circus, the theater and the amphitheater, and the great baths (*thermae*) so essential to imperial Rome, challenged the engineering ability of the builders. Here huge crowds must
be accommodated, sometimes in the out-of-doors, sometimes within,
with an appearance of luxury and display commensurate with the taste
of the day. The *Colosseum* (FIG. 285) was one of these places of amusement. The vast size of the structure prevented extensive use of stone and
led to the use of concrete faced with brick on the interior, with hard
stone at points of stress, and an exterior of travertine masonry set with
no mortar but clamped by iron dowels. The design consists of a system
of arches both parallel to and at right angles to the outer circumference.
The exterior consists of three stories of arches and a solid attic. Between
the arches of each story are engaged columns that support a continuous
entablature. The engaged columns add to the rhythm, and the entablature not only unifies the arched openings and binds them into
a firmly felt unity but also forms a fine single sweep of curve which,
repeated on each story, accents the basic geometric form. The effect
of the building without this decoration can be seen on the right side
of the illustration, where a bare monotony results from the loss of
the rhythm and of the accent of the vigorous curves. The combination of structural solidity and effective decoration has created a building imposing in dignity and magnificence. On the ground story the
columns are of the Doric order, on the second of the Ionic, and on
the third of the Corinthian, an arrangement known as superimposed
orders. The fourth story is ornamented by flat Corinthian pilasters.
The *Colosseum* is a conspicuous example and a possible justification of
the Roman practice of using a structural member for a nonstructural
and purely esthetic purpose.[1] For, constructionally, the columns do
not carry the load.

The impression of material power, at times grandiose, is felt in high
degree in the thermae that provided the Roman not only with his

[1] A point which leads to infinite debate and no absolute conclusion. "*De gustibus
non est disputandum.*"

Fig. 275. Pont du Gard. Nîmes. Augustan Age.

Fig. 276. Maison Carrée. Nîmes. I or II cent. A.D.

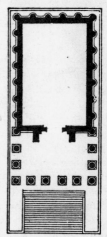

Fig. 277. Plan of the Maison Carrée.

daily bath, hot, warm, or cold, but with his library and lounging-place, for the numerous recreation rooms had the same function as the modern athletic club. A ground plan (FIG. 283) gives us some conception of the great extent of these baths and also of the orderly planning that characterizes the organization of multitudinous parts into a single whole. FIG. 284 reconstructs one hall of the *Baths of Caracalla*. The impression is of vast spaciousness and, in the rich marble facings, carvings, and coffered ceilings, of magnificence and splendor. Here, as in the *Pantheon*, the Roman builder conquered space, that is, he so inclosed a great volume of unbroken space as to make one standing within it conscious of it. And this he accomplished, as we have described, by the use of the vault and the dome. How impressive today are even the ruins of these huge vaults; indeed they are probably even more impressive than when

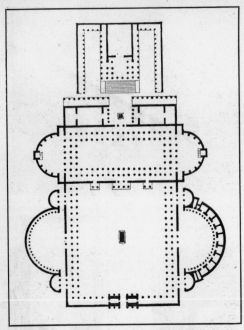

Fig. 278. Plan of the Forum of Trajan.

they were decked out with marble and gilded coffers. As in the aqueducts, the sheer engineering, the great simple moving masses and surfaces, are some of the most powerful expressions of the Romans.

Commemorative monuments — tombs, altars, rostra, columns, arches — are peculiarly characteristic of the realistic Roman who established, in the triumphal arch in particular, a type that has survived for centuries. In the *Arch of Titus* (FIG. 286) the great central opening is flanked by solid masses of masonry with engaged columns that rise from a plain base to support the entablature, which has a sculptured frieze uniting the three parts. The decoration is restrained, and confined chiefly to the arch. The *Arch of Constantine* illustrates the more elaborate triple arch with more sumptuous sculptural decorations.

Ornament the Roman used lavishly; frequently, in the attempt to obtain magnificence, he overloaded his buildings and concealed the structure. The restraint of the Greek in the use of moldings and decoration was too severe to suit the Roman taste, which loved display, and preferred the Corinthian capital to the more austere Doric and Ionic. In his best work, however, the Roman proved himself a master of a certain kind of decoration. This we can see best in the *Ara Pacis* (FIG. 287). From a central group of acanthus rises a vertical foliate form and curving stems that branch off so as to cover the surface with spiral forms that terminate now in a leaf, now in a flower or rosette; near the top a swan with outspread wings has alighted. While naturalistic representation has formed the basis of the decoration, the ultimate effect is dependent partly upon the delicacy and precision of the carving and partly upon the carver's restraint in keeping his design a clear decorative pattern. The motif of the foliate spiral rising from a bed of acanthus, known as the *rinceau* (FIG. 290), became one of the most popular in Roman decorative art, especially as applied to pilasters and borders, and later formed the basis of much Renaissance ornament.

With the Flavian emperors, this naturalistic ornament sacrificed decorative quality to a greater illusion of actual appearance. Details of plant and bird forms were copied from nature, and the cutting of the marble followed the irregularities of nature instead of retaining definite planes of stones; an almost atmospheric effect is produced, as in the rose columns on the *Tomb of the Haterii* (Lateran) and the marble pilasters of FIG. 291. The same tendency is discernible in the figure reliefs. In the procession of men, women, and children on the *Ara Pacis* [1] (FIG. 288) the relief is higher in the foreground figures and lower in the

Fig. 279. Pantheon. Rome. Originally the walls were faced with marble and stucco and the dome covered with bronze plates. 120–124 A.D.

Fig. 280. Pantheon. D. and H. 142 ft. From an engraving by Piranesi.

background, giving one a distinct sense of depth and atmosphere. Details are worked out to a greater extent and there is a considerable amount of portraiture in the faces; in fact we feel the individual figures here quite forcibly. The purpose has been to give an illusion rather than an organized expression of a procession, as in the *Parthenon Frieze* (FIG. 217). This realistic tendency is carried still further in the reliefs on the inner side of the *Arch of Titus*, in which architectural

---

[1] For a detailed description and reconstruction of the *Ara Pacis* see Albert Grenier, *The Roman Spirit in Religion, Thought, and Art*, Knopf, 1926.

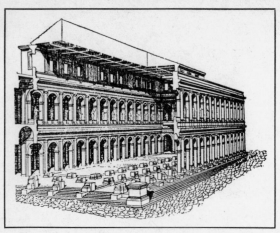

Fig. 281. Basilica Julia. Restored. Rome. (Huelsen)

details contribute a pictorial quality; and the tendency reaches a climax in the *Column of Trajan*, in which a detailed pictorial record of military campaigns spirals around the shaft from the base to the summit.

Another medium of ornament used most effectively by the Romans was stucco (FIG. 289) applied as a finish to the rough concrete vaults and walls. The surface was divided by moldings into geometric patterns that frequently inclosed figures; or was filled with naturalistic spirals or other ornaments and dainty figures. The addition of marble dust made the stucco both durable and fine in texture. The moldings and the figures were worked in the wet stucco partly by stamps, noticeably in the moldings, and partly by freehand. As in the fresco technique, the rapidity with which plaster dries requires rapid workmanship; and the figures depend for their effect not so much upon careful modeling as upon spontaneity, ease of workmanship, and freely flowing line.

An additional note of magnificence as well as comfort in imperial Rome was supplied by the system of parks and gardens, including perhaps thirty great parks around the city, with lawns, trees, gardens, and fountains, made possible by the unparalleled water supply. Every Roman of sufficient means had a villa set in a park, perhaps on the outskirts of the city or in the Alban or Sabine hills near by.

Domestic architecture featured prominently. The palaces and villas of the emperors, now in fragmentary ruins, rivaled the thermae in size and sumptuousness: huge groups of rooms about courts, rooms of state and private apartments, gardens and baths. Sometimes, as in the *Palace of Domitian*, the units of the establishment were related to a central axis as were the thermae and the *Forum of Trajan;* sometimes, as in the *Villa of Hadrian*, quite irregularly placed because of the character of the topography.[1]

[1] The *Palace of Domitian* on the Palatine in Rome, the *Villa of Hadrian* near Tivoli, and the *Palace of Diocletian* at Spalato are examples of Roman imperial palaces. See Anderson and Spiers, *op. cit.*, Chapter VIII, for descriptions and reconstructions.

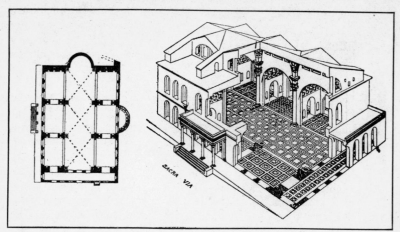

Fig. 282. Basilica of Maxentius or Constantine. Rome. 306–312 A.D. Plan, and
section of a reconstruction.

Probably [1] the average person lived, in the crowded city, in an
apartment house (*insula*), which was several stories high, a habitation
to each story, with windows and loggias on the street and on the
courtyard, about which several insulae were sometimes grouped. As
the Roman lived largely in the open, about the public buildings, in
the places of amusement, and in the porticoes and parks, he may have
been content with his crowded living-quarters if only they provided
him a corner for sleeping and a protection for his lares and penates.
The homes of the well-to-do away from the congested metropolitan
areas are the atrium type found at Pompeii and Herculaneum, many
of which, protected by the volcanic ash and lava in which they were
buried, are extraordinarily well preserved, with their mural decorations
still fresh and sometimes with their equipment and household utensils
undisturbed. The house stood flush with the sidewalk. Through a
narrow entrance, one entered a vestibule (FIG. 293) that led to a court
known as the *atrium* (1), roofed over along the four sides so as to leave
an opening in the center, with a corresponding sunken place in the
floor to collect the rain water; along the sides were small rooms except
at the end, where the atrium extended the full width of the building,
forming two wings, *alae* (2). Behind the atrium was the *tablinum* (3),
in which the family archives and statues were kept, and which could
be shut off or could afford a passage to the *peristyle* (4), a large colon-

[1] On the analogy of houses found at Ostia, Rome's seaport. The *Casa di Diana*
is a typical insula. For a reconstruction see Anderson and Spiers, *op. cit.*, PL. XC;
D. S. Robertson, *A Handbook of Greek and Roman Architecture*, Macmillan, 1929, pp.
308–09.

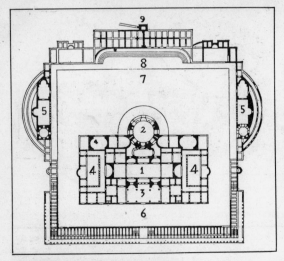

Fig. 283. Baths of Caracalla. Rome. 211–217 A.D. The central building is 750 x 380 ft. (1) *tepidarium*, or warm lounge; (2) *calidarium*, or hot room; (3) *frigidarium*, or cooling room with a swimming pool open to the air; (4) open peristyles; (5) lecture rooms and libraries; (6) promenade; (7) garden; (8) stadium; (9) aqueduct and reservoirs.

Fig. 284. Baths of Caracalla. Central Hall, restored by Spiers. 211–217 A.D. Rome. (Anderson and Spiers)

naded court with fountains and garden, about which were grouped the private apartments of the family, the atrium serving more as a reception room or a room of state. At the back there was sometimes a garden (5); the small rooms along the outer sides (s) opening on the street were shops. It is clear that the house faced inward, depending upon its courts for light and air; and when opened its entire length (FIG. 292) afforded a charming vista of open court with colored marbles, gardens, fountains and statues, and brightly painted walls. This type of house, with its small number of doors and windows, offered considerable stretches of wall space for decoration; with the result that an originally plain, almost cell-like room not only became gaily brilliant in color, but appeared to open up vistas of garden or landscape. As we see in FIG. 294, the wall space has assumed an architectural appearance. Columns and windows have been painted on the surface in perspective, to give them an appearance of relief. In the center, this framework incloses a large painting; on the

Fig. 285. Colosseum, or Flavian Amphitheater. Rome. 70–82 A.D. (Alinari)

sides, architectural openings lead the eye to the landscape in the distance, which gives an air of spaciousness to the room.

These paintings are executed in fresco. The plaster at Pompeii was laid very thick, and by keeping moist for a considerable length of time enabled the painter to work with greater leisure than in the Renaissance, when the thin coating necessitated rapid work. The colors were bright — red or black to throw the panels or figures into relief, with rich creamy white in the borders. A certain brilliance of surface that enlivened the effect the Roman obtained by a careful preparation of the wall surface; the plaster, which was specially compounded with a mixture of marble dust and laid on layer after layer, was

Fig. 286. Arch of Titus. Restored on the sides. A bronze four-horse chariot surmounted the arch. Rome. 81 A.D. (Alinari)

beaten with a smooth trowel until it became very dense, and then was polished until it assumed an almost marblelike finish.

In the frescoes of the *Villa Item* (*Villa of the Mysteries*) near Pompeii (FIG. 295) the feeling of the wall is much more definitely retained and the figures move within a very shallow space, as in a relief. The figures are constructed in light against a darker ground and are generally flat, though there is an extraordinary grasp of the structure of the figure and of its place within the shallow space in relation to the adjoining figures. Expressive drawing and a slight use of shadow suggest

Fig. 287. Ara Pacis (Altar of Peace). Erected in 13 B.C. to commemorate the victories of Augustus in Spain and Gaul. Detail of decoration. Terme (National) Museum, Rome.

both volume and structure with much the same result as that accomplished by line alone in FIG. 262. In the *Villa of Livia*, however, the surface of the wall has been composed to create the illusion of a garden, as if the side of the room opened out upon the garden represented (FIG. 296). A low fence separates the spectator from the scene and also gives solidity and unity to the composition, where trees, plants, and vines in cool green-grays stand out against a blue sky with bits of bright color in the flowers, fruits, and brightly plumaged birds flying about or enjoying the fresh water of the fountains. It is a charming bit of nature brought in from the out-of-doors to delight the life lived inside; in spirit it is closely akin to the naturalistic carvings of which the Roman was so fond.

C. SCULPTURE

Statues in great profusion stood in the forums, and in both public and private buildings. Villas and huge baths were perfect museums of Greek sculpture, originals,[1] copies, or adaptations to suit Roman taste. Such, however, are not Roman art. Authentic Roman sculpture is best represented in the portraits. In the late Greek period, the generalization that distinguished the earlier portraits had given way to some surprisingly individualistic work. The Roman's desire for literal facts together with his custom of keeping in his house, always before his eye, the *imagines*, or wax masks, of his ancestors, influenced the sculptor still further to accentuate this individuality. In the head

[1] We read of 285 bronze and 30 marble statues brought from Corinth in 145 B.C.; of 500 bronzes brought from Delphi by Nero — two illustrations only of the ransacking of Greece to deck Rome.

of an *Unknown Roman* (FIG. 297), for example, one is struck by the intensely alive quality. The bony structure of the head, the keen eye, the sparse hair, the sagging skin beneath the chin, all the lines and wrinkles that designate the peculiar characteristics of an individual — all these qualities combine to give us a realistic portrait of one of those rugged men of dominant will who helped, in the days of the Republic, lay the foundations of Rome's greatness.

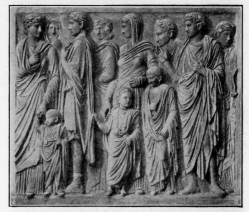

Fig. 288. Ara Pacis. Detail of procession. Uffizi, Florence.

But when we turn to the statue of *Augustus* (FIG. 299), the feeling is different. The Emperor stands easily. He wears an elaborately decorated metal cuirass with leather fringe over his linen tunic and carries his military cloak thrown over his left arm.

Fig. 289. Stucco Decoration. Tomb of the Valerii, Via Latina, Rome. I cent. A.D. (Alinari)

In every part of the costume is seen skill in the rendering of texture: the soft and heavy quality of the cloths, the rigidity of the metal, and the tough nature of the leather. In his left hand he holds the scepter; his right is lifted in the direction of his glance as if addressing his troops; for Augustus himself had led the army on his conquests. But the face does not characterize Augustus in detail, as does the head of the *Unknown Roman*. There are no individual lines to indicate personal idiosyncrasies. It is rather a generalized type distinctly reminiscent of Greek work. If we recall that the Augustan age was a period when the acquisition of Greek statues and the influence of Greek art was at its height, we can easily see why Roman realism had given way. The same general characteristics are found in the bronze statue of a *Roman Boy* (FIG. 300). He wears the Greek cloak rather than the Roman toga; and while there is sympathy for the boy nature, the expression of it is

Fig. 290. Roman Rinceau. Lateran Museum, Rome.

Fig. 291. Pilaster. Marble. I–II cent. A.D. Metropolitan Museum, New York. (Metropolitan Museum)

not realistic but, as in the *Augustus*, generalized and reserved. There is great beauty of execution in the modeling of the nude parts and also in the drapery, which is arranged in broad, simple folds, near in feeling to Greek work.

The sympathetic understanding of youth and childhood is frequently to be seen in Roman sculpture. In the *Portrait of a Child* (Fig. 298) the soft flesh and the rounding features that distinguish the child are well indicated; but even more remarkable is the artist's ability to understand the workings of the child mind and to depict that characteristic moment of hesitation between a laugh and a cry that reveals itself so clearly in the quiver about the mouth. In these portraits of the youthful aristocrats of Rome we discern the real feeling of the child, now bashful, now eager and alert.

The generalizing tendency of the Augustan age did not maintain itself long against the Roman love for literal fact. Thus the spirited portrait of *Vespasian* (Fig. 301) is an individualistic expression of the rugged soldier that we know Vespasian to have been, an expression not so detailed as the Republican portraits nor so trenchant. The incisiveness and linear quality of the latter has softened to a gradual blending of detail producing the same atmospheric quality to be found in the Flavian reliefs. When we come to such a portrait as that of *Caracalla* (Fig. 302), certain elements have been added to achieve greater illusion of life. The large bust that includes shoulders and arms, the turn in the head that heightens greatly the vivacity, the rough mass of hair that contrasts with the smoothly finished face, the naturalistic treatment of the

Fig. 292. Vista of a Pompeian House from the Atrium.

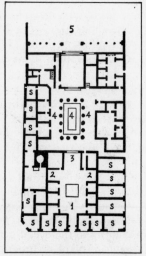

Fig. 293. House of Pansa.
Pompeii. (1) atrium; (2) alae;
(3) tablinum; (4) peristyle; (5)
garden; S, shops.

Fig. 294. Wall Decoration of a
Pompeian House. Architectural
style, creating an illusion of depth.
(Anderson)

Fig. 295. Frescoes in the Villa Item (Villa of the Mysteries), near Pompeii. Augustan Age.

eyes, deep-set in the shadow of heavy brows — all these means have combined to create an illusion of natural appearance in conjunction with convincing characterization.

D. PAINTING

While we know that independent paintings served a variety of purposes — votive pictures for temples, portraits for libraries and for private houses — and that great quantities of Greek paintings as well as statues were taken to Rome from Greece, practically nothing remains except the mural paintings, a few in Rome, the great majority in Pompeii and Herculaneum. Probably many of the panel pictures in these murals were copies of famous Greek works. Even when not copying, the painters, many of whom were Greeks, were working in the Hellenic tradition. In the best of these we see, besides the largeness of design and a certain measured reposefulness, a knowledge of perspective, a consistent use of light and shade and of the cast shadow, and a unity of the figure with the landscape or architecture — all fundamental principles that had been worked out by the Greek. Some of the individual figures in Pompeian painting are charmingly spontaneous in their "impressionistic" effect, impressionistic in the sense of merely suggesting rather than actually presenting to the eye. Such are the *Cupids* in the *House of the Vettii*, and the *Flora* (Naples Museum), in which there is nothing profound in theme or monumental in form — only a charming momentary action expressed in a rapid spontaneous sketch filled with atmosphere, lyric in its appeal, and consistent in its mode of expression with the subject matter.

E. MINOR ARTS

The skill of the Romans in the use of metal we see not only in the casting of large sculpture but also in the small bronzes such as the

Fig. 296. Frescoes from the Villa of Livia. Prima Porta. (Stoedtner)

candelabra stands, furniture supports, and a great variety of household utensils that have been found at Pompeii. But the wealth and splendor of life made demands upon the goldsmith and the silversmith as well to furnish fine plate for luxurious tables. Much of this, of course, was looted by thieves at the time of the catastrophe or by the barbarians in later ages, but a few finds of such treasure,[1] hidden away, have come to light to give us a glimpse of the lavishness displayed at the famous Roman feasts. The silver crater from Hildesheim (FIG. 303) for mixing the wine is finely shaped, with handles so adjusted that one feels their unity with the structural lines of the vase. Low reliefs, done in repoussé, give a play of delicate light and shade over the surface, adding richness without overloading; at the base the relief is higher, more elaborate, and more compact, thus strengthening the support. The design here consists of two griffins back to back in balanced position, from which rises a conventional plant form; from this and from the sweeping wings of the griffins delicate spirals rise and spread over the surface, terminating in naturalistic forms. Clinging to the stems and tendrils are tiny children attacking, with tridents, the sea animals that intertwine among the spirals. In a two-handled silver cup from Boscoreale (FIG. 307), we see the Roman love of realism; for here sprays of fruiting olive have been wreathed about the cup, a charming idea giving one quite the illusion of natural appearance, since the fruit is molded in the

[1] One of the rich finds of silverware was at Hildesheim, Germany; this is now in the museum at Berlin and is known as the *Hildesheim Treasure*. Another, the *Boscoreale Treasure*, most of which is in the Louvre, was discovered at Boscoreale near Pompeii.

Fig. 297. Unknown Roman. Terra cotta, with traces of color. I cent. B.C. Museum of Fine Arts, Boston. (Boston Museum)

Fig. 298. Portrait of a Child. Marble. I cent. A.D. Museum of Fine Arts, Boston. (Boston Museum)

Fig. 299. The Emperor Augustus Addressing His Army. Marble, originally painted, found in the Villa of Livia, wife of Augustus, at Prima Porta. Vatican, Rome.

Fig. 300. Roman Boy. Probably a Julian Prince. Bronze. I cent. A.D. Metropolitan Museum, New York. (Metropolitan Museum)

204

Fig. 301. Vespasian. Marble.
69–79 A.D. Terme (National)
Museum, Rome.

Fig. 302. Caracalla. Marble. 211–217 A.D.
Berlin. (Berlin Museum)

round. This ornamentation, however, not only obscures the structural lines of the cup but by attracting interest to itself destroys the harmony that results when decoration is kept subordinate.

In Roman pottery the most conspicuous accomplishment was the *Arretine* bowl, made of a fine reddish clay, with the decoration stamped in relief on the outside by means of molds in which the design was cut in intaglio. Then a reddish glaze was added. A sacrificial scene is represented in FIG. 305 in which winged figures are decorating an altar to which women clad in diaphanous drapery are bringing offerings. These figures remind one of the stucco reliefs in their dainty charm and, being in very low relief, are unobtrusively decorative.

The Roman lapidaries of the Augustan age were skilled in cameo-cutting, which consists of carving a design in relief from a striated stone, such as sardonyx, in such a way that each layer — and the layers usually are alternately light and dark, numbering from two to nine — shall be utilized in working out the design.

The cameo technique was carried by the Roman into the craft of the glassworker, as we see in the *Portland Vase* (FIG. 304). Up to the second or first century B.C. glass had been molded, a laborious process. About that time the blowpipe was invented, causing a rapid growth of the glass industry; thus glass supplanted, to a large extent, the more usual pottery for everyday use. In making such a vase as the *Portland*,

Fig. 303. Silver Crater from the Hildesheim Treasure. Probably Augustan age. Berlin. (Giraudon)

Fig. 304. Portland Vase. H. c. 10 in. I cent. A.D. British Museum, London. (Mansell)

the glassworker shaped the deep-blue vase with his blowpipe and then dipped it into opaque white liquid glass. The handles were molded separately and added. When thoroughly hard, the white layer was cut away, leaving the raised white figures in relief against the deep-blue ground. The subject is not understood. At the left a young woman is reclining on some rocks beneath a fig tree, in the usual attitude of sleep; at the right another young woman is seated on a pile of rocks, holding a scepter. The figures are carved with characteristic naturalism. The mask beneath the handle is more decorative.

Another very effective use of glass we find in the *Millefiori* or "thousand-flower" bowls (FIG. 306), which, when held up to the light, give an impression of rich mosaic and hence are sometimes called mosaic glass. The process was as follows: Threads of different-colored glass were fused together into a larger thread, drawn out, and then cut into small pieces that were fitted into a mold and fused into a solid mass. By carefully regulating his color and pattern, the glassworker could create a color harmony of surpassing richness.

F. SUMMARY

The tonic effect of the vital Etruscan art persisted in Rome notwithstanding its Hellenization. The bold vigor of Etruscan stone construction on the arch principle in the hands of Roman engineers in urban, cosmopolitan Rome, and under the stimulation of an imperial ideal, produced structures of large conception and daring engineering — bridges, temples, palaces, theaters, baths, basilicas, triumphal arches.

Fig. 305. Arretine Bowl. 40 B.C.–60 A.D. Metropolitan Museum, New York. (Metropolitan Museum)

Fig. 306. Millefiori Bowl. Metropolitan Museum, New York. (Metropolitan Museum)

Engineering in fact was just another manifestation of that Roman impulse toward order which found expression also in law and governmental organization. By means of vaulting the Romans solved the problem of inclosing great space without intermediate support, though they usually concealed the construction with lavish ornament to suit the taste of the day. Thus the great baths are characteristically Roman in their combination of mechanical and esthetic engineering with glittering sumptuousness. Again it may have been the Etruscan inheritance, combined with the Roman passion for literal fact rather than for abstractions, that led to a realistic portraiture of great vitality. In the wall paintings, too, the practical Roman sought his objective directly: if the room is small and stuffy enliven it and open it to the outside in imagination if not in actuality! If these wall paintings are debatable as mural decoration, they at least have a clear raison d'être.

Fig. 307. Silver Cup from Boscoreale. Louvre, Paris. (Alinari)

BIBLIOGRAPHY

Alexander, Christine, *Jewelry, the Art of the Goldsmith in Classical Times*, Metropolitan Museum of Art, New York, 1928

Amelung, Walther, and Holtzinger, Heinrich, *Museums and Ruins of Rome*, tr. by Mrs. S. A. Strong, Dutton, 1906, 2 vols.

Anderson, W. J., and Spiers, R. P., *The Architecture of Ancient Rome*, rev. by Thomas Ashby, Scribner, 1927

Bailey, Cyril, ed., *The Legacy of Rome*, Oxford Press, 1923

Breasted, J. H., *Ancient Times*, 2d ed. rev., Ginn, 1935

Chase, G. H., *Greek and Roman Sculpture in American Collections*, Harvard University Press, 1924

Grenier, Albert, *The Roman Spirit in Religion, Thought and Art*, tr. by M. R. Dobie, Knopf, 1926

Gusman, Pierre, *L'art décoratif de Rome*, Paris, 1908, Vols. I–III

Huelsen, C. C. F., *Roman Forum*, tr. by J. E. Carter, Stechert, 1909

Lamb, Winifred, *Greek and Roman Bronzes*, Dial Press, 1929

Lanciani, R. A., *Ancient Rome in the Light of Recent Discoveries*, Houghton Mifflin, 1888

Laurie, A. P., *Greek and Roman Methods of Painting*, Putnam, 1910

Lukomsky, G. K., *L'art étrusque*, Paris, 1930

McClees, Helen, *The Daily Life of the Greeks and Romans*, Metropolitan Museum of Art, New York, 1925

Mau, August, *Pompeii: Its Life and Art*, tr. by F. W. Kelsey, new ed. rev., Macmillan, 1902

Platner, S. B., *A Topographical Dictionary of Ancient Rome*, completed and rev. by Thomas Ashby, Oxford Press, 1929

Poulsen, Fredrik, *Etruscan Tomb Paintings, Their Subjects and Significance*, tr. by Ingeborg Andersen, Oxford Press, 1922

Richter, G. M. A., *Handbook of the Classical Collection*, Metropolitan Museum of Art, New York, 1927

Rivoira, G. T., *Roman Architecture*, Oxford Press, 1925

Robertson, D. S., *A Handbook of Greek and Roman Architecture*, Macmillan, 1929

Rodenwaldt, G. M. K., *Die Kunst der Antike*, Berlin, 1927

Showerman, Grant, *Eternal Rome*, new ed., Yale University Press, 1925

—— —— *Rome and the Romans*, Macmillan, 1931

Strong, E., *Art in Ancient Rome*, Scribner, 1928, 2 vols.

—— —— *Roman Sculpture, from Augustus to Constantine*, Scribner, 1907

Swindler, M. H., *Ancient Painting*, Yale University Press, 1929

Walters, H. B., *The Art of the Romans*, Macmillan, 1911 and reprints

Wickhoff, Franz, *Roman Art*, tr. by Mrs. S. A. Strong, Macmillan, 1900

Weege, Fritz, *Etruskische Malerei*, Halle, 1921

See also the General Bibliography, pp. 749–751.

Part Four

MEDIEVAL ART

CHAPTER VIII

Early Christian Art in the West
(Fourth to Sixth Century A.D.)
Byzantine Art (Fourth to Fifteenth Century A.D.)

A. HISTORICAL BACKGROUND

About the year 300 A.D. we see Rome still outwardly splendid — a highly organized despotism, internally decayed and externally hard pressed by barbarians or by cultivated indigenous peoples struggling for self-expression. Meanwhile the Christian Church, growing at first in secret, and strengthened by persecution, emerged victorious as the real successor of Rome. Constantine, by changing the capital in 330 A.D. to Byzantium, which he renamed Constantinople, cut the Empire into two rather sharply divided parts, the East and the West. Let us note a few of the important movements in each.

The lands about the eastern Mediterranean had always been Hellenic rather than Roman at heart. In many places the traditions of the older civilizations, such as those of Egypt and of Babylonia-Assyria, were still dominant. Long before Christianity became officially the state religion, vigorous Christian communities began to flourish in Persia, Egypt, Asia Minor, and in Syria, that great highway of war, commerce, and ideas. Under the stimulus of the new faith, brilliant creative work began in church-building and was unhampered by the weakening of Roman power. But Constantinople, because of its wealth and prestige, became the point at which the various Eastern influences coalesced with the Hellenic and Roman to form what is known as Byzantine art, or, as it has well been called, the Christian art of the East. In the reign of Justinian (527–565 A.D.) this art reached its first climax under the patronage of the Church and the court. But some of the forces that were shaping it — the prejudice of the early Christian against everything pagan and of the Semitic peoples against the repre-

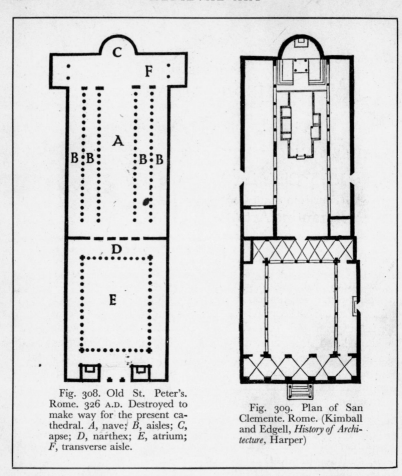

Fig. 308. Old St. Peter's. Rome. 326 A.D. Destroyed to make way for the present cathedral. *A*, nave; *B*, aisles; *C*, apse; *D*, narthex; *E*, atrium; *F*, transverse aisle.

Fig. 309. Plan of San Clemente. Rome. (Kimball and Edgell, *History of Architecture*, Harper)

sentation of sacred personages; the influence of Islam; [1] and the impersonal, mystic attitude of the East — these forces inevitably led to the iconoclastic (image-destroying) controversy (726–824 A.D.), which guided creative impulses into the channels of rich ornamentation based upon floral and geometric motifs, and into a dependence upon richness of color and texture. But a compromise eventuated, under Basil I and his successors, in a second climax of Byzantine art, whose purpose was "to render visible the mysteries of the supra-natural world. . . . If God might be painted after all, not only in innocence and majesty but in the commonplace and degradation of earthly life, then painting

[1] See Chapter XI.

Fig. 310. Section of an Early Christian Basilica. Restored. (Dehio and Bezold)

should be worthy and attempt the highest." [1] Hence arose "a mystical renunciation of the transient phenomena of earth for the universal in-being Reality — enshrined in a fixed iconography whose rigid apportionment of subject and space alone could put intelligible bounds to so immeasureable an aim." [2]

The western half of the empire presented a different picture. For centuries the barbarians had been threatening the Rhine and Danube frontiers, and the decaying government could no longer hold out against the strong vitality of the North. On all sides the uncouth barbarians poured in, finally reaching Rome; and though they may have had some reverence for the magnificence they saw, with no capacity for appreciation they cared little for its maintenance. The *Colosseum* was merely a mine from the stones of which could be drilled out the iron clamp to tip the spear of a Goth. The one power to hold firm was the Church, the earnestness and zeal of whose leaders, such as Saint Augustine and Saint Gregory, laid the foundations for its supremacy in the Middle Ages.

Although the history of the two halves of the Roman Empire ran so differently, there were close relations between them. The establishment of the exarchate at Ravenna brought a flow of Byzantine work westward. Byzantine builders came to Italy at the summons of patrons whose own country was no longer producing trained artists. The iconoclastic outbreak drove artists to Italy to seek employment; while

[1] Bréhier, *L'art chrétien*, quoted by Robert Byron and David Talbot Rice, *The Birth of Western Painting*, Knopf, 1931, p. 15.
[2] *Ibid.*

Fig. 311. Santa Maria in Cosmedin. Rome.
Late VIII cent.; Campanile, XII cent.

pilgrims and traders brought with them such portable objects as enamels, ivories, manuscripts, and textiles.

B. ARCHITECTURE

Rome, notwithstanding its pitiable condition,[1] offered ample incentive for building. Here were the sacred places, the sites of martyrdom and burial of saints. Thus hither came pilgrims from all Christendom, throngs so great, even in the days of no regular transportation, that men and women were trodden under foot. And ample material was at hand to be had for the taking — the finely cut stones, columns, and marble veneers of the huge Roman structures. With the emergence of Christianity from secrecy we observe a type of church established — the basilica — which, though known in the East,[2] became predominant in Italy.

FIG. 308 illustrates the plan of the basilica, a rectangular building entered through an open colonnaded court, the atrium (A), one side of which (B) forms the narthex or vestibule; the body of the church consists of a nave (C), aisles (D), apse (E), and a transverse aisle or transept (F) inserted between the nave and the apse and slightly projecting beyond the walls, making the plan T-shaped. FIG. 309 is simpler, with single aisles and no transept, but shows the place of the altar immediately in front of the apse, and the choir with two pulpits occupying about half of the nave. The nave walls rest directly on columns (FIG. 310) and rise higher than the side walls, forming a clerestory for lighting (FIGS. 312, 315) and leaving a great wall space

[1] See Grant Showerman, *Eternal Rome*, new ed., Yale University Press, 1925, for a good description.
[2] Particularly in Syria. See H. C. Butler and E. B. Smith, *Early Churches in Syria*, Princeton University Press, 1929.

between the colonnade and the windows. Both the nave and the aisles of such a basilica carried wooden roofs, but the apse was usually vaulted. The origin of the basilica is difficult to determine. In many respects it is close to the classical basilica, the name of which it carries; yet certain elements, such as the atrium and the transverse aisle, seem to be derived from the Roman private house, where the early congregations met in secret and whose whole arrangement suited the liturgical needs of the service.

Fig. 312. Santa Maria in Cosmedin. Rome.

Santa Maria in Cosmedin (FIG. 311) well illustrates a modest basilica.[1] Its plain exterior shows an unadorned narthex, above which rises the clerestory of the nave. The interior (FIG. 312) is a rectangular

Fig. 313. Sant' Apollinare in Classe. Ravenna. 534–538 A.D.

space so designed that interest focalizes upon the altar standing in high relief against the rich mosaics of the apse. The columns supporting the walls are different in size and in design and well illustrate the practice of these builders to secure their material from the structures of pagan Rome. Should one ruin fail to supply enough columns for a basilica, another would be stripped of its material with apparently little concern for the matching of the columns. It was even the practice

[1] Built in the sixth century A.D.; enlarged in the eighth century; restored in the twelfth. The bell tower (campanile) is Romanesque. The church has frequently been remodeled, notably in the late Renaissance, when a Renaissance façade was added; and it was restored in 1894–99 to its eighth- and twelfth-century form. This continuous remodeling of churches, especially in Rome, each in the style of the period of the remodeling, makes many churches a confusing composite of Early Christian, Romanesque, Renaissance, and Baroque, and leaves but few in the original style of their building.

For a sensitive understanding of the formal relationships in *Santa Maria in Cosmedin* see Le Corbusier, *Towards a New Architecture*, pp. 160 ff.

Fig. 314. St. Paul's Outside the Walls. Rome. Founded 386 A.D.; rebuilt after the fire of 1823 which destroyed almost all except the transept.

to prop up small columns with additional bases to the required height. Thence also were procured the fine marbles of the choir rail, pulpits, and floor. The choir, for the clergy who participated in the service, with its two flanking pulpits, one for the reading of the gospels and one for the epistles, occupied a considerable part of the nave (see also FIG. 309). The walls were originally covered with frescoes and the simple wooden roof brightly painted. A large and elaborate basilica is that of *St. Paul's Outside the Walls* (FIG. 314), built over the tomb of St. Paul, very resplendent in colored marbles, gilded coffered ceiling, and mosaics.

Thus the interior of a basilica was colorful. Of the many mediums used to obtain color, mosaic transcended all. By means of mosaic the Byzantine builders clothed the surfaces of the apse and often of the walls too, if economic affluency permitted, with mural decoration of unsurpassed splendor, equally satisfactory for decorating a dim interior and for conveying the ideas of Christian mysticism. Its forms are conventional because of the nature of the medium, and symbolic because of the nature of the ideas expressed. By *mosaic* is meant a design worked out by means of small pieces of colored glass or stone called *tesserae*, set in cement with a slightly undulating surface. It is clear that to carry out a design in this medium, the artist must make the drawing so simple that the form becomes almost a flat pattern, with sharp contours and little light and shade. It affords ample opportunity, however, for broad massing of color and for deep glowing tones, especially when gold is used liberally either as a background for the figures or as a backing for the tesserae (FIGS. 315, 317, 330–332).

As the basilicas in Rome have been so repaired and remodeled that few give an adequate picture of their original appearance, those at Ravenna will serve to illustrate how relatively barren, yet impressively frank and rugged, was the exterior of the early basilica (FIG. 313); relatively, we say, in contrast to the interior (FIG. 315), where the half-light from translucent marble panels and perforated marble windows discloses rich colors, gold, carvings, and stately hieratic figures. Here is the atmosphere of another world, of infolding peacefulness and mystic calm. With symbolism prominent in the mental outlook of the age, one wonders whether the early Christian thus symbolized the hard externals of his life with the beauty of the inner spirit.

Early Christian art, both in the East and in the West, was an art of symbols: the fish, not only an acrostic but a symbol of water, baptism, and in general of the Faith; the ship (Latin *navis*, whence "nave"), symbol of the Church in which the faithful were carried over

Fig. 315. Sant' Apollinare in Classe. Ravenna.

the sea of life; the vine, symbol of Christ; animals, especially the sheep, and the shepherd; the stag, the soul thirsting for baptism; and the peacock, emblem of immortality, an illustration of how the early Christians infused pagan symbols (the peacock was the bird of Juno) with new meaning. Thus symbols constitute a language, and as they tend to isolate and emphasize some dominant element of the person or thing symbolized they tend in their form toward the highly generalized and the abstract and thus are more than likely to be peculiarly decorative as well as expressive of intense inner significance.

The mosaics of the apse and triumphal arch [1] of *Sant' Apollinare in Classe* (Fig. 315) do not pretend to picture on the walls an illusion of nature, but to decorate the surface and at the same time to carry a message symbolically. Against the gold ground is a great blue medallion, with gold stars and a jeweled cross; just above, the hand of God is seen issuing from the clouds, in which Moses and Elias are floating; below are three sheep looking upward. The scene symbolizes the Transfiguration, the three sheep representing the three disciples who accompanied Christ to the foot of the mountain. Below, in the midst of green fields with trees, flowers, and birds, stands St. Apollinaris with uplifted arms, accompanied by twelve sheep, symbolizing the twelve Apostles, and forming, as they march in regular file across the

[1] The arch which frames the apse opening.

Fig. 316. The Tomb of Galla Placidia (in the foreground) and San Vitale (in the middle background). Ravenna.

apse, a wonderfully decorative base. The grandeur of the conception, the austerity of the figures, and the splendor of deep color produce an emotion akin to that evoked by music. The side walls of *Sant' Apollinare Nuovo* above the columns and between the clerestory windows glow with rich colors and gold, from which emerge figures, stately and hieratic, moving along in rhythmic order almost as purely architectural as the columns below.

At Ravenna we meet the other important type of church building, the central, which, though not unknown in Rome,[1] seemed less at home there than it did in Ravenna, which had direct connections with the East, where this type of building reached its highest development. A simple form we find in the *Mausoleum of Galla Placidia* (FIGS. 316, 317), which is built in the form of a Greek cross with a dome over the intersection of the two arms that is inclosed and concealed from the exterior view by a low rectangular tower. It is of the plainest brick construction and unadorned except for the blind arcades and dentils along the cornices. But as one steps within he finds himself enveloped in mellow light and quietly rich color. Above the yellow marble paneling blue-ground mosaics sheathe the entire surface: deeptoned blues with accents here and there of other hues and with a restrained use of gold. The same incredibly rich interior we find in a church of the central type, *San Vitale* (FIGS. 316, 318). The brick construction, presenting an almost barnlike appearance on the outside, is entirely concealed on the inside by marbles and glowing mosaics.

This central type of building reaches its culmination, as we have said, in the East, specifically in *Santa Sophia* (FIG. 319).[2] A study of the

[1] *Santa Costanza* and *San Stefano Rotondo* are examples.
[2] More strictly, *Hagia Sophia*, meaning *Church of the Holy Wisdom.*

ground plan (FIG. 320) reveals that the building combines the features of the domed central type with those of the basilica. The plan is rectangular, with side aisles separated from the nave by columns; there is an apse, a narthex (double here), and an atrium. The length of the nave necessitated the addition of half-domes to supplement the great central dome. The exterior view [1] shows a very compact mass of brick, of great solidity at the corners, covered with a low lead-covered dome and half-domes. But as one enters (FIG. 322) he stands amazed at the wonderful spaciousness, obtained through the simple but daring design of the building, which consists of a harmonious ar-

Fig. 317. Tomb of Galla Placidia. Ravenna. c. 450 A.D.

rangement of arches and half-domes moving rhythmically with increasing size and volume until they unite in the all-embracing dome, which seems to rest easily and lightly over the great space — the sky of its own universe. Organized space is the first impression; then, sumptuousness. The richest materials of all kinds were used — rare marbles of all colors and literally acres of gold-ground mosaics [2] — yet every detail is subordinate to the powerful space-organization. Let us listen to Procopius, a writer of the period, who says in describing the church: "The entire ceiling is covered with gold; but its beauty is even surpassed by the marbles which reflect back its splendor. One might think one had come to a meadow of flowers." And the poem of Paulus Silentiarius, court poet of Justinian, written to commemorate the dedication of the church, thus describes it: "About the center of the church, by the eastern and western half-circles, stand four mighty piers of stone, and from them spring great arches like the bow of Iris, four in all; and,

[1] The minarets and heterogeneous buildings about the base were added by the Muhammadans when they converted the church into a mosque after the capture of Constantinople in 1453; and the atrium no longer exists.

[2] The mosaics, which were largely painted over by the Moslems, are now being uncovered. See Thomas Whittemore, *The Mosaics of St. Sophia at Istanbul*, Oxford Press, 1933.

Fig. 318. San Vitale. Looking
toward the apse. 526 A.D.

as they rise slowly in the air, each separates from the other to which it was at first joined, and the spaces between them are filled with wondrous skill, for curved walls touch the arches on either side and spread over until they all unite above them. . . . The base of the dome is strongly fixed upon the great arches . . . while above, the dome covers the church like the radiant heavens. . . .

"Who shall describe the fields of marble gathered on the pavement and lofty walls of the church? Fresh green from Carystus, and many-colored Phrygian stone of rose and white, or deep red and silver; porphyry powdered with bright spots; emerald-green from Sparta, and Iassian marble with waving veins of blood-red and white; streaked red stone from Lydia, and crocus-colored marble from the hills of the Moors, and Celtic stone, like milk poured out on glittering black; the precious onyx like as if gold were shining through it, and the fresh green from the land of Atrax, in mingled contrast of shining surfaces.

"The mason also has fitted together thin pieces of marble figuring intertwining tendrils bearing fruit and flowers, with here and there a bird sitting on the twigs. Such ornament as this surrounds the church above the columns. The capitals are carved with the barbed points of graceful acanthus all gilt; but the vaulting is covered over with many a little square of gold, from which the rays stream down and strike the eyes so that men can scarcely bear to look." [1]

The decoration of *Santa Sophia*, however, is by no means merely abstract. It is filled with meaning. The subject matter of the mosaics was determined by the Church, and the characters or episodes move in hieratic succession from the more human scenes on earth, scenes relating to the life of the Virgin and of Christ, through the figures of angels, saints, and prophets on the walls, to the four cherubim in the

[1] W. R. Lethaby, "Santa Sophia, Constantinople," *Architectural Review*, April, 1905, p. 122.

Fig. 319. Santa (Hagia) Sophia. Istanbul. 532–537 A.D. The minarets are later Muhammadan additions. (Publishers' Photo Service)

pendentives, and finally to the Pantocrator, the Ruler of the Universe, in the crown of the dome: "Know and behold that I am." Thus the movement of lines and volumes is paralleled by a literary movement of ever increasing sanctity and awe culminating in the symbol of the heart and mystery of the Faith.

The dome, as we have said, appears to rest lightly and without effort, yet we know that it exerts a tremendous weight, which is met by the massive masonry that we noticed at the exterior corners. For the dome of *Santa Sophia* differs from that of the *Pantheon* structurally in that its load is concentrated at four piers rather than distributed along a circular wall. The triangular segments that carry the load to the piers are known as pendentives and a dome so constructed is called a dome on pendentives (Fig. 321). This structural method solved the problem of erecting a perfect dome over a square area and of keeping the space free of load-carrying walls; or, in other words, of concentrating the load at the fewest possible points, thereby creating a largely unbroken interior space. Though the origin of this solution of the structural problem is uncertain as to date and place, it appears to have been the result of many experiments in vaulting by the builders of the Near East and passed on by them to the West, where we meet it in *St. Mark's* in Venice, in the Romanesque churches of southern France, in the domed cathedrals of the Renaissance such as *St. Peter's*, and in many domed buildings of modern times.

The stone carvings in *Santa Sophia*, though often based upon the

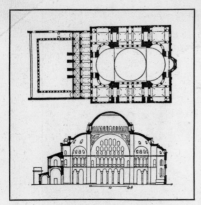

Fig. 320. Plan of Santa Sophia, and longitudinal section (without the atrium).

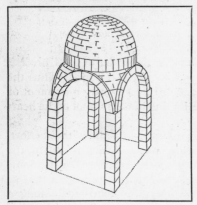

Fig. 321. A dome on pendentives, the Byzantine solution of the problem of transferring a circular load to four piers. This solution enabled the builder to erect a dome over a square area and thus secure a lofty, unobstructed interior space (Fig. 321).

acanthus and other classical motifs (Fig. 323), differ from the classical in their insistence upon the surface which they decorate (contrast Fig. 248). For the stone is undercut, not to model and produce an illusion of depth but just enough to provide a dark background for the flat pattern. This type of carving appears to be Eastern in origin, as is apparent in the *Mshatta Frieze* (Fig. 324). Richly carved moldings finish the edges of a long border that is decorated with a zigzag and rosettes, which, together with the entire background, are luxuriantly carved with acanthus and vine scrolls in which are interwoven vases, animals, centaurs, and other fantastic beings. Here, as in *Santa Sophia*, the carving is done by means of drilling into the background and leaving the original flat surface cut into a pattern, rather than by modeling with the chisel, leaving an uneven relief surface, as did the Greeks and Romans. The zigzag and rosettes add vitality and rhythm to the delicate all-over pattern.

Stone-carving played a large part in early Christian and Byzantine ornament and was applied to capitals, screens, railings, and pulpits. Byzantine capitals (Figs. 318, 325) appear to be derived from the classical Corinthian type, though they afford a great variety of detail. From the square abacus, the carver gradually merged his stone into the circular shape of the column and covered the surface with carvings — the basket type, so called because of its basketlike interlacings; the melon type, in which the stone is cut in ridges like those of a melon; the wind-blown acanthus style, with its classical acanthus realistically swaying; or that with the interlaced circle motif which is so frequently found in medieval ornament. An entirely new feature, however, is the

impost block, of much
the same shape as the
capital itself, inserted
between the abacus
and the springing of
the arch. The purpose
of this is not quite
clear. It may have
been to obtain greater
height, or to bring the
weight of the arches
directly upon the shaft
rather than on the
outer edge of the aba-
cus. Sometimes the
impost block was
richly carved; some-
times it bore simply a
monogram (FIG. 325);
and sometimes it was
omitted, as in *Santa
Sophia* (FIG. 323). The
stone railings afforded
a large area for deco-
ration. They were
carved with patterns
very much like those
on the capitals; or

Fig. 322. Santa (Hagia) Sophia. (Drawing by
J. B. Fulton in the *Architectural Review*)

with animals and birds in a balanced bilateral arrangement, a scheme
of decoration that probably originated in the Near East and found
great favor in all the arts.

The central type of church on the Greek-cross plan continued,
modified, in the second golden age of Byzantine art (FIG. 327). The
angles of the arms were filled in and frequently covered with domes;
the domes themselves became more conspicuous by being lifted up
on high drums (FIG. 328); external decoration found a place, in the
form of patterned brickwork, sometimes polychrome, as well as in
carvings. On the interior, colored marbles and mosaics or frescoes
covered the walls (FIG. 326). Even more strict now was the control
over the iconographic scheme, the guides or manuals prescribing in
detail the place of each subject, the composition, and the forms, even
to the detail of the color of the Virgin's hair. Hence arose the similarity
of type and composition quickly seen in all Byzantine painting. Such

Fig. 323. Santa (Hagia) Sophia. Carvings of capitals and spandrels. Marble.

Fig. 324. Frieze from Mshatta, a Palace in the Syrian Desert. H. 15 ft. IV–VI cent. A.D. Berlin. (Berlin Museum)

Fig. 325. Byzantine Capitals.

a procedure precluded any study of nature and insisted upon continual copying and recopying until the figures were so fixed in the mind that they could easily be reproduced from memory. In other words, the painters were using a language understood by all and at the same time extraordinarily effective in its austere splendor. Add to this the iconostasis [1] with its elaborate decorations and icons, the gold, ivory, and enamels in the vessels, and the rich stuffs in the vestments, all seen in a dim light with incense and flickering candles, and one feels that the Byzantine artists did not fall short of their objective: "to render visible the mysteries of the supra-natural world."

C. PAINTING

The function of the painter in the early Christian and Byzantine world was to decorate the walls of the churches with mosaics and frescoes, to paint panels for the iconostases of private chapels, and miniatures to illustrate books.[2] The early paintings are strongly Hellenistic or Roman. The early Christians, before the emergence of the

[1] The panel or partition, found in Eastern (Orthodox) Catholic Churches, which separates the sanctuary from the nave. Only the clergy may enter the sanctuary.

[2] A *miniature* is a small picture that illustrates a manuscript, and is derived from the Latin verb *miniare*, to decorate with vermilion, for that was the color most popular with the painters. As the pictures were always small, the meaning has been extended to apply to a small portrait, usually on ivory or porcelain, and to anything small. To *illuminate* means to decorate with gold, silver, and bright color, especially the initial letters. An illuminated manuscript may or may not contain miniatures. See Charles Diehl, *La peinture byzantine*, Paris, 1933, for a series of fine plates arranged chronologically, thus providing a general survey of the field.

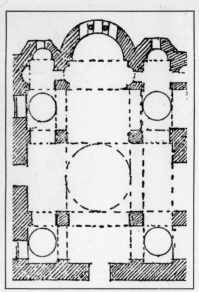

Fig. 326. Church of the Monastery of Xenophontos, Mt. Athos. XI cent. (Millet, *Monuments de l'Athos*)

Fig. 327. Plan of a Byzantine Church of the Second Golden Age.

Fig. 328. Church at Daphne, Greece. Late XI cent.

Fig. 329. Joshua before the Walls of Jericho. Detail from the Joshua Roll. V–VI cent. A.D. Vatican, Rome. (Muñoz)

Church from secrecy, decorated the walls of the catacombs with frescoes such as the vine, which is an echo of the carved floral pattern so common in Roman ornamentation and was a favorite theme because of the frequent symbolic use of the vine in the New Testament. They also used figures, such as those representing brotherly love that are close to the Pompeian frescoes of Cupids and Psyches in the *House of the Vettii.* Thus there was no break in the classical tradition on the part of those who forsook the pagan faith; the early Christian painter merely gave the traditional forms new meaning. Among the mosaics, the apse of *Santa Pudenziana* (Rome) of the late fourth century well illustrates the Hellenistic phase, as does the *Joshua Roll* [1] among the miniatures. FIG. 329 reproduces a detail in which Joshua, near the walls of Jericho, is prostrating himself before the angel, in obedience to command; in the lower right-hand corner is a female figure crowned with a tower, the personification of the city. Though the subject is Christian, the method of expression is Hellenic — the personification of the city, the naturalism of the figures, the way in which they fit into the landscape, and the perspective in the architecture. But soon a change occurred in the character of the forms, a trend away from Greco-Roman naturalism toward a conventional, highly abstract expression. In the *Good Shepherd* mosaic (FIG. 330) in the *Tomb of Galla Placidia*

[1] This manuscript was originally a continuous roll 32 ft. long and 1 ft. wide, with pen-and-ink and color illustrations from the life of Joshua, which occupy most of the space, interspersed with the text in Greek. It has now been cut into sections and mounted for preservation. The manuscript belongs to the period when the long roll used by the Egyptians, Greeks, and Romans was being superseded by the *codex,* that is, a book made of separate pages bound together, the usual modern method. The change was probably due to practical considerations, since passages can be found much more readily in this form.

Fig. 331. Mosaic of the Apse of Sant' Apollinare in Classe. Ravenna (Fig. 315). (Alinari)

Fig. 332. Theodora and Her Attendants. Mosaic, San Vitale. Ravenna (Fig. 318). (Alinari)

the landscape is flattening out, though there is still some depth and some use of shadow in the rocks and sheep to indicate volume. The complete reduction into one plane and to abstract form we find in the apse of *Sant' Apollinare in Classe* (FIG. 331), and in the *Theodora* and *Justinian* portrait groups in *San Vitale* (FIG. 318). In the *Theodora* (FIG. 332) we see the wife of Justinian with her attendants carrying a gold chalice for the performance of some ceremony, possibly in connection with the dedication of the church. She stands in front of a shell niche with a nimbus about her head, is dressed in royal purple, richly embroidered, and wears a jeweled crown. The head has some of

Fig. 333. Pietà (Lamentation). Xenophontos, Mt. Athos. 1544. (Millet)

the individual characteristics of a portrait, with its slender neck, long nose, and thin lips. Her attendants also wear gorgeous robes and jewels. But under the straight folds there are no real bodies. As a matter of fact, the artist does not pretend to represent nature. The long stiff row is made up of gorgeous symbols of bodies highly decorative because of their very flatness, and because of the shimmer, throughout the design, of the rich colors of the embroideries and jewels.

The effect of the iconoclastic controversy we have already noted. A rigid iconography; materials rich in color, texture, and gold; impersonal forms far removed from an illusion of the actual world; abstract representations of this world and symbols of another world — all these combined to produce mosaics and frescoes which were monumentally austere but perfectly definite in their objective. "The pictures have the same object as the liturgy; they possess the same sacramental character and form the requisite setting for the mystery of the Eucharist." [1] Such we find in the mosaics of *St. Luke of Stiris*.

Mosaic met perfectly the Byzantine requirement of splendor of effect, but was costly. Fresco, it is frequently supposed, was used

[1] Bréhier, *L'art chrétien*, quoted by Byron and Talbot Rice, *loc. cit.*

Fig. 334. Christ and Apostles. Fragment of a sarcophagus. IV–V cent. A.D. Berlin. (Berlin Museum)

when economic conditions demanded a cheaper substitute. One wonders, however, whether the tedious, limited technique of mosaic proved too irksome to one who wished to find expression in a swifter, more fluid line, as did the Greek vase-painter when he forsook the black-figured technique for the red-figured, or the Egyptian when he abandoned the relief and painted directly on the wall. Whatever the reason, there developed a great school of Byzantine painting that paralleled the mosaics,[1] both of which were strongly affected by a revival of the study of Plato and of Greek humanism in general. Forms became less austere, more human; otherworldliness partook somewhat of this earth. For three centuries, from the thirteenth to the fifteenth, the Byzantine painters covered the walls of the churches and monasteries of Greece with frescoes in which the forms, though humanized, are still abstract, built up of light and color.[2] In the *Lamentation over the Body of Christ* (FIG. 333) a dramatic subject is expressed with emotional intensity through "a tempestuous rhythm of light and dark." The faces, the garments, the body of Christ, and the rocks are constructed into various patterns of light and dark, sharply darting areas of light against dark, a contrast emphasized by the juxtaposition of complementary hues as well as by values; and these individual patterns are organized into long sweeping curves and sharp angles.

D. SCULPTURE

Monumental sculpture was produced only to a very limited extent in early Christian art, because the statue in the round was even more

---

[1] *Daphne* in Greece (eleventh century), *Palermo* in Sicily (twelfth century), *Kahrie Djami* in Istanbul (fifteenth century) are examples of mosaics.

[2] For a detailed exposition see Byron and Talbot Rice, *op. cit.*

Fig. 335. Sarcophagus of Theodore. VII cent. A.D. Sant' Apollinare in
Classe, Ravenna. (Alinari)

closely akin than painting to the graven images of the pagan. In a
rare example, the *Good Shepherd* of the Lateran Museum (Rome), we
recognize an archaic Greek motif, imbued with a new significance.
This again is a striking example of the continuity of the old tradition.

One of the chief expressions of sculpture we find in the sarcophagi.
In some the surface is entirely covered with reliefs representing scenes
from the Old and New Testaments, crowded together one upon another
for the purpose of narration, with little regard for design, a continuity
again of Roman third-century style, and the use of classical figures
to express Christian ideas. In another type well illustrated by an
example in the Berlin Museum (Fig. 334), Christ and two apostles
are in niches with spirally fluted columns and elaborate carving. The
pose of the figures and carving of the drapery are Hellenic; the decoration of the niche drilled in flat relief, Eastern.

A third kind of sculpture is represented by the *Sarcophagus of Theodore*
(Fig. 335). Here there is no crowded relief, in fact no figures, but a
piece of beautiful decoration composed of symbols, each of which by
itself and in conjunction with the others carries a clear, definite message.
In the center of the side is the sacred monogram [1] in a circle, facing
which are two peacocks, symbols of eternity. Behind them are scrolls
of fruiting vines and birds; on the lid are three wreaths inclosing sacred
monograms and the inscription; rather plain moldings frame the design.

[1] This monogram consists of the first two letters in the Greek name of Christ,
chi and rho; in the side angles formed by the chi are the Greek letters alpha and
omega, frequently used to symbolize the divinity of Christ. See Fig. 416.

Fig. 336. Bishop's Chair, Called the "Throne of Maximian." Wood, inlaid with ivory panels and borders. VI cent. A.D. Archiepiscopal Palace, Ravenna.

E. MINOR ARTS

Great demands were made upon the craftsmen in this period by the luxurious courts of the East and by the Church. Both needed fine fabrics for costumes and for hangings; jeweled ornaments; books, which, to suit current tastes, might be written in gold letters upon purple-tinted vellum or decorated with bright miniatures on gold grounds, and bound in gold, ivory, enamel, and jewels; vessels for the service,[1] which must be of the finest material and workmanship to be worthy of the Church. Under such patronage the minor arts flourished.

The ivory-carver is important, not only for the intrinsic quality of his work but also because his craft carried on the tradition of sculpture until its emergence as a major art, hundreds of years later, about the portals of the churches. The carved figure followed at first the general idiom of the Hellenic style, as one sees in the *Angel* (FIG. 337) carved on one side of a consular diptych.[2] He is standing in a richly carved niche at the top of a flight of steps, holding in his right hand an orb surmounted by a jeweled cross, in his left hand, a long staff. The Hellenic naturalism seen here in the drapery, for example, and in the carvings of the niche — all carved with a very sure-handed craftsmanship — was already yielding to Eastern influence, which is very pronounced in the so-called *Throne of Maximian* (FIG. 336), an episcopal chair covered with panels of richly carved ivory. On the front are five niches containing figures of St. John the Baptist and four Apostles which have markedly individual

[1] See W. R. Lethaby and Harold Swainson, *The Church of Sancta Sophia, at Constantinople*, Macmillan, 1894, for a description of the great quantities of sumptuous vessels used in this church.

[2] A two-leaved book of ivory, carved on the outside and provided with wax for writing on the inside, like the classical writing-tablets found in Pompeii. They were ordered by the consuls upon election, as gifts for friends and important officials — hence *consular*.

Fig. 337. Ivory Leaf of a Diptych. H. 16 in. IV cent. A.D. British Museum, London. (British Museum)

Fig. 338. Christ Crowning Romanus and Eudocia, Rulers at Constantinople. 1068-71. Ivory. Bibliothèque Nationale, Paris. (Giraudon)

characteristics, vary in pose and drapery, and appear to have been studied from nature. Though they lack the serenity and refinement of the *Angel* on the ivory leaf and the figure of Christ on the sarcophagus, they are akin to both. The borders above and below, however — with the monogram, and spiraling vines which inclose figures of peacocks and various animals, and with the rampant lions flanking a central vase (in the lower panel) from which issue vines interspersed with animals — recall in their flat patternlike forms against a dark ground the stone carvings of *Mshatta* (Fig. 324) and of *Santa Sophia* (Fig. 323).

The effect of iconoclasm upon the ivory-carvers was much the same as upon other branches of art, as one sees by comparing *Christ Crowning Romanus and Eudocia* (Fig. 338) with the *Angel* (Fig. 337). In the center, Christ, with the halo of divinity, standing on a dome-shaped pedestal fringed with windows like the dome of *Santa Sophia*, is placing crowns upon the heads of the emperor and empress, who stretch out their hands as if in acknowledgment of his sovereignty. The royal pair are dressed in rich ceremonial costumes very different from the simple

Fig. 339. Chalice. XI cent. Treasury
of San Marco, Venice. (Alinari)

robe of Christ. Yet compare this robe with that of the *Angel*, in which the carver attempted to imitate the accidental folds in the drapery that envelopes the figure and to show the depth of the folds. In the *Romanus* panel nature is basic, yet an illusion of natural appearance is not the objective of the carver. Conventions and symbols with both a meaning and a formal beauty irrespective of meaning constitute a language by which the artist conveys his ideas. How direct and clear the meaning is because of these formal relationships — the placing of the group as a whole without crowding into the round-topped inscribed panel; insistent verticals balanced by equally insistent horizontals; long unbroken lines with calligraphic beauty suggesting, without copying, folds of cloth; square and round motifs with bead and zigzag borders, taken from rich fabrics, playing all through the panel like musical motifs in a composition, tying it together and also providing broken moving areas to balance those unbroken and quiet. Originally these relationships stood out even more definitely through the use of color. For the ivories could not remain uncolored in a total cultural expression that was so colorful. The idiom of the day determined that.

Another craft to contribute color and sumptuousness was that of the enameler. Most of the Byzantine enamels are of the *cloisonné* type. The process is as follows: First the design is outlined by soldering strips of thin gold about a thirtieth of an inch wide, called *cloisons*, to a metal base usually gold. The cells formed by the cloisons are then filled with enamel, a vitreous compound, colored or uncolored, translucent or opaque, which when subjected to heat fuses with the metal base. A second coat of enamel is sometimes added to fill any concavities, frequently covering the cloisons. This must be ground away until the surface becomes perfectly smooth, showing all the cloisons, and polished to a glasslike finish, a very laborious process yet one upon which depends much of the rich effect.

Because of the precious material used and the long, tedious process, the enamels were small and were used chiefly to adorn larger objects (FIG. 339). To an even greater extent than the mosaic-worker, the enameler must reduce his design to its simplest terms, for the beauty of the finished product is dependent upon its line, pattern, color, and texture. To attempt to represent the human figure in so difficult a medium is daring; for the technique requires not only the utmost economy of line but, even within that, the greatest precision in placing the cloisons — a slight deviation in the face, for example, would bring about a ludicrous expression. Yet the Byzantine craftsman did not hesitate, as is seen in the plaque representing *St. Peter* (FIG. 340), in which a surprising amount of character has been expressed in the face framed by the white hair and beard. Geometric or

Fig. 340. Saint Peter. Enamel and gold plaque. D. 4 in. X cent. Metropolitan Museum, New York. (Metropolitan Museum)

more abstract design, however, emphasizing as it does the massing of color and texture, was usually found more suitable to this medium. These enamels are so satisfactory because the Byzantine craftsman in enamel, as in mosaic, never overstepped the severe laws that govern the technique.

The application of enamel plaques to larger objects is illustrated by a chalice (FIG. 339) made of sardonyx, mounted in silver and decorated with enamels, gilt, and pearls — an illustration of the sumptuousness of the age.

Together with the ivories and enamels, textiles formed an important branch of the minor arts and proved very influential in the art of western Europe. In the early centuries of the Christian era, the Coptic textiles of Egypt show patterns in wool upon linen, sometimes woven directly in the garment or hanging, and sometimes on borders or medallions to be appliquéd. In FIG. 342 the design is made up of a vine scroll with leaves and fruit, at which birds are pecking, on a black ground. In both the plant and the bird forms there is a fine underlying observation of nature; yet all the forms have been subordinated to the decorative scheme, so that the birds, the leaves, and the grapes have been flattened out, simplified, and so massed that they are splendidly adapted to fill without crowding the spaces made by the wave line of the stem. This same fundamental principle one observes in a hunter medallion (FIG. 341), probably a Persian motif. In the center is a mounted horseman with a running hound, with no accessories of detail or landscape; the inclosing border is made of interlacing bands which form circles filled with lions, plants, and baskets

Fig. 341. Coptic Textile. Tapestry woven in wools, chiefly purple.
H. 12½ in. IV–V cent. A.D. Victoria and Albert Museum, London.
(Victoria and Albert Museum)

of flowers. The forms are expressed with great vigor, and with a lively sense of the decorative quality.

Silk fabrics, however, were the most important textile product of the East and were used for garments, hangings, vestments, and furnishings, wrappings for the dead and for the bones and other relics of numerous saints, which must be shrouded in the finest material procurable. For several centuries before the time of Justinian, Persia had held a monopoly on the silk industry, controlling not only the manufacture of these fabrics but the sale as well. Because of this monopoly in the trade of an article much desired by the wealthy Byzantines, Justinian introduced the industry into the empire with the help of two monks, so the story goes, who smuggled the eggs of the silkworm out of China in hollow staves. A hunting scene is frequently found on these stuffs and is evidently of Persian origin. The design is a medallion repeat pattern within which the hunters and game offer materials for a symmetrical composition of flat decorative units. In all these textiles the pattern reveals its dependence upon the basic technique of any textile — the creation of a surface by interlacing fibers at right angles.

F. SUMMARY

Byzantine art was a natural consequence of the fusion of the East and the West: the impersonal, mystic East whose ideal was transcen-

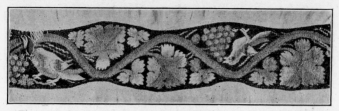

Fig. 342. Coptic Textile. Linen, with tapestry weaving in colored wools on black. W. 3¾ in. IV or V cent. A.D. Victoria and Albert Museum, London. (Victoria and Albert Museum)

dental and whose forms were abstract; the individual, anthropocentric West, whose ideal was humanistic and whose forms were naturalistic. In this fusion originated an art based upon nature yet with no intention of producing an illusion of natural appearance; it consisted of a convincing formalism free from the accidents of actuality and in perfect accord with the ideals of the Church: "to render visible the mysteries of the supra-natural world." It was a hieratic and aristocratic art, in the service of the Church and of the gorgeous Byzantine court, and always sumptuous. The symbols and abstract forms through which it spoke contributed to its high decorative beauty, as did the lavish use of splendid stuffs, gold mosaics, fine marbles, rich color, gold and jewels. At its best, under the spiritual power and driving force of a new faith all its expression aimed to interpret this faith and to evoke its spirit of otherworldliness.

BIBLIOGRAPHY

Anthony, E. W., *A History of Mosaics*, Porter Sargent, 1935.

Bayley, Harold, *The Lost Language of Symbolism*, Lippincott, 1913, 2 vols.

Breasted, J. H., *Oriental Forerunners of Byzantine Painting*, University of Chicago Press, 1924

Butler, H. C., and Smith, E. B., *Early Churches in Syria*, Princeton University Press, 1929

Byron, Robert, *The Byzantine Achievement*, Knopf, 1929

—— —— *The Station, Athos: Treasures and Men*, Knopf, 1928

—— —— and Talbot Rice, David, *The Birth of Western Painting*, Knopf, 1931

Cunynghame, H. H., *European Enamels*, Putnam, 1906

Dalton, O. M., *Byzantine Art and Archaeology*, Oxford Press, 1911

—— —— *East Christian Art*, Oxford Press, 1925

Diehl, Charles, *L'art chrétien primitif et l'art byzantin*, Paris, 1928

—— —— *Byzantine Portraits*, tr. by Harold Bell, Knopf, 1927

—— —— *History of the Byzantine Empire*, Princeton University Press, 1925

—— —— *Manuel d'art byzantin*, 2d ed. rev., Paris, 1925–26, Vols. I–II

—— —— *La peinture byzantine*, Paris, 1933

Diez, Ernst, and Demus, Otto, *Byzantine Mosaics in Greece*, Harvard University Press, 1931

Frothingham, A. L., *The Monuments of Christian Rome from Constantine to the Renaissance*, Macmillan, 1908

Glück, Heinrich, *Die christliche Kunst des Ostens*, Berlin, 1923

Hamilton, J. A., *Byzantine Architecture and Decoration*, Scribner, 1934

Hauttmann, Max, *Die Kunst des frühen Mittelalters*, Berlin, 1929

Jackson, Sir T. G., *Byzantine and Romanesque Architecture*, 2d ed., University of Chicago Press, 1920, 2 vols.

Jameson, A. B., *Sacred and Legendary Art*, Houghton Mifflin, 1911, 2 vols.

Lanciani, Rodolfo, *Pagan and Christian Rome*, Houghton Mifflin, 1893

Lethaby, W. R., *Mediaeval Art*, new ed., Scribner, 1913

—— and Swainson, Harold, *The Church of Sancta Sophia at Constantinople*, Macmillan, 1894

Lowrie, Walter, *Monuments of the Early Church*, Macmillan, 1923

Maskell, A. O., *Ivories*, Putnam, 1905

Millet, Gabriel, *Le monastère de Daphni*, Paris, 1899

—— —— *Monuments byzantins de Mistra*, Paris, 1910

Morey, C. R., *Christian Art*, Longmans, 1935

Munro, D. C., and Sellery, G. C., eds., *Medieval Civilization*, Century, 1904

Muratof, P., *La pittura bizantina*, Rome, 1928, "Valori Plastici" (French translation, *La peinture byzantine*, Paris, 1928)

Peirce, Hayford, and Tyler, Royall, *Byzantine Art*, Stokes, 1926

Pfister, Kurt, *Katakomben Malerei*, Potsdam, 1924

Porter, A. K., *Medieval Architecture*, Yale University Press, 1909, 2 vols.

Rivoira, G. T., *Roman Architecture*, Oxford Press, 1925

Schultz, R. W., and Barnsley, S. H., *The Monastery of Saint Luke of Stiris*, Macmillan, 1901

Sherrill, C. H., *Mosaics in Italy, Palestine, Syria, Turkey and Greece*, London, 1933

Showerman, Grant, *Eternal Rome*, new ed., Yale University Press, 1925

Strzygowski, Josef, *Origin of Christian Church Art*, tr. by O. M. Dalton and H. J. Braunholtz, Oxford Press, 1923

Talbot Rice, David, *Byzantine Art*, Oxford Press, 1935

Van Millingen, Alexander, *Byzantine Churches in Constantinople*, Macmillan, 1912

—— —— *Byzantine Constantinople*, Scribner, 1899

Victoria and Albert Museum, *Catalogue of Textiles from the Burying-Grounds of Egypt*, London, 1921–23, 3 vols., Vol. I, *Graeco-Period*

Warner, G. F., *Illuminated Manuscripts in the British Museum*, London, 1904

Whittemore, Thomas, *The Mosaics of St. Sophia at Istanbul*, Oxford Press, 1933

See also the General Bibliography, pp. 749–751.

CHAPTER IX

Medieval Russian Art

A. HISTORICAL BACKGROUND

Whence came the original Slavic peoples of Russia? This is a moot question. The peoples who early colonized along the Black Sea and who roamed the great steppes were Hellenic or Iranian. Whatever their origin, these early pagan Russians were settled in Kiev and other cities along the western rivers when Vladimir I (about 956–1015) through close relations with Constantinople accepted Eastern (or Greek) Catholicism as the state religion and imposed this faith upon his subjects.

Russia at this time consisted of a group of loosely federated cities situated on the great water trade route between the Baltic and the Black seas. This route lay along the Dnieper and northern lakes and rivers, with Kiev the chief city of the south and Novgorod of the north (Fig. 343). In this land of illimitable areas — vast steppes in the south and unmeasured swamps and woodlands in the north — the natural trade routes of long navigable river systems connected by short portages determined the city sites. These great distances, as well as differences of climate and geography, on the one hand militated against unity, political and cultural, but on the other, enabled the northern cities to remain comparatively independent and out of reach of the Asiatic invaders who were surging west over the great steppes.

At first Byzantine influence was strong. But inevitable expansion eastward (eleventh and twelfth centuries) into the valley of the Volga, another great trade route, and the change of the capital from Kiev to Vladimir (1109) brought the Russians into relations with Caucasia and Transcaucasia. In the thirteenth century the great cultural development at Vladimir was halted by the invasion of the Mongols (1238),[1] who held sway over Russia until the rising principality of Muscovy at first defied and then defeated the invaders (1480) and finally under Ivan the Terrible, expelled the last of them (1552).

In the meanwhile northwestern Russia, centering at Novgorod, free from the Tatar domination, developed its native arts, into conformity

[1] The same westward movement of the Mongols under Jenghiz Khan which captured and destroyed Baghdad in 1250 and set up the Mongol dynasties in Persia. See Chapter XII.

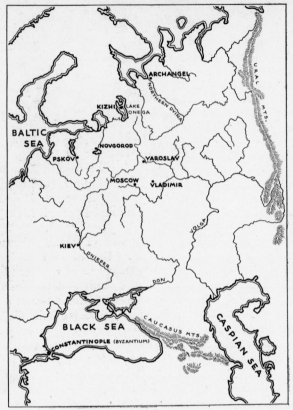

Fig. 343. Russia.

with which it brought the imported Byzantine traditions. Though
Novgorod was a member of the Hanseatic League and was on the
direct trade routes to the East, still it was in a comparative isolation,
so far as cultural influences were concerned, that the arts evolved.
In the fifteenth century, with the eviction of the Tatars, Russia again
established close relations with the Byzantine Empire. Byzantine
painters came to Novgorod and Moscow, and Novgorod painters
and Pskov builders helped build the new Moscow. So that as Moscow
became a cultural as well as political center, a truly Russian style
emerged which translated borrowed forms into its own modes of
expression.

B. ARCHITECTURE

The architecture [1] of medieval Russia was ecclesiastical, at first strongly under the influence of Constantinople, if not actually produced by Greeks. Such are *Santa Sophia* at Kiev and a similar though less pretentious *Santa Sophia* at Novgorod. Both are built on the post-iconoclastic plan of the Byzantine church (FIG. 327), that at Kiev with five apses and some very fine Byzantine mosaics; [2] that at Novgorod with three apses, bulbous domes, and frescoes instead of mosaics — for Novgorod was not so affluent as Kiev, not being the seat of royalty. At Novgorod and at near-by Pskov the bulbous dome [3] vividly colored had already appeared, as had external galleries, covered stairways, and separate bell towers — all characteristic features of Russian churches.

Fig. 344. Church of St. Nicholas the Wonder-Worker. Panilowo, Gov. Archangel. 1600. (Grabar)

Two churches at or near Vladimir, *St. Dmitri* (FIG. 345) and the *Church of the Intercession*, are built on the typical plan of a square inclosing a Greek cross and crowned with a dome (FIG. 346), in these churches a single dome on a high drum. They are built of stone, which is rare in Russia, where brick, stucco, and wood are the usual materials. With very few openings, the wall spaces are decorated effectively with moldings, some of which, rising unbroken from the ground to the roof, divide the wall into panels; others, much shorter, form blind arcadings. At *St. Dmitri* the surface within the arcadings is elaborately carved in low reliefs peculiarly adapted to stone, and in

[1] The only book in English which adequately treats medieval Russian architecture is D. R. Buxton, *Russian Mediaeval Architecture*, Macmillan, 1934, to which the author is largely indebted for the material in this section. The basic authority on Russian art is the history by I. E. Grabar, which unfortunately has not been translated from the Russian but which is invaluable for its illustrations and to which the author is indebted for many of the illustrations in this chapter.

[2] Only the central part of the present church at Kiev, with apses, belongs to the original church of 1037.

[3] Apparently a native Russian form the origin of which is uncertain, though a plausible explanation is that it sheds the snow.

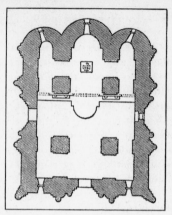

Fig. 346. Plan of a Russian Church of the Type of St. Dmitri.

Fig. 345. Church of St. Dmitri. Vladimir. View showing the three apses. 1194–97. (Grabar)

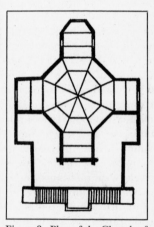

Fig. 348. Plan of the Church of the Transfiguration. Kizhi.

Fig. 347. Church of the Transfiguration. Kizhi, Lake Onega. Early XVIII cent. (Grabar)

subject matter and form close to Sassanian and other west-Asiatic carvings.

A truly native style of church building originated in the north in the vast rural districts dotted with villages where timber was abundant. Free from Byzantine and Eastern influences and undisturbed by Mongol invaders, the Russian evolved out of his simple domestic buildings constructed of tree trunks laid horizontally the type of church seen in the octagon, "tent-roofed" church of *St. Nicholas* (Fig. 344), of which the *Church of the Transfiguration* at Kizhi (on an island in Lake Onega) is an elaboration (Fig. 347). In the latter the octagon plan has been con-

Fig. 349. Church of the Ascension. Kolomenskoe (near Moscow). 1532. (Grabar)

verted into a cross by extending four of its sides (Fig. 348) and the mass of the church is as compact as its plan, notwithstanding the fantastic covering of roofs, which look like horizontally extended bulbous domes. Each roof carries a dome, and together they mount vivaciously to the crowning members — an extraordinary grouping of twenty-two domes into a compact conical mass.[1]

So deeply traditional was this native wooden type that when requirements of greater permanency demanded brick or stone, the type was translated quite literally into the new medium, as one sees in the *Church of the Ascension* (Fig. 349) at Kolomenskoe (near Moscow), and reaches a fantastic expression in *St. Basil* of Moscow, in which all the elements noted above are used in excess, in exaggerated form and with intense color. Yet "a rare beauty of proportion emerges from apparent confusion — an impression of tranquility, not chaos," es-

[1] Though these timber churches all date after 1600, Mr. Buxton feels that they are the culmination of a long tradition, the earlier expressions of which have been lost through the perishable nature of the material and particularly through fire.

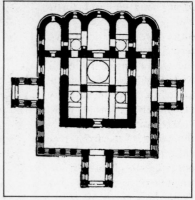

Fig. 351. Plan of the Church of St. John the Baptist. Yaroslav.

Fig. 350. Church of St. John the Baptist. Yaroslav. 1687.

pecially when "seen from the distance in some happy play of sun or moonshine."[1]

The fusion of Byzantine, astern, and native timber styles[2] took place in Muscovy, where at Moscow and Yaroslav one finds, from the fifteenth to the seventeenth century, the climax of the national style. The *Cathedral of the Annunciation* (FIG. 352) is an example. It is built on a square plan with eastern apses and is covered with five bulbous domes, one over each angle between the arms of the cross and a central one over the crossing; around three sides run external galleries approached by covered stairways; on the roof, leading up to the domes are "encorbeled" arches.[3]

In 1650 an edict of the Patriarch of Russia standardized ecclesiastical architecture by requiring for all churches the square plan with five domes. Already Italian architects had been coming to Moscow bringing Western forms into construction and details. At Yaroslav, however, a great trade center still free from foreign influence, the church

[1] Buxton, *Russian Mediaeval Architecture*, p. 44.

[2] The relation of the timber style to that of Moscow, like the origin of the bulbous dome, is controversial, as are, in fact, many points of origin and influence connected with this art, which has received but little attention up to the present time.

[3] This extraordinary external decorative feature originated in a structural device, on the part of builders in Pskov, of superposing corbeled arches above the four great arches of the crossing in order to make the transition from the square base to the dome — a problem solved by the Byzantine builders with pendentives.

of *St. John the Baptist* (Figs.
350, 351) is consistently Russian. Notable here are the external brickwork; the glazed
tile decoration around the
windows; the fine porches;
and the general magnificence
of the church as a whole.

We have spoken only of
the exteriors of these Russian
churches. As their window
openings are few and small,
the interiors are dim. However, their great wall spaces
lend themselves to mural decoration, as did their prototypes, the later Byzantine
churches (Fig. 326). A few
wealthy churches used mo-

Fig. 352. Cathedral of the Annunciation.
Moscow. 1482–90.

saics, the others fresco, but in either case according to a strict iconography. The truly Russian feature was the iconostasis (Fig. 353), the
many-tiered screen that separates the sanctuary from the main body
of the church, with three doors, the central one — the royal door —
reserved for the priests only. The iconostasis contains the sacred images
(icons, hence the name) arranged according to rigid regulation. It is
decorated elaborately with carvings, gilding, and metalwork, and before it hang magnificent candelabra. Very resplendent is such an interior, its very dimness adding to the effect. The audience stands; the
liturgy contains long chants and a cappella music, with frequent cens-
ing; in flickering candlelight and through clouds of incense the rich
vestments of the clergy combine with the brilliant color and ornament
of the iconostasis to create a focal point, which is surrounded by dim
walls covered with figures that rise in hieratic succession to the Pantocrator of the dome. Thus every element contributes to an effect
which would seem to be the climax of the Byzantine aim to bring to
human perception by means of human sensations "the mysteries of the
supra-natural world."

C. PAINTING

To decorate the walls of the churches, to paint icons for private
shrines and for the iconostasis and miniatures for the sacred books,
were the functions of the painter. Again, it was an ecclesiastical art.

Fig. 353. Iconostasis. Uspenski Cathedral, Moscow.
XVII cent.

Like the buildings, the early mosaics, frescoes, and icons are Byzantine in style. Some icons were probably imported from Constantinople
or Greece, as seems true of the *Vladimir Madonna* (FIG. 355), one of
the most sacred icons because of a belief in its efficacy to protect the
Russians against the Mongols. For this reason it held a place of honor
in the lowest tier of the iconostasis of the church at Vladimir. It is
a typical Byzantine painting,[1] in which two figures are compactly
united into a majestic group that fills the panel with its flat pattern,
a silhouette with unbroken sweep of virile contour within which the
figures are tied together both as to form and as to sensitive feeling.

The development of the iconostasis into the elaborate screen with
upwards of five tiers had an important effect on icon-painting. For
the purpose of these paintings was to enable the worshiper to read
pictorially. Clear pictorial legibility in wavering candlelight and
through clouds of incense required strong pattern, firm lines, and intense color. For this reason the relatively sober hues of the early Byzan-

[1] There are at least six layers of repainting; only the faces show the original surface. As the icons were quickly blackened by the incense, it was a usual practice
to repaint them, which was often done, unfortunately, by a low-rate painter. For
the extraordinary accomplishment in the cleaning of this and many other icons by
the Central National Restoration Workshops of the Soviet Government, see M. S. Farbman, ed., *Masterpieces of Russian Painting*, London, 1930.

Fig. 354. Rublëv. Old Testament Trinity. Trinity Cathedral in the Monastery of Sergievo. c. 1410. (A. H. Barr, Jr.)

tine paintings give way to the more characteristically Russian colors, intense and contrasting.

This style we find in the work of the Novgorod and Pskov painters, in the *St. Basil* (Fig. 356), for example, which is dynamic in feeling, startling in its angularity and contrasts. The sharp angles and strong curves repeated in every detail, the precise outlining of the parts of the head and of the features, the sharp color-contrasts, the elongated proportions — each of these elements contributes to an abstract pattern of brusk forcefulness and vigorous movement that is little concerned with a representation of visual perception.

As in architecture, it was the assimilation of outside influences with this native dynamism that produced a Russian style. As in architecture, again, with the waning of the Mongol domination, during which Byzantine influence was cut off, Greek painters again appeared at Novgorod and Moscow, among them Theophanes, a painter from Mistra. Under this renewed Byzantine influence and through the re-

Fig. 355. Vladimir Madonna. XI cent. Historical
Museum, Moscow. (A. H. Barr, Jr.)

quirements of the iconos-
tasis, which was just at
that time reaching its highest development, a climax
of Russian painting was
reached in the work of An-
drei Rublëv (about 1370–
1430) whose monumental
Old Testament Trinity (FIG.
354) is a masterly design
in line and color. About
a table are seated the three
angels who appeared to
Abraham near the oaks of
Mamre. The figures, each
framed with a halo and
sweeping wings, nearly fill
the panel, and are clearly
and definitely related to
each other and to the space
by a design of horizontals
and peculiarly suave
curves, free from clashing
oppositions, which pro-
duces a tranquillity like
that of the *Vladimir Ma-
donna.* Yet sufficient angularity in the table,
chairs, and folds of the garments provides contrasting motifs. These
forms are constructed of color, each detail an area of color which is
frequently intensified by the juxtaposition of a complementary hue.
The intense blue and green folds of the cloak of the central figure
stand out starkly against the deep-red robe and gilded orange wings.
In the figure on the left the high lights of the orange cloak are a pattern of opalescent blue-green: " . . . one is amazed at a recurrent
gamme of color different from any that Western art has produced or
attempted to produce until recent years, in the extraordinary copy of
Rublëv's Trinity, the unforgettable Saint Demetrius robed in vermilion
with a vermilion shield, the black-winged archangels, Michael and Gabriel. The dominant scale of color is distinctly Oriental — parchment
white, golden buff, turquoise, blue, vermilion, malachite green, an occasional note of plum heightened by the uncompromising accent of un-
relieved black. It could be matched by grouping Chinese, Korean, and

Persian ceramics. The enamel-like purity and brilliance of the pigment constitute an almost unparalleled triumph in the technique of painting." [1]

D. MINOR ARTS

One should not forget in considering this rich ecclesiastical art of medieval Russia the indispensable part played in the entire ensemble by the minor arts: the carvings and rich metalwork of the iconostasis and the finely wrought jeweled halos and other ornaments on the icons; the candlesticks and candelabra; the miters and ecclesiastical robes stiff with gold, embroidery, and jewels; the illuminated books bound in gold or ivory inlaid with jewels and enamels; the crosses, croziers, sacred vessels, and processional banners. Each contributed with its amazing richness of texture and color to the total effect.

E. SUMMARY

The common objective of Russian art in the Middle Ages — to create visibly and emotionally an effect of transcendent otherworldliness — produced one of the loftiest expressions of Eastern Christianity. It was an art that took much from other cultures yet by adapting these borrowings to its own vernac-

Fig. 356. St. Basil the Great. Right half of a pair of royal doors. XIV cent. Museum of Tver. (A. H. Barr, Jr.)

ular produced something strangely individual. In the quiet, if not monotonous, landscape a vivid, picturesque mass of domes and steeples "gleams like a jeweled clasp on a sober robe," while the dim resplendent interior, to whose effectiveness builder, painter, and craftsman contributed, is perhaps the most complete expression of the common objective.

BIBLIOGRAPHY

Barr, A. H., Jr., "Russian Icons," *The Arts*, February, 1931
Buxton, D. R., *Russian Mediaeval Architecture*, Macmillan, 1934

---

[1] Lee Simonson, Metropolitan Museum of Art, *Bulletin*, January, 1931, p. 6.

Eliasberg, Alexander, *Russische Baukunst*, Munich, 1922

Farbman, M. S., ed., *Masterpieces of Russian Painting*, London, 1930

Grabar, I. E., *Istoria Russkago Iskusstva*, Moscow, 1909–16, 6 vols.

Hallé, F. W., *Altrussische Kunst*, Berlin, 1920

Kondakov, N. P., *The Russian Icon*, tr. by E. H. Minns, Oxford Press, 1927

Lukomsky, G. K., *Alt-Russland: Architektur und Kunstgewerbe*, Munich, 1923

Maskell, A. O., *Russian Art and Art Objects in Russia*, Scribner & Welford, 1884

Metropolitan Museum of Art, *A Catalogue of Russian Icons*, with introduction by I. E. Grabar, Metropolitan Museum, 1931

Muratov, P. P., *Les icones russes*, Paris, 1927

—— —— *La peinture byzantine*, tr. by Jean Chuzeville, Paris, 1928

Newmarch, H. J., *The Russian Arts*, Dutton, 1916

Olsufiev, Y. A., "Development of Russian Icon Painting from the Twelfth to the Nineteenth Century," *Art Bulletin*, December, 1930

Réau, Louis, *L'art russe des origines à Pierre le Grand*, Paris, 1921–22

Talbot Rice, David, ed., *Russian Art: An Introduction*, London, 1935

CHAPTER X

Muhammadan Art [1] (622 A.D. to date)

A. HISTORICAL BACKGROUND

When we think of the Muhammadans, we think not of a nation in the modern sense of the word, with sharply defined geographical boundaries, but of groups of people of varying cultures, widespread geographically but bound together by a burning and at times fanatical religious faith. The Muhammadans call this faith Islam, which means obedience to the will of Allah (God); and their creed is embodied in the prayer chanted by the muezzin from the minaret as he calls the faithful to worship: "God is great, God is great, God is great. I bear witness that there is no god but God. I bear witness that there is no god but God. I bear witness that Muhammad is the Apostle of God. I bear witness that Muhammad is the Apostle of God. Come to prayer. Come to prayer. Come to security. Come to security. God is great. God is great. There is no god but God." This religion, originating in Arabia, spread both east and west with amazing rapidity, chiefly by means of the sword; for the Moslem became an invincible soldier because of his fatalistic belief in the will of Allah, and because he was lured by the promise of immediate entrance into the Garden of Paradise if he died upon the field of battle fighting for the Faith.

Because of geographic extent and lack of traditional unity, Muhammadan art has manifested itself in diverse ways, strongly affected by local traditions, sometimes merely grafting upon the native art

[1] Also called Mohammedan, Moslem (Muslim), or Islamic.

Fig. 357. Mosque of Ibn Tulun. Cairo. 876–878 (Photo. Creswell)

Fig. 357. Mosque of Ibn Tulun. Cairo. 876–878 (Photo. Creswell)

a few of its requirements. At first the Moslem conquerors, Arab nomads, with no arts of their own,[1] did just what the Persians under Cyrus did when they conquered the older civilizations — adapted or borrowed what they found at hand. For example, when they conquered Constantinople they converted the church of *Santa Sophia* into a mosque by merely inserting a niche, whitewashing the mosaics containing figure work, and erecting the minarets. Soon, however, they so transformed the adaptations with their own means of expression that Muhammadan art became a strikingly individual thing. Because of this

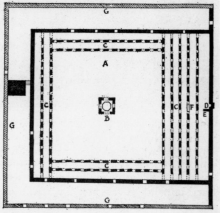

Fig. 358. Plan of the Mosque of Ibn Tulun. Cairo. *A*, court; *B*, fountain; *C*, covered arcades; *D*, niche (*mihrab*) indicating the direction of Mecca; *E*, pulpit (*mimbar*); *F*, tribune (*dikkeh*); *G*, girdle wall. The court is 300 ft. square.

diversity we shall confine our discussion, in this chapter, to one location, Egypt,[2] and there note some of the characteristic features of Islamic art.

Egypt was a province of the Byzantine Empire at the time of its conquest by the Moslems in 641 and already the early Christians of Egypt, the Copts, had evolved from the strongly intrenched Hel-

[1] No visual arts. Pre-Muhammadan Arabic poetry is of a high order.

[2] Although possibly the finest early mosques and fortified palaces important for their stone construction are to be found in Damascus and Aleppo. For Moslem art in Persia see Chapter XI.

Fig. 359. Mosque of Sultan Hassan. Cairo. 1356–59.
The dome indicates a tomb-mosque.

lenistic art centered at Alexandria a very vital non-materialistic expression much more consistent with their own traditions. It was an expression augmented by influences from the East, as we saw in their textile designs (Fig. 342). Ruled first by governors appointed by the caliphs of Damascus or Baghdad, Egypt finally set up an independent government under the Tulunids (868–904), which continued under the Fatimids (969–1171), who founded a new capital at Kahira (Cairo) in 969 and reached, in their art expression, a climax of refinement and dynamic vitality. Succeeding them as rulers were the Mamelukes (1252–1517), Tatar slaves of the sultan who rose from servitude to become for nearly three hundred years independent Moslem sovereigns of Egypt. Politically it was an age of intrigue and murder. The Mamelukes were still barbarians and merciless cut-throats; rarely did a Mameluke reign more than a few years, and very few died a natural death. Yet the arts flourished with an amazing vigor and displayed a rare and refined taste — one of the startling contrasts of history, as Mr. Lane-Poole suggests.

Against sumptuousness and license of all kinds the Koran decreed puritanically. Yet the Muhammadans, particularly the Mamelukes, with their Oriental love of color, of fine silks, jewels, and richly inlaid vessels, managed in various ways to circumvent these decrees. With great wealth at their command, they adorned their homes, and even their traveling tents of gold-shot silk, with rich hangings, fine rugs and, at least a few exquisite utensils; and they clothed themselves in the most splendid apparel. In spite of many fastings, prayers, and pilgrimages demanded by the Koran, life was gay with festivals, feasts, and sports.[1]

[1] For a picture of Muhammadan life, see Stanley Lane-Poole, *Art of the Saracens in Egypt*, London, 1888, Chapter I.

Fig. 360. Mosque of Sultan Hassan. Court, looking toward
the sanctuary.

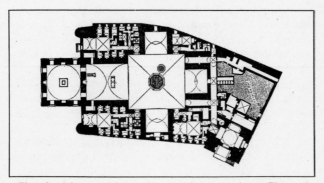

Fig. 361. Mosque of Sultan Hassan. Cairo. 1356–59. The angles
formed by the recesses of the court are filled with rooms for schools,
offices, and apartments for the attendants. The exterior of this
mosque is built of stone from the Pyramids of Gizeh; the interior,
except the great arches, of brick stuccoed. (Franz Pasha)

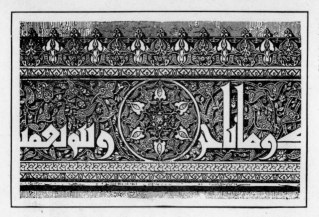

Fig. 362. Decorative Border with Arabesques and Kufic Lettering. Mosque of Sultan Hassan (Fig. 360).

B. ARCHITECTURE

Since the Muhammadan was fanatical in religious belief and at the same time zealous in the pursuit of pleasure, it is natural to find his architecture devoted chiefly to the mosque and the palace. So far as worship was concerned, his needs were simple: a secluded place, away from the noise of the streets, where a fountain provided water for ablution (for he must bathe before going to worship), and a place protected from the hot sun where, with face turned toward Mecca, he could pray. This direction was indicated to him by a niche in the wall of the mosque, beside which was a pulpit from which the Friday (the Muhammadan Sunday) sermon was preached; a little in front of these stood the raised platform from which the Koran was recited and prayers were chanted. These constitute the sanctuary of a mosque (FIGS. 358, 365).

The early cloistered mosque of *Ibn Tulun* (FIGS. 357, 358) adequately supplies these needs. It consists of a great open court with a fountain in the center, surrounded by covered arcades two deep on three sides but five deep on the sanctuary side, the special place of prayer, that is, the end facing toward Mecca; and a girdle wall, standing fifty feet outside the mosque walls on three sides, which gives the building added seclusion. The exterior presents a plain, massive wall with a row of small windows and simple unadorned doorways, the only decoration being a crenelated parapet. At one side rises the minaret, the tower from which the muezzin calls to prayer; it is rectangular, partaking of the same simple boldness and massiveness as the rest of the mosque. An external ramp provides a means of ascent, which carries the mind back to the ramp towers of Babylonia (FIG. 108).

Fig. 363. Tomb-Mosque of Sultan Kait Bey. In the environs of Cairo. 1472–76.

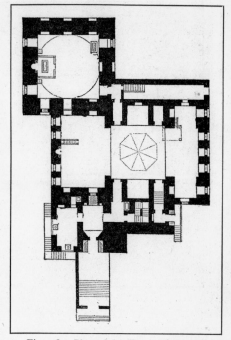

Fig. 364. Plan of the Tomb-Mosque of Kait Bey.

The mosque of *Sultan Hassan* (FIG. 359) is more complex in plan (FIG. 361). On each side of the court is a barrel-vaulted recess (*liwan*) with pointed arch, the largest constituting the sanctuary, behind which is the dome-covered tomb. The angles of the recesses are filled with rooms for schools, offices, and apartments; for Moslem educational institutions are usually connected with the mosque. This mosque is an austere mass of stone (appropriated from the *Pyramids of Gizeh* just as the early Christians appropriated stone and marbles from the classical Roman buildings to build their churches), with decoration concentrated at the lofty portals and in a frieze beneath the crenelation. The interior (FIG. 360), except the great arches, is made of brick stuccoed with decorative carvings and a particularly fine border (FIG. 362) at the spring of the vault.

Smaller mosques enabled the builders to decorate more lavishly; as we see in the mosque of *Kait Bey* (FIG. 363), whose small size, lightness, and elegance contrast with the grandeur and unadorned simplicity of *Ibn Tulun* and *Sultan Hassan*. The mosque with its minaret and the tomb with its dome are massed asymmetrically, as is indicated in the nonaxial plan (FIG. 364). The tall arched portal, so characteristic a feature of the mosque, is elaborately ornamented with carvings and

Fig. 365. Tomb-Mosque of Kait Bey (Figs. 363, 364). Sanctuary, showing the pulpit (*mimbar*), the niche (*mihrab*), and the richly colored glass
windows; at the upper left is a segment of the horsehoe arch.

stalactites; shallow recesses inclosing the windows break up the wall
surface. The slender, graceful minaret, with projecting galleries from
which stalactites depend, is ornamented with niches and carvings; the
contrasting dome with its virile sweep of line is covered with arabesque
carvings. The usual crenelation finishes the walls, for the overshadowing cornice rarely finds a place in Muhammadan architecture. In this
mosque the place of ablution is a small room at the left of the entrance;
the court is roofed with a hexagonal lantern rich in color and gold,
and on it opens the sanctuary, with a pointed horseshoe arch of alternating light and dark stone (Fig. 365). The floor is paved with
marble slabs, and the lower part of the walls is faced with variously
colored marbles through which gleams mother-of-pearl. The niche is
ornamented sumptuously with marble and mosaic and the pulpit with
carvings; above, the wall is pierced with small windows of brilliantly
colored glass. From the ceiling are suspended chains that originally
held inlaid metal or enameled glass lamps. The impression of such
a sanctuary with its subdued light is one of great richness of material and splendor of color.

Even a superficial glance at Islamic art, not building only but all
the arts, discloses its love of an ornament which impresses one with

Fig. 366. Wood Door Panel. Carved with arabesques and the heads of two horses. XI cent. Metropolitan Museum, New York. (Metropolitan Museum)

Fig. 367. Pulpit of Kait Bey. Door. Wood and ivory. H. 24 ft. Late XV cent. Victoria and Albert Museum, London. (Victoria and Albert Museum)

its dynamic vitality and decorative beauty. Its motifs were very limited. Islam forbade the representation of human and animal figures, and though the decree was not followed except by the orthodox and except in the case of objects used in the mosque, still it turned the eye of the artist to geometry and the world of nature for subject matter. From plant life — no one has discovered just where or when — was derived the arabesque, that universal Moslem motif which is one of the most characteristic marks of the style. The arabesque is a flowing, spiraling, interlacing pattern with palmette- or half-palmette-like motifs, suggestive but not at all imitative of leaf forms (FIG. 366). It was adaptable to almost every material, and with its capacity for spiraling with infinite variations well satisfied the Moslem's strong impulse to cover surfaces. For a *horror vacui* possessed him. Another universal motif in Islamic ornament was Arabic calligraphy. Writing was a fine art and both styles, Kufic and Neskhi,[1] revealed decorative possibilities,

---

[1] *Kufic:* the older, formal, angular style, so called from the city of Kufa in Mesopotamia, where the best calligraphers lived. *Neskhi:* a cursive script. Kufic was used

Fig. 368. Carved Wood Panel. From the mosque-hospital of Sultan Kalaun, Cairo. 1284. (After Prisse d'Avennes)

the Kufic (FIGS. 362, 374) providing contrasting angularity, the Neskhi flowing into the curves of the arabesques (FIG. 370). A third Islamic motif found from Spain to India was the stalactite, a pendant architectural ornament, used with a particular effectiveness in the mosque portal.

Plaster, used wet, was a particularly adaptable medium for the freely flowing line that distinguishes Muhammadan ornament, for here the hand could move easily and spontaneously. It appears in the earlier buildings, for example, about the arches in the mosque of *Ibn Tulun*, but was largely replaced by stone or marble about the fourteenth century. The Kufic frieze (FIG. 362) that decorates the sanctuary of the mosque of *Sultan Hassan* well illustrates stucco ornament. The bold, angular letters are particularly monumental and contrast effectively with the delicate floral arabesques from which they emerge.

Though plaster and stone were used largely in architectural ornament and even occasionally for a pulpit, wood was the material most favored for decorating the furnishings of both mosques and palaces. It was not only carved but frequently inlaid with ivory and ebony. This is well illustrated by the mosque pulpit, which stands at the right of the niche, as one faces the sanctuary (FIG. 365). Approached by a high door, it consists of a stairway that leads to a small covered platform surmounted by a cupola. Elaborate decoration, geometric, floral, and stalactite, covers the surface. A door from one of these pulpits (FIG. 367) illustrates the abundance of the carving. Arabesques, with panels inserted for the inscriptions, cover all the surfaces except the

for inscriptions and for copying the Koran, though later Neskhi was used for the latter purpose, with Kufic reserved for chapter headings.

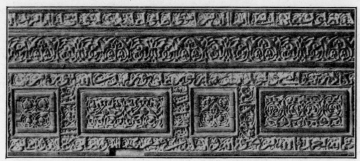

Fig. 369. Carved Wood Panel from the Tomb of a Sheikh. Detail. On the upper border and about the panels are inscriptions from the Koran and benedictions for the dead; otherwise the carving is based upon the arabesque. 1216. Victoria and Albert Museum, London. (Victoria and Albert Museum)

panels of the doors, which are filled with geometric patterns whose incisive angularity affords a happy contrast to the gliding lines of the rest of the carving. The geometric patterns are made up of many small polygons, each framing a floral motif and finished with a molding. The polygons are ingeniously fitted together so as to allow for warping, which is expected in the Egyptian climate. In these geometric designs we see the same fertility of invention as in the arabesque.

In an example of Fatimid woodcarving which is notable for the virility of its design (FIG. 366) the wood is undercut so as to create a light pattern on a dark ground, thus bringing into prominence its strong central motif terminating in horses' heads, and its integration, carried out with such inevitability, into the lighter rapid arabesques. Another panel (FIG. 368), from the *Hospital of Kalaun*, makes greater use of human and animal figures, some of which are suggestive of Eastern textiles. Broad sweeping bands form a heart-shaped motif repeated with variations and playing into the narrower spirals. Thus two systems of movement interplay throughout the panel. Broadly sweeping lines intertwine and knot, now terminating in floral forms that fill the ground and now forming geometric areas that contain human, bird, animal, and griffin forms. In the large central medallion is a kneeling man carrying a slain deer on his shoulders; above him are two eagles in balanced position, and at the sides two cockatoos whose long sweeping tails repeat the curves of the scrolls; the four circular medallions are filled with griffin or deer on whose backs are eagles with outspread wings. Details are omitted, and the forms are flattened out, simplified, and pleasingly adapted to the curving lines of the geometric areas.

A particularly rich and beautiful example of arabesque with in-

Fig. 370. Brass Bowl. Inlaid with silver. The inscription reads: "His Excellency, generous, exalted, lordly, great Amir, wise, ruler, leonine, fighter for the Faith, warden of Islam (liegeman) of El-Melih En-Nasir" (a Mameluke ruler of XIV cent.). British Museum, London.

scriptions is the panel from a sheik's tomb (FIG. 369), in which the carving is varied in motif and height of relief, and emphasized by the contrastingly unadorned moldings.

Color and gilding played an important part in the ornament of the Muhammadan. Both stucco and woodcarvings were vividly painted. Another method of obtaining color was by marble inlay and stained glass. Panels of variously colored marbles — red, yellow, black, green — perhaps combined with blue tile, or bordered with a geometric pattern of colored glass and mother-of-pearl, faced the sanctuary of the mosque or formed a dado around the palace room. A most brilliant effect of color came from the windows, which were made by filling a wooden frame with plaster about an inch thick, scooping out a pattern in the plaster while it was still soft, and then filling in the perforations with bits of colored glass. In FIG. 371 the design consists of a palm tree with spreading branches that curve to fit into the arch in which it stands; below are plane trees and flowers. The process is very simple and crude in comparison with the leaded windows of the Gothic period (FIG. 435); but the harmonious masses of color when penetrated by the Egyptian sunshine are rich and jewel-like in their effect.

The Cairene palace or house was, and it is today, a flat-topped structure of several stories built about an open court — the typical Mediterranean house plan — with one part reserved for the women, who live in seclusion. It stands flush with the narrow street and often has a carved, metal-studded wooden door and overhanging windows with infinitely varied wooden lattice. Although provided with these

windows, the house faces the court, which in
the better homes is a garden with fountains.
The furnishings are extremely simple, but
the carpets and cushions, inlaid metal, and
carvings produce the same richness of effect
that we have observed in the mosque.

C. MINOR ARTS

With both painting and sculpture forbidden, how could the orthodox Moslem satisfy
his love of rich and sumptuous effects? As
the mosque or the palace with its furnishings
constitutes the range of his expression, he
must needs depend upon the carvers in stone
and wood, the mosaicists, the workers in
various metals, the glassmaker, and the
weaver to satisfy his needs. The same motifs

Fig. 371. Window. Stucco
and glass. H. 30 in. Victoria
and Albert Museum, Lon-
don. (Victoria and Albert
Museum)

— the arabesque, floral and geometric designs and interlacings, calligraphy — appear in all the crafts, and are a revelation of the flexibility
of this narrow range of ornament, for rarely does one find exact du-
plication.

Islamic metalwork maintains the high quality that has characterized
this art in the Near Eastern lands throughout the ages. Basins, often
huge in size, ewers, candlesticks, trays, perfume-burners, jewel cases,
writing-boxes — many objects for use in the mosque and the home
— were made of wrought copper or brass, engraved and inlaid with
silver,[1] with the base sometimes covered with a black substance to
set forth the silver inlay more sharply and thus create a resplendent
effect. In FIG. 370, for example, effective use is made of the Arabic
calligraphy; the chief band of decoration consists of an inscription in
large letters, broken by rosettes which are made of a central whorl
surrounded by a ring of flying ducks, a frequent motif in the metalwork. A narrower band of scroll pattern, broken at intervals by whorls,
separates the broad band from the diaper pattern of flowers and birds
on the bottom.

Very brilliant was the enameled glass, particularly effective in the
mosque lamps. The glass of these lamps is blown, with many bubbles
and streakings, and is usually slightly yellow or green. In FIG. 373,
the broad, tall neck tapers toward the rather squat body, which carries
six loops or handles for the silver chains by which it was suspended to
the beam or ceiling of the mosque. The surface is covered with bands of

[1] That is, damascened. See note, p. 118.

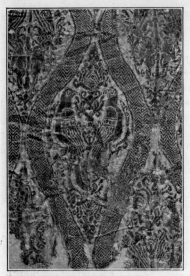

Fig. 372. Fatimid Silk Textile. XIII cent. Metropolitan Museum, New York. (Metropolitan Museum)

Fig. 373. Mosque Lamp. Enameled glass. H. 13 in. The inscription on the neck from the Koran reads, "In the house that God hath permitted to be raised for His name to be commemorated therein, men celebrate his praises morning (and evening)." XIV cent. Victoria and Albert Museum, London. (Victoria and Albert Museum)

arabesques and arabesque-entwined inscriptions worked in enamel — blue, white, yellow, green, red — with a liberal use of gold. Inside the lamp a small glass vessel, with the oil and wick, is hooked to the rim, so that the light brings out the decorations with a rich soft glow. The effect of a considerable number of these lamps in such a sanctuary as that of *Kait Bey* must have been magnificent.

Woven fabrics and leather were of great value for their contribution of texture and color. When the Arabs came into Egypt the weaving craft had already reached a high level of attainment among the Copts, as it also had in Sassanian Persia,[1] whose fine silks not only were highly prized but dominated textile design throughout the Near East.[2] At first the Arabs employed the Copts to work for them, and from these expert weavers they learned the craft. By the time of the Fatimids Arab fabrics were famous (FIG. 372). The fabrics were made usually with a fine linen warp and silk weft and the patterns were based upon the usual Islamic motifs, the arabesque and calligraphy, and upon

[1] See Chapter XI.

[2] It is interesting to note how many of our names for textiles originate in Near East weaving centers — *damask*, *muslin*, and *taffeta* are examples — indicating the fame of these centers for producing fabrics.

Coptic and Sassanian designs
of interlaced circles containing birds and animals or two
bilaterally balanced figures.

The calligrapher, we have
already noted, was one of the
most important of Islamic
artists. We have seen his
finely shaped letters used
decoratively in every branch
of Muhammadan art. But his
own creative work was, literally, the writing of books, and
most specifically the sacred
book of Islam, the Koran
(Qur'an). His work consisted
not only in the shaping of the
letters but also in illumination as rich as the decoration
of the mosque sanctuary
(FIG. 374). The first and last
two or three pages generally
contain a richly decorated

Fig. 374. Illuminated Page from a Koran.
1368–88. Khedivial Library, Cairo. (Moritz)

panel with the usual inscription — "Let none touch it save the puri-
fied" — in Kufic letters, and a margined medallion. Frequently the
text is written in gold letters. Vivid blue predominates, with a little
red and white, black or green, and a great deal of gold "like sunshine
on rippling seas." The splendor of the effect is perhaps equaled by the
delicacy of the infinite detail, even more intricate than the carvings
and engravings, for the brush is more facile than the carver's tools.

D. SUMMARY

Among the Muhammadans we find an art with unusually narrow
restrictions. The mosque with its sparse furnishings illustrates the range
of art expression. There is a conspicuous absence of pictures and sculpture and few representations of the human or animal figure except for
secular use, and then infrequently. In their stead are delicate carvings
of stone, stucco, wood, and ivory or marble inlay, rich stuffs, fine
rugs, brilliantly colored glass, and resplendent metal. Everywhere
is line, pattern, and color. The minor arts are inextricably interwoven
with the major, not only in creating the ensemble but in the interchange of ideas and motifs; for the geometric inlay on the helmet

finds its way to the carvings of the dome; the stone or stucco carved band on the mosque, to the pages of a Koran; and the textile design, to the silver inlay of a bowl. The very restrictions of this art, however, seem to be responsible for its particular bent. For with concentration upon decoration, and that, too, dependent upon a few fundamental geometric and floral motifs, the Muslim created an endless variety of carvings, now the angular geometric pattern, now the smoothly flowing, intricate arabesque. But in the best period each work, no matter what the medium, is apparently a fresh and vital creation, displaying, in spite of narrow bounds, great inventiveness and amazing exuberance.

BIBLIOGRAPHY

Arnold, Sir T. W., *Painting in Islam*, Oxford Press, 1928

—— and Guillaume, Alfred, eds., *The Legacy of Islam*, Oxford Press, 1931

Bourgoin, Jules, *Les éléments de l'art arabe: Le trait des entrelacs*, Paris, 1879

Briggs, M. S., *Muhammadan Architecture in Egypt and Palestine*, Oxford Press, 1924

Creswell, K. A. C., *Early Muslim Architecture*, Oxford Press, 1932, Vol. I

Dimand, M. S., *A Handbook of Mohammedan Decorative Arts*, Metropolitan Museum of Art, New York, 1930

Fry, R. E., *Vision and Design*, Coward-McCann, 1924, "The Munich Exhibition of Mohammedan Art"

Glück, Heinrich, and Diez, Ernst, *Die Kunst des Islam*, Berlin, 1925

Grousset, René, *The Civilizations of the East*, Knopf, 1931, Vol. I

Hobson, R. L., *A Guide to the Islamic Pottery of the Near East*, British Museum, London, 1932

Kendrick, A. F., *Catalogue of Muhammadan Textiles of the Medieval Period*, Victoria and Albert Museum, London, 1924

Koechlin, Raymond, *Les céramiques musulmanes*, Paris, 1928

—— and Alfassa, Paul, *L'art de l'Islam*, Paris, 1928

Lane, E. W., *Account of the Manners and Customs of the Modern Egyptians*, Ward, Lock, 1890

Lane-Poole, Stanley, *Art of the Saracens in Egypt*, London, 1888

Migeon, Gaston, *Les arts musulmans*, Paris, 1926

Nicholson, R. A., *Translations of Eastern Poetry and Prose*, Macmillan, 1922

Pézard, Maurice, *La céramique archaïque de l'Islam*, Paris, 1920

Rivoira, G. T., *Moslem Architecture*, tr. by G. McN. Rushforth, Oxford Press, 1918

Ross, Sir E. D., ed., *The Art of Egypt through the Ages*, Studio, 1931

See also the General Bibliography, pp. 749-751.

CHAPTER XI

Persian Art

1. SASSANIAN PERSIAN ART (226–641 A.D.)

A. HISTORICAL BACKGROUND

In the third century A.D. a new power had arisen in Persia, the Sassanian, so called from a priestly Iranian family who lived in a secluded part of southern Persia and there maintained the old traditions and religion of their race. Having conquered the Parthians, the Sassanians, notwithstanding the welter of Hellenistic, Roman, Parthian, and early Christian influences in the Valley of the Two Rivers, brought about a revival of Iranian culture, especially of the ancestral faith of Zoroaster. This Sassanian empire, with capitals at Istakhr (near Persepolis) and at Ctesiphon (near Baghdad), reached a climax under Chosroes (Khosrau) I (531–579 A.D.) and Chosroes (Khosrau) II (590–628), when Ctesiphon became a fabulously rich city and one of the most influential centers of the Near East. These rulers were great patrons of the arts and encouraged all workers in the crafts, particularly the weavers of fine silk textiles, which were in demand by the luxurious Byzantine court and which, through their introduction into the West, became a strong influence in the evolution of European ornament. When Justinian, in his zeal to propagate the Christian faith, closed the pagan schools of Athens, the artists and scholars fled to the court of Chosroes, carrying with them the classical traditions and learning, with the result that the Sassanian court was one of the broadest and most enlightened of the Near East. But, notwithstanding its power and vigor, this empire was short-lived, for it was one of the first to fall before the Moslem invaders (641 A.D.).

B. ARCHITECTURE

Sassanian art is a further example of the great assimilative capacity of the Iranian. Whatever he took he translated into his own idiom and infused with his own dynamic vitality. As with the Achaemenids, the palace is the type building, of which the *Palace at Ctesiphon* (FIG. 375) is the outstanding example. Though the columnar Hellenic style had penetrated the East through the conquests of Alexander the Great and had continued under Roman and Parthian rule, the Sassanian

Fig. 375. Palace at Ctesiphon. Sassanian (Sarre and Herzfeld)

revived the native tradition of vaulted construction, though Western influence is seen in details. What little is left of the *Palace at Ctesiphon* is eloquent of monumental grandeur, and when one recalls the stucco decorations and — upon reading of the booty taken by the Moslems — the marvelous carpets and furnishings, he easily becomes credulous of its fabulous magnificence. An imposing elliptical barrel vault of brick which roofs the throne room dwarfs human beings by the magnitude of its scale. It is buttressed by a solid façade, decorated with engaged columns and blind arcadings, which do not follow the superimposed system of the Roman style, but show a striking variety of arrangement in the stories that reveals an unhampered versatility.[1]

C. SCULPTURE

Monumental vigor through largeness of design distinguishes Sassanian rock-cut sculpture: the colossal equestrian reliefs of Ardashir I and Shapur I at Naksh-i-Rustum near Persepolis, and of Chosroes at Tak-i-Bostan, a villa near the modern Kermanshah that was a famous park in Sassanian times. Here, in an arched recess cut in a rock at the base of a cliff which borders a small lake, is the statue of Chosroes. His charger Shabdiz (a name meaning "Black as Night") is heavily caparisoned, and the rider clothed in armor. Though the statue has been badly mutilated by the Moslems, it still impresses with its monumentality, with its feeling for stone, and with the virility of every line and detail, which are so carved that they imbue the entire figure with an intense vitality as well as surface decorative beauty

[1] Recent excavations at Ctesiphon have brought to light a large number of fragments of stone and stucco ornament and other objects. See the Metropolitan Museum of Art, *Bulletin*, August, 1932. See also reports of excavations by the University Museum at Damghan and by the Oxford-Field Expedition at Kish.

Fig. 376. Carving with Winged Griffin. Detail from a relief of Chosroes II.
(Sarre)

Fig. 377. Silver Cup. D. 10 in. IX–X
cent. Bibliothèque Nationale, Paris.
(Giraudon)

— qualities that are evident also in the
recently discovered stucco fragments
of horses and decorative panels.

D. MINOR ARTS

This same pulsating vitality combined with a sensitive relationship of
forms controls the work of the silversmiths and weavers. Behind the Sassanian metalworker lay a long tradition of extraordinary quality which
his own cups and plates maintain.
The winged griffin is a popular motif,
in early examples expressed with all
Fig. 378. Silver Plate. Sassanian.
III–IV cent. Hermitage Museum,
Leningrad.

the vigor of the carvings (FIG. 376). Later it acquires more elaboration,
elegance, and ease of line, as in the shallow cup with a plumed griffin in
the Victoria and Albert Museum. An easy facility of line combined with
a vigor of conventional form is seen in another cup (FIG. 377), which
is decorated with a lithe animal walking along the banks of a river,
indicated by swirling lines, from which rise lotus flowers to fill the
vacant spaces. Another popular motif is the hunter. In FIG. 378 four
figures are composed into a unit determined by a circular space. Dynamic curves and countercurves, now flowing together, now meeting
at sharp angles, create a forceful pattern through which conventional
motifs for drapery, muscles, manes, and fur carry rapid minor rhythms.

Weaving, we have said, reached a high stage of accomplishment.

Fig. 379. Silk Textile with the Hunter Motif. Sassanian, c. 600. Kunstgewerbe Museum, Berlin. (Lessing)

The silk-weaving craft had made its way westward from China and became a flourishing industry in Persia, where the craftsmen wove fabrics not only for home use but for Europe as well. So popular were their designs that they were imitated in the West throughout the Middle Ages. An all-over pattern based upon large medallions connected by small ones is a distinctive feature of these stuffs. In FIG. 379 the hunter motif appears. Two kings on winged horses, arranged with perfect bilateral balancing, are holding aloft the cubs of the lioness that they have been hunting. The forms of all the figures are so highly generalized that they have become decorative patterns splendidly adapted to the circular space. The astounding amount of vigor in the forms, and the highly simplified drawing necessary for a successful textile pattern, are harmonized with extraordinary skill in the Sassanian fabrics.

E. SUMMARY

The recent discoveries, which are adding much needed material to our limited resources for the study of Sassanian art, only strengthen the original impression of its vitality and exuberance, its grandeur and monumentality. A peculiar power seems to have penetrated the age-long Mesopotamian tradition of brick vaulting and of the animal arts, the latter in the form of metal and textiles. The result was that although the political life of Sassanian Persia was short, the dynamism of its art continued to dominate the Near East and to penetrate western Europe notwithstanding the conquests of Islam.

2. MUHAMMADAN PERSIAN ART (641–1736 A.D.)

A. HISTORICAL BACKGROUND

The kingdom of the Sassanids was short-lived because of the invincible fighting power of the Moslems, who swept eastward in their conquests in the seventh century A.D. and in 762 established Baghdad as the seat of the caliphate, a final blow to the life of Ctesiphon. Bagh-

Fig. 380. Royal Mosque, Isfahan. 1612. (Photo Arthur Upham Pope)

dad became the center not only of a gorgeous and pleasure-loving court, the famed city of the Thousand and One Nights, but also of a culture and art that was ostensibly Islamic but at heart Iranian. For it was the age of the Iranian Abbasids, of that famed ruler Harun-al-Rashid (786–809); the age of Firdousi (940–1020), the great epic poet who gathered together the heroic legends of the Iranian people into the *Shah-nama* or *Book of Kings;* of Nizami (1141–1203), the famous romantic poet of Persia; and of Omar Khayyám (died 1123), who took for the setting of his quatrains the luxurious, pleasure-seeking aspect of life.

Meantime the Mongols, or Tatars, who had been moving westward under Jenghiz Khan (1162–1227), captured Baghdad in 1258, and came to rulership, bringing with them the traditions of China. Thus Persia has been the melting-pot of many influences which have centered there in the wake of conquering armies: the Babylonian, Assyrian, and Achaemenian with an admixture of Egyptian; through the conquests of Alexander and the Romans, the Hellenic influence, the Roman, and their successor the Byzantine; after the revival of the Iranian by the Sassanids, the Islamic influence; and with the Mongol invasion, the Chinese. But despite these converging influences, one feels the constancy and tenacity of the Iranian tradition. The Mongol rulers of the thirteenth and fourteenth centuries, with their capital at Samarkand, accepted Islam. The dynasty of the Timurids

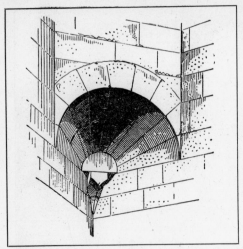

Fig. 381. A Squinch. This constructional device consists of filling the corner (here with arched masonry) to make the transition from a square to a polygonal base.

Fig. 382. Detail of the Royal Mosque (Fig. 380) showing glazed tile. (Photo Arthur Upham Pope)

(1396–1500), founded by Timur (Tamerlane), was a period of prosperity and wealth, and under their patronage were produced some of the finest books, carpets, and metal. The Safavids (1502–1736) at the time of Shah Abbas I (1587–1628) reached another climax. But already overelegance, easy grace, and a naturalistic trend were foretelling the decline.

B. ARCHITECTURE

In Islamic Persia it is the mosque as well as the palace that engages the builder. And the garden assumes extraordinary importance in this semi-desert land, an importance that finds expression in poetry as well as in painting and in the garden carpets. For Persian art "is inseparable from the very land of Persia, where, against an ever-present background of mauve and golden desert, set in a frame of rosy mountains, a few dead mountains standing out against the horizon like some landscape in the moon, a slender stream of water, a few poplars, and an old crumbling wayside inn suddenly assume a totally unexpected artistic value.

"And in addition to this incessant reminder of the desert there is the light air of the high plateaus with its incomparable purity, which adds an unvarying delicacy to every tone. Against this sky of a tender blue the favorite colors of the Persian architects acquire an extraordinary value — the mellow tone of the brick of the ancient mosques of Hamadan and Varamin or the fairy-like blue of the great domes of Isfahan or the gold of the dome of Qum, brooding and solitary in the infinite space of the desert. A profound harmony exists between this country and its art, an intimate re-

Fig. 383. Bullock. From a Manafi al-Hayawan (Bestiary). Late XIII cent. Pierpont Morgan Library, New York. (Metropolitan Museum)

lation which transcends human factors and will survive them, for here ruin assumes the aspect of the very soil of the country, while the desert itself possesses the tones and appearance of its ruins." [1]

The *Royal Mosque* (*Masjid-i-shah*) of Isfahan (FIG. 380) reflects this description. It faces a great open square about which are located the imperial palace, mosques, and markets. Rising from a group of subsidiary cloisterlike buildings and courtyards with gardens and fountains, it presents a composition of pointed, bulbous dome, pointed arches framed by rectangles, and cylindrical minarets — all sheathed in brilliantly colored glazed tile. There are evident here several traditions of the Valley of the Two Rivers: brick, with a limited use of stone, for material; the arch system of construction; and intensely colorful ceramic decoration. Structurally the erection of a dome on a rectangular or polygonal plan brings the problem of the transition from angular to spherical volumes, a problem met by the Byzantine builders with the pendentive (FIG. 321), by the Persian with the squinch (FIG. 381).

The ceramic decoration at Isfahan (FIG. 382) is a continuation of the tradition we have followed in the Valley of the Two Rivers from the blue tile of the sanctuary of the *Ziggurat* at *Ur* (FIG. 108) by way of *Khorsabad* (FIG. 124) and the *Ishtar Gate* (FIG. 132) to *Susa* (FIG. 138) and *Persepolis*. The motifs are geometric patterns, arabesques, or inscriptions, sometimes slightly in relief, and the colors rich blues of many tones, green and yellow, black and white — now used with strong contrast, such as a white arabesque on the deepest blue or

[1] René Grousset, *The Civilizations of the East*, Knopf, 1931, Vol. I, p. 393.

Fig. 384. Mirak. Laila and Majnun. XVI cent. Metropolitan Museum, New York. (Metropolitan Museum)

black ground, now more nearly in the same key. Yet whatever the color combination and however intricate the design, the surfaces are never broken. The clear, definite organization of a few simple masses, with the help of the shadows in the arched recesses, keeps the rich surface decoration entirely subordinate, just as in *Santa Sophia* (FIG. 321), where the rhythmic movement of arches and domes holds under control the sumptuous detail.

C. PAINTING

Although frescoes are by no means unknown,[1] our chief criterion of Persian painting and probably its greatest expression is found in the miniatures. The shahs were great lovers of fine books. They spared neither time nor money to obtain them and maintained trained calligraphers and painters at the court, among whom often were the most famous artists of the day. Among the early books, in addition to the splendid copies of the Koran written in the monumental Kufic calligraphy by the famous copyists of Kufa, are the copies of the *Manafi al-Hayawan* (or Bestiary), in which the paintings of the animals are monumental in scale and directly powerful in design (FIG. 383). The bold conventional patterning, Sassanian in feeling, contrasts happily with the almost naturalistic grass foliage and birds, lightly painted in the Chinese style of ink painting, which came to Persia with the Mongols.

The truly Persian style and some of the greatest triumphs of Persian painting are found in the secular books of the Timurids and Safavids, such as the poems of Firdousi and Nizami illustrated by a whole galaxy of painters, famous among whom were Bihzad (about 1440–1553); Mirak and Sultan Muhammad, court painters of Shah Tahmasp (1524–1576), a great art patron. Although the shahs were Moslems, orthodox Islamic restrictions regarding the figure did not affect

[1] For the recently discovered frescoes at Isfahan, see *Persian Fresco Paintings*, American Institute for Persian Art and Archaeology, New York, 1932.

their secular arts, so that
the gay scenes of their life
of pleasure — the hunt, the
battle, the feast, flowers,
music, and romance — fill
the pages of their books.
As one looks at them, he
feels the luxury, the splendor, and the fleeting happiness of Omar. The cool
gardens with fruit trees always blossoming and tall
slender palm trees waving
gently against the blue
sky; the palace or mosque
that gleams with enamel-
like walls of lustrous faïence; or the rocky hillsides
where the hunters or war-
riors dash by on slender
horses — these form the
setting for these tales.

From one of Nizami's
romantic poems is the
Laila and Majnun (FIG.
384). The scene represents

Fig. 385. Equestrian Portrait of a Prince and His
Servant. Attributed to Sultan Muhammad. XVI
cent. Coll. Louis Cartier. (Metropolitan Museum,
New York)

a school, apparently in a mosque. Seated on a rug is the turbaned
priest, the teacher, lash in hand, listening to a youth reading; round
him are other youths studying, all seated on their knees and heels or
with one knee raised, the customary sitting postures in the East. Here
and there are the cross-legged book rests; in the foreground one boy is
pulling his companion's ear, and at the left, near the large water jar, two
are playing ball. In the middle distance are the lovers Laila and Majnun, obviously aware of the other's presence. There is a good deal of
vivacity in the narrative element. The figures are drawn expressively
with delicate, flowing lines; but they are flat, with no chiaroscuro, and
with but a hint of perspective; the tiles in the court and the rugs on the
floor appear to be hanging vertically. The painting is conceived from
the point of view not of natural appearance but of pattern and vivid
color. To this end the tones are kept bright and clear. The decorative quality of the miniature is emphasized by the broad margins of
the page, which is tinted pale blue and flecked all over with gold.
The opposite page of the book is designed to harmonize with the il-

Fig. 386. Ewer. Brass inlaid with silver, and ornamented with inscriptions and festal scenes. H. 11 in. 1232. British Museum, London. (British Museum)

lustrated page, for the area containing the writing is equal to that of the miniature and the margins are of the same gold-flecked pale blue. The writing, a beautiful example of the Arabic script, is the work of a famous calligrapher who says in the colophon that the book was "finished with God's help by the hand of the poor and obscure Sultan Muhammad Nur"; and the binding is an example of the rare skill of the craftsman in gold-tooled leather.[1]

In FIG. 385, a *Portrait of a Prince*, in the style of Sultan Muhammad, everything extraneous has been eliminated. The mounted prince and his servant create the loveliest of surface patterns. Each detail of the figures and the costumes, drawn with the surest yet most delicate lines, is a contributing element of shape or color, and the wealth of minute detail is balanced by the large unbroken areas.

D. MINOR ARTS

The tradition of the metalworker, as we have said, is very old in the Valley of the Two Rivers and appears never to have ceased in spite of the rise and fall of dynasties and the influence of foreign invaders. In the twelfth and thirteenth centuries, after a period of suppression at the hands of orthodox Moslems, there appears to have been a revival of this work, probably due to the coming of the Tatars, who though converted to Islam still held but slight regard for its decrees. The center of the craft was at Mosul, near great copper mines, from which it spread to other localities, appearing in Egypt in such a work as the brass bowl (FIG. 370), in which inscriptions and arabesques furnished the motifs of decoration. In the Mosul products, however, figure work is an important element, as we see in a ewer (FIG. 386) in which the figures of men, animals, and birds in hunting, fighting, and feasting scenes are inlaid in silver on an engraved brass ground. On the silver also were engraved details such as features, drapery, plumage of the birds, and manes of the horses, so that the effect of the contrasting metals and the delicate chasing is one of rich splendor.

[1] See Gardner, *Understanding the Arts*, pp. 253 ff., for a description and illustrations of this book.

Fig. 387. Rhages (Ray or Rayy) Bowl Showing a Court Scene. XIII cent. Metropolitan Museum, New York. (Metropolitan Museum)

Fig. 388. Lustered Rhages (Ray) Bowl. c. 1200. Metropolitan Museum, New York. (Metropolitan Museum)

Behind the products of the ceramist, as of the metalworker, lay a long tradition, including ceramic wall decoration on a large scale as well as the more usual smaller products. And as the former made the walls of mosques and palaces glow with color, so the latter provided accents of texture and color to the interior. For shape and color were the potter's objective, and to its realization he brought a spontaneity and an ease of expression based upon an innate sensitivity and a technical ability handed down from generations. In short, these Persian potters were master ceramic designers. Their shapes — bowls, cups, bottles, pitchers, plates, jars — are usually true clay shapes, not sharply precise like metal, and their decorations in every detail relate to the shape. The vital lines and contours are in perfect harmony with and in purposeful contrast to the rim of a plate (FIG. 388) or to the curving surface of a pitcher; and all appear to be dashed on the surface spontaneously and with great ease, yet with a perfect conviction of their exact rightness.

The coarse base of most of this pottery required a slip or coat of opaque enamel to provide a surface for the painting. In the *Rhages* (Ray) [1] bowl of FIG. 387, the ground is turquoise blue on which are painted in many colors, with dull red and blue predominating, and a little gold, a sultan on his throne with courtiers on each side and seated figures in the surrounding compartments. About the rim runs a Kufic inscription, and on the outside, in cursive hand: "Glory, triumph, power and happiness, generosity and safety, to the owner."

[1] So called from the city of Rhages, near Teheran, a great center of pottery-making, and one of the most splendid cities of Persia before its destruction by Jenghiz Khan in the thirteenth century.

Many of the jars and plates have a creamy glaze with decorations in a soft brown that has a peculiarly fleeting charm when covered with a transparent luster.[1] For when viewed at a certain angle there appears an iridescence of violet, dull gold, and copper. Move slightly, and the sparkling color disappears. Thus it produces a subtle, evanescent form of decoration that is highly suggestive of the joy of the passing hour. There is none of the sobriety of Egypt or China, or of the intellectuality of Greece, but rather the restless joy of Minoan art. Delight in the happiness of the present hour expresses itself in the sparkling, fleeting beauty of the luster vases.

This pottery was an aristocratic art, and like the books and many of the fine carpets was produced under royal patronage. Carpets, however, are peculiarly expressive of the people as a whole. The land itself produces all the necessary materials, and the need of protection against the winter cold makes them indispensable both in the nomad shepherd's tent and in the shah's palace. And in each case the intimate relation of the carpet to its makers and to its function determines its design, as one realizes in comparing a small shepherd rug of bold primitive pattern with the huge royal carpets of subtle richness. In the houses and palaces of Persia, built of brick, stone, plaster, and glazed tile, the carpets contribute a contrasting texture as floor and divan coverings and wall hangings.

The success of a carpet, then, will result from color massing and texture. The royal *Ardebil Carpet* (FIG. 389), a large example of the medallion type, depends for its effectiveness upon a simple massing of large elements of design enhanced by a wealth of subordinated detail. These main elements are the single unifying tone of the field, the central and corner medallions, and the finishing borders. The field is a rich blue and is covered with flowers and leaves attached to a framework of delicate stems which weave a spiral design over all the field. The central medallion is of yellow, surrounded by small oval panels of yellow, red, and green, from one of which is suspended a mosque lamp; quarter-sections of this medallion group fill the corners. The broad border has alternating medallions of red and yellow on a deep purple ground; the narrow borders make a happy transition from field to border.

In the *Ardebil Carpet* there are no human or animal figures, since it was made for a mosque; but another carpet (FIG. 390) from Ardebil illustrates how these weavers used the animal form. Lions and other animals are attacking spotted gazelles, while boars are running rapidly away; other animals, peonies, and various flowers fill the field. All

---

[1] *Luster* is a very thin, transparent, metallic film added after the vessel has been glazed and decorated; the vessel is then fired again at a low temperature.

Fig. 389. Ardebil Rug. Detail. Wool. 34½ × 17½ ft. Made by Shah Tahmasp for the tomb-mosque of his family at Ardebil. Victoria and Albert Museum, London. The inscription at the bottom of the field reads:

"I have no refuge in the world other than thy threshold,
There is no place of protection for my head other than this door.
The work of the slave of the threshold, Maqsud of Kashan, in the year 926 [1540 A.D.]."

(Victoria and Albert Museum)

these forms, whether flora or fauna, show an extraordinary combination of simplified naturalism, for each can be clearly identified. The decorative pattern thus enables the weaver to mass shapes and colors into an underlying abstract design whose movement is confined by the borders, each of which contains in its motifs rhythmic movements of varying tempo around the central field.

Carpet-weaving was an inherited craft among the Persians, attained through generations of effort. Many a pattern, or perhaps the secret of making a particularly fine dye, was handed down from father to son. The wool was obtained from the sheep which grazed on the mountain sides of this rugged country; and the dyes, few in number, from plants. When the weaver had strung the warp on his primitive loom he would begin putting in a horizontal row of knots (Fig. 391); then one or two lines of weft, pressing it down firmly with a comblike implement when he had woven several rows. Thus he continued

Fig. 390. Wool Animal Rug. Detail. c. 1520–30. Metropolitan Museum, New York. (Metropolitan Museum)

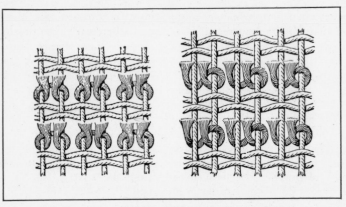

Fig. 391. Two Methods of Knotting a Persian Carpet. (Kendrick and Tattersall)

putting in rows of knots and weft, varying his color according to his pattern. As the knots were of uneven length, the surface was cut, leaving an even pile that concealed both the warp and the weft. Pile weaving is a slow process at best, and since a great royal carpet like the *Ardebil* often has more than three hundred knots to the square inch, such a carpet was probably the product of a group of weavers. It has been estimated that it would have taken one skilled worker about twenty-four years to weave a carpet of this size, a length of time Shah Tahmasp would not have waited.

E. SUMMARY

Persian art in all its manifestations — the mosque, the carpet, the illuminated page, the *Rhages* bowl, the inlaid metal — reveals its delight in the massing of color to obtain brilliant effects. It is not interested in producing an illusion of nature, but it delights in the flat pattern suggested by the human, animal, or plant form and seen as an element of decorative power. We feel this in the hastily sketched figures on the pottery, in the silhouettes of the slender-legged horses that dash across the page of the manuscript, in the flat swaying palm trees, in the infinitely varied flowers of the rugs, and in the inscriptions of silver that shine forth from the dark metal ground. Nor are there, in this art, profound abstract expressions. It is rather a frank reflection of a life of luxury, splendor, and romance, delighting in the pleasures of the present, lively, joyous, worldly, and transitory. It is the spirit of Omar Khayyám expressed by the potter, the painter, and the metalworker. Influences from all directions converged upon Persia, where great highways crossed. But the Iranian race, though it assimilated certain elements, preserved its identity and continued to manifest its innate sensitivity in intense and subtle color harmonies and in masterly decorative designs.

BIBLIOGRAPHY

Arnold, Sir T. W., *Painting in Islam*, Oxford Press, 1928
—— Wilkinson, J. V. S., and Gray, Basil, *Persian Miniature Painting*, Oxford Press, 1931
Blochet, Edgar, *Musulman Painting, XIIth–XVIIth Century*, tr. by C. M. Binyon, London, 1929
Bode, Wilhelm von, *Antique Rugs from the Near East*, tr. by R. M. Riefstahl, Weyhe, 1922
Dimand, M. S., *A Guide to an Exhibition of Islamic Miniature Painting and Book Illumination*, Metropolitan Museum of Art, New York, 1933
Firdousi, *The Shāh-nāmah*, described by J. V. S. Wikinson, Oxford Press, 1931
Glück, Heinrich, and Diez, Ernst, *Die Kunst des Islam*, Berlin, 1925
Gray, Basil, *Persian Painting*, London, 1930
Hannover, Emil, *Pottery and Porcelain*, Scribner, 1925, 3 vols.

Hawley, W. A., *Oriental Rugs, Antique and Modern*, tr. by Bernard Rackham, Dodd, Mead, 1913

Jackson, A. V. W., *Persia Past and Present*, Macmillan, 1906

—— and Tattersall, C. E. C., *Fine Carpets in the Victoria and Albert Museum*, London, 1924

Kendrick, A. F., *Catalogue of Muhammadan Textiles of the Medieval Period*, Victoria and Albert Museum, London, 1924

Koechlin, Raymond, and Migeon, Gaston, *Oriental Art; Ceramics, Fabrics, Carpets*, tr. by Florence Heywood, Macmillan, 1928

Martin, F. R., *The Miniature Painting and Painters of Persia, India, and Turkey*, London, 1912, 2 vols.

Mayer, L. A., *Saracenic Heraldry*, London, Oxford Press, 1933

Mumford, J. K., *Oriental Rugs*, new ed., Scribner, 1915

Nizami, *Poems*, described by Laurence Binyon, Studio, 1929

Pope, A. U., *An Introduction to Persian Art since the Seventh Century*, Scribner, 1931

Ross, Sir E. D., and others, *Persian Art*, London, 1930

Sarre, F. P. T., and Trenkwald, Hermann, *Old Oriental Carpets*, tr. by A. F. Kendrick, Vienna, 1926–29, 2 vols.

Tattersall, C. E. C., *Notes on Carpet-Knotting and Weaving*, 2d ed., Victoria and Albert Museum, London, 1927

Victoria and Albert Museum, South Kensington, *Brief Guide to the Persian Embroideries*, London, 1929

—— —— *Brief Guide to the Persian Woven Fabrics*, London, 1922

—— —— *Guide to the Collection of Carpets*, with an introduction by A. F. Kendrick, 3d ed. rev., London, 1931

See also the General Bibliography pp. 749–751.

CHAPTER XII

Romanesque Art

(about 500–1150 A.D.)

A. HISTORICAL BACKGROUND

While the long-continued Byzantine tradition was following a more or less unbroken course in the East, chaos ruled in the West from about the year 500 to 1000 A.D. Through the close relations of Constantinople with Venice and Ravenna, and through trade and pilgrimages, especially the Crusades, interchange was constantly bringing Byzantine ideas westward. During this period of chaos the elements that were to form the foundation of western Europe were meeting and mingling — Roman, Byzantine, barbarian, and Christian. Rome, through its provincial system, had built cities over a large part of western Europe, connected them by magnificent roads, and there had established its customs and culture. In swept waves of barbarians, illiterate but of the fresh, vigorous blood of the North. In their new environment they continued to govern by tribal methods instead of accepting Roman

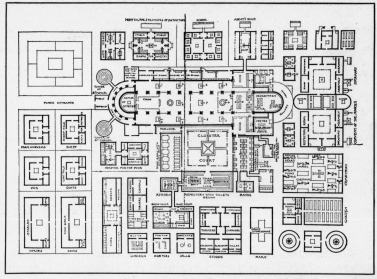

Fig. 392. Monastery of St. Gall. Switzerland. Plan, drawn from a manuscript. The various activities indicated here constitute a complete social unit. (Porter, *Medieval Architecture*, Yale University Press)

law; and when this law ceased, and with it order — for the kings were usually powerless — a natural outcome was feudalism; for people of necessity bound themselves to anyone who could provide some measure of safety from the dangers and outrages of the times.

The one power to remain strong was the Christian Church. Steadily it was perfecting its organization and increasing both its spiritual and its temporal power. At the head of each unit of its organization stood the bishop, who lived in the largest city of his diocese. In the church of this city was the bishop's chair, called the *cathedra*. Hence his church was known as the *cathedral*. As feudalism was the ruling power, the bishop became practically a feudal baron. With the increase of its power and wealth, the Church was weakened by elements of decay, and in protest against its degradation arose the monastery. This institution with its triple vow of poverty, chastity, and obedience had originated in the East; it was introduced into Italy by St. Benedict in 526; and thence spread rapidly over western Europe. At the head stood the abbot, and his church was known as the abbey church. In Fig. 392 we see the plan of a typical monastery of the period. In the center, dominating the group, is the abbey church, of basilican type with an apse at either end and a cloister at the side. About it are grouped the living-quarters, bakehouse, storerooms, shops for the goldsmith, the

Fig. 393. Sant' Ambrogio. Milan. Early XII cent. A rare example of the survival of the atrium. (Alinari)

blacksmith, the fuller, and other craftsmen, gardens and cattle yards, hospitals and schools — a complete community in itself where daily needs were supplied without communication with the outside world. As a protection against robbers and feudal barons, some monasteries were surrounded by a fortified wall. Thus the monastery was much more than a church. In it centered most of the learning of these centuries, for it was the industrious monks who kept alive whatever ancient culture had survived. It was, in fact, the church, the school, the library, and the hospital all in one; and, furthermore, it was the steadying hand throughout this whole formative period.

With the exception of the large cities, which could withstand the attacks of the barbarians, there were few towns up to about the year 1000. The people lived in rural communities, attached, practically as serfs, to the estate of some feudal lord, abbot, or bishop; and because of the dangers of travel there was little intercommunication or commerce.

But the members of medieval society mentioned above — the feudal lord, the bishop, and the abbot — were not stable. There was constant warfare. The strife between the bishops and the abbots, who were jealous of each other's power, added to the turmoil. The one brilliant spot was the reign of Charlemagne, when for a short time order was restored, education and learning were revived, and the arts stimulated. But after his death Europe descended to its lowest level, and even the Church sank to deepest degradation, from which it was ultimately rescued through the influence of such monasteries as that of Cluny, which was established in 909 and for two hundred years served as the spiritual guide of Europe.

About the year 1000 a new spirit began to infuse Europe. We hear of uprisings against the feudal barons, the establishment of towns, the opening-up of communication, the organization of trade guilds, and the growth of commerce. Religious faith developed into religious enthusiasm of great vitality, and culminated in the First Crusade,

Fig. 394. Sant' Ambrogio. Nave. (Alinari)

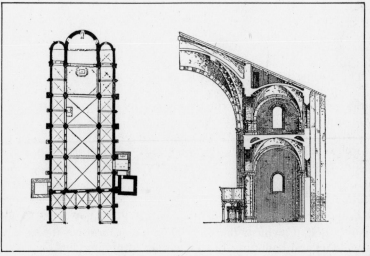

Fig. 395. Sant' Ambrogio. Milan. Plan (with but one bay of the
atrium) and section. (Dehio and Bezold)

Fig. 396. Cathedral. Pisa. XI–XII cent.

which, though participated in by many for the sake of adventure, nevertheless was an indication of the religious faith of the age. The consequence of this new spirit was a vigorous artistic activity which swept all Europe.[1]

Universities and schools of learning were founded. The various vernaculars were becoming mediums of literary expression. The troubadours were singing their songs at the gay feudal courts of southern France, while the Song of Roland and the legends of the Grail were stirring men with the ideal of chivalry.

Thus, while five centuries were years of chaos, during which the different basic elements were fusing, the eleventh and twelfth centuries were the early flowering of this fusion, a powerful archaic age with institutions and art forms, centered in the monastery and the feudal court, peculiarly expressive of the entire outlook of the age as well as a prelude to the full flowering of medieval culture in the Gothic age.

B. ARCHITECTURE AND SCULPTURE

As the monastery was the predominating power during the Romanesque period, it is chiefly the abbey church that furnishes the examples of building and sculpture. In fact, with its furnishings and equipment, it illustrates the entire range of the arts, as does the mosque in Islamic

[1] Note that this synchronizes with the second Byzantine golden age; and it now seems probable that not only the stimulation but also many of the forms in building, sculpture, and especially the minor arts are directly attributable to the East.

Fig. 397. Marble Pavement. Baptistery, Florence. (Alinari)

Fig. 398. Pulpit Decorated in Cosmati
Work. Ravello. XIII cent. (Alinari)

art. Before the year 1000 there was little building, as the barbarians
were incapable, and the Latins inactive because of the disorder. But
the new spirit discernible about that year was an incentive to church-
building.

In studying the architecture of the Romanesque period, one important fact must always be kept in mind — very little remains in
its original condition; there are few structures with no additions or
restorations of a later period. Another important fact is that the architecture is not homogeneous, but manifests itself differently in different
parts of Europe. Hence we shall look at a few examples in several
countries, beginning with Italy.

In the sixth century the Po Valley had been occupied by the Lombards, whose name to this day designates this part of Italy. Of the
buildings that they erected in the eleventh century, the most important is *Sant' Ambrogio* (FIG. 393). It is a plain building, with an unbroken sloping roof which shows that there is no clerestory. The
façade, which is approached through an atrium, consists of a two-
storied arcade, flanked on either side by a sturdy square tower. The
decoration consists of a corbel table along the cornices and on the
tower. The whole design is one of dignity, with no suggestion of
elaboration, and is saved from heaviness by its reserved decoration.

As we look at the ground plan (FIG. 395), we see a Christian basilica
without a transverse aisle. Now the early Christian basilica had a
wooden roof which, the builders realized, was neither permanent nor

Fig. 399. San Miniato. Florence.
Façade of marble inlay and mosaic.
Begun 1013. (Alinari)

fireproof. Hence a central problem of
the Middle Ages was to roof over the
basilica with a vault. This means two
things — to construct the vault and to
support it adequately. In studying Roman architecture, we found that the
Romans constructed great barrel and
groin vaults (FIGS. 274, 284) that rested
upon massive walls, heavy enough to
withstand the thrust of the vault. The
Byzantine builders preferred a domical vault on pendentives (FIGS. 321,
322) and the Persians, a domical vault
on squinches (FIG. 381). The Byzantine type, though found in western Europe,[1] did not appeal to the medieval
builders so much as did the basilica.
Let us see how this problem is met
in *Sant' Ambrogio*. As we look at the
nave (FIG. 394) we see that instead
of carrying a long barrel vault it is divided into sections, or bays, by
transverse arches or ribs; and that each bay is covered by a groin vault
with four diagonal ribs built along the lines of the groins. Why are
these ribs here, and of what value are they in the construction of the
building?

In building a barrel or groin vault, a large amount of centering,
that is, wooden scaffolding to hold the vault during its erection, is
necessary. Soon the builders discovered that by separating the long
barrel vault into bays by transverse arches, they could vault one
section at a time, thus economizing on the centering. Next they
noticed that these arches offered a convenient ledge on which to rest
the vaulting; and then it occurred to them that it would be equally
convenient to build ribs diagonally across each bay, following the lines
of the groins and intersecting at the crown, on which to rest the four
sections of the vault. Thus they discovered that they could erect a
skeleton of ribs to support the vaulting, which could be made of much
lighter material than that used in a barrel or groin vault without ribs,
and hence afford much greater freedom in construction. In fact, the
application of the rib vault to the roofing of a basilica was the greatest
constructional discovery of the Middle Ages. The builders now had the
means of lightening and raising the skeleton framework, until, two
hundred years later, it reached the majestic height of the nave of

[1] *St. Mark's*, Venice; *Angoulême* and *Périgueux*, France.

the Gothic cathedral (FIG. 424). But they were not guided by the structural problem alone. With a sensitiveness to design, they appreciated the rhythm and decorative effect of the ribs. Compare, for example, the heaviness and barrenness of the barrel vault with the lightness, rhythm, and emotional uplift of the Gothic nave.

We have now studied the principles on which the vault in *Sant' Ambrogio* was constructed. Let us see

Fig. 400. Marble Inlay on the Façade of San Michele. Lucca.

how it is supported. In FIG. 394 it will be noticed that the transverse arch springs from a pilaster rising from the floor; the diagonal rib, from an engaged column also rising from the floor; the longitudinal rib that incloses the double arcade separating the nave and aisle, from a thin pilaster; and the smaller arches of the arcade, from pilasters or engaged columns. That is, each rib of the skeleton frame of the vault is supported by a member rising either from the floor or from the second story, all of which unite in forming a compound or clustered pier.

These piers, however, are not adequate of themselves to support the weight of the roof. Cross walls are built over the transverse arches of the aisles at right angles to the clustered pier, where the thrust of the vault is concentrated (FIG. 395). These, together with the vaulted aisles, carry the thrust to the outer thick walls, which in turn are reinforced by pier buttresses at the points where the cross walls meet them. Thus while we have in *Sant' Ambrogio* a structural principle worked out for constructing the vaults, we still have the heavy walls for buttressing them. How this latter problem was met, we shall see later in France.

Sant' Ambrogio is important, therefore, because it is an early example of rib vaulting and clustered pier. These innovations, however, did not appear at once. The rib was known to the Roman and to builders in the East, and possibly its use was a rediscovery rather than a discovery. First these principles were tried out timidly in the aisles, then finally some courageous builder ventured to apply them in the nave. Even here at *Sant' Ambrogio* the timidity is seen in the fact that there

Fig. 401. St. Trophime. Arles. Portal. XII cent.

is no clerestory, as if the builder did not dare raise the ribs high enough
to allow for that. Hence the interior is low and dark.

These important structural innovations, however, did not develop
further in Italy. The Lombards themselves seemed too much embroiled
in political strife to continue a development so splendidly begun, while
the rest of Italy appeared to be more interested in decoration. An
example of this is the *Cathedral of Pisa* (FIG. 396), a basilica with vaulting over the aisles and a small dome over the crossing but a wooden
roof over the nave. The group as a whole — the cathedral, campanile
("Leaning Tower"), and baptistery (chiefly Gothic) — impresses one
with its splendor when compared with the more rugged *Sant' Ambrogio*. Blind arcades with colored marbles fill the ground story, and
open arcadings, subtly irregular in height and spacing, the stories
above.[1] It is not surprising to find arcading on many of the Italian
churches, for this was one of the most characteristic elements of Roman
architecture, and the numerous examples of it in Italy could hardly
fail to impress the Northerners and to suggest to them its use as a
means of impressive decoration.

External embellishment and attention to proportions transformed the
campanile, or bell tower, from the almost unbroken cylinder at *Sant'
Apollinare in Classe* (FIG. 313) into the generally rectangular (though
round at Pisa) towers, still free-standing, lightened by openings and
enlivened by moldings and color, which are one of the most stirring
forms in Italy in their fine balance between solidity and grace.

[1] See Ruskin's detailed analysis in his *Seven Lamps of Architecture*.

Fig. 402. Church at Moissac. Tympanum of the south portal. c. 1100.
Contrast, in style, with the tympanum of Fig. 401. (Giraudon)

Marble inlay is characteristic of this central Italian work. In *San Miniato* (Fig. 399) and the *Baptistery* of Florence both the exterior and the interior are decorated in geometric designs worked out in dark marble on white. In the arcades of the cathedral of *San Michele* at Lucca (Fig. 400) some of the columns are carved, and others are covered with various designs in marble inlay — spirals, zigzags, checker — while the spandrels are somewhat heterogeneously filled with geometric, and also grotesque, animal figures in white marble on a dark ground. The interesting play of light and shade in the galleries, combined with this free and vigorous type of decoration, produces a rich, almost fantastic effect, peculiarly characteristic of the imaginative vigor of the age.

Marble inlay as a floor decoration (Fig. 397) shows a great variety of patterns, including animal as well as geometric forms, some of which, especially the bird or animal figures inclosed in circles, closely resemble the textiles of the Near East (Fig. 379). A somewhat more elaborated form of inlay is found in the *Cosmati* work [1] (Fig. 398), which consists of colored marble slabs surrounded by borders, frequently interlacing, made up of small pieces of marble and glass cut into various shapes.

[1] So called from the Cosmati family in Rome, who were particularly skillful in this technique.

Fig. 403. St. Peter. On the jamb of the south portal of the church at Moissac (Fig. 402). Contrast with the static figures of Fig. 401.

Even the spiral flutings of columns are so decorated. The vigor of the curving borders, the exquisite detail of the inlays, and the rich colors brought out by the light marble into which they are set produce an ornamentation both rich and highly effective.

Turning to France and Spain,[1] here again we find widespread and diverse building in the Romanesque period. The southern part of France had been thoroughly Latinized by the Romans. Flourishing cities existed at Nîmes, Arles, and Orange, whose theaters, arches, temples, and baths could not but influence the medieval builders. We see their influence in the churches of *St. Gilles* (Gard) and *St. Trophime* (Arles). In plan *St. Trophime* is basilican with a cloister, as is usual in abbey churches, and is roofed with a barrel vault, as are the covered passages of the cloister. This plan and constructional system, with variations, is common in southern and central France as in the *Madeleine* (Vézelay), which has transverse arches with groin vaulting. Another plan and construction is illustrated by *St. Front* (Périgueux), the central type with the Greek cross roofed with domes on pendentives; or by *St. Pierre* (Angoulême), basilican in plan, and roofed with a series of domes.

To return to *St. Trophime,* the façade (FIG. 401) reveals the basilica

[1] The similarity of the Romanesque style in France and in Spain is largely due to the famous pilgrimage route to the shrine of St. James the Great at Santiago de Compostela, along which artistic conceptions and forms, if not actual copies, were conveyed by the pilgrims and by the builders and craftsmen who accompanied them. See A. K. Porter, *Romanesque Sculpture of the Pilgrimage Roads*, Marshall Jones, 1923, 10 vols., text, pp. 171 ff., for a discussion of the pilgrimage as one of the most vivid and influential institutions of the Middle Ages.

type with nave, clerestory, and lower side aisles, and is quite barren except for the richly carved portal. Above the plain base runs a broad band of decoration with columns resting on the backs of lions or grotesques, and with statues of saints in niches tied together by a continuous frieze. Above the door a sculptured tympanum surrounded by concentric, slightly pointed arches breaks the upper part and accents the entrance; a bracketed cornice parallel to the roof finishes the design. Thus the builder divided his space effectively, concentrating his ornament on the central band like a piece of embroidery on a plain garment, and setting it off by the contrasting plain surfaces about it and by the vigorous arches above the door. A closer inspection of the details shows that the brackets of the cornice, the Corinthian capitals, the fluted pilasters, the acanthus, and the fret are classical; the figures in the niches, the tympanum, and the friezes are related stylistically to Byzantine ivories and miniatures.

Fig. 404. Romanesque Ornament.

In the tympanum is the seated figure of Christ, surrounded by an aureole, one hand holding a book, the other raised in blessing. About him are grouped the four beasts of the Apocalypse, which symbolize the four evangelists — the winged man, St. Matthew; the winged lion, St. Mark; the winged ox, St. Luke; and the eagle, St. John. On the lintel below are the twelve Apostles, seated; to the left are the blessed going to heaven; to the right the damned, chained together and being led to hell. The representation of Christ surrounded by the symbolic beasts had already become a conventional representation in Christian art and is found very frequently, not only over the doorways of the churches but in the illuminated manuscripts, the ivories, and the enamels. For art in the Middle Ages was subject to the authority of the Church. As in Byzantine art, certain subjects must be represented

Fig. 405. St. Pierre. Angoulême.
1105–28. Note the domical vaulting.
See p. 284, note 1.

Fig. 406. Church at Saintes. Detail
of the carvings about the doorway.
XII cent. (Baudot)

in a certain way and placed in a certain position on the building, and the authorized use of symbols and attributes be strictly followed. Yet while the medieval sculptor or painter was limited by convention, still he could use his individual imagination to a surprising extent.

To illustrate this let us look at the south portal at *Moissac* (FIG. 402), which consists of a vestibule covered by a barrel vault, with both doorway and sides richly carved. In the tympanum we find the same subject and the same general arrangement as at *St. Trophime*, except for the addition of the angels and of the twenty-four elders arranged in zones below and on each side of the central group. But at *Moissac* the figures are filled with life and movement; they are even twisting and writhing; the draperies are fluttering, and the elders are straining their necks toward the figure of Christ. Thus, while the subject matter, the arrangement of the figures, and such details as the attributes are the same in both, yet the feeling is diametrically opposed. *St. Trophime* is tranquil and static, with all parts harmoniously related and balanced. *Moissac* is energetic and dynamic, with forceful oppositions in the movement surging through; the lower relief has a lineal quality (a mark of Northern art) peculiarly fitted in its dynamic rhythms to express the fervor of the Northerners, and for the sake of which the figures are twisted and distorted. A comparison of the *St. Peter* (FIG. 403) on the door jamb with one of the saints of *St. Trophime* will illustrate the difference perfectly, though in both styles the forms are

Fig. 407. St. Etienne, or Abbaye-
aux-Hommes. Caen. 1064–77.

Fig. 408. St. Etienne. Nave. Vaulting reconstructed c. 1135.

archaic, and the drapery, clouds, hair, and other details are expressed
by conventions with a linear beauty which adds to their decorativeness.

In looking at Romanesque portals one needs to recall that almost
no monumental sculpture had been produced since about 500 A.D.
The evolution of the figure arts and of Christian iconography had been
in the hands of the mosaicists, the fresco and miniature painters, and
the ivory-carvers. And when about 1100 sculpture on a large scale
began to revive, it took as a starting-point the forms of these craftsmen.

At *Angoulême* (Fig. 405) the sculpture, instead of being concentrated
at the portal, is more widely spread over the surfaces and with the
blind arcadings enriches the broad unbroken surfaces and at the same
time, because it is carved in the actual masonry, retains a unity with
it. *Angoulême*, like most Romanesque churches, is solid, firmly rooted,
and presents a picturesque massing of volumes — a rectangular basilica, domes, and a bell tower which is incorporated into the structure rather than free-standing, as in Italy.

Romanesque ornament (Figs. 403, 404, 406) is always spirited, infinitely varied, and highly decorative. On the lintel of the doorway
of *Moissac* (Fig. 402) we see, at each end of the lintel, a chimera-like
creature, reminiscent of the East, from whose mouth issue cords that
inclose finely carved rosettes, all slightly different and unequally spaced;
their ground is carved with various motifs. Fantasy manifests itself
particularly in the "storied capitals," where characters from the Bible,

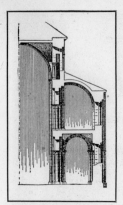

Fig. 409. St. Etienne. Caen. Section of the nave and aisle. (Dehio and Bezold)

and creatures of the imagination, centaurs, and hunters, many of Eastern origin, find a place, often intertwined with scrolls and foliage. Strikingly effective are many of the Romanesque recessed portals, about which was concentrated much of the decorative carving. One notes in particular that all this carving is an integral part of the stone capital or the stone masonry. In fact it *is* the stone, with its original surface retained but enlivened by the vigorous carving of conventional motifs of a calligraphic character organized into a highly decorative pattern.

Turning to northern France, we recall that this part of the country had been occupied by the Normans, who, like the other barbarians, had no notable arts of their own. Furthermore, the dwellers in northern France, unlike those in the southern part of the country, had no large Roman cities to teach them. Their own accomplishment, in which they were probably aided by builders from Lombardy who settled there, is illustrated by the *Abbaye-aux-Hommes* (FIG. 407).[1] The first impression of the church, as we think of *St. Trophime* and *Angoulême*, is its plainness and its rugged vigor. We notice that the façade with its two flanking square towers is divided into three vertical sections separated by pilaster buttresses and emphasized by a triple doorway, indicating a triple division on the interior — a nave and two side aisles — while the doorways and two rows of windows indicate that the structure is three stories high. Notice also the almost entire lack of decoration except the arcading in the upper stories of the towers. There is no monumental portal, no figure sculpture.

As we look at the interior (FIG. 408) we realize that here is something that we have not seen since we left *Sant' Ambrogio* in Milan (FIG. 394). There is a similarity in the principles of structure, such as the ribbed vaulting, the division of the nave into bays, and the clustered pier. But the most distinctive difference lies in the height of the vaults. At *Sant' Ambrogio* the builder, in his timidity, omitted the clerestory; in the *Abbaye-aux-Hommes* the Norman with the daring blood of the old Vikings in his veins had the courage to add it and thus to obtain both height and light.[2]

[1] The spires are a later addition. The original towers rose but three stories above the roof.

[2] The present vaults of the *Abbaye-aux-Hommes* are later than the original roof, but the arrangement of the piers indicates that the original plan must have been on the Lombard principle.

Fig. 410. Carved Doorway. Wood. c. 1200. Oslo Museum.

Fig. 411. Doorway of the Church at Kilpeck. XII cent. (The County Studio, Monmouth)

Let us see how the Norman buttressed his vaults. A cross section of this abbey (FIG. 409) shows us that the principle adopted was similar to that of *Sant' Ambrogio* (FIG. 395), that is, the heavy vaults and cross walls of the aisles are strong enough to hold the nave vaulting. But in the *Abbaye-aux-Hommes*, instead of a complete barrel vault over the aisle, a half-barrel vault springs from the outer wall to abut on the nave wall. Here it is evident that the builders realized that the thrust from the nave vaults was not equally distributed along the entire length of the nave wall, but concentrated at the points where the ribs converged, that is, at the clustered pier. Hence it followed in their understanding that much of the half-barrel buttressing vault was unnecessary; so when they built a neighboring church, the *Abbaye-aux-Dames*, they cut away, as it were, the unnecessary parts, leaving those sections only that abutted on the nave wall where the piers stood, and thus created a rudimentary flying buttress. But it was still concealed under the sloping roof of the aisle.

Thus in Normandy we find further development of the principles established at *Sant' Ambrogio*. The nave vaults have been lifted higher, admitting the clerestory as a means of lighting; the principle of the

Fig. 412. Cathedral. Bamberg. 1185–1274. For the plan of a church with two apses see Fig. 392.

flying buttress has been applied, making the whole structure much lighter; the triple façade, with its two flanking towers and triple portal, has become an acknowledgment of the internal structure. These principles, we shall see, reach their culmination in the Gothic cathedral.

The Norman builders carried with them to England the principles evolved in northern France and there built such massive, sturdy structures as *Durham Cathedral*, usually in a picturesque setting and characterized by a massive rectangular tower over the crossing. Norman ornament, developing apart from the highways of trade — which, as we have said, are always highways of ideas — was used at first very sparingly, and consisted of conventional motifs of which the zigzag, with variants, was important. In England, the Norman builders produced some very delightful doorways, such as those at *Iffley* and *Kilpeck* (FIG. 411). The thick Norman wall permitted a deeply recessed doorway, with a series of decorated shafts in the jambs and several orders of decorated arches surrounding the semicircular tympanum.

In Germany, the Rhine Valley became a very active center of building as well as of other arts, for the German has always been preëminent as a thorough craftsman. An abundance of excellent building stone led him early toward vaulted structures, although the great forests of Germany tempted him to wooden roofs. The cities of the valley were strongly organized politically and economically, and had rapidly become a firm stronghold of Christianity, with many abbey churches, such as the *Church of the Holy Apostles* at Cologne (twelfth to thirteenth century), and cathedrals, such as *Speyer* (eleventh to twelfth century), *Mainz* (chiefly thirteenth century), and *Bamburg* (FIG. 412). As the Rhine Valley was one of the great trade routes between northern and southern Europe, close relationships with Italy, especially Lombardy, are reflected in the fine vaultings based upon the Lombard system;

and also in the exterior arcadings reminiscent of *Pisa*. These cathedrals show not only structural excellence but a massive, picturesque appearance that results from the multiplicity of structural elements boldly and interestingly grouped. For the apse and towers are frequently used at both ends of the nave; [1] a polygonal tower rises over the crossing and also at the west end of the nave. But when the apse is repeated it deprives the building of the spacious portals that so distinguish the façade designs of the French cathedrals.

Fig. 413. Stave Church of Gol. 1000–1500. Now in the Bygdoe open air museum near Oslo.

Mention at least should be made of an individual variant of the Romanesque basilica in another material, the stave churches of Norway (FIG. 413). The wealth of timber in the forest-covered mountains of this land led to its almost exclusive, in fact prodigal, use in both secular and ecclesiastical building. With the coming of Christianity about 1000 the basilica plan was adopted, to which was added a low inclosing passage, like an extended narthex. The church was of solid timber construction, strong posts providing support with upright planks (staves) between, a vertical timber construction in contrast to the horizontal used in secular buildings and in the wood architecture of northern Russia (FIG. 344). Externally the building emphasizes verticality in its proportions and in its steep-pitched roofs. The additional passage affords not only ample gathering-space and protection for the supports of the building against rain and snow, but also repeats the roofs above, makes the building more compact and the base broader and more solid. About the portals the heavy timber is carved into low relief of great decorative beauty and of a peculiarly architectural quality, for it is carved in practically two planes and retains an extraordinary feeling of identity with the doorpost (FIG. 410). The designs are frequently very intricate, and combine natural, geometric,

[1] The reason for the double apsidal plan of the German Romanesque churches has not been satisfactorily explained.

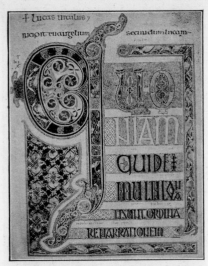 

Fig. 414. Quoniam Page from the Book of Lindisfarne (St. Cuthbert's Gospels). H. 13½ in. c. 700. British Museum, London. (British Museum)

Fig. 415. Page from the Liber Vitae. H. c. 10 in. XI cent. British Museum, London. (Herbert)

and zoömorphic motifs into rhythmic linear patterns similar in style to Celtic work. The roof lines were made fantastic by affixing conventionalized dragon heads and tails, the same motifs that the Viking builders and carvers attached to the prows and sterns of their ships.

C. PAINTING

While great series of frescoes decorated the stretches of wall space in the Romanesque churches, they have so progressively disappeared [1] that very little can be judged of them, except that they show the same type of work that we see in the illuminated manuscripts of the period, which therefore serve as the best criterion of Romanesque painting.

D. MINOR ARTS

As we looked at the ground plan of the monastery of *St. Gall* (FIG. 392), we noticed that rooms or separate buildings were provided for the various craftsmen, so that while some of the workers were clearing

[1] A considerable number of Romanesque paintings have been recovered from overpainting and whitewash, especially in Spain. Easily accessible are the frescoes from the apse of *Santa Maria de Mur*, Catalonia, now installed in the Boston Museum of Fine Arts.

Fig. 416. Monogram Page from the Book of Kells. H. c. 13 in. c. 700. Trinity College, Dublin.

the land, planting the gardens, and tending the cattle, others were carving the ivory crosiers, shaping gold chalices and reliquaries, and decorating them with jewels and enamels; others were copying and illuminating manuscripts, painting miniatures to illustrate the text, and fashioning splendid covers for them of gold and silver, ivory, jewels, and enamel. The point of view of these monks, and the relation of their art to their religion, are seen in a treatise on painting, enameling, metalworking, and other crafts written by a monk called Theophilus in the eleventh or twelfth century. The prologue of the third book reads:

"David, that most excellent of prophets . . . collecting himself with all the attention of his mind to the love of his Creator, uttered this saying among others: 'Lord I have loved the beauty of Thine house.' And — albeit a man of so great authority and of so deep an understanding called this house the habitation of the court of heaven, wherein God presideth over the hymning choirs of angels in glory that cannot be told . . . yet it is certain that he desired the adornment of the material house of God, which is the house of prayer. . . . Wherefore, most beloved son, make thou no long delay, but believe

Fig. 417. Gospel Cover. Of oak covered with plates of gold set with enamels and stones. H. 10 in. XII cent. Victoria and Albert Museum, London. (Victoria and Albert Museum)

in full faith that the Spirit of God hath filled thine heart when thou hast adorned His house with so great beauty and such manifold comeliness . . . Work therefore now, good man, happy in this life before God's face and man's, and happier still in the life to come, by whose labour and zeal so many burnt-offerings are devoted to God! Kindle thyself to a still ampler art, and set thyself with all the might of thy soul to complete that which is yet lacking in the gear of the Lord's house, without which the divine mysteries and the ministries of God's service may not stand; such as chalices, candelabra, thuribles, chrism-vases, crewets, shrines for holy relics, crosses, missals and such like, which the necessary use of the ecclesiastical order requireth. Which if thou wouldst fashion, begin after the manner thus following." [1] The spirit of devotion and reverence that characterizes this prologue of Theophilus not only permeated the monastery but was basic in the social solidarity of the community as a whole.

The manuscripts were largely religious in subject — copies of the Bible, in whole or in part, prayer and liturgical books — and were written in Latin.

A highly individual kind of illumination was that of the Celtic monks of Ireland and northern England, who had a preference for intricate initial letters that sometimes cover an entire page, as we see in the *Quoniam* page of the *Book of Lindisfarne* [2] (FIG. 414). The circular part of the Q is decorated with particularly fine spirals, while the motif of the all-over pattern filling the irregular space below is made by

[1] G. G. Coulton, *A Mediaeval Garner*, London, 1910, p. 166; see also A. P. Laurie, *Materials of the Painter's Craft in Europe and Egypt*, Lippincott, 1911, p. 152.

[2] This page contains the Latin word *Quoniam*, with which the Gospel of St. Luke begins. The *Book of Lindisfarne* is also known as *St. Cuthbert's Gospels*, because it was written in honor of St. Cuthbert, bishop of Lindisfarne.

interlacing four birds. The stems of
the letters and the borders are filled
with spirals, interlacing birds, and
elongated dogs, with dottings and
delicate diaper patterns as a background for the letters.

In the monogram page of the *Book
of Kells* [1] (FIG. 416) the background
and also the panels within the letters
are filled with various forms of decoration, some geometric, such as the
interlaced bands and knots, spiral
and quatrefoil; others naturalistic,
such as foliage, birds, reptiles, grotesques, and occasionally a human
form. All are interwoven with a
facility, an intricacy, and a fine
sweep of line that leave one as-
tounded at the possibility of such
execution, and also at the vigor,
fancy, and infinite variety found
in one initial. Comparable with
this illumination in intricacy of design and delicacy of brush work are

Fig. 418. Cover of the Psalter of
Melisenda. Ivory, set with turquoise and
rubies. H. 9 in. 1131–34. British Museum, London. (British Museum)

some of the *Korans* (FIG. 374). But in comparison with the latter,
the Celtic work is more varied, more sweeping in its linealism, and
more restrained in effect because it employs almost no gold. And one
should mention the fact that like the *Korans* these Celtic manuscripts,
in particular the *Book of Kells*, contain some of the most beautiful
calligraphy of the Middle Ages. The motive for the incredible patience
and utter disregard of time which must have characterized these artist-
monks is well epitomized in the colophon of the *Book of Lindisfarne* —
"For the love of God and St. Cuthbert."

Important work was produced also at Canterbury, and particularly
at Winchester, then the capital. Some of the illuminations are close
to Byzantine models and some, illustrated by the *Liber Vitae* [2] from

[1] The *Book of Kells* is a book of gospels and miscellaneous matter that came from
the monastery of Kells in Ireland. Records tell of a gold cover now lost. The monogram page contains the first three letters of the Greek word for Christ, chi, rho, and
iota (see p. 229, note 1). The chi occupies most of the space; the rho and iota, much
smaller, are found in the lower part.

[2] Literally *The Book of Life*, a book showing the rewards of good and evil, here
seen in the action of St. Peter, who in the upper row welcomes the blessed at the gate
of heaven; in the middle row, he rescues a soul from the clutches of a devil whom he
assails with his great key; below, he securely locks in hell the devils and the damned.

Fig. 419. Ardagh Chalice. Of silver, brass, and gilt bronze, with decoration in gold and silver filigree with enamels, blue glass, and amber. D. 9½ in. c. 700. Royal Irish Academy, Dublin. (Royal Irish Academy)

Winchester (FIG. 415), show an art of vigorous penwork with light washes of color, in which the figures have the same twisting movements, elongations, energy, and linear decorativeness as those in the carvings at *Moissac* (FIG. 402).

The covers for these books were as rich as possible, for the liturgical books were as sacrosanct as the vessels used on the altar. In FIG. 417 the rich effect is obtained through the combination of many materials. In the center panel is the figure of Christ, done in gold repoussé, surrounded by a narrow border containing an inscription in cloisonné enamel in opaque white on a luminous blue ground; the wider border is decorated with a conventionalized floral pattern, and both are set with stones irregular in size, shape, and color. The broad outer border is made up of alternating gold plaques with various jewels and filigree and enamel. The shimmering gold, enhanced by the massing of color, the luminous blue of the enamel that is all the deeper because of the opaque white and the rich color of the other stones, produce a richly decorative effect.

Another book cover, that of the *Psalter of Melisenda* (FIG. 418), is made of ivory, carved with a design of six interlaced circles surrounded by a border, and set with turquoise and rubies. The circles contain scenes from the life of David, and the intervening spaces, figures of the Vices and the Virtues. The border is composed of vine scrolls issuing from vases, interspersed with dolphins, birds, and interlacings, arranged with a great variety in details which contributes vitality to the design. The interlacings, for example, are not placed in the same relative position on the two long sides, but are varied on the right so as to accommodate the clasps; and the foliate motifs in the corners are quite different. The little figures, both in the circles and in the intermediate spaces, are depicted with dramatic power, quite characteristic of this age of the Crusades. Life is creeping into the outworn conventions of the Byzantine carvers, just as we have seen it infusing the work of the stone-carvers and the miniaturists.

Among the metalworkers, and they were many and important, the Celtic craftsman again produces individual work in style akin to the illuminations, with regard for difference of medium. Brooches, staffs, and ecclesiastical vessels of all kinds were constructed of various materials and decorated with enamels, jewels, repoussé, and filigree. The *Ardagh Chalice* (FIG. 419), for example, is a round bowl shape with two handles, a short stem, and a broad base, a design of strength rather than of elegance. The rich ornamentation neither overloads nor interferes with the structural lines, being concentrated about the handles, on the two disks on the body of the chalice, and in the borders that decorate the top and the foot. In examining the details we discern the spirals and the interlaced animal forms

Fig. 420. Chalice and Plate. Gold, with enamels, filigree, and vari-colored uncut stones. X cent. Nancy Cathedral. (Neurdein)

of the *Book of Kells* executed in gold and silver, worked both in repoussé and in filigree of almost incredible finesse.

Boldness rather than intricacy appears in the gold chalice and plate in the cathedral of Nancy (FIG. 420). The center of the plate is decorated with a five-lobed pattern and jewels; the border is made up of alternating enamel plaques, of both geometric and animal figures, and stones set in filigree work, and is finished on the inside with a tiny beading and on the outer edge with a braid pattern. The same general scheme of border decoration is carried out on the chalice, more slender in its proportions than the *Ardagh Chalice*, with a more narrow foot and more elaborately shaped handles. The stones are unevenly matched in shape and color, and together with the deep, luminous enamels form a scheme of decorative quality that expresses as clearly as the church at *Angoulême* the sturdy vigor of Romanesque times.

The bronze and iron workers of Hildesheim in Germany were another group of great craftsmen. Their bronze church doors and candlesticks were particularly famous for both their spirited designs and their masterly execution.[1]

[1] See the doors of *St. Michael* at Hildesheim, and the large Paschal candelabra at South Kensington, London, and in Milan.

E. SUMMARY

In every aspect of the Romanesque period we have observed enthusiasm, experimentation, accomplishment. Out of the chaos that marked the early part of the period order was emerging, largely through the steadying hand of the monastery. The barbarians, Christianized, were going to school to the old traditions of the Mediterranean civilizations, but were transforming them with the fresh vitality of the North. North, South, and East were mingling. As Ralph Adams Cram says: "The awe of the dark forests and fierce seas was still on them [the Northerners], and strange apocryphal beasts, fantastic herbage, impossible flowers, all knotted and convoluted in runic designs, became the substance of their decorative sculpture. There is something of terror and much of grotesque in their work, but above all a brilliant decorative sense and a quality of wild freedom that, curbed at last by sound law, became the noble liberty of Gothic art." [1]

In a certain sense, Romanesque is a preparation for Gothic, an archaic prelude to an accomplished climax. Yet like every archaic art it displays its own kind of accomplishment in the power and decorative beauty of its forms. In this expression of a newly awakened Europe the force of the Northerners manifests itself in a dynamic, highly decorative linealism, an abstract force that permeates and re-creates traditional forms.

BIBLIOGRAPHY

Aars, Harald, ed., *Norsk kunsthistorie*, Oslo, 1925–27, Vols. I–II
Adams, Henry, *Mont-Saint-Michel and Chartres*, Houghton Mifflin, 1913
Allen, J. R., *Celtic Art in Pagan and Christian Times*, Jacobs, 1908
Baltrušaitis, Jurgis, *La stylistique ornementale dans la sculpture romane*, Paris, 1931
Baum, Julius, ed., *Romanesque Architecture in France*, Dutton, 1912
Belloc, Hilaire, *The Book of the Bayeux Tapestry*, Putnam, 1914
Clapham, A. W., *English Romanesque Architecture*, Oxford Press, 1931–34, 2 vols.
Coffey, George, *Guide to the Celtic Antiquities of the Christian Period*, Dublin, 1910
Coulton, G. G., ed., *A Mediaeval Garner*, London, 1910
Cunynghame, H. H., *European Enamels*, Putnam, 1906
Dawson, Mrs. Nelson, *Enamels*, McClurg, 1908
Focillon, Henri, *L'art des sculpteurs romans*, Paris, 1931
Hammett, R. W., *Romanesque Architecture of Western Europe*, Architectural Book Publishing Co., 1927
Hauttmann, Max, *Die Kunst des frühen Mittelalters*, Berlin, 1929
Jackson, Sir T. G., *Byzantine and Romanesque Architecture*, University of Chicago Press, 1913, 2 vols.

---

[1] "The Architecture of the Middle Ages," in American Institute of Architects, *The Significance of the Fine Arts*, Marshall Jones, 1923, Pt. I, p. 75.

Jameson, A. B., *Sacred and Legendary Art*, Houghton Mifflin, 1911, 2 vols.

Lethaby, W. R., *Mediaeval Art*, new ed., Scribner, 1913

Maritain, Jacques, *Art and Scholasticism*, Scribner, 1930

Markham, V. R. (Mrs. James Carruthers), *Romanesque France*, Dutton, 1929

Maskell, A. O., *Ivories*, Putnam, 1905

Millar, E. G., *English Illuminated Manuscripts from the Xth to the XIIIth Century*, Paris, 1926

—— —— *English Illuminated Manuscripts of the XIVth to XVth Centuries*, Paris, 1928

—— —— ed., *The Lindisfarne Gospels*, Oxford Press, 1924

Porter, A. K., *Medieval Architecture*, Yale University Press, 1912, 2 vols.

—— —— *Romanesque Sculpture of the Pilgrimage Roads*, Marshall Jones, 1923, 10 vols.

Ricci, Corrado, *Romanesque Architecture in Italy*, Brentano's, 1925

Rindge, A. M., *Sculpture*, Harcourt, Brace, 1929

Robinson, S. F. H., *Celtic Illuminative Art*, Dublin, 1908

Saunders, O. E., *History of English Art in the Middle Ages*, Oxford Press, 1932

Strzgowski, Josef, *Early Church Art in Northern Europe; with Special Reference to Timber Construction and Decoration*, Harper, 1929

Sullivan, Sir Edward, *Book of Kells*, London, 1920

Swartwout, R. E., *The Monastic Craftsman*, Cambridge, England, 1932

Warner, Sir G. F., *Illuminated Manuscripts in the British Museum*, London, 1899, 1900, series 1–2

See also the General Bibliography, pp. 749–751.

CHAPTER XIII

Gothic Art

(about 1150–1550 A.D.)

A. HISTORICAL BACKGROUND

The word "Gothic," in the sense of "barbarian," was a term of reproach applied to medieval buildings by the architects of the Renaissance, who found their only ideal in the architecture of Greece and Rome. The Gothic cathedral, however, is the highest expression of an age that was vigorous in its civic life, intensely religious, and profoundly intellectual. Rising in the midst of the houses that huddled closely about it (FIG. 422), not only did it dominate the town, but it stood as a center for the activities of the people, all of whom it was large enough to hold when the whole town gathered for the Christmas or Easter celebration, or to see a mystery play. The market place, the shop, and the home were situated literally in the shadow of the great church; and so interwoven were religious and secular activities in the Middle Ages that life presented a unified whole rather than the segregations of modern times. Let us look at some of the factors in the civilization which thus manifested itself.

Politically stronger kings, such as Philip Augustus (1180–1223) and

Fig. 421. Château of Coucy.
Restored. (Viollet-le-Duc)

Louis IX (St. Louis; 1226–70), were holding in check the feudal lords, though here and there such a baron as the Sieur de Coucy, protected by moat, thick walls, and a great donjon (Fig. 421), could support his boast, "I am not king, nor prince, nor duke, nor even count; I am the lord of Coucy." In distinction from the Romanesque period, when life was chiefly rural and monastic, the Gothic age was one of towns, with their merchant guilds, growing in number and power. Revolting from the feudal domination of the baron or the bishop, one by one they became independent communes, robust and vigorous with a growing sense of freedom and expansion, resulting from the opening-up of intercourse with neighboring countries and the Near East through the Crusades. Economically, this intercourse stimulated commercial activity and brought wealth.

Religiously, the thirteenth century saw the culmination of enthusiasm that had been developing since the year 1000. Under a strong line of popes, such as Innocent III, the Church reached the pinnacle of temporal as well as of spiritual power. The monastery, having fulfilled its purpose of reforming the Church from within, declined in power, while attention was focused upon the churches of the towns where the bishops lived. Hence we see the rise of the great cathedrals. The higher clergy had developed the creed and the ritual until they had become subtle and complex, far above the comprehension of the mass of the people, whose religion nevertheless was intense, manifesting itself in the mystery and miracle plays and in the worship of relics. Many of the latter were believed to be miracle-working and, carefully protected in reliquaries (Fig. 460) of gold and silver inlaid with precious stones and enamels, were carried through the land, curing the sick and obtaining large sums of money for the erection of the church to house the relic. So intense was the enthusiasm that at Chartres, for example, all the people, old and young, prince and peasant, hitched themselves to carts and dragged great loads of stone to build the cathedral.[1]

But a new far-reaching element was altering religious ideas — the

[1] For a full account, see the letter of Haymo, an eyewitness, as translated in A. K. Porter, *Medieval Architecture*, Yale University Press, 1912, 2 vols., Vol. II, pp. 151 ff.

Fig. 422. Chartres, the Town and the Cathedral. (N. D. Photo)

Fig. 423. Cathedral of Notre Dame. Chartres. Chiefly XII–XIII cent. (N. D. Photo)

Fig. 424. Chartres. Nave, looking east. L. 418 ft.; w. 110 ft.; h. 118 ft.

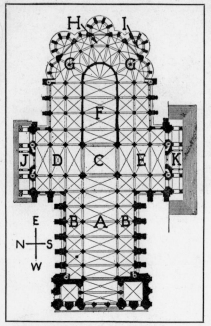

Fig. 425. Chartres. Plan. As is usual, the cathedral faces west. *A*, nave; *B*, aisles; *C*, crossing; *D*, north transept; *E*, south transept; *F*, choir; *G*, chevet; *H*, ambulatory; *I*, apsidal chapel; *J*, north porch; *K*, south porch.

Franciscan movement. In 1210 St. Francis of Assisi, in protest against the growing internal degradation of the Church, clad in a rough peasant's cloak, barefoot, with no money, began traveling about, with his small band of followers, preaching the creed of poverty, chastity, and obedience and inspiring the people with his own gentleness and radiant love for all life. The birds, the animals, the crickets, the trees, and the sun — everything in nature was a part of God's great universe, a brother, to be loved and respected. Gradually there came about a change in point of view — a change from the medieval ideal of focusing upon the life to come, for which this life was but a preparation, to a realization of the value of this life for itself, for the beauty to be seen all about and for a legitimate joy in nature. Such a realization turned men's eyes toward an observation of nature that revealed itself early in the Gothic age, and found its culmination in the individualism and secularization of the Renaissance.

Another aspect of medieval life reveals itself in the cathedral — the intellectual. It was a period of great learning. Universities were springing up, and the passion of the age for encyclopedic knowledge we observe in the work of Vincent of Beauvais, who attempted to classify all knowledge under four headings, which he called *The Four Mirrors:* first, the mirror of nature, which included scenes of creation, vegetable and animal ornament, monsters and grotesques; second, the mirror of science or instruction, which included human labor, the handicrafts, and the seven arts; third, the mirror of morals, which revealed the vices and virtues; and, fourth, the mirror of history, which related the stories of the Old and New Testaments, the tales of the apocryphal books, and the lives of the saints. And the age, not content with gathering this knowledge into a book, carved it all in stone on the

Fig. 426. Cathedral of Chartres.

portals of the cathedral, on the capitals, and high up on the buttresses and towers; and pictured it in vivid colors in the windows.[1]

Everyday life in the towns was vigorous and democratic, each person contributing to the life of the community. To be sure, the streets were narrow and dark; and there was little sanitation, so that plagues, once started, easily wiped out great masses of mankind. At the feudal courts life was festive and gay, and from hall to hall the troubadours traveled, singing their songs of love and adventure.[2]

B. ARCHITECTURE AND SCULPTURE

As we have said, the highest achievement of the age was the cathedral, which is an epitome in stone of medieval life. Unlike Romanesque architecture, which was diverse and widely scattered, the Gothic is distinctly French and in its purest form narrowly restricted to the Île de France, though it manifested itself in varying forms in other localities.

To understand the cathedral, let us travel about fifty-five miles

[1] For a fuller description and symbolic meaning, see Emile Mâle, *Religious Art in France, XIIIᵗʰ Century*, Dutton, 1913.

[2] Vivid pictures of life in this period are found in the manuscripts, especially the calendars, in which the activity typical of the month is illustrated — the feast and the hawking party, sowing and reaping, and hunting the wild boar for the Christmas feast (Fig. 455). Henry Adams, *Mont-Saint-Michel and Chartres*, Houghton Mifflin, 1930, is especially recommended for its sympathetic insight into the spirit of the age.

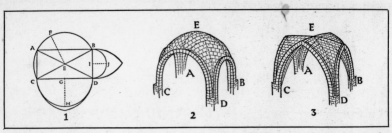

Fig. 427. The Value of the Pointed Arch. (1) *ABCD* is an oblong bay to be vaulted. *BC* is the diagonal rib; *DC*, the transverse; and *BD*, the longitudinal. If circular ribs are erected, their heights will be *EF*, *GH*, and *IJ*. The result will be a domical vaulting (2) irregular in shape because of the unequal height of the ribs; and with the longitudinal arch too low to admit of a clerestory. A building so vaulted is low and dark, like *Sant' Ambrogio* (Fig. 395). The problem, then, is to bring the crowns of all the ribs to the same height as that of the diagonal rib *E*. This can be done by pointing the lower ribs. The result is a lighter, more flexible system, affording ample space for a clerestory (3).

southwest of Paris to Chartres and there study in detail, as a typical example, the cathedral of *Notre Dame de Chartres*.[1] As we approach (FIG. 422), we notice how it looms above the compact town, a bulky mass culminating in two spires. A nearer view (FIG. 423) reveals the façade, with a dominant note of quiet strength and majesty, for it is simple and sincere and, with the exception of the northern tower, sober in decoration. The façade is divided vertically into three parts — a central division marked by the portal, three lancet windows, a rose, and an arcade; and two flanking towers that reach up into tall spires. The design, however, is not symmetrical, the most striking irregularity being in the towers, one of which is sturdy and plain, the other higher, more slender, and ornate; and the division into stories is not uniform. These irregularities, however, which are due to different periods of building, do not disturb the balance of the composition.

Of the towers, the south, or *Old Tower*, is much the simpler and sturdier of the two, harmonizing better with the general composition than does the slenderer, more ornate north tower built in the style of three hundred years later. The effect of the *Old Tower* is marred by the arcading and the rose, which bring the central part of the façade higher than was originally planned; for the tower was intended

[1] The present cathedral dates from the fire of 1134, which destroyed the old basilica on the site. The west façade was built by 1150. To gain space in the nave (FIG. 424), this façade, which had been built behind the towers, was moved forward until flush with the west end of the towers, its present position. The south tower was completed between 1180 and 1194, when a great fire destroyed all the church except parts of the western end. Rebuilding proceeded rapidly and the new cathedral, the present one, was dedicated in 1260. The northern and southern portals were added during the thirteenth century, and the northern spire between 1506 and 1512.

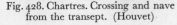

Fig. 428. Chartres. Crossing and nave
from the transept. (Houvet)

Fig. 429. Chartres. Section of the nave
showing the "flying buttresses."

to rise freely from the third story and hence is "hunched up by half
a rose and a row of kings." [1] But we instinctively feel its sober strength,
quiet harmony, and reposeful lines and proportions. It rises from a
firm, square base and is decorated with blind arcades, splayed windows,
and pilaster buttresses. At the point of transition from the square
tower to the octagonal spire — and this is the most difficult problem
of the builder — the work becomes lighter, with more frequent openings and small pinnacles that lead directly to the towering spire; but
so skillfully is this transition made that one is quite unaware how gradually and subtly it took place.

Before studying the decoration of the façade, let us look at the structural principles that produced such a cathedral. The ground plan
(FIG. 425) is that of an elaborated early Christian basilica. By bringing the transept near the center of the nave and lengthening out the
choir, the T-shaped plan of the early basilica (FIG. 308) has become
cross-shaped. The apse has developed into a complicated form called
the *chevet*,[2] which includes not only the apse itself but the surrounding
aisles, known as ambulatories, or apsidal aisles, and the chapels opening from them (FIG. 426).

With this plan in mind, we enter the cathedral (FIG. 424). In the

[1] Adams, *op. cit.*
[2] Note that the apse is the full height of the nave, but the ambulatories and chapels,
though vaulted, are but one story high and over them spring the flying buttresses.
See also FIG. 441.

Fig. 430. Chartres. Western, or Royal, Portal. So called because on the central tympanum is represented Christ as King of Kings. c. 1145. (Houvet)

quiet and subdued light, one is overwhelmed by a feeling of mystery
and exaltation; for by swiftly rising verticals, rhythmically repeated
down the deep vista of the nave, one is lifted as if in an effort to reach
heights just beyond the mysterious shadows high up in the vaults; and
another note of exaltation is added by the rich color of the windows,
spreading its radiant luminosity over the gray of the stone. Mechanical
skill alone could not have produced such a nave. Everywhere one is
aware of the sincere religious conviction that inspired it.

As we think back to *Sant' Ambrogio* (Fig. 394), low, dark and heavy,
and even to *St. Etienne* (Fig. 408), where advance over *Sant' Ambrogio*
came about through the daring of the Normans, we ask ourselves what
enabled the Gothic builders to erect their lofty naves. It was three
things primarily — ribbed vaulting, the pointed arch, and the flying
buttress — by means of which they produced a building that was not
only uplifting in emotional appeal, but highly intellectual in organic
unity.

Let us explain this term "organic unity" more fully. As we look again
at the nave of *Chartres*, we recognize the ribbed vaulting, but we see that
the arches are pointed rather than round. By studying Fig. 427 we
understand why the pointed arch could give height and light where the
round one could not; and that was what these builders were trying to

Fig. 431. Chartres. Western Portal: A Queen. (Houvet)

Fig. 432. Chartres. Western Portal: July. (Houvet)

secure — height for expression, and light because of the dull Northern climate.

Given, then, a method of securing these two essentials, how is the vaulting stably supported in its lofty position? In FIG. 428 we see that the great piers at the crossing are of the clustered or compound type such as we saw in *Sant' Ambrogio*, that is, each rib of the vaulting, diagonal, transverse, and longitudinal, has its individual supporting member in the clustered pier. The consistent application of this principle makes a massive pier at the crossing necessary to support the tower over the crossing that the original plans called for but which was never built. It also affords an effective accent at this part of the cathedral. Along the nave and transept, however, the builders used a single shaft with four engaged columns (FIG. 428) — quite adequate to carry their load — three of which rise one story only to support the arches of the ground-story arcade and the transverse arches of the aisle; the fourth, that facing the nave or the transept, rises from the base to the vaulting, interrupted by stringcourses only, and at that point meets the downward thrust of the great transverse ribs of the nave. Smaller shafts, which carry the diagonal and longitudinal ribs, rise from the capitals of the ground-story arcade.[1] The same deviations from regularity that

---

[1] A comparison of the piers of several of the great cathedrals, such as *St. Denis, Senlis, Sens, Paris, Amiens*, and *Reims*, will reveal an interesting variety of methods of treating the problem of the compound pier.

Fig. 433. Chartres. Western Portal: Kings and Queens. (Monuments Piot)

are found in the buildings of many peoples — in the *Ziggurat of Ur*, the *Parthenon*, the arcades of *Pisa*, to cite a few — appear in Gothic in the unequally spaced piers, and in the curved stringcourses.

A study of one bay in detail indicates a clearly marked division into three stories: the ground-story arcade that separates the aisle from the nave; the triforium, a low second story pierced with four arched openings separated by colonnettes;[1] and the clerestory, which consists of tracery filled with glass, reaching to the crown of the vaulting (FIG. 428). An obvious characteristic of the system is the relatively small amount of wall space in comparison with the openings. The long reaches of uninterrupted surface in the basilica have given way to this light, open arrangement, with the clerestory entirely filled with apertures for the admittance of the light. But this suppression of wall also eliminated any space for mural decoration such as the frescoes or mosaic that so enriched the interiors of the early Christian churches. Compensation for this the Gothic builders found in stained glass, which was just reaching a climax in its development. Eagerly seizing upon its possibilities, they substituted great areas of glass for stone, producing a decoration of deep, glowing color, richer and more luminous even than the Byzantine mosaics.

We have now explained the pointed ribbed vaulting and the clustered pier from which it springs. The third vital element involved, if the vault is to stand, is efficient buttressing; otherwise the thin walls will be pushed out by the great weight and the whole structure will collapse, like a house of cards. We have already learned that buttressing is needed only at the points where the thrust of the vault is concentrated. This thrust, which exerts pressure both downward and outward, is concentrated partly on the piers and partly at a point about a third of the way up the curve of the rib, a point called the *haunch*, so that here the

---

[1] As this story frequently had three openings, it became known as the *triforium*, meaning *three-pierced;* sometimes a gallery is built here over the aisles.

thrust must be met by
a counterthrust. This
is the function of the
flying buttress.

With this in mind
let us study the but-
tresses (FIGS. 426, 429).
From the ground rise
massive pier buttres-
ses, each on the axis of
a clustered pier, in
line with the trans-
verse arches of both
the nave and the aisle
(FIG. 425). They di-
minish in thickness as
they rise, and from
each spring two half-
arches, the flying but-
tresses, which abut on
the nave wall, one at
and slightly above the
capital of the pier, and
the other at the crown
of the ribs. The lower

Fig. 434. Chartres. Northern Porch, detail.
c. 1205-70. (N. D. Photo)

arch is double with an open arcade between, an unusual feature. Furthermore, the nave wall between is stiffened by engaged columns. The
buttresses of the *Abbaye-aux-Hommes* (FIG. 409), hidden beneath the roof
with their place of abutment too low, have here come out into the open,
frankly revealed and efficiently constructed. Thus the thrusts of the
vaults are counterbalanced and the whole structure is dynamically
stable.[1]

Organic structure alone, however, though fundamentally important,
deals with but one aspect of the Gothic cathedral. Decoration plays
an equally important part. Two kinds of ornament the Gothic artists
used primarily — sculpture and stained glass. The purpose of the
former was chiefly to enrich the portals; of the latter, to form a luminous decoration for the interior.

Turning again to the western façade of *Chartres*, we see that upon the

[1] As in the case of the clustered pier, no two cathedrals show the same treatment
of the flying buttress, though the underlying structural principle is the same. *Sant'
Ambrogio*, *Abbaye-aux-Hommes*, *Abbaye-aux-Dames*, *St. Germer de Fly*, *Soissons*, *Chartres*,
Amiens, *Notre Dame de Paris*, *Reims*, and *Beauvais* illustrate the general evolution. The
trend is toward lightness without sacrifice of structural stability.

Fig. 435. Tree of Jesse Window.
Detail. Chartres. XII cent.

Fig. 436. The Goat, a Sign of the
Zodiac. Western Portal, Chartres.

triple portal (FIG. 430), which occupies the central division only of the
façade, is concentrated the elaborate sculpture, carved of the same
material, which enlivens the stone masonry and accents the entrance.
The first impression is that of perfect architectural unity. In the central
tympanum is the figure of *Christ* surrounded by the four beasts of the
Apocalypse, in every respect very close to *St. Trophime* (FIG. 401). The
linealism of its conventional forms contributes to its decorative value,
while the austerity of the central figure combined with benevolence
and pity for the humanity whom he is blessing conveys to one entering
the church the innermost meaning of that for which the Church stood.
In the rows of kings and queens on either side of the doorway [1] (FIG. 433)
we see elongated figures standing rigidly erect, compact, with arms
close to the body, never projecting beyond the contour. The long lines
of the drapery are predominantly vertical, reminiscent of flutings, so
that the whole effect is that of a column. And this is what the artist was
striving for — to use the human figure to adorn a column and yet not
lose the feeling of the column. This effect is still further enhanced by
the background of rich carvings on the pedestals and intermediate
shafts. As representations of kings and queens, they are richly clad in
embroidered robes, befitting royalty; each carries a scepter, a book,

[1] The unequal height of the figures is probably due to the fact that they were
assembled, after the fire, from different parts of the building. The plain shafts indicate repair.

Fig. 437. Notre Dame. Paris.
1163–1235.

Fig. 438. Notre Dame. Amiens.
1220–88.

or a scroll, and many wear crowns. In the heads are expressed great variety and marked individuality. One of the kings shows a "mingling of firmness, dignity, shrewdness, even a little levity and vanity in the arched brow, but also intelligence and coolness in time of peril," while the queen (Fig. 431) is an epitome of gracious nobility. At the same time these figures are primarily of stone, of the same material and texture as that of the building itself and carved in a manner that is suitable to a rather coarse stone. The sculptors have consistently carved this stone to serve a definite function and not to produce a realistic representation of kings and queens.

Throughout the portal, then, first, there is the feeling for function as seen in the restraint and conventionalization of the figure so as to adapt it to the place that it was to occupy; second, there runs through the figures a living quality of marked individuality, with a serene emotionalism born of sincere religious conviction.

Two details of the left and right doorways we must notice. Upon the orders of the arches about the left tympanum is carved a calendar. Why should such a subject be represented upon a cathedral? Recalling the *Four Mirrors* of Vincent of Beauvais, we read in the *Mirror of Instruction* that while man can be saved only through a redeemer, still he can prepare himself for redemption by labor and knowledge. Hence the sculptor pictures man's typical occupation for each month together

Fig. 439. Notre Dame. Reims.
1211–90.

with the appropriate sign of the zodiac (FIG. 436). *July*, for example (FIG. 432), is represented by a man cutting corn. In type he probably represents the peasant whom the carver saw every day in the fields; he wears a tightly fitting round cap with a plaited border; standing knee-deep in the stubble, he is cutting the grain with his sickle; behind him are two decorative trees, admirably filling the space. In the niche at the right stands *April*, wreathed with flowers. In all these little pictures there is a mingling of the fanciful and the simple homely scenes of everyday life, very spontaneous, and very close to the heart of the people.

Another glance at the ground plan of *Chartres* (FIG. 425) shows that the transepts terminate in deep porches approached by a broad flight of steps. In FIG. 434 we see the north porch, a large open portico, each of its triple divisions vaulted over and capped with a pediment. As on the western portal, rows of figures flank the doorways; the tympana are filled with sculptured reliefs; all the orders of the arches are carved with figures and the intervening spaces decorated with trefoil ornament. The south porch is similar in general design. Both form effective entrances, rich in detail and harmonious in design with the whole façade.

The subject matter of the sculpture of the north porch is taken from the Old Testament and the life of the Virgin, fitting subjects for that portal which looks to the cold and dark of the North, forming a prelude to the life of Christ that finds its place on that portal which faces the warmth and sunshine of the South. On both porches are found representations of scenes from the creation, the Vices and Virtues, and the lives of saints and martyrs, thus continuing the illustrations from the *Four Mirrors*.

As we look at some of the figures from these north and south portals (FIG. 434), we realize that this is a different art from that of the western portal. The figures are well proportioned; they appear to stand upon their feet and turn their bodies and heads so that we feel that a bodily structure exists beneath the drapery, which falls in naturalistic folds. So, too, the carvings on the capitals and bases reveal a tendency away from the conventional to the naturalistic. During the century that in-

tervened between the building of the
western and the side portals, the Gothic
sculptor had been turning to nature,
and in his eagerness to imitate it had
sacrificed that complete subordination
to architectural needs which characterized the western portal. He has not
lost his sense of design, however. The
beautiful long sweeping lines of the
drapery give the figures something of
the architectural feeling; but they are
not so impressive or so essentially a
part of the building as are the kings
and queens at the western doorway. In
the *Visitation* particularly do we notice
the sweep of line in the delicate, almost
clinging drapery.

Beneath each statue or underneath
the bracket upon which it stands are
small figures which not only are decorative but also bear some symbolical
or historical relation to the statue
above. Beneath the feet of *Christ*, for
example, are the lion and the dragon:
"The young lion and the serpent shalt

Fig. 440. Rouen Cathedral. From
c. 1200; façade, 1507–30. The tower
on the right is the Tour de Beurre
(Butter Tower), so called because it
was built with funds secured in return for permission to eat butter during Lent, 1485–1507.

thou trample under foot." These little figures are added to symbolize
Christ's conquest over evil. Thus we see on these portals not only the
stories from the Bible and the legends, and the illustrations from the
Four Mirrors, but interwoven with them all a whole world of figures
and attributes which are symbolic.[1]

Sculpture, we have seen, was used chiefly on the exterior, to adorn
the portals. The second factor in decoration, the stained glass, ornamented the interior. As we stand in the nave of *Chartres* and look up at
the three lancets and the rose window of the western façade, we are
aware of a mass of the richest color imaginable, glowing like a cluster
of brilliant gems, chiefly deep reds and blues like rubies and sapphires,
relieved by a little white or lighter hue. Upon closer inspection, however, we find that these windows are carefully worked out pictures full
of meaning and symbolism. To illustrate this we shall study the *Tree
of Jesse* window (FIG. 435). In the lowest panel Jesse is lying upon a
couch; from his loins rises the stem of a tree that branches out into
somewhat conventional scrolls inclosing seated figures of the ancestors

[1] For the symbolic interpretation of Gothic sculpture, see Mâle, *op. cit.*

Fig. 441. Reims. North Side. Reims, as planned, would have carried seven spires, two at each of the portals and one, the highest, over the crossing. (N. D. Photo)

of Christ; the next to the upper panel contains the Virgin, and the upper, the figure of Christ, with the dove descending from above. On either side of the panels in semicircular spaces are prophets who foretell the coming of Christ. A border of interlacing lines and conventionalized flowers resembling those in the central panel completes the design. The first and greatest impression that this window makes is one of radiant, harmonious decoration. Its chief characteristics are the lack of background, of landscape, or any feeling for distance; all is linear in one plane, with a considerable amount of simplification and conventional representation, both in the human figures and in the forms of nature. The purpose of the glassmaker was not to give a naturalistic representation with background and distance, but to keep his design flat with all details subordinated to design and color harmony.

Let us follow a glassworker as he makes such a window. With the dimensions of the window in hand, he draws his design in full size upon the whitened boards that form the bench upon which he is building up his window, indicating with heavy black lines the iron bars that are necessary to hold the window firmly; for a large sheet of glass and lead is too pliable to withstand the force of storms. These bars must play into the design and not obstruct it; hence by cutting the space into small areas they determine the main lines of the composition. Having drawn in the figures to fill these areas, he begins putting in the glass. At hand he has sheets of glass which has been colored, not by being painted, but by having coloring matter, chiefly metal, added while the glass was in a molten state. From these sheets, with

Fig. 442. Reims. Buttress of the chevet,   Fig. 443. A Pinnacle with
spanning a double aisle.   Crockets and Finial.

his hot iron or diamond point, he cuts tiny pieces, usually not more than an inch long, to fit his designs, a separate piece for each color or shade of color. He pieces them together with strips of lead, because this metal is soft and pliable; and solders the strips where they join. Thus he builds up his design, piece by piece, always mindful first, as he works in his reds and blues with whites, yellows, and greens, of the harmony that will result when the light penetrates the window and blends the tiny pieces into a unified whole. Hence he does not hesitate, when his design calls for an illustration of the Prodigal Son feeding the swine, to make one pig green, two blue, and one red, because it is more important for the final effect to have those colors at certain spots than to follow the color of nature. And again, with the final effect in mind, when he wants a rich purple he does not always make purple glass, but places side by side small bits of red and blue, allowing the eye to mix them at a distance, and so obtaining a much richer hue than by coloring the glass purple. Thus the twelfth-century glassmakers used the same principle as the French Impressionists of the nineteenth century who juxtaposed their red and blue pigment on the canvas for the eye to mingle into purple from afar. Here and there in the designs he needs somewhat larger pieces of glass on which must be painted a face, a hand, or a bit of drapery. With a brownish

Fig. 444. Detail from the Southern Transept, Notre Dame, Paris.

Fig. 445. Smiling Angel. Reims, detail of the Western Portal. XIII cent. Contrast with Fig. 433.

enamel, in fine, firm strokes, he draws these details and fires the pieces (thus fusing the enamel with the glass) and then leads them into the design. Thus the glassworker was guided by the same principle as the sculptor, namely, decorative value determined by architectural needs. At the same time, a vital content coheres with visual effectiveness.

While sculpture and stained glass formed the chief decorative elements of the cathedral, polychromy and certain accessories also played an important part. Color and gilding were applied, apparently, to any available wall space, to capitals, ornamental details, and statues. Of this, because of time and the destructive Northern climate, nothing but faint traces now remains. Furthermore, accessories of the service — the rich robes of the clergy, the gold and silver jeweled crosses, reliquaries, and chalices, the carved ivory crosiers, and the great tapestries — testify to the love of color and contribute to the magnificence expressive of the religious exaltation of the times.

Many other great Gothic cathedrals were built, particularly in the thirteenth century in France, noteworthy of which were *Notre Dame* in Paris (FIG. 437), *Amiens* (FIG. 438), and *Reims*[1] (FIG. 439). Each was constructed on the same basic principles as *Chartres*. Only in detail and ornamentation do they differ. All are incomplete, and the impression of squatness produced in some observers would have been eliminated had the towers been carried up by spires to the intended

Fig. 446. Capital of a Clustered Pier. Reims. (Giraudon)

height. In façade composition, the tendency is toward elaboration. *Notre Dame* (FIG. 437) has sobriety and repose due to the almost classic balance of line and the quiet unadorned spaces of wall and buttress; at *Amiens* (FIG. 438) there is richness of detail, effective interplay of line, and richness of light and shade; at *Reims* (FIG. 439) decoration has become excessive and the vertical line predominant; at *Rouen* (FIG. 440) ornamentation is supreme. We notice in all of these façades the decorative beauty and the suggestion of welcome in the deeply recessed portals that extend the width of the façade. The flying buttress also developed from the simple, robust type of *Chartres* into the lighter and more elaborate type of *Reims*, which, with its niches, pinnacles, crockets, and finials (FIGS. 441, 442, 443), contributes to the soaring quality of the cathedral.

The sculpture of these great thirteenth-century cathedrals, while akin to that of the north and south portals of *Chartres*, still shows marked differences. The *Vierge Dorée*, a gracious virgin, stands holding the child and playfully smiling; three angels, two in rapid movement, hold the shell-adorned nimbus. She stands so that the figure is built on a great sweeping curve; the drapery, girded high, falls in broad folds. The delicate naturalistic carvings and the fluttering angels enhance the graciousness of this gentle, smiling queen. In his tendency toward naturalism, the sculptor has altered his type, and for the austerity and dignity symbolic of the queen of heaven of the eleventh and twelfth centuries has substituted elegance and the serene joy of the more human type of mother and child. Possibly the most characteris-

---

[1] As each of these cathedrals bears the name *Notre Dame*, it has become the habit to designate them by the towns in which they are located, with the exception of the Paris example, which has persisted to a greater degree than the others in retaining its original name.

Fig. 447. Church of Notre Dame.
Louviers. South Porch. 1494.

Fig. 448. An Ogee Arch with
Flamboyant Detail.

tic figure to illustrate the temperament of these sculptors is the *Smiling Angel of Reims* (FIG. 445). The tall, slender figure stands in an attitude of ease and grace; the swing of the body is accentuated by the long sweeping curves of the drapery. The tilt of the head, the movement of the uplifted hand, the sweep of the wings that frame the head — all these lend charm to this angel who is so tender and so joyful. While the statue is not so impressively architectural as the kings and queens of the western portal of *Chartres*, it still retains with its naturalism a sense of decorative fitness; with the exception of the wings, it stands within the space bounded by the two engaged columns, the straight verticality of which, repeated in the fold of the cloak, acts as a foil to the dominant curves of the design.

Although the subject matter, general treatment, and location of the major sculpture of the cathedrals were dictated by the Church,[1] the imagination of the carvers found free play in the carvings on the capitals, on pedestals, up on the towers — in all the nooks and corners. This decorative carving, as well as the statues of the portals, reveals a return to nature. The capitals of the clustered piers of *Reims* (FIG. 446) are covered with foliage in which animals and fantastic figures are intertwined; the leaves, deeply undercut or standing out in the round, appear to have been just fastened up on the stone. Naturalism has destroyed the surface of the stone and has supplanted the organization

[1] See Mâle, *op. cit.*, for a full exposition of this.

Fig. 449. Glouces-
ter Cathedral. Tran-
sept and Choir (Fig.
452). 1331–37.

of stone as stone with an illusion of natural
appearance. The grotesques (FIG. 444) that
live high up on the balustrades of the towers peering out over the city — half man,
half beast, crow, elephant, the three-headed
Cerberus — were born probably of pure
fancy, and show that the fantastic and chi-
merical forms of the world of imagination
also belonged to the mirror of nature, and
for this reason are found tucked away in
the corners all over the cathedral.

The Gothic cathedral reached its culmination in the thirteenth century, continuing
in the fourteenth without great change.
The fifteenth-century cathedrals, however,
such as *Rouen* (FIG. 440), reveal quite a
different aspect. The feeling of structural
significance has given way to lightness and
elegance and an overemphasis upon decoration for its own sake. In the lacelike carving of the portal of *Louviers* (FIG. 447) the
restless line finds recurrent expression in the

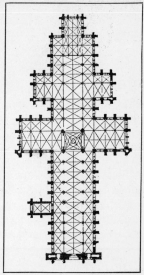

Fig. 450. Salisbury Cathedral. The cloister at the right
is not shown. See Fig. 451.

ogee arch (FIG. 448) which is not structurally an arch but is formed
by two moldings with reversed curves that unite and terminate in a
finial. So too the foliage, departing from the naturalism of *Reims*, now
twists and turns in wavy, flamelike lines, so that the work of the late
Gothic period became known as flamelike or Flamboyant.

Although Gothic architecture was primarily French, its influence
spread to England, the Low Countries, Germany, Spain, and Italy,

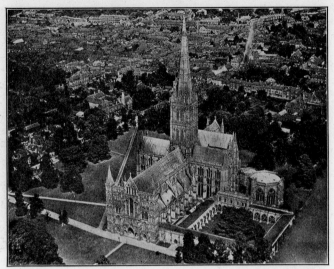

Fig. 451. Salisbury Cathedral. 1220–58. (Aerofilms Ltd., London)

with variations according to local conditions. The English Church
was long monastic, and thus, in contrast with the French, was originally
situated apart from the town in the open country (Fig. 451) and included a close and a cloister, forms so ingrained in the English tradition that they were used with the secular cathedrals as well. The plan
(Fig. 450) shows a long nave, a square end, probably a Saxon inheritance, and deep, usually double transepts, which provide material
for a complex massing of volumes that culminate in the rectangular
tower over the crossing (Fig. 449), sometimes, as at *Salisbury* (Fig. 451),
crowned with a spire. One misses in the English church that characteristic French feature, the flying buttress. For the English is not so consistently organic a style because many of the churches were rebuilt
Norman (Romanesque) structures whose solid walls and pier buttresses
were sufficient support for the vaultings. Where the flying buttress was
used, it was insignificant and often concealed beneath the roof. Thus
the English cathedral retains considerable of the Romanesque sturdy
solidity and seldom shares the French restless, emotional, aspiring
quality.[1] But the need for light tended to increase the size of the open-

[1] Most English cathedrals show various periods of building and rebuilding and
thus are seldom homogenous in style. *Canterbury* and *Winchester* are excellent examples
of all styles, which are: Late Norman or Romanesque (twelfth century), *Durham;*
Early Gothic (thirteenth century), *Lincoln* nave and Chapter House, *Canterbury,*
Salisbury, the *Angel Choir* of *Lincoln;* Decorated (fourteenth century), *Gloucester,*
Canterbury nave, *Winchester* nave; Perpendicular (fifteenth to sixteenth century), *Oxford*

ings and to stimulate the development
of tracery to hold huge areas of glass
(FIGS. 449, 452, 453).

In window tracery and vaulting the
English builders overstepped structural requirements in favor of decorative elegance. In the choir of *Gloucester*
(FIG. 452) for example, the composition is based upon the vertical line;
the piers rise without interruption even
on stringcourses from floor to rib; the
stone paneling harmonizes, as does
the stone tracery of the eastern end
that holds the great area of glass. In
the vaulting the ribs spread out in
great sweeping lines from the capital,
and with the help of intermediate ribs
weave an elaborate design on the ceiling — a system known as lierne vaulting. A few of these ribs are structural,
but most of them are decorative. The

Fig. 452. Gloucester Cathedral.
Choir. Rebuilt, 1331–37, on the lines
of the older Norman cathedral with
thick walls.

climax of multiplying nonfunctional ribs, as in the *Oxford Divinity School*
(FIG. 454), is reached in the fan vaulting of the *Chapel of Henry VII*.

In the low Countries, particularly Flanders, although typical Gothic
churches were built, the most individual expression was the secular
building, especially the town halls and the cloth halls of Flanders.[1]

In Germany, Gothic building was generally imitative of the French.
In the Romanesque period the builders in the Rhenish cities had developed a particularly virile, original style of church architecture. The
Gothic was arbitrarily accepted rather than naturally evolved. Hence
Cologne Cathedral (1248–1880), although it imitates *Amiens* quite consistently, lacks the imagination and spontaneity of the French cathedrals. The most original accomplishment of Gothic Germany was the
Hallenkirchen or *Hall Churches*, in which the vaults of the aisles equaled in
height those of the nave, giving the building a simple outline and mass.

In Spain, the Gothic style — *Burgos* (founded 1226, spires begun
1442) and *Seville* (begun 1401) may be taken as typical — shows distinct
contrasts with the French, due partly to different climatic conditions.
The hot, dry climate did not require the steeply pitched, protecting
roofs; hence the vaults were either left exposed or covered with tiles,

---

Divinity School, Gloucester Lady Chapel, Windsor Chapel of St. George, Chapel of Henry VII,
Westminster.

[1] See Chapter XVI and FIGS. 575, 576.

Fig. 453. Chapter House. Westminster Abbey. Begun 1250. (From an engraving)

giving a flat or low-sloping shape to the roof. Because of the hot, brilliant sunshine, the large number of openings needed in the North was diminished, thus increasing the plain wall space. Frequently the clerestory was omitted or the windows blinded, making the interior gloomy. Decoration, especially in the late period, shows characteristic Spanish exuberance and love of overloading, especially about the choir and the altar, and frequently combines Moorish and Christian motifs.

In Italy the essentially Northern Gothic was still less at home than in Spain. In the hill towns of Assisi, Orvieto, and Siena are found characteristic examples which in some respects seem more Romanesque than Gothic. Possibly more successful adaptations of the style were the secular Gothic buildings, the town halls of Florence and Siena, and the polychrome Venetian palaces.[1]

C. PAINTING AND THE MINOR ARTS

Because of the elimination of the wall space, the Gothic style offered but little opportunity for mural painting. Hence book illustration was the chief function of the painter. The craft of bookmaking no longer centered in the monastery. A flourishing school had developed in thirteenth-century Paris, where the university was attracting men of learning. Although secular books such as treatises on medicine, romances, and histories were appearing, the most usual volumes were

[1] See pp. 342–44.

still liturgical and theological, such as the psalter and the book of hours, a varied collection of calendars, lessons, prayers, and psalms for private devotional use.

A culmination of bookmaking was reached in France in the fourteenth and fifteenth centuries. In looking at the manuscripts of the time (Color Plate II, opposite p. 328), one is impressed with the glowing color, probably influenced by the stained-glass workers, the shimmer of gold over the page, the fine spacing, and the exquisite delicacy and refinement of every

Fig. 454. Divinity School, Oxford. 1445–80. A transitional stage between lierne and fan vaulting.

part. The ivy was a popular form of border decoration. Its foliated sprays were seminaturalistic, spreading out in delicate curves to form a flat pattern. Occasionally a single leaf was covered with gold slightly raised, giving a delicate richness to the page. In among the sprays one frequently finds tiny figures of animals, birds, and grotesques that are another evidence of the fancy of the medieval artist that revealed itself in the cathedral grotesque.

The tendency toward naturalism that we saw in sculpture appeared in painting also. The miniature representing *December* from the *Très Riches Heures* (FIG. 455) gives us a naturalistic and intimate picture of the boar hunt in preparation for the Christmas feast. In the foreground the hunters in gay costumes with their dogs are closing in upon the boar; behind them is a dense forest with leaves in their autumn color of golden bronze, above which rise, in the distance, the towers of one of the Duke's châteaux, over against a deep blue sky. Above the miniature, in a semicircle, is the chariot of the sun with winged steeds, surrounded by the sign of the zodiac for the month. The gold back-

Fig. 455. Pol de Limbourg and His Brothers. December, from the *Très Riches Heures* (the *Very Rich Book of Hours*) made for the Duc de Berri, c. 1416. Musée Condé, Chantilly. (Giraudon)

ground of the illuminations of earlier centuries has given way to landscape. Naturalism is there, but only in so far as it is consonant with the feeling of decoration.

Out of the school of the illuminators, independent painting as a major art began to arise,[1] and soon the miniature school waned as the coming of the printing press impinged upon its very life, the life of one of the most vigorous and beautiful arts of the Middle Ages.

Besides the bookmaker, many other craftsmen — metalworkers, enamelers, and weavers — were needed to supply both ecclesiastical and rapidly increasing secular needs. Notwithstanding the revival of sculpture and the consequent relegation of the ivory-carver to secondary importance, the services of this craftsman were still in demand for small shrines and for statuettes such as the *Virgin* (FIG. 456). With one arm she holds the child, who is standing on her lap, playing with the cord on her mantle, and on whom she looks with a playful smile — a happy group of a mother and child. The figure still retains a great deal of the original conventional color that was applied to the surface — blue, red, and gilding; for it was the usual practice to conceal the texture of the ivory in this way. Secular subjects as well occupied these carvers. Ivory covers for the little mirrors that the ladies carried attached to their girdles by gold or silver chains were decorated with love scenes, very popular among which was the storming of the Castle of Love. These little pictures were carved with all the freshness and spontaneity of the love songs of the troubadours.

The work of the woodcarvers we see in the furniture, both secular and ecclesiastical. Gothic furniture impresses one with its sturdy simplicity and strength. Great oak forests furnished an abundance of timber of superior quality and massiveness; one feels to what an extent this medium has determined the general character of the product.

[1] See Chapter XXI.

II. PAGE FROM A BOOK OF HOURS

With a Miniature of Saint Eutropius. French, First Half of the Fifteenth Century.
Collection of C. L. Ricketts, Chicago.

Fig. 456. Ivory Statu-
ette of the Virgin and
Child. Painted. XIII cent.
Villeneuve-les-Avignon.

Fig. 457. Gothic Chair. Metropolitan Museum, New York.
(Metropolitan Museum)

Fig. 458. Choir Stalls. Amiens. 1508–19.

Fig. 459. Chalice of St. Remi. Gold, with cloisonné enamels, gems, and filigree. H. 7 in. Late XII cent. Reims. (N. D. Photo.)

There were not many kinds of furniture made. The rooms were rather bare, one piece — a great oak chest, for example — serving not only as a receptacle but also as a seat and a bed. The chair in FIG. 457 combines the function of chair and chest, and its simple massiveness seems the direct result of the use of heavy timber. The carved panels on the back and base are clearly derived from late Gothic tracery and ornament.

In ecclesiastical furniture, the choir stalls (FIG. 458) gave the woodcarver ample opportunity to exercise his craft. The carving of the canopy and the background is flamboyant, with the ogee arch predominating. In the misericords and the arm rests particularly, the carver gave free rein to his fancy and fashioned the knoblike rests to represent the Washerwoman, the Baker, and Reynard the Fox.

The ceremonial vessels needed for the church rites demanded especially the skill of the metalworker. Chalices we have noted in each period since the founding of the Christian Church (FIGS. 339, 419, 420). The *Chalice of St. Remi* (FIG. 459) in comparison with these reveals a departure from the ruggedness of the earlier examples toward a greater elegance in shape and proportion, a certain regularity and precision of detail. In this chalice a larger amount of the surface is decorated than in the earlier ones, for the filigree, stones, and cloisonné enamels cover a considerable amount of the broad base, stem, and cup. The shimmer of the gold, the light and shade in the filigree bands, deepened by the rich color of the stones and the deep luminous tones of the enamels, make this chalice a superb example of the skill of these goldsmiths.

Cloisonné enameling was still used, but another, the *champlevé*, was practiced very successfully. The process was as follows: On a metal plate the design was drawn in a fine line and then the metal cut away to a depth of from a sixteenth to a thirty-second of an inch, leaving a narrow raised metal ridge to indicate the outline of the design. The depressions were usually roughened so as to hold the enamel more securely, and then filled with the enamel, usually opaque, which was

fused and polished as by the
cloisonné method. The reliquary seen in Fig. 460 is
made by this process. It is
architectural in form, suggesting the steep roofs of this
Northern country. In the
long panel are the figures of
Christ in an aureole and four
saints in niches above, angels
on either side of a circle containing a lamb and the cross.
The figures are in dark blue,
light blue, green, and red
enamel on a delicately
chased metal base. In general there is more boldness
and vigor in the champlevé
method, more delicacy and
elegance in the cloisonné, a
difference naturally resulting from the difference in the
early stages of the process,
for greater facility is possible
with cloisons than with the
more rigid lines left by cutting away the metal field.

Fig. 460. Reliquary. Limoges champlevé
enamel on copper. XIII cent. Metropolitan
Museum, New York. (Metropolitan Museum)

Fig. 461. Iron Hinge. XIII cent. Notre
Dame, Paris.

Another metal used with
highly artistic results was
iron, which when hammered
partakes of the pliability of
softer metals and is free from the feeling of rigidity which results from
casting in a mold. A fine example is found in the iron hinges of *Notre
Dame* (Fig. 461). Here the elaborate, elegant design, like that of the
Chalice of St. Remi (Fig. 459), has retained just enough reserve to save
it from the weakness of overdecoration. The fine, strong scrolls, uniting firmly with the main stem, suggest the strength that should characterize a hinge. Within and about these scrolls, but subordinate to
them, are minor details of naturalistic decoration, such as birds and
serpents, which reveal again the fancy of their designers.

Of great importance were the large tapestries which added color
to the interior of the cathedral when hung, on festal occasions, from
the triforium, and which decorated the great stone halls of the châteaux

Fig. 462. Tapestry. The Lady and the Unicorn. Early XVI cent.
Cluny Museum, Paris.

and with their firm texture [1] helped retain whatever warmth was afforded by the fireplace. They were often made in sets, as in *The Lady
and the Unicorn* series of six, one of which FIG. 462 reproduces. In
the center stands the lady, gowned in rich stuff and jewelry, with her
pet dog and falcon. She dips her hand into a cup held by her attendant, also richly costumed. On one side is a lion, on the other a unicorn, each holding a standard with a heraldic device. These animals
with their standards and the trees frame the central group and a great
ellipse unites them. The space within the ellipse as well as the background is filled with plants and many varieties of flowers and with
animals — rabbits, birds, a fox, a dog, a monkey, and others. All are
drawn with the greatest freedom and naturalism and yet, as in the
Persian carpets, each functions as one unit in a harmonious massing
of rose, blue-greens, warm ivories, and browns — a frankly decorative
design which could well be relied upon, with its contrasting texture
and color, to enrich a stone wall.

D. SUMMARY

The cathedral is the summation of the Gothic age. All the enthusiasm of a vigorous town life in which civic pride and religious fervor
were inextricably interwoven poured itself into the erection of the

[1] For the technique of tapestry-weaving, see Gardner, *Understanding the Arts*, Pt. 9.

cathedral, which thus became the symbol of the town's social solidarity, in which individuals as such, great personalities though they often were, were submerged. Its frankly expressed organic structure, a stone framework of piers, ribs, and buttresses with little wall space, but open arcades and huge areas of tracery and glass; its decorative sculpture and glass, which are purely architectural in form and filled with meaning both direct and symbolic — these elements in combination created a form that communicates the feeling of the Middle Ages. This feeling reveals itself in the predominantly vertical lines and repeated pointed arches, restless and upreaching; in the ever increasing height of the nave lost in mysterious purple shadows; in the radiant beauty of the glass with its own note of exaltation; in the sculpture, architecturally satisfying and profoundly significant; in all the multitude of accessories, "the adornment of the material house of God," and in the liturgy, with its plainsong. Though the involved theology of the Church lay beyond the intellectual grasp of the people, they were offered a visible evidence of its meaning that enabled them to share the feelings of the Abbé Suger when he said as he entered *St. Denis*, his own cathedral, upon whose structure and decoration he had labored earnestly: "When the house of God, many-colored as the radiance of precious stones, called me from the cares of the world . . . I seemed to find myself, as it were, in some strange part of the universe, which was neither wholly of the baseness of the earth, nor wholly of the serenity of heaven; but by the grace of God, I seem lifted in a mystic manner from this lower, toward that upper sphere."

BIBLIOGRAPHY

Ackerman, Phyllis, *Tapestry, the Mirror of Civilization*, Oxford Press, 1933
Adams, Henry, *Mont-Saint-Michel and Chartres*, Houghton Mifflin, 1913
American Institute of Architects, *The Significance of the Fine Arts*, new ed., Marshall Jones, 1926
Arnold, Hugh, *Stained Glass of the Middle Ages in England and France*, Macmillan, 1926
Bond, Francis, *The Cathedrals of England and Wales*, Scribner, 1912
—— —— *Introduction to English Church Architecture*, Oxford Press, 1914, 2 vols.
Bridaham, L. B., *Gargoyles, Chimères, and the Grotesque in French Gothic Sculpture*, Architectural Book Publishing Co., 1930
Bushnell, A. J., *Storied Windows*, Macmillan, 1914
Coulton, G. G., *Art and the Reformation*, Knopf, 1928
—— —— ed. and tr., *Life in the Middle Ages*, Macmillan, 1928–30, Vols. I–IV
Cram, R. A., *The Substance of Gothic*, Marshall Jones, 1925
Cunynghame, H. H., *European Enamels*, Putnam, 1906
Davis, W. S., *Life on a Mediaeval Barony*, Harper, 1923
Day, L. F., *Stained Glass*, Scribner, 1904
Delaporte, Yves, *Les vitraux de la cathédrale de Chartres*, Chartres, 1926, 3 vols.
Ffoulkes, C. J., *Decorative Ironwork from the XIth to the XVIIIth Century*, Doran, 1914

Francis of Assisi, *The Little Flowers of St. Francis*, Dutton, 1917 (Everyman's Library)

Gardner, Arthur, *French Sculpture of the Thirteenth Century*, Stokes, 1915

—— —— *Medieval Sculpture in France*, Macmillan, 1931

Gardner, Samuel, *English Gothic Foliage Sculpture*, Macmillan, 1927

Herbert, J. A., *Illuminated Manuscripts*, Putnam, 1911

Houvet, Etienne, *Cathédrale de Chartres*, Chelles, 1921, 7 vols.

Hulme, E. M., *The Middle Ages*, Holt, 1929

Jackson, Sir T. G., *Gothic Architecture in France, England, and Italy*, University of Chicago Press, 1915, 2 vols.

Jameson, A. B. M., *Sacred and Legendary Art*, Houghton Mifflin, 1911, 2 vols.

Karlinger, Hans, *Die Kunst der Gotik*, Berlin, 1927

Lethaby, W. R., *Mediaeval Art*, new ed., Scribner, 1913

Macquoid, Percy, *History of English Furniture*, Putnam, 1904–05, 4 vols.

Mâle, Emile, *Art et artistes du moyen âge*, Paris, 1927

—— —— *L'art religieux du XIIe siècle en France*, Paris, 1922

—— —— *Religious Art in France, XIII Century*, Dutton, 1913

Marriage, M. S. and Ernest, *The Sculptures of Chartres Cathedral*, Putnam, 1909

Martin, M. R., *Les peintres de manuscrits et la miniature en France*, Paris, 1909

Maskell, A. O., *Ivories*, Putnam, 1905

—— —— *Wood Sculpture*, Putnam, 1912

Moore, C. H., *Development and Character of Gothic Architecture*, 2d ed., Macmillan, 1899

Muratov, P. P., *La sculpture gothique*, Paris, 1931

Pollen, J. H., *Ancient and Modern Furniture and Woodwork*, rev. by T. A. Lehfeldt, Vol. I, London, 1908

Read, H. E., *English Stained Glass*, Putnam, 1927

Salzman, L. F., *English Life in the Middle Ages*, Oxford Press, 1926

Saunders, O. E., *History of English Art in the Middle Ages*, Oxford Press, 1932

Sherrill, C. H., *Stained Glass Tours in England*, Lane, 1909

—— —— *Stained Glass Tours in France*, Lane, 1908

Smith, H. C., *Catalogue of English Furniture & Woodwork*, Victoria and Albert Museum, London, 1923, Vol. I, *Gothic and Early Tudor*

Street, G. E., *Some Account of Gothic Architecture in Spain*, Dutton, 1914, 2 vols.

Taylor, H. O., *The Mediaeval Mind*, 4th ed., Macmillan, 1925, 2 vols.

Thomson, W. G., *History of Tapestry*, Putnam, 1906

Victoria and Albert Museum, *A Picture Book of English Mediaeval Wall Paintings*, London, 1932

Villard de Honnecourt, *Album de Villard de Honnecourt, architecte du XIIIe siècle*, Paris, 1895

West, G. H., *Gothic Architecture in England and France*, Macmillan, 1911

Worringer, Wilhelm, *Form in Gothic*, tr. by Herbert Read, Putnam, 1927

See also the General Bibliography, pp. 749–751.

Part Five

RENAISSANCE ART

CHAPTER XIV

The Renaissance in Italy
(about 1300–1600 A.D.)

A. HISTORICAL BACKGROUND

Renaissance (literally, "Rebirth") is the accepted though too restricted name given the complex movement that began stirring Italy in the thirteenth and fourteenth centuries, reached a climax there in the fifteenth and sixteenth,[1] and spread with different manifestations over Europe. Out of its complexity at least two general aspects emerge which affect its art expression: the discovery and enjoyment of the individual and his world, and the revival of classical culture. The trend in the Gothic age from the transcendent to the empirical, manifested in an increasing naturalism, and given great impetus in Italy by St. Francis and the Franciscan movement, eventually turned the tide of thought from the medieval point of view, which focused upon a future life, to a realization of the value of man in his actual present and to a vision of the delights and beauties of this life. This humanistic and individualistic point of view found a great source of stimulation in the Humanistic classical literature, philosophy, and art, whose study was one of the intense passions of the day.

The Renaissance, then, meant essentially a new attitude toward life, which led to a development of the individual, a greater freedom of thought, and a consequent curiosity about man and his world. Hence we find ourselves in an age of scientific research and invention. The introduction of gunpowder, probably early in the fourteenth century, changed methods of warfare; the invention of the printing press, about the middle of the fifteenth century, meant the gradual substitution of printed books for manuscripts. Interest in man's surroundings naturally led to voyages of travel and discovery such as those of Columbus

---

[1] The evolution of the Renaissance falls roughly into divisions marked by the centuries in their Italian names: Dugento (thirteenth), Trecento (fourteenth), Quattrocento (fifteenth), Cinquecento (sixteenth).

Fig. 463. Italy.

(1492–1504), which had been prompted by the earlier journeys of Marco Polo in China (1260–1295) and by the tales that he brought back of the fabulous riches of the East. The result of such voyages was a wider knowledge of geography; colonization; the development of commerce, with the wealth that followed. Leonardo da Vinci (1452–1519), with insatiable curiosity about man, animals, plants, and mechanical devices as well, attacked great engineering problems, even discovering some of the principles of flying machines and submarines. Copernicus, the Polish astronomer (1473–1543), rediscovered the revolution of the Earth and the planets about the Sun, a concept that had been lost since the Greeks; and Galileo (1564–1642), watching a swaying lamp in the cathedral of Pisa, deduced from its movement the law of the pendulum.

Fig. 464. Cathedral of Florence, or Santa Maria del Fiore (St. Mary of the Flower). So called because of the lily in the coat of arms of the city. 1296–1462. The present façade was added 1875–87.

This freedom of thought was often opposed by the Church, which saw in it the undermining of its authority. The early Renaissance, largely medieval, shared still the fervor of the preceding centuries under the stimulation of the two great monastic orders founded in the thirteenth century — the Franciscan and the Dominican; and the religious and the secular were inseparably interwoven. But with the new freedom secularization and revolt against authority, especially in the face of the pomp and circumstance and at times intrigue and profligacy of the papal court, brought about on the one hand reform within the Church and on the other skepticism; a definite break in the social solidarity of the Middle Ages; and a growing emphasis upon secular life.

Socially, democratic tendencies led toward an equalization of classes and with the advent of cheap printed books more nearly equal opportunities for education. The social ideal was the many-sided gentleman, and towards its attainment were produced such remarkable individuals as Leon Battista Alberti [1] and Leonardo da Vinci.

Politically, it was an age of turmoil. For the communes found it necessary to ally themselves with one or the other ruling power, the Papacy or the Empire; they fought each other fiercely for commercial

[1] For a brief statement, see J. C. Burckhardt, *The Civilization of the Renaissance in Italy*, Harper, 1929, pp. 149 ff.; for a contemporary discussion of this ideal, see Baldassare Castiglione, *The Book of the Courtier*, Scribner, 1903.

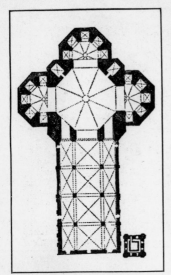

Fig. 465. The Cathedral of Florence.

advantage, and within their own walls kept up local warfare over the lordship of the commune. These lords — tyrants, as they were known — were frequently enlightened paternal rulers; frequently they were not. In either case, many of them were remarkable personalities with equal capacity for war, business, and culture.

Notwithstanding the enthusiasm and prolific accomplishments of the Renaissance, its contributions to science, its great outburst of expression in literature, music, all the arts, and in the amenities of outward life, there is the contrasting picture of its brutality and violence, profligacy, treason, poisonings, and assassinations.

The heart of the Renaissance was Florence (FIG. 463): "Fair and gay Florentine city, fount of valor and joy, flower of cities, Fiorenza . . . [yet in appearance] proud and dark and threatening . . . one hundred and fifty towers and battlemented walls surrounded by moat, against a somber background of hills not yet brightened by houses and olive orchards but covered with cypresses, oak, ash, and fir trees." [1] This walled, compact city with narrow streets and tall threatening towers was a thriving commercial center, and its bankers and cloth-finishers were known all over Europe for their shrewdness as well as for their products. Florence prospered amazingly though it fought continuously, if not with Pisa and Siena for commercial supremacy, at home over local politics, for it had no gift for managing its civic affairs. Whatever stability it had was due largely to its highly organized guilds,[2] whose power extended far beyond the limits of industry. The noble families, each keen for the power, kept the city in a turmoil with their feuds, not at all deterred by the sight of the bodies of the vanquished hanging in the public square or, hardly less gruesome, painted on the walls of the palace of the chief magistrate. This last became the custom, so that one artist commissioned to paint these effigies after one of the periodic uprisings won for himself the name "Andrea of the Hanged."

[1] Guido Biagi, *Men and Manners of Old Florence*, McClurg, 1909, p. 16.
[2] See J. E. Staley, *Guilds of Florence*, McClurg, 1906, for a full description of the guilds as well as interesting illustrations.

Fig. 466. Sant' Andrea. Mantua. Alberti, architect. 1472.

Fig. 467. Medici-Riccardi Palace. Florence. Built for the Medici, 1444, and later taken over by the Riccardi family.

Fig. 468. Cassone. c. 1475. Florentine. Metropolitan Museum, New York. (Metropolitan Museum)

Fig. 469. Davanzati Palace. Restored. The Great Hall. XIV–XV cent. Florence. (Alinari)

In spite of these frequent upheavals, the various activities of life continued uninterrupted and with amazing vitality. The people were industrious and ambitious; intellects were keen and quick; anything mediocre failed to satisfy.[1] Thus the great sculptor Donatello refused to remain in Padua after he had completed his commissions there with great success, because, he said, he was too much praised by Paduans, and felt the need of the continual censure of the Florentines as an incentive to greater excellence.

Thus the city flourished materially and flowered culturally. Outwardly, life was festive.[2] The great palaces of the nobles (FIG. 467), though massive and fortresslike for defense, contained many comforts and luxuries. Festivals and pageants of various kinds were frequent.[3] Now we hear of an Adoration of the Magi or an Annunciation; now of an Age of Gold or the Car of Death. Jousts and weddings not only furnished entertainment for the people, but together with the pageants kept the artists busy decorating banners, fashioning jewelry, painting the marriage chests, designing the scenery, costumes, and cars for the festivals — all of which in turn quickened the fancy.

Thus with the Church, the nobles, and the wealthy merchants in constant need of his wares, the artist's place was as well defined and natural as that of the silk merchant, the butcher, or the baker. Supply and demand offered no problem. An artist was a versatile craftsman and specialization was the exception, not the rule. His shop was a place where a patron could come to consult about building a palace or carving a statue or painting an altarpiece or decorating the walls of a chapel; where he could order a jewel set in a miter, a chest carved and painted, a banner decorated with the family heraldic device, cos-

---

[1] Read the introductory paragraphs to Vasari's life of Perugino.

[2] George Eliot's *Romola* furnishes a fairly accurate picture of Florentine life in the fifteenth century. For contemporary illustrations of everyday life, see Paul Kristeller, *Early Florentine Woodcuts*, London, 1897; Burckhardt, *op. cit.*; Julia Cartwright, *Isabella d'Este*, Dutton, 1903, 2 vols.; and J. A. D.-G. Ross, *Florentine Palaces and Their Stories*, Dutton, 1905.

[3] See G. B. Brown, *Fine Arts*, Scribner, 1927, Pt. I, Chap. III, for a description.

Fig. 470. Carving from the Ducal Palace, Urbino. 1468–82. (Alinari)

tumes and properties made for pageants and Church festivals, books illuminated, and tapestries designed for a palace or a church.

Training for such versatility was acquired through the apprentice system.[1] Each well-known artist had a shop, a *bottega*, as it was called — there may have been from twenty to thirty in Florence — and to the artist a boy was apprenticed when he was ten or twelve years old. He spent his time grinding the colors, preparing the gold, transferring the cartoons (the master's preliminary drawings) to the panel or wall, preparing the panel of seasoned wood for a painting. Thus years were spent in laying a solid foundation of craftsmanship. As the apprentice became proficient in the fundamentals of these crafts, he was permitted to work somewhat more independently and even trusted to paint minor parts of a great altarpiece or to make the jewel-set brooch, according to his master's design; and finally, after many years of such training he might leave his master's shop to set up one of his own.

For the public and officialdom, art was a matter of civic interest and enthusiasm. The archives of fifteenth-century Florence reveal to us what a great amount of time the council spent upon art projects, such as the competition for the dome to be erected on the *Cathedral*, or the bronze doors for the *Baptistery*, or the location of Michelangelo's statue of *David*. And the people as a whole felt and appreciated art as a vital part of life, so that much of the art criticism came from the masses. When Ghiberti was making his plaque in the competition for the doors of the *Baptistery*, he invited people to come to his shop and criticize his work as it progressed. When Duccio's *Majestà* was completed there was a holiday in Siena, and a great procession of priests

[1] See Cennino Cennini, *The Book of the Art of Cennino Cennini*, London, 1922; Brown, *op. cit.*, sections on a Florentine workshop, Pt. I, Chap. III; and E. H. and E. W. Blashfield, *Italian Cities*, new ed., Scribner, 1912, "The Florentine Artist."

Fig. 471. Doorway from the Ducal Palace, Urbino. Showing door of inlaid wood. 1468–82. (Alinari)

and citizens in holiday dress, with candles, and with the sound of bells and musical instruments, carried the altarpiece to its place in the cathedral. And when Leonardo had made his cartoon of the *Madonna with St. Anne*, "the chamber wherein it stood was crowded for two days by men and women, old and young; a concourse, in short, such as one sees flocking to the most solemn festivals, all hastening to behold the wonders produced by Leonardo and which awakened amazement in the whole people."

The general appearance of the city had a stimulating effect upon both the people and the artists. In their love for it and in their pride, the Florentines adorned their city with works by the greatest artists, many of which were placed in view of the public along the thoroughfares and in the open squares. Here, at the entrance of the municipal palace facing the piazza, stood Michelangelo's *David*; niches in *Giotto's Tower* and *Or San Michele* held statues made by Donatello, Ghiberti, and Verrocchio; Ghiberti's *Gates of Paradise* faced the cathedral piazza, in the heart of the city; along a narrow street was a lunette filled with a Luca della Robbia *Madonna and Child* in rich blue-and-white glazed terra cotta, or a painted terra-cotta *Nativity* by Donatello; just inside the churches and the monasteries were great cycles of mural paintings; while above all soared the powerful lines of Brunelleschi's dome. With mind and eye trained by daily acquaintance with all these, it is little wonder that the average Florentine was a keen art critic.

B. ARCHITECTURE

During the Dugento and the Trecento, and well into the Quattrocento,[1] the Gothic style of architecture prevailed, modified by climatic conditions and by the tenacity of the Romanesque because of its pecul-

[1] See p. 335, note 1.

477. Farnese Palace. Rome. Architects, Antonio da San Gallo, 1530–34; Michelangelo, 1546, designed the cornice; and Giacomo della Porta, completed the palace c. 1580.

Fig. 478. Farnese Palace. Court.

ozzo (1396–1472), is a simple massive structure whose strength is accentuated by the use of rusticated stone on the ground story.[1] Its division into stories by unbroken horizontal moldings, its great cornice decorated with dentils, egg and dart, and acanthus, show classical influence; the mullioned windows flush with the wall, the great unbroken wall areas, medieval influence. In the *Rucellai Palace* (Florence) by Alberti, classical entablatures were added to each story, and pilasters between the windows. Thus in secular building as well as in ecclesiastical the fifteenth century was a century of transition, in which medieval forms were evolving, under the impact of the revival of the classical culture and classical forms, into a new style.

A typical room in one of these Florentine palaces such as the great hall of the *Davanzati Palace* (FIG. 469) had spaciousness and simple dignity. The beamed ceiling was brightly painted, and the plastered walls, whose openings were without trim, furnished an unobtrusive background for the color accents of painted decorations or the tapestries and majolica. An emphatic note was the fireplace with a high sloping hood. The furniture was simple and massive and consisted of but a few pieces, most important of which was the great chest or

[1] The great arches on the ground story, originally open entrances to a loggia, were later filled with windows in the style of the High Renaissance. The *Strozzi Palace* well illustrates an unbroken ground story.

Fig. 472. Iron Grille. Palazzo Pubblico, Siena. 1445.

Fig. 473. Iron Lantern. Guadagni Palace, Florence. (Alinari)

Fig. 474. Ca d'Oro. Venice. XV cent.

Fig. 475. Vendramini Palace, Venice. Pietro Lombardo, architect. 1481. Contrast this open design with the solidity of the Florentine palace (Fig. 467).

iar suitability to Italy.[1] In the fifteenth century the builders, whose eyes opened to the material remains of the ancient civilization that lay everywhere about them, began studying these ancient monuments as the Humanists were eagerly perusing the literature of the same culture. When the young Brunelleschi went to Rome with his friend Donatello,[2] he was struck with amazement and eagerly spent day and night among the ruins, drawing ground plans, vaults, cornices, and moldings. As a result of this new interest in classical remains, the architects began to introduce into their buildings classical decorative motifs, cornices, and horizontal moldings, and thus freely intermingled the old and the new with a freshness and at times a daring that are indicative of the free attitude of the early Renaissance.

This daring is characteristic of the young Filippo Brunelleschi (1379–1446) in his design for the dome of the *Cathedral of Florence* (FIG. 464), which though not original in construction,[3] bears a distinctive new note in its scale and external effectiveness. To roof a structure with a dome had been accomplished successfully many times before, notably in the *Pantheon* (FIG. 279) and *Santa Sophia* (FIG. 319); but a comparison of these two domes with that at Florence reveals at once a sharp difference, namely, that the former are partly concealed from the exterior view and aim at interior effect chiefly; the latter purposely emphasizes the exterior, to dominate not only the cathedral but the city. This dome is octagonal in shape, and rises from an octagonal base and drum which is pierced with circular windows for light. The great stone ribs rise with a curve of great beauty and strength to con-

verge on the circular apex holding the lantern. Because of its size and its simple design, the dome dominates by its grandeur. It does not possess the mystic, aspiring quality of the Gothic cathedral, nor yet the perfect equilibrium of the Greek temple, but rather the frankly pagan note of the mastery of power. But its effectiveness is external only, for

Fig. 476. Cancelleria, or P
Rome. Attributed to

the interior effect of well-designed space such as o
theon and *Santa Sophia* is lost when a long nave re
small segment of the dome (FIG. 465. See FIG. 481
and 322). A realization of this failure led the arch
aissance to abandon the basilica plan of church in f
type, which found its fullest expression in *St. Peter'*
the essentially medieval *Cathedral of Florence* states, wi
of the inner problems of church architecture of the

More characteristically Renaissance in design, and
inspiration from classical art, are the *Pazzi Chapel* of B
Croce, Florence); *San Francesco* (Rimini), and *Sant' A
by Alberti (1404–1472). In these one sees the classi
vertical and horizontal; round arches and arcadings; cl
tures, pediments, and details; the combined use of the
systems; and in *Sant' Andrea* the Roman triumphal-arch
triple division (FIG. 466). Ornament is used sparingly
subordinate to the quietly restrained design.

Another departure from medieval tradition was the g
tion given secular architecture, for, with the point of view
aspiration for the future to a consideration of the present
and civic buildings claimed equal attention with the ecclesi
early Renaissance is best illustrated by the Florentine pa
powerful piles of stone, not only dignified but stern, for whil
menaced a palace must serve as a fortress as well as a dwelli
compact city it stood flush with the street, and as a rule
doorway and a few small windows in the massive ground s
for light and air it was built about an inner court. The *Medi*
Palace, for example (FIG. 467), built for Cosimo de' Medici b

---

[1] Commerical expansion and material prosperity in the thirteenth and fourteenth centuries stimulated a large amount of building, civic as well as ecclesiastical: *San Francesco*, Assisi; *Cathedral* and *Palazzo Pubblico*, Siena; *Cathedral, Santa Croce, Santa Maria Novella, Bargello*, and *Palazzo Vecchio*, Florence; *Ducal Palace*, Venice; *Milan Cathedral*.

[2] Read the account of this in Vasari's lives of Brunelleschi and Donato (Donatello).

[3] Read the account of the building in Vasari's life of Brunelleschi.

Fig. 472. Iron Grille. Palazzo
Pubblico, Siena. 1445.

Fig. 473. Iron Lantern.
Guadagni Palace, Florence.
(Alinari)

Fig. 474. Ca d'Oro. Venice. XV cent.

Fig. 475. Vendramini Palace, Venice. Pietro Lombardo, architect. 1481. Contrast this open design with the solidity of the Florentine palace (Fig. 467).

iar suitability to Italy.[1] In the fifteenth century the builders, whose eyes opened to the material remains of the ancient civilization that lay everywhere about them, began studying these ancient monuments as the Humanists were eagerly perusing the literature of the same culture. When the young Brunelleschi went to Rome with his friend Donatello,[2] he was struck with amazement and eagerly spent day and night among the ruins, drawing ground plans, vaults, cornices, and moldings. As a result of this new interest in classical remains, the architects began to introduce into their buildings classical decorative motifs, cornices, and horizontal moldings, and thus freely intermingled the old and the new with a freshness and at times a daring that are indicative of the free attitude of the early Renaissance.

This daring is characteristic of the young Filippo Brunelleschi (1379–1446) in his design for the dome of the *Cathedral of Florence* (FIG. 464), which though not original in construction,[3] bears a distinctive new note in its scale and external effectiveness. To roof a structure with a dome had been accomplished successfully many times before, notably in the *Pantheon* (FIG. 279) and *Santa Sophia* (FIG. 319); but a comparison of these two domes with that at Florence reveals at once a sharp difference, namely, that the former are partly concealed from the exterior view and aim at interior effect chiefly; the latter purposely emphasizes the exterior, to dominate not only the cathedral but the city. This dome is octagonal in shape, and rises from an octagonal base and drum which is pierced with circular windows for light. The great stone ribs rise with a curve of great beauty and strength to con-

[1] Commerical expansion and material prosperity in the thirteenth and fourteenth centuries stimulated a large amount of building, civic as well as ecclesiastical: *San Francesco*, Assisi; *Cathedral* and *Palazzo Pubblico*, Siena; *Cathedral*, *Santa Croce*, *Santa Maria Novella*, *Bargello*, and *Palazzo Vecchio*, Florence; *Ducal Palace*, Venice; *Milan Cathedral*.

[2] Read the account of this in Vasari's lives of Brunelleschi and Donato (Donatello).

[3] Read the account of the building in Vasari's life of Brunelleschi.

verge on the circular apex holding the lantern. Because of its size and its simple design, the dome dominates by its grandeur. It does not possess the mystic, aspiring quality of the Gothic cathedral, nor yet the perfect equilibrium of the Greek temple, but rather the frankly pagan note of the mastery of power. But its effectiveness is external only, for

Fig. 476. Cancelleria, or Palace of the Chancellor. Rome. Attributed to Bramante. 1495.

the interior effect of well-designed space such as one finds in the *Pantheon* and *Santa Sophia* is lost when a long nave renders visible but a small segment of the dome (FIG. 465. See FIG. 481; contrast FIGS. 280 and 322). A realization of this failure led the architects of the Renaissance to abandon the basilica plan of church in favor of the central type, which found its fullest expression in *St. Peter's* (FIG. 481). Thus the essentially medieval *Cathedral of Florence* states, without solving, one of the inner problems of church architecture of the Renaissance.

More characteristically Renaissance in design, and revealing direct inspiration from classical art, are the *Pazzi Chapel* of Brunelleschi (*Santa Croce*, Florence); *San Francesco* (Rimini), and *Sant' Andrea* (Mantua) by Alberti (1404–1472). In these one sees the classical balance of vertical and horizontal; round arches and arcadings; classical entablatures, pediments, and details; the combined use of the arch and lintel systems; and in *Sant' Andrea* the Roman triumphal-arch design with its triple division (FIG. 466). Ornament is used sparingly and is quite subordinate to the quietly restrained design.

Another departure from medieval tradition was the greater attention given secular architecture, for, with the point of view shifted from aspiration for the future to a consideration of the present, the palace and civic buildings claimed equal attention with the ecclesiastical. The early Renaissance is best illustrated by the Florentine palaces, those powerful piles of stone, not only dignified but stern, for while feuds still menaced a palace must serve as a fortress as well as a dwelling. In the compact city it stood flush with the street, and as a rule had but a doorway and a few small windows in the massive ground story; and for light and air it was built about an inner court. The *Medici-Riccardi Palace*, for example (FIG. 467), built for Cosimo de' Medici by Michel-

Fig. 477. Farnese Palace. Rome. Architects, Antonio da San Gallo, 1530–34; Michelangelo, 1546, who designed the cornice; and Giacomo della Porta, who completed the palace c. 1580.

Fig. 478. Farnese Palace. Court.

ozzo (1396–1472), is a simple massive structure whose strength is accentuated by the use of rusticated stone on the ground story.[1] Its division into stories by unbroken horizontal moldings, its great cornice decorated with dentils, egg and dart, and acanthus, show classical influence; the mullioned windows flush with the wall, the great unbroken wall areas, medieval influence. In the *Rucellai Palace* (Florence) by Alberti, classical entablatures were added to each story, and pilasters between the windows. Thus in secular building as well as in ecclesiastical the fifteenth century was a century of transition, in which medieval forms were evolving, under the impact of the revival of the classical culture and classical forms, into a new style.

A typical room in one of these Florentine palaces such as the great hall of the *Davanzati Palace* (FIG. 469) had spaciousness and simple dignity. The beamed ceiling was brightly painted, and the plastered walls, whose openings were without trim, furnished an unobtrusive background for the color accents of painted decorations or the tapestries and majolica. An emphatic note was the fireplace with a high sloping hood. The furniture was simple and massive and consisted of but a few pieces, most important of which was the great chest or

[1] The great arches on the ground story, originally open entrances to a loggia, were later filled with windows in the style of the High Renaissance. The *Strozzi Palace* well illustrates an unbroken ground story.

cassone that served as a clothes closet, a storage place for the family plate or books, a seat, a bed, a table if high enough, and a trunk if small enough. The early *cassoni* were very much like the Gothic chests in their almost severe rectangularity with simple carved decoration. In the example seen in FIG. 468 this severity is modified by the bracketlike carved ornaments, which are covered with gesso and gilded, by the cornicelike projection of the lid, and by the brightly painted panel on the front. Rarely has an important piece of furniture attained the splendor and dignity of the Italian *cassoni*. The panels were frequently painted by the best artists of Florence.[1]

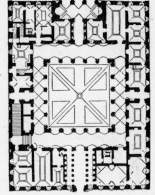

Fig. 479. Farnese Palace. A covered arcade surrounds the court. The ground floor of the Renaissance palace was generally used for storage and business; the second and third stories, for living-rooms that opened off the court. At the rear was a garden. (Anderson)

Wealth of ornament increased as the fifteenth century advanced. Frescoes covered the walls of palaces[2] as well as of the churches. Carved pilasters, lintels, and cornices framed doors of inlaid wood (FIG. 471). The motifs were chiefly classical — the acanthus, the rinceau, candelabra, garlands, Greek molding — and, like the classical, naturalistic in form. They were carved crisply and spontaneously as if by one who was finding his first delight in rich and varied effects of light and shade (FIG. 470).

Another feature of Renaissance architecture, equally functional and decorative, merits more than passing attention — the wrought-iron work. The strength of the metal makes it valuable for grilles and gates where strong protection, and at the same time light and air, are needed. Technically, it can be worked by several processes, for it can be hammered, molded, welded, carved, chased, and stamped. The necessary tools are few and simple — a forge and bellows, hammer and anvil, tongs and chisels. An important fact in designing in this medium is that the metal must be worked in the plastic state, that is, at red or white heat, and must be worked quickly. Hence virility and breadth must control a successful design, though the chased ornament may be added at greater leisure. This harmony of material, process, and design is well seen in the palace gates and chapel grilles (FIG. 472); and in the standard-holders and lanterns of the palaces. The lantern of

---

[1] Many of these panels have been stripped from the chests and now hang as isolated pictures in galleries and museums.

[2] The gay frescoes of Benozzo Gozzoli in the chapel of the *Medici Palace*, for example.

Fig. 480. St. Peter's Cathedral. Rome. View from the west. 1506–1626.

Fig. 481. St. Peter's Cathedral. Rome. Nave.

the *Guadagni Palace* (FIG. 473), for example, with its curving branches, is fittingly strong and architectural in feeling; and its decoration, done by fine chiseling, is entirely in keeping with the main design.

The Venetian palace forms a class by itself. Venice, in its isolation, was slow to accept the influence of the Renaissance; and, being free from internal feuds because of its remarkably stable government and also free from external foes because of its geographic location, it did not need to make its palaces fortresslike, as did the Florentines. The Gothic style with its light, open tracery, as in the *Ducal Palace* and the *Ca d'Oro* (FIG. 474), its warm color, and its rapid movement of light and dark reflected in the canals was peculiarly adapted to the geographic situation. In the *Vendramini Palace* (FIG. 475) we see the same influences at work that we saw in Florence, the ordering of the elements into a classically balanced symmetrical design and a substitution of classical detail for medieval. The ground story, with the door in the center, serves as a base for the lighter construction above, which consists to a large extent of two-light rounding windows with circular tracery. Each story carries a cornice, the upper, more widely projecting, serving to finish and unify the entire design. The double shafts of the superimposed orders divide the façade into three parts, the central division containing three groups of windows separated by single columns, balanced on either side by a single group with double columns at the ends. Thus through the symmetry, proportion, and rhythm of parts the façade presents an effective design. The windows with their mullions and tracery are Gothic, while the superimposed orders, cornices, and decorative detail are classic.

With the sixteenth century, the center of building activity shifts from Florence to Rome, where under the leadership of a large group of architects [1] working chiefly for the papal court and the Roman nobles, Renaissance style reached a climax known as the High Renaissance. This was an accomplished age, one of splendor and magnificence in which wealthy popes and princes created a great demand for churches and palaces, villas and gardens, all of which in their scale, in their princely dignity and splendor, reflect the worldly grandeur of the High Renaissance.

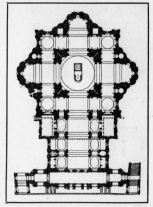

Fig. 482. St. Peter's Cathedral. Rome. The dotted line shows approximately the front line of the building according to the plans of Bramante and Michelangelo.

One palace, the *Farnese*, illustrates this sixteenth-century type, and the *Cancelleria* (Fig. 476) is an interesting transition from the fifteenth-century Florentine to the sixteenth-century Roman. The princely dignity of the *Farnese Palace* (Fig. 477) is the direct result of a design calculated to attain just that effect — a design of classical balance and symmetry. The long rectangle of the smooth façade wall is framed by quoins and a cornice, and across it march the long lines of windows, whose regularity is broken by the strong central accent of the doorway built of rusticated stone and surmounted by a balcony and the Farnese coat of arms. The windows are no longer flush with the wall, as in the *Medici Palace* (Fig. 467), but project beyond the surface, producing depth in the design; each window is a complete unit with engaged columns, entablature, and pediment. The different treatment of these units on each of the three stories, and the alternating round and triangular pediments, contribute the necessary variations to so symmetrical a design. The court (Figs. 478, 479) is strongly classical in design, combining, like the *Colosseum*, the arch and lintel systems, and using superimposed orders, Doric engaged columns on the ground floor, Ionic on the second, and Corinthian pilasters on the third, each order being finished with a complete entablature. But the windows with their pedimented niches are peculiarly Renaissance.

The interiors of these palaces are consistently regal, depending for

---

[1] Donato Bramante (1444–1512); Raphael (1483–1520); Baldassare Peruzzi (1481–1536); Antonio San Gallo the Younger (1482–1546); Michelangelo (1475–1564); Giacomo Barozzi da Vignola (1507–1573); and others.

their effect upon gilded coffered ceilings, sometimes containing painted panels, frescoes, and painted and gilded stucco.[1] The ceiling and the cornice received especial emphasis, as seen in the hall of the *Farnese Palace*, while the richest of stuffs in the furnishings — velvets, brocades, damask, taffeta —contributed another note of sumptuousness, or overstepped into the pompous and grandiose.

As these wealthy princes sought the cooler air of the hills during the hot season, the villa assumed importance, and particularly its garden, a formal garden consisting of beds of flowers

Fig. 483. Gardens of the Villa d'Este. Tivoli. 1549.

laid out geometrically, and usually, for the enjoyment of the color, situated near the house. Beyond these flower beds were regular compartments of greenery with closely clipped hedges of box; masses of trees, ilex or pines, or a stretch of wooded land in its natural state that served as a background for the formal parts and also afforded the desired shade; statues and stone benches; and, with especial emphasis, water: pools, fountains, cascades (Fig. 483). All these elements were used architecturally as integral parts of a formal whole to which each, including the villa itself, contributed form, color, and texture.

Ecclesiastical building of the High Renaissance culminated in *St. Peter's*, the cathedral which replaced the early Christian basilica on

---

[1] See the *Piccolomini Library* of the *Siena Cathedral* and the *Borgia Apartments* of the Vatican for paintings, and the *Villa Madama* at Rome, decorated by Raphael, for stucco.

the same site. With the realization that a dome could not produce its full interior effect in a church built on the basilica plan, the Renaissance architects reverted to the central or Greek-cross type,[1] the basic plan of *St. Peter's* (FIG. 482), which consisted, as planned by Bramante and Michelangelo,[2] of a compact base so designed that the dome could dominate effec-

Fig. 484. The Basilica, or Town Hall. Vicenza. Andrea Palladio, architect. 1549. A medieval building remodeled in Renaissance style.

tively both the exterior and the interior, an objective later frustrated by the lengthening of one arm of the cross to gain space and by the addition of the wide inharmonious façade. Thus it is that only the western, or back, view of the cathedral gives some conception of the complete unity of masses which underlay Michelangelo's sculpturesque design [3] (FIG. 480). The plan consists of a Greek cross with the corners made by the arms of the cross filled in (compare FIGS. 320, 327), and with apses on three sides and the entrance on the fourth side — a plan that is extraordinarily compact. As a volume the cathedral consists of a closely knit unit of cube and half-cylinders, which in their volumes, surfaces, and contours form a harmonious base for the great dome that rises like a majestic symbol of universal authority. On the base gigantic pilasters carry an entablature which ties the parts into a unity. One wonders whether Michelangelo had in mind the *Colosseum* (FIG. 285), in which cornices tie the arches together in a similar way. In *St. Peter's*, however, the cornices are not continuous, as in the *Colosseum*, but are broken. By advancing and receding they create movement in depth as well as laterally. This movement in depth, a three-dimensional quality, becomes stronger in the drum of the dome, where deeply projecting pairs of colonnettes

[1] The conception of formal unity in a domed building, in which the body of the building serves as a base for the dome, is seen in Bramante's *Tempietto* of *San Pietro in Montorio*, Rome.

[2] Ten architects worked upon this cathedral. The plan is essentially that of Bramante, somewhat modified by Michelangelo, who designed the dome, which was completed from his drawings after his death. The façade was built by Maderna (1606–1626) and the great court with double colonnades by Bernini (1656–1663).

[3] See Le Corbusier, *Towards a New Architecture*, for a formal analysis from this point of view.

Fig. 485. Nicola d'Apulia. Pulpit in the Baptistery of the Cathedral of Pisa. 1260. (Alinari)

crowned with a sharply broken cornice not only serve as bases for the great ribs of the dome but carry the eye inward and outward as it sweeps around the drum.

Structurally the cathedral offers no new problems, no new solutions, as is true of most Renaissance building. The arms of the cross are covered with barrel vaults and the dome rests upon pendentives.

The interior view (FIG. 481), because of the lengthened nave, precludes any such impression of admirable space design as one receives in the *Pantheon* and *Santa Sophia*. Everything is scaled to colossal size. Gigantic pilasters support broken cornices, as on the exterior. Colored marbles, painted and gilded stucco reliefs, richly gilded cofferings, adorn all the available space. When to these is added the colorful pageantry and music of the religious festivals, the effect is overwhelmingly magnificent, for the bizarre decoration is somewhat mitigated by the great spaciousness. In imagination one can realize that had the original plan of Bramante and Michelangelo been left untampered with, it would have produced a building of the highest dignity and majesty.

This striving for effect, ceaseless movement, colossal scale, and three-dimensional design soon became the objective of building; and the baroque style,[1] foreshadowed if not actually begun in *St. Peter's*, supplanted the truly Renaissance. It was not without opposition, however. For another school, called the Academic, held fast, even rigidly, to the canons of building set forth by the one whom they believed an infallible guide, the Roman Vitruvius, whose treatise on architecture had been discovered in the fifteenth century. This school is best represented by the work, at Venice and Vicenza, of Palladio (1518–1580). His *Basilica* (FIG. 484) was a Gothic town hall which he remodeled on the lines of a Roman basilica, hence its name. The building has a two-storied arcade around it with superimposed orders, Doric on the first story and Ionic on the second, thus combining in the Roman fashion the arch and lintel systems. The intercolumniations, however,

[1] See Chapter XV.

are not spanned by the arch alone, but contain smaller columns set two deep from which the arch springs.[1] The bays, whose width was determined by the old building, are unusually wide for their height, but in reducing the width to be arched by the insertion of the smaller columns Palladio not only attained superb proportions for his arches but also brought about a rich play of light and shade where the smaller columns group around the larger pier. In both stories the entablature breaks about the columns, thus making more insistent the vertical lines, which form the main accents of the horizontal rhythm and also carry the eye upward to the statues adorning the balustrade. At the corner, Palladio narrowed the intercolumniation, but not the arch, by placing the smaller shafts nearer the large, and he doubled the columns at the cor-

Fig. 486. Arnolfo di Cambio. Detail from the Baldacchino of St. Paul's Outside-the-Walls (Fig. 314), Rome. 1285.

ners, thus giving a feeling of solidity at this point. In the *Villa Rotonda*, Palladio established the classical two-storied portico, later so popular.

C. SCULPTURE

In the thirteenth and fourteenth centuries sculpture was largely medieval and thus architectural, that is, an integral part of the structure. Yet new forces were already affecting its character, far earlier than that of the building itself. For Nicola d'Apulia or Nicola Pisano (about 1206–1278), a sculptor who had been trained in southern Italy, where one of the earliest of classical revivals was in full swing, began working in Pisa, Siena, and Perugia. In his *Pisan Pulpit* (FIGS. 485, 487) his work is partly Romanesque in its large architectural masses, which, though crowded, are entirely subordinated to the frame of the pulpit rail. The quiet imposing figures, flattened to maintain the frontal plane, achieve a clearly decorative quality. The stolid types

[1] A form that has become known as the Palladian window. It is found frequently in American Colonial architecture, whither it came by way of England.

Fig. 487. Nicola d'Apulia. Crucifixion. From the pulpit in the
Pisan Baptistery (Fig. 485).

seem Roman [1] but a fresh observation of nature and a certain solidity
in the figures are new notes.

In the work of Nicola's son, Giovanni (about 1250–1330), the discretion of Nicola, so truly sculptural in its effect, was submerged in
tumultuous movement [2] (FIG. 488). Through the restless groups rapid
movement rushes hither and thither. In detail each figure, compared
with Nicola's is small in scale, and dynamically alive. Here Gothic
naturalism and intricate linealism burst the bonds of architectural
necessity but contributed to the evolving tradition a dynamic living
quality.

Quite in contrast to Giovanni's confused agitation are the clarity,
calm rhythms, and architectural fitness in every detail of the tombs
and ciboria of Arnolfo di Cambio (died 1302; FIGS. 314, 486), which
show a perfect unity of various materials and forms — Gothic motifs,
colorful Cosmati work and colored marbles, and highly decorative refined sculpture. Gothic linealism, again, marks the work of Lorenzo
Maitani (about 1275–1330) in the low reliefs on the façade of the
Orvieto Cathedral (FIG. 489).

Sculpture seemed more actively pursued outside of Florence until
another Pisano, Andrea (about 1270–1348), was called by the Florentines to make a set of bronze doors for the *Baptistery* (FIG. 490). Andrea

[1] Nicola's immediate inspiration appears to have been late-Roman sarcophagi,
examples of which were to be seen in Pisa.
[2] Note the style of both these Pisani in the *Siena Pulpit* and in the *Perugia Fountain*,
on which they collaborated.

Fig. 488. Giovanni Pisano. Crucifixion. From the pulpit at
Pistoia. 1298–1301.

made his doors decorative by means of a repeated geometric motif,
one found in Gothic sculpture and illuminations, within which he
placed low reliefs of simple composition with smoothly flowing lines,
admirably adapted to the spaces, and in no way detracting from the
main decorative pattern. In his reliefs on the *Campanile* of the *Cathedral* one feels the largeness of Nicola's style and the dynamic force
of Giovanni's plus an accomplishment in design not met before. The
adequacy of design to material as illustrated in the bronze reliefs of
the *Baptistery Doors* is paralleled by the stone carvings of the *Campanile*
(Fig. 491). The amplitude of the forms, which are based upon a
direct observation of nature, their clear placement in shallow space,
and their highly sensitive relation to the hexagonal shape seem to
point to an influence upon Andrea of his contemporary Giotto, who
designed the *Campanile* and probably carved some of the reliefs.

Something of the imposing breadth of Nicola's style combined with
a robust energy marks the work of a Sienese sculptor, Jacopo della
Quercia (1375–1438). His *Allegorical Figure* (Fig. 492) made for the
Fonte Gaia of Siena is a powerful form whose vitality is repeated by
the opposing movements in the massive, deeply cut folds of the cloak.
A broad naturalism underlies this robust work, whose energy assumed,
in some of the reliefs of *San Petronio* in Bologna, an intensity that fore-
shadows Michelangelo, yet quiets to a placid stillness in the *Ilaria del
Carretto* (Fig. 493), if indeed this sepulchral monument is the work of
Jacopo. Ilaria lies easily with her head upon a double cushion and at

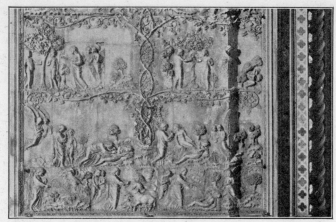

Fig. 489. Lorenzo Maitani (?). Scenes from Genesis. Façade of
the Orvieto Cathedral. Early XIV cent.

her feet a dog, the symbol of fidelity; her face, with its exquisite oval
framed by the turban and the high collar, is perfectly serene. The
effectiveness of the monument is due to the insistent repetition of unbroken horizontals and to the long undulating rhythm in the reposeful drapery, interwoven with quicker rhythms noticeable in the winged
putti with weighty garlands.

Thus the same confusion of the medieval style with new forms, uneven and uncertain, as we saw in architecture, marks the sculpture
of the thirteenth and fourteenth centuries. But with the coming of the
fifteenth century and in particular in the person of Donatello (1386–
1466) we are carried with an onward rush of adventurous spirit into
that wholehearted search for new forms to express new ideas which
Donatello shared with Brunelleschi and Masaccio [1] and which definitely marks the Renaissance. In the early *St. George* [2] (FIG. 494) this
spirit already declares its daring. The youthful knight clad in armor
stands firmly on both feet and with furrowed brow looks keenly to the
left. The naturalistically tied cloak, whose folds contrast with the rigid
armor, and the shield simplify the contour and render the mass more
compact. But though the figure is firmly rooted to the ground, there
is a turn in the torso as well as in the head; in fact there courses through
the statue a great rhythm, visually stressed by the sweep of the cloak,
which follows the turn in the pose. This movement controls the mass

[1] See p. 388.
[2] St. George was the patron saint of the Guild of the Armorers, who commissioned
the statue for a niche on the exterior of the church of *Or San Michele*. The original
statue has been removed to the Bargello (the National Museum), and a reproduction
placed in the niche.

as a whole and is by no means the same thing as the sweeping surface rhythms of Gothic sculpture (FIG. 445). To quote Vasari, "Life seems to move within the stone." This young knight is spiritedly alive, and his chivalry is expressed as much by the formal relations within the mass of stone as by descriptive details such as the expression of the face and the costume.

Donatello, with Brunelleschi had steeped himself at Rome in a study of all the classic remains available. Of sculpture there were not as yet many examples; a large number of those well known today were then still buried in the ruins. Only small objects such as gems and coins were at all common. In fact Donatello and Brunelleschi while digging around the ruins in Rome,

Fig. 490. Andrea Pisano. South Doors of the Baptistery, Florence. Bronze. In the panels are scenes from the life of St. John, and allegorical figures. 1330. (Alinari)

according to Vasari, found an ancient vase full of coins and thereafter were known as the "treasure-seekers"; but their real treasure was the stimulating ideas by which Brunelleschi was enabled to build the great dome of the *Cathedral* and Donatello to carve statues that were filled with energy and vitality. The lesson that the antique taught Donatello was to return to nature. Only by a careful observation of nature could he emulate what, to him, were the superlative accomplishments of the ancients. To his undying credit, he did not copy the Greeks. On the contrary, he learned from them how to make visual perception a starting-point. But his realism was not mere description; rather it was a means toward the creation of a formal organization that should convey a spiritual significance.

In the *Zuccone*, for example (FIG. 495), we see an eccentric-looking old man walking forward, ugly and sad. He wears a heavy mantle that falls from the left shoulder in massive folds which are realistic yet

Fig. 491. Andrea Pisano. Weaving, from the Campanile of the Cathedral, Florence. 1334-38.

Fig. 492. Jacopo della Quercia. Allegorical Figure. 1409-19. Siena Museum. (Alinari)

Fig. 493. Jacopo della Quercia (?). Tomb of Ilaria del Carretto. 1406. Lucca Cathedral. (Alinari)

Fig. 494. Donatello. St. George. Marble. 1416. Originally on the exterior of Or San Michele; now in the Bargello, Florence.

Fig. 495. Donatello. Zuccone, meaning "Pumpkinhead." 1416–35. Campanile, Florence. (Alinari)

of great formal power. The bared right shoulder droops and the fingers are thrust into a sling with an almost convulsive movement of the wrist, revealing the bodily structure in a most convincing way. In fact, the modeling of the throat, the bared shoulder, and the arm reveal an intimate study of the human figure as an organic structure, not, however, as an end in itself but as a means for the expression of a character. The wrinkled face with its large mouth, the inclination of the head toward the uplifted left shoulder, the slouching right shoulder, and the bent wrist, the awkward movement of the figure — all these combine to express vividly the individuality of this curious old man. "By the faith that I put in my Zuccone," was Donatello's way of expressing strong conviction on any subject.

Accentuation of essentials for the expression of inner meaning lies at the base of Donatello's expression of child life as seen in the *Cantoria* (Fig. 499). Within an architectural framework of carved marble

Fig. 496. Donatello. Erasmo da Narni, called Gattamelata, a nickname meaning "Honeyed Cat." Bronze. c. 1446. Padua. (Alinari)

Fig. 497. Ghiberti. Temptation of Christ. Bronze. Panel from the North Doors of the Baptistery. 1403–24. Florence. (Alinari)

Fig. 498. Donatello. The Mule before the Host. Bronze. Altar of Sant' Antonio, Padua. 1446–48.

Fig. 499. Donatello. Cantoria, or Singing Gallery. 1433 to c. 1440.
Museum of the Florence Cathedral.

and gold mosaic a group of putti swings from side to side. The active poses of infinite variety, each a careful observation of nature, impress one chiefly as contributing elements in the surging rhythms whose objective is an expression of the spontaneity and exuberance of children at play. But these figures, notwithstanding their riotous activity, are confined within regulated planes of depth and their movements are both controlled and emphasized by the framework with its static classical motives and its gold mosaic ground, and particularly by the colonnettes, which both in form and in material contrast with and stress the surging movement behind them.

The bronze monument to Erasmo da Narni, a famous condottière, known as *Gattamelata* (FIG. 496), seen in silhouette, composes into a design built on curves with a dynamic diagonal in the sword and baton and related effectively as an architectural unit to its site in the square of *Sant' Antonio*. Seen as a three-dimensional design it composes into closely knit masses of man and horse set upon a lofty elliptical stone base; and possessed of a wealth of detail in the armor and saddle, subordinated to a deliberate emphasis upon monumental form to express a powerful personality. Thus one feels not only in the features but even more convincingly in the bearing of the helmetless rider, and in the massive solidity and inevitable relationships of the forms, a quietly strong, masterful leader.

How Donatello's adventurous spirit attained sculptural control over a narrative subject is illustrated by his small bronze reliefs on the high altar in *Sant' Antonio*. In the *Mule before the Host* (FIG. 498) the principles controlling the relief of the *Cantoria* (FIG. 499) still operate in a more complicated situation. The single clear impression of the incident, which involves a great crowd of people, is due to the under-

Fig. 500. Ghiberti. "Gates of Paradise." Bronze. The scenes represented are taken from the Old Testament. 1425–52. Baptistery, Florence.

lying abstract design. The varied complex movements of the crowd are kept within regulated parallel planes of shallow depth, are chiefly lateral, and are confined to a well but not mechanically defined band less than half the height. These movements are united and controlled by a forceful architectural setting of three great barrel vaults. Thus the impression of the crowd is thrice real because its expression is driven home by an organization of compelling rhythms.

The influence of Donatello, which together with that of Brunelleschi and Masaccio constituted the modern movement of the fifteenth century, did not entirely overwhelm the conservative Gothic style, which lived on beside the new, as is inevitable in any age of transition, and found its highest expression in the work of Lorenzo Ghiberti (1378–1455). In the second *Doors of the Baptistery* [1] Ghiberti followed the all-over pattern of Andrea Pisano (FIG. 490). In the *Temptation* (FIG. 497) we see that the sculptor was concerned chiefly with the swing of line and with the beautiful pattern that his figures could weave within the inclosed space, a pattern built on arcs of circles that approach but do not meet, symbolizing both a physical and a spiritual separation between Christ and the Devil. We may notice the Gothic sway of line particularly in the drapery of the Devil, and the exquisite manner in which his wings are adapted to fill the space and to balance the group of ministering angels. Ghiberti, through the use of line and pattern, has succeeded not only in creating a beautiful design but also in exhibiting a great amount of dramatic power.

Ghiberti, however, was not untouched by the naturalistic movement

[1] There are three sets of bronze doors to the *Baptistery* at Florence: the first (FIG. 490), made by Andrea Pisano for the eastern doorway, which faced the cathedral, were moved to the south door to make way for those made by Ghiberti in 1403–24 (FIG. 497); these in turn were moved to the north door in order that the second pair made by Ghiberti, the famous *Gates of Paradise* (FIG. 500), might be placed in the eastern, the most important entrance.

Fig. 501. Ghiberti. Episodes from the Life of Abraham. From the
"Gates of Paradise" (Fig. 500).

of the day. Paradoxically, he was a great lover and collector of classical marbles, bronzes, and coins, evidence of which appears in his work.
In the niche on the right of Fig. 501, for example, is a nude figure that
appears to have been copied from some classical Heracles.

In the *Gates of Paradise* (Fig. 500) Ghiberti abandoned the all-over
pattern of the earlier doors and divided the space into rectangular
panels, each containing a relief set in plain moldings. These reliefs,
when gilded, produced with their scintillating movement an effect of
great elegance.[1]

Taking one panel in detail (Fig. 501), we find several episodes welded
into one design, not an uncommon practice in Renaissance art. In the
upper right-hand corner Abraham is about to slay Isaac on the altar
when the angel appears to stay his hand; at the foot of the hill the
servants and the ass are waiting for the master; on the left Abraham
kneels before the three angels who appeared to him before his tent
near the oaks of Mamre; in the background Sarah stands at the door
of the tent. These groups Ghiberti has united with astonishing ease.
Emphatic lights and darks, as in the rocks and trees, and planes receding at angles to the foreground, as in the angels, the foreshortened
ass, the rocks at the right, carry the eye upward and inward; so also

[1] It may have been this that called forth from the grim stonecutter Michelangelo
the remark, "They are so beautiful that they might fittingly stand at the gates of
Paradise."

Fig. 502. Luca della Robbia. Madonna. Glazed terra cotta. Kaiser-Friedrich Museum, Berlin. (K.-F. Museum)

do the higher relief in the foreground figures with sharper transitions of light and shade and the lower relief in the group of the sacrifice with gentler transitions. Thus is produced an effect of aerial perspective, a pictorial quality that shows an influence upon Ghiberti of the contemporary naturalistic movement, an influence seen again in the modeling of the figures in the lower right corner, while the angels, near by, with the subtly flowing lines in their drapery and wings carry one back to the angels of *Amiens* and *Reims* (FIG. 445). By a comparison of this panel and Donatello's *Mule before the Host* (FIG. 498) one realizes how sculptural is Donatello's conception in contrast to the pictorial quality in Ghiberti's work.

If the first half of the fifteenth century was dominated by Donatello, with Ghiberti as a late flower of the Gothic style, the second half also was under the influence of the former, though the sculptors may be divided into two rather well defined groups. There was the gentle Luca della Robbia (1400–1482), whose simple unaffected naturalism has a certain appeal. He is best known, however, for his introduction into Italian sculpture of the medium of glazed terra cotta, which was desirable both on grounds of economy, in comparison with stone and bronze, and on account of its color. The intense blues, yellows, greens, and purples with ivory-white made a very decorative note when used in a lunette over a doorway in a dull Florentine street. Luca's figures are the simply and broadly modeled clay forms necessary for glazing, and his types are appealing for their serene wholesomeness and tenderness, which is neither profound nor sentimental (FIG. 502).

In addition to Luca, there was a whole group of stonecutters who, though pupils or followers of the forthright Donatello, were interested primarily in securing exquisite surface effects, in catching a charming momentary pose of a youthful Tuscan aristocrat, in carving marble surfaces into beautifully cut patterns. Probably Desiderio da Settignano (1428–1464) best illustrates the group.[1] The alluring charm of

[1] Others were Antonio Rossellino (1427–1478); Mino da Fiesole (1430–1484); and Benedetto da Maiano (1442–1497).

his *Laughing Boy* (FIG. 504) or *Marietta Strozzi* results from subtle carving and exquisite surface modulation; from an impression of momentary alertness or of gracious personality. The uncompromising realism and formal structure of Donatello have given way to surface delicacy and technical virtuosity.

Nor is this smiling charm absent in the tombs designed and carved by Desiderio. Florence honored its dead — statesmen, humanists, artists, churchmen — with burial in its churches and with monumental tombs made by the greatest artists. In the *Tomb of Carlo Marsuppini* (FIG. 503) the sarcophagus, with an effigy of the dead reclining on a bier, stands in a niche formed by two fluted pilasters that rise from a decorated base to the entablature, whence springs a round arch surmounted by a candelabrum, from which garlands are suspended. The back of the niche is filled with four panels of colored marble, which balance the horizontal line of the sarcophagus and base and afford with their plain surfaces a rest-

Fig. 503. Desiderio da Settignano. Tomb of Carlo Marsuppini. c. 1455. Santa Croce, Florence. (Alinari)

ful contrast to the rich, delicate ornament, carved in low relief so that the light and shade flits over the surface gently with no great contrasts, and produces an effect of elegance and refinement without a feeling of overloading. But the figures at the corners and the garlands, evidence of a superrealistic tendency, mar that perfect architectural unity found in Arnolfo's tombs (FIG. 486).

A lone sculptor who stood apart from the generally naturalistic trend of the Renaissance was Francesco Laurana of Zara (about 1425–1502), who penetrated beneath the superficial surface beauty of the Desiderio group and at the same time substituted for the terse reality of the Donatello tradition the "proud unreality" of an austere architectural form. In the head of a *Princess* (FIG. 505) the shoulders are one with the base from which they rise and their solid mass and unbroken impeccable contour support the slender neck and spherical head. Every detail is a unit in a pattern; from the front view, of repeated curves, horizontals, and a strong vertical axis, with diagonals, sharp angles,

Fig. 504. Desiderio da Settignano. Laughing Boy. Benda coll., Vienna.

Fig. 505. Laurana. A Princess of the House of Naples. Berlin. (Clarence Kennedy)

Fig. 506. Antonio Pollaiuolo. Heracles and Antaeus. Bronze. Bargello, Florence. (Clarence Kennedy)

Fig. 507. Verrocchio. Colleoni, a condottière, or military leader. Bronze. 1481-88. Venice.

and definitely broken surfaces in the embroidered dress. Within this formal organization are the subtlest surface modulations, not used as ends in themselves or as naturalistic renderings of flesh or fabric but as contributory elements in a compelling abstract design.

Working side by side with the Desiderio group of sculptors was another, the direct descendants of Donatello. Of especial importance was Antonio Pollaiuolo (1429–1498), who is an excellent illustration of the eager zeal of these Florentine artists in their search for the fundamentals of figure expression. In the case of Antonio, it was the figure in movement based upon an intensive study of anatomy. In his bronze statuette of *Heracles and Antaeus* (FIG. 506) the two figures with tensely strained muscles are surcharged with vitality, and are so interlocked that their opposing movements and sharp angles, accentuated by the clear-cut contours and reflections of the dark bronze, produce an almost abstract expression of titanic conflict.

Fig. 508. Michelangelo. Bound Slave. Marble. c. 1513. Louvre, Paris. (Alinari)

Another important sculptor of this group was Andrea Verrocchio (1435–1488), who is best represented by the equestrian statue of *Colleoni* (FIG. 507), one of the greatest soldiers of the age and at the same time a prince of great wealth, living part of the time in the midst of camp hardships, and part of the time in the luxury of a magnificent court. We see Colleoni in full armor sitting rigidly in the saddle, from which he seems to be half rising, the feet pressing firmly upon the stirrups which bear the weight of the body, in marked contrast to *Gattamelata*, who relaxes into the saddle. The violent twist of the figure, the grim face and piercing eyes, and the angularity of the group contribute to the impression of impetuosity; and every detail contributes to a dramatic expression of forceful energy.

Through the mediation of such sculptors the uncompromising reality of Donatello and his use of plastic means for the expression of what was significant in man or event was bequeathed to Michelangelo Buo-

Fig. 509. Michelangelo. Tomb of Giuliano de' Medici. 1524–33. New Sacristy, San Lorenzo, Florence.

narroti (1475–1564). To it was added, in its passage, the results of the intensive study of this group of sculptors in the structure and plastic possibilities of the human figure. The important problems had been solved, and it was left to Michelangelo to bring a great intellect to bear upon the application of these solutions, and to carry to a climax that "harmony of structural plastic sequences" which Donatello had originated. "Either the spirit of Donatello lives in Michelangelo," said Borghini, "or that of Michelangelo already lived in Donatello." Marks of his fully developed style are already apparent in his early *Moses*,[1] in the pose with its restless movement backward and forward, the opposing movements in the drapery and beard. Yet the figure is extraordinarily compact and its restless movement is sternly confined within the ideal space determined by the block of stone from which it was carved. The detailed modeling (here perhaps too intent upon anatomical accuracy) later became broader, and plastically as well as structurally organi , as in the *Bound Slave* (FIG. 508). This figure is not so restless as the *Moses* and every part is subservient to one great rhythmic movement which rises from the foot to the uplifted arm, where it is turned back into the figure and flows, by means of the hand, into another movement around the figure visualized by the tight band about the breast. Both of these movements traverse in their spiraling the entire space determined by the four planes of the stone block.

All of Michelangelo's sculpture was architectural, that is, was de-

[1] The *Moses* was carved to decorate the tomb of Pope Julius II that was never completed as planned. The horns on the head, traditional in representations of Moses, are due to an incorrect interpretation of the passage in Exodus that describes the rays about the head of the prophet as he came down from Mt. Sinai.

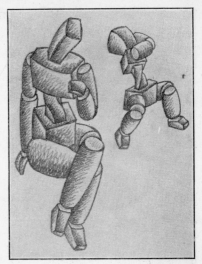

An analysis of the spiraling volumes in
Fig. 510.

Fig. 510. Michelangelo. Medici Madonna. New Sacristy, San Lorenzo,
Florence.

signed as a definite part of an architectural setting, a relationship
illustrated by the *Medici Tombs* [1]
(FIG. 509). The three figures form
a triangle within a framework of
verticals, horizontals, and curves;
not within one plane, however, but
in a series of planes with movement
backward and forward as well as
lateral. In the *Tomb of Giuliano de'
Medici*, Giuliano is seated in a niche in such a pose as to make one
distinctly aware of space,[2] as do the figures of *Day* and *Night* upon
the sarcophagus, each of which with its complicated movements seems
to be revolving about its central axis.

Giuliano, seated with head turned to his left, is clad in a suit of
magnificent armor, and holds a marshal's baton somewhat listlessly.
The whole figure, with its generalized features, is more a symbol of
ineffectuality than a portrait of the Prince. Also symbolic are the two
figures below. The Titanic *Day* has aroused himself and peers out

[1] In the *New Sacristy* of *San Lorenzo*, Florence. Michelangelo had entire charge
over the whole design, both building and sculpture, revised it several times and left
it quite incomplete as was true of all his gigantic projects.
[2] Contrast the two-dimensional organization of the *Marsuppini Tomb* (FIG. 503).

Fig. 511. Benvenuto Cellini. Saltcellar. Of gold with chasing and enamel; the base is of black ebony with figures in gold. Vienna. (Plon)

upon the world with keen gaze. The head rises vertically erect above a mighty shoulder and a muscular arm that swings around the body and thus opposes a strong horizontal movement to the verticality of the head. Parts of the figure, such as the back and shoulder, are highly finished, revealing the anatomical structure with scrupulous care; other parts, such as the head and the left hand, are still in the rough, giving one the feeling that this vigorous giant is trying to wrest himself from the block of stone. Yet such details are subordinate to the powerful rotation of masses about a central axis, which results in a design of utmost movement within the limited space marked off by the block from which it was carved. The same restlessness permeates the *Night*, whose head droops upon the bent arm, thus bringing the face effectively into the shadow. Despite the presence of the owl beneath the bent knee and a poppy wreath to symbolize slumber, the uneasy sleep of the restless figure is more truly symbolized by the mask whose open eyes follow one with fascination.

In such figures as the *Bound Slave*, *Day*, and *Night* one realizes Michelangelo's purpose. His perfect understanding of and control over the figure as an organic structure even in the most complicated movements enabled him to use the figure not as an end in itself but for the creation of plastic designs which by their formal value as well as representational content translated into visual form the conceptions of a great imagination and intellect. The *Bound Slave*, for example, may suggest the futility of struggle and the *Night* the hopeless search for rest. Interpretation of sculpture, as of poetry, is not always satisfactory. But one notes that nowhere is there tranquillity. Something of his own tortured spirit [1] permeates the tortuous movement of his designs.

[1] One needs to recall the general background of the Counter-Reformation and Michelangelo's deep concern for the Church, to which he was devoutly loyal.

Perhaps the summation of interlocking movements is found in the unfinished *Madonna* of the *New Sacristy* (FIG. 510) in which the two figures spiraling in opposite directions nevertheless compose into a unit of the utmost compactness.

D. MINOR ARTS

One of the most striking characteristics of the Renaissance artist was his versatility, the result of an apprenticeship system of education in a shop where many kinds of work were always going on. For the

Fig. 512. Orazio Fontana. Majolica Plate. XVI cent. Metropolitan Museum, New York. (Metropolitan Museum)

demands upon an artist's shop were various. All through the Middle Ages fine vessels and books were made of the most precious material for the Church service, jeweled regalia for the clergy, and tapestries to decorate the cathedral. This need still continued; and to it were added the needs of wealthy nobles and merchants as secular life became more important and the mode of living more luxurious and ostentatious. Carvings, tapestries, and painted decorations were in demand for the palaces, as well as more elaborate furniture and gold and silver plate, and fine cloths, velvets, and brocades for costumes, and jewelry and fine armor. Books in particular, with the widening of knowledge, scientific research, and passion for the literature of Greece and Rome, assumed an importance unknown before. As most of these things came from some *bottega*, it is easily seen that the artist must be versatile; and as public taste was of a high order, he must produce works of quality both in design and in technique.

Metal — bronze, iron, gold, silver — was an important medium, and skill in casting,[1] molding, chasing, and engraving was essential. The use of iron in buildings and bronze doors and in sculpture we have already seen. Among smaller objects in bronze the commemorative medal became important as the individualistic strain was manifesting

[1] For an account of bronze-casting as practiced by the Renaissance sculptors, see Benvenuto Cellini's dramatic account of how he cast his *Perseus*, in his *Memoirs*, Dutton, 1906 (Everyman's Library), pp. 402 ff.

Fig. 513. Brocaded Velvet. Italian, XV cent. Metropolitan Museum, New York. (Metropolitan Museum)

itself in portraiture. It reached a climax in the work of Antonio Pisano, known as Pisanello (about 1395–1455), in the medals of Leonello d'Este, Marquis of Ferrara.

The goldsmith was important. In fact it was as a goldsmith that many a painter and sculptor began his career. The processes used were substantially the same as those employed in the Middle Ages — repoussé, chasing, jewel-setting, and enameling; and the character of the work in the early Renaissance had the same quality of sound design, with decoration subordinate and contributory, as in the best medieval work. But increasing luxury and desire for display in all aspects of life are reflected in the changed taste seen in the late Renaissance. Of this period, the famous bronze and gold worker, Benvenuto Cellini (1500–1571), is typical, and the saltcellar (FIG. 511) with figures representing the *Sea* and the *Land* that he made for Francis I well illustrates his work.[1] There is no question about the superb technical skill here shown, the great ease and facility of handling the medium and of finishing it. But who would conceive of this exquisite bit of work as a container for salt and pepper? Here is a lack of sound craftsmanship. To astonish and delight by exquisite finish or decoration and to surprise by ingenious motifs seems to be the aim. It is as baroque in design as the Jesuitical churches, and like them very characteristic of the age that produced it.

The potter and the weaver contributed to the rich colorfulness of the age, the potter with his majolica,[2] which is earthenware covered with a whitish opaque glaze on which the decoration is painted. The colors used were intense, and their effect was heightened by rich transparent overglaze and by a luster of amazing brilliancy. A particularly fine majolica was made in the sixteenth century at Urbino, illustrated by a plate by Orazio Fontana (FIG. 512), in which borders with winged lions, birds, and half-human figures combined with garlands and scrolls surround a central medallion containing a mythological scene closely related in style to the paintings of Raphael. If one questions the use of three-dimensional painting as ceramic decoration, in the border

[1] See the artist's own description, *ibid.*, p. 340.
[2] The name is probably derived from Majorca, one of the Balearic Islands, a calling-place of the ships that brought to Italy the glazed and lustered wares of Spain.

designs at least he will find the fanciful motifs used as decorative color-units against the creamy glaze.

Fig. 514. Liberale da Verona. Aeolus. Historiated initial from a choir book. Piccolomini Library, Siena. (Alinari)

From the weaver's shop came the fine fabrics — silks, velvets, brocades, tapestries — which were in such demand, as the paintings show,[1] for costumes, both ecclesiastical and secular, and for hangings. We have seen how Persia had been a center for weaving, especially of fine silks; how Justinian introduced the craft into Europe; and how the Muhammadans became expert weavers. In their conquests westward the Moslems brought the craft with them to Spain, to Sicily, and thence to Italy, where luxuriant stuffs were woven which in pattern, color, and motifs were entirely of the tradition of the Near East. In the fifteenth century, however, the Italian weavers, quite in accordance with the spirit of their times, broke with this old tradition, and introduced into their fabrics a pomegranate motif (FIG. 513) used with many variations. The richness of color and vigor of pattern, in their velvets and brocades in particular, are in harmony with Renaissance art as a whole.

In the field of bookmaking, the Italians made valuable contributions. We have been following the evolution of the book from the long rolls of the Egyptians, Greeks, and Romans to the codex, which became in the early Christian era very sumptuous in its writing, decoration, and binding, and throughout the Middle Ages remained a work in whose making a whole group of artists collaborated. Probably the highest expression of the Italian scribes and illuminators is seen in the great choir books that reached their culmination in the late fifteenth century. The most characteristic part of their decoration is the initial letter, painted in bright colors with white tracery, foliate orna-

[1] See particularly the paintings of Domenico Ghirlandaio, Benozzo Gozzoli, the Bellini, Crivelli, Titian, and, in fact, most of the Venetian painters, whose works reveal so clearly the love of the Venetians for fine stuffs.

POLIPHILO QVIVI NARRA,CHE GLI PAR VE AN-
CORA DI DORMIRE,ET ALTRONDE IN SOMNO
RITROVARSE IN VNA CONVALLE,LAQVALE NEL
FINE ER A SER A T A DE VNA MIR A BILE CLA VSVR A
CVM VNA PORTENTOSA PYRAMIDE,DE ADMI-
RATIONE DIGNA,ET VNO EXCELSOOBELISCO DE
SOPR A,LA QV ALE CVM DILIGENTIA ET PIACERE
SVBTILMENTE LA CONSIDEROE.

Fig. 515. Page from the *Hypneroto-machia Poliphili*, or *Strife of Love in a Dream*. Printed by Aldus at the Aldine Press in Venice, 1499.

ment, and gold; and frequently be-cause of its large size historiated, that is, adorned with a miniature within the form of the letter. Many of these were painted by well-known artists, as was the *Aeolus* (FIG. 514). Within the letter and wonderfully adapted to the shape is a representation of Aeolus sweeping forward with all the energy of the north wind. The use of a classical subject is interesting here, as is the spontaneous, naïve concep-tion so characteristic of the fifteenth-century attitude toward Greek and Roman subjects. The rich foliate decoration surrounding the initial is typical of Italian work, which often became too heavy and florid to have the perfectly decorative quality of the French manuscripts.

Meanwhile, one of the most far-reaching inventions was about to bring to an end the handmade book: printing, an invention not of one man or at one place, but the growth of centuries. Some of the under-lying practices, such as using a stamp for initial letters, had long been known. Paper was becoming common in the fourteenth century, mak-ing inexpensive books possible, though vellum and parchment were long used for fine books. What we know is that in the decade from about 1450 to 1460 printing with movable type became established at Mainz, and by the end of the fifteenth century was being practiced in all the countries of western Europe. The early books (incunabula) closely re-sembled the manuscripts of the period in composition, form of letters, and decoration. In fact printing was used for the small letters only; the initials and the decorations were added in color by hand after the printing was done, so that the general effect of the page was the same as that of the manuscript.

For nearly a century the printed book very closely followed the tradition of the manuscript. It had no title page, no chapter heading, no running title, no pagination. The early printed books of Italy show clearly the Italian sensitiveness for unity of design (FIG. 516), which appears especially in the small pamphlets issued at Florence, known as *Rappresentazioni* because they reproduced the plays given on saints' days. In place of a title page, they had a woodcut with the representation of an angel as a herald to announce the play, and perhaps a characteristic scene from the life of the saint who was being celebrated. These Florentine books are among the most successfully illustrated books ever made, because the illustration illustrates and at the same time harmonizes with the letterpress. Its purpose was to elucidate the text or to emphasize some point by visualization, and not to call attention away from the text to itself as an end. The Florentine realized that to keep this unity his illustration should harmonize with the printing, and that nothing could accomplish this end so adequately as purely linear work. The *Hypnerotomachia Poliphili* (Fig. 515) illustrates these practices on a more elaborate scale. Its high quality does not lie in the content of the text, which is dull and long drawn out, nor in the woodcuts alone, but in the complete and satisfying unity of letterpress, margins, type, and illustrations, a unity as important in bookmaking as it is in picture-making, unless one looks upon a book merely for its content and not as a work of art. As in the Florentine pamphlet, so in the *Hypnerotomachia*, the linear quality of the woodcut adds variety to the printed page and at the same time maintains the unity of the page composition.

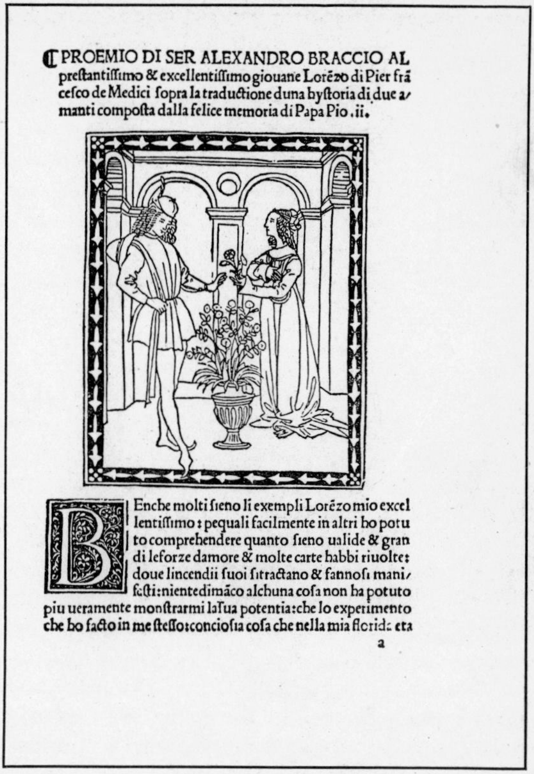
¶ PROEMIO DI SER ALEXANDRO BRACCIO AL prestantissimo & excellentissimo giouane Lorẽzo di Pier frã cesco de Medici sopra la traductione duna hystoria di due amanti composta dalla felice memoria di Papa Pio .ii.

BEnche molti sieno li exempli Lorẽzo mio excellentissimo: pequali facilmente in altri ho potuto comprehendere quanto sieno ualide & grandi leforze damore & molte carte habbi riuolte: doue lincendii suoi sitractano & fannosi manifesti: nientedimãco alchuna cosa non ha potuto piu ueramente monstrarmi laSua potentia: che lo experimento che ho facto in me stesso: conciosia cosa che nella mia florida eta

a

Fig. 516. Title Page of the *Story of Two Lovers*. XV cent. Florence. (Metropolitan Museum)

Another kind of illustration used by the Italians was the *engraving*. The process is as follows: A copper plate is beaten smooth and highly polished; on this the engraver incises his design with a sharp instrument called the *burin*. The plate is then inked by passing over it an inked roller that fills the incised lines of the design. Then it is wiped and a sheet of paper is laid on it and subjected to pressure that sucks the ink out of the plate, leaving the design in raised lines on the paper. The fact that many printings, or impressions, can be made from one plate made the process appeal to the Italians as a practical method of making many copies of a design to serve as models for their apprentices. The origin of engraving, as of printing, is uncertain. The Netherlands, Germany, and Italy claim priority in its use. Not many of the first-rate Italian painters made use of the medium, though two notable exceptions were Antonio Pollaiuolo (FIG. 529) and Mantegna, both of whom were interested in an intensive study of form that found expression primarily in line.

E. SUMMARY

The Renaissance meant a change in point of view, the emergence of new ideas, and consequently the need of new forms for their expression. The social solidarity of the Middle Ages and the predominantly ecclesiastical outlook began to give way before an advancing individualism and secularization, with parallel changes in the art expression. Hence the early Renaissance was primarily an age of transition in which Romanesque and Gothic forms first admitted classical details, only to disappear themselves eventually in the face of an increasing enthusiasm for the revived classical style. Symmetry in plan and design, domes, classical orders and ornament appeared, but these traditional forms were combined into new unities under the inquiring and adventurous spirit of the fifteenth century, until a truly Renaissance style emerged, both ecclesiastical and secular, based upon classical forms yet individual in their use. Interest centered not on problems of construction, but upon basic abstract forms, though ornament engaged both builder and sculptor, for architecture and sculpture were closely allied, so that a similar evolution is discernible in sculpture. Romanesque and Gothic decorative sculpture began to feel the influence of the Humanistic classical art earlier than architecture, and to create forms based upon a visual grasp of nature and upon a scientific study of the structure of the figure. Starting with what the eye saw and the mind learned about the human figure as an organic structure, the sculptors sought to translate both intellectual and visual facts into an esthetically satisfying form.

BIBLIOGRAPHY

Anderson, W. J., *The Architecture of the Renaissance in Italy*, Scribner, 1927

Baum, Julius, *Baukunst und decorative Plastik der Frührenaissance in Italien*, Stuttgart, 1926

Biagi, Guido, *Men and Manners of Old Florence*, McClurg, 1909

Blashfield, E. H. and E. W., *Italian Cities*, new ed., Scribner, 1912

Bode, Wilhelm von, *Die Kunst der Frührenaissance in Italien*, 2d ed., Berlin, 1926

—— —— *Florentine Sculptors of the Renaissance*, Scribner, 1909

Burckhardt, J. C., *The Civilization of the Renaissance in Italy*, tr. by S. G. C. Middlemore, Harper, 1929

Cartwright, Julia (Mrs. Ady), *Beatrice d'Este*, Dutton, 1903, 2 vols.

—— —— *Isabella d'Este*, Dutton, 1903, 2 vols.

Castiglione, Baldassare, *Book of the Courtier*, tr. by L. E. Updycke, Scribner, 1903

Cellini, Benvenuto, *Autobiography*, tr. by J. A. Symonds, Modern Library, 1927

Cruttwell, Maud, *Verrocchio*, Scribner, 1904

Faure, Gabriel, *Wanderings in Italy*, Houghton Mifflin, 1919

Fortnum, C. D. E., *Maiolica*, London, 1882

Geck, F. J., *Bibliography of Italian Early Renaissance Art*, University of Colorado, 1932

—— —— *Bibliography of Italian High Renaissance Art*, University of Colorado, 1933

—— —— *Bibliography of Italian Late Renaissance Art*, University of Colorado, 1934

Gilman, Roger, *Great Styles of Interior Architecture*, Harper, 1924

Gromort, Georges, *Italian Renaissance Architecture*, tr. by G. F. Waters, Helburn, 1922

Herbert, J. A., *Illuminated Manuscripts*, Putnam, 1911

Hill, G. F., *Portrait Medals of Italian Artists of the Renaissance*, London, 1912

Holroyd, Sir Charles, *Michael Angelo Buonarroti*, Scribner, 1904

Jackson, Sir T. G., *The Renaissance of Roman Architecture*, University of Chicago Press, 1922, 2 vols., Vol. I, *Italy*

Kristeller, Paul, *Early Florentine Woodcuts*, London, 1897

Marquand, Allan, *Luca della Robbia*, Princeton University Press, 1914

Meyer, A. G., *Donatello*, Lemcke & Buechner, 1904

Moore, C. H., *The Character of Renaissance Architecture*, Macmillan, 1905

Odom, W. MacD., *History of Italian Furniture*, Doubleday, Page, 1918–19, 2 vols.

Orcutt, W. D., *The Book in Italy in the Fifteenth and Sixteenth Centuries*, Harper, 1928

Pollard, A. W., *Early Illustrated Books*, new ed., Empire State Book Co., 1927

Ricci, Corrado, *Architecture and Decorative Sculpture of the High and Late Renaissance in Italy*, Brentano's, 1923

Ross, J. A. D.-G., *Florentine Palaces and Their Stories*, Dutton, 1905

Ruskin, John, *Stones of Venice*, Estes, 1913, 3 vols.

Schubring, Paul, *Die Kunst der Hochrenaissance in Italien*, Berlin, 1926

Scott, Geoffrey, *The Architecture of Humanism*, 2d ed., Scribner, 1924

Solon, L. M. E., *History and Description of Italian Majolica*, Cassell, 1907

Staley, J. E., *Guilds of Florence*, McClurg, 1906

Symonds, J. A., *Short History of the Renaissance in Italy*, Holt, 1894

Taylor, H. O., *Thought and Expression in the Sixteenth Century*, Macmillan, 1920

Triggs, H. I., *The Art of Garden Design in Italy*, Longmans, 1906

Vasari, Giorgio, *The Lives of the Painters, Sculptors and Architects*, tr. by A. B. Hinds, Dutton, 1927, 4 vols. (Everyman's Library)

Venturi, Adolfo, *A Short History of Italian Art*, tr. by Edward Hutton, Macmillan, 1926

Young, G. F., *The Medici*, Modern Library, 1930

Fig. 517. Duccio. Majestà. Detail of the center. Originally it had an elaborate Gothic frame. 1308–11. Siena Cathedral Museum. (Alinari)

F. PAINTING IN SIENA AND FLORENCE

If sculpture in the early Renaissance was definitely architectural, painting was equally so. When not actual mural decoration, mosaic or fresco, for which Italian buildings with their large areas of unbroken walls were peculiarly adapted, it was an altarpiece or a panel commissioned for a definite site possessing a definite lighting. The painters were still working in the provincial "Italo-Byzantine," style which was a decadent form of early Byzantinism, though the contemporary Greek culture of the second climax with its great schools of painting seems also to have been felt in Italy, while in Rome a faint thread of Roman naturalism appeared now and then. Thus, as in architecture and sculpture, we find in early Renaissance painting medieval styles which through the impacts of new attitudes and new ideas evolved, after an age of transition, into a new style.

It is in Siena that the older style of the East blossomed into its finest flowering in Italy; in Florence that the new style was initiated and led to a brilliant climax. At least some reasons for this difference are not difficult to find. Siena, though situated only about thirty miles from Florence (FIG. 463), always remained in temperament close to the mystic East,[1] and too conservative to admit the new ideas and classical influences, as is illustrated by the story of the statue of Aphro-

[1] See the life and letters of St. Catherine, the most adored saint of Siena.

Fig. 518. Duccio.
Three Marys at the
Tomb. A panel from
the back of the Ma-
jestà. Siena Cathe-
dral Museum. (Ali-
nari)

dite that was discovered near the city and set up to decorate the public fountain. Since a long series of disasters subsequent to the coming of Aphrodite was laid to her malevolent presence, the council decreed not only her removal but, in naïve faith, her burial far enough away from the city to be within the boundaries of the commune of its great foe, Florence.

Not only by temperament but by geographic situation Siena was destined to be out of the current of the Renaissance. In its lofty site on a triple hill it suffered a tragic disadvantage in comparison with the cities in the valleys on the great natural trade routes, as was Florence. Though important commercially in the twelfth and thirteenth centuries, and in close contact through Pisa with the East, it fell eventually but gloriously before mightier Florence, and the Renaissance swept by leaving it, in its emotional intensity and mysticism, isolated and still medieval.

Here, then, was congenial soil for Byzantinism, which reached a climax in Duccio di Buoninsegna (1255–1319), whose great altarpiece, the *Majestà* or *Madonna in Majesty* [1] (FIG. 517), stood facing the nave on the high altar of the cathedral. In its original elaborate Gothic frame, with a liberal use of gold in the backgrounds and details, in the clear massing of large areas of color and definitely linear quality it must have shared somewhat the sumptuous effect of a gold-ground mosaic.

---

[1] For an account of the festive occasion when this altarpiece was carried from the shop to the cathedral, see Langton Douglas, *A History of Siena*, Dutton, 1902, p. 336.

Fig. 519. Simone Martini (assisted by Lippo Memmi). Annunciation.
1333. Uffizi, Florence. (Alinari)

The Madonna and Child, of majestic size, seated on an elaborate
Cosmati throne and surrounded by four angels who bend over the
throne and by row upon row of saints and angels, provide a clear
central accent in a symmetrical, severely simple composition. Through
clear areas of resplendent color gleams the gold of the ground, of the
exquisitely tooled halos and of small details — a beautiful example of
tempera painting.[1] The majesty of otherworldliness is combined with

---

[1] The foundation of a tempera painting was a panel of carefully selected wood,
often covered with linen, on which was laid a thin coat or several coats of *gesso*, that
is, fine plaster of Paris mixed with glue. This was rubbed down until the surface
was marblelike. A detailed preliminary drawing, called the *cartoon*, was made to size
and transferred to the panel. The pigments, in dry powder form, were mixed with
egg and slightly thinned. First a coat of underpainting in green or brown was put
in, with shading to model the form. Over this were added the local colors applied
in small strokes and with painstaking care, for the pigment dried quickly to a hard
surface finish and gave no opportunity for making changes such as are possible when
oil is used. The results of this method were definite outlines, slight shading, a hard
enamel-like surface, and a generally decorative effect. The unpleasantly greenish
tone of many Italian paintings is due to the wearing away of the surface pigments,
leaving the underpainting exposed. Also the brownish tone found in so many paintings
even down to the present is due to the fact that the brown underpainting controls
and unifies the hues applied over it. See A. P. Laurie, *The Materials of the Painter's
Craft in Europe and Egypt*, Lippincott, 1911; Sir C. J. Holmes, *Notes on the Science of
Picture Making*, new ed., Stokes, 1928; James Ward, *History and Methods of Ancient and
Modern Painting*, Dutton, 1913–17, 3 vols.

monumental splendor through the type of design that Duccio has used for a large altarpiece placed in a half-light.

Upon the reverse of the altarpiece was a series of small panels illustrating scenes from the life of Christ which show not only Duccio's power of narration — for these little pictures were meant to be read, as were the windows of *Chartres* — but also how, as in the front panel, he built his forms of light and color and organized them into a design whose very character achieved lucidity of statement and beauty of decoration. The composition of *The Three Marys* (FIG. 518), for example, as a whole and of the figures in detail is traditional in Byzantine art,[1] elements of a widely known pictorial language. The triangular pattern of the angel's figure framed by the triangular hill and resting upon a rectangularly paneled base

Fig. 520. Sassetta. Marriage of St. Francis and Poverty. 1444. Musée Condé, Chantilly.

is opposed to the blocklike group of the three Marys accented by a blocklike hill, and through both groups play curves and countercurves, and sharp angles. While the three figures produce an effect of solidity and the sculptured hills one of a considerable feeling for space, the sharply defined areas of color, often of contrasting hues, and the flat gold background and halos leave one with the impression of a sumptuously decorative panel, and at the same time with an unmistakable statement of the incident.

In many of Duccio's figures one notices a limited use of light and shadow to suggest volume, naturalistic folds of drapery, some feeling for solidity and space — hints of the entrance, even into Siena, of the new naturalism which swept Europe in the thirteenth century, instances of which we noted in the sculpture at *Chartres*, and in the work of the Pisani and Arnolfo. On the whole, however, these evidences of the new approach do not alter the essentially Byzantine character of Sienese painting.

The followers of Duccio we find focusing now upon one aspect,

[1] See Byron and Talbot Rice, *The Birth of Western Painting*, PL. 59.

Fig. 521. The Arena Chapel. Padua. Decorated with frescoes by Giotto, 1305. (Alinari)

now upon another, of his all-inclusive style. Simone Martini (about 1285–1344) created exquisite surfaces — gold grounds, with marvelously tooled borders, through which play gliding linear rhythms and charming color-patterns. His *Annunciation* (FIG. 519), when seen in the dim light of the chapel in the Siena Cathedral for which it was painted (now in the Uffizi), has a mosaiclike, sumptuous, decorative quality, exquisite and lyrical rather than epically monumental, as is Duccio's *Majestà* (FIG. 517) near by. The angel has just alighted and eagerly presses forward with the olive branch to deliver his message to the Virgin, who, interrupted in her reading, shrinks away, thus affording the painter, by her pose, an opportunity to combine the suave curves and countercurves of her figure in its dark robe into a charming pattern of blue against the gold ground, and to carry the movement, with the help of the arches of the frame, back to the angel. Here the rapid movement in the fluttering draperies and in the broken patterns of the gold brocade, wings, and cloak offers an effective contrast to the quiet dark silhouette of the Virgin; while the vase of flowers, the olive branch, and the floor, as well as the gold ground, unite the disparate elements. With practically no reference to visual perception Simone wove symbols of figures into this charming, almost abstract pattern whose very loveliness of form intensifies the idea to be conveyed.

This delight in the loveliness of surface and sinuous line given such impetus by Simone was one of the constant elements in Sienese painting and is by no means lacking in an entirely different follower of Duccio, Ambrogio Lorenzetti (active 1323–1348), whose robust figures, humanized from the hieratic Duccio type, vigorous color contrasts, and equally vigorous straight lines, as well as a lucid organization within a realized space,[1] are evidences of the fact that he worked in Florence and there came into contact with the Humanistic and naturalistic movement of Giotto.

When the fifteenth-century Sienese painters could scarcely avoid some influence from the powerful new movement permeating all Italy,

[1] See Ambrogio's frescoes in *San Francesco*, his narrative panoramic style in the *Palazzo Pubblico*, Siena; compare his *Majestà* of Massa Maritima with Duccio's *Majestà*.

it was still the traditions of their great Trecento forbears that dominated their work, onto which the new naturalism was weakly grafted. To take the *Mystic Marriage of St. Francis* (FIG. 520) by Sassetta (1392–1450) as an example, though the gold ground has disappeared before a landscape and terrestrial spaciousness, the slender Gothic figures provide an excuse for the use of rhythmically repeated calligraphic lines and a primary interest in pat-

Fig. 522. Giotto. Pietà. Fresco. 1305. Arena Chapel. Padua. (Alinari)

tern in which the use of space as an element of balance is matched only by the great masters of handling space, the painters of China and Japan. In the fifteenth-century Sienese painting the monumental archaic form of Duccio was transformed into a frail loveliness that betokened a declining age.

In the invigorating air of cities in a ferment of changing ideas, the Byzantine style could hardly suffice as a means of expression. Cimabue (about 1240–1301) in the face of this inadequacy attempted to revitalize its forms by infusing them with a new energy. Cavallini of Rome (active 1250–1330) in both his mosaics and frescoes attempted to meet the problem in a revival of Roman naturalism, that is, by modeling his figures in light and graduated shadow and by making their garments deep folds of actual stuffs instead of flat linear constructions, and by imbuing the figures with a stately dignity. Cavallini was something of a Nicola d'Apulia in painting, as Cimabue, at least in his emotional content, was a Giovanni Pisano.

Here, then, were two general lines of approach which confronted the youthful Giotto (1276–1336) when he came to Assisi to assist in the decorative scheme of *San Francesco*, which had been going on since its erection.[1] And here was the very heart of one of the dynamic forces

[1] This church well illustrates Cimabue's work in the *Crucifixion* (Upper Church) and the *Madonna and St. Francis* (Lower Church); see also his *Madonnas* (Uffizi and Louvre). The *Isaac* series (Upper Church) represents the Roman school; for Cavallini, see the mosaics in *Santa Maria in Trastevere* (Rome) and the frescoes of *Santa Cecilia in Trastevere* (Rome).

Fig. 523. Giotto. Obsequies of St. Francis. Fresco. c. 1320.
Santa Croce, Florence. (Alinari)

of the Renaissance — St. Francis and the Franciscan movement. At
Assisi Giotto seems to have created a mode of expression which he set
forth fully developed in the *Arena Chapel* [1] (FIG. 521) at Padua a few
years later. Here one senses at once a great gulf between the old and
the new despite Giotto's artistic ancestry in both Byzantine and Roman
styles and his continued use of traditional Byzantine iconography and
composition, his use of the contemporary fresco technique, and the
usual practice of covering walls with narratives which served a combined didactic and decorative purpose.

The great difference between Giotto's work and that of his immediate
predecessors and contemporaries is the difference between two widely
divergent attitudes in painting.[2] With the one, represented by the latter
painters, forms are constructed of purely formal elements — line, light
and dark, color — with little or no regard for the natural appearance
of what is represented; its tendency is toward abstraction and if carried
to its logical conclusion would result in pure geometry. This is the
Byzantine attitude. With the other, represented by Giotto, forms are
constructed with direct reference to visual perception and spatial rela-

[1] So named because it stands on the site of an ancient Roman arena or amphitheater. It is also called the *Scrovegni Chapel* because Enrico Scrovegni, the son of
a wealthy Paduan who was so avaricious that Dante placed him in the seventh circle
of hell among the usurers, had built the chapel as if to atone for the reputation of
the family.

[2] These two attitudes, which roughly divide all painting into two groups, with
many border cases, of course, are highly important for an understanding of the evolution of European painting and particularly for its twentieth-century phase.

Fig. 524. Masaccio. Tribute Money. Fresco. c. 1425–28. Brancacci
Chapel of Santa Maria della Carmine, Florence. (Alinari)

tions; its tendency is toward naturalism and its logical conclusion is
a photographic copy. Now what particularly impresses one about
Giotto's work, in comparison with the Byzantine, is its actuality, its
wholehearted grasp of an actuality based upon visual perception.
Other painters had groped in this direction. Perhaps Tuscany inherited more than its name from the Etruscans of long ago. Perhaps
there still existed a slight thread of their own vital human reality.
One likes to feel this when looking at Cimabue's *Crucifixion*. But Giotto
was the first to turn definitely to visual actuality, and so definitely
that he set painting on the path of visual investigation that it was
to travel for five hundred years.

Take the *Pietà* (FIG. 522) as an example. The body of Christ is
held and surrounded by mourners who are actual people, with real
bodies, in clearly defined space, united in their expression of intense
human grief; in fact the entire fresco is permeated with this emotional
quality. There is the mere suggestion of a barren landscape — a rocky
hillside and a dead tree — while the sky is filled with angels who are
giving themselves up to unrestrained grief. The center of interest is
the head of Christ, on which all the lines converge — the curves of the
bending figures, the line of the hillside, which is broken by one of the
figures and hence not too obvious, the vertical folds of the drapery just
above the Virgin, and even the glance of the two upright figures on
the right, whose function is to balance the group on the left and to
form, in an almost architectural way, a framework for the central
group. Every figure in the panel plays its part as if it were an architectural member of an abstract construction to which every gesture
and detail is a contributing element. Looking at the individual figures,
we see with what economical means yet how convincingly the bodies
are realized as masses existing in space, and with what discrimination

Fig. 525. Paolo Uccello. Battle Piece. c. 1456. National Gallery, London.

Fig. 525 (*a*). Analysis of depth. The foreground and background are organized in depth by means of linear perspective. But they are not united by the middle distance, which is more or less a void as far as space is concerned.

Fig. 525 (*b*). Analysis of planes. The main elements of the painting are composed into planes generally parallel to the picture plane and the movement is lateral.

their simplest aspects only are expressed. With slight use of shadow and line which defines the mass,[1] each figure is so placed in depth that in addition to the linear pattern there is felt a movement in depth which radiates from the focal point elliptically, for the opportunity of movement is chiefly lateral, since the shallow depth is abruptly terminated by the blue ground. This blue, however, used consistently in all the panels in the chapel, serves as a unifying element in the decorative scheme.

An even more perfect cohesion is found in the *Obsequies of St. Francis* (FIG. 523), which though similar to the *Pietà* in subject matter and basic composition is expressive of intense calm, due to an emphasis upon symmetry, upon the vertical and horizontal, while in the *Pietà* the stress lay upon asymmetry and

Fig. 526. Andrea del Castagno. Pippo Spano. Former convent of Sant' Apollonia, Florence.

a forceful diagonal.[2] In fact almost every painting by Giotto shows his inventiveness, for each presents a different problem of integrating visually perceived figures and objects into just that type of abstract organization which would convey the spiritual significance of the event in terms of human actuality.

Giotto's unique and powerful art produced imitators only, without his power of lucid synthesis. Sienese painting was at its climax, for Duccio and Giotto were contemporaries and Ambrogio Lorenzetti was painting in Florence about the time of Giotto's death. Thus the painters of the second half of the Trecento vacillated between an attempt to copy Giotto's forms and a maintenance of the traditional medieval style, which was much more popular and more easily understood than Giotto's.

Hence it was not until the fifteenth century that the movement

[1] This kind of drawing might be called sculptural, and is found in the drawings of those artists who see and feel masses in three dimensions and thus is to be distinguished from the calligraphic line of such painters as Simone Martini and the Persian miniaturists. Roger Fry calls attention to the fact that when we realize the great significance of Giotto's line, the famous story of Giotto's O seems credible. For this story see Vasari's life of Giotto. See also Bernhard Berenson's essay stressing "tactile values" in *The Florentine Painters of the Renaissance*, Putnam, 1909.

[2] For an analysis of the *Obsequies*, with analytical drawings, see Gardner, *Understanding the Arts*, pp. 214 ff.

Fig. 527. Baldovinetti. Madonna. c. 1460. Louvre, Paris. (X Photo)

Fig. 528. Antonio Pollaiuolo. Heracles Slaying the Hydra. 1460. Uffizi, Florence.

initiated by Giotto found further expression in Masaccio (1401–1428),[1] whose frescoes in the *Brancacci Chapel* of the *Carmine* (Florence) dominated the Florentine school of the fifteenth century as did the sculpture and building of Brunelleschi and Donatello, their contemporaries. To illustrate by the *Tribute Money* (FIG. 524), one sees a group in a rugged barren landscape of great depth and spaciousness, not abbreviated or symbolic as in Giotto, into which the figures fit as in the world of actuality visually perceived. The disciples are gathered about Christ, who is directing Peter to go and cast his line, saying that in the mouth of the first fish he will find a coin with which he is to pay the tax. In the foreground, with his back to the spectator, stands the publican. The two concluding incidents are also shown in the panel, for at the left Peter is seen dragging the fish from the water, while at the right he is giving the publican the coin. The visual reality of the scene is what Vasari felt when he said that Masaccio was the

[1] Masaccio's real name was Tomaso; but because of his careless disregard for his personal affairs, his forgetfulness of his debtors and equally of his creditors, he won the nickname Masaccio, a shortened form of Tomasaccio, meaning "Clumsy Tom." The Florentines frequently gave expression to their fun-loving disposition by applying appropriate nicknames to their citizens, which became so current that they have taken precedence over the real name. Thus in the case of Donatello, this sculptor's name was Donato, to which the suffix -*ello*, denoting endearment, was added, signifying the loving esteem felt by the Florentines for him. For the life of Masaccio, see Vasari.

Fig. 529. Antonio Pollaiuolo. Battling Nudes. Between 1465 and 1480.
Coll. Paul J. Sachs, Cambridge, Mass. (Paul J. Sachs)

first artist to attain to the imitation of things as they are. But the scene is not merely an imitation of nature; it is an exceedingly dignified and monumental conception. Christ is the central figure among the disciples who encircle him in a broadly sweeping compact group that is related in many details to the background. The figure on the right, for example, repeats the verticals of the house and the outstretched arm near the left, the diagonals of the hills. Again the figures are tied together and to the landscape by a consistent use of light and, if one can judge despite overpaintings, a feeling of an all-pervasive atmosphere. Not only is the group convincing because of its monumental dignity, its relation to the landscape, and its largeness of design, but the individual figures give one a sense of massiveness and of existence in space, as did Giotto's, and also a sense of bodily structure. In this respect Masaccio advanced beyond Giotto. This may be noted particularly in the figure of the publican, in which there is real expression of a structural organism. One feels that there is a bony framework, muscles, joints, and articulations which enable this organism to support itself and move. As Vasari said, "Masaccio made his figures stand upon their feet."

With Masaccio we enter the early Renaissance with its eager enthusiasm for inquiry. The world of actuality, curiosity about man and his world, led to fresh observations and to a compelling need for new forms in which to express them. The supranatural grandeur of Byzantinism arose from an entirely different world from that in which the

Fig. 530. Unknown artist. Portrait of a Lady. c. 1460. Poldi Pezzoli, Milan. (Anderson)

Fig. 531. Luca Signorelli. Last Judgment, detail. 1500–04. Orvieto Cathedral. (Anderson)

men of the Quattrocento found themselves. Thus arose a scientific search for a more adequate type of expression; this involved the study of anatomy for the structure of the figure; of light and shadow to show its volume; of linear and aerial perspective to determine its place in space; and of new technical methods of mixing and applying pigment.

Paolo Uccello (1397–1475) displayed his compelling enthusiasm for perspective in his battle pieces (FIG. 525), but not as an end in itself. The foreshortened figure, spears, and miscellany in the foreground carry one directly and insistently across space into the middle distance, whence the roads and diminished figures continue the movement into the far distance. Thus is carved out a space for the action. A mass of soldiers accented by their spears moves in from the left, a movement balanced by the road moving forward diagonally from the depth at the right. The "impressionistic" crowd becomes more and more clearly defined until in the foreground simple trenchant forms of horsemen stand fixed, their movement transmuted into immobility. Each form is clearly defined of itself and in space by juxtaposing highly contrasting values and by the sharp delineation of the forms by line. Thus an incident of complex movement becomes a clearly coördinate organization of formal and decorative beauty, in the search for which science was used only as the means to an end. In fact all the artists

Fig. 532. Piero della Francesca. Visit of the Queen of Sheba to King Solomon. Fresco. 1452–66. San Francesco, Arezzo. (Alinari)

of this "scientific" group to which Paolo belonged sought scientific knowledge of the visual world for this purpose, and because they were primarily great artists "their facts had to be digested into form." [1]

Important members of this group were Andrea del Castagno (1397–1457), whose portrait of *Pippo Spano* (FIG. 526) reveals Andrea's tense incisiveness and also the emergence of portraiture, inevitable in a day of dynamic individuals; Domenico Veneziano (1400–1461), an important innovator in the field of oil glazes; Antonio Pollaiuolo (1429–1498); Andrea del Verrocchio (1435–1488); Alesso Baldovinetti (1425–1499); and the Umbro-Florentines, Piero della Francesca (1416–1492) and Luca Signorelli (1441–1522).

Baldovinetti's workshop was an important center for the group about the middle of the century. Secular subject matter, especially classical, was recommending itself to them. Experiments were going on in the use of oil as a freer, more slowly drying medium than the tempera; and experiments in aerial as well as linear perspective, as one gathers from Baldovinetti's painting, the Louvre *Madonna* (FIG. 527), for example, but, as in Uccello, not for an illusionistic purpose primarily. The figure of the Madonna is realized as mass and as an organic structure, yet it is constructed as tersely as Uccello's horses. Though

[1] R. E. Fry, *Vision and Design*, Coward-McCann, 1924, "The Art of Florence."

Fig. 533. Fra Angelico. Coronation of the Virgin. c. 1430. San Marco, Florence. An example of beautiful tempera painting: gaily colorful, luminous, effectively organized in shallow space. The intense colors of the robes, interspersed with the gold of the halos and details, set against the gold ground produce the effect of a magnified cloisonné enamel.

it rises majestically into a great spaciousness, it bears no natural relationship to the landscape behind it. Yet the two tie into an organic design of complementary sharp angles and suave curves, of slow movements in unbroken contours balanced by the rapid rhythms of veil, hair, and meandering streams. These motifs are repeated all through the canvas with unmistakable clarity because of the sharp juxtaposition of lights and darks which contributes to the generally decorative effect of the panel. Antonio Pollaiuolo, trained first, like many Florentine artists, as a goldsmith, became equally successful as a sculptor, particularly in bronze (FIG. 506), as a painter, as an engraver, and as a designer of tapestries. In a small panel representing *Heracles Slaying the Hydra* (FIG. 528) Heracles is rushing upon the monster, grasping one of the heads in the left hand, and about to bring down his club with the right. The two figures nearly fill the panel and stand out against a low-lying landscape with winding rivers in much the same way as in Baldovinetti's *Madonna*. In Heracles' figure we feel the tenseness of the muscles and the articulation of the joints as every part of the anatomy responds to the demand of the moment. One leg is bent to a right angle and firmly placed, with toes clutching the ground, the other is stretched to its utmost as he concentrates his energy upon the attack. As Berenson says, Antonio Pollaiuolo was "one of the greatest masters of movement that there ever has been and one of the ablest interpreters of the human body as a vehicle of life-communicating energy and ex-ulting power." We know that he made searching studies in perspective and in anatomy, especially through dissection. What interested him par-ticularly was how the human figure would act in violent movement. For this reason he usually selected subjects that gave an opportunity for action. In his engraving of the *Battling Nudes* (FIG. 529) each figure is an epitome of intense energy, a grimly realistic expression of human ferocity. Yet what a superb pattern these figures weave against the curtainlike back-ground of plants and trees! This bal-ance between the visual perception and formal organization is well illus-trated in a charming portrait (FIG. 530), possibly by Antonio, a beautiful

Fig. 534. Fra Filippo Lippi. Ma-donna and Child with Two Angels. C. 1457. Uffizi, Florence.

example of tempera technique with exquisite modulations and a deco-rative effect that results from the fine, precise brush strokes and the sharply defined edges.

Piero della Francesca, from a small town in Umbria, worked in Florence in conjunction with the scientific group, a relationship one is keenly aware of as he looks at the Arezzo frescoes. In a detail from the *Visit of the Queen of Sheba to Solomon* (FIG. 532), the Queen, sur-rounded by her attendants, is kneeling before a bridge,[1] the whole group being accentuated by the tree behind them. The kneeling Queen is emphasized by the contrasting tall, erect figures of the attendants. From the one to the other the eye is carried by the alternating light and dark masses, and by the long sweeping lines of the drapery to the group on the left, that of the grooms and horses, also accentuated by a tree. Here the white horse turns the movement inward, where it is caught by the light hat, the black horse, and is taken up by the undulating hills, whose quiet rhythm is accented by the staccato of the trees. Every figure fits inevitably into the ample spaciousness, which is cut off in the middle distance, keeping the wall rather flat. Even the illimitable sky is held by the decisive trees. A profound calm

[1] This fresco is a detail from a series that illustrates the story of the cross on which Christ was crucified. In this scene the bridge before which the Queen is kneeling was made from the tree that was destined to furnish the wood for the cross.

Fig. 535. Botticelli. Birth of Venus. c. 1485. Uffizi, Florence. (Alinari)

devoid of human emotion pervades the austere figures, in which Piero shows a lofty disregard of an illusion of natural appearance yet communicates a deeply convincing feeling of actuality. Every figure and every object in itself austerely simplified is placed with mathematical precision in space and in relation to every other figure — a relationship indicated precisely by the shapes and movements of contrasted light and dark color-masses with sharply defined edges and tied together by an all-pervading cool tonality. "The lofty expanse of sky is an intense, unforgettable blue, not medievally flat, not filled with realistic clouds and haze, but varied a little in tone, so that it seems to recede into infinite distance. Its hue condenses to a deeper turquoise in some of the robes, and its pale dry light descends to reveal every figure with unflickering crystal clarity. It fills both highlights and background with a fresh, cool atmosphere, against which garments of deep red, green and gold stand out here and there in warmer contrast." [1]

If in Piero scientific knowledge of mathematics, perspective, and anatomy was distilled to its essence and objectified in cool, impersonal, abstract forms infinitely precise in their relationships, in his pupil Signorelli (1441–1523) this knowledge manifested itself in dramatic intensity, in a tingling life, in energy, and in a harsh realism in the expression of structure, as one sees in the frescoes of *The Last Judgment* (FIG. 531) in the *Cathedral of Orvieto*. Yet these seething groups

[1] Thomas Munro, *Great Pictures of Europe*, Coward-McCann, 1930, p. 133. This book is excellent for clear concise statements on color.

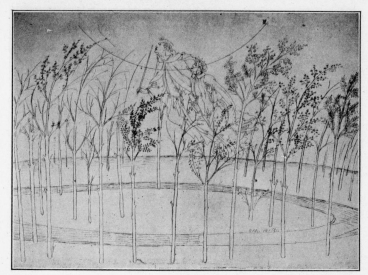

Fig. 536. Botticelli. Drawing to Illustrate Dante's *Divine Comedy, Paradiso I.*
1492–97. (Lippmann)

as wall decorations are adapted with skill to the lunette-shaped spaces they fill. This truculent art, like that of Pollaiuolo, one of its progenitors, was powerful in its challenge to the sixteenth-century figure-painters and wall-space organizers, particularly Michelangelo.

In this group of experimenters lay the fire of the Quattrocento. Yet it did not comprise all the painters in Florence. As in Ghiberti among the sculptors, the medieval style persisted in a more reactionary group, illustrated by Fra Angelico (1387–1455). As his name implies, he was a *frate*, a monk, brought up in the medieval tradition fostered in the monasteries. In his *Coronation of the Virgin* (FIG. 533) Christ and the Virgin are represented seated upon a throne of clouds from which radiate golden rays, and about which circle angels and saints. The panel is a beautiful pattern of bright colors and gold organized by sweeping lines. We mark how effectively the drapery of the angels nearest the central group encircles it; how the rhythm is repeated in the outer circle of angels and saints, and relieved by the kneeling saint in the left foreground and the angel with the harp on the right; and how the long trumpets very effectively fill the space above.

While in a general way the painters fell into the two groups typified by Masaccio and Fra Angelico, many did not, for the output of the shops, in this experimental age when life was all eagerness and spirits ran high, was too prolific, varied, and uneven to be so definitely pigeon-

Fig. 537. Botticelli. Calumny. Uffizi, Florence.

holed. There was Fra Filippo Lippi (1406–1469), who profited from contact with Masaccio even if the calligraphic line of Fra Angelico found its way into his work. His own liking for the gracious, charming types and aspects of life which he saw in Florence led him to imbue the traditional religious themes with a gracious humanity (Fig. 534). Benozzo Gozzoli (1420–1498) in the refreshingly gay decorations of the private chapel in the palace of the Medici represents ostensibly the *Journey of the Magi* but in reality a vivid pageant of the Medici court. Domenico Ghirlandaio (1449–1494) in *Santa Maria Novella* makes scenes from the New Testament excuses for the family portraits of rich merchants — a vivid picture of the "men and manners" of fifteenth-century Florence. The popular, narrative style of this group with its gaiety and easy charm, infused though it is at times with the sterner aspects of the scientific group, is quite analogous to that of the Desiderio group of sculptors which emphasized surface loveliness and decorative charm.

Thus this vividly alive century moves into its last quarter. Certain youths, then apprentices, were partly to continue its spirit of investigation and partly to take the results of its researches and by the strength of their individualities mold them into the more unified style of the sixteenth century — Botticelli, Leonardo, Raphael, Michelangelo, Fra Bartolommeo, Andrea del Sarto.

Sandro Botticelli (1444–1510), whose individual bent for calligraphic

line was not crushed but rather was developed by his grounding in the realistic
school, was a unique product of the Florentine school because he was out of its
main current. Instead of accepting his
visual perceptions as something to reproduce he "conceived the visual world as
an architecture of rhythmic line," [1] not
Giotto's sculptural line which defines
masses but something akin to that of the
Persian miniaturists. In *The Birth of Venus*
(Fig. 535) a classical goddess stands
lightly on a shell that is being blown to
the shore amid a shower of roses by two
vigorous zephyrs; at the right a nymph
is hurrying with a mantle to meet her.
The composition is built on a great arc
that rises along the figures of the winds,
reaches its crown in the head of Venus,

Fig. 538. Leonardo. Drawing of
Madonna and Child. Pen and ink.
Louvre, Paris. (Giraudon)

follows the fluttering hair, and is carried down by the arm of the nymph
and the line of the mantle. This arc is repeated in the upper curve of
the shell, and about it play quick nervous movements in the drapery,
hair, wings, and water. The tall, slender figure of Venus with its long,
quiet lines, standing somewhat isolated against a low horizon, is rather
flat, and the contour lines, while they model the form, as long graceful
curves have a beauty of their own, and are emphasized by the movement in the great mass of hair twisting and fluttering and framing the
drooping head, whose expression of wistful melancholy is so characteristic of Botticelli. The flying locks lead to the nymph, where the
impatient, whimsical curves of the drapery are all the more restless
in contrast with the straight lines of the tree trunks, the little prom-
ontories, and the horizon. After all, the significance lies in the line
and pattern. While the lines model, in so far as they express the essentials of form, still they have a quality of their own. Now they are
long and quiet, now short and capricious, now whimsical, and always
rhythmic. "My fancy is never checked: as the zephyr it flows smoothly
along the gull-like pattern of waves on the green sea, along the facile
lines of Venus' golden hair. You will soon forget the actual picture
and you do not notice it: it is so evanescent and shy, as rare as a
dream." [2]

[1] Yukio Yashiro, *Sandro Botticelli and the Florentine Renaissance*, Hale, Cushman &
Flint, 1929 — a very sympathetic interpretation from the point of view of an Oriental.
[2] *Ibid.*

Fig. 539. Leonardo. Adoration of the Magi, central figure. 1481. Uffizi, Florence.

This evanescent dreamlike quality perhaps finds its highest expression in the drawings for the *Divine Comedy* (FIG. 536). "The daintiest trees ever drawn wave softly over a smooth meadow"; through the circle that they form Dante and Beatrice rise toward heaven, their upturned faces filled with ecstasy. The trees and figures are drawn with a few exquisitely delicate lines. The drawing does not give us a reproduction, an illusion of nature, or a conventionalization of natural form; nor is it a sympathetic illustration of the *Divine Comedy*, for the temperament of Botticelli was altogether different from Dante's, which was profound, majestic, and dramatic. These drawings are made of the same "stuff" as music. That is, they evoke the same exquisite emotion as does a delicate melody when drawn by a master from a rare violin.

The waning of medieval religious fervor and the increasing popularity of secular and particularly classical themes, especially under the stimulation and patronage of the court of the Medici, is well illustrated in Botticelli. The *Calumny* (FIG. 537), for example, is an attempted reconstruction, with the help of classical literature, of a famous painting of the Greek Apelles. Calumny and Envy accompanied by Treachery and Deceit drag the innocent victim before the Judge into whose asses' ears Ignorance and Suspicion are whispering; at the left, naked Truth protests in isolation while Remorse looks to Truth as she moves toward the vindictive group. Apart from its subject matter, however, this painting is an excellent example of a freer asymmetrical balance (contrast Perugino's *Crucifixion*, FIG. 547) and particularly of the use of color in the tempera painting of the fifteenth century. One feels that this is primarily drawing to which color has been added as a decorative element. Each object is a crystalline-clear color-unit defined by sharp contours. Together with bright colors freely interspersed with gold, they produce a rather flat, vivacious, and very decorative effect and a surface texture that is smooth, hard, and luminous.

Contemporary with though far different from Botticelli was Leonardo da Vinci (1452–1519), an epitome of the "myriad-minded" man of the Renaissance. For centuries Europe had been breaking away from the dogma and authority of the Middle Ages. Finally, with the help of the newly discovered Humanistic classical culture, an entirely new world lay before man. It was not in view of everyone, but it strongly aroused the keen observation and eager curiosity of such a truly scientific spirit as Leonardo, whose myriad-sided curiosity is revealed best in his notes — comprising more than five thousand pages — jottings and studies, liberally interspersed with sketches, on botany, geology, zoölogy, optics; on hydraulic and military engineering and all kinds of physical and mechanical sciences; on Latin and Italian grammar; on animal lore; on

Fig. 540. Leonardo. Mona Lisa. 1503–06. Louvre, Paris. (Alinari)

perspective, light and shade, color, anatomy; and on man — structural, emotional, and intellectual. Nothing of man and his world seems omitted. Painting and sculpture were merely two of a multitude of interests.[1]

In his notebook jottings on painting [2] Leonardo says of the purpose of painting, "A good painter has two chief objects to paint — man and the intention of his soul. The former is easy, the latter hard, for it must be expressed by gestures and movements of the limbs. . . . A painting will only be wonderful for the beholder by making that which is not so appear raised and detached from the wall," that is, modeling with light and shadow is the heart of painting, and particularly a somewhat diffused light. "Towards evening or in bad weather I have noticed the features of men and women in the streets and marked what grace and softness can be seen thereon." For Leonardo combined with his scientific attitude a very subtle esthetic sensibility, and a predilection for the gracious aspects of the world.

Very early, perhaps while still in Verrocchio's shop as an apprentice, he seems to have become a master in transferring his images to paper with the greatest freedom and spontaneity. In Fig. 538 line alone models the baby form with its folds of soft flesh and also expresses

[1] See the remarkable letter of self-recommendation which Leonardo wrote to the Duke of Milan in Osvald Sirén, *Leonardo da Vinci*, Yale University Press, 1916, p. 59.
[2] Later collected from all his manuscripts and put together into what is now known as his *Treatise on Painting*.

Fig. 541. Leonardo. Last Supper. c. 1495–98. Refectory of Santa Maria delle Grazie, Milan. (Alinari) The doorway in the foreground was cut through later. The ruined condition of the Last Supper is due partly to careless restoration and vandalism and partly to the fact that in this painting Leonardo appeared to be experimenting, as was his habit, in media, and painted upon a wrongly prepared surface.

a single moment of delightful intimacy between the mother and child, "the intention of the soul" as well as Leonardo's predilection for "grace and dignity."

In the unfinished *Adoration* (FIG. 539) [1] Leonardo has placed the Madonna in the center, contrary to tradition, somewhat back from the frontal plane, a position emphasized by the inward movement of the kneeling king on the right, and has encircled her with the group of adorers. In this painting he has posed and partly solved a spatial and a psychological problem: the formal unity of a dramatic group in space all of whose movement focalizes upon the quiet, somewhat isolated central figures; and an emotional unity that binds the dramatic figures together in the adoration of the central figures. The background is filled with miscellaneous objects, horsemen, ruined architecture, trees and landscape, and bears little compositional relation to the compact foreground group except that the large trees help tie them both together. Complete organization in deep space has not yet been attained.

Formally and emotionally, a great similarity exists between the *Adoration* and the *Last Supper* (FIG. 541), except that in the latter the highly dramatic action is made still more emphatic by the placement of the group in a quiet setting. In a simple, spacious room, at a long

[1] The underpainting, in browns, has been laid in, a few of the heads and the Child's figure quite completely modeled in light and shadow, the Virgin's and kings' sketched only. The painting would have been completed by continuing the modeling and then adding the local color, either in tempera or in the newer oil medium which Leonardo used in his later works.

table set in the foreground parallel to the picture plane, Christ and the twelve disciples are seated. Christ, with outstretched hands, has just said, "One of you will betray me." At this statement a wave of intense excitement passes through the group as each asks, "Is it I?" The force and the lucidity with which this dramatic moment is expressed are due to the abstract organization. In the center is the figure of Christ, in perfect repose, isolated from the disciples, framed by the central window at the back, emphasized by the curved line over the

Fig. 542. Sistine Chapel. Vatican, Rome. (Anderson)

opening (the only curved line in the architectural framework), and the focal point of all the lines in the composition. Into this reposeful framework are fitted four groups of agitated disciples, united within themselves and also to each other by a movement of the hand, a gesture of the arm, or a turn of the head. The two figures at the ends are more quiet, as if to frame in the movement, which grows more intense as it approaches the figure of Christ, whose quietude at the same time halts and intensifies it. All this movement is lateral and confined to a plane parallel to the picture plane and but slightly removed from it in depth.

The ruined condition of the *Last Supper* makes it advisable to turn to other paintings, such as the *Madonna of the Rocks*, to illustrate the increasing depth and mystery of the shadows and their tendency to break up the unity of the design. Contrast the perfect clarity and architectural function of every detail in Piero's frescoes (FIG. 532). Leonardo's predilection for high lights and deep shadows must have been highly stimulated by the use of oil as a medium, with its capacity for

Fig. 543. Michelangelo. Sistine Ceiling, detail. 1508–12.

subtle nuances such as are found in the *Mona Lisa*, which have a loveliness of their own and at the same time a capacity for recording in
the face enigmatic "intentions of the soul."

Mona Lisa (FIG. 540) is seated in an armchair on a loggia whose
stone rail and columns frame a misty landscape. She is simply dressed,
with no ornaments, and her hair, falling in loose ringlets, is covered by
a thin veil. The composition recalls Baldovinetti's *Madonna* (FIG. 527)
— a pyramidal mass sensitively related to the space and to the background. The powerfully realized figure with strong, almost unbroken
contours rises against a vague dreamlike landscape whose elusive movement repeats itself in the subtle nuances of the face; sharp high lights
in the crumpled satin folds act as a foil to the extraordinarily subtle
modeling of the hands. This interaction of the definite and the indefinite, the psychological and the formal, controls the composition.
A definitely felt vertical axis falls from the forehead to the crossed
hands, connecting the two masses of interest, the face and the hands,
each of which is an example of Leonardo's technical ability to objectify his visual perception realistically by means of infinitely gradual
transitions from light to shadow. By this means also he could depict
in the face that elusive expression [1] which reflects fleeting emotions
into the mysteries of which Leonardo's curiosity led him to delve.

[1] Read Walter Pater's famous passage in his essay on Leonardo in *The Renaissance*.

Fig. 544. Michelangelo. Creation of Adam. Sistine Ceiling.

With Michelangelo, on the other hand, we meet a man who was interested only in big generic ideas and who, building upon the researches of the scientists of the fifteenth century, in painting and sculpture alike used the figure as a vehicle for the expression of these conceptions. He considered himself a sculptor; and when Pope Julius II ordered him to decorate the ceiling of the *Sistine Chapel* [1] (FIG. 542) he rebelled. But the Pope was insistent. The result looks as if Michelangelo had said, "Well, if the Pope will have his ceiling, let him have it; but," as Wölfflin suggests, "he will have to stretch his neck to see it." As a scheme of decoration, this ceiling is an absurdity, a penance alike to the artist while he painted it and to the spectator who wishes to look at it. A vast complex of humanity thunders down upon him, drowning out everything else, and the frescoes on the walls pale before it. Though the first impression is bewildering, a brief study easily resolves the mass into a great pattern, the motifs of which are rhythmically repeated and inextricably coördinated (FIG. 543). The eye is carried from human figure to human figure; prophets and sibyls sit in niches flanked by pilasters on which are putti who serve, Caryatid-like, to hold up the painted cornice which runs the length of the vault

[1] Frescoes in three chapels form epochs in the history of Italian painting: those in the *Arena Chapel* by Giotto, about 1305; in the *Brancacci Chapel* by Masaccio, 1424–26; in the *Sistine Chapel* by Michelangelo, 1508–12.

Fig. 545.   Michelangelo.   Jeremiah.
             Sistine Ceiling.

and forms a framework for the central panels and a connecting link between the prophets and the panels; for on this cornice rest the blocks on which the nudes are seated, a pair at each corner of the smaller panels, holding between them, by means of bands, round medallions. These figures serve a decorative and unifying purpose, each pair with the help of the medallions carrying the eye, by their repeated rhythmic pattern, from the larger to the smaller panels all the length of the ceiling.

The marvel of gathering so many figures into a harmonious unit would have been impossible except for the extremely simple, though strongly marked, architectural framework, in monochrome, which holds the mass together, so that the eye can wander about among the figures and yet feel the unity of the whole. It is always the human figure, sharply outlined against the neutral tone of this architectural setting or the plain background of the panels. Why did Michelangelo decorate the ceiling in this way? It was because to him the most beautiful, the most expressive thing in the whole world was the human figure. It was beautiful not only because of its form but because of the spiritual and ethical significance, the state of mind or soul that its form could so successfully express. He represented it in its most simple, elemental aspect, that is, the nude or simply draped, with no background, no ornamental embellishment, and with an idealized physiognomy. It was upon the sheer power of definitely related masses that he depended. "Simple people," he called the prophets. *Jeremiah* (FIG. 545), to take an example, sits with head bowed upon his uplifted hand, sunk in deep thought. The related masses of the figure are powerfully expressed by broad brush strokes reminiscent of the sculptural drawing of Giotto, except that in the *Jeremiah* the figure, instead of consisting of one mass, is a unit of organically related masses of the legs, torso, arms, and head. With what ease and inevitability, for example, the prophet's left arm, as a mass, crosses and unites with the left leg as a mass. These backward and forward movements are stabilized by the sweeping contour of the shoulders repeated in the drapery across the lap and by the insistent verticals in the beard and drapery. The pose of the figure — with the drooping right shoulder, the weight of the head on the right hand, the limp left hand, the ponderous weight of the whole — is determined by a desire to convey an impression of deep thought. There are no details to individualize this prophet; everything is so generalized that we feel that this is not only Jeremiah brooding over Israel, is not only Michelangelo himself, pondering in isolation and melancholy, but is every human being who, probing with his own soul beneath the surface of things, loses himself in the contemplation of the problems and mysteries of life.

Fig. 546. Michelangelo. Decorative Nude. Sistine Ceiling.

It was probably in the twenty *Nudes* that Michelangelo was happiest, for here he had the opportunity of reveling in his ideal — the human nude conceived sculpturally. Although all serve the same decorative purpose (FIG. 543), still they are very different, each, perhaps paradoxically, a more or less realistic rendering of the human figure and at the same time an expression of a definite inner state of mind. In FIG. 546 strain and stress are symbolized by the mighty back, the thrust-out arm and shoulder, the violent contrasts in the direction of movement, the tousled hair, the sharp profile with open mouth; in others, ease and complacency, lyric joyousness, the weight of burden-bearing.

As an illustration of Michelangelo's composition, the *Creation of Adam* (FIG. 544), one of the larger panels of the ceiling, is divided into two masses, which stand out clearly against the flat background. Adam, on a hillside — the hill is merely suggested, again a Giottesque quality — is just awakening. The physical potentialities of the reposeful figure are suggested in the balancing of broken jagged contours with those that are unbroken and suavely curving; and the balancing of parts in movement — the thrust-back shoulder, the turned head, the sharply bent leg — with the relaxed outstretched arm and leg. This comparatively quiet figure is opposed to the second group, that of God and his attendant spirits, which is full of vigorous movement; and the two are united by the two hands, each expressive of the mood of its possessor — Adam's limp and lifeless, God's tense with creative power.

In most of these figures on the ceiling, one can hardly fail to feel their inherently sculptural quality, their effect of being, as it were, "painted sculpture." Michelangelo himself says in a letter written while he was

Fig. 547. Perugino. Crucifixion. 1493–96. Santa Maria Maddalena
dei Pazzi, Florence. (Anderson)

discouraged and depressed about the ceiling: "This is not my profession.
I waste time without any results. God help me." In all his work one
looks in vain for quietude, and everywhere is made to feel restlessness
or violence — something of the bitterness and conflict which distracted
this artist's soul.

In Michelangelo we reach a climax in painting so powerful that it
overwhelmed the artists of the time, who forsook their own paths to
follow in his — with the result that we have empty copying of his forms
entirely lacking in the creative spirit. Hence came the decadence which
followed his death.

In Raphael (1483–1520) we find an increasing ability to organize
crowds of people into space. An Umbrian, a pupil of Perugino, he
early acquired a feeling for spaciousness, characteristic of that master,
a feeling that perhaps was partially acquired from the influence of the
actual open reaches of this gently rolling hill country. [1] In Perugino's
Crucifixion (FIG. 547), for example, there is a dominant note of quiet
repose, though the subject matter is dramatic and tragic. The painter
has divided the wall space into three sweeping arches, which of themselves create a quiet rhythm. Into these the figures, uninteresting and
even sentimental, are fitted as architectural units to form a triangle
with long base, while behind, unifying the whole composition, stretches
a landscape of hills, valleys, rivers and trees, above which are reaches
of sky, whose spaciousness is suggested by the tall slender trees at the
left. The lines of this landscape are far-extending and quiet, and the
distance is immersed in a bluish haze. Apart from this Umbrian in-

[1] See Gabriel Faure, *Wanderings in Italy*, Houghton Mifflin, 1919, Pt. III, p. 141

Fig. 548. Raphael. Disputà. 1509–11. Vatican, Rome. (Alinari)

Fig. 549. Raphael. School of Athens. 1509–11. Vatican, Rome.

Fig. 550. Raphael. Madonna known as "La Belle Jardinière." 1507–08. Louvre, Paris.

heritance of what Mr. Berenson calls "space composition," Raphael was a product of the Florentine school. With great powers of assimilation he profited not only from his contemporaries, Leonardo and Michelangelo, but from Masaccio, Donatello, Pollaiuolo.

The whole series of Raphael's Madonnas, from the *Granduca* to the *Sistine*, is indicative of the way in which the Florentine masters were shaping this docile Umbrian talent. In *La Belle Jardinière* (FIG. 550), for example, the influence of Leonardo appears in the compact pyramidal grouping of the figures;[1] that of Michelangelo, in the restless twisting pose of the Christ Child.[2] The group is set naturalistically into, not in front of, a charming landscape with the Umbrian feeling for tranquillity and spaciousness. In fact there is a compelling realization of this spaciousness, though the Madonna dominates the picture. The *Sistine Madonna*[3] derives its effect from the carefully studied design in depth with its effective use of contrasts. The traditional pyramidal arrangement is there; the Madonna and Child, grouped and balanced, are all the more majestic because the saints on either side are kneeling; the figure of one saint is turned inward, the other, by his gesture, outward; one looks down, the other up.

Raphael's accomplished design is best revealed in his Vatican frescoes. In the *Disputà* (FIG. 548) two approaching arcs are cut vertically by a central axis about which all parts are balanced symmetrically. The upper arc incloses the scene in heaven with Christ between the Virgin and St. John, surrounded by saints, angels, and cherubim, with God the Father above, and the dove below. The lower arc marks a varied group, each figure contributing by its pose or gesture to the movement toward the four Fathers of the Church gathered about the altar on which stands, silhouetted against the highest light and on the vertical axis, the monstrance, symbol of the mystery of the faith and focal point of the design. A serene Umbrian landscape with great open

[1] See Leonardo's *Madonna of the Rocks* (Louvre), and the *Madonna with St. Ann* (Louvre).

[2] See Michelangelo's *Madonna and Child* (Bruges).

[3] Painted for the Sistine monks of Piacenza and called *Sistine* because of their ownership and the prominent figure of Pope Sixtus II.

reaches of sky serves to unite the two groups. Particularly noteworthy here is Raphael's architectural sensitivity seen in the relation of his design to the room as a whole and in the way in which he incorporated in his design the actual door which cuts into the wall area.

Perhaps more imposing and more facile in composition is the *School of Athens* (FIG. 549). An effective architectural setting which in form, scale, and dignity is quite at one with sixteenth-century ideals [1] furnishes a framework into which the figures are so placed that an elliptical movement swings from the front to each side and thence back to the figures of Plato and Aristotle framed by the series of arches.

Fig. 551. Andrea del Sarto. Madonna of the Harpies (from the figures of Harpies on the pedestal). 1517. Uffizi, Florence. (Alinari)

A supplementary movement inward directly from the picture plane to the focal point is carried by the receding lines of the inlaid floor, the steps, and the two seated figures.

The imposing dignity and plastic unity that we found in the architecture and sculpture of the High Renaissance thus finds its counterpart in painting: in the great series of frescoes of Raphael and Michelangelo and in such panel paintings as those of Fra Bartolommeo and Andrea del Sarto (1486–1531). In Andrea's *Madonna of the Harpies* (FIG. 551) the stately figures almost fill the canvas. One finds an echo of the traditional symmetrical pyramidal grouping, but not the diffused lighting, sharply defined contours, and generally lateral movement of the Quattrocento. Instead he sees dark shadows in which details are lost, blurred edges and movements backward and forward in a complete organization in depth which controls each figure as a single unit (note the rotary movement in the Madonna unit) and as one unit of the group.

[1] Bramante was at this time working on the plans for the new *St. Peter's* and Raphael himself was about to assist in this great undertaking.

G. SUMMARY

Of the Italian painters of the thirteenth and fourteenth centuries, all of whom were working primarily in the Byzantine tradition, the Sienese remained rooted in that style which they brought, with some modification because of the general naturalistic movement, to a climax in Italy — an art of exquisite surface patterns with suavely flowing calligraphic lines and areas of vivid color and gold; an art whose forms were imaginatively and conventionally constructed with but little regard for a visual perception of actuality. The Florentines, on the contrary, set themselves to the task of investigating the world of visual perception — the figure itself, its place in space, and spatial relations — not for the purpose of providing a perfect copy of man and his world but for the expression of the essential, monumental aspects of form and of the outward manifestation, through form, of generic or abstract conceptions. It was a figure art, at first of religious subjects, for such was commissioned by the Church, the nobles, and the guilds, all of whom were the art patrons of the time; then increasingly secular because of the growing secularization of the whole cultural fabric. It was an art of the draftsman, with color largely a decorative adjunct, for drawing was the most suitable means of expressing the scientific facts of anatomy and perspective that were the passion of the fifteenth century. Yet this enthusiasm did not overwhelm esthetic demands, for the Florentine always "digested his facts into form," and by the sixteenth century he had attained an accomplished style of great dignity and of great mastery over the figure itself, over spatial relations and the expression through them of what was spiritually significant.

For Bibliography, see p. 427.

H. PAINTING IN NORTHERN ITALY

Among the cities of northern Italy (FIG. 463) — Venice, Milan, Verona, Mantua, Ferrara, Bologna, Padua — Venice was chief. The islands on which it was built in the midst of salt marshes near the head of the Adriatic Sea had offered a refuge for the peoples of northern Italy from the barbarian invaders of the fifth century. Thus isolated and segregated from the rest of Italy, it developed quite independently. The Venetians early became a seafaring people, establishing close relations with the East and sending their artists to execute commissions at the court of Constantinople. Venetian markets were full of the rich brocades, silks, jewels, metal goods, and slaves of the Near East. Politically, Venice was sound; and, though autocratic, it was peaceful and free from the periodic feuds that were constantly rending other Italian cities. Religiously, too, Venice was more independent. Safely remote from the papal power at Rome, it centered its religious life independently about the worship of its patron, St. Mark.

Venetian life was the antithesis of Florentine, for it was dominantly gay and luxurious. A fervid patriotism made strong demands upon the citizens for the glorification of the state. There were gorgeous pageants and ceremonies, both religious and civil, besides private banquets and pompous balls (see the paintings of Giovanni Bellini, Carpaccio, Tintoretto, Veronese), the richest costumes of stiff brocades, gold embroidery, and lavish lace and jewels. This extravagance and love of display was not conducive to intellectual pursuits. A humanist was shabbily treated and even starved in Venice, and a profoundly religious man found no sympathy there.

Gay and isolated as it was, however, its art did not remain uninfluenced by the great stirrings that were revolutionizing Italian art, though it clung longer than Florence to the Gothic style in painting just as it did in architecture. Up to the fifteenth century Venetian painting was strongly Byzantine and Gothic, with the love of color a predominant quality, as one might expect in a city so closely connected with the East as well as one located in a naturally colorful setting. Nevertheless it received strong enough influences from other Italian centers, particularly from Florence, to affect its art powerfully without changing its essentially Venetian character.

A new spirit first appears in the work of the so-called father of Venetian painting, Jacopo Bellini (died 1470). In his notebooks of drawings [1] we are struck by his fancy, and by his lively joy in nature — trees, hills, flowers, animals particularly, both real and fantastic. Jacopo had been touched by the naturalistic movement, and also by the growing passion for classical subjects, for sheet after sheet in these notebooks shows drawings of architectural details, antique statues, centaurs, and satyrs.

A still greater influence upon Venetian painting came from near-by Padua, an old Roman colony which had always had strong intellectual and religious strains in its culture. Its pride in being the birthplace of the great Roman historian Livy stimulated an enthusiasm for things classical; and its religious fervor led it to respond easily to St. Bernard. Furthermore, Giotto had decorated the *Arena Chapel* about 1305; Paolo Uccello in the first half of the fifteenth century was working in this general locality; and in 1443 Donatello came to decorate an altar and to make the equestrian statue of *Gattamelata*. Under such influences Padua became an important center. The northern Italians to be sure

[1] See Corrado Ricci, *Jacopo Bellini e i suoi libri di disegni*, Florence, 1908.

Fig. 552. Mantegna. Crucifixion. 1459. Louvre, Paris. (Alinari)

had come under the wave of naturalism but, unlike the Florentines, they did not "digest their facts into form." Instead, they (Pisanello, for example) took great delight in every newly discovered object, adding it to their decorative patterns without reference to those basic structures and interrelations of forms which constitute the basis of Florentine painting.

The painter who was most influential in infusing the more descriptive northern Italian style with something of the stern realities of Florence was Andrea Mantegna (1431–1516), who as an apprentice in Padua came under the influence of Donatello's realism and the Paduan passion for the classical culture. In his *Crucifixion* (FIG. 552) [1] we see both influences working. In the foreground on a rocky hill stand three crosses and two groups of spectators, the Romans and the friends of Christ. The scene as a whole is organized by two diagonal planes that recede from the two corners (an obvious exercise in perspective) and intersect behind the central cross, which thus receives additional emphasis to that given by the repeated verticals of the rocky hills and the soldier's spear, and the spacious sky against which it is silhouetted. Mantegna's

---

[1] This small picture is part of the predella of Mantegna's *San Zeno Altarpiece*. The predella was the long, narrow panel that rested directly upon the altar and served as a decorative base for the altarpiece. It consisted usually of several small paintings related in subject matter to the large painting above. Many of these predellas were scattered when the altarpieces in course of time were dismembered. An example of an altarpiece that still retains its predella is the *Annunciation* of Fra Angelico at Cortona.

Fig. 553. Mantegna. Gonzaga Family. A tablet in the room bears the following inscription: "To the illustrious Marquis Lodovico II, most worthy prince, invincible in the faith, and to his illustrious Lady Barbara of incomparable renown; their Andreas Mantegna of Padua has completed this humble work to their honor in the year 1474." Castello, Mantua.

passion for everything Roman here finds opportunity to use Roman types and costumes; and his almost harsh realism reveals itself in the figures on the crosses, though he has not entirely broken from the Gothic linear patternizing.

Mantegna's penetrating observation and uncompromising fearlessness in recording facts is evident in the portraits painted on the walls of the castle at Mantua for the Gonzagas, whom he served for many years as court painter. In the *Gonzaga Family* (Fig. 553) the group is placed rather compactly in a shallow space between two pilasters and a very naturalistic curtain drawn aside and twisted about the pillar as if to present a view to the spectator. At the left sits the Marchese Ludovico Gonzaga, holding in his hand a letter just brought to him by his secretary, to whom he turns as if giving some direction. At the right the Marchesa sits rather stiffly, looking toward the Marchese as if with some concern as to the contents of the letter; a little girl holds up an apple toward her, without attracting her attention; at her left is a dwarf whose task was to furnish amusement; grouped about are members of the family and court. Here is a quiet family scene, dignified and serious. The incident of the letter is a minor matter. What impresses the spectator is the exceeding reality of all these people, a reality that brings out sternly and incisively the character of each one, with no idealizing. The Marchese is a lofty-minded man, a conscientious and

Fig. 554. Mantegna. Ceiling of the Camera degli
Sposi. Castello, Mantua. 1474.

successful ruler; his secretary, with his squint-
ing eyes and huge nose,
a clear-headed, shrewd,
and capable assistant;
the stately Marchesa, a
thoroughgoing house-
wife and helpmeet. But
while each portrait in
itself is an astonishingly
forceful character-
ization, as a whole the
group lacks unify-
ing formal relationships.
Throughout the *Camera
degli Sposi* on whose walls
the group was painted
Mantegna carried his
realism to the point of
breaking down the walls
and substituting an al-
most complete illusion of space, especially in the ceiling (FIG. 554),
where by boldly foreshortened figures standing on the ledge, by others
peering over, and by a light sky with clouds he creates a perfect illusion
of an opening to the sky, an illusionism that was to reach a climax in
seventeenth-century baroque.

In this austere and searching study of form, Mantegna accomplished
for northern Italy what Donatello and Masaccio did for Florence.
Classical sculptures, examples of which he had in his own collection,
served as his models, and though at times his passion for archaeology
dominated his art, he nevertheless brought a tonic influence to schools
whose predominant interests lay in the splendor of color, the texture
of fine stuffs, the pride of their city, or the mood of the sunset hour.

Another energetic realist sojourning in northern Italy was Antonello
da Messina (1430–1479), whose origin is uncertain but whose contact
with northern European art is evident. His intensely real portraits
have convincing mass, and his *St. Jerome in His Study* is an unusual
example of interest in genre and interior-lighting effects. In addition
he brought a great stimulation to the already growing use of the oil
technique, the capacities of which for securing rich color and surface
effects he had learned from the Northerners.

While Mantegna was still in Padua, Jacopo Bellini and his family
had traveled thither, with the result that Mantegna married Jacopo's

daughter and through his friendship with the sons brought the stern realities of his art directly into Venice. As Gentile Bellini's interest lay, apart from his portraits, in following his father's narrative turn, his expositions of Venetian pageants constitute his chief work.

This narrative interest finds a climax in the far more imaginative Vittore Carpaccio (1460–1522). For the staid groups of Gentile's pageants became full of lively action, as in the *St. Ursula Series*

Fig. 555. Carpaccio. Dream of St. Ursula. 1495. Academy, Venice.

(Venice), a vivid picture of contemporary Venetians whose costumes of magnificent stuffs provided an excuse for the use of vivid color-spots organized into a vivacious design and flooded with sunshine. In the *Dream of St. Ursula* (FIG. 555), how real is the space of the room and the interplay of the outside and interior lighting which fills the room and with its varying values produces a feeling of the reality of the space! A very quiet design — a simple organization of vertical, horizontal, curve, and a sparse use of diagonal — is in harmony with the mood of the scene.

To return to the Bellini family, it is Jacopo's son Giovanni (1428–1516) who strikes out along new paths. In an early *Pietà* (FIG. 556), a profound emotional quality combined with a terse, almost harsh drawing and cold color are evident. A low-lying landscape and an expanse of sky marked by horizontal cloudlets form a quiet background for concentration upon the tragic grief expressed by the three figures represented half-length in the foreground, just behind a parapet. The Virgin and St. John are supporting the body of the dead Christ, whose head is turned toward the Virgin's. The figures are brought together into a compact unity both formal and spiritual. Despite the angularity and the hard schematic lines and shadows there is an intense searching for form and a relating of mass that is almost sculptural. Giovanni's

Fig. 556. Giovanni Bellini. Pietà. c. 1460. Brera, Milan. (Alinari)

Fig. 557. Giovanni Bellini. Madonna. 1488. Church of the Frari, Venice. (Alinari)

Fig. 558. Giovanni Bellini. Allegory, possibly from a medieval poem, the Pilgrimage of the Soul, and representing in the foreground the earthly paradise. c. 1490. Uffizi, Florence. (Alinari)

Fig. 559. Giorgione. Fête Champêtre. Late. Louvre, Paris.

evolution, however, was to be more Venetian, neither so profound in feeling nor so monumental in form as this early work. This truly Venetian quality becomes evident in the frankly gorgeous *Frari Madonna* (Fig. 557). The composition suggests a scene in a church. In the center is the apse, decorated in gold brocade, where the Madonna sits on a lofty throne. On each side two saints turning toward her are standing in the aisles that surround the apse, separated from it by columns. Thus the architectural unity suggested by the church building, and the psychological unity of the two groups of saints with the Madonna, bring about a singleness of effect. The elaborate frame covered with typically Renaissance carvings, the rich chiaroscuro, the sumptuous stuffs, and the mellow, harmonious color produce a picture of truly Venetian splendor.

An important tendency not only in Giovanni but in the Venetian school as a whole is seen in a small *Allegory* (Fig. 558). Here, in the foreground is a paved inclosure in the center of which are children playing around a tree; men and women stand about apparently without unity of action. The rest of the panel is filled with a landscape in which is a mountain lake surrounded by rocky hills. Here is a grasp of out-of-door space, not met before, in which the foreground with the figures is tied naturalistically with the landscape, a unity attained not only by the all-incorporating horizontal plane on which every object takes its place inevitably, by the movement of other planes and lines, but particularly by the consistent scintillating light and by the enveloping atmosphere, which blurs the contours and unites all objects with its mellow tone.

Into the shop of Giovanni came the two youths who were to add new elements to Venetian painting and to bring it to a culmination — Giorgione and Titian. Giorgione (1478–1510) left but few paintings, for he died young. His *Castelfranco Madonna* (Color Plate III, on opposite page) forecasts if not entirely attains the tranquil mood so characteristic of Giorgione. In the center on a lofty throne are the Madonna and Child; on the sides in front of an inclosing wall, two saints, Francis and George;[1] behind the wall a landscape stretching into the distance over which is the glow of early-morning light. The three figures form a triangle set over against the rectangular framework of the wall and throne. The long diagonal of the banner, repeated in the right side of the triangle, in the Virgin's robe, and in the shadows on the pavement, cuts sharply across one side of the triangle, and breaks the otherwise too precise symmetry; it also helps construct the interlocking triangles and rectangles of the pattern, and serves to connect the foreground with the background. The tranquillity of this surface pattern is repeated in the quiet recession of parallel planes into the distance: the

[1] It is a moot point whether the figure of the warrior is St. Liberalis or St. George.

Fig. 560. Titian. Portrait of an Unknown Man ("Young English-man," or "Duke of Norfolk"). c. 1540–45. Pitti, Florence. (Alinari)

Fig. 561. Titian. The Man with the Glove. Early. Louvre, Paris. Compare with Fig. 560 for contrasting units of composition: sharp angles and diagonals versus curves and verticals.

floor patterning takes one directly to the saints, thence by the receding throne to the Madonna, to the middle distance, and to the horizon; while a tranquil mood pervades the figures and the landscape equally. The warmth of rich reds and rose concentrated in the figure group is relieved by cooler greens and blues in the tiling of the floor and in the landscape, though they are united by a pervading atmosphere and glowing light.

Truly Giorgionesque and Venetian is the *Fête Champêtre* (FIG. 559). Here the basic organization is much less obvious, less symmetrical, more subtle. The surface pattern consists of a quiet framework of verticals in the standing figure, the trees and houses; of horizontals in fountain, lute strings, background, and sky; of two sets of opposing diagonals, repeated in arms, legs, contours of the hills, and many details; and of sweeping curves of foliage and figures. These organizing lines in contrast to those in Botticelli's *Calumny* (FIG. 537) or Raphael's *School of Athens* (FIG. 549), are intuitively felt rather than clearly visible, for most of the edges are blurred by atmosphere or lost in shadows. Yet the organization is as compelling as in the *Calumny* and the *School of Athens*, even if less evident at first glance and accomplished by different means — chiefly by spots of color of varying hues and values.

But this organization is by no means a surface pattern only. Here is a grasp of space and an organization in space particularly emphasized by the great plane that wedges in diagonally from the front on which the main figures are placed, yet without any lack of unity with the

Fig. 562. Titian. Education of Cupid. Late. Borghese Gallery, Rome.

middle and far distance. As in the *Castelfranco Madonna*, a warm, intense color, in particular the red velvet sleeve of the lute-player, marks the center of interest, about which radiate somewhat less warm and cool hues. An additional richness of effect results from the varying textures of stuffs, flesh, stone, foliage, but all are tied into a rich tonal unity by that pervasive "golden glow" which is a characteristic mark of Venetian painting. Color is no longer used as a decorative element to enhance the unity of the design but functions as an inseparable element in the construction of form. This richness of color and surface texture, the soft blending of light and dark, and the enveloping blurring atmosphere were made possible by substituting for the tempera technique the oil technique, whose potentialities were peculiarly favorable for the expression of Venetian ideals.

One more element in the *Fête Champêtre* is both Giorgionesque and Venetian — a profound sensitivity to an idyllic charm and a tranquil brooding mood. Among the Italians it was the Venetian school that first expressed a love for nature and a realization of its potentialities for the painter, though this school never reached the point of eliminating entirely some figure interest.

The youthful Titian (1477–1576) followed rather closely, at first, in the style of Giorgione, as is evident in the *Concert* (Pitti, Florence), which may have been a collaboration of the two. But Titian's naturally robust, exuberant nature soon found more congenial expression in a more vigorous subject matter and more striking design, as in the *Bacchus and Ariadne* (National Gallery, London), the magnificent *Assumption*

Fig. 563. Titian. Entombment. 1559. Prado, Madrid.

of the Virgin and *Pesaro Madonna* (Frari, Venice), and the *Entombment* (Louvre), though the means he employed were much the same as in the *Fête Champêtre* — organization by deep, rich color masses, light and dark, warm and cool, which harmonize, contrast, and merge into sumptuous effects quite in tune with the Venetian love of pomp, splendor, and worldliness. Such surfaces were secured by a long patient building-up, usually upon the tempera ground painting, of layer upon layer of thin coats of pigment mixed with oil, some opaque, some transparent, with dryings and bleachings in the sun at every stage. The ground, in Titian often a warm red-brown, served to bind all the local colors into a dominant tonal unity.

It was not long however before Titian began restricting his hues and weaving them into more subtle organizations, as in some of the portraits. In the *Young Englishman* (FIG. 560), so called for the identity of the subject is unknown, we see a young man represented half-length, dressed in a black costume relieved only by the heavy gold chain and the delicate white ruffles at the throat and wrists. His right hand holds his gloves; his left is held somewhat restlessly on his hip. With the greatest simplicity and reserve, Titian reveals the pride and aristocracy of this young man, and his fine sensitive nature. The half-length figure admirably fills the square frame; the eye travels back and forth with

Fig. 564. Tintoretto. Miracle of St. Mark. 1548. Academy, Venice.

the help of the chain and the contours of the arms from the face to the hands, which are as expressive of this young man's character as the face itself. In this portrait and particularly in *The Man with the Glove* (FIG. 561) a very restrained color scheme with close values conveys a restrained impression. Yet the figure exists in an ample spaciousness made very real by the background, which vibrates with infinitely subtle variations. The characterization in these portraits is accomplished not only by expression of the face and by characteristic details of costume, pose, or accessory that contribute to the creation of an environment which is as expressive of the individual as is the face itself, but is accomplished also by a basic design that says abstractly what features and details say concretely. For example, contrast the effect of the curves and the vertical of the *Young Englishman* with that of the sharp triangles in the *Man with the Glove*. For a group, one may take the *Pope Paul III and His Grandsons* (Naples), in which Titian's penetrating vision and intellectual grasp of individual character and of the psychology of a situation find inescapably clear expression because of the perfect cohesion of every means available to the painter. Facial expression, pose, gesture, costume, line, color — each is one element definitely related to every other to attain the objective.

In his later works, such as the *Education of Cupid* (FIG. 562), the late *Pietà* (Venice Academy), the late *Entombment* (FIG. 563), and the *Crown*

Fig. 564 (A). Analysis to show the S-curve organization.

ing of Thorns (Munich), the forms, which melt into a golden glow, are constructed of light and color with a use of pigment that foreshadows the great painters of Spain and northern Europe even into the days of Impressionism.[1]

As distinction and poise, even in movement, and elegance and grace, even in tragedy, were a manifestation of Titian's individuality, so dramatic force, impetuous movement, and vivid contrasts of color reflect the vehement Tintoretto (1518–1594); both, albeit, true Venetians. In the *Last Supper* (FIG. 565) dramatic contrasts of light and dark control a design that is organized with a fully three-dimensional expression of deep space. The eye is guided by these startling high lights along an imaginary line of direction from the two figures in the left-hand lower corner across the foreground and back to the group of angels in the background, while the same distance into space is reached more directly by the long table. In the *Miracle of St. Mark* (FIG. 564) the same energetic movement is subordinate to a great S-curve swinging backward and forward in space through the downward sweeping figures of St. Mark, the executioner, and the slave; and another movement in depth swings from the judge on the right, back through the group of spectators and forward to the lofty figures on

[1] See Munro, *Great Pictures of Europe*, pp. 170–71.

Fig. 565. Tintoretto. Last Supper. 1594. San Giorgio Maggiore, Venice.

the left. Along the entire course of these single controlling rhythms the
eye is guided by light and dark spots of rich warm color, accented by
the cooler hues of the quiet background, but all united tonally.

Tintoretto's flashes of light, brushed in with apparent spontaneity
and disregard for detail, were not haphazard but often the result of
many trials of a design and of single figures, as is seen in his drawings
in the British Museum. And in his more direct method of painting he
is closer to the modern school than any of the other Italians.[1]

Truly Venetian in his expression of worldly brilliant pageantry,
whether the subject was sacred or secular, and in his facility in handling
pigment to create a magnificent surface was Veronese (1528–1588).
The narrative and descriptive painting of Carpaccio, naïvely joyous
and clearly organized, became in Veronese a colossally grandiose and
unimaginative expression of Venice's sophisticated pageantry. Into an
imposing architectural framework, as in the *Feast in the House of Levi*
(FIG. 566), he placed animated groups of many figures all in movement, thus creating an impression of constant vibration of spots of
color with little internal organization and little accent upon the focal

[1] Tintoretto's impetuosity and his habit of working directly upon the canvas without preliminary sketches is well illustrated by Vasari's tale of the decoration of
the ceiling of the *Scuola di San Rocco*. This confraternity had commissioned three
painters, Tintoretto among them, to present competitive designs for the ceiling.
When the council assembled to judge of the design and award the commission, they
found that Tintoretto had painted his directly on a full-sized canvas and already
had it put into place, saying that that was his way of doing it and if they did not
wish to recompense him he would make them a gift of the painting.

Fig. 566. Veronese. Feast in the House of Levi. 1573. Academy, Venice.

point, which is difficult to find. As a unit, however, this movement is quite under the control of the dominant rhythm of the architectural framework. The surface texture in Veronese's canvases is subtly varied, and his color, perhaps owing to his early training in Verona, is less warm than Titian's and Tintoretto's, with more blue, less red, and less suffusion of warm golden tonality. A cool, more diffused luminosity and less contrast between light and dark stress the decorative aspect.

While Titian and Tintoretto were still youths, a painter who lived in comparative isolation in and around Parma, Correggio (1494-1534) was painting altarpieces of a certain lyric charm — when not too sweet and sentimental — and was experimenting in artificial and concentrated lighting, as in the *Holy Night*, or in the mythological panels, such as the *Danaë* (Rome), creating a delicate kind of painting, not of rich surface textures like those of most of the Venetians, but of almost imperceptible modulations of light, filled with half-tints and of a cool silvery tonality. In the *Assumption* (FIG. 567) in the dome of the *Parma Cathedral*, one is carried from the moderate movement in the pendentives, where saints and Church Fathers with angels are seated upon clouds, by way of a balustrade to which vigorous upward-gazing Apostles cling, into a whirling ecstatic flight of innumerable figures, an illusion of swift movement into infinite heights quite regardless of the material limitations of the stone dome. This illusion Correggio created partly by foreshortened figures but largely by the emotional force of a swirl of radiant light and color.

In these Parma frescoes, one is carried back to the boldly foreshortened figures and the illusionistic effect of Mantegna's *Camera degli Sposi* (FIG. 554). In fact in all Correggio's work there are evidences of Michelangelo's drawing, of Raphael's types sentimentalized, of Leonardo's chiaroscuro, and of Titian's design and color, though cooler.

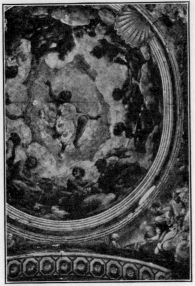

Fig. 567. Correggio. Assumption. 1520–24. Dome of S. Giovanni Evangelista, Parma.

Such eclecticism normally follows a period of such masters as those produced in Florence, Rome, and Venice in the sixteenth century. The Eclectics, or Mannerists, were centered at the art school which they established at Bologna. They attempted to combine into a perfect art the best qualities of the great masters — the drawing of Michelangelo, the noble types and composition of Raphael, the color of Titian, and the chiaroscuro of Correggio. Such a method, which copies external appearance and fails to grasp fundamental principles, is destined to become pedantic, or rhetorical, or melodramatic, as were many of the paintings of the Bolognese, particularly those of the Caracci.

The other tendency was that of the realists, chief of whom was Caravaggio (1569–1608), who, in revolt against the weakness of the Mannerists, selected his types from the lowest classes, and painted figures and scenes with a realism that at times approaches the photographic. His chiaroscuro, based upon that of Correggio in such a painting as the *Holy Night*, consists of picking out a detail here and there and sinking all else into shadow.

Chiaroscuro we have seen developing in Italian painting from Giotto, who, though he used the shadow for modeling, still expressed both mass and space chiefly by line. The early fifteenth-century painters of Florence — Masaccio, Fra Angelico, Baldovinetti, and Pollaiuolo — used it moderately to express the structure and volume of the figure in space, so that their work, whether in fresco or in tempera, had an even tonality without strong contrasts of light and shade. This was due partly to the medium and partly to interest in the structural line, for the Florentines were principally draftsmen. Leonardo with the help of the oil technique carried contrasting light and dark with soft transitions much farther in his attempt to secure a high-relief-like quality. Giorgione, Titian, and Tintoretto subordinated line and organized by light and dark color-masses in which figures and objects are constructed of light and color. Visible line hardly exists, though organizing lines of direction are clearly felt; edges are blurred and all figures are united by an enveloping atmosphere of dominant tonality. Michelangelo's remark that Titian could not draw, which might well have elicited the retort that Michelangelo could not paint, simply reflects a different way of seeing, feeling, and expressing form. To Michelangelo, the figure was an organic structure whose volumes arouse tactile sensations and can best be expressed by lines which indicate the movement of planes defining these volumes. To Titian, the figure was a mass perceived by light, which is color, and enveloped by atmosphere.[1]

I. SUMMARY

Quite in distinction from the Florentines, who were primarily interested in the scientific study of form as a means for the expression of ideas and emotions that were largely abstract, the Venetians, wealthy, worldly, closely connected with the colorful Near East, frankly strove to set forth their own sumptuous magnificence and gorgeous pageantry. Such an impression the painters were able to create by complex designs in deep space in which the chief organizing means were the richest colors tied together by an all-embracing glowing light, a use of pigment made possible through the development of oil as a medium. Of all the Italians the Venetians were most truly painters, not only in their construction of figures from color and light but particularly in their realization of the potentialities of pigment for creating surfaces that in color and texture have a distinctly emotional appeal in themselves, quite without regard to the subject matter. Another important contribution of the Venetians, seen early in their idyllic landscape backgrounds, was a revelation of nature; and though they never eliminated the figure interest, they opened up the great possibilities of nature as material for the painter.

BIBLIOGRAPHY

Berenson, Bernhard, *The Central Italian Painters of the Renaissance*, Putnam, 1897
——— *The Florentine Painters of the Renaissance*, Putnam, 1909
——— *The Italian Pictures of the Renaissance*, rev. ed., Oxford Press, 1932
——— *The North Italian Painters of the Renaissance*, Putnam, 1907
——— *Essays in the Study of Sienese Painting*, F. F. Sherman, 1918
——— *Study and Criticism of Italian Art*, Macmillan, 1901–02, 2 vols.
——— *The Venetian Painters of the Renaissance*, 3d ed., Putnam, 1897
Borenius, Tancred, *Florentine Frescoes*, Nelson, 1930
Brown, A. V. V., and Rankin, William, *A Short History of Italian Painting*, Dutton, 1914

---

[1] For an exposition of these contrasting attitudes towards form see Heinrich Wölfflin, *Principles of Art History*, Holt, 1932.

Brown, G. B., *Fine Arts*, Scribner, 1927

Byron, Robert, and Talbot Rice, David, *The Birth of Western Painting*, Knopf, 1931

Cecchi, Emilio, *Sienese Painters of the Trecento*, tr. by Leonard Penlock, Warne, 1931

Cennini, Cennino, *The Book of the Art of Cennino Cennini*, tr. by C. J. Herringham, London, 1922

Conway, Sir Martin, *Giorgione*, London, 1929

Crowe, Sir J. A., and Cavalcaselle, G. B., *History of Painting in North Italy*, ed. by Tancred Borenius, new ed., Scribner, 1912, 3 vols.

———— *New History of Painting in Italy*, ed. by Edward Hutton, Dutton, 1908–09, 3 vols.

Cruttwell, Maud, *Antonio Pollaiuolo*, Scribner, 1907

Douglas, Langton, *Fra Angelico*, 2d ed. rev., Macmillan, 1902

———— *A History of Siena*, Dutton, 1902

Edgell, G. H., *A History of Sienese Painting*, Dial Press, 1932

Faure, Gabriel, *Wanderings in Italy*, Houghton Mifflin, 1919

Francis of Assisi, St., *The Little Flowers . . . of St. Francis*, Dutton, 1910 (Everyman's Library)

Fry, R. E., *Giovanni Bellini*, Longmans, 1901

———— *Vision and Design*, Coward-McCann, 1924

Gronau, Georg, *Leonardo da Vinci*, tr. by Frederic Pledge, Dutton, 1903

———— *Titian*, tr. by A. M. Todd, Scribner, 1904

Hagen, O. F. L., *Art Epochs and Their Leaders*, Scribner, 1927

Hollanda, Francisco de, *Four Dialogues on Painting*, tr. by A. F. G. Bell, Oxford Press, 1928

Holmes, Sir C. J., *Raphael and the Modern Use of the Classical Tradition*, Dutton, 1933

Holroyd, Charles, *Michael Angelo Buonarroti*, Scribner, 1903

Horne, H. P., *Alessandro Filipepi, Commonly Called Sandro Botticelli*, London, 1908

Jameson, A. B. M., *Sacred and Legendary Art*, Houghton Mifflin, 1911, 2 vols.

Konody, P. G., and Wilenski, R. H., *Italian Painting*, Nelson, Toronto, 1929

Kristeller, Paul, *Andrea Mantegna*, Longmans, 1901

Longhi, Roberto, *Piero della Francesca*, tr. by Leonard Penlock, Warne, 1930

Marle, Raimond van, *The Development of the Italian Schools of Painting*, The Hague, 1923–31, Vols. I–XV

Mather, F. J., Jr., *A History of Italian Painting*, Holt, 1923

Merezhkovsky, D. S., *The Romance of Leonardo da Vinci*, tr. by B. G. Guerney, Modern Library, 1928

Munro, Thomas, *Great Pictures of Europe*, Coward-McCann, 1930

Offner, Richard, *Italian Primitives at Yale University*, Yale University Press, 1927

Pater, W. H., *The Renaissance: Studies in Art and Poetry*, Modern Library, 1919 (first published in 1878)

Phillips, E. M., *Tintoretto*, Scribner, 1911

Ricci, Corrado, *Antonio Allegri da Correggio*, tr. by F. Simmonds, Scribner, 1896

———— *Art in Northern Italy*, Scribner, 1911

Rolland, Romain, *Life of Michelangelo*, tr. by Frederic Lees, Dutton, 1912

———— *Michelangelo*, tr. by Frederick Street, 4th ed., Duffield, 1927

Ruskin, John, *Stones of Venice*, Estes, 1913, 3 vols.

Sabatier, Paul, *Life of Saint Francis of Assisi*, tr. by L. S. Houghton, Scribner, 1928

Schevill, Ferdinand, *Siena*, Scribner, 1909

Sirén, Osvald, *Giotto and Some of His Followers*, Harvard University Press, 1917, 2 vols.

———— *Leonardo da Vinci, the Artist and the Man*, Yale University Press, 1916

Strutt, E. C., *Fra Filippo Lippi*, Macmillan, 1906

Taylor, H. O., *The Mediaeval Mind*, 4th ed., Macmillan, 1925, 2 vols.

Taylor, R. A., *Leonardo the Florentine*, new ed., Harper, 1930

Thiis, J. P., *Leonardo da Vinci*, Small, Maynard, 1914

Venturi, Adolfo, *A Short History of Italian Art*, tr. by Edward Hutton, Macmillan, 1926

Venturi, Lionello, *Pitture italiane in America*, Milan, 1931

Vinci, Leonardo da, *Note-books*, tr. by Edward McCurdy, Scribner, 1906

Voss, H. G. A., *Die Malerei der Spätrenaissance in Rom und Florenz*, Berlin, 1920, 2 vols.

Wölfflin, Heinrich, *The Art of the Italian Renaissance*, new rev. ed., Putnam, 1913

——— ——— *Principles of Art History*, tr. by M. D. Hottinger, Holt, 1932

Yashiro, Yukio, *Sandro Botticelli and the Florentine Renaissance*, Cushman & Flint, 1929

See also the background books of the bibliography on p. 377; and the General Bibliography, pp. 749–751.

CHAPTER XV

Baroque Art in Italy in the Seventeenth Century

Baroque is an excellent example of the necessity of seeing the culture that is responsible for a style of art and the reasons for the character of that culture. The coming of the seventeenth century marked the decline of the Renaissance in Italy, as the sixteenth marked its maturity and the fifteenth, its youth. Hence one expects to find complexity and contradiction, technical virtuosity, and theatrical realism. A secular life centered in display found its needed stimulation in a grandiloquence that surprised and overwhelmed the senses. A complacent, decadent Church, threatened with disintegration by the progress of the Reformation in northern Europe, aroused itself into reform through the Counter-Reformation, and saw in the pomp and circumstance of the rising baroque style a type of expression that could overawe with splendor. And this with the help of the Jesuits, recently established in Spain, whose influence was powerful not only in missionary endeavor but also in holding adherents loyal in the face of powerful heresies. Hence the motivation of both secular and religious interests was to feed strained emotionalism with grandiloquent brilliance. One is not surprised to find Italian opera developing rapidly, and the aria, with much florid embroidery, the vogue of the day; or the rise of the viol family among instruments, culminating at Cremona in the creations of the Stradivarius family.

Yet the seventeenth century was not completely unified in this objective. Its complexity admitted many contradictory elements, such as the emergence of the truly scientific spirit. For stimulated by the Ren-

Fig. 568. Santa Maria della Pace,   Fig. 569. Santa Maria della Salute.
          Rome. 1655–57.   Venice. 1631–82.

aissance ideal of complete objectivity, men's minds turned from magic
and the authority of the Church to independent observation. On the
one hand the church warmly reasserted the mystery of the Faith; on
the other, Descartes with his "Cogito, ergo sum" displaced medieval
faith with reason. It was the century of Galileo and Francis Bacon;
of the invention of the telescope, the microscope, and the thermometer;
of the discovery of the circulation of the blood. In other words, as the
cycle of the Renaissance declines, the modern scientific age is being
born.

Rome was the fountainhead of the baroque style, partly because
of the religious situation in the city of the mother church and partly
because the seeds of the style, sown in the sixteenth century, particularly in the work of Michelangelo, naturally grew quickly in native
soil. But it spread rapidly to Naples and to northern cities, especially
Venice, Genoa, Turin, barely touching, however, that stronghold of
the early Renaissance, Florence. Great scale, restless movement, organization in depth, Michelangelo had held within bounds. With him
relationships in all the parts were clear and definite. With the baroque
artists, movement became an end in itself. In a typically baroque
church it is not the clear precise relationship of every part that the
artist strives to set forth but the total effect of many parts half seen,
moving, incoherent provided the total effect is a "spectacle of never-
ending movement"; not stability but flux.

Because of the powerful religious motivation it was a great age of

Fig. 570. Andrea del Pozzo. St. Ignatius Carried into Paradise.
c. 1685. Sant' Ignazio, Rome.

Fig. 571. Great Hall. Farnese Palace (Fig. 477). Decorated by the
Caracci, 1600–05.

431

Fig. 572. Stairway from the Piazza di Spagna to Santa Trinità de' Monti, Rome. XVIII cent.

church building and remodeling.[1] Such a façade as that of *San Carlo alle Quattro Fontane* or of *Santa Maria della Pace* (FIG. 568) [2] is organized in several planes so that there runs through it an advancing and retreating movement. Various architectural forms — columns, pilasters, pediments, carvings — are used to carry movement laterally, vertically, and in depth — a continuous flowing movement with occasional staccato accents, as in a broken or repeated pediment.[3]

The central type of church with a dome still prevailed. Its external possibilities for expressing solidity and compactness of mass are best seen in *Santa Maria della Salute* in Venice (FIG. 569), because of its open site at the head of the Grand Canal. It is octagonal in plan, with a great central dome and a smaller one over the chancel, which are the climax of a restless design with complicated patterns and movements, and with indefinite broken upper contour because of the free-standing sculpture and great scrolls, which, however, unite the polygonal base with the circular dome. From this restless base rises the clear-cut mass of the dome above which is repeated, in the lantern, the half-defined pattern below.

But the central type of church afforded opportunity for even more dazzling effects on the interior than on the exterior. For not only were all kinds of materials used to secure an effect of richness and all available spaces loaded extravagantly with marbles, reliefs, bronzes, gilding, and paintings, but the dome became the point at which crowds of figures soar in a breath-taking sweep upward through the violently foreshortened architectural framework, which creates an illusion of reaching up to infinite heights (FIG. 570). Here is the climax

[1] This practice accounts for the baroque façade of *St. John Lateran* and of other early basilicas and for the refurbishing of many interiors, some of which are, fortunately, being restored. *Santa Maria in Cosmedin* (FIG. 311) is one such case.

[2] *San Carlo* by Francesco Borromini (1599–1667), *Santa Maria della Pace* by Pietro da Cortona (1596–1669). See also the façade of *Il Gesù* by Giacomo della Porta (1541–1604); the façade of *St. Peter's* by Maderna (1556–1639); and the external collonades and the baldachino of the altar of *St. Peter's* by Bernini (1598–1680).

[3] Contrast the single plane and quiet movement of the façades of the fourteenth- and fifteenth-century churches and palaces of Florence.

of the illusionism of Mantegna (FIG. 554) and Cor-
reggio (FIG. 567).

Secular architecture dis-
played the same general
grandiose character as religious. Imposing stair-
ways, both external and
on the interior, were a
fertile motive toward this
end, as is illustrated by the
Aldobrandini Villa at Frascati, or by a sketch of the
Scuola di San Marco in
Venice by *Francesco Guardi*
(1712–1765) which catches
the whole spirit of the
baroque as well as its
forms. The Great Hall of
the *Colonna Palace* in Rome
or of the *Farnese Palace*
(FIG. 571) is typical of the
extravagance of ornament

Fig. 573. Bernini. The Episcopal Chair of St. Peter with the Four Doctors of the Church. St. Peter's, Rome. 1656.

to convey a feeling of pomp and circumstance: paintings and gilded
stucco ornament with statuary below; above, rising from a heavy cornice, a cosmos of figures, statues, and paintings.

Besides the churches and palaces the supplementary piazzas, such
as the great piazza fronting *St. Peter's,* with its gigantic fountains and
imposing colonnades of single sustained rhythm; monumental fountains combining architecture, sculpture, and water; imposing stairways, such as that of *Santa Trinità* (FIG. 572) — all are structures that
in scale as well as form contribute to a general aspect of sumptuousness.

In sculpture, the dominating personality was Giovanni Lorenzo Bernini (1598–1680), architect as well as sculptor. To be a consistent part
of an imposing, even theatrical building, sculpture must partake of
similar qualities. The *Shrine* for the bishop's chair in *St. Peter's* (FIG. 573)
well illustrates the dependence upon materials for their richness of color
and texture, for the baroque sculptors freely combined colored and
white marble and gilding. The indistinct half-realized forms — figures,
clouds, rays — show a technical virtuosity in handling materials but
an almost impudent disregard for their limitations — clouds and rays
of light made of bronze. Yet the dazzling energy of this host of people,
half sculptural, half pictorial, is held by an all-incorporating sustained

Fig. 574. Bernini. The Ecstasy of Santa Teresa.
1646. Santa Maria della Vittoria, Rome.

rhythm and by the vast spaciousness in which it is placed and within which it therefore becomes a focal point. Bernini's papal tombs in *St. Peter's*, that of *Alexander VII*, for example, and his *Santa Teresa* in *Santa Maria della Vittoria* (Fig. 574) are prime examples of theatricality, manifesting the same kind of technical virtuosity and entire loss of feeling for stone that characterizes late Greek work. Intense facial expression, melodramatic poses, pictorial background, agitated voluminous draperies of white marble in juxtaposition to huge folds of variegated red marble, all contribute to the desired effect. Michelangelo had expressed the utmost movement in his figures (Figs. 509, 510) but always sternly within the ideal space created by the original block of stone. Bernini abandoned this ideal space and allowed the figure to burst forth in all directions with an energy that is intensified by voluminous draperies, and by a pictorial use of light and shade. The truly sculptural ideal was too limited and stern for the baroque artists, who attempted, in meeting the requirements of the day, to force it into the more tractable field of painting.

Baroque painting involves carrying to a climax, at times to an extravagant climax under the stimulation of melodramatic ideals, many of the tendencies of the sixteenth century. Correggio is as truly, though less extravagantly, baroque in his *Parma Cathedral* frescoes as are the frescoes in the domes of *Il Gesù* and *Sant' Ignazio*, and in the *Barbarini Palace* in Rome. Caravaggio's realism and violently contrasted light and dark and the Mannerists' types become more sweetly sentimental. Tintoretto's conquest of space design set the three-dimensional organization as the normal type, with one or two great rhythms holding complex detail within their dominating sweep; and his rapid, more direct method in his brush work was peculiarly suited to the expression of half-defined, dramatic effects. Veronese's use of a cooler, more silvery light and largeness of decorative quality reappears in Giovanni Battista Tiepolo (1696–1770), with whom we are still in the baroque yet largely in the eighteenth century, when dramatic intensity eases into flowing grace.

To enter for a moment the field of the minor arts, Benvenuto Cellini's fantasies in gold and enamel, the saltcellar (FIG. 511) or the shell-shaped dish (Metropolitan Museum), are as characteristically baroque as the *Baldachino* and *Episcopal Chair* of *St. Peter's*.

A. SUMMARY

The consistency of the baroque style in all the arts, the perfect harmony of its forms and ideals, mark it as a style that consciously used a certain type of expression because no other could suitably serve its objective. Its technical virtuosity, the result of centuries of endeavor, now became an end in itself. Its hysterical striving for effects, its theatricality — if these qualities are the object of unfavorable criticism, it should be criticism aimed at the age itself, at those forces which demanded in the declining years of the Renaissance cycle a type of expression that the artists must inevitably supply. When the exuberance of baroque was under control, its capacity for subordinating a multiplicity of complex movements into the sweep of an all-incorporating rhythm and its magnificent conquest of space in three-dimensional design were contributions of great value to the European tradition.

BIBLIOGRAPHY

Briggs, M. S., *Baroque Architecture*, McBride, Nast, 1914
Fry, R. E., *Transformations*, Coward-McCann, 1927
Hagen, O. F. L., *Art Epochs and Their Leaders*, Scribner, 1927
McComb, A. K., *The Baroque Painters of Italy*, Harvard University Press, 1934
Ricci, Corrado, *Baroque Architecture and Sculpture in Italy*, Dutton, 1912
Scott, Geoffrey, *The Architecture of Humanism*, 2d ed., Scribner, 1924
Sitwell, Sacheverell, *Southern Baroque Art*, Knopf, 1924
Voss, H. G. A., *Die Malerei des Barock in Rom*, Berlin, 1925
Weisbach, Werner, *Die Kunst des Barock*, Berlin, 1924
Wölfflin, Heinrich, *Principles of Art History*, tr. by M. D. Hottinger, Holt, 1932
—— —— *Renaissance und Barock*, München, 1926

Part Six

RENAISSANCE AND POST–RENAISSANCE ART IN NORTHERN AND WESTERN EUROPE AND IN THE UNITED STATES

CHAPTER XVI

Art in Flanders

(Fourteenth to Seventeenth Century)

A. HISTORICAL BACKGROUND

While the Renaissance was evolving its normal cycle from archaic beginning to baroque decline, the rest of Europe, each country with local variations, was pursuing the Gothic tradition to its flamboyant decadence, which was reached when the Renaissance was but maturing — in the fifteenth century. Even that century, late, saw evidences of a centrifugal movement on the part of the Renaissance to all parts of Europe; but the sixteenth, seventeenth, and eighteenth centuries brought its direct impact. Sometimes its influence was assimilated; often it entirely transformed the native art or robbed it of its individuality. Frequently it was imposed by arbitrary monarchs, for the eighteenth century in particular was the heyday of the monarch and the aristocracy, under whose influence art, and especially Italian art, became an artificial fashion rather than a genuine expression with vital significance. But the Renaissance had a far wider influence than this. The love of independent thought that was the heart of the movement permeated religious life, bringing about a revolt from the Catholic Church and the establishment of Protestantism. It stimulated scientific activities, laying the foundation of observation and critical thinking that has resulted in unparalleled scientific development; in industrial and economic revolution; and politically, in the overthrow of absolutism and the coming into power of the middle classes and the masses. In the nineteenth century Europe and America were still struggling with the effects of the Renaissance as they began to emerge into the era of the present day. To watch the large aspects of this movement — for its complexity is too great to treat it in detail in one volume — we shall begin with the flourishing Gothic art of the fifteenth-century Netherlands.

The lowlands facing the North Sea near the mouth of the Rhine were the home of an industrious people, hardy because of their continual struggle with nature for self-preservation. Their knowledge of the sea and their courage in braving it early made them traders and manufacturers. Their ships not only brought raw wool but carried away the fine woolen cloth famous throughout Europe. Of the several provinces included in the Lowlands or Netherlands, Flanders up to the seventeenth century was the most important, with many great manufacturing centers such as Ghent, Louvain, and Ypres, and with Bruges not only the chief market of the Lowlands but one of the great trade centers of Europe. For an arm of the North Sea, now silted up, reached inland to Bruges as late as the fifteenth century. Some of its trade went overland by the Rhine and the Brenner Pass; some by sea around western Europe through Gibraltar.

Bruges (meaning the "City of Bridges") was the typical Flemish city of medieval times, large, industrious, and wealthy. "In the fifteenth century buyers and sellers from every land resorted to Bruges for their trade. The merchant of Venice and the Jew of Lombard Street encountered one another on her quays and in her exchanges. Sailors and traders from all parts of the world made her streets lively with the varied colouring of their bright costumes. They came and went, and each left something behind him. The wealth of England met the wealth of the East in the market-halls of Bruges. The representatives of twenty foreign princes dwelt within the walls of this capital of the Dukes of Burgundy, at the crossroads of the highways of the North. 'In those days,' says Mr. Weale, 'the squares [of Bruges] were adorned with fountains; its bridges with statues of bronze; the public buildings and many of the private houses with statuary and carved work, the beauty of which was heightened and brought out by gilding and polychrome; the windows were rich with stained glass, and the walls of the interiors adorned with paintings in distemper or hung with gorgeous tapestry.' " [1]

Though technically Flanders was a fief now of a duke and now of a king, these great Flemish industrial cities were only loosely united, for each was a strong civic unit, thoroughly organized through its merchant guilds, which were not only industrial but social, religious, and political as well. The cult of the individual, so prominent in Italy in the fifteenth century, had not yet reached Flanders. To pursue

[1] Sir W. M. Conway, *The Van Eycks and Their Followers,* Dutton, 1921, p. 85; for an excellent picture of Flemish life in the Middle Ages see Chaps. VII and VIII.

Fig. 575. Cloth Hall. Ypres. XIII cent. Destroyed, 1914,
in the Great War.

a craft, a man must belong to the guild controlling that craft, the
painter, for example, to the Guild of St. Luke, which included the
saddlers, and glassworkers and mirror-workers as well. To secure mem-
bership in the guild, the boy was apprenticed early to a master, with
whom he lived as a son, and who taught him the fundamentals of
his craft — how to make implements, how to prepare the panels with
gesso, and how to mix colors, oils, and varnishes. When the youth
had mastered these problems — for there was no supply house where
a painter could purchase ready-made pigments and implements —
and had learned to work in the traditional manner of his master, he
usually spent several years as a journeyman, traveling about from city
to city, observing and gaining ideas from other masters. He was then
eligible to become a master of his craft and was admitted to the guild.
Through the guild he obtained commissions; the guild inspected his
painting for honest, craftsmanlike materials and workmanship; and
the guild secured him adequate payment.[1] The result of such a system was the sound craftsmanship that characterizes the best work of
Flanders.

By the end of the fifteenth century Bruges was losing its prestige
because of the silting-up of its harbors and because of political dis-
turbances. Antwerp now became its successor as the center of the
political, industrial, and artistic life of Flanders. Antwerp was more
cosmopolitan than Bruges, and more eager to receive the stimulation
to trade that was being felt because of the discoveries in the New World

[1] For the guild system see Conway, *op. cit.*

Life became more exuberant, and more sympathetic toward the new ideas that were penetrating northern Europe from Italy. Just at this time, however, Flanders, as a fief of the Spanish crown, was drawn into the religious wars. The Renaissance in northern Europe had emphasized the right of the individual in religious matters as opposed to the authority of the Catholic Church. Many of the provinces of the Lowlands had turned Protestant. Spain, strongly Catholic and Jesuitical, directed against these heretics the Spanish Inquisition. Antwerp, the center of the struggle, lost much of its wealth and vigor in these wars. In the seventeenth century, however, after the Peace of Westphalia, a renewed vitality under a stimulation from Italy produced the last great school of Flemish art.

Fig. 576. Town Hall. Brussels. 1401–55.

B. ARCHITECTURE

Flanders in the fourteenth and fifteenth centuries was thoroughly Gothic; and though the Flemish built fine cathedrals, their most characteristic buildings were the town halls and belfries, the guild and cloth, or market, halls, such as those at Bruges, Ghent, and Ypres. The *Ypres Cloth Hall* (FIG. 575), of great vigor and dignity, is [1] a large rectangular building with a steeply pitched roof, four small turrets with spires at the corners, and a massive tower with turrets which crowns the building. The small amount of decoration is inconspicuous. The impressiveness of the hall is due to the symmetrical massing of simple units — the rectangular body with pointed roof and the rectangular tower — to the quiet rhythm of repeated pointed arches and pointed turrets, and to the unbroken expanse of the roof, which balances the large number of openings below.

This sturdy, restrained design became more slender, more elegant, and more ornate in the *Brussels Town Hall* (FIG. 576) — an example of the same evolution of style that we saw in the cathedral. We note this in the tower and turrets, in the roof broken by frequent dormers, and in the light and shade of the façade made rich by the carvings and niches, the original statues of which were painted and gilded.

[1] More accurately "was," for this building was destroyed in the World War, 1914.

C. PAINTING

Fig. 577. Hubert and Jan van Eyck. Ghent Altarpiece, or Adoration of the Lamb. Central Panel. W. 8 ft. 1415-32. Church of St. Bavon, Ghent.

In northern Europe no great wall surfaces offered the painter an opportunity to develop a monumental kind of wall decoration such as the Italians produced in their mosaics and frescoes. For the evolution of the Gothic aimed ever to eliminate the wall by reducing the structure to a framework of piers and vaulting and by filling the open spaces with glass, the great mural decoration of the North. Hence the Northern painter's activity in the Gothic age was confined chiefly to painting miniatures and illuminations, unless one includes also the making of windows, which is handling of color, though not with the brush. In fact the windows in their colors, composition, backgrounds, and drawing bear close relation to the miniatures despite the difference of medium.

Suddenly, in the early fifteenth century, painting on a major scale appeared in the work of the Van Eyck brothers, Hubert (about 1370–1426) and Jan (about 1385–1440). Not that miniature-painting ceased. In fact the Flemings, Pol de Limbourg and his brother, at the court of the Duke of Burgundy, were producing such books as the *Très Riches Heures* (FIG. 455) at just about the time that the Van Eyck brothers were painting the *Ghent Altarpiece* (FIG. 577).[1] This altarpiece is a good example of the folding altarpiece typical of the North. When closed it

---

[1] This was commissioned of Hubert in 1415, left unfinished at his death in 1426, and completed by Jan in 1432. It seems impossible to disentangle the work of the two brothers.

presents in mono-
chrome the Annunci-
ation and also, equal
in scale and impor-
tance, realistic por-
traits of the donors;
when opened, there is
presented an intensely
colorful rendering of
the medieval concep-
tion of the redemption
of man. In the center
of the large lower
panel, the *Adoration of
the Lamb*, in a meadow
gay with violets, lilies,
daisies, and cowslips
stands the altar with
the Lamb, from whose
heart flows a stream
of blood into a chal-
ice; around it are
kneeling angels; in
front is the fountain of
life surrounded by
kneeling Apostles.

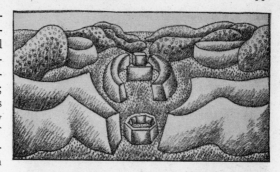

Fig. 577 (A). Analyses of the Adoration of the Lamb
to show: (*a*) the organization of depth and the play
upon texture; (*b*) the use of a sharp triangle as a basic
unit shape.

Toward the center from the four corners great throngs of people approach, clad in rich robes, through a country where rosebushes and
vines are laden with flowers; in the background stretches a varied landscape with richly wooded hills, rivers, and towns, and above this an early-
morning sky. Over the altar appears a dove from which rays descend to
all the groups below. Above are the majestic figures of God the Father,
John the Baptist, and the Virgin, who sits tranquilly, reading a book.
Her hair falls loose over her shoulders; her elaborate crown is decorated
with rubies, topaz, and pearls, with roses, lilies, and harebells, symbols
of her virtues; seven shining stars scattered over the inscriptions of the
arch form a supercrown. Her robe of blue is trimmed with an elaborately jeweled panel of gold and black brocade. The soft texture of
the hair, the luster of the pearls, the gleam of the other jewels, in fact
all the details, are indicated with extraordinary realism. But despite
these realistic renderings of the detail, the *Adoration* scene is subordinate
to a simple symmetrical organization with the Lamb as a focal point.
The altar is placed on the vertical axis and about it swing two con-

Fig. 578. Jan van Eyck; also attributed to Hubert.
Madonna of Chancellor Rolin. H. 27 in. c. 1432.
Louvre, Paris. (Alinari)

centric planes, the inner marked by the kneeling angels, the outer by the kneeling Apostles, the edge of the hosts, and the dove; from this outer circle the hosts radiate toward the four corners, while the wavelike horizontal of the landscape unites all the elements.

This minutely literal rendering of objective appearance strikes one forcibly in Flemish art if he approaches it with Italian painting in mind. Soon, however, he realizes that all these details and all the varying textures create a unity in which line and color are important organizing means. Here is a smooth enamel-like surface of deep resonant color that has a strong linear quality, for the pigment is used with a precision that seems to be born of an innate sensitivity to line. It is, in fact, Gothic linealism.

In the small jewel-like *Madonna of Chancellor Rolin* (FIG. 578) the wealth of detail is equally well controlled and organized. In a loggia with tiled floor, rich carvings, and stained glass the Madonna is seated, heavily draped in a richly bordered mantle which spreads in great folds over the pavement about her; and an angel is holding a gold crown above her head. On the left, Chancellor Rolin, the donor of the picture, dressed in the richest stuffs, kneels before a prayer desk. Through the columns one looks out on a garden with flowers and birds to a parapet where two passers-by are looking over toward the town on both sides of a winding river, where people walk about the square and across the bridge; beyond this scene the landscape fades into distant blue hills. The eye delights in the rich color-harmony as it wanders from detail to detail, from texture to texture — stone, tile, glass, gold, hair, stuffs, flowers — but this wandering of the eye feels the coördinating influence of the arches and columns of the loggia and of the consistently hard luminous surface. From a painter of this kind we might expect portraits of great realism. In the *Esquire of the*

Order of St. Anthony (Berlin) we see an unprepossessing man who wears a fur-trimmed coat, with a bit of brocade and fine linen showing at the throat, and a high, broad-brimmed beaver hat; about his neck is a chain with the insignia of the order of St. Anthony; in his right hand he holds three wild pinks. Jan has observed his model keenly and has placed upon the panel a literal record of the face and hands set off against the broadly painted coat, hat, and flat ground.

The quality of color, the surface texture, and the enduring quality of these paintings — for they are in an extraordinary state of preservation — are due to the technical methods of

Fig. 579. Jan van Eyck. Jean Arnolfini and His Wife. 1434. National Gallery, London.

the Van Eycks, who, while they did not invent the oil medium, seem to have brought earlier experiments to a climax. The preliminary stages in painting such a picture were the same as in tempera, that is, coating the wooden panel with gesso upon which the figures were drawn and modeled in light and shadow. Upon this groundwork were added successive coats of glazes, though the exact vehicle used is not known, until a lustrous, hard, enduring surface was produced.[1]

In the work of the Van Eycks we are witnessing the same exploitation of the visible world, the same break from the imagery and symbolism of the medieval world, that we saw in Italy, except that in the North it took the form of a passionate interest in all the minutiae of objective nature and an equally passionate desire to translate these details into a painting. In details, we see an exact copy of nature; in their unity, we see an organization not found in nature. The idea of using everyday life as subject matter for the painter was novel. The

[1] See the unfinished *St. Barbara* (Antwerp) by Jan Van Eyck to illustrate the preliminary stages. On the technique of the Flemings consult Laurie, *The Materials of the Painter's Craft in Europe and Egypt.*

Fig. 580. Rogier van der Weyden. Descent from the Cross. 1435–50. Escorial, Spain.

Ghent Altarpiece is thoroughly medieval; in the *Madonna of the Chancellor Rolin* the religious subject matter is hardly more than an excuse; while in the *Jan Arnolfini and His Wife* (FIG. 579) a thoroughly genre scene shows the ability of Jan not only to satisfy the popular demand for realism but also to organize realistic detail into a coherent design in an interior space, partly by the subtle values of the space-defining and unifying light and partly by the pattern of line and unit shapes that repeat, contrast, and center upon the hands.

Rogier van der Weyden (about 1400–1464), whose home in the Walloon country in southern Flanders brought him into contact with the French, at times reveals a subordination of details and a predominant sense of design based upon sweeping line and balance of mass. In his *Descent from the Cross* (FIG. 580) the eye is not lured from detail to detail, but is focused upon the central figure of Christ, to which the rhythmic sweep of line and mass inevitably leads it. There is no landscape background. Against a flat surface the figures stand out in strong relief, and through the group runs a common intense emotion that unites them psychologically. Capacity for selecting essentials and setting them forth with emphasis enabled Rogier to paint portraits of forceful directness.

Another painter who retained the Flemish craftsmanship, lustrous color, and fine surface texture yet who shows an unusual organizing ability was Dierick Bouts (1410–1475) who in his *Passover* (FIG. 581) carves out the space of the room, set within which is a table that he surrounds with a stiff row of columnlike figures — all of which produce an impression of astonishing reality of space; while through the scene runs the interplay of squares, circles, and triangular motifs, sharply set forth by juxtaposed light and dark colors.

In the second half of the fifteenth century quite definite influences from Italy [1] brought into Flemish painting something of the suavity of

[1] Hugo van der Goes (about 1440–1482) painted for Tommaso Portinari, agent of the Medici banking house at Bruges, an altarpiece (Uffizi, Florence) whose advent in Florence is responsible for the realistic shepherds in Ghirlandaio's *Adoration of the Shepherds* (Uffizi). Florentine painters were making cartoons for tapestries to be woven in Flanders. These are but two of many mutual relationships between the two countries.

certain Italian paint-
ers of that half-cen-
tury. The linealism of
the Van Eycks and
Rogier van der Wey-
den was softened and
the types were sweet-
ened in Hans Memlinc
(about 1430–1494), yet
without loss of the
Flemish rich color and
enamel-like texture. In
the *Marriage of St.
Catherine* (FIG. 582) the
Madonna and Child
are enthroned in the
center, a panel of rich
damask behind them
and a fine Oriental
rug on the floor; saints
and angels are grouped
symmetrically on each
side. At the top of the
panel two small angels
are floating down with

Fig. 581. Dirk Bouts. Passover. 1464–68. Church
of St. Peter, Louvain.

a crown to place on the Virgin's head; on both sides are kneeling angels,
one with a musical instrument, the other holding open a book, the leaves
of which the Madonna is turning over. At the right St. Barbara with
her tower sits reading intently; at the left St. Catherine reaches out her
hand to receive the ring from the Christ Child; behind stand St. John
the Baptist with the lamb and St. John the Evangelist with his poison
cup; through the columns and piers we catch glimpses, in typical
Flemish surroundings, of scenes from the lives of these saints. We feel
the Northern realism here, in the detailed painting of the pattern and
texture of the fine rug, the rich brocade of the panel, the angel's robe
and St. Catherine's dress of black and gold brocade, the red velvet of the
sleeves, and the delicate veil, so exquisite that it is scarcely discernible
in a photograph. Still the total impression is not so much an insistence
upon minute detail as one upon the suave rhythms that control the
detail and upon sweetness and grace. St. Catherine, with her gorgeous
raiment, is the daintiest of figures. The whole conception of this mystic
marriage is lyrical and far removed from the austerity of the *Ghent
Altarpiece.*

Fig. 582. Memlinc. Marriage of St. Catherine.
1479. Hospital of St. John, Bruges.

It is apparent, from even a cursory study of a group of fifteenth-century paintings, that there are certain well-defined types that govern the appearance of the figures, except in the case of an actual portrait. The Madonnas, for example, are much alike. The face with its high forehead, long nose, and small mouth is conventional. The Child is like a diminutive man with a large head, a face as mature as the Madonna's, and a wizened body quite without structure.

These expressions are largely conventional, a part of the tradition of the school. Form as an organic structure is something in which the early Flemings were not interested, as were the Italians.

The great century of true Flemish painting was the fifteenth, as we have seen it in the work of the Van Eyck brothers, Rogier van der Weyden, and Memlinc, centering chiefly in Bruges. During this century communication between Flanders and Italy was becoming much more frequent. Not only did these countries have a common trade interest, but the Flemish artists began to journey more frequently to Venice and Florence. Evidences of this contact we see creeping into Flemish art — an interest in the figure as expressed in the nude; Renaissance architecture and architectural details replacing Gothic in backgrounds; Italian types and landscape. With the coming of the sixteenth century Bruges lost its industrial prestige with the silting-up of its harbor, and the center of industry as well as of art shifted to Antwerp, an alert, more cosmopolitan city in which the new ideas of the Renaissance found more fertile soil than in conservative medieval Bruges. Thus the sixteenth century saw two main currents of art: first, the native tradition with its insistence upon realism which, when severed from the religious subject, became genre, sometimes charming, sometimes satirical of contemporary life, and in the hands of some painters displaying

Fig. 583. Bruegel. Hunters in the Snow. 1565. Vienna.

a tendency to sink into the vulgar and repulsive; second, the Italian imitation, which resulted in paintings that were neither Mediterranean nor Gothic but a curious combination in which both racial styles were used, unassimilated.

The native tradition, on the other hand, proved far more healthy and showed in Pieter Bruegel (or Breughel) the Elder (1525?–1569) how it could accept increments from other traditions without impairing its own integrity. Bruegel, when a journeyman, traveled widely, particularly in Italy, and while in *Hunters in the Snow* (FIG. 583), for example, one feels something of the Italian selective and organizing power, the Italian universalizing of the theme, and familiarity with the science of linear and aerial perspective, yet every influence has been thoroughly assimilated. The eye takes in the scene and the mood at a glance, so directly and so naturally is it presented. A few moments' careful observation, however, reveals that this apparent directness and naturalness are the result of a very precise organization that controls every detail. A cold blue-green dominant color with warm accents here and there, as in the fire and in the hunters and dogs, sets forth the mood, as well as the visual appearance of a village in winter. A clearly enunciated diagonal movement, marked by dogs, hunters, and trees, starts from the lower left-hand corner and continues, less definitely but none the less surely, by the road, the row of small trees, and the church far across the valley to the jutting crags of the hills. This movement is countered by an opposing diagonal from the lower

Fig. 584. Bruegel, the Elder. The Wedding Dance. 1566. The
Detroit Institute of Arts. (The Detroit Institute)

right, marked by the edge of the snow-covered hill and repeated again
and again in details. Verticals, prominent in the trees and houses, and
horizontals in the skating-ponds stabilize the diagonals, as do the rectangular motif of the ponds, the sharp triangles in the hunter group,
in the branches of the trees, in the roofs and the hills.[1]

The roistering peasant life of his own environment absorbed Bruegel,
and whatever the theme, its vivid reality, at first glance so casually
natural, is not the recording of visual perceptions, as with many
Flemings, but the marshaling of them into an abstract design which
by distilling the merely perceived renders it far more effective to the
eye. Particularly is this true in handling a large crowd, as in *The
Wedding Dance* (FIG. 584). The individuals in the foreground, while retaining all the actualities of type, costume, and environment, at the
same time are drawn with such economy and emphasis at vital points
that each becomes an abstract expression of the rhythm of the dance.
The group as a whole is firmly knit into interlocking curves in depth
— movements that are carried partly by line and partly by shapes and
values of color areas — which are held and accented by static trees and
standing figures.

There was however but one Pieter Bruegel the Elder. Italianization
seemed inevitable, and by it the truly Flemish art perished, while the
Italianate form reached a pinnacle because of the sheer genius of Peter

[1] Compare with Giorgione's *Fête Champêtre* (FIG. 559); a similar basic design.

Paul Rubens (1577–
1640), who lived in
Italy for eight years as
the court painter of
the Duke of Mantua
before he returned
to Antwerp. Antwerp,
after the religious
wars, regained its
wealth and prestige
and, still loyal to the
Church, was ready to
accept the expression
of the Counter-Refor-
mation, the baroque.
Jesuit churches, pat-
terned after their Ital-
ian prototypes, rose in
Antwerp, Louvain,
and Brussels, with pul-
pits, as in *St. Gudule* in
Brussels, of truly ba-

Fig. 585. Rubens. Rape of the Daughters of
Leucippus. 1619 or 1620. Munich.

roque fantasy though hardly at ease in a severe Gothic interior; and
Guild Halls were remodeled to accord with the fashions of the day.

The exuberant painter Rubens was in perfect tune with this environment.[1] Gifted in the handling of pigment, he brought painting
to a climax in the history of painting in Europe that was a powerful influence for succeeding centuries. With an energy like that of
Tintoretto he wisely chose dramatic themes, whether the subject was
religious or mythological, landscape, portrait, or genre.[2] In the *Rape
of the Daughters of Leucippus* (FIG. 585), to take an example from the
mythological pictures, the surface pattern consists of areas of extraordinarily rich contrasting textures — soft luminous flesh, silky hair, lustrous satin with scintillating reflections, swarthy masculine flesh, armor
and heavy cloaks, the hide of the horses, the sky and landscape — and is
organized by intersecting diagonals and strong verticals; by light masses
surrounded by dark. Yet it is not primarily surface pattern but a tightly
knit group of solid masses existing definitely in space, with movement

[1] Compare a similar situation with Titian and a contrasting one with Leonardo
and Michelangelo.
[2] The huge number and uneven quality of pictures attributed to Rubens is due
to his well-known practice of composing or perhaps partly painting a picture and
leaving the completion to some of his assistants, a great number of whom were employed in his large popular shop.

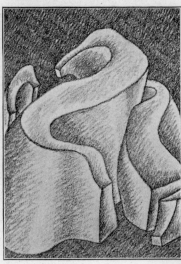

Fig. 586. Rubens. The Adoration of the Magi. Antwerp Museum. 1624. An example of Rubens' S-curve organization.

backward and forward in a truly baroque type of three-dimensional design (see also FIG. 586). Each unit of this design is built up of color and light as in Titian's late works; it is not drawn, in the Florentine sense of draftsmanship.[1]

Whirling movement carried on a diagonal off into space, quieted, and then brought back into a whirl is illustrated in the *Kermess* (FIG. 587). Units of swirling movements made up of two or three figures or of the still life in the foreground keep swirling and at the same time are carried, by every kind of compositional device — line, light and dark, color, aerial perspective — from the lower left-hand corner to the distant right and thence inward by the lines of the hills and sky and by the strongly patterned trees and house back to the starting-place. The exuberant movement of the dancers is offset by the quiet spaciousness of the distance and by the solidity and repeated verticals of the trees and house.

In Anthony van Dyck (1599–1641) we pass from the dazzling richness, impetuosity, and frequent coarseness of Rubens, his master, to a sobriety and refinement which, by comparison, is at times rather soft and empty. In his portraits, his chief work, he at times created a quietly rich surface of the textures of the rich fabrics, fine lace, jewelry, and feathered fan. Even the well-known portraits of the chil-

[1] See Munro, *Great Pictures of Europe*, pp. 217 ff., for excellent notes on Rubens use of color in this and other pictures.

Fig. 587. Rubens. Kermess (Village Dance). c. 1623.
Louvre, Paris.

dren of the court of Charles I in their overelegant satins and lace furnished Van Dyck an opportunity for beautiful passages in the painting of stuffs. He displays in his figures no vigor either of character or of form, but, rather, an aristocratic detachment and somberness. For his sitters — much of his work was done for England's nobility, who invited him thither to paint portraits, to decorate their mansions, and to perpetuate their family pride — his sitters were a stately, elegant, self-centered people whose life was superficial. And Van Dyck was not a satirist, like Goya.

D. MINOR ARTS

The carefully worked out details in the painting of Flanders serve to illustrate the minor arts of the Flemish, whose versatility and skill made them famous and influential throughout Europe. As in painting, everything was produced under the control of the guilds, with a like result of sound craftsmanship. The crowns and miters, jewels, and ceremonial vessels reveal the same skill of the goldsmith that we saw in the Gothic period. The pages of the illuminated manuscripts, glowing with color and gold, richly decorated initial letters, and miniatures, rival the panels of the altarpieces. Their skill in the carving and paneling of wood made a wide market for their furniture and carried their workers to many parts of Europe to execute orders on the ground. But it is perhaps in the craft of tapestry-weaving that the Flemings showed their greatest skill.[1] In the Gothic tapestries (FIG. 462) we saw that the

[1] There were two important centers for tapestry-weaving: Arras and Brussels. Arras was the chief center from early in the fourteenth century until 1447, when

same fundamental principles controlled the weaver that controlled the sculptor and the glassworker, namely, decorative fitness through the insistence upon line, pattern, and color. Although the tendency toward naturalism was making itself felt and a love of minute detail was inherent in the Flemish artists, still they composed their figures skillfully into large units for the decorative effect, and kept detail subordinate. The tapestries became very large, and more complicated in composition. Classical, historical, and pastoral subjects entered. Dyes of intermediate tones, which were now becoming available, enabled the weavers to obtain more brilliant color and more pictorial effects. The borders become wider and more complicated and often give delightful representations of foliage, fruit, and flowers as well as heraldic devices and inscriptions.

E. SUMMARY

In contrast to southern, or Mediterranean, man with his search for the underlying principles of an expression of form and structure that is clear, definite, with all parts precisely related, symmetrical, and reposeful, "Northern man knows nothing of repose; his entire power of configuration concentrates itself on the representation of uncontrolled, boundless agitation. The storm spirits are his nearest kin." [1] Thus the Gothic style, with its incessant movement, its unattained aspiration, is the most fitting expression of the North, though the baroque, with similar indefiniteness and movement, found there a congenial home. Therefore in Flanders a splendid secular architecture, symbolic of the vigorous industrial and civic life, clung to the Gothic style; and out of the flourishing school of Gothic miniature-painters rose a school of painting whose strong linealism controlled its matter-of-fact actuality and literal presentation of the details of visual perception. The soundest of craftsmen, these Flemish painters, by creating magnificent surfaces of glowing color, hard and enamel-like, made an important contribution to the evolution of the oil medium, while their fellow craftsmen, through the rigid control of the guilds, maintained an equally high quality in the fields of bookmaking, metalwork, and weaving. With the inevitable movement of the Renaissance to northern

Louis XI seized the town. The Arras hangings were famous all over Europe, and some of them were designed by the Van Eycks and Memlinc. After the fall of Arras, Brussels became the center of the craft, which there operated under royal patronage. Painters such as Rogier van der Weyden and Rubens made cartoons for the weavers. Charles V required that the tapestries be signed by the master weavers. Of these Willem de Pannemaker was the most famous, and his signature appears on the great series made for Charles, such as the *Conquest of Tunis* in the Royal Palace at Madrid.

[1] Wilhelm Worringer, *Form in Gothic*, Putnam, 1927, p. 83.

Europe, a period of unsuccessful assimilation was followed by a complete control, in the hands of Rubens, of both Northern and Southern elements and a complete fusion into a great climax in European painting.

BIBLIOGRAPHY

Ackerman, Phyllis, *Tapestry, the Mirror of Civilization*, Oxford Press, 1933
Barker, Virgil, *Pieter Bruegel the Elder*, Arts Publishing Corp., 1926
Conway, Sir W. M., *The Van Eycks and Their Followers*, Dutton, 1921
Friedländer, M. J., *Die altniederländische Malerei*, Berlin, 1924–33, 11 vols.
—— —— *Die niederländischen Meister des 17. Jahrhunderts*, Berlin, 1923
Fromentin, Eugène, *The Masters of Past Time*, Dutton, 1913
Fry, R. E., *Flemish Art*, Coward-McCann, 1927
Glück, Gustav, *Die Kunst der Renaissance in Deutschland, den Niederlanden, Frankreich, usw.*, Berlin, 1928
Hourticq, Louis, *Rubens*, tr. by Frederick Street, Duffield, 1918
Hunter, G. L., *Tapestries, Their Origin, History and Renaissance*, Lane, 1912
Lambotte, Paul, *Flemish Painting before the Eighteenth Century*, Studio, 1927
Munro, Thomas, *Great Pictures of Europe*, Coward-McCann, 1930
Rooses, Max, *Art in Flanders*, Scribner, 1914
—— —— *Rubens*, tr. by Harold Child, Lippincott, 1904, 2 vols.
Taylor, H. D., *Thought and Expression in the Sixteenth Century*, 2d ed. rev., Macmillan, 1930, 2 vols.
Valentiner, W. R., *Art of the Low Countries*, tr. by Mrs. Schuyler Van Rensselaer, Doubleday, Page, 1914
Weale, W. H. J., *The Van Eycks and Their Art*, with the coöperation of M. W. Brockwell, Lane, 1913

See also the General Bibliography, pp. 749–751.

CHAPTER XVII

Art in Germany
(Fourteenth to Sixteenth Century)

A. HISTORICAL BACKGROUND

In the Middle Ages we noted the vigor of the Rhenish craftsmen in many of the arts. They built finely constructed and vaulted churches of bold picturesque mass and contour. Among the crafts their textiles and metalwork and woodcarving were equal to any produced in Europe. The impulse toward independent thought that was basic in the Renaissance movement in Germany touched chiefly religious and intellectual life, and resulted in a revolt from the authority of the

Fig. 588. Peller House. Nuremberg. 1605. An application of the Renaissance style to the high gabled house of the North.

Church of Rome and the establishment of the Protestant Church. The result of this Reformation was hostility to Rome and perhaps unconsciously, to all things Italian. Probably for this reason the tradition of the Middle Ages persisted so long in Germany.

It was not until the sixteenth century that German Renaissance expression reached a climax in Dürer, Holbein, and Cranach. Almost immediately after this Germany was plunged into a series of disastrous religious wars which so drained its energy and its resources that it was unable to make any notable contribution to the art of Europe. In the eighteenth and nineteenth centuries, however, there rose the other great expression of its people, perhaps its loftiest — the music of Bach, Händel, Mozart, Beethoven, Wagner.

B. ARCHITECTURE

German buildings always appeared to have a predilection for the picturesque — irregular outlines, abnormally high, steeply pitched roofs with dormers, and abundant decoration in the form of bright color, gilding, and carvings. When the influence of the Renaissance came — late, as we have said — it came in the form of the baroque, which with its extravagance, vague form, and unceasing movement made a strong appeal to German taste. It was in secular architecture particularly, the town halls and the houses of the wealthy merchants, that this influence made itself felt. The reformed Church had little zeal for building. In the houses — the *Peller House* in Nuremberg (Fig. 588) is a typical example — the high gable has retained the essentials of the old traditions but has accepted some of the outward forms of Italy. The arrangement of the doors and windows has become symmetrical; the doorway is placed in the center and is emphasized by a bay above it; the stories with superimposed orders to frame the openings continue up into the gable and are decorated fantastically with scrolls, pinnacles, and statues.

C. PAINTING AND GRAPHIC ARTS

German painting, like that of Flanders, evolved from miniature-painting and the making of stained-glass windows, and appeared early in the multiple altarpiece, which was usually the gift of some wealthy burgher and painted to please his taste and that of his friends. The *Isenheimer Altarpiece* (Colmar) by Matthias Grünewald (1485–1530)

summarizes several important traits. There is something savagely grim, brutally realistic, in much of the early German painting; intense

Fig. 589. Dürer. St. Christopher. Woodcut. 1511. Contrast with Fig. 590 for difference between woodcut and engraving.

color, at times as harsh as the portrayal of the incident. Crucifixions and scenes of agony were popular, and the *Danse Macabre* was peculiarly Germanic. Yet fairy gardens with the Madonna seated in the midst of roses in a mellow radiant light may be the scene upon which the wings open. But in all this painting there is never absent the controlling, intricate linealism of the North.

In the sixteenth century, however, Dürer, Holbein, and Cranach were able to soften the crassness of the native style without sacrificing its vigor, to infuse a feeling of structure into the forms, to eliminate much of the detail in favor of emphasis at essential points, without, however, loss of the restless intricate Gothic line with its own abstract, musical quality.

It was Albrecht Dürer (1472–1528) who first showed this reconciliation. While Dürer was still a young man, the printing press was beginning to make books available. Paper was becoming better in quality and cheaper in price. Illustrations began to be used commonly in printed books as early as about 1475. The extraordinary technical ability of the German in woodcarving and his feeling for line as the chief means of creating form, as well as for its intrinsic calligraphic possibilities, were preëminent potentialities for successful illustration. Thus Dürer's inherited tradition together with his individual ability fitted him to supply the illustrated religious books that were in demand because of the religious ferment of the Reformation. His conceptions, like those of Hubert Van Eyck, were of the Middle Ages, and his convictions were as sincere and intense as his imaginative powers, to take the *Apocalypse* series as illustration.

Fig. 590. Dürer. St. Jerome in His Study. Engraving. 1514. Light is the real theme as well as the chief element of organization.

Fig. 591. Dürer. Four Preachers, detail. 1526. Munich.

Technically, Dürer used both the woodcut and the engraving. In the former the design is drawn on a block of wood and then enough wood is cut away to leave the lines in relief so that when the block is inked and the sheet of paper pressed upon it the design will be transferred to the paper. It is, in fact, pictorial printing. Such a process demands elimination of detail on the part of the designer, and patience and skill on the part of the cutter.[1] In the *St. Christopher* (FIG. 589) the crisp lines create a surface pattern of large units of black, white, and intermediate gray in which the sweeping curves of the hills and the cloak hold in subordination the short, broken, jagged lines, which maintain a constant rapid movement.

The *St. Jerome in His Study* (FIG. 590) is a print from an engraving on copper in which the lines are engraved on the plate by the burin. Here is a delightful atmosphere of peace, quiet, and orderliness — an atmosphere conducive to meditation. The sun streams warmly through the little round panes and envelops everything in the room with varying tones of light, thus tying them into unity. The Saint sits at his desk

[1] Some illustrators cut their own blocks; others do not. In Dürer's case it seems probable that this part of the work was done by a professional cutter.

Fig. 592. Holbein the Younger. Dance of Death: The Old Man. Woodcut. c. 1526. Metropolitan Museum, New York. (Metropolitan Museum)

Fig. 593. Holbein the Younger. Man in a Broad-brimmed Hat. Drawing with washes of color in the hair and face. Basel Museum.

absorbed in work, quite disregardful of the movement of the sands in the hourglass behind him. The lion and the dog are dozing in perfect repose. The books, the cushions, and even the slippers underneath the bench suggest relaxation and comfort. In fact a mood as well as a light suffuses and submerges all the infinite detail, which, however, with its varying materials — knotty wood, glass, metal, fur, stuffs — creates a surface of interplaying textures. All the details feel the control of certain emphatic unifying elements, such as the beams of the ceiling, the arch of the window, the shadow on the floor repeating the curves in the animals.

Like Leonardo, Dürer was an inquirer. In his eager curiosity about everything he belonged to the Renaissance. He traveled in Italy, and was much impressed with the painters and with the beauty of the country. "How I shall freeze after this sun!" he wrote to his friend at Nuremberg. But Dürer's fiber was too strong for him to be lured away from native traditions, as were many Northerners, to their destruction. In a late painting, never finished, the *Four Preachers* (FIG. 591), the conception is Northern, of the Reformation; but the treatment shows definite Italian influences. These powerful monumental figures are of Northern type and detailed individuality in the heads, and Mediterranean in their scale, as they fill the panel, and in the sculpturesque feeling in the broad, deep, massive folds of drapery.

Hans Holbein the Younger (1497–1543), like Dürer, belonged to Renaissance Germany. But in his greatest work, his portraits, Holbein

Fig. 594. Holbein. Catherine Howard, Fifth Queen of Henry VIII. 1540–41. Toledo Museum. (Toledo Museum)

alone of his nation had the selective ability, the capacity to extract from the total visual impression a definite linear motif to which he subordinates whatever detail he uses. In *Catherine Howard* (FIG. 594), for example, notice how he states the dominant curve motif in the large brooch, repeats it again and again in the face and headdress, expands it in the embroidery of the sleeves, and opposes it by the sharp angles of the collar. His lines are clear-cut and sustained, not broken, indefinite, and restless as in many Northern painters. Technically Holbein belongs to the fifteenth-century Flemish tradition, for the surfaces of his paintings are as lustrous as enamel; flat, for he uses shadow sparingly; and highly decorative.

Holbein's keen vision, his control over line, and his ability to select a pose, a costume, and a motif of composition that will emphasize characteristic aspects of personality are evident in his drawings, which are largely preliminary studies for the long series of portraits painted for the English court, whither he was called by Henry VIII. Drawn in red or black chalk, or with a silver point, with a light wash of color here and there or a few minutely worked details of pattern or color, the line is sometimes light, as in the designs for metalwork and jewelry; sometimes it is a strong continuous sweep; often it is broken or wavering; usually it is definite, and it always attains its objective unerringly. In the *Man in a Broad-brimmed Hat* (FIG. 593) the strong silhouette of the hat not only is interesting as pattern but serves to emphasize the sensitive face and keen eyes, and the suave curves in hat and hair are consistent with the almost effeminate character of the subject. The forty-one woodcuts known as the *Dance of Death* (FIG. 592) not only illustrate Holbein's lucid thought and expression but disclose a remarkable dramatic power and an exuberant inventiveness. Death, in the form of a skeleton imbued with natural life and alert movement, always plays his part with grim irony as he mockingly enters into the activity of each individual.

Lucas Cranach the Elder (1472–1553), an accomplished engraver and

Fig. 595 (A). Analysis of the Crucifixion for Light and Dark Organization.

Fig. 595. Cranach. Crucifixion. 1538. C. H. Worcester coll. Chicago. (Art Institute of Chicago)

well as a painter, remains more German in his harsh realism, detailed individual heads, strong unmodulated color, and emphatically linear design. In the *Crucifixion* (FIG. 595) the massing of the lights and darks — the three figures against the dark sky, the heads and spears against the light, the light masses of the horses and of the group of the Virgin — suggest an engraver's design. But the crass realism is permeated by a spiritual quality that results from the isolation of the crosses, as in Mantegna's *Crucifixion* (FIG. 552), and from the symmetrical spatial organization that radiates from the central cross. The horses cut like wedges through the informally massed crowd with its indefinite, intricate, unending linear movement, which is echoed in the nervous drapery above.

D. SUMMARY

In the graphic arts and in painting, which remained essentially Gothic, the German found an expression most in harmony with his nature. For in these arts line — with a reality of its own quite apart from its use in demarking areas and defining planes — abstract, intricate, interweaving line produced an indefinite, never-ending movement that found a counterpart in the polyphonic music of Bach, especially in the fugue. Thus the typically Northern minute realism, intense, often harsh in feeling, was saved by its rhythmic lineal pattern and its stimulating color, so consistent in mood with both the content and the pattern. Their superb technical ability combined with love of decoration often led the artists to load with ornament not only their buildings, but the altars, grilles, and even the pages of their early printed books. Technical virtuosity rather than esthetic effectiveness seemed to be their objective, though such masters as Dürer, Holbein, and Cranach, from contacts with the Mediterranean cultures, infused structure and organization into Northern lineal realism. After the sixteenth century, production became negligible, because of the devastating religious wars, until creative activity again manifested itself in another form, the music of the eighteenth and nineteenth centuries.

BIBLIOGRAPHY

Carrington, FitzRoy, ed., *Prints and Their Makers*, Houghton Mifflin, 1916
Davies, G. S., *Hans Holbein the Younger*, Macmillan, 1903
Dickinson, H. A. S., *German Masters of Art*, Stokes, 1914
Dürer, Albrecht, *Records of Journeys to Venice and the Low Countries*, ed. by R. E. Fry, Merrymount Press, 1913
Ganz, Paul, *The Work of Hans Holbein*, Brentano's, 1913
Glaser, Curt, *Lukas Cranach*, Leipzig, 1923
—— —— *Les peintres primitifs allemands*, Paris, 1931
Glück, Gustav, *Die Kunst der Renaissance in Deutschland, den Niederlanden, Frankreich, usw.*, Berlin, 1928
Hagen, O. F. L., *Art Epochs and Their Leaders*, Scribner, 1927
Hind, A. M., ed., *Albrecht Dürer, His Engravings and Woodcuts*, Stokes, 1911
Horst, Karl, *Die Architektur der deutschen Renaissance*, Berlin, 1928
Moore, T. S., *Albert Dürer*, Scribner, 1905
Pollard, A. W., *Fine Books*, London, Putnam, 1912
Taylor, H. O., *Thought and Expression in the Sixteenth Century*, 2d ed. rev., Macmillan, 1930, 2 vols.
Weitenkampf, Frank, *How to Appreciate Prints*, 3d ed. rev., Scribner, 1921
Wölfflin, Heinrich, *Principles of Art History*, Holt, 1932

See also the General Bibliography, pp. 749–751.

CHAPTER XVIII

Spanish Art
(Fifteenth to Eighteenth Century)

A. HISTORICAL BACKGROUND

Spain, because of its geographic position and the mountainous character of its territory, is more isolated than most of the other countries of Europe. Yet it has been particularly the prey of the foreign conqueror — Roman, Goth, and Moor — and of foreign influences, from Flanders, Italy, France, and the Near East. The coming of the Moor and his long residence in the peninsula were a provocation to the Christians, whose long struggle against the infidels, combined with native conservatism, made them grim fighters for the faith and severe dealers with all forms of heresy. The Church, of a narrow conservative type and with a fanatical priesthood, has always been the dominating power in Spain. Hence the Inquisition could flourish in Spain as in no other country of Europe. This constant struggle and religious fervor made the Spaniard brutal and fanatical on the one hand and emotional and mystical on the other.

It was not until after the fall of Granada in 1492 that any semblance of unity in the peninsula was possible. By the sixteenth century, largely through marriage and inheritance, Spain had become a first-rate power, holding large sections of Europe in fief and acquiring great wealth through its newly discovered possessions in America. Through Seville, the trade center of southern Spain, flowed the gold and silver from the New World. Here, too, nature was less austere than in the barren, mountainous plateaus of the central part of the peninsula. The warm sunshine, fertile soil, and romantic temperament were more conducive to geniality. Southern and eastern Spain were also closer to Italy because of possessions in Naples and Sicily, and the great commercial seaports carried on a brisk trade with the East. But constant wars, mismanagement, and shortsighted policies controlled by a bigoted Church rapidly exhausted Spain's wealth. Its religious fanaticism led to the expulsion, in 1609, of the Mudéjares and Moriscos, and deprived the country of its chief industrial class and its most skillful craftsmen, thus crippling the nation both economically and artistically. By the beginning of the seventeenth century the greatest days of Spain were past.

B. ARCHITECTURE, SCULPTURE, THE MINOR ARTS

Fig. 596. University of Salamanca. Portal. C. 1530.

Spain, like other European countries, accepted the influence of the Renaissance upon its architecture, adapting it to local conditions and bringing about a particularly ingenious fusing of it with the native temperament, especially in the matter of ornament. In the early Renaissance, when the continuity of the Gothic tradition in structure was still unbroken, a new spirit revealed itself in the plateresque style,[1] which is well illustrated by the *Town Hall in Seville* and by the entrance of the *University of Salamanca* (FIG. 596). Plateresque ornament was often concentrated about the doors and windows and its decorative value increased by the plain surfaces that surrounded it. At the *Salamanca* entrance a richly decorated panel rises above the double portal. The ornament is arranged in three zones separated by double stringcourses and crowned by an elaborate cresting. Engaged clustered shafts frame the panel and furnish the needed vertical lines. The carvings increase in depth and boldness as they rise and are broken by portrait medallions, heraldic emblems, and a sculptured group. The motifs include putti, masks, and grotesques, and predominantly the rinceau, showing an influence from Italy. More typically Spanish is the ornament of the *Archiepiscopal Palace* at Alcalá. The walls of the patio (the open court) give one the impression of richness and quiet taste. At first sight they appear to be rusticated, but on close inspection are found to be carved in low relief with animals, birds, masks, griffins, and putti expressed in vigorous movement that is characteristically Spanish.

The plateresque was the most original accomplishment of the period, and its short life of only about half a century was due to external causes. It was still vigorous and spontaneous when Philip II came to the throne in 1556. But it was too imaginative, too exuberant, too emphatic in its ornament to please that austere, morose monarch. So, by royal order,

---

[1] A name derived from *platero*, a silversmith, and applied to the style because of the delicate execution of its ornament.

a cold, unadorned classic ideal was imposed upon Spain, and the warm, typical Spanish style gave way to a grim and solemn majesty exemplified by the *Escorial*, a monastery built by Philip thirty miles from Madrid. The Spanish love of luxuriant ornament, however, did not long bow to this severe ideal; and the baroque style, which appealed both to the native temperament and to the religious zeal of the people, succeeded the cold severity of the purely academic style, revealing itself particularly in extravagantly ornate altar screens and highly realistic sculpture.

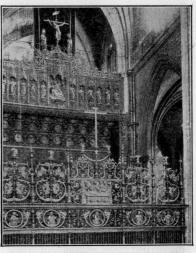

Fig. 597. Retable. Upper part, showing the crest of the reja (Fig. 599) in the foreground. Seville Cathedral.

Spanish sculpture is quite definitely a part of the church, either as architectural sculpture or as religious equipment. Of prime importance was the retable, or choir screen, developed in Spain to a size and magnificence met nowhere else in Europe. Its origin was in the simple altarpiece. But the native love of splendor and decoration and the native extreme religiosity seemed to pour itself forth in expanding the altarpiece until it spanned the bay or nave and lifted its crest well up into the vaulting. Sometimes it was carved of stone, more frequently of wood; invariably it was gorgeously painted and gilded, thus furnishing the richest possible background for the altar. In the retable of the *Seville Cathedral* (FIG. 597) vertical shafts and horizontal bands divide the space into panels with elaborately carved niches and figure sculpture. The motifs are chiefly Gothic, but mingled with them are Moorish domes and arabesques. The impression of overloading with no contrasting reposeful surface perhaps finds partial compensation in the position of the retable in a spacious cathedral with unadorned surfaces and dim light.

Wood was always a popular material with Spanish sculptors, being plentiful and cheap and offering a good surface for the painting, which was considered to be of equal importance with the carving if we may judge from the fact that well-known painters were employed for this part of the work and specialists developed, such as flesh-painters, drapery-painters, and gold-painters.

The advent of Italian influence is illustrated by Alonso Berruguete

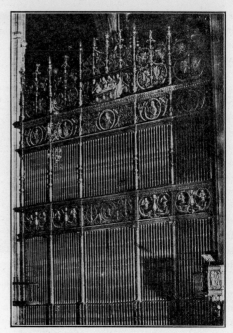

Fig. 598. Custodia. Re-
stored. Gold and silver.
1513. Cordova.

Fig. 599. Reja. Of hammered iron, gilded.
H. 21 ft. 1518–33. Seville Cathedral.

(about 1486–1561), who studied in Rome not only sculpture but architecture and painting, was a pupil of Michelangelo, and on his return
to Spain produced a melodramatic Michelangelesque style in which
the controlled movements of the Italian were transformed into un-
controlled contortions that suited the Spanish love of realism and intense emotionalism. Somewhat less emotional than some is the *St. Peter*
(Fig. 601), though even in this figure there is a brittle tenseness in the
lean, almost skeletonlike hands and feet and the expressive face. The
drapery sweeps about the figure in massive folds, their broad simplicity accentuating the emaciation of the body. This high relief is a
detail of the elaborate choir stalls, which, like the retable, were a part
of the church equipment that the sculptors carved lavishly.

The fervid piety of the Spaniard and his love of realism often led him
to extravagant extremes, as in a wholly naturalistic polychromy, the
use of actual hair and garments on figures, and glass tears. Restrained,
by comparison, yet fervid in its emotional appeal is the *St. Francis*
(Fig. 602) of Pedro de Mena (1628–1688). The long monk's robe and

Fig. 600. Mudéjar Wood Ceiling. Archbishop's Palace, Alcalá.
XIV cent. (Moreno)

hood completely clothe the quiet figure, and frame a face which in its
expression of asceticism is typically Spanish. The compact cylindrical
shape, the deeply cut hood, and the manner of the carving are peculiarly indicative of the material, wood.

Another craftsman who contributed to the richness of the church
was the metalworker. Spain was rich in mines of gold, silver, iron,
and jewels that supplied it with material even before the vast resources
of America were opened to it. An important contribution of the silversmith, the *platero*, was the *custodia*, the large templelike receptacle that
contained the monstrance and was carried in processions. The *custodias*
made before the Renaissance well illustrate the Spanish love of ornament (Fig. 598). From a polygonal base this gold and silver structure — for the design is primarily architectural — rises lightly and
delicately, gradually diminishing in circumference. It is all decoration — reliefs with representations of both sacred and secular subjects,
figure work, and Gothic ornament, all executed with great technical
skill. Whether or not overloading with ornament is ever justifiable, it
is done here with a fairylike grace that almost disarms criticism.

The ironworker too attained the highest skill, especially in the *reja*,
or grille, which inclosed a chapel or altar in such a way that it could
protect the treasures within and still leave them visible. To make such
a grille it was necessary for the craftsman not only to work his material
dexterously but also to have a sense of architectural fitness in his de-

Fig. 601. Berruguete. St. Peter. 1543. From the choir stalls of Toledo Cathedral.

Fig. 602. Pedro de Mena. St. Francis. Wood. Toledo Cathedral.

sign. The reja of the *Capilla Mayor* (FIG. 599) of the *Seville Cathedral*, reaching from pier to pier, incloses the altar and the great retable (FIG. 597), and appears "glittering in the dim light like vast bits of gold lace heavy enough to stand of themselves on edge." Together with the rich colorful retable, it makes an ensemble of great splendor. The design is arranged in two stages, with decorative borders and a cresting. Vertically the reja is separated into five panels, the central one wider than the others. The vertical shafts on the lower stage are colonnettes covered with delicate reliefs reminiscent of silverwork, and carrying capitals; in the second tier they are carved balusters, and in the cresting, candelabra. In the decorative borders the chief motif is the scroll containing figures, while the intervening space is filled with the typically Renaissance rinceau; similar motifs appear in the cresting with flying angels and cherub heads. The artistry of such a reja consists of the happy balance of vertical and horizontal lines; of great richness of detail held in strict subordination to the main lines of the design; the architectural fitness of the design; the fitness of the material for the purpose; and the visible evidences of the hammer and tongs on the material when in a tractable state, and of the chisel, when hard.

Besides the metalworkers, the craftsmen in leather, the woodworkers, and the potters added notes of color and texture to the stone and stucco buildings, more particularly in domestic and civic buildings. The leatherworkers of Cordova provided sumptuous painted and gilded leathers for hangings, cushions, furniture, and coverings for chests. The leather was moistened, and the designs were worked up in relief like repoussé by means of molds, the details added by engraving, and color applied — red, green, blue, black, and white. If silver or gold was used, the sheet metal was applied with oil sizing to the leather before the relief was stamped, so that the silver or gold relief stood out against the natural color of the leather or the brighter pigments. The Spanish love of color, stimulated by trade contacts with the East and

Fig. 603. House at Sitjes (Barcelona). A typical Catalan interior.

by the long presence of the Arabs in the peninsula, found a means of satisfaction in polychrome woodwork and tiles. The Mudéjares were expert workers in wood and perhaps their supreme accomplishment, besides their fine furniture, is found in their ceilings, which were sometimes simply crossbeamed, sometimes coffered, or open-raftered, or three-planed, or of segments that simulated a dome. They were painted, gilded, carved largely with Moorish geometric ornament, and frequently served as the focal point of a room (FIG. 600).

Balancing this colorful richness above, in a stone or stucco room with few openings, were tapestries and colored tiles below, or simple massive furniture with upholstery and cushions of sumptuously gilded and painted leather. The tilings, reflecting the influence of the ceramic tradition of the Arabs, were often of interlacing geometric pattern or arabesque, or of animal and figure motifs — all painted in vivid colors on tin enamel with a spontaneous dashing quality. Climatic conditions favored a wide use of this cool material for interiors (FIG. 603). The Hispano-Moresque pottery, which included plates, bowls, and jars with foliate and heraldic decorations painted in an exuberant colorful style and often heightened with luster, constituted a great industry in the Mediterranean coastal provinces, especially in Malaga and Valencia, and furnished the commercial cities with one of their important articles of trade. Cobalt and manganese on white enamel combined with a golden or iridescent luster, in designs that maintain surface continuity, produce a decorative accent that is highly colorful and peculiarly Spanish.

In Spain as in Italy, the minor arts were so closely interwoven with the major that the distinction here implied did not exist, for all artists

Fig. 604. El Greco. Assumption of the Virgin. 1577. Art Institute of Chicago. (Art Institute)

Fig. 604 (A). Analysis for Three-dimensional Form and for the Combination of Cylindrical and Cubical Shapes.

were craftsmen. As among other peoples, the trade guilds were of paramount influence. "The formula of admission to a Spanish brotherhood was very quaint in its punctilious and precise severity. . . . It was required that the candidate for admission should be a silversmith, married in conformity with the canons of the church, a man well spoken of among his neighbors, and not a recent convert to the Christian faith. The day prescribed for choosing or rejecting him was that which was consecrated to Saint John the Baptist, coinciding with the festival of Saint Eligius or San Loy, 'the patron and representative' of silversmiths, who in life had been a silversmith himself." [1] We hear of Berruguete assisting in the decoration of the palace at Alcalá, carving wooden panels for the choir stalls at Toledo, as well as making marble tombs for counts and cardinals and statues for altarpieces. Juan de Arfe is equally famous for the delicate workmanship of his silver *custodias* and for his bronze sepulchral statue of *Don Cristobal*. The famous makers of iron grilles were sculptors and architects as well.

[1] Leonard Williams, *Arts and Crafts of Older Spain*, McClurg, 1908, 3 vols., Vol. III, p. 222.

Fig. 605. El Greco. Burial of the Count of Orgaz. c. 1584. Santo Tomé, Toledo. (Anderson)

Fig. 606. El Greco. Pentecost. 1604–14. Prado, Madrid.

C. PAINTING

Thus a very close interrelationship and unity of style existed among the builders, sculptors, and various craftsmen. Spanish painting in its highest expression, on the other hand, seems more like sporadic outbursts in the hands of strong individuals, often working in alien traditions rather than a normally evolving national expression. Before the sixteenth century locally differentiated groups of painters produced miniatures, frescoes (for Spanish churches, like Italian, provided large wall areas), and panels, largely religious, in a medieval style that was strongly Byzantine. They were painted in tempera with a lavish use of gold and frequently with details molded in relief in the gesso, and in their dramatic quality and grim realism are perhaps the most truly Spanish paintings. Foreign influence played an important rôle, now from Siena by way of Avignon, now from Flanders, now from France.

Suddenly in the sixteenth century a great expression appeared in a foreigner who found a congenial home in Toledo — Domenico Theotocopuli, known as El Greco, "The Greek" (1541–1614). His origin, highly important for an understanding of his art, appears to have

Fig. 607. Velásquez. Surrender of Breda. 1639 or 1641.
Prado, Madrid.

been in a Greek, that is, a Byzantine, family long established in Crete;
and his training, in Byzantine art of the second golden age, at Cretan
monasteries. When a young man he sailed for Italy; after a few years
in Venice and Rome he left, for some unknown reason, for Spain,
where he spent the rest of his life at Toledo.

A double, and almost irreconcilable basis, late Italian and Byzantine, is evident in his early *Assumption of the Virgin* (FIG. 604). Some
of the figures, in particular that of the kneeling disciple, in pose and
drawing suggest Michelangelo, and the composition obviously is based
upon Titian's painting of the same subject, though the three-dimensional baroque organization is close to Tintoretto. The panel is divided
into two parts. Below, the disciples are grouped about the empty tomb,
in a circle from which, above, the Virgin is rising in a floating, slightly
spiraling movement, which nothing impedes but which, on the contrary, every detail accentuates: the sharp point of the sarcophagus
lid, the break in the circle of disciples, the uplifted hands, the horns
of the crescent moon, the long slashes of light on the Virgin's robe.
As she rises she is surrounded by a group of angels whose lightness
and agitation contrast with the solidity of the firmly rooted figures
below. As surface pattern, sharp triangles furnish the dominant motif,
marked chiefly by the sharp edges where color areas meet. For everywhere the eye is guided by abrupt transitions from color to color,

from light to dark. This sharp cutting of areas and planes, often by the juxtaposition of complementary colors, boldly at variance with the Venetian practice of soft transitions, enveloping atmosphere, and dominant tonality, is evidence of El Greco's Byzantine training in building forms out of color and light and integrating them into a design that by its own abstract power makes forceful the inner significance of the incident.[1]

In the *Burial of the Count of Orgaz* (FIG. 605) we find a like division of a large curved panel into two parts, the one devoted to

Fig. 608. Velásquez. Maids of Honor. 1656–57. Prado, Madrid. (Anderson)

the scene upon earth, the other to that in heaven. As the priest is reading the service, St. Stephen and St. Augustine miraculously appear clad in gorgeous vestments, to take charge of the burial. The three figures form a compact circular group about which are massed, at the right, the priest who is reading the service, clad in a robe stiff with rich embroidery and holding a gold, jeweled cross, and beside him another of the clergy, in filmy robe, standing with outstretched hands, transfixed by the vision above; at the left in balanced position, two monks, wondering at the miracle; and behind them a row of mourners dressed in black robes, with lacy ruffs about the neck and wrists. There is much solid painting in this lower group, and fine characterizations in the highly individual portraits, which appear realistic in comparison with the painting above. A restrained mood suffuses the group, though the design is somewhat agitated in its sharp angles and dynamic contrasts of light and dark, in the rapid jagged movement of the ruffs and in the long sensitive fingers, and in the streaks of the filmy robe and of the torches, which help, with the drab color, to unite the two

[1] To see the logical conclusion of this point of view applied to this subject matter, see the late *Assumption* (*San Vincente*, Toledo), in which the forms are completely etherialized in an attempt to objectify the ultimate essence in an ecstatic swirl of unearthly light and color.

Fig. 609. Velásquez. Innocent X. 1650.
Doria Gallery, Rome.

dissimilar parts. Above swift lines leap up to the crown of the arch, creating an impression of tremendous movement and intense emotion. Here is the scene of the reception of the soul of the Count into heaven. Everywhere is restless movement, expressed by the same means that we saw in the *Assumption* — sharp cutting of planes, and high lights sharply picked out against the dark background with the unexpected, startling effect of lightning.

As El Greco's emotional intensity became more concentrated, his design became more clearly abstract. His palette was often very restricted, as in the *View of Toledo* (Metropolitan Museum); again somewhat rich, as in the *Pentecost* (FIG. 606). This panel is high and very narrow, curved at the top. At the head of a stairway is the Virgin seated, and grouped about her are the disciples and the other two Marys, upon whom the Spirit, symbolized by the dove, is descending in tongues of fire. The spectator is carried at once into that realm of fiery emotion which the group as a whole is experiencing. The figures form a rectangle inclosing a triangle made of the two foreground figures and the Virgin, and its upper edge is broken by the uplifted arm, which also connects the group with the effective space above that emphasizes the descent of the Spirit and is singularly suggestive of the meeting-place of the uplifted spirit of man with the descending spirit of the divine. At the same time the group exists in space with agitated rhythms that move inward and outward in true baroque fashion. Visible line has practically ceased to exist. Light and color remain as organizing means and are used not naturalistically to represent form — its volume, structure, texture and surrounding atmosphere, that is, an illusion of visual perception — but as something eerie, imaginative, entirely nonnaturalistic as a means of "rendering visible the mysteries of the supra-natural world." Thus the figures are signif-

icant partly for their representational values but largely as units in
an abstract design, and hence are
elongated or distorted, when necessary, to fulfill their function in the
framework of light and color whose
purpose is the expression of an ecstatic emotional experience. And in
this mystic quality El Greco is at
home in the intensely religious
Spain of the Inquisition.

In Diego Velásquez (1599–1660),
on the other hand, we perceive a
cool, objective, impersonal attitude
toward objective visual appearance.
In his *Surrender of Breda* [1] (FIG. 607)
Justin of Nassau, the Flemish governor, is handing to Spinola the keys
of the town. The two commanders,
elaborately dressed for the occasion
and accompanied by their retinues,
occupy the foreground against a
hazy background of lowland country with marching troops, winding
rivers, and smoke from conflagra-
tions. Such an organization provided an opportunity to mass clear
warm colors and varying textures

Fig. 610. Murillo. Immaculate Conception. 1655–65. Prado, Madrid.

against cool blue-greens with a decorative, tapestrylike effect. While
each figure is objectively and naturalistically seen, the basic organization of repeated verticals, horizontals, and prominent diagonal in the
central group and the flag, through which play wavelike movements in
the men and horses, combined with the color organization and with a
selection and emphasis of the essentials of the incident — these raise
it above the level of a mere historical document.

As court painter to Philip IV, Velásquez spent a large part of his
life recording, in his cool, detached way, the objective appearance of
this rigidly conventional royal household, with little interpretation but
with the keenest eye for selecting what was important for pictorial

[1] During the struggle between Spain and the Netherlands in the seventeenth century, the town of Breda, a key to Flanders, was still in possession of the Flemish.
To the Marquis of Spinola the Spanish king Philip II had said, "Spinola, you must
take Breda!" After a siege that was brilliant alike for defense and offense, the town
surrendered.

Fig. 611. Goya. Family of Charles IV. 1800. Prado, Madrid.

expression and with a control of paint to secure exactly the desired effect. Through acquaintance, while in Italy, with the work of Caravaggio and through contact with the Spaniard Jusepe de Ribera (1588–1656), he learned something of the potentialities of a very limited palette, black and neutrals, as is evident in many of his portraits, which are subtle harmonies of grays and blacks.

The *Maids of Honor* (Fig. 608), which summarizes Velásquez' attack upon spatial problems, represents an apparently casual interior scene in which the little Infanta Margarita, accompanied by her maids of honor, by dwarfs and a dog for amusement, is posing for her portrait, which Velásquez himself is painting on a large canvas at the left. In the background at an open door the grand marshal of the palace is pushing aside a curtain; the King and Queen stand in the same position as we, the spectators, and their likeness is reflected in the mirror in the background. Behind the casualness of this intimate scene is an organization built around the Infanta, upon whom the light falls from the window at the right and in relation to whom each figure takes its place in space, producing an impression of extraordinary reality of the space from the Princess to the out-of-door light behind the marshal and from

the floor to the lofty ceiling. This intense reality of the space is partly the
result of a precise observation and the
recording in pigment of the exact
amount of light that each object receives and the effect of the light upon
the distinctness of the form and its contours. Yet combined with and dominating this accuracy in the observance
of values are the relationships among
the different parts. The foreground
group forms an S-curve in depth from
the dog to the painter and is filled with
bright light, color, and movement
painted in dashing strokes, now of thin
pigment, now of thick, which define
exactly each texture and quality of
light. This vivacious group is played
off against a large quiet spaciousness
of gray-green with quietly proportioned

Fig. 612. Goya. Portrait of His Wife.
1811–14. Prado, Madrid. (Anderson)

rectangles repeated on the walls, each detail of which is toned as precisely as the foreground group. And the two parts, which act as a foil to
each other, are united by the enveloping light and also by the prominent edge of the canvas at the left.

In painting these royal portraits, whatever interpretation he made or
whatever emotional reaction he experienced Velásquez kept to himself.
Royalty, courtliness of the most rigid character, it was his task to
portray, not individual personality. But the portrait of *Innocent X*
(Fig. 609) leads one to suspect that there might have been more interpretation had the painter been free to express it. For in this Roman
portrait there is not only objective reality in its tersest essentials, an
arresting design of curves and angles, a masterly use of pigment in a
play upon reds and whites in contrasting textures of satin, lace, velvet,
and metals, but also a piercing penetration and forceful presentation
of a personality. Through his practice of using pigment as it is used in
the *Maids of Honor* and in the *Innocent X*, in short or long, thin or thick,
apparently hasty and spontaneous but actually most skillfully calculated strokes, Velásquez was a forerunner of the modern practice of
direct painting.

The stark barren northern plateau around Madrid slopes down into
the luxuriant colorful Andalusian plain of southern Spain, where, at
Seville, a school of painting arose in which were interwoven the warm
southern Spanish "flavor" and a strong Italian influence. It was

Fig. 613. Goya. Caprice: "Why Hide Them?" (Calvert)

necessarily a religious art appealing strongly to the native pious fervor through subject matter and dramatic quality; for with the impossibility of using the nude because of religious prejudice, no figure art could develop, as it did in Italy. Ribera, who lived long in Italy, brought to Spain a style, based on that of Caravaggio, which pleased the Spaniards with its dramatic and realistic portrayal of morbid scenes painted in somber color. But the true favorite, the true expression, of the Andalusian was Bartolomé Esteban Murillo (1618–1682), who showed the Andalusians, in his Madonnas, how charming and peaceful were the Sevillian types. Despite a too frequent soft, sentimental prettiness, Murillo revealed a technical ability in creating a surface of vibrating color, in bathing the canvas in a delicate glowing light; and in one or two of his *Immaculate Conceptions* — the most popular subject matter of Andalusia — an organizing power of some strength (FIG. 610).

After the seventeenth century there is little that is noteworthy in Spanish painting until it flames up once more in Francisco Goya (1746–1828), who for a considerable part of his life was the favorite painter of the Spanish court. In the *Family of Charles IV* (FIG. 611) we see Goya as realistic as Velásquez; but in contrast to Velásquez' impersonal poise, Goya paints into these portraits his high scorn of this sham court degenerate in both body and mind. Prominent in the foreground is Charles, much bedecked with regalia, "the pompous futility of a king," and his queen Maria Luisa, masterful and dominating, surrounded by the other members of the royal family, whose elegance of costume only heightens their weakness. At the left in the background stands the painter at his canvas. How an artist who was so fearless of truth and so bold in his expression of it could be tolerated at such a court is a puzzle. Either Charles was too stupid to understand or he was too lazy to resent. Besides the caustic satire of the portrait, we here discern Goya's power to paint exquisitely the silks, jewels, velvets, and lace, each with a brush stroke suitable to the texture represented and productive of a delicately colorful vibrating surface. The spatial problem here is not unlike that of Velásquez in the *Maids of Honor* (FIG. 608). "There are no lines in nature," said Goya, "only lighted forms and forms which are in the shadow, planes which project and planes which recede." So each figure in the group takes its own place backward or forward in relation to its neighbor; and the group as a unit, filled with atmosphere, with varying lights and shadows which play over the richly colored textures, is set off against the quiet spaciousness of the room.

A contrasting characterization, as warm in its sympathy as the family portrait was bitter in its satire, we find in the *Portrait of His Wife* (FIG. 612), who is sitting stiffly with conventional propriety, her gloved hands folded over her lap. The sharp triangles of the figure and the ground are opposed to the rounding motifs of the head, the shoulder, and the back of the chair. Over the surfaces of the solidly realized figure a light movement runs through the delicately painted hair, the transparent shawl, and the stuffs of the dress and upholstery.

But nowhere else do we appreciate Goya's insight into the life about him and his fearlessness in expressing it so clearly as in the *Caprices*. In this series he pictures with stinging satire the weakness of the State, the greed and corruption of the Church, the hypocrisies of the people, and the social rottenness. In the foreground of *Why Hide Them?* (FIG. 613) a miser with snarling face tightly clutches his money bags, bending over them as if to protect them from the four men who stand laughing at him. He is probably one of the clergy, for the great wealth and greed of the Church at that time were commonly known. Goya's draftsmanship is as incisive as his satire is biting. With a few economical lines and a dynamic patterning of black and white he has set forth the significance of the situation with amazing lucidity and startling power.

D. SUMMARY

The Spanish "national temperament, somber as it is, is a baroque temperament, full of fancies and extravagances, warlike, religious to the verge of superstition, yet inconsequential, and in Spain even the baroque style, carried to a degree of ornateness unparalleled elsewhere in Europe, compels admiration for its dignity and splendor." [1] The exuberant love of ornament was held in restraint in the short-lived plateresque style but burst forth in the baroque retables, choir stalls, metalwork, and vestments in the creation of which the Spaniard was extravagantly lavish of both time and material. At the same time he was never free to develop a normal self-expression, limited as he was by a bigoted Church and a rigid court and with his energy occupied

[1] R. R. Tatlock, ed., *Spanish Art*, London, 1927, p. 97 (Burlington Magazine Monograph).

in assimilating or combating aliens and alien influences. Particularly true is this in the field of painting. However, in El Greco's construction of form in light and color; in Velásquez' detached observation of "the pictorial possibilities of life," his limited palette, and his abrupt brush work combined with subtle niceties of values to organize space; and in Goya's trenchant satire, enhanced by a consistently dynamic form, whether in pigment or in the graphic arts — in these masters at least Spanish painting played a brilliant rôle in the evolution of painting in Europe.

BIBLIOGRAPHY

Barber, E. A., *Hispano-Moresque Pottery in the Collection of the Hispanic Society of America*, Hispanic Society of America, 1915
Beruete y Moret, Aureliano de, *Goya as a Portrait Painter*, tr. by Selwyn Brinton, Houghton Mifflin, 1922
—— —— *School of Madrid*, tr. by Mrs. Stuart Erskine, Scribner, 1909
—— —— *Spanish Painting*, ed. by Geoffrey Holme, Lane, 1921
—— —— *Velasquez*, tr. by H. E. Poynter, Scribner, 1906
Byne, Arthur, and Mildred, *Decorated Wooden Ceilings in Spain*, Putnam, 1920
—— —— *Spanish Architecture of the Sixteenth Century*, Putnam, 1917
—— —— *Spanish Interiors and Furniture*, Helburn, 1921–25, 3 vols.
—— —— *Spanish Ironwork*, Hispanic Society of America, 1915
Byron, Robert, and Talbot Rice, David, *The Birth of Western Painting*, Knopf, 1931
Caffin, C. H., *The Story of Spanish Painting*, Century, 1910
Calvert, A. F., *Goya*, Lane, 1908
—— *Sculpture in Spain*, Lane, 1912
—— and Gallichan, C. G. H., *El Greco*, Lane, 1909
Dieulafoy, M. A., *Art in Spain and Portugal*, Scribner, 1913
Justi, Karl, *Diego Velasquez and His Times*, tr. by A. H. Keane, Lippincott, 1889
King, G. G., *Mudéjar*, Longmans, 1927
Mayer, A. L., *El Greco*, 3d ed. enl., Munich, 1916
Meier-Graefe, Julius, *The Spanish Journey*, tr. by John Holroyd-Reece, Harcourt, Brace, 1927
Munro, Thomas, *Great Pictures of Europe*, Coward-McGann, 1930
Peers, E. A., ed., *Spain, a Companion to Spanish Studies*, Dodd, Mead, 1929
Post, C. R., *History of Spanish Painting*, Harvard University Press, 1930, 3 vols.
Riaño, J. F., *The Industrial Arts in Spain*, London, 1890
Rothenstein, William, *Goya*, Longmans, 1904
Rutter, F. V. P., *El Greco*, Weyhe, 1930
Stevenson, R. A. M., *Velasquez*, Macmillan, 1899
Stokes, Hugh, *Francisco Goya*, Putnam, 1914
Tatlock, R. R., ed., *Spanish Art*, Weyhe, 1927 (Burlington Magazine Monograph)
Tyler, Royall, *Spain: Study of Her Life and Arts*, Kennerley, 1909
Van de Put, Albert, *Hispano-Moresque Ware of the XVth Century*, Lane, 1904
Whittlesey, Austin, *The Renaissance Architecture of Central and Northern Spain*, Architectural Book Publishing Co., 1920
Williams, Leonard, *Arts and Crafts of Older Spain*, McClurg, 1908, 3 vols.

See also the General Bibliography, pp. 749–751.

CHAPTER XIX

Dutch Art of the Seventeenth Century

A. HISTORICAL BACKGROUND

The country now commonly called Holland constituted the northern and eastern part of the group of provinces known as the Lowlands or the Netherlands, while Flanders occupied the southern and western part. There was a racial difference between the two, the Hollander being closer to the German, the Fleming to the French. Like Flanders, these northern provinces were the fief now of one lord and now of another. At the time of the religious and political struggle with Spain, however, the northern provinces, which had quite generally accepted Protestantism, revolted from the Spanish crown, forming the nucleus of modern Holland, whose independence was recognized by Spain in the Peace of Westphalia in 1648. Under the early part of the Spanish rule the Dutch, like the Flemish, had flourished. The East India Company had been formed and the discovery of the New World had opened up to them further opportunities for trade and colonization. Their great commercial cities, such as Haarlem and Amsterdam, had thus been stimulated, and were rapidly acquiring great wealth. Life was not unlike that in the neighboring Flemish cities. Civic pride was strong, and supervision by guilds and similar organizations effective.[1]

Religiously, however, there was a great difference. Protestantism gained a strong hold among the Dutch and with its puritanical attitude toward art banned sculpture, religious pictures, pagan myths, and even historical subjects. As we think back over the art of the Middle Ages and of the Renaissance, we realize that to eliminate the religious subject means to eliminate most of the art and one of its chief motivations. What then was left for these wealthy Hollanders, under the stimulation of their recently won independence, their national pride, and their religious convictions? Fromentin has answered the question thus: 'A writer of our time, very enlightened in such matters, has wittily replied that such a people had but one thing to propose — a very simple and bold thing, . . . and that was to require that they [the artists] should paint its portrait. This phrase says everything. Dutch painting, it is quickly perceived, was and could be only the portrait of Holland,

---

[1] See G. B. Brown, ed., *Rembrandt*, Scribner, 1907, Chap. III, for a picture of Holland in the seventeenth century; also H. W. Van Loon, *Life and Times of Rembrandt: R. v. R.*, Garden City Publishing Co., 1932.

Fig. 614. Hals. Laughing Cavalier.
1624. Wallace coll., London.

Fig. 615. Hals. Young Man with
a Slouch Hat. 1660. Cassel.

its exterior image, faithful, exact, complete with no embellishment. Portraits of men and places, citizen habits, squares, streets, country-places, the sea and sky — such was to be, reduced to its primitive elements, the programme followed by the Dutch school, and such it was from its first day to the day of its decline." [1]

B. PAINTING

Thus it came about that the Dutch painters pried into the pictorial possibilities of this everyday life, yet with an eye to their patrons, the middle-class burghers who were acquiring wealth and position and wanted paintings to hang on the walls of their houses as an evidence of their prosperity, and also to enjoy, with their inherited appetite for realism, a copy of actual appearance. What the artists supplied was a compromise, if it suited at all.

In the field of portraiture Frans Hals (1580–1666) met the demand, at least for part of his life, through the sheer drive of his style, which combined a slashing directness in the use of pigment and a robust naturalism with a knack of terse characterization and a contagious spirit of laughter and jollity. Thus in the *Laughing Cavalier* (FIG. 614) a self-confident soldier with a suggestion of bravado looks out at us with a very direct glance, while over his face ripples a momentary expression difficult to analyze. The unbroken surfaces of the flaring black hat and of the cool blue-gray ground act as a foil to the ostentatious coat with

[1] Eugène Fromentin, *The Masters of Past Time*, Dutton, 1913, p. 130.

its fine lace collar and cuffs, silk sash, and rich embroidery of warm red-browns and yellows, all dashed in with a vigorous brush work. The simple pattern of sweeping curves and sharp angles, the color scheme, and the contrast of cool quiet and warm vivacious areas are in harmony with the nonchalance and the bravado of the subject.

Fig. 616. Rembrandt. Young Girl at an Open Half-Door. 1645. Art Institute of Chicago. (Art Institute)

Momentary surface expression, caught in passing and frequently of a jovial nature, is characteristic of much of Hals's work, and his technical methods are particularly suitable to his purpose. How much he could say by means of a few of his vigorous brush strokes, the *Young Man with a Slouch Hat* illustrates (FIG. 615). He is sitting in a chair with his arm over the back; his eyes sparkle; an infectious jollity spreads over the face, which the easy, unconventional position of the body and the angle of the hat accentuate. The right-angle motif of the informal pattern and the planes that define the figures are indicated by broad, bold brush strokes, and their lights and darks meet abruptly.

Goya's artistic creed might well be applied here, "A picture is finished when its effect is true," and the effect of sparkling vivacity, of a passing moment, could hardly find a more consistent mode of expression. In his group portraits painted for the Civic Guards the figures are so grouped that each is equally visible and each head an individualized portrait — otherwise it probably would not have been accepted. But the artist has managed to tie them into a loose pattern and to rely largely upon creating a sparkling vivacious surface by his vigorous painting of the textures of lace, velvet, satin, metal.

In Rembrandt van Rijn (1606–1669) we find an entirely different type of mind from that of Hals, a totally different method of using paint, and a refusal to compromise with the ideals of the Dutch burghers, who failed to grasp his imaginative conceptions and could not understand his formal means. The immediacy of effect in Hals and the clear literalness of some of his minor contemporaries suited the current taste better. Consequently the *Night Watch*[1] was refused and hooted at and the artist eventually ruined financially.

[1] For an analysis which very lucidly explains the artistic problem involved, see

Fig. 617. Rembrandt. Supper at Emmaus. 1648. Louvre, Paris. Compare with Fig. 604 for a similar organization in the lower part. (Giraudon)

For a single figure, the *Young Girl* (FIG. 616) illustrates Rembrandt's attitude toward objective reality and his means for expressing it. His subject matter was of great importance to him, both in its visual appearance and in its inner significance: the character of the form of the *Young Girl* and the interpretation of her personality. She is standing at a Dutch door with her hands resting on the lower part, and faces the spectator directly, though her glance is averted to her right. She wears a tightly fitting bodice with a linen guimpe gathered closely about the throat, and a full skirt, and about her neck a double string of beads. Her youthful awkwardness rather than grace, and her shyness and reserve — which is not unfriendly, one judges from the suggestion of a smile about the mobile mouth — Rembrandt has pictured with an appropriate simple directness. A brilliant illumination concentrates upon the side of the face, one hand, and the wall behind

Munro, *Great Pictures of Europe*, pp. 267–69; then compare with Hals's *Archers of St Adrian*.

Fig. 618. Rembrandt. Christ Healing the Sick, Called the Hundred Guilder Print. c. 1649. Art Institute of Chicago. (Art Institute)

the figure, against which the arm is sharply silhouetted, and submerges the other parts in shadow. A glowing light and shadow envelop the figure and blur its outlines. The most subtle gradations of tone within a very few hues — reds, red-browns, and yellows — create a deep space, define the volume of the figure, and place it exactly in that space. Light, then, is Rembrandt's basic means of expression, as line was Botticelli's — a light, usually warm, that throbs with infinite variations quite opposite to the cold, darting, untoned light of El Greco. This light penetrates the shadows as well, for they too throb with color in infinite variations and subtle gradations and are as alive with atmosphere as are the highest lights.

The *Supper at Emmaus* (FIG. 617) is also organized in space by the same means — light. Four men are grouped about a table, Christ in the center. The disciple at the left sits with hands folded in adoration as he recognizes the guest; the one at the right has made a quick movement as recognition dawns, but remains transfixed as if still doubting; the stolid serving boy hesitates, puzzled at the scene. The room is dim except for the brilliant light that falls on the tablecloth and the face and hands of Christ, touches the hands of the disciple at the left, and brings out the faces and hands of the two at the right. It plays upon surfaces — the chairs, tablecloth, garments, stone — bringing out their textures. The highest light, about the figure of

Fig. 619. Pieter de Hooch. Pantry Door. H. 27 in. 1658. Rijksmuseum, Amsterdam.

Christ, holds the eye to the center of interest and plays into the other figures, tying them into a psychological as well as a formal unity before it melts into the shadow. One sees here a typically baroque, asymmetrical balance (note the relation of the central figure and the arch to the vertical axis of the panel); a strongly felt linear pattern of verticals, horizontals, curves, and a dynamic diagonal, blurred, to be sure, by light; and a closely knit group of figures which are tied together into a semicircular volume that swings around the rectangular table. All these visual elements are suffused with a warm vibrant yellow relieved with cooler grays.

One may question here why, after what has been said about the aversion of the Dutch Protestants to representing sacred themes, we have as the subject an incident from the life of Christ. Rembrandt, as individual in religious thought as in artistic creed, evidently cared little for the dogma of the times and the decrees of the Church. The fierce struggle of the Jesuits and the Calvinists did not trouble him. His representation of the Bible story was human and realistic, and in terms of contemporary Dutch life. Many of the religious paintings of the Italian Renaissance, with their splendor and idealism, were made at the command of the Church as outward manifestations of its power. In the baroque painters, the Church, in its attempt to stem the tide of the Reformation, became pompous and grandiloquent. How very simple and sincere then, in contrast, is Rembrandt's everyday story told in the language of everyday man!

The use of line as a means for the expression of form was not unknown to Rembrandt, as his etchings show. The process of the etcher is this: Upon a polished copper plate is laid a thin coating of a mixture of wax, gum, and rosin called the *ground*, in which the etcher draws his design with a sharp needle, exposing the copper below. This plate he then immerses in an acid, known as the *mordant*, which bites the copper along the lines exposed. The ground is then removed and a print made as in engraving. The difference between the processes of engraving and etching is that greater ease and facility can be obtained by the needle working freely in the soft wax than by the burin cutting directly into the hard metal. These two processes are analo-

Fig. 620. Ter Borch. The
Concert. Berlin.

Fig. 621. Vermeer. Head of a Young
Girl. H. 18½ in. The Hague.

gous to the two techniques of the black- and red-figured Greek vases,
in which we saw that the Greek abandoned the black for the red in
order to attain greater freedom in drawing.

That this use of line appealed to Rembrandt is clear from the large
number of etchings that he made. His subject matter he took from
the life round about him — the landscape of Holland, the beggars of
Amsterdam, peasants, and the common folk of all kinds, even when
the title was religious, as in the *Hundred Guilder Print* [1] (FIG. 618). The
center of interest is the figure of Christ, a concentrated mass of brilliant light set against a dark ground. Christ is raising his hands in
welcome to the woman carrying a little child whom Peter is attempting
to push aside; just behind her comes another woman with a baby, urged
on by an eager child. In the crowd at the left in the open diffused
light are the fat, supercilious Pharisees and the sneering crowd; one
youth, however, sits on the ground with his head resting on his hand,
pondering deeply. At the right are grouped the sick, a great crowd
of them coming through the opening in litters and wheelbarrows,
or limping along with the help of friends. The pictorial effect of this
side of the print is due to the same use of illumination that we have
seen in Rembrandt's paintings. The light accentuates now one form
and now another before it blends into the shadow. On the left side
of the print his method is different; with line only, with a few essential strokes, he expresses not only form and texture but as penetrating

[1] The subject of the print is *Christ Healing the Sick*. *Hundred Guilder Print* is a title
probably derived from the price that the print brought at an auction sale.

Fig. 622. Vermeer. Young Woman at a Casement. H. 18 in. Metropolitan Museum, New York. (Metropolitan Museum)

a characterization as we found in his portraits. The two contrasting parts of the print he merges by using intermediate tones in the central group.

Contemporary with Hals and Rembrandt was a group of painters who were supplying the Dutch with another kind of small picture to hang on their walls, pictures of their homes, their courtyards, their streets, and their everyday activities. Genre, as subject matter for the painter, was infrequent [1] before these "Little Dutchmen" of the seventeenth century [2] not only popularized it but usually kept it on a high level of artistic treatment as well. In the *Pantry Door* by Pieter de Hooch (FIG. 619) we are in one of these Dutch homes, and see a young woman just outside the pantry handing a small jug to a little girl. There is the usual beamed ceiling and tiled floor; in the room beyond, a chair, and above it a portrait near the half-open window where the light and air pour in, flooding the room and permeating even the darker corners of the foreground. There is nothing monumental, nothing of profound spiritual significance, about the picture but much that is quietly human. What interests us is the masterful way in which the artist makes us feel the interior. The bright outside light coming through the windows emphasizes, by contrast, the dimmer light inside, and so true are the artist's values here that we get a living impression of the air-filled space and distance. The two figures are placed effectively against the wall and break the almost monotonous angularity of the design.

[1] Note Carpaccio's *Dream of St. Ursula* (FIG. 555); Van Eyck's *Jan Arnolfini and His Wife* (FIG. 579); Dürer's *St. Jerome in His Study* (FIG. 590); and Velásquez' *Maids of Honor* (FIG. 608).

[2] Important in the group are Pieter de Hooch (1629–1677); Jan Steen (1626–1679); Gerard Ter Borch (1617–1681); Jan Vermeer (1632–1675); Jacob Ochtervel (1634?–1708?).

Fig. 623. Ruisdael. Swamp. Hermitage, Petrograd.

The textures of various objects afforded these painters opportunity to create interesting surfaces. Ter Borch, for instance, shows extraordinary craftsmanship in the painting of lustrous satins and velvets, and heightens their quality by surrounding them with contrasting hues and textures, and with subtly modulated light organizes them into deep space (FIG. 620).

In Vermeer of Delft we reach, probably, a climax of Dutch genre painting. In his *Young Woman at a Casement* (FIG. 622) there is pictured an everyday scene of purely human significance; not merely an illusion of visual perception but the organization of the elements of visual perception into a formal unity: the human connotation, and the abstract form; neither the one nor the other alone, but the perfect union of the two. A young woman is standing at a partly open window by a table, one hand resting on the window, the other holding a pitcher. There is perfect poise and serenity in the picture and a feeling of great coolness and restfulness. The informal, asymmetrical design is based upon rectangles, in window, map, table, and still life, countered by the curves of the figure, the pitcher, and the basin; and upon the interplay of various textures and inherent qualities of the materials represented: smooth rigid glass and metal, stiffened linen, a thick rug that weighs down solidly. The light from the window falls upon the wall with the subtlest gradations of tone, fills the room, unifying all objects with its generally blue tonality. The dress is deep blue; the cloak thrown over the back of the chair is lighter blue; blue plays through the linen headdress and the window glass. A cool white with infinite modulations covers the wall, while the map and the rich red rug on the table furnish complementary notes of warmth and strength.

In the *Head of a Young Girl* (FIG. 621) the girl looks over her shoulder toward the spectator with a momentary glance, and her frank questioning eyes and the parted lips give to the face an expression of ingenuousness and wonder. Her turbaned headdress of blue and yellow set over against a warm ground states the color notes upon which the artist plays in a pattern composed of curves with a strong vertical in the loose end of the turban, of ovals and triangles, set with typically Northern asymmetry in the square space. Through the elimination of details, the high simplification of all parts, and the clear-cut contours and definition of planes expressed by modulation of tone, the head takes its exact place as a volume in space as well as a striking pattern of color and texture.

In the field of landscape, the Hollanders made a great contribution in that they saw in their native landscape, unidealized, as great possibilities for pictorial expression as in their homes. In the *Swamp* (FIG. 623) of Jacob van Ruisdael (1628?–1682) we are looking across a marshy place in the woods, surrounded by great gnarled trees whose trunks are reflected in the open stretch. Water plants fringe the edge of the swamp and float on its surface; a duck flies off to the left where two others are swimming; the light illumines a great log half in the water, a slender birch sapling, and a gaunt oak; behind the trees the clouds roll up with an impression of movement in space. The calm and stillness, tinged with melancholy, reveal the artist's sympathy and intimacy with nature, which have enabled him to interpret rather than merely transcribe its appearance. Despite an overattention to realistic detail Ruisdael has massed his darks strongly at the corners, allowing the light and air to penetrate freely in the center, while the high lights strike important accents and unify the scene. The color is somber, browns and greens predominating both in the light and in the shadow.

C. SUMMARY

It is in the field of painting primarily and there for a brief century only that Holland's creative activity produced magnificently and prolifically. The sturdy independent Dutch Protestants, who banned everything classical and Italian, made demands upon the painters that produced, besides portraiture, a new subject matter — genre and intimate landscape — in which unpretentious scenes found artistic expression through beautiful surface textures and spatial organization by tonal values. The general tone of sincerity and sobriety in the painter is only occasionally lighted up with imagination or poetry, except in Rembrandt, but they are superlative craftsmen, who had a capacity to see everyday things as forms organized in space, as harmonies of textures and colors, and not merely as visual perceptions to be faithfully copied.

BIBLIOGRAPHY

Baker, C. H. C., *Dutch Painting of the XVIIth Century*, Boni, 1926

Bode, Wilhelm von, *Great Masters of Dutch and Flemish Painting*, tr. by M. L. Clarke, Scribner, 1909

Brown, G. B., ed., *Rembrandt*, Scribner, 1907

Caffin, C. H., *The Story of Dutch Painting*, Century, 1909

Coulton, G. G., *Art and the Reformation*, Knopf, 1928

Davies, G. S., *Franz Hals*, Macmillan, 1902

Fromentin, Eugène, *The Masters of Past Time*, Dutton, 1913

Hind, A. M., *A History of Engraving and Etching*, 3d ed. rev., Houghton Mifflin, 1923

————— *Rembrandt*, Harvard University Press, 1932

Holmes, C. J., *Notes on the Art of Rembrandt*, London, 1911

Knackfuss, Hermann, *Rembrandt*, 9th ed. rev., Leipzig, 1906

Laurie, A. P., *Brush-work of Rembrandt and His School*, Oxford Press, 1932

Lucas, E. V., *Vermeer of Delft*, 2d ed., London, 1922

Michel, Emile, *Rembrandt*, tr. by Florence Simmonds, new ed., Scribner, 1904

Robins, W. P., *Etching Craft*, Dodd, Mead, 1923

Valentiner, W. R., *Art of the Low Countries*, tr. by Mrs. Schuyler Van Rensselaer, Doubleday, Page, 1914

Van Loon, H. W., *Life and Times of Rembrandt: R. v. R.*, Garden City Publishing Co., 1932

Wilenski, R. H., *An Introduction to Dutch Art*, Stokes, 1929

See also the General Bibliography, pp. 749–751.

CHAPTER XX

English Art
(Sixteenth to Nineteenth Century)

A. HISTORICAL BACKGROUND

Though the accomplishment of England in the fine arts since the Gothic age has been supreme in literature and admirable in some of its architecture, in painting it has seldom risen to the first level and its attempts in sculpture have been negligible, for the British have not evinced any marked feeling for sculptural form. Much of the fine vigorous art of the Middle Ages in England — cathedrals, carvings,

Fig. 624. Compton Wynyates. 1520. Warwickshire, England.

illuminated manuscripts, embroideries — had been created under the stimulus and patronage of the Church. But when, in the sixteenth century, Protestantism secured a strong hold and the monasteries were destroyed, this patronage ceased and England was deprived of a large class of skilled craftsmen. Protestantism in general was averse to religious representation, as in Holland; and its attitude became extreme among the Puritans, even iconoclastic under the Commonwealth. The Restoration, however, gave added zeal to the aristocracy, whose wealth and position, increased greatly through the acquisition of large colonial holdings, stimulated the building of fine mansions on great estates, and the production of fine furnishings and portraits. Except in building there was so great a dearth of native talent that the kings and lords were forced to turn to foreign countries for artists. This need is especially noted in the field of portrait-painting. It was not until the eighteenth century, a hundred years after the Renaissance had begun to influence architecture, that a British school of painting evolved. This, like that of the Dutch, was devoted to portraiture and landscape; but, unlike the Dutch, it was strongly under the influence of Italy and existed for the aristocracy.

The eighteenth century also initiated a revolution that was far-reaching in its effects upon the arts not only of England, but of the world — the Industrial Revolution. For at that time machinery, driven by steam, began to replace the handmade or literally *manufactured* product. The movement spread rapidly to France, America, and other countries, and vitally affected all the arts; for it took away from the vast majority of the workers the creative faculty and the ideal of craftsmanship that was vital because it was a part of life. Art was now confined chiefly to building, to painting, and to sculpture, and was fast becoming something apart, something that was looked upon as a luxury

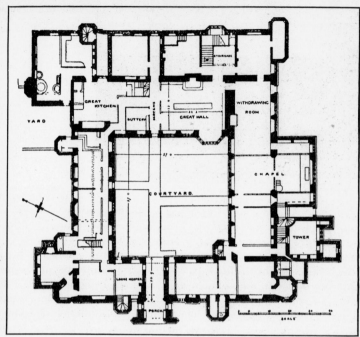

Fig. 625. Compton Wynyates. c. 1520. Notice the irregularity of the plan. At the left are the rooms of service; at the right, the great hall that served as the chief living-room of the household. At one end was a raised dais where the lord and lady dined, while the servants and retainers occupied the space below; the hearth was often in the center of the room. Beyond the great hall were the private apartments of the owner, and the chapel. (Garner and Stratton)

to be enjoyed at certain times and in certain places rather than as an integral factor of life. In the period of readjustment due to this new situation, which affected life socially and economically as well, taste declined. In 1857, when William Morris and Burne-Jones installed themselves in London as "artists" (a profession then looked upon as odd and hardly respectable) and attempted to furnish their rooms, all the furniture and hangings that could be purchased were so ugly that they were driven to make everything themselves — the designs, the dyes, the textiles, and the furniture. Thus began the Morris movement, which was essentially a protest against the artificiality of the times and against the spiritually unhealthy conditions under which the creative impulse of those who were engaged in making everyday things was trying to express itself.

Fig. 626. Longleat.
1567–80. England.

B. ARCHITECTURE

Gothic art in England was strong, versatile, and long-lived. The first suggestions of the Renaissance were seen in decorative details, and in the greater symmetry of ground plan and of design, especially in the great houses of the Tudor age. For with the coming of Protestantism church-building almost ceased. At the same time the greater security throughout the country and the increasing wealth of both nobles and merchants from confiscated properties of the monasteries and from colonial possessions encouraged the building of country places. The typical Gothic manor, such as *Compton Wynyates* (FIG. 624), is set in a great park with stretches of green lawn, masses of elms and oaks, and gardens, all carefully designed with an informality that is patterned after nature. There is an air of comfort, geniality, and freedom from conventionality about both the manor and the surrounding park that is peculiarly English. The variety of materials used in the construction — brick, wood, stone, and plaster — and the irregularity of the exterior and the plan (FIG. 625) give the manor a picturesque appearance. In the early Renaissance, the Tudor age, a terrace was sometimes substituted for the outer side of the court and the rooms were grouped symmetrically on either side so that the plan assumed an H-shape.[1]

The Renaissance influence reveals itself more clearly in such a house as *Longleat* (FIG. 626). The plan shows how balance and symmetry, fundamental principles of the Renaissance, were controlling the arrangement. The exterior, with its flat roof, superimposed orders, regularity, and proportions, is due to the Italian influence; the large number of openings, the bays, and the mullioned windows are due to the medieval English tradition.

The interiors of these English houses indicate the wealth of the coun-

[1] *Montacute House* and *Hatfield House* are good examples of this plan.

Fig. 627. Hampton Court. Great Hall. 1515–40. London. (Nash)

try in timber — oak and other hardwoods — and also the taste and skill with which it was used. The open timber ceiling, the wainscoting, and the stairways were perhaps the three most characteristic uses. The hammer-beam ceiling,[1] which is the ceiling and roof combined, is seen fully developed in *Westminster Hall* and in its most elaborate form in the *Great Hall* of *Hampton Court* (FIG. 627). The room is two stories high and of fine proportions. At the end and along the sides are large windows filled with perpendicular tracery, placed high, thus leaving space below for the tapestries that provided warmth and added color and texture; at the left is an oriel entirely filled with tracery and covered with fan vaulting; above is the highly decorative hammer-beam ceiling, rich in fine sweep of curved line,

Fig. 628. Hammer-Beam Ceiling. Westminster Hall, London. (Viollet-le-Duc)

in tracery, and in carvings. It is a hall of conservative good taste and dignified magnificence.

A fine example of wainscoting is found in the *Bromley* room [2]

[1] An open timber ceiling in which pairs of hammer beams (short beams that project from the top of the walls and are supported by brackets) support large brackets that rise to the collar beam (a short tie beam connecting the rafters near the top of the roof). The hammer beam acts as a lever and dispenses with the tie beam between the lower rafters, thus affording height and spaciousness to the interior. It frequently terminates in some decorative carving, and the space above is usually filled with tracery (FIG. 628).

[2] The palace is now destroyed, but this room has been reërected in the Victoria and Albert Museum, London.

Fig. 629. State Room from Bromley-le-Bow. 1606. Victoria and Albert Museum, London. (Victoria and Albert Museum)

(FIG. 629). The walls are entirely sheathed in panels of a fine quality of oak in a simple, restful design. The center of interest in the room is the great fireplace with its carved stone lintel, above which rises the overmantel elaborately ornamented with the royal coat of arms. The ceiling of molded plaster harmonizes with the mantelpiece and adds another element of richness. Although the flat plaster ceiling had taken the place of the vault, it still retained the most obvious feature of the lierne vaulting (FIG. 452), that is, the intricate design made by the ribs.

When the Renaissance came as an effective force, it came quickly and in a purely academic form, chiefly that of Palladio. This was due very largely to the dominating personality of Inigo Jones (1573–1652). The new style is evident in the *Banqueting Hall* of *Whitehall* (FIG. 630). The façade is designed in two orders superimposed, with columns in the center and pilasters near the ends, doubling at the corners; the entablature of both orders breaks about the supporting members and is finished with a balustrade. All these characteristics are suggestive of Palladio's *Basilica* (FIG. 484). The window treatment is peculiarly Renaissance, with alternating rounding and triangular pediments on the ground story and horizontal cornices supported by scroll consoles on the second. The rusticated masonry gives a feeling of strength and solidity; and the ample window openings furnish the light needed in a Northern climate. Inigo Jones, then, availing himself of the elements and principles of the Renaissance architects, combined and adapted them to the needs of London. Like all accomplished designers of buildings, he has kept his decoration subordinate. Everywhere there is fine proportion, dignity, and restraint.

The second great architect of the English Renaissance was Sir Christopher Wren (1632–1723). Wren, like Inigo Jones, fell under the spell of Italy, as we see in *St. Paul's Cathedral* (FIG. 631). Here the emphasis has been placed upon an effect of picturesqueness and majesty rather than upon a frank expression of structure. The artist realized that a church located in the heart of London with no open space as a setting but viewed from the irregular streets leading to it, and in a city whose climate is uncertain, dull, and foggy, if it were to dominate must be vigorous,

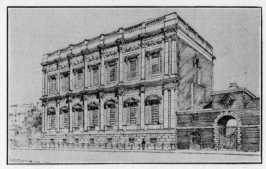

Fig. 630. Whitehall Palace. Banqueting Hall. Inigo Jones, architect. 1619–22. London. (Blomfield)

bold, and even picturesque in its composition. Wren used the basilica plan with a great dome spanning both the nave and the aisles. The classical portico shows some baroque tendencies in its superimposed colonnades, in their saliency, and in the inward and outward movement of the turret colonnades, which repeat the motif of the encircling colonnade of the drum of the dome and of the portico below. The two stories, which are carried consistently about the building, hiding the vaults, are rusticated and are decorated with coupled pilasters, and with strongly profiled and ornamented cornices to give the needed shadow. *St. Paul's* is an interesting example of a discreet and skillful artist's use of the classical style with a frank acceptance of conditions of location and climate different from those of its original home.

The small city churches of London, a demand for which resulted from the London fire of 1666, provided a new problem for the builders; for the congested conditions predetermined a plan that would be conformable to the restricted plot of land and also led the builder to place emphasis upon that part of the structure which would set the building apart from its crowding neighbors, that is, upon the tower. Wren's *St. Mary-le-Bow* (FIG. 632) would seem nonexistent were it not for the tower, which begins at the street level as a strong square structure no more pretentious than its secular neighbors. As it overtops these it takes on a more elegant character, evolves into increasingly slender polygonal and circular forms with encircling colonnades, and finally terminates in a slender spire. Thus it proclaims its symbolism above the roof level of the city. James Gibbs's *St. Martin-in-the-Fields* (1722), on the contrary, because of its open site on Trafalgar Square makes an effective use of a lofty classical portico, consistent with the contemporary classical revival but inconsistent with the functionalism of the tower, which appears perched on the sloping roof.

Fig. 631. St. Paul's Cathedral. London. Sir Christopher Wren, architect. 1668–1710.

Fig. 632. St. Mary-le-Bow. London. Sir Christopher Wren, architect. 1680.

Characteristic of this period that followed the Restoration were the mansions and country houses of the aristocracy, which vary from the great palaces such as Wren's addition to *Hampton Court* (1689–1703), *Chatsworth* (1681), *Blenheim* (1705–24), and *Somerset House* in London (rebuilt 1776–79) to the modest manors whose setting in great parks contributes much of their charm. Renaissance styles were popular, particularly the Palladian design of the *Villa Rotonda* at Vicenza, in which a two-storied portico surmounted with a pediment formed a dominating feature of the design (*Prior Park*, near Bath, and *Chiswick House*). This late-Renaissance style was followed in the late eighteenth century and the first half of the nineteenth by the classical revival, illustrated by *Kedleston* (1761–65) in domestic architecture and by the *Bank of England* (1788–1835) and the *British Museum* (1825–47) in civic.

The interiors of the palaces and manor houses are perhaps more characteristic of the elegant formality of the times than the exteriors. Lofty proportions and fine materials contribute to their stateliness; classical sculpture, one of the passions of the aristocratic classes, fills the niches; and family portraits, perhaps by Reynolds or Gainsborough, stimulate family pride as well as decorate panels of the wall. The hall at *Houghton Hall* (Fig. 633) illustrates the consistently monumental scale, the Renaissance treatment of the strongly salient doors, mantel,

Fig. 633. Stone Hall. Houghton Hall, Norfolk. Built entirely of white stone. 1722–35. (A. Stratton, *The English Interior*, Batsford, London)

Fig. 634. Dining-Room. Detail. Designed by Robert Adam. London. (Swarbrick)

and ornament; and the hall at *Kedleston* with its great height, alabaster colonnades, and rich ornament has the grandiloquence of Italian baroque. Thus the desire for a dignified effect at times led to extravagant pomposity, a reaction to which found expression, in the late Georgian age,[1] in the work of Robert Adam (1728–1792), an influential architect and designer. Adam retained the characteristic spaciousness but lightened the detail. Consonant with the classical revival, and with Roman stucco decoration (FIG. 634) in mind, he based his stucco ornament upon classical motifs — garlands, scrolls, vases, candelabra — kept it low, light, and delicate, and arranged it in panels, frequently oval, for curved lines predominated and the room was frequently designed on an oval plan. White was the prevailing hue, or the pale tones of green, tan, and gray. Invigorating color was supplied by the rugs, the hangings of velvet and chintz, and the mahogany of the furniture.

The furniture of the late eighteenth century, *Chippendale*, *Hepplewhite*, and *Sheraton*,[2] was made under the influence of Robert Adam, and

[1] The period from about 1720 to 1780, covering roughly the reigns of the Georges.
[2] Thomas Chippendale (died 1779) and George Hepplewhite (died 1786) were cabinetmakers with shops of their own; Thomas Sheraton (about 1751–1806) was primarily a designer, famous chiefly for his publications of designs for furniture.

Fig. 635 Chippendale Chair. Metropolitan Museum, New York. (Metropolitan Museum)

Fig. 636. Hepplewhite Chair. Metropolitan Museum, New York. (Metropolitan Museum)

harmonized perfectly with the architectural setting. The *Chippendale* chair (FIG. 635) shows solid construction, and at the same time lightness and finely carved decoration, for Chippendale was a skillful woodcarver. The legs often are straight and efficient in appearance, though sometimes the front ones are cabriole, that is, curved, much like those of the French furniture (FIG. 654). The back has an openwork splat extending from the top to the seat and variously designed, sometimes after Gothic window tracery. The *Hepplewhite* chair (FIG. 636) is contrastingly delicate, and more severe in its lines. The legs taper. The heart-shaped back does not meet the seat. The decoration is unobtrusive, frequently consisting of inlaid wood instead of carving. Of a more extreme delicacy and severe balance is the *Sheraton*, which has inlays of various kinds of wood and dainty paintings of floral decoration.

C. PAINTING

In the field of British painting one feels an insularity that was due partly to its separation from the vitalizing influences current throughout the Continent, and partly to its frequent dependence upon foreign artists, whose influence lay, but little assimilated, on the surface, while a contemporary native style was practiced weakly by its side. Not until the time of Reynolds did the art of painting become thoroughly professional. Then too, "the English temperament does not take kindly to the creation of monumental design in terms of three-dimensional form; but prefers a narrative and descriptive art based on close observation of nature, given a whimsical or dramatic turn, and put in terms of color and linear rhythm." [1] These characteristics mark the source and one of the highest accomplishments in the graphic arts, the English and Irish medieval illumination and miniature, and some

[1] W. G. Constable in the catalogue of the College Art Association, *International 1933*, p. 37.

wall and portrait painting, such as the Westminster *Portrait of Richard II* (FIG. 637), all of which was essentially linear, flat, and decorative.

No school of British painting, however, evolved from this medieval basis, as in Flanders and France. To be sure, the miniature portraits painted by the Oliver family and others in the sixteenth and seventeenth centuries and the group of portraits, chiefly of royalty, by unknown painters of the fourteenth century to the sixteenth mark a beginning of great promise, over which swept the tidal waves of imported styles. First Holbein, in England from 1531 to 1534 at the invitation of Henry VIII, then Van Dyck, summoned in 1632 by Charles I, and Sir Peter Lely (1618–1680) set the styles in portrait-painting that were accepted by the chief patrons — the royal family and the aristocracy.

In the eighteenth century a sporadic expression of a more independent character was that of William Hogarth

Fig. 637. King Richard II. Late XIV cent. Westminster, London.

(1697–1764). A wide social gulf separated classes in seventeenth- and eighteenth-century England. The portrait-painters, whether native or imported, supplied the demands of the aristocracy, as did the builders and furniture-makers. On the wave of classicism and consequent antiquarianism many classical statues and paintings by "old masters" found their way into manor and town houses; and a certain unity resulted from the unity of life within the limits of a given social class, such as existed in France under the Louis. But it was not in this social stratum that Hogarth found his interest. His "moralities" were aimed at the London middle classes whom he knew so well, and were strongly narrative and realistic. It was the age of Addison and Steele, the *Spectator*, and the early novelists. The middle classes had been growing in power at the expense of the court. Of the former class were the Puritans, whose life was drab and intolerant; and of the latter, the Cavaliers, who were trivial, artificial, and licentious. In the life and manners of these eighteenth-century people Hogarth, like Addison, found his subject matter. The dramatic situation, recalling stage productions,

Fig. 638. Hogarth. Shrimp Girl.
National Gallery, London.

focuses attention upon narration, and its satire, though apparent, has a weakness of formal organization that prevents it from affecting the spectator with the unforgettable force of a Goya or a Daumier.

Evidence of Hogarth's feeling for pigment, however, is found when he was off guard, forgetful for a moment of his narrow moralizing. In a few portraits, notably in the *Shrimp Girl* (FIG. 638), there is the sureness of a swift perception, and a sparkle and verve in its expression, attained through a spontaneous, swift, and vigorous use of pigment — an artistic kinship with Hals — however rightly one may point to its lack of form, and to its lack of evidence that "the artist is preoccupied with purely visual values" (Roger Fry), both of which are permanent weaknesses of British painting.

It was the portrait-painting of Reynolds, Gainsborough, and their followers, however, that was the popular expression of the aristocracy. Sir Joshua Reynolds (1723–1792), despite a romantic sentimental vein and a futile attempt to adopt an Italian style, restored to painting, in his *Discourses* and his professional standards, acquired largely through study in Europe, the solid professional base which had been lost since the breakup of the medieval schools at the closing of the monasteries. More a theorist than an artist, overwhelmed by the color harmonies of the Venetians, he built up a "grand style" in which he painted the fashionable people of the day. An artificial society found in him its artificial painter, satisfied with superficial description containing little interpretation, structure, or organization, though he apparently saw these qualities in the prototypes he professed to follow.

Thomas Gainsborough (1727–1788), though he too painted the fashionable people of the time, tended to give their artificiality artistic expression (FIG. 639). His portraits are usually composed after a Venetian formula with masses of foliage, or a column, with a distant landscape in the background. But light and air play about the figures, which take their place in space in relation to the whole composition. Spontaneity and ease of line, and the textures of satin, lace, velvet, and plumes delicately brushed in with glowing iridescent color, together produce charming passages of surface. But it is largely surface painting, which in the followers [1] of Reynolds and Gainsborough weakened eventually into sweet prettiness.

If the British portrait-painters attained only a superficial excellence, the landscape school made definite contributions. The work of Richard Wilson (1714–1782), with its close dependence upon elemental nature, and of John Crome (1768–1821), with its quiet spaciousness filled with light and air, its direct and intimate relation to nature, often expressed with greater breadth and simpler realism than in Hobbema, by whom he was influenced — the work of these men was a prelude to the climax of British landscape-painting in Constable and Turner.

Fig. 639. Gainsborough. Morning Walk. Lord Rothschild's coll., Tring Park.

John Constable (1776–1837), like the Dutch and like Wilson and Crome, found delight in a direct contact with his native landscape — in the light and warmth of the sunshine, the cool of shadow, and the movement of the wind and rain. The *Hay Wain* (FIG. 640) reveals the quiet charm of the countryside in a composition that is informal and unconventional. In the foreground a hay wagon is fording a stream near a house behind which are luxuriant trees that cast cool shadows; at the right stretch the meadows glowing in the sunshine; masses of clouds move rapidly through the spacious sky. Something of the vibrant quality of light and air that was lacking heretofore appears in this picture, and a rich varied texture rather subdued in color tonality. These effects Constable secured by substituting for the traditional smooth surface of greens, grays, and browns, short thick strokes or dots of pigment of various hues laid over the ground color, a method known as *divisionism*, or broken color. Thus he gained not only a vibrating quality of light and air but a rich texture of surface, which he sometimes enhanced by manipulating the pigment with the palette knife as well as with the brush.[2]

Joseph Mallord William Turner (1775–1851) was also interested in

[1] George Romney (1734–1802); Sir Henry Raeburn (1756–1823); John Hoppner (1759–1810); Sir Thomas Lawrence (1769–1830).
[2] To illustrate Constable's technical innovations, contrast his early painting of *Salisbury Cathedral* (Victoria and Albert Museum), exact in its descriptive details, with the later Salting and Ashton examples of the same subject.

Fig. 640. Constable. Hay Wain. 1821.
National Gallery, London.

Fig. 641. Turner. Fighting Téméraire. 1839.
National Gallery, London.

light and air. But in contrast to Constable's intimacy with and rather close transcription of nature, to the solidity of his forms and the reticence of his expression, Turner, after a preliminary direct study of nature, was swept off into a world of imagination, into limitless space filled with light in which forms lost structure and solidity and existed merely for the sake of the golden misty light and air which enveloped them. His subject matter was as dramatic as his color, and whatever its literary title, the majesty of the sun, sky, sea, and mountains and the vastness, power, and grandeur of light-filled space were his actual themes. Since he was enormously prolific — there exist thousands of oils, watercolors, drawings, the *Liber Studiorum* — the selection of two or three is obviously inadequate. In the *Fighting Téméraire* and in the *Ulysses Deriding Polyphemus* he is preoccupied with titanic nature. In the *Fighting Téméraire* (FIG. 641) the old battleship, in the light of a brilliant sunset and a rising moon, is being towed down the harbor to the wrecking-yards by an efficient, puffing tug. Here a romantic subject has found a consistent expression, with structure and organization present, though freely unconventional. While in these paintings the human interest associates itself with the landscape in a highly imaginative way, later paintings reveal almost abstract visualizations of space and light. In *Rain, Steam and Speed* (National Gallery) the structure and solidity of all objects are lost in the effect of the swift movement of the train through a driving rain — an effect secured by using a rather thick pigment in broken color. In *San Benedetto: Looking toward Fusina* everything melts into a golden misty light with a strongly defined gondola in the foreground for stability; and in the watercolor *Norham: Sunrise* (National Gallery at Millbank) phantom shapes float in the opalescent mist as a result of the thinnest washes of transparent color drawn over a masterly, lightly sketched outline.

A solitary in English painting was William Blake (1757–1827), the mystic who lived the largest part of his life in the world of his visions (FIG. 642). "There assuredly never was a more singular,

Fig. 642. Blake. When the Morning Stars Sang Together. From the Book of Job. 1825. Metropolitan Museum, New York. (Metropolitan Museum)

more inexplicable phenomenon than the intrusion, as though by direct intervention of Providence, of this Assyrian spirit into the vapidly polite circles of eighteenth-century London. The fact that, as far as the middle classes of England were concerned, Puritanism had for a century and a half blocked every inlet and outlet of poetical feeling and imaginative conviction save one, may give us a clue to the causes of such a phenomenon. It was the devotion of Puritan England to the Bible, to the Old Testament especially, that fed such a spirit as Blake's directly from the sources of the most primeval, the vastest and most abstract imagery which we possess. Brooding on the vague and tremendous images of Hebrew and Chaldean poetry, he arrived at such indifference to the actual material world, at such an intimate perception of the elemental forces which sway the spirit with immortal hopes

and infinite terrors when it is most withdrawn from its bodily conditions, that what was given to his internal vision became incomparably
more definite, more precisely and more clearly articulated, than anything presented to his senses. His forms are the visible counterpart
to those words, like *the deep, many waters, firmament, the foundations of the
earth, pit* and *host*, whose resonant overtones blur and enrich the sense
of the Old Testament." [1] With an intuitive sensitivity for linear
rhythms, he objectified these internal visions in linear designs — woodcuts, engravings with a wash of color added, wash drawings — composed of symbols by which he wished to objectify the elemental forces
with which he lived. His drawings and paintings are not illustrations
of an incident, but objectifications of an experience of a man who has
seen through the incident to its fundamental implications and who
struggles for a form suitable for their expression. In his claim that the
Byzantine style was revealed to him one discerns a realization that his
own objective and that of the Byzantines were similar — "to render
visible the mysteries of the supra-natural world." [2] Yet his style of
drawing shows affinity with contemporary neoclassic art.

A movement in English painting that is perhaps of greater value
historically than for the intrinsic worth of its expression was the Pre-
Raphaelite Brotherhood, and its sympathizers. In 1848 seven young
men [3] formed this brotherhood, whose purpose was to break away from
the bad taste and empty artificiality of the times, and to substitute real
ideas, a sincere study of nature, and sound craftsmanship. The brotherhood sought to regain the spirit of the ages that preceded Raphael and
to bring back the old ideal of the craftsman who could make things not
only useful but beautiful in shape, line, pattern, and color. This group
of men worked as craftsmen along various lines: they made stained
glass windows, textiles, dyes, and furniture; decorated walls; painted
panels; designed cartoons for tapestry and wallpaper; and printed and
illustrated books. The value of the movement lay chiefly in its protest
against the bad results of the segregation of art from life, and in its
efforts to make art again a vital, spontaneous expression manifesting
itself in the chair and the book as well as in the building and the statue.
The chief figure in this aspect of the movement was William Morris
(1834–1896), who in the zeal of his unstinted endeavor made an important contribution toward the solution of the still unsolved problem —
the place of art in contemporary civilization.

[1] Fry, *Vision and Design*, p. 214, by permission of the publisher, Coward-McCann.
[2] See p. 210.
[3] Best known of the group were Dante Gabriel Rossetti (1828–1882) and William
Holman Hunt (1827–1910); in close sympathy were Ford Madox Brown (1821–
1893), Sir Edward Burne-Jones (1833–1898), and William Morris. A champion of the
cause was John Ruskin (1819–1900).

D. SUMMARY

In England we meet a people who had developed strong native traditions in all lines of art during the Middle Ages and who through their natural conservatism and tenacity were not easily influenced by Italian styles. The architecture of their churches and especially of the great manor and city houses shows a fusion of the Renaissance and native traditions without, on the whole, too great a sacrifice of taste and design. Sculpture was negligible and painting extraordinarily limited in content — portrait and landscape — and tending on the whole toward illustration rather than toward form and formal relations. It showed a constantly recurring predilection, inherited from the great schools of miniature-painters of the Middle Ages, for linear pattern rather than an interest in three-dimensional organization. The land-scape school of the nineteenth century, however, made valuable con-tributions to the technique of oil painting. While in England there began the world-wide Industrial Revolution that together with the baneful aspects of the decadent Renaissance has well nigh overwhelmed true spontaneous art expression, also in England there have arisen against this unhealthy condition strong protests, which, if not always justifiable in detail, in the main have done much to turn attention toward higher standards and to stimulate the ideal of honest craftsmanship.

BIBLIOGRAPHY

Armstrong, Sir Walter, *Art in Great Britain and Ireland*, Scribner, 1909
—— —— *Gainsborough and His Place in English Art*, Scribner, 1906
Baker, C. H. C., *British Painting, with a Chapter on Primitive Painting by Montague R. James*, Hale, Cushman & Flint, 1934
—— and Constable, W. G., *English Painting of the Sixteenth and Seventeenth Centuries*, Harcourt, Brace, 1930
Binyon, Laurence, *The Engraved Designs of William Blake*, Scribner, 1926
—— —— *The Drawings and Engravings of William Blake*, Studio, 1922
—— —— *English Water-Colours*, Macmillan, 1933
Blomfield, Sir R. T., *A History of Renaissance Architecture in England, 1500–1800*, Macmillan, 1897, 2 vols.
Brown, G. B., *William Hogarth*, Scribner, 1906
Cescinsky, Herbert, *The Old-world House, Its Furniture and Decoration*, Macmillan, 1924, 2 vols.
Dobson, Austin, *William Hogarth*, new ed., Lippincott, 1902
Figgis, Darrell, *Paintings of William Blake*, Scribner, 1925
Fry, R. E., *Reflections on British Painting*, Macmillan, 1934
—— and others, *Georgian Art (1760–1820)*, Scribner, 1929 (Burlington Magazine Monograph)
Gotch, J. A., *Early Renaissance Architecture in England*, Scribner, 1914
Grundy, C. R., *English Art in the Eighteenth Century*, Studio, 1928
Hind, C. L., *Landscape Painting from Giotto to the Present Day*, Scribner, 1923, 2 vols.

Holmes, C. J., *Constable*, Dutton, 1903

Jackson, Sir T. G., *The Renaissance of Roman Architecture: II, England*, University of Chicago Press, 1922

Johnson, Charles, *English Painting from the Seventh Century to the Present Day*, Dial Press, 1932

Macartney, M. E., *English Houses and Gardens in the 17th and 18th Centuries*, Scribner, 1909

Macquoid, Percy, *A History of English Furniture*, Putnam, 1904–08, 4 vols.

Mulliner, H. H., *The Decorative Arts in England, 1660–1780*, London, 1924

Richardson, A. E., *Georgian England*, Scribner, 1931

Speed, Harold, *Science and Practice of Oil Painting*, Scribner, 1924

Swarbrick, John, *Robert Adam and His Brothers*, Scribner, 1916

Tallmadge, T. E., *The Story of English Architecture*, Norton, 1934

Triggs, H. I., *Formal Gardens in England and Scotland*, Scribner, 1905, 3 pts.

Turner, J. M. W., *Golden Visions*, comp. by C. L. Hind, Nelson, 1925

Vallance, Aymer, *Old Colleges of Oxford*, Scribner, 1912

Victoria and Albert Museum, *Panelled Rooms*, London, 1914–24, Vols. I–VI; Vol. I, *Bromley Room;* Vol. II, *Clifford's Inn Room;* Vol. V, *Hatton Garden Room*

—— —— *Catalogue of English Furniture and Woodwork*, London, 1923–31, Vols. I–II, IV; Vol. I, *Gothic and Early Tudor*, by H. C. Smith

Wilenski, R. H., *Masters of English Painting*, Hale, Cushman & Flint, 1934

See also the General Bibliography, pp. 749–751.

CHAPTER XXI

French Art
(Fifteenth to Eighteenth Century)

A. HISTORICAL BACKGROUND

Up to the sixteenth century France was still Gothic, and each community was still a unit of civic and religious elements which found free expression in the work of the artists. But cosmopolitanism was taking the place of medieval local solidarity. The exchange of commodities and of ideas was establishing a broader attitude toward life. Political interrelations were taking the French kings to Italy and ended in bringing Italian ideas to dominate France. There is little wonder that the warmth and splendor of Italy captivated the Northerners, even those who came primarily on political missions, as did Charles VIII, who during his expedition to Italy in 1494 lived for some time in the Medici Palace in Florence. Even more influential was Francis I (1515–1547), a great patron of all the arts, who not only brought ideas from Italy but induced Italian artists such as Leonardo da Vinci and Benvenuto Cellini to come to France, and there execute commissions for him.

For it was the king
and not the Church
who now held the bal-
ance of power in
France. The religious
art of the Middle Ages
was being superseded
in the attempt to glo-
rify the State and to
flatter the monarchs,
who were now arbi-
trary and now whim-
sical, and usually
under the spell of
Italy. Hence upon the
native artists the kings
usually imposed a
foreign art.

Fig. 643. Château of Blois. Wing of Francis I.
1515–19. (N. D. Photo)

Politically, socially, and economically, the rapid tendency toward the
final suppression of the feudal lords and toward the concentration of
power in the hands of the monarch reached its climax in the famous
statement of Louis XIV, "I am the State." The burden of religious
wars and persecutions, of unendurable taxation, and of the injustices
of class privilege on the one hand, and on the other, a new mental
outlook in which reason and the laws of nature challenged medievalism,
combined in the great outburst of the French Revolution, one of the
important signs pointing to a new era based upon a new social order.

B. ARCHITECTURE

The tendency in France from religious toward secular interests, even
before the coming of a direct influence from Italy, brought about a
greater demand for châteaux and civic buildings. Protection, an important function of the medieval château (FIG. 421), was no longer
necessary. Yet some of its features, such as the towers and battlements,
had become so traditional that they still persisted. Climatic conditions
also determined several features characteristic of Northern buildings
— steep roofs, a large number of windows, chimneys and fireplaces.
The Italian influences we see emerging at *Blois* (FIG. 643), in the
wing built by Francis I. The steep roof with its dormers and chimneys,
the large windows with mullions, the niches containing statues, the
gargoyles — these are French. The Italian reveals itself in the greater
regularity of design, the greater repose that comes from the balance

Fig. 644. Château of Chambord. 1526–44.
(N. D. Photo)

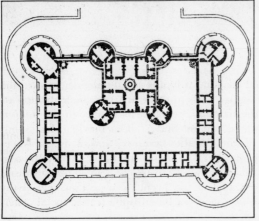

Fig. 645. Château of Chambord. In the central
building were the rooms of state; in the side wings, the
servants' quarters, kitchens, and pantries. There was
little in the way of convenience or sanitation. The
stables were near the living-rooms and the kitchens far
from the dining-room. (Du Cerceau)

of vertical and horizontal lines, and the classical pilasters and carvings. Traditional love for the Gothic verticality, however, has made the builder break his entablatures with pilasters.

Typical of the early Renaissance châteaux is *Chambord* (FIG. 644). It stands out on the open plain, as did most of these châteaux; for they were great country places usually built near a forest so as to serve as hunting lodges. Its plan (FIG. 645) shows regularity and symmetry — a central square building with four rounded towers at the corners, set in a court, surrounded on three sides by an outer line of rooms with towers at the corners, all surrounded by a moat. The exterior design shows marked regularity of spacing and balance in the lower stories, with a strongly felt horizontality of stringcourse and with pilasters for the only ornament. To compensate for this restraint, the roof rising from a rather elaborate cornice presents a fantastic group of steep surfaces, with dormers and chimneys, about a central lantern.

The rooms of the early Renaissance châteaux (FIG. 646) were large; the ceilings, when not vaulted, showed the structural wooden beams, which were richly painted; the walls, whether of stone or plaster, were covered with tapestries that served two purposes — decoration and warmth. The only source of heat in this cold climate was the huge fireplace, which not only served this utilitarian purpose but was also a center of decorative interest; for the overmantel that usually reached to the ceiling was elaborately carved, giving a strong accent to the design and a note of elegance to the entire room.

Thus the architecture of the early Renaissance, as illustrated by *Blois* and *Chambord*, is still French at heart.

Fig. 646. Chaumont. Dining-room, restored. (Saint-Saveur)

Afterward, in the reign of Henry II (1547–1559), came translations of treatises by Italian architects and even the architects themselves; and study and travel in Italy by the French. This brought about a more thoroughgoing revolution, though it never entirely eliminated some French elements. The building that best illustrates this period is that part of the *Louvre* (Fig. 647) which was built by the architect Pierre Lescot (1510?–1578) and the sculptor Jean Goujon (died before 1568). The typically French charm and grace of this façade are somewhat lost in the large court that it now faces, four times the size of the original one; for the projections, the shadows, and the detail are too delicate to carry a great distance. Each story forms a complete order, the pilasters no longer breaking through the entablature as at *Blois*. The cornices project enough to furnish the balancing horizontal line. The projecting central and corner pavilions that characterize all parts of the *Louvre* are partly a reminiscence of the traditional tower pavilions and central gate of the early fortresslike château, especially where they terminate in high roofs, and partly a development of the projecting end bays of the Roman palace (Fig. 476). The arcading on the ground story is the French use of the Roman combination of the arch and lintel; artistically, it is recessed enough to produce more shadow than the upper stories, thus strengthening the base of the design. On the second story the pilasters rising from bases, and the alternating curved and triangular pediments supported by consoles, have direct antecedents in the Roman palace; but the lower height of the stories, the larger size of the windows, and the sloping roof are Northern. Sculptured

Fig. 647. Louvre. Court, showing the façade of Lescot and Goujon. 1546–76. Paris.

Fig. 648. Hôtel des Invalides. Chapel. Mansart. 1692–1704. Paris.

Fig. 649. Louvre. Façade of Perrault. 1665. Paris.

Fig. 650. Gardens of Versailles. Basin of Latona from the terrace
of the château. (Rigaud)

decoration verging on overornamentation plays a large part in the
composition. This decoration is delicately carved in low relief and is
distinctly architectural in its design. In this façade we have the best
of French Renaissance architecture, showing masterly design both in
the balance and in the proportions of the large elements, as well as
delicacy, charm, and fine taste in the details and ornamentation.

A more literal dependence upon Renaissance design is evident in
the façade of the *Louvre* (FIG. 649) built by Claude Perrault (1613–
1688) for Louis XIV. This effective composition has strongly influenced columnar façade design ever since. The general impression is
one of imposing nobility combined with quiet restraint. There are
five divisions, bilaterally balanced — the projecting central pavilion,
emphasized by a great arched doorway and crowned with a pediment;
the two projecting end pavilions; and the two connecting colonnades.
The unifying line is the horizontal of the cornices, relieved by the projecting pavilions and pediment. The severely plain ground story with
its light, unbroken surfaces not only serves as a base but emphasizes
by contrast the richness of the broken light and shade of the colonnade.
This varying light and shade is carefully regulated — deepest in the
colonnades because of the open loggia behind the columns; lighter
in the center, where the columns stand close to the walls; and lightest
on the corners, where the columns are engaged or supplanted by pilasters, with a shadow accent in the central niche. Thus there comes
about a varying degree of light and shade, like the different values
in a painting, that adds richness and unity to the design.

In ecclesiastical architecture as well as in secular, the seventeenth
century saw Paris definitely, not half-heartedly, transformed from
Gothic to Renaissance; and this was true in sculpture and painting as

Fig. 651. Versailles. Galerie des Glaces. Louis XIV.

Fig. 652. Hôtel Soubise. Louis XV. Paris.

well as in architecture. Everything Italian was the vogue of the day. In the chapel of the *Hôtel des Invalides* (Fig. 648), which is typical of a large group of churches, we find a thoroughly Renaissance base surmounted by a dome that derives obviously from *St. Peter's*. Here the greater saliency in the parts of the façade, through their organization in several planes, the more exaggerated play upon light and dark, the superimposed orders, and the broken cornices and ornament of the dome — all these elements show the influence of the baroque.

The French gardens that formed an integral part of the plan and the life of the château were as formal as the age itself. Those laid out at *Versailles* (Fig. 650) by André le Nôtre (1613–1700), the landscape artist employed by Louis XIV, illustrate how magnificent the gardens had become. Water played an important part and its use demanded a knowledge of hydraulic engineering. Garden design called for great basins to catch the reflections of the buildings, and for fountains, large and small, cascades, and canals. Statues of river gods and of playing children and great ornamental vases of lead served as accents in the fountains or against the tall clipped hedges that bordered the gardens. Broad walks and long avenues afforded fine vistas and great masses of trees framed the design.

While the exteriors of these buildings were so purely imitative of the

Fig. 653. Table. Louis XIV. Of wood with metal ornamentation. Metropolitan Museum, New York. (Metropolitan Museum)

Fig. 654. Console. Louis XV. Metropolitan Museum, New York. (Metropolitan Museum)

Italian Renaissance, the interiors were a freer expression of the personal taste of the monarch. This is particularly true of the buildings erected during the reigns of Louis XIV and Louis XV. Louis XIV (1661–1715) was a great builder who paid special attention to decoration and to furnishing, with the result that the ensemble was an unusually harmonious unit. Louis was able to do this because of the centralization of the arts in the Gobelins' establishment, purchased for him in 1662. At that time it did not limit its productions to tapestries but made furniture, metalwork, jewelry, and textiles. The Grand Monarch's ideal was somber dignity and magnificence; and as artists were at the service of the state for the purpose of pleasing and glorifying the monarch, the palace at *Versailles* in all its aspects, from the architectural design of the buildings to the metal decorations of the furniture, is sober, symmetrical, and stately. The *Galerie des Glaces* or *Hall of Mirrors* (FIG. 651) is magnificent in its dignity and in its sober color enriched by brilliantly painted ceilings, by hangings of silk, velvet, and tapestry, and by an abundance of ornament, such as colored marbles, plaster relief painted and gilded, carvings, and metal fittings. The furniture is consistently heavy and rich (FIG. 653), of simple, massive construction but elaborately veneered with fine woods and usually decorated with metal ornaments of various alloys.

At the death of Louis XIV, the nobility threw off this heavy dignity, and turned to the gaiety, frivolity, and sparkling lightheartedness that characterized the reign of Louis XV. The age found a perfectly harmonious expression in the rococo.[1] Dainty rooms for conversation or card-playing or boudoirs are typical (FIG. 652). Slender proportions and never-ending movement in easy curves with a definite avoidance of straight lines and angles; light color with much gilding; the use of

[1] From *rocaille*, the rockwork or shellwork found frequently in rococo ornament.

Fig. 655. Sèvres Porcelain. Metropolitan Museum, New York. (Metropolitan Museum)

many mirrors to add vivacity with their reflections — such, in general, constituted the rococo style, the light, sparkling, thoroughly French version of baroque. Such a room, however, is incomplete without the people for whom it was built, with their elegant costumes of lustrous satins and brocades, their equally elegant manners, and their sparkling wit. The furniture (FIG. 654) shows a design based entirely upon curved lines. Its slender proportions, its dainty decorations of flowers and garlands, and its gray-white color form a harmonious part of the rococo style. So also the paintings of a whole galaxy of painters of court life — Watteau, Boucher, Nattier, Fragonard, to mention a few — the brocaded satins, the Sèvres porcelain, music and literature, together constituted a unified expression, produced under the lavish patronage of the court and the nobility, that points to a unity and consistency in Parisian court life of the eighteenth century.

C. MINOR ARTS

The centralization of all the arts in the Gobelin factory forced the artists who were in the employ of the ruling aristocracy into the state-controlled system. This resulted in standardization and artificiality on the one hand and a high standard of craftsmanship and great unity on the other. The fine furniture made during the reigns of Louis XIV, Louis XV, and Louis XVI,[1] with its inlays of various fine woods and tortoiseshell, and gilt bronze mountings, was the work of artists as well known as the painters and sculptors: André Charles Boulle (1642–1732), for example, and Jacques Caffieri (1678–1755). Likewise the royal Sèvres porcelains were the products of potters who were masters of ceramic technique; and they harmonized with the artificial elegance of the interiors. Chinese porcelains had made their way to Europe perhaps as early as the eleventh or twelfth century, and because of their thinness and translucency they were greatly admired. But it was not until the eighteenth century that the potters in both Germany and

[1] The Wallace collection in London is particularly rich in the arts of eighteenth-century France.

France discovered the nature of true porcelain. A typical Sèvres vase (FIG. 655) is elegant in shape, is covered with a deep-blue enamel, flawless in its finish, and is heavily ornamented in gold. On the body of the vase in a reserved panel is a naturalistic painting of figures and landscape. Thus despite its display of technical virtuosity and its perfect harmony with the table on which it stood, like some products of the Gobelins it fails to possess, because it vies with the art of the painter, that integrity of medium which is the mark of the finest ceramic products.

This same transgression of the limitations of a medium is seen in the great tapestries made at the Gobelin establishment, which since its purchase for Louis XIV had been a center for the finest production. The tapestries of this period were of great size. Their subjects were taken chiefly from history and mythology, and the compositions were designed by the most important artists of the day. Technically, they show the great skill of the weavers in their complicated compositions, the large number of colors and tones used, and their elaborate borders. But artistically many of them fail to attain their purpose of decorating the wall, as the Gothic tapestries so successfully did, because they are fashioned not so much to produce a decorative color harmony as to create an illusion of reality, after the fashion of a painting, by the use of distance, perspective, light and shade.

Fig. 656. Goujon. Panel from the Fountain of the Innocents. 1547–49. Paris.

Some of the other textiles reveal a more consistent textile design. The large repeat pattern that originated in the Near East began to break up into a lighter framework and by the time of Louis XV had taken the form of a delicate pattern of vines, garlands, flowers, and ribbons that well harmonized with the interior decoration and the furnishings of the period. These brocades and silks were made largely at Lyon, an important textile center; and, like the tapestries, they show the great technical skill of the weavers.

D. SCULPTURE

Sculpture too follows the graph of style. Yet the native grace and swing of line in Gothic carving (FIGS. 444, 454) still dominated in the

Fig. 657. Houdon. Voltaire. 1781.
Comédie-Française, Paris.

somewhat Italianate and more naturalistic architectural sculpture of Jean Goujon (died before 1568). On the decorative panels of the *Fountain of the Innocents* (Fig. 656) nymphs are carved in low relief. The easy grace of the "rhythmic figures, bending here, curving there, haunting but elusive," the elongation of the proportions to obtain free sweep of line, the soft clinging drapery that suggests the flow of water, the emphasis upon the sinuous line accentuated by the rigid verticals of the fluted pilasters that frame the figures — all this reveals Jean Goujon as a master of decorative sculpture, as we saw in his sculpture on the *Louvre.*

Much of the sculpture of the seventeenth, eighteenth, and into the nineteenth century is feminine both in subject matter and in feeling — figures of goddesses all ease and grace and with exquisite surface finish expressive of the texture of flesh or fabric, too often mere superficial prettiness. This was the result of the autocracy of the French Academy, which narrowly restricted the subject matter and the technical methods of the painters and sculptors. An outstanding figure is Jean Antoine Houdon (1741–1828), who used the current baroque and rococo forms with independent vigor, especially in his portraits, which constitute his best work. In the *Voltaire* (Fig. 657) baroque qualities — restlessness, momentary pose, realism, the dependence upon heavy draperies for pictorial effect — are modified by the usual French poise and suave flow of line. In the terra-cotta portrait of *Louise Brogniart* (Fig. 658) the vivacious turn of the head, the quick glance of the eye, and the mobile expression about the mouth are spontaneously caught and expressed in clay, the medium so suitable for momentary expressions, and held permanent by baking the clay. Such sparkling portraits find their counterpart in the rococo paintings and furnishings of the late eighteenth century and thus represent the sculptural phase of the rococo style.

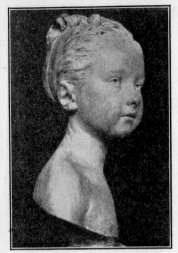

Fig. 658. Houdon. Louise Brogniart. Baked clay. Louvre, Paris.

Fig. 659. Jean Clouet. Charlotte of France. c. 1540. Max Epstein coll., Chicago. (Art Institute of Chicago)

E. PAINTING

French painting of the fourteenth and fifteenth centuries is largely in the Gothic style, which originated in miniature- and glass-painting, with the altarpiece the most conspicuous form until portraits began to appear as the individualizing tendency was permeating the social structure. The French painter, though naturalistic, was not so insistent upon detail as the Flemish and the German. He was possessed of a larger, more selective way of seeing his world and a greater facility for organization; and his racial predilection for poise and gravity, for an easy flow of line, and for suave rhythms lent an air of graciousness to his paintings. Activity was localized in a number of sites, particularly around Paris; in Burgundy, for the Dukes of Burgundy were great art patrons; in Touraine; and at Avignon, where Italian influence was strong because of Italian painters at the papal court. So long as the demand for handmade books continued, well-known painters, such as Jean Fouquet (about 1415–1481) painted miniatures as well as altarpieces and portraits. From some unknown painter of southern France comes a *Pietà* (FIG. 660) whose scale and monumentality show an influence of the Sienese frescoes in Avignon. Above a low-lying landscape, with the towers of Jerusalem at the left, three figures rise against a gold background: the Virgin, with Mary Magdalen and John on

Fig. 660. Pietà. Middle of XV cent. Louvre, Paris. (Giraudon)

either side, bending over the dead body of Christ, which lies gaunt and angular, across the lap of the Virgin; in the left corner is the kneeling figure of the donor. The picture is filled with an intense emotion, expressed not by a realistic rendering of agonized grief in pose and facial expression, as in many Northern paintings, but by purely formal qualities: a large, striking pattern of light and dark masses of sober color and gold; great sweeping curves opposed by dynamic diagonals and sharply defined right angles; and quieting horizontals.

The vital late Gothic art continued, in the sixteenth century, in the portraits of the Clouets and of Corneille de Lyon, in face of the Italianizing school fostered, if not arbitrarily imposed, by the French court. Ironically enough the monarch, when it came to portraits of himself and his family, seems to have preferred the native traditional style, while the school at Fontainebleau was producing pictures in an eclectic Italian style under the direction of masters imported from Italy. *Charlotte of France* (FIG. 659), for example, by Jean Clouet (working about 1516–1546) is a relatively flat pattern of light and dark color areas of varying textures and shapes — curved shapes effectively opposed to angular — and sharply defining edges. Hence there results a strongly linear quality not unlike that of Holbein.

In the seventeenth century, as the Italianizing style continued into a baroque phase under Simon Vouet (1590–1649) and Eustache Le Sueur (1616–1655), the Le Nain Brothers (Antoine, 1588–1648; Louis,

Fig. 661. Louis le Nain. Peasant Family. Louvre, Paris.

Fig. 662. Poussin. Funeral of Phocion. Louvre, Paris.

Fig. 663. Claude Gellée (Lorrain). Egeria. 1669. Naples. (Anderson)

Fig. 664. Watteau. Embarkation for the Island of Cythera. 1717. Berlin.

1593–1648; Mathieu, 1607–1677) were producing for the bourgeoisie a popular genre art similar to that of the Flemish and the Dutch.[1] Yet in this painting, to take the *Peasant Family* of Louis Le Nain (FIG. 661) as an illustration, is a smaller unit of visual perception than in the Dutch and consequently a larger scale of figures. With the sober color of a limited palette, chiefly grays and red-browns, and with the skillful handling of light, both natural illumination and firelight, the painter has constructed solid, almost sculptural forms placed firmly in space. Thus Le Nain shows a greater concern for massive forms related in space than he does for a description of the multitude of details present in unselective visual perception. At the same time he has recognized all the human values of the subject, and has portrayed both their immediate expression and their wider implications with a sincere directness.

In the field of landscape the French made a contribution through two painters, Poussin and Claude, who however, lived most of their lives in Italy and whose paintings are markedly Italian Renaissance in their quiet architectonic structure, which is counter to the contemporary baroque of Rubens (FIG. 586) and to the intimate realism of

[1] See R. H. Wilenski, *French Painting*, Hale, Cushman & Flint, 1931, pp. 47–48, for the influence of a colony of Dutch and Flemish painters at St. Germain-des-Prés.

Ruisdael (FIG. 623). In both, the figure and title interest (usually mythological or religious) is submerged, almost lost, in a true land-scape feeling, imaginative to be sure and based on the Italian and classical. Nicolas Poussin (1594–1665) in his figure painting was an eclectic derived from Italian masters, chiefly Raphael and Titian. In his landscape he carved out space, a deep spaciousness that is con-structed by a few definite planes insistently stated and repeated with variations. In the *Funeral of Phocion* (FIG. 662), for example, each figure, tree, and building is set firmly upon the basic horizontal plane or its variations, a plane which stretches from the foreground to the distant mountains; and each is constructed clearly of light and color with its component planes meeting rather sharply. Very definitely one is guided through the landscape by these lights and darks and by the shapes which they form — the angular patterns of the buildings and the rounding masses of the trees. In comparison with the melting at-mospheric quality in Claude, Poussin's landscapes have a precise clarity often emphasized by an abrupt, almost clashing passage of color.

Claude Gellée (1600–1682), also called Claude Lorrain, though he too builds up nature imaginatively, with classical subject matter, constructs an "architecture of tone masses." In the *Egeria* (FIG. 663) Claude has massed his trees and buildings to serve as a framework for the opening through which we are carried into a vast spacious-ness by the light, whose highest value is here concentrated and thence radiates throughout the picture and ties together all parts by its en-veloping tonality. At the right is a group of classical ruins, so usual in Claude, and in the distance on a hill a ruined castle, the dark mass of which carries the eye inevitably into luminous space. The trees on the right perform this same function by silhouetting interesting patterns against the high light. In fact, the composition is largely the skillful, balanced arrangement of light and dark masses, one which despite its formality gives an impressive sense of heroic grandeur and infinite spaciousness.

While Poussin and Claude were painting their ideal landscapes in Italy, art in France was becoming more and more the monopoly of the privileged class. The establishment in 1648 of the French Academy of Sculpture and Painting gave official sanction to the dictates of the autocracy which ruled France during the seventeenth and eighteenth centuries to further its own selfish interests. The pompous dignity of the court of Louis XIV and the elegance and light gaiety of that of Louis XV and XVI it was the business of the painters to portray. For the former there were Pierre Mignard (1610–1695) and Hyacinthe Ri-gaud (1659–1743); for the latter, Antoine Watteau (1684–1721); Jean-Baptiste Pater (1696–1736) and Nicolas Lancret (1690–1743); François

Fig. 665. Chardin. Saying Grace.
Louvre, Paris.

Boucher (1703–1770); and Jean-Honoré Fragonard (1732–1806). Fragonard's typically rococo *Swing* (Wallace collection, London) or Watteau's *Embarkation for Cythera* (FIG. 664) is representative of its spirit. In the latter, in the delightful cool shade of a park couples are idly loitering; winged loves hover about, cling to a statue of Venus, and dance around a dainty, gilded ship toward which the couples are making their way to journey to the island of love far away in the golden, misty distance. All is lightheartedness and gaiety, grace and elegance. But Watteau was too much of an artist to express merely this idea. Here are revealed his excellent feeling for balance; for the interesting pattern of trees against the luminous distance; for the easy rhythm of the S-curve that begins in the figure of Venus, follows the groups across the canvas, and then turns inward again in the rollicking cherubs in the sky at the left; and, perhaps most of all, his feeling for the harmony of exquisite color which the textures of the elegant stuffs gave him opportunity to exploit, put on in light touches that melt in the enveloping glow.

Apart from this whole galaxy of court painters, whose pictures in theme and in style were in perfect harmony with court life and the rococo spirit, was a somewhat isolated artist who drew his subject matter from a different social stratum and sphere of life, Jean-Baptiste Siméon Chardin (1699–1779). Not only in theme but in attitude toward form Chardin seemed to continue the tradition of the Le Nain brothers and the "Little Dutchmen" of the seventeenth century. Sometimes it is the interior of the French middle-class home, which Chardin, like the Dutch painters, saw as raw material with pictorial possibilities (FIG. 665). The sober dusk of the small room provided an opportunity so to modulate the light that it would create a space in which to place the figures that catch the high light from an open door, and form a cylindrical mass cut across by repeated diagonals. The warm, vibrating brown ground modulates the rose, green, and yellow of the striped upholstery and garments; a contrasting note is the cool gray-blue, of large mass in the apron balanced by smaller areas in the details. The

Fig. 666. Chardin. Still Life. Louvre, Paris.

colors are not used with the light sparkling dash of Watteau but with a sober deliberation. Chardin's primary interest in genre as pictorial material for its own sake, exclusive of associational values, appears in his frequent use of still life. In Fig. 666 one large rectangular box, cutting into space on diagonals that are repeated in the pipestems and shadows, counters a number of cylindrical objects. Or as pattern, straight lines and angles oppose curves and ellipses; warm color, cool color; light texture, dark texture. With all the means at the painter's disposal these objects are built into an organization whose unity and harmony have a power of their own quite separate from the representational content.

F. SUMMARY

The late Gothic age saw France still vigorous in all the fine arts, though the heightened fervor of the Middle Ages had somewhat cooled. A strong school of native painting had grown out of miniature-painting and a school of independent sculpture had developed, both of which showed a tempered naturalism and a sincere feeling for fine design. Upon this native art the Renaissance was imposed by arbitrary monarchs who had been captivated by the Italian style. By the eighteenth century the centralization of the government was followed by the centralization, under government control, of all the arts, which thereupon existed to serve the court. Notwithstanding their general artificiality and formalism, these arts reveal a high standard of craftsmanship, as required by state supervision, and an extraordinary unity, and stand as a consistent reflection of the mood of the court of whichever monarch they served.

BIBLIOGRAPHY

Barnes, A. C., and Mazia, Violette de, *French Primitives*, Barnes Foundation, 1931

Blomfield, Sir R. T., *A History of French Architecture from the Reign of Charles VIII till the Death of Mazarin*, Macmillan, 1911, 2 vols.

—— —— *A History of French Architecture from the Death of Mazarin till the Death of Louis XV*, Scribner, 1921, 2 vols.

Brownell, W. C., *French Art*, Scribner, 1892

Cox, Trenchard, *Jehan Foucquet, Native of Tours*, London, 1931

Dilke, Lady E. F. S., *French Architects and Sculptors of the 18th Century*, Macmillan, 1900

—— —— *French Furniture and Decoration in the XVIIIth Century*, Macmillan, 1901

Fourreau, Armand, *Les Clouets*, Paris, 1929

Fry, R. E., *Characteristics of French Art*, Coward-McCann, 1932

—— —— *Vision and Design*, Coward-McCann, 1924

Furst, H. E. A., *Chardin*, Scribner, 1911

Glück, Gustav, *Die Kunst der Renaissance, in Deutschland, der Niederlanden, Frankreich, usw.*, Berlin, 1928

Gromort, Georges, *Histoire abrégée de l'architecture de la Renaissance en France (XVI, XVII, XVIII siècles)*, Paris, 1930

Hind, C. L., *Landscape Painting from Giotto to the Present Day*, Scribner, 1923, 2 vols.

Hourticq, Louis, *Art in France*, Scribner, 1911

Huizinga, J., *The Waning of the Middle Ages*, Longmans, 1924

Jackson, Sir T. G., *The Renaissance of Roman Architecture*, University of Chicago Press, 1922, 3 vols., Vol. III, *France*

Konody, P. G., and Lathom, M. X., *An Introduction to French Painting*, London, 1932

Moore, C. H., *The Character of Renaissance Architecture*, Macmillan, 1905

Munro, Thomas, *Great Pictures of Europe*, Coward-McCann, 1930

Osborn, Max, *Die Kunst des Rokoko*, Berlin, 1926

Royal Academy of Arts, *Commemorative Catalogue of the Exhibition of French Art, 1200–1900*, Oxford Press, 1935

Speed, Harold, *Science and Practice of Oil Painting*, Scribner, 1924

Terrasse, Charles, *Les peintres français de la Renaissance*, Paris, 1932

—— *Les primitifs français*, Paris, 1931

Tilley, A. A., *The Dawn of the French Renaissance*, Putnam, 1918

Victoria and Albert Museum, *Panelled Rooms*, London, 1914–24, Vols. I–VI; Vol. III, *Boudoir of Mme de Sérilly*

Ward, W. H., *Architecture of the Renaissance in France*, 2d ed., Scribner, 1926, 2 vols.

Wilenski, R. H., *French Painting*, Hale, Cushman & Flint, 1931

CHAPTER XXII

Art in the United States:
Colonial and Early Republican Art
(Early Seventeenth Century to about 1830)

A. HISTORICAL BACKGROUND

The century and a half succeeding the arrival of the colonists in the New World was spent in transplanting a deep-rooted culture to conditions at first quite primitive, and adapting it to the needs of an evolving culture with many different basic factors. Along with the developing institutions of self-government arose locally differentiated economic and social bases: manufacturing, trading, and shipping in the conservative theocratic New England; tobacco- and cotton-growing in the genial Cavalier South; both shipping and agriculture in the colonies between; while an early trek across the mountains established the freehold farmer.

In this pioneering stage the infrequency of contact with original sources forced the colonists into an idiom of their own. When this stage had passed, in the East about 1725, the economic basis was firmly enough established to enable creative activity to come into play. This development was possible because of demands of the colonists for churches and homes that were not merely shelters, and because of the leisure and financial resources at their disposal for making or purchasing even luxurious furnishings. In addition, a justifiable pride in a century of remarkable success in colonization manifested itself in a desire for buildings, furnishings, and a pattern of living commensurate with this success.

This rapid growth was checked temporarily by the War of Independence, which was followed by an age of ferment of ideas, engendered partly by the high feeling, confused to be sure, in the local situation and partly by the repercussion of events in Europe: the French Revolution and the Industrial Revolution with the consequent upheavals in thought, politics, society, and economics. Pioneering continued in the Mississippi Valley, where rose an agrarian culture with simple ideals, a culture that paralleled in time the aristocratic, more complex society of the Eastern seaboard, patterned more or less after the European prototype, for transatlantic travel was becoming fairly common.

Fig. 667. Peirce-Nichols House. Salem. c. 1790. (Essex Institute)

Fig. 668. Woodlands. Philadelphia. Rebuilt 1788–89. (Copyright by Detroit Publishing Co.)

B. ARCHITECTURE, THE MINOR ARTS

The earliest churches and homes were naturally built in the style with which the colonists were familiar — the middle-class-English Gothic or Elizabethan in New England, Dutch in New Amsterdam, Jacobean of the Cavalier class in the South. All of these were kept fresh in mind by European building manuals, which the builders used as guides. With timber as the chief building material in the North, stone in the middle colonies, and brick in the South, we find simple, massive, rectangular structure in both the buildings and their furnishings, structural in every detail and sparse of ornament.[1]

Better economic conditions and more frequent contacts with Europe in the eighteenth century were reflected in a change to the late-Renais-

[1] The *Fairbanks House*, Dedham (1636), the *"Old Ship"* *Meeting House*, Hingham (1681), and the *Whipple House*, Ipswich (about 1650) are among the few existing buildings of the seventeenth century.

Fig. 669. Peirce-Nichols House. East Parlor. An example of the woodwork of Samuel McIntire. (Essex Institute)

sance or Georgian style, then the vogue in England, translated into a provincial timber form [1] and frequently in its forthright vitality and unity of furnishings more effective than the overelegance of the European prototype. Such a house is the *Peirce-Nichols House* of Salem (Fig. 667). Its symmetry of plan and elevation reflects the Renaissance. The regularity of spacing in the façade, the symmetrical balance, the accent upon each window as a unit, the corner pilasters, the cornice and roof balustrade — all these elements of design can be traced, by way of England, to a distant ancestor such as the *Farnese Palace* (Fig. 477) and, like that, produce an impression of dignity and well-being, even though austere.

In the middle colonies, as at *Woodlands* (Fig. 668) and in the Southern, as at *Westover* (Virginia) a somewhat different type is found. The general impression is one of dignity and stateliness, like that of the *Peirce-Nichols House*, but more genial. In opposition to the austere life in New England, life in the Southern colonies was gay and more luxurious. A warmth of welcome and a note of hospitality are felt in the two-story pedimented portico with its lofty columns. The strict regularity is broken by the circular bays on the sides and by the great arched window of the ground story, Palladian in its design. Most of the houses of the period were placed with careful regard for natural surroundings. Trees, hedges, spacious lawns, and gardens contributed to the qualities of the building itself.

The churches,[2] like the homes, were largely reproductions in wood, with modifications, of London city churches (Fig. 632). Though this

---

[1] Baroque Georgian, 1725–50; Classic Georgian, 1750–90; Adam influence, chiefly in the North and the central colonies, about 1790–1825.

[2] *St. Paul's*, New York (1764–66; steeple 1794); *St. Michael's*, Charleston (1732–61); *King's Chapel*, Boston (1749–54; portico 1790).

Fig. 670. Paul Revere. Silver Creamer. H. 7 in. 1799. Museum of Fine Arts, Boston. (Boston Museum)

provincial Georgian style suited well both functionally and esthetically, a new style appeared shortly after the War of Independence, the classical. Its coming was due partly to the break with England and consequently with the English style, partly to the classical wave that was sweeping Europe, and partly to the personal influence of Thomas Jefferson. Whatever the causes, here was an arbitrary acceptance of a historic style taking the place of a style that naturally evolved from cultural conditions, the first in a series that was to dominate American architecture until the modern age.

A Colonial or Early Republican interior shows not only refined taste but sensitive relationships among all the interior elements (FIG. 669). Fine woodwork was set off by, and itself set off, the walnut or mahogany furniture. Pine, found in abundant quantities and especially adaptable to carving because it is rather soft and fine-grained and at the same time durable, was used extensively for paneling, fireplaces, and stairways; it was painted white or a pale tint. Stairways and fireplaces furnished important accents. The stairway, because of its conspicuous position in the center of the house near the entrance, received especial attention in the way of carved balusters or mahogany rail. Likewise the fireplace provided a focal point for the living-room, and about it were often found the finest carving of the room, the ancestral portraits, and brasses. The woodwork of Samuel McIntire, one of the best-known carvers, reflects that of Robert Adam (FIG. 634) in the delicacy of its low-relief carvings. The ceilings were usually plain, and the general effect was much less stately and more modestly domestic than the English prototype.

Current European fashions dictated the furniture as well as the building design — Chippendale, Hepplewhite, Sheraton, French rococo — though much of the furniture was the work of American craftsmen; and the products of some of the cabinetmakers' shops in Boston, New York, and Philadelphia were equal in design and craftsmanship to those imported from London. Such a shop was that of Duncan Phyfe of New York.

Into this framework of the room and its furniture the products of various craftsmen contributed notes of color and texture — iron, brass, pewter, silver, glass, textiles, and, by no means the least, the people themselves and their costumes. Despite its European derivation a new spirit infuses this interior architecture, welding it into an extraordinary unity of vigor, restraint, and fine taste, with little or no trace of eighteenth-century European prettiness. Thus while the various items and general design are European, their organization reflects frankly the "mental outlook" of the youthful American republic.

Especial mention perhaps should be made of the silver.

Fig. 671. Unknown. Mrs. Freake and Baby Mary. Coll. Mrs. W. B. Scofield and Mr. A. W. Sigourney. (Worcester Art Museum)

For, in the absence of banks, family wealth often consisted of silver objects, and the family silver, the pride of the family for generations, proclaimed both its social and its economic position. Thus the silversmith held a more distinctive place in the community than the other craftsmen, and an exceptional quality was demanded in his products. A pitcher by Paul Revere, for example (FIG. 670), has an architectural quality in the fine relationships of its mass and contour, the subordination of the restrained ornament to a direct clarity of form, and a fine balance between the smooth unbroken and the rough broken surfaces.

C. PAINTING

Another object found almost universally in these Colonial and Early Republican homes was the portrait. The painter at first found little demand for his products. What few pictures there were had been brought over from Europe. In Puritan New England strong religious prejudice against art, born of the Reformation in Europe, confined the practice of this craft to such activities as coach- and sign-painting.

To surmount this prejudice, however, became none too difficult for the wealthy colonists, who wanted portraits not only to decorate their walls but also to hand on to posterity "lest their efforts to found families

Fig. 672. Copley. Lady Wentworth. 1765. New York Public Library. (New York Public Library)

and states be forgotten." [1] Hence arose a demand for the portrait that was met by untrained enthusiasts or low-rate limners, or face-painters, who had come to the New World perhaps for adventure. The Cavaliers of the South, however, in closer contact with England, had their portraits painted in London, with personal sittings if possible, otherwise by verbal description. European painters, learning of this need, began to arrive to meet it. They not only painted portraits themselves but stimulated the development of the art by bringing engravings of European paintings and by giving instruction to the untrained local face-painters. Those who came from Holland to New Netherlands showed evidence of descent from Hals; those from England, the influence of the English portrait school.

An early arrival was John Smibert of Edinburgh (1688–1751) as "professor of drawing, painting, and architecture in the college of science and art which Berkeley proposed to found in Bermuda for the benefit of the American Indian" [2] — a Utopian dream soon blasted. Smibert's group portrait, *Bishop Berkeley and His Entourage*, in comparison with the work of the limners shows a certain amount of professional resourcefulness in drawing, handling pigment, and composition notwithstanding his rather mediocre ability. The works of the local limners, however, often reveal a certain vigor, frank objectivity, and intuitive capacity, as one sees in such a portrait as *Mrs. Freake and Baby Mary* (FIG. 671) by an anonymous painter.

Besides John Smibert other painters arrived to contribute at least to the accumulating local endeavor, which reached a climax in John Singleton Copley (1737–1815). Beyond help in rudiments from his stepfather and opportunity to see some paintings and engravings,

---

[1] Mather, F. J., Morey, C. R., and Henderson, J. H., *The American Spirit in Art*, Yale University Press, 1927, p. 4.
[2] F. W. Bayley, *Five Colonial Artists of New England*, privately printed, 1929, p. 336.

Copley was self-educated in his pre-European work. In his *Lady Wentworth* (FIG. 672) he shows some grasp of the figure, whose stiffness is an evidence partly of propriety and partly of a lack of ease on the part of a painter untrained professionally. There is a generally hard effect and an overemphasis upon contrasting lights and darks, and an inability to fuse them or to utilize them as pattern; a fondness for the texture of satin, laces, and other fine stuffs; and an intentional realism in details, for straightforward objectivity was the painter's purpose. Copley established his permanent residence in England after 1774; and in proportion as he gained

Fig. 673. Stuart. Mrs. Yates. 1793. Thomas B. Clark coll., New York.

professionally he lost in forthright candor of characterization. For despite their technical weaknesses the portraits of his Colonial period possess an unpretentious directness and sheer force of characterization. Such an accomplishment, had it been grounded in the needed professional training might conceivably have produced a truly indigenous art of high quality. But the potentialities of provincial life as a motivation of art expression passed unnoticed. Copley's choice to remain in England meant an increased facility in handling pigment, but a general weakening of his genuine ability, and was the first of a long series of similar choices that have throttled a normal evolution of art expression in this country.

Instead, "To London" filled the air. To be sure it was necessary for technical training. But at that few stopped. Benjamin West (1738–1820), for example, after an adventurous and now legendary youth, set out for Italy in 1760 through the financial assistance of a rich patron and came to London at the time when Sir Joshua Reynolds was the revered president of the Royal Academy. Falling into the current styles, West became popular and wealthy, made a grandiloquent gesture by refusing knighthood, and upon the death of Sir Joshua in 1792 became president of the Academy. His studio was a mecca for American students during and for a generation after the War of Independence and thus brought American painting into close affiliation with English traditions. In addition West introduced historical, mythological, and religious subjects in the "grand manner," an influence of French Romanticism, but with none of the fire of a Delacroix and, in fact, with little or no conviction.

Portrait-painting continued in the colonies, more and more under the influence of the English school, and also under that of the French.[1] Gilbert Stuart appears the most individual of the generation, and despite long residence in London, freer from imitating the styles with which he came in contact. With a real feeling for his medium he built up a vibrant surface of loose virile strokes that has its own esthetic value. *Mrs. Yates* (FIG. 673), for example, illustrates his sureness of technique and his use of it to set forth his subject with objective reality and interpretive probity.

BIBLIOGRAPHY

American Folk Art, Museum of Modern Art, New York, 1932

Art in America, from 1600 to 1865, University of Chicago Press, 1934

Avery, C. L., *Early American Silver*, Century, 1930

Barker, Virgil, *A Critical Introduction to American Painting*, Whitney Museum of American Art, New York, 1931

Beard, C. A. and Mary, *The Rise of American Civilization*, Macmillan, 1927, 2 vols.

Briggs, M. S., *The Homes of the Pilgrim Fathers in England and America, 1620–1685*, Oxford Press, 1932

Caffin, C. H., *American Masters of Sculpture*, Doubleday, Page, 1913

—— —— *The Story of American Painting*, Stokes, 1907

Clarke, T. B., *Portraits by Early American Artists of the Seventeenth, Eighteenth and Nineteenth Centuries*, The Museum of Art, Philadelphia, 1928

Cornelius, C. O., *Early American Furniture*, Century, 1926

—— —— *Furniture Masterpieces of Duncan Phyfe*, Doubleday, Page, 1922

Cousins, Frank and Riley, P. M., *The Colonial Architecture of Philadelphia*, Little, Brown, 1920

—— —— *The Colonial Architecture of Salem*, Little, Brown, 1919

—— —— *The Wood-Carver of Salem: Samuel McIntire, His Life and Work*, Little, Brown, 1916

Eberlein, H. D., *The Architecture of Colonial America*, Little, Brown, 1915

—— and McClure, Abbot, *The Practical Book of Early American Arts and Crafts*, Lippincott, 1916

Embury, Aymar, Jr., *Early American Churches*, Doubleday, Page, 1914

Foote, H. W., *Robert Feke, Colonial Portrait Painter*, Harvard University Press, 1930

Halsey, R. T. H., and Cornelius, C. O., *A Handbook of the American Wing*, Metropolitan Museum of Art, New York, 1932

Hamlin, T. F., *The American Spirit in Architecture*, Yale University Press, 1927 (*Pageant of America*, Vol. 13)

[1] Ralph Earle (1751–1801); Matthew Pratt (1734–1805); Charles W. Peale (1741–1827); and Gilbert Stuart (1755–1828).

Isham, Samuel, *The History of American Painting*, rev. by Royal Cortissoz, Macmillan, 1927

Jackman, R. E., *American Arts*, Rand, McNally, 1928

Kimball, S. F., *American Architecture*, Bobbs-Merrill, 1930

—— —— *Domestic Architecture of the American Colonies and of the Early Republic*, Scribner, 1922

La Follette, Suzanne, *Art in America*, Harper, 1930

Laughton, L. G. C., *Old Ship Figure-heads and Sterns*, Minton, Balch, 1925

Lee, Cuthbert, *Early American Portrait Painters*, Yale University Press, 1929

Mather, F. J., *Estimates in Art, Series II*, Holt, 1931

Morey, C. R., and Henderson, J. H., *The American Spirit in Art*, Yale University Press, 1927 (*Pageant of America*, Vol. 12)

Mumford, Lewis, *Sticks and Stones: A Study of American Architecture and Civilization*, Boni, 1924

Murrell, William, *A History of American Graphic Humor*, Whitney Museum of American Art, New York, 1934, Vol. I

Neuhaus, Eugen, *History and Ideals of American Painting*, Stanford University Press, 1931

Park, Lawrence, comp., *Gilbert Stuart*, with an appreciation by Royal Cortissoz, Rudge, 1926, 4 vols.

Sherman, F. F., *Early American Painting*, Century, 1932

—— —— *Early American Portraiture*, privately printed, 1930

Taft, Lorado, *The History of American Sculpture*, rev. ed., Macmillan, 1924

Tallmadge, T. E., *The Story of Architecture in America*, Norton, 1927

Weitenkampf, Frank, *American Graphic Art*, new ed., Macmillan, 1924

See also the General Bibliography, pp. 749–751.

Part Seven

PRIMITIVE ART

CHAPTER XXIII

The Art of the American Indian

The advent of primitive art among the arts of the world is recent; likewise the recognition of its high esthetic quality. And the strong influence that it is exerting on the arts of today is by no means a mere fad but the revelation of a definite esthetic kinship. By "primitive art" is meant the art expression of peoples in a generally primitive state of culture. Such an art may be of a very high order, however illiterate or barbarian its creators. It is widespread over space and time and far too varied in character to admit of generalizations. It may be simple and childlike or sophisticated and adult; representational or geometric; realistic or abstract. Each culture that produced it is a unit with indigenous habits of living, thinking, feeling, believing, with local materials and art patterns that are the result of the whole cultural pattern.

The origin of the primitive peoples of the Americas is uncertain, though migrations from Asia (possibly 25,000 to 10,000 years ago) seem probable, a series of migrations of Neolithic nomads with possibly no arts except stonecutting and perhaps basketry. By slow stages, of which we know almost nothing, they moved southward and at some date, estimated variously from 1500 to 3000 B.C., some of them settled down as an agricultural people on the Mexican plateaus, where they had learned to cultivate maize by domesticating the wild grasses native to this arid highland. Others settled in the humid tropical lowlands of Central America, where they raised a variety of maize and other crops adapted to that climate.

Out of the shadowy background where fact and legend mingle confusedly, focal points of culture emerge — the Mayan of the lowlands of what is now Guatemala, Honduras, and the plateau of Yucatan; the Zapotec and Mixtec on the southern Mexican plateau near Oaxaca; the Totonacan in central Vera Cruz; the Toltec and Aztec on the Mexican plateau around Mexico City; the pre-Inca and Inca in Peru; the Pueblo and nomad Indians of the Southwest and of the plains;

and the Indians of the Northwest coast (FIG. 674). The relationships among these cultures have been worked out in but a few spots. The epochal events that vitally affected, if they did not destroy, most of these cultures were the Spanish conquests and other European colonizations from the early sixteenth century. In some places a fusion of the Spanish and Indian took place; in others, some contributions on the part of the Spaniard without fundamental cultural changes; in some places which because of geography and climate are peculiarly inaccessible the indigenous culture appears to have survived. On the whole, so recently and so unevenly has the field been studied that definite statements and conclusions are not possible. However, the present renascence of the arts in Mexico and among some of the Indians of the Southwest seems to point to the fact that these indigenous cultures have retained their vitality and esthetic power in spite of the chaos that resulted from the European colonization of the Americas. They are now receiving the recognition due them as one of the world's great art expressions, and are again producing works of art in direct line with their own vital long-lived traditions.

Fig. 674. The Americas, Showing Important Centers of Art Activity among the Aboriginal Americans.

1. MEXICAN AND CENTRAL AMERICAN INDIAN ART

A. HISTORICAL BACKGROUND

For a brief survey, Mexico and Central America constitute a unit known as Middle America. Here we find a great variety of geographic

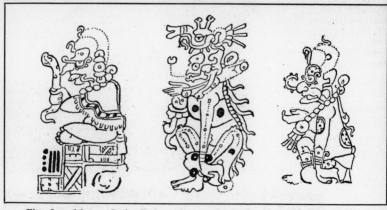

Fig. 675. Mayan Gods. From a manuscript in Dresden. The Long-Nosed God of Rain, the Death God, and the Sun God. (Spinden)

Fig. 676. Section of a Typical Mayan Building. (Holmes)

and climatic conditions. The country lies in the belt of dry and rainy seasons. Great reaches of arid plateau land, fertile for raising maize and wheat wherever water can be secured, rise to heavily forested mountain slopes and thence, at some places, to perpetual snow; or they descend to the moist tropical jungles of the coastal plains, which are marvelously rich agriculturally if man can only clear the land and steadily pursue his battle against the rank luxuriousness of nature.[1] The country is a volcanic region; the volcanic rock, now coarse and now fine-grained, together with plentiful limestone furnished abundant material both for building and for carving. Of the Middle American cultures, the Mayan appears to have been among the first to evolve beyond an early primitive stage and to have reached the highest point of development. In the early centuries of the Christian era the Maya were in possession of moist lowlands in Central America and were at a stage of civilization that

[1] The value of the airplane and air photography in archaeological research is well illustrated by the work in Central America. See the account of the Lindbergh air expedition, in the *Pan American Union Bulletin*, December, 1929.

Fig. 677. El Castillo, Pyramid Temple of Kukulcan Chichen Itzá. H. 105 ft.; the base covers one acre. XIII or XIV cent. (Carnegie Institution, Washington)

Fig. 678. Temple of the Warriors. Chichen Itzá. (Carnegie Institution, Washington)

Fig. 679. Chichen Itzá. El Castillo, center; Temple of the Warriors, center right. (Carnegie Institution, Washington)

537

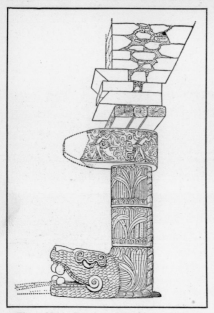

Fig. 680. Feathered-Serpent Column. Restored. H. 7 ft. 9 in. Chichen Itzá. (Holmes)

presupposes a development of centuries. The first climax of the Mayan culture came between 450 and 700 A.D. at such centers as Copán, Palenque, and Quiriguá. After a period of civil war, decadence, and shift of habitation to northern Yucatan, a second climax was reached between about 990 and 1200 A.D., with Chichen Itzá and Uxmal as influential centers, after which the Maya came under the dominance of the more powerful Toltecs (about 1200–1458) and were in decline at the time of the Spanish conquest.

Though the Maya were an agricultural people, all the activities of life were dominated by religion. The government was in fact a theocracy, and the cities were great centers where gorgeous ceremonies and the display of magic power overawed the people. The gods, such as the sun god, the wind god, the maize god, and the death god (FIG. 675), personified the processes of nature. Some of these gods represented the powers of evil and some the powers of good. They were constantly at war with each other, and at times the good, unless supported by other powers of good, might fall a victim to some evil like that of death. In form these gods combined human, bird, and animal features. A very important deity, Kukulcan, for example, called Quetzalcoatl [1] by the Aztecs, was a combination of the quetzal, a plumed bird, with the serpent, the coatl. In his bird manifestation he appeared to typify the winds and thus had to do with the sky and the four directions; in his serpent manifestation he was connected with water and rain. Sometimes he had the teeth of the jaguar and in his mouth a man's head, all of which involves an intricate symbolism, not entirely understood. Apparently another means of symbolic expression was color — blue for the sky god, yellow for the sun, green for the sea, and red for war.

[1] Quetzalcoatl appears to have been a historical and legendary personage, a great Toltec king who came to live among the Maya and brought them many of the elements of their culture.

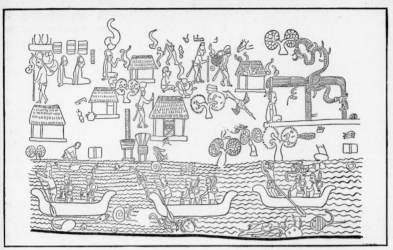

Fig. 681. A Seacoast Mayan Village. Drawing of a reconstructed fresco in the
Temple of the Warriors. (Carnegie Institution, Washington)

An important factor in the Mayan culture is the system of hieroglyphs. This tribe quite early developed an intricate method of
reckoning time, that is, a calendar, the purpose of which, apart from
agricultural necessities, was chiefly to assist the priests in their elaborate
systems of religious observances and festivals. Another surprising fact
is that these people at their climax and even at the time of the Spanish
conquest were in a Stone Age culture. Metal tools, if known at all,
which is doubtful on account of the rarity of copper, were negligible.

West of the Mayan country were Mt. Albán and Mitla, sites of the
Zapotecs and Mixtecs,[1] different from though influenced by the Maya.
To the north were the Totonacs, whose art seems to be related to the
Mayan and also to the cultures on the central plateaus of Mexico.
Apparently the first tribe to reach a comparatively high stage of civilization on these arid plateaus was the Toltec (about 750–1050 A.D.),
about whose power and splendor there is much legend but little known
fact. Though the Toltec culture was maintained in some localities,
their power was broken by decay and civil war and the supremacy
passed to the intensely warlike Aztecs, who set up their capital at
Tenochtitlan (now Mexico City), and dated their rule from their first
warrior king in 1370 A.D. Like most of the Indians, the Aztecs were
predominantly religious; but more than any other tribe they carried

[1] Very little is known of these tribes. But highly important excavations at Mt.
Albán and an intensive study which aims to decipher their inscriptions undoubtedly
will soon add greatly to our knowledge of these peoples.

Fig. 682. Temple at Mitla. Detail of the façade, showing stone mosaic decoration in geometric patterns.

Fig. 683. House of the Governor. Detail of the façade, showing stone mosaic decoration. L. 320 ft. Uxmal.

religious fanaticism to a hideous extreme of human sacrifice. After conquering the Toltecs and other tribes they settled in the region as an agricultural people, assimilating the culture they found there, and developing a state that was wealthy and peaceful, though in many respects barbarous and never reaching the level of culture attained by the Maya.

B. ARCHITECTURE

As the highest state of culture reached by the Middle American tribes seems to have been that of the Maya, we shall study the buildings of this people chiefly.[1] Since religion was the dominating power, the temple was important, though there are so-called palaces, buildings composed of groups of rooms evidently used for habitation, perhaps by the priests or the nobles. The homes of the people were probably thatched huts. An abundance of excellent building material favored the Maya, who, we remember, were still in the Stone Age. They had quarries of evenly grained limestone that could be cut with stone tools, and an abundance of stone already weathered by vegetation and climate into small pieces convenient for making ce-

[1] The rank vegetation of Yucatan has been the great enemy of these structures. Plants began to grow around and over the temples almost as soon as they were abandoned, and roots have pried the stones apart and loosened them, so that today it has been necessary to cut away dense jungles to extricate the ruins.

ment and concrete. Great forests of wood furnished ample timber and also firewood for the preparation of lime.

The most characteristic building was the pyramid temple (FIGS. 676, 677, 679), a temple standing upon a high pyramidal base and approached by a broad flight of steps on each side. The base was a solid mass of concrete faced with stone; the thick walls were concrete faced with stone blocks smoothed on the outer face but left roughly pointed on the inner, to hold more tenaciously in the concrete. On the interior the courses projected inward, forming two corbeled arches that sprang from wooden lintels. Rooms so constructed could not be more than about twelve feet wide, but might be of unlimited length. Hence the temples consisted of two long, narrow compartments, the inner one of which, the sanctuary, was sometimes divided into smaller units. Above the flat roof rose, in some buildings, a false front or a pierced roof-crest for decoration. The construction of

Fig. 684. Stone Mosaic Patterns. Mitla. (Holmes)

such a building — the quarrying of the stone, the transporting and lifting of it to its high position — represents a prodigious amount of labor. The stone tools were primitive, and there were no transportation facilities, not even beasts of burden. Decoration played an important part in these temples. Stucco, stone carvings and mosaic, all brilliantly colored, as well as wall paintings in black, blue, red, yellow, and several shades of green, adorned the broad exterior surfaces, the columns, lintels, and interior walls.

The *Temple of the Warriors* (FIG. 678), a temple of Kukulcan, the patron god of Chichen Itzá, to take a specific illustration, rises from rows of finely spaced massive rectangular piers carved in low relief. The temple itself rests on a base of four terraces, each with a carved frieze, and is approached by a broad stairway with carved stone balustrades; at the entrance are feathered-serpent columns. The cor-

Fig. 685. Stucco Ornament with Figure in Ceremonial Costume. Palenque. (Maudslay)

Fig. 686. Great Dragon or Turtle of Quiriguá. Carved stone monolith. View of the top. W. 11½ ft. (Maudslay)

beled roof, now gone, was supported by rectangular piers carved with figures of warriors, priests, and other figures which fill the entire space and were painted in bright colors; on the interior walls were frescoes of domestic, military, and religious scenes.

Thus the whole decorative scheme was elaborate and brilliant. The feathered-serpent columns belong to a type common in Mayan architecture (Fig. 680) in which the base is formed of the head, the shaft of the body with feathers carved in low relief, and the capital of the tail with rattles, for here the rattlesnake appears to be represented. Fig. 681 reproduces one of the wall paintings that is as informative in subject matter as it is decorative as a mural. Here is a *Seacoast Mayan Village* with village folk going about their everyday life in their boats on the sea and around their huts on the land. The figures and objects are strongly outlined areas of contrasting color, placed one above the other, covering the surface without crowding and keeping it unified in one plane. Thus results an extraordinarily decorative pattern, informal in composition, made up of the conventions for water, boats, fish, trees, roofs, people, clearly differentiated because of the contrasting color yet definitely united because closely keyed in tone. The convention for trees lends itself particularly to repetition with variety, for it consists of a trunk dividing into two branches which support two circular areas of foliage different in detail to indicate different kinds of leaves.

Another kind of decoration consisted of stone mosaic as in the so-

Fig. 687. A Mayan Sculptured Lintel. From Piedras Negras. A ceremonial scene in relief with a border of Mayan hieroglyphs. Museum, the University of Pennsylvania. (Eldridge R. Johnson Expedition of the University Museum and the Guatemalan Government)

called *Governor's House* at Uxmal (FIG. 683). This long rectangular building carries a boldly designed decorative band of fret against a lattice ground, with an elaborate ornament surrounding a human figure over the doorway. This border, except for the door ornament, is made of stone mosaic in relief; that is, small pieces of stone were cut and fitted, each individual piece to its own place, and set in mortar, a process involving an enormous amount of patient labor. This stone mosaic covers the walls of tombs and the panels of the temples of the Zapotecs and Mixtecs (FIGS. 682, 684). Here, for some inexplicable reason, mythological and naturalistic subjects and sculpture were entirely eliminated, and all the decoration, both exterior and interior, is purely geometric and seems to be based upon textile designs. The tough yet easily worked stone of this vicin-

Fig. 688. Young Maize God. From Copán. Peabody Museum, Harvard University, Cambridge. (Peabody Museum)

ity lent itself well to the technique. The small pieces of stone, at most a few inches in size, were carefully cut and finished on the face, which projected only about one and a half inches, with the back left rough and deeply triangular so as to adhere more firmly to the mortar bedding.

Another kind of ornament, stucco, was used very skillfully by the Maya, particularly at Palenque, where the native stone was usually too hard to work with stone tools. Commonly it was employed to secure a smooth surface over roughly pecked stone. But it was also used plastically for decorating bases, piers, and crests. When the

Fig. 689. Drawing from a Mayan Vase. (Joyce, *Mexican Archaeology*,
G. P. Putnam's Sons)

relief was high, the rough wall was covered with plaster in which
small stones were set to give a framework for the figure. Holes were
sometimes cut in the foundation stone to give a firm hold for this stone
skeleton. On this the plaster was molded; and the final coat of fine
quality was polished and painted so that the surface was brilliant and
shining. Typical of this work is a relief from Palenque (FIG. 685), in
the center of which stands a figure in ceremonial costume and plumed
headdress, carrying a staff surmounted by the conventionalized serpent, and two seated figures. The brilliant color of the relief was probably determined by symbolical as well as artistic criteria.

C. SCULPTURE

Logically sculpture can hardly be separated from building, for most
of the sculpture is architectural, chiefly decorative reliefs on buildings,
altars, and steles; and the small amount of sculpture in the round that
has been found is strongly four-sided in character, and reveals the
same sensitive relation of simplified masses of stone that one finds in
Egyptian sculpture, and also the same vitality. And this the Maya
accomplished with but the most primitive tools. Clay also was used
and with a fine feeling for its plastic qualities in distinction from stone,
as is seen on the Totonacan *Smiling Heads*. The decorative reliefs on
the temples, steles, and altars, in which the carving frequently covers
every inch of the space — for unused space with the Middle Americans,
as with the Hindu but in marked contrast to the Chinese, was a *horror*
— may at first impress one as unjustifiably overcrowded. There is a
teeming luxuriance in this decoration, as in India. Yet when the struc-

Fig. 690. Double-
Headed Serpent. Mosaic.
L. 17½ in. Probably Aztec.
British Museum, London.

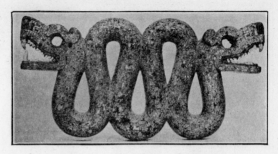

ture is seen as a whole in the midst of a luxuriant tropical setting, a
place for the performance of elaborate rites and ceremonies by priests
in still more elaborate costumes, when one sees the surfaces of these
geometrically simple sculptural masses lightly broken by a decoration
whose teeming richness is organized, unified, and given emphasis by
its linear quality and particularly by a conventional use of color[1] —
when one sees and takes all these considerations into account he realizes the entire unity and consistency of the whole. The *Corn-Sower* stele
and the lintels from *Piedras Negras* (FIG. 687) show an asymmetrical
space-filling tendency held in restraint. The *Dragon of Quiriguá*, on the
other hand, tends to floridity, for it is entirely covered with intricate
carvings in both high and low relief. The most conspicuous part of
the design on the north face is the human figure, dressed in rich garments with an enormous elaborate headdress, and seated in the mouth
of a great dragon. The placing of a human figure in the jaws of a
reptile is quite common in Mayan art and undoubtedly had a symbolic
meaning, possibly the endowing of the serpent with human intelligence, thus combining in the god the highest type of mind with any
type of material body. The top of the altar (FIG. 686) presents an
intricate decorative design based upon a highly conventionalized form
of the serpent in which the virile lines that indicate the features stand
out from the intricate decoration about them with a dominating
power.

Important points in the decorative scheme received emphasis through
the use of high relief, as in the figures over the doorway at *Uxmal*
(FIG. 683). Such may have been the use of the head, practically in
the round, of the *Maize God* (FIG. 688), carved from trachyte, a hard,
roughly cleaving volcanic stone. The quiet spiritual intensity is all
the more profound because of the monumental simplicity of the form,

[1] For color reproductions see E. H. Morris, Jean Charlot, and A. A. Morris, *The
Temple of the Warriors at Chichen Itzá, Yucatan,* Carnegie Institution, 1931, 2 vols. An
abbreviated account, with two color plates, is given in the *News Service Bulletin* (School
ed.) of the Carnegie Institution, Vol. II, Nos. 17–21.

Fig. 691. Gold Pendant. Mixtec. From Monte Albán. Oaxaca Museum.

Fig. 692. Mayan Vase. From Copán. Peabody Museum, Harvard University. (Peabody Museum)

which consists of a clear direct statement of proportions and relationships clearly grasped, such as the oval of the face repeated in the radiating locks and the countercurving plume.

D. PAINTING

Mural decoration seems to have been the chief function of the painter, though he illustrated manuscripts and drew and painted figures on pottery. His forms and apparently much of his color were conventional, with possibilities, however, of a wide range of expression. His people may be thin or fat, old or young, at times of astonishing reality; his trees extraordinarily varied within the visual symbol which means "a tree." FIG. 689 illustrates his capacity as a draftsman. Here is represented a chief receiving a visit from an inferior. The former, wearing an elaborate headdress, is seated on a dais, bending toward the visitor with outstretched hand; the latter is kneeling and offering a pouch of copal; behind him stands an attendant. The interesting and surprising thing here is not only the quality of the line, so sure-handed and firm, but particularly the skill shown in foreshortening that is seen in many details, and in the ability of the painter to express with line alone the mass of the figure and the movement of planes in depth.

E. MINOR ARTS

Ceremony and ceremonial costume would naturally create a demand for objects of many materials and fine craftsmanship. Thus in Middle

Fig. 693. Pottery of Central America. Yale University. *A.* and *B.* Armadillo ware. In *A* the armadillo is used as shoulder ornaments. In *B* the neck is decorated with alternating groups of armadillo tail and eye motifs. *C.* A Chiriquian ware decorated by wax painting. (MacCurdy, *Chiriquian Antiquities*, Yale University Press)

America developed extraordinary craftsmen: the carvers of stone and bone, the goldsmiths, potters, and probably weavers. The skill of the stoneworker was unbelievable one judges from the finds in the recently discovered Mixtec tombs at Mt. Albán near Oaxaca — vessels of hard rock crystal and obsidian as well as onyx, marble, jade, turquoise, and bone fashioned by primitive tools into objects of high esthetic worth. It seems probable, though not yet proved, that all this material was native. Small objects of all kinds, many apparently sacrificial, and articles of adornment were carved from these stones, though the turquoise was used chiefly for incrustations. The long bone objects, for example, found at Mt. Albán, whose use is unknown, were not only covered with intricate designs in relief but some were inlaid with turquoise to emphasize the design. Entire objects were incrusted with turquoise tesserae fixed to a foundation with gum. In a large breast ornament representing the *Double-headed Serpent* (FIG. 690), perhaps a ceremonial ornament of a priest, the coils are of turquoise and other stones; about the head are massed red and white shell; the holes for the eyes were probably filled with disks of glowing stone. The ornament shows a splendid vigorous design both in line and in massing of color. These tesserae were cut and polished probably with stone implements only.

Gold mines furnished a lavish amount of metal which the goldsmith worked by molding, hammering, wax-process casting, and engraving into pendants, necklaces, anklets, and other ornaments that were used

Fig. 694. Greater
Chavin Stone. H.
6 ft., Museo Nacional.
Lima.

not only for personal adornment but as amulets to charm away evil spirits, for burial with the dead, and for sacrifices to the gods. They are fashioned after various forms — butterfly, crocodile, toad, birds, lizards, monkeys, human figures. In all these objects the form has been highly conventionalized. In general it is the pattern suggested by the form that is used rather than any naturalistic representation of it. In the Mt. Albán tombs a great wealth of jewelry was discovered — rings, armlets, necklaces, earrings, breastpieces — of extraordinary craftsmanship and much of it of a reserved impeccable taste (FIG. 691).

The Middle American potter had no knowledge of the wheel but constructed his pottery by hand molding, coiling, or by the use of a mold. Nor did he know of glazing but obtained a polish and a certain amount of imperviousness by rubbing. The cylindrical vases of the Maya are boldly vigorous and richly warm in color, black against a yellow or orange ground, with details of red, brown, and white. Borders of hieroglyphs are frequent, as in FIG. 692, in which the chief decorative motif is derived from the quetzal. Again the decoration may be representational and narrative (FIG. 689). Farther south among the Chiriqui, or Talamancans, several fabrics were produced, the *Armadillo* ware (FIG. 693 A–B), bowls with handles or tripod feet, named from the fact that the armadillo furnished the chief decorative motif. Another ware (FIG. 693 C) illustrates an unusual technique of decoration. The vase was shaped and then covered with a cream slip upon which the design was painted in wax; the whole vase was then covered with black paint and boiled; as the wax melted it carried off with it the paint from the parts it had covered, leaving the design in the original cream ground color against the now black ground.

2. SOUTH AMERICAN INDIAN ART

A. HISTORICAL BACKGROUND

In South America, both on the coast and on the highlands, there developed a series of cultures which may have originated in migrations from Central America. South America, like Middle America, presents great contrasts of climate and geography (FIG. 674). The

narrow western coastal plain is a
hot desert, habitable only along
the rivers that bring water from
the mountains. Of the numerous
settlements of this coastal strip,
two stand out prominently —
Nazca in the south and Chimu
in the north. Since air-dried
brick constituted the building
material, with the result that
little is left of their architecture,
pottery and weaving furnish the
chief evidence of their culture.
The highlands of the Andes contain two physical conditions of
life — the high, bleak regions
and the intermediate valleys,
where climatic conditions are
less stern and more conducive to
the development of a high state
of culture. Both on the coast and

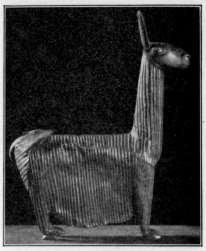

Fig. 695. Alpaca. Silver. H. 9 in. Inca.
American Museum of Natural History, New
York. (American Museum of Natural
History)

in the highlands the cultures we have noted were developing contem-
poraneously during the first five centuries of the Christian era. The
Tiahuanacan culture [1] on the highlands expressed itself in an art that
was starkly austere, conventional, and limited in color. On the coastal
strip the early Chimu developed a naturalistic style, and the early
Nazca a highly imaginative, richly colorful style tending to abstractions. From about 600 to 900 A.D. the Tiahuanacan Empire dominated
both the highlands and the coast, and through mutual influences produced an art of the highest quality. With the disintegration of this
empire a renascence of Nazca and Chimu cultures took place from
about 900 to 1400. In the meantime the Incas, a small highland tribe,
began to develop into a place of power and authority, until they had
established an empire with its capital at Cusco, over what is now
Peru, Bolivia, Ecuador, nothern Chile, and western Argentina, an empire which was at a climax at the time of the Spanish conquest in
1530.

Although the Inca is the best known of these cultures, largely because of the Spanish chroniclers (for no one of the South American
primitive peoples evolved a system of writing), it does not illustrate
the climax of culture attained. Its place is analogous to that of the

[1] So called because of important remains at Tiahuanaco near Lake Titicaca in
Bolivia.

Fig. 696. Chimu Portrait Head. H. 8½ in. Gaffron coll., Berlin. (Lehmann)

Fig. 697. Nazca Pottery. Gaffron coll., Berlin. (Lehmann)

Aztec, for, like the latter, it shows a warlike tribe conquering and taking over the older civilizations, but never itself attaining their artistic level.

B. ARCHITECTURE AND SCULPTURE

Since clay served for a building material on the lowlands, it is only on the highlands that we find monumental building that has lasted. An abundance of fine hard stone was at hand for these highland Peruvian builders, who were master masons in the cutting and joining of hard stone, as is to be observed in the great *Gate of the Sun* at Tiahuanaco, in the lava walls at Cusco, and in the granite walls of the Inca city of *Machu Picchu.*[1] This city, with palaces, temples, fountains, baths, stairways, and terraces, was built upon the crest of a mountain that rose in a secluded and almost inaccessible mountain valley about sixty miles from Cusco. The work shows not only great engineering ability but also astonishing skill in cutting the stone both for rectangular and for round buildings, and laying it without mortar in courses that gradually decrease in width as they rise, making a wall that is marvelous in its solidity, texture, and finely cut angles.

The decorative carvings, which appear to have been used only at emphatic points such as an entrance, are in low relief, and their angularity, severe austerity, and symmetry contrast markedly with the curvilinear design, rich luxuriousness, and asymmetry of Mayan reliefs. The carving about the *Gate of the Sun* is an illustration, and both the

[1] For illustrations of *Machu Picchu*, see Hiram Bingham, "In the Wonderland of Peru," *National Geographic Magazine*, April, 1913.

Fig. 698. Peruvian Textile. Slit tapestry weave. Museum of Fine Arts, Boston. (Boston Museum)

gateway, a monolithic structure of lava, and its decorative carving seem to partake of the bold massiveness of the surrounding mountains. Another example is the *Greater Chavin Stone* [1] (FIG. 694). The first impression is of an elaborate conventional pattern consisting of a central vertical motif from which radiate diagonal lines terminating alternately in spirals and serpent heads, the whole forming a perfectly bilateral design. Closer study reveals that at the base is a figure, in frontal view, short, and built on rectangular forms except for the arms and legs, which are slightly modeled; the features are so highly conventionalized that it is difficult to identify them; in each hand is held a bunch of staves. The panel above this figure is occupied by three masks with protruding decorated tongue and fangs. To see them it is necessary to reverse the illustration. The first and lasting impression of this carving is its severely formal character, its angularity, its highly abstract and decorative quality.

C. MINOR ARTS

In three fields in particular the peoples of South America created works on a lofty artistic level — in metal (FIG. 695), for the country is rich in gold and silver, in pottery, and in weaving.

In pottery, the north-coastal people with their bent toward realism produced, among a varied group of pottery shapes frequently including representational genre, many portrait heads (FIG. 696), which seem to be clay sculpture rather than pottery, though they may have originated as pottery. Some were made in molds and some were freely modeled, the tool marks being plainly visible. As portraits they are highly individual. Emphasis upon sculptural form in clay, representational and restrained in color, marks early Chimu work. Nazca pottery (FIG. 697), on the contrary, is brilliantly colorful, largely abstract,

[1] A carved monolith found at Chavin, a town in central Peru.

Fig. 699. Peruvian Textile. American Museum of Natural History, New York. (American Museum of Natural History)

freely exuberant in its manner of covering the surface with highly conventionalized figures painted in a wide range of color — white, yellow, black, violet, blue-gray, and intermediate tones — on a ground of white, red, or black.

Possibly it is in his textiles that the Peruvian attained his climax, both technical and esthetic. The women were the weavers and their productions not objets d'art but the articles of everyday use — pouches, girdles, tunics, borders of garments — which have survived because of burial in dry alkaline soil. With the most primitive type of loom and the wool of the native llama, alpaca, and vicuña, these weavers produced an astonishing variety of weaves — tapestry, pile, gauze, embroidery, with tapestry predominating — some of which are of incredible fineness and practically all of the highest quality of textile design. The range of hues is rather narrow — red, brown, blue, and green — and the motifs geometric or stylized forms of puma, fish, bird, and man; very rarely of plants and flowers (FIGS. 698, 699).

3. THE INDIAN ART OF THE SOUTHWEST AND OF THE PLAINS

Of the origin of the Indians of the Southwest and of the Plains, the Pueblo tribes of the upper Rio Grande in New Mexico and Arizona, and their seminomad neighbors the Navaho, the nomad Sioux and Dakotas of the northern plains, and the various tribes of California — of the origin of these tribes we know almost nothing. The Pueblo or village, people can be traced back some four thousand years. The historical tribes, which seem to be the result of tribal intermingling

Fig. 700. Pomo Basket. National Museum, Washington. (National Museum)

Fig. 701. Zuñi Jar. (Laboratory of Anthropology, Santa Fe)

were a settled agricultural people, organized into a democratic society, who built communal houses of stone or adobe in the cliffs, on mesa tops, or on the plains near the citadel-serving mesa. Such a house, usually several stories high and containing as many as eight hundred rooms, housed the tribe, while subterranean chambers (*kivas*), served for religious ceremonial functions. Theirs was an arid land and the water from springs and that stored up from summer rains hardly sufficed for the maturing of their crops of corn, beans, squash, and fruit. Hence the necessary propitiation of the gods, especially the rain gods, with suitable rites was the origin of one of their highest expressions — the ceremonial festivals and dances.

Not only the dances but all their arts were functional: containers for food and water, weavings for clothing for protection or for personal adornment or for ritualistic requirements. Yet in all their arts the esthetic significance is as great as the functional. The most ancient of these arts may have been basketry, the most primitive form of weaving, and a craft suitable for nomads in contrast to pottery, whose fragile character precludes any usefulness among a roving people. Desert plants, such as the yucca, provide tough fibers as well as coloring matter; and the light, strong character of the basket makes it ideal as a container for dry stuffs, for storage and for transportation as well as for ceremonial use.

Excellent basketry is found among several tribes in Arizona, particularly the Pima and Hopi Indians, and very fine work among the California tribes, some of whose products, notably those of the Pomo Indians, are unusually fine in weave, extraordinary in size, and reserved in their color scheme of black, brown, and tan (FIG. 700). The highly abstract decorative motifs, whose marked angularity shows an adjustment to the requirements of the weaving technique, appear

Fig. 702. Hopi Jar,
National Museum,
Washington. (Bureau
of Ethnology, Smith-
sonian Institution)

purely geometric; but a large number of them have specific names —
butterfly, arrowhead, quail plumes, striped water snake — and thus
like the pottery carry a meaning, if not symbolic at least rooted in
the daily life of the weavers. Technically, these Indians use both
coiling and twining and find their materials at hand: willow for the
warp, with wefts of yellow pine or sedge.

Close kin to the art of basketry is that of pottery. Its function is
the same, household and ceremonial use, though broader because of
its impervious character. Jars for containing and cooling water are
one of the great needs of an arid land. This art points to a settled
agricultural people and it is among the Pueblos of the upper Rio
Grande that we find some of the finest examples of the potter's art.
These craftsmen had no knowledge of the potter's wheel but constructed their shapes — and still do — by coiling ropes of clay until
the desired form is reached (a process singularly like that of basket-
weaving) and then smoothing the surface with gourd scrapers. Nor
did they use a glaze to finish the surface and render it impervious,
but instead covered it with a slip and then polished it with a very
smooth flint pebble, so making it slightly porous to permit enough
evaporation to cool drinking-water. Thus with the most primitive tools
and with an equally primitive method of firing the Pueblo potters
have attained high results.

Both shape and decoration vary among the tribes but the decoration
in general is nonnaturalistic, highly conventionalized, and if not symbolic at least associated with religious concepts or related to some
activity.[1] A preponderant number of decorative motifs have to do with

---

[1] Ruth L. Bunzel, whose *Pueblo Potter*, Columbia University Press, 1929, is important for an interpretation.

Fig. 703. San Ilde-
fonso Black Ware.
(Laboratory of An-
thropology, Santa Fe)

the clouds, rain, wind, lightning, with everything that is associated
with these people's greatest need — rain. The primary concern of the
potter [1] appears to be utilitarian — art for art's sake does not exist
among primitive peoples — and the finished product is the fusion of
a form dependent upon use and a decoration which relates fittingly
to the shape and at the same time carries a meaning that is rooted
in their immediate life. The *Zuñi Jar* (FIG. 701) is well shaped as a
container and is decorated with a large-scale dark pattern in red and
black on a white slip. The large sunflower pattern follows closely the
curvature of the surface, as do the curving motifs which inclose the
deer; the decoration on the neck, though harmonious, is quite distinct and separated from that of the body by the broken life-line.[2] A
characteristic *Hopi Jar*, the Sityatki ware (FIG. 702), is low and wide
and the broad upper surface not only offers the only suitable place for
decoration but limits its character to the character of its shape — a
circular band about a circular opening. On the warm yellow ground
usually found in this ware, the boldly drawn motifs are painted in
red, brown, and black, and united by the broad band below and
the broken life-line above. The best traditions of this ware have
recently been revived in the work of Nampeyo, a potter of Hano
pueblo. At San Ildefonso in addition to polychrome ware is the black
ware of Marie and Julian Martinez, whose efforts in reviving the fine
traditional quality of the old work as well as inventing this new style
have notably stimulated the ceramic industry of the Southwest. In
this black ware (FIG. 703) shape, proportions, and beauty of surface
through the contrast of polished and dull black, textures secured
through a special method of firing, are the objectives of the potter.

[1] Pottery-making is the prerogative of the women.
[2] The "life-line" or "road," a broken or unjoined line, is found in much of the
pottery and basketry of the Southwest. According to R. Bunzel, *op. cit.*, it symbolizes
the span of life. "When I finish it, I shall finish my life," says the Indian. Thus the
line is left unjoined.

Fig. 704. Navaho Blanket, Detail. Museum of the American Indian, Heye Foundation, New York. (Museum of the American Indian, Heye Foundation)

The neighbors of the Pueblos, the Navaho, are shepherd nomads. The sheep they obtained from the Spaniards; since that time they have developed especially an art which makes use of this raw material, meets a daily need, and can be pursued under the circumstances of a changing habitation. That art is weaving. The log loom is set up in the open, often attached to a supporting pole of the summer tent; and, until the present use of aniline dyes, the few colors used besides the natural black, white, and gray of the wool were obtained from local plants and minerals. The blankets and rugs are tapestry weave, usually interlocked, thick and strong — for their purpose is utilitarian — and the patterns boldly geometric, straight and angular (FIG. 704), endless in their variety and, like the designs on the Pueblo pottery, largely symbolic, though some appear to be purely decorative even if they originated in a meaning now lost.

In the sand paintings of the Navaho we find a unique art with elements of ancient religious significance and high esthetic value inextricably intermingled. They are created as a part of that elaborate ceremonial so characteristic of primitive peoples, out of colored sands secured by grinding stones from the colored cliffs of this desert country. Their highly abstract designs, apparently infinite in variety, are traditional and retained by memory, as are the dances, songs, and chants. The painter, with an incredible poise and dexterity, makes these paintings from memory and by free hand, squatting on the ground and dropping the colored sand, which he holds between his thumb and forefinger, on to a smoothed surface of ordinary sand. "The design, and every smallest part of it, is wholly symbolic. It has an archetypal, elemental significance. However intrinsically beautiful, its beauty to the Indian is in its meaning. It represents a philosophic conception of life. Its purpose is to convey this philosophy, and, once it has been used in the ceremonial ritual that follows, the painting is entirely erased and destroyed with the same ceremonial precision with which it was made. This is the spirit of Indian art — difficult to explain because it is so different from our modern individualistic conception of art. It belongs to a world where expression is subservient to the 'idea' — where the forms of art are never collected or hoarded as such, but the idea or image is tenaciously held and preserved through centuries." [1]

The Plains Indians farther north were also nomad tribes and hence were limited in their art expression to portable objects, to decorating their clothing and tepees, their moccasins and bags, with designs of dyed porcupine quills and feathers and later with beads, which they first obtained from the European and American traders. Here again we find simple geometric patterns — triangles, squares, rectangles — and the human or animal figure, if used at all, highly stylized.

Fig. 705. Indian Village Street Showing Totem Poles. British Columbia. (American Museum of Natural History)

4. THE NORTHWEST COAST INDIAN ART

The Indians of the coasts of British Columbia and southeastern Alaska are a fishing and hunting people who live on an irregular rocky coast from which heavily timbered mountains rise abruptly. This timber, largely cedar, which grows to an enormous size, and the products of their hunting provide them with the raw materials not only for food, clothing, houses, and canoes, but for all those objects

[1] A. C. Henderson, "*Modern Indian Painting*," in *Introduction to American Indian Art*, Exposition of Indian Tribal Arts, New York, 1931, Pt. II, p. 3, by permission of the publishers.

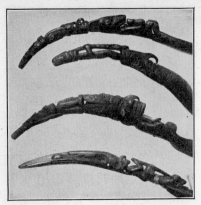

Fig. 706. Carved Spoon Handles. Northwest Coast Indian. American Museum of Natural History, New York. (American Museum of Natural History)

Fig. 707. Carved and Painted Wooden Chest. Haida Indian. National Museum, Washington. (National Museum)

of everyday and ceremonial life which constitute their art expression. Shell, bone, horn, and skins are abundant, but above all wood, and as a result these Northwest Coast tribes are the best woodworkers in America.

How this material shall be used is definitely determined by their religious and especially by their social patterns; and their decorative designs, though infused with religio-social symbolism, derive from their own immediate realm of nature — beaver and seal, hawk and eagle, killer whale and shark, bear, wolf, frog, snail, raven, and dragon fly. It is a highly conventional, in fact highly stylized, art. "This art style can be fully understood only as an integral part of the structure of Northwest Coast culture. The fundamental idea underlying the thoughts, feelings, and activities of these tribes is the value of rank which gives title to the use of privileges, most of which find expression in artistic activities or in the use of art forms. Rank and social position bestow the privilege to use certain animal figures as paintings or carvings on the house front, on totem poles, on masks and on the utensils of everyday life. Rank and social position give the right to tell certain tales referring to ancestral exploits; they determine the songs which may be sung. . . . A similar relation, although not quite so intimate, prevails in the relation of religious activities and manifestations of art. It is as though the heraldic idea had taken hold of the whole life and had permeated it with the feeling that social standing must be expressed at every step by heraldry which, however, is not confined to space forms alone but extends over literary, musical and dramatic expression." [1]

[1] Franz Boas, *Primitive Art*, Harvard University Press, 1928, by permission of the publishers, p. 280.

Fig. 708. A Killer Whale Design. The conventionalization and synthesis of natural forms into an abstract pattern.
(American Museum of Natural History, New York)

Fig. 709. Bear De-
sign. Painting on a
house front.

Notwithstanding its conventionality and heraldic significance, it is
a purely utilitarian art. The largest of the trees are scooped out into
canoes, at times forty or more feet in length, which serve as the chief
means of transportation for both hunting and pleasure. The Haida
Indians of Queen Charlotte Islands are particularly famous for their
canoes, which are not only seaworthy but shaped with a feeling for
proportion and for the quality of line in their curving prows and sterns,
which, in addition, are carved or painted with the heraldic devices
of the owner, who considers his canoe one of his most-prized possessions.
From the abundant timber they built also their sturdy wooden houses,
for which they cut planks sometimes sixty feet long and single poles
nearly a hundred feet high to be carved with totems, that is, with
heraldic designs — derived usually from animals or birds — that are
the mark and prerogative of the family or clan, or which illustrate
a story or myth (FIG. 705). In carving these poles the cylindrical mass
and rounding surface of the pole are never lost. Only enough is cut
away to leave clearly defined, with the help of conventional color, the
totems, which are large in scale and imposing in their simplified conventional form. Frequently additional totems are painted on the front
wall of the house.

Another closely allied field for the woodcarver is the making of the
masks which serve purposes of magic and play an important part in
the ceremonial dances that often are dramatic presentations of legends.
These masks are sometimes human, more often birds or animals or
legendary monsters. They are frequently very large in size, are made
of several parts, and so contrived mechanically that they can be manipulated with strings, thus enabling the actor to achieve strange effects
of opening the mouth of one monster only to disclose another within.
As for their esthetic significance, some possess a superior quality as

Fig. 710. Chilkat Blanket with Bear Design. Of goat's hair and cedar bark. (American Museum of Natural History, New York)

woodcarving, in which conventional color has been used as an additional element to clarify and accent.

In the furnishings of their houses, the Indians' first regard is for the purpose of the object, its material, and the rank of the owner. With pottery unknown, wood again is the chief material, and out of single pieces are carved killing clubs, grease and food trays, bowls, spoons, and ladles, large for ceremonial use, small for everyday (FIG. 706). Since fat is an important item in the diet of these Northerners, the grease dish for the fish and seal oil is more elaborate than the other dishes and is often elaborately carved, painted, and inlaid with abalone and other shells. Spoons and ladles sometimes have horn handles or are made entirely of the horn of the mountain goat by boiling the horn until it is pliable and then shaping it in a mold and finally carving the handle with totemic designs. Among their sparse furnishings boxes and chests play an important part, and even in large chests the four sides are made of one plank, which has been steamed by very primitive methods until pliant, and then bent to form the corners. These boxes and chests are carved and painted in red, black, and blue (FIG. 707). The blue is used least, since the material from which it is made is rare and difficult to obtain.

In these carvings, whether on wooden dishes, spoon handles, boxes, or totem poles, a unity of style is apparent, a common attitude toward the forms of nature that serve as the raw material of the artist. For it is not the animal's appearance from which he draws his material but his knowledge of its essential parts, each of which he has reduced to a conventional unit and combined according to the space to be filled. Each unit is based upon its most characteristic aspect quite regardless of a consistent point of view; some from front view, some profile, some from above. For example, in the killer whale design

Fig. 711. Tlingit Basket, Alaska. Museum of the American Indian, Heye Foundation, New York. (Museum of the American Indian, Heye Foundation)

Fig. 712. Indian in Ceremonial Costume. (American Museum of Natural History, New York)

(FIG. 708) the essential features — the large, long head with large mouth and prominent teeth, the dorsal fin, the body, the tail — have been reduced to almost geometric patterns and combined to fill a rectangular space: the full-face head in the center at the top flanked on each side by the dorsal fin; below, the head in profile repeated bilaterally; at the bottom, the tail, body, and dorsal fin repeated and combined. So conventionalized are these parts that cedar stencils are made for each unit, allowing a great variety of grouping, dependent upon the shape and size of the space to be filled. In a similar way the head of an animal may be shown front view and the body cleft into two parts and spread out laterally (FIG. 709), again forming a highly decorative pattern. So conventional a style is translatable into various mediums. Hence the similarity of style between the carvings and the paintings on skins and in the woven blankets.

In the field of weaving the *Chilkat Blankets*, of wild goat's wool and cedar bark, are woven in designs similar to those found in the carvings and usually with totemic significance. FIG. 710 has the bear design, woven in yellow, white, blue, and black. The central panel contains the front view of the face and various parts of the body; the side panels contain the profile view, stylized to the point of unintelligibility, at times even to the Indian, as in the case of the Pueblo pottery designs. These blankets are used only on ceremonial occasions and are worn about the shoulders over a tunic woven with a similar pattern; leggings of skins are painted and decorated with bits of bone or ivory which clink with the movements of the dance; and there is an elaborate head-dress of abalone shell and ermine — a costume of elegance and taste and worthy of upholding the dignity of the family or the clan (FIG. 712). These blankets are woven by the women on the most primitive looms according to designs drawn on boards by the men.

The *Tlingit Baskets* (FIG. 711), exclusively the work of the women, are woven from grasses and fern stems and are used for various house-hold purposes, for berrying in particular, and are woven finely and tightly enough to serve as drinking-cups. They are all decorated, by varying the weave or by the introduction of colored weft, or by wrap-ping colored grasses aroung the weft strand on the outside. The deco-rative motifs thus worked out look geometric but have names, showing that originally they had a meaning, although it has frequently been lost. Many of these baskets, especially those used for berrying, are cylindrical in shape with the decoration concentrated in zones.

BIBLIOGRAPHY

Middle American

American Sources of Modern Art, Museum of Modern Art, New York, 1933
Davis, E. C., *Ancient Americans*, Holt, 1931
Gann, T. W. F., *Ancient Cities and Modern Tribes*, Scribner, 1926
—— and Thompson, J. E., *The History of the Maya from the Earliest Times to the Present Day*, Scribner, 1931
Holmes, W. H., *Archaeological Studies among the Ancient Cities of Mexico*, Field Columbian Museum, 1895–97, issued in pts.
Joyce, T. A., *Central American and West Indian Archaeology*, Putnam, 1916
—— —— *Maya & Mexican Art*, Studio, 1927
—— —— *Mexican Archaeology*, Putnam, 1914
MacCurdy, G. G., *Study of Chiriquian Antiquities*, Yale University Press, 1911
Mason, Gregory, *Columbus Came Late*, Century, 1931
—— —— *Silver Cities of Yucatan*, Putnam, 1927
Morris, E. H., *The Temple of the Warriors*, Scribner, 1931
Saville, M. H., *The Goldsmith's Art in Ancient Mexico*, Museum of the American Indian, Heye Foundation, 1920
—— —— *Turquois Mosaic Art*, Museum of the American Indian, Heye Foundation, 1922
Spinden, H. J., *Ancient Civilizations of Mexico and Central America*, American Museum of Natural History, 1922
—— —— *A Study of Maya Art*, Peabody Museum, Cambridge, Mass., 1913
Thompson, J. E., *Mexico Before Cortez*, Scribner, 1933
Totten, G. O., *Maya Architecture*, The Maya Press, 1926

Tulane University, *Expedition to Middle American Tribes and Temples*, Tulane University, 1927, 2 vols.
Willard, T. A., *Bride of the Rain God*, Burrows Bros., 1930
————— *City of the Sacred Well*, Century, 1926

South American

American Sources of Modern Art, Museum of Modern Art, New York, 1933
Joyce, T. A., *South American Archaeology*, Putnam, 1912
Lehmann, Walter, and Doering, Heinrich, *The Art of Old Peru*, Weyhe, 1924
Markham, Sir C. R., *The Incas of Peru*, 3d ed., Dutton, 1912
Means, P. A., *Ancient Civilizations of the Andes*, Scribner, 1931
————— *Peruvian Textiles*, Metropolitan Museum of Art, New York, 1930
————— *A Study of Peruvian Textiles*, Museum of Fine Arts, Boston, 1932
————— *A Survey of Ancient Peruvian Art*, Yale University Press, 1917
Schmidt, Max, *Kunst und Kultur von Peru*, Berlin, 1929

Southwest, Plains, and Northwest Coast Indian

Amsden, C. A., *Navajo Weaving*, Fine Arts Press, 1934
Boas, Franz, *Primitive Art*, Harvard University Press, 1928
Bunzel, R. L., *The Pueblo Potter*, Columbia University Press, 1929
Chapman, K. M., *Decorative Art of the Indians of the Southwest*, Laboratory of Anthropology, Santa Fé, N. M., 1932
Cossio, M. B., and Pijoan, José, *Summa Artis*, Madrid, 1931–00, Vols. I–V, Vol. I
Cushing, F. H., comp., *Zuñi Folk Tales*, Knopf, 1931
Gillmor, Frances, and Wetherill, Louisa, *Traders to the Navajos*, Houghton Mifflin, 1934
Guthe, C. E., *Pueblo Pottery Making*, Yale University Press, 1925
Hewett, E. L., *Ancient Life in the American Southwest*, Bobbs-Merrill, 1930
Introduction to American Indian Art, Exposition of Indian Tribal Arts, New York, 1931
James, G. W., *Indian Blankets and Their Makers*, McClurg, 1914
Kidder, A. V., *An Introduction to the Study of Southwestern Archaeology*, Yale University Press, 1924
Krieger, H. W., *Aspects of Aboriginal Decorative Art in America*, Smithsonian Institution, Annual Report, 1930, Washington, 1931
Mason, O. T., *Aboriginal American Basketry*, Smithsonian Institution, Annual Report, 1902, Washington, 1904
Matthews, Washington, comp. and tr., *Navaho Legends*, Houghton Mifflin, 1897
Wissler, Clark, *North American Indians of the Plains*, American Museum of Natural History, New York, 1912

CHAPTER XXIV

African and Oceanian Art

1. AFRICAN ART

In west-central Africa (FIG. 713) — on the coast, in the river basins of the Niger and the Congo, in the southern reaches of the Sudan — live a great number of primitive tribes whose origin and history are largely unknown. Some are nomadic or seminomadic herdsmen on the grasslands fringing the forests; some are settled agriculturalists in clearings of the heavily forested regions of the river valleys; all are hunters and fighters. With an animistic religion they people all forms of nature with spirits for whose placation or supplication fetishes are in great demand. Dancing and chanting, to the accompaniment of a boldly rhythmic music, elaborate and awe-inspiring costumes, in which masks feature prominently, are important in their ritual.

The exigencies of their life, in which a primitive hut serves for a dwelling, and the materials at hand have given rise to a remarkable art of woodcarving practiced for centuries: [1] the making and embellishing of objects of everyday and ceremonial use out of the abundant native timber during the abundant leisure time that this way of life affords. Occasionally the carvers have used stone and more frequently ivory or bronze, the technique of whose working the Benin people learned from the Europeans.

As these African tribes vary in language, customs, religion, and social organization, so the styles of their carving vary, a fact that precludes generalizations that are applicable to all, except that one point of view seems to obtain for their carvings. Practically none of it has a copy of nature as its objective. Just as in the Northwest Coast Indian designs (FIGS. 707, 708, 709), the African dissected and distorted the parts of the human or animal figure and reassembled them, not according to nature but according to an esthetic pattern related to the material he was using, the space to be filled, and the function of the object. The carving has nothing to do with a verisimilitude of natural appearances, though occasionally it may tend thither; but it presents a type of visualization that is traditional and thoroughly intelligible to both the artist and his public, however far removed it is from the

---

[1] The best work was produced before the nineteenth century. Contact of the African with the civilization of the white man has probably been the chief reason for the deterioration in his work.

Fig. 713. Africa, Showing the Regions (inclosed by a
dotted line) Where Negro Sculpture Is Produced.

European type, which before the twentieth century was relatively close
to visual perception.

"Every part in a typical, fully realized negro statue functions as an
element in plastic design: an embodiment, a repetition in rhythmic,
varied sequence, of some theme in mass, line or surface. To be transformed into a design, the human figure must be regarded in a way
quite different from that of ordinary life and of most sculpture. It
must not be seen as an inviolable whole, treated as one unit and merely
posed in this attitude or that. The figure must be dissociated into its
parts, regarded as an aggregate of distinct units: the head, limbs,
breasts, trunk and so on, each by itself. So distinguished and usually
marked off by a surrounding groove or hollow, each part can be
moulded into a variation of some chosen theme — a sharp, slender
projection, or perhaps a smooth, bulbous swelling — never exactly the
same as its neighbors, for that would be monotonous; never too far
from nature, or completely abstract, for that would destroy its interest
as representation, its relevancy to the world of human experience. In
the same figure an artist may introduce two or more radically different
shapes, perhaps repeating and slightly varying each one. Such contrast gives, as in music, an arresting and interesting shock to the observer. It carries with it a possible loss of unity; the whole piece may

Fig. 714. Figure Supporting a Table.
Wood. Congo. XVII cent. Barnes coll.,
Merion, Pa. (Morgan Photo)

seem to fall apart, to be confusingly
unrelated. Then the genius of the
artist consists in finding means to
weld the contrasting themes together by some note common to
both.

"Constructed like a building of
solid blocks, a typical negro statue
is itself a solid, a full, substantial
block, set with convincing, massive
reality in its own space." [1]

Take for example the table with
a figure support (FIG. 714). The
cylindrical piece of wood, from
which just enough has been cut
away to allow the figure to emerge,
is clearly felt as a determinant of
the basic design; its section is retained in the top and base and its
diameter maintained in the horizontal reach of the arms; and its
shape is repeated in the torso, neck,
and arms. The figure, compressed
into a kneeling position, emerges
from, yet remains rooted in, the
semi-ovoid base through the flattening and distorting of the feet, thus
bringing unity and stability to the table as a whole. It then rises through
a series of outward- and inward-moving masses conoidal in shape and
thus with a zigzag contour, to support the top firmly by the head
and uplifted arms, and by this action secures a vertical as well as a
horizontal balance. This play upon masses — ovoids, conoids, cylinders — is repeated in the surface treatment, in which highly polished
surfaces contrast with carved. Thus the table as a whole is basically
a three-dimensional abstraction in which the parts are as closely related, structurally and esthetically, as in any building.

This three-dimensional organization so markedly characteristic of
Negro sculpture is based upon a generally cylindrical mass, at times
starkly geometric, as in the Gabun figures; at times with rich surface

[1] Paul Guillaume and Thomas Munro, *Primitive Negro Sculpture*, Harcourt, Brace,
1926, p. 35, by permission of the publishers. This book presents a lucid exposition
of the artistic qualities of Negro sculpture with detailed analyses of individual pieces.
See also Roger Fry, *Vision and Design*, "Negro Sculpture."

Fig. 715. Ivory Coast Mask. Wood. XIV cent. Barnes coll., Merion, Pa. (Morgan Photo)

Fig. 716. Portrait of a Benin King. Bronze. Originally surmounted by a large carved tusk. University Museum, Philadelphia. (University Museum)

treatment by carving. In contemplating these compositions upon the theme of the cylinder, one ponders on the influence of a naturally cylindrical material upon the carver, on his daily life among the trees, which furnish him with a material that is soft and easily carved in comparison with stone, and whose continuous rounding surfaces suggest movement in depth to both his visual and his tactile perception. How different will be the work of a carver confronted with a four-sided block of hard, weighty stone that resists every stroke of the chisel and hammer! Most of the African carvings are relatively small, and while extraordinarily firm and stable have none of the mighty solidity of stone sculpture.

After the perplexity or even aversion felt by a non-African upon first seeing these carvings has given way to a desire for insight and at least a partial understanding, he becomes aware of their intense vitality. Likewise he recognizes a superb craftsmanship, and a design which may be entirely abstract to the foreigner but so obviously filled with intense meaning to the African that it is bound to impress the unprejudiced observer, however little he may grasp its full import. The masks are an excellent illustration. Masks serve the same function, or rather

Fig. 717. Bushman Paintings. (Obermaier and Kuhn, *Bushman Art*, Oxford
University Press)

contribute to the same objective, a
the ceremonial chant and dance
They are one of the visual parts of
a ritual whose purpose is to inspire
awe or fear and thus must presen
to the eye of the observer a form
that will function to that end
Since the masks are actually worn
they are life-sized or larger, and
are highly simplified arrangement
of the parts of the face, combined
perhaps with a headdress; and
though in relief only, they show
the same attitude toward natura
forms as the carvings in the round

In Fig. 715, for example, there is an interplay of the oval — in the
face and its details repeated on a small scale in the headdress —
and of the sharply angular zigzag on a large scale above and smal
below. Likewise the strong vertical accent balances a rhythmic repe
tition of horizontals.

Metal was used to a limited extent and in primitive ways by the
Africans, but in Benin (Fig. 716) the metalworkers, having learned
from the Portuguese the more advanced process of cire perdue, created
as fetishes, bronze heads which probably were ancestor portraits and
were surmounted by elephant tusks elaborately carved with representa
tions of the king and his attendants. Since ancestor worship was a
essential part of religious belief and rites, these heads with tusks stood
on the altar and symbolized the spirits of the ancestors who were poten
in bringing good or evil into the lives of their descendants, and t
whom therefore sacrifices were made for supplication or for placation
In these heads one discerns not only a great vitality but a sensitivity t
material in the rounding forms with flowing surfaces, the interplay o
smooth and broken surfaces and rounding and angular motifs.

Among the Bushmen of the Kalahari Desert south of the Congo
who were very primitive nomad hunters living in a naturally poo
land, paintings on the rocks have been found of a character quit
different in point of view from the African art of which we have bee
speaking and strangely like that of the Paleolithic cave painters o
France. A visual perception of their world reduced to essentials an
expressed with directness and economy seemed to be their objectiv
(Fig. 717). These are not generalized men and animals and move
ments but individualized men and animals in an infinite variety o
naturalistic poses, even those involving foreshortening such as front an

three-quarters view, which indicates an extraordinarily keen
vision and memory.[1]

2. OCEANIAN ART

The peoples of Oceania are
a mixed race compounded of
the aboriginal inhabitants of
the islands and Asiatics who
migrated. While Paleolithic
and Neolithic remains in Java,
Sumatra, and Celebes carry
human habitation far back into
prehistoric times, migrations
from the continents appear to
be relatively recent, some possibly as late as a few centuries B.C.
So vast is the ocean area covered by these islands and so
varied the race and life pat-

Fig. 718. Tapa. From Samoa. Chauvet
coll., Paris.

terns and art forms that no generalizations can be made even in one of
the main divisions into which they are grouped: Polynesia, Melanesia,
and Micronesia.

The Polynesians are a finely built brown people organized socially
into the family and the clan with the chiefs, of attributed divine birth,
as rulers. Their religion consists of spirit and ancestor worship, infused
through and through, as is their social system, for the social and
religious are hardly separable, with a highly developed system of taboo
(*tapu*), which means "prohibited" for sacred or objectionable reasons.
"The true inwardness of the word *tapu* is that it infers the setting apart
of certain persons or things on account of their having become possessed
or infected by the presence of supermaterial beings." [2] Magic too plays
a considerable part in the ceremonial, often highly elaborate, which
attends many of their everyday activities, their fishing for example.[3]
Economically fishing ranks first; agriculture is important where possible, and warfare employs a considerable part of their time.

The art forms of such a people are dependent upon the materials
at hand and the tools they have evolved; and they are inextricably

[1] See Fry, *op. cit.*, "The Art of the Bushmen," for a discussion of perceptual and
conceptual images.
[2] Field Museum of Natural History, *Ethnology of Polynesia and Micronesia*, p. 147.
Continue this quotation for a detailed account of *tapu*.
[3] See *Ibid.*, p. 27, for a detailed description.

Fig. 719. The Carved Prow of a Canoe. Polynesian. British Museum, London. (British Museum)

Fig. 720. Head of an Orator's Staff. Maori. University Museum, Philadelphia. (University Museum)

knit into the whole pattern of everyday life. The chief material is wood from the rich growth of timber that supplies building material for houses and canoes, and for furnishings of all kinds, and pulp and fibers for bark cloth and mats; the feathers of colorful tropical birds for feather ceremonial robes; bone for carvings; and abalone and other shells for inlays. They have no metal and no pottery. Their tools are very primitive, an adz with a blade of jade or shell, knives of flaked obsidian or set with a row of shark's teeth, drills with points of stone, shell, or shark's teeth.

Their buildings of wood and thatch, adapted to the climate of the southern Pacific and unusually craftsmanlike in details of construction, reach a climax in the *Moari Council Houses,* particularly because of their carvings. The chief Polynesian art expression, however, consists in the making and decorating of articles for everyday or ceremonial use — mats, baskets, bark cloth for garments and hangings, paddles, clubs, spears, and other implements of warfare, all kinds of woodenware for housefurnishing — and in decorating their own bodies by tattoo and scarification. On the whole it is a richly decorative art, at times symbolic with a magic purpose. Most of the designs, as in aboriginal American art, have specific names which relate them closely to the milieu of their makers.

Mats are an important article of furnishing because they serve for floor and wall coverings as well as for beds and sails. Mat-making is done by the women, who obtain their material from sedge and from the leaves of the pandanus tree; and by a change in the plaiting or in the width of the fiber or by the introduction of colored fibers they create an infinite variety of patterns. Bark cloth, or *tapa*, which is used for clothing and hangings, is not a textile, for it is made by beating

together strips of the inner bark of the paper mulberry tree until they form a sheet
of fabric sometimes thirty feet long by fif-
teen feet wide. The sheet is then painted,
the finer pieces by hand, in bold geometric
designs in black, yellow, or red-brown. The
simple geometric pattern of FIG. 718 is filled
with unexpected variations as if the creative
activity was too vital and prolific to repeat
itself, though it adheres sternly to the basic
pattern.

The boldly free and varied brush work
in the tapa-painting shows the same understanding of materials and techniques as
does the woodcarving, which is probably
the highest expression of the Polynesian
people. Boxes and food dishes, paddles and
staves both ceremonial and utilitarian, killing clubs and weapons of warfare — all
these objects of daily and ceremonial life
are carved lavishly. Frequently the entire
surface is covered with an intricate pattern
of curving motifs, inlaid with abalone shell,
and reveals a great virtuosity in carving,
especially when one recalls the primitive

Fig. 721. Melanesian An-
cestral Shield. Chauvet coll.,
Paris. (Ryerson Library)

tools with which it is done. In FIG. 719 the carving covers the surface
almost too exuberantly with a continuous movement in spiraling motifs like the unending rhythm of a tom-tom. In the orator's staff of
FIG. 720 (extempore oratory about gods and legends accompanied by
the wielding of this ceremonial object is a privileged art expression
among the Maori nobles) the carving is confined to the upper part, is
adjusted in scale to the part that it decorates, and serves to enhance
rather than to obliterate the form and its surfaces.

In contrast to the suavely elegant, accomplished carvings of the
Polynesians are the starkly decorative carvings and paintings of the
Melanesians, a Negroid race of lower civilization, a cannibalistic people
but one of an extraordinary esthetic sensibility. It is a boldly decorative art, at times purely ornamental, at times with totemic significance,
that is lavished upon wooden shields and commemorative tablets,
carved coconut-shell cups, bamboo boxes, bark belts, wooden spatulas,
paddles, spears, dancing-shields and dancing-sticks, ceremonial masks
— all objects of everyday and ceremonial use. In the great *ravi*, or
men's house (for the women and children live in small family houses)

Fig. 722. Carved Cocoanut Shell. Melanesian. Field Museum of Natural History, Chicago. (Field Museum)

hang many of the shields and tablets (FIG. 721), elliptical in shape and painted or carved in designs which commemorate some event or have a totemic meaning. Ample timber provides suitable material, which is felled and roughly shaped by stone axes, adzes, and chisels and finally carved by stone, shell, teeth, or boar's tusk. The boldness of the ornament results partly from the designs themselves and partly from the use of contrasting color. For after the wood is carved it is painted red or black and the incisions are filled with lime. The masks are made from the bright feathers of tropical birds; or from bark cloth (the tapa of the Polynesians) stretched over a light frame and painted in black, white, red, and yellow — colors which are obtained from the native soil and from shells and charcoal. These masks play a prominent part in initiation ceremonies and at religious festivals, where they represent ancestors or bear a totemic significance. Rising loftily above the mass of shredded palm leaves or grasses that covers the figure of the wearer they produce a startling effect in the tropical surroundings. The decorative motifs used by the Melanesians show an almost constant use of spiraling motifs opposed to sharp dentils and chevrons; of the human or animal face highly conventionalized; and of an infinite variety of geometric shapes and variations thereof adapted most skillfully to the space to be filled, with a sensitive regard for scale (FIG. 722).

BIBLIOGRAPHY

Bell, Clive, *Since Cézanne*, Harcourt, Brace, 1922
Burkitt, M. C., *South Africa's Past in Stone and Paint*, Macmillan, 1928
Clouzot, Henri, and Level, André, *L'art nègre et l'art océanien*, Paris, 1920
Cossio, M. P., and Pijoan, José, *Summa Artis*, Madrid, Vols. I–VI, 1931–00, Vol. I
Einstein, Karl, *Afrikanische Plastik*, Berlin, 1922
Fry, R. E., *Vision and Design*, Coward-McCann, 1924, "The Art of the Bushmen"; "Negro Sculpture"
Guillaume, Paul, and Munro, Thomas, *Primitive Negro Sculpture*, Harcourt, Brace, 1926
Haddon, A. C., *The Decorative Art of British New Guinea*, London, 1894
Holmes, J. H., *In Primitive New Guinea*, Putnam, 1924
Lewis, A. B., *Carved and Painted Designs from New Guinea*, Field Museum of Natural History, Chicago, 1931

Lewis, A. B., *Decorative Art of New Guinea: Incised Designs*, Field Museum of Natural History, Chicago, 1924

Obermaier, Hugo, and Kühn, Herbert, *Bushman Art*, Oxford Press, 1930

Portier, André, and Poncetton, François, *Les arts sauvages*, Paris, 1929, 2 vols.

Sadler, Sir M. E., *The Arts of West Africa*, Oxford Press, 1935

Sweeney, J. J., ed., *African Negro Art*, Museum of Modern Art, New York, 1935

Sydow, Eckart von, *Die Kunst der Naturvölker und der Vorzeit*, Berlin, 1923

—— —— *Handbuch der afrikanischen Plastik*, Berlin, 1930, Vol. I

Tongue, M. H., and Balfour, Henry, *Bushmen Paintings*, Oxford, 1909

Part Eight

ORIENTAL ART

CHAPTER XXV

Indian Art

A. HISTORICAL BACKGROUND

India [1] comprises the substance of a continent within itself, surrounded by water except on the northern boundaries, the only gateway for invaders until recent times. The country divides geographically into three units: first, the wall of the Himalayas, a barrier and also a source of vital river systems, and the traditional home of the gods; second, the northern river valleys, generally known as Hindustan, including the basins of the Ganges and the Indus, very fertile, densely populated, the home of the Aryan invaders and the seat of the strongest political powers; third, peninsular India, comprising the Deccan and the Tamil states, the home of the Dravidian races, tropical tablelands south of the northern river basins and naturally separated from them by mountains and forests (FIG. 723).

Among these divisions are great extremes of climate and of geography, from tropical heat to perpetual snow and glaciers; from desert conditions to the heaviest rainfall in the world. Economically, greatest poverty stands opposed to greatest wealth — wealth still kept in the form of the family treasure, gold and jewels. The northern river basins have a wonderfully productive soil and the mountainous regions are rich in stone, woods, ivory, gold, and precious stones.

Likewise, among the people, numbering nearly three hundred million, there is great diversity of race, language, and custom. Politically India has always been divided into many minor principalities and only rarely in its long history has any considerable area been unified for more than a brief time.

Unity is not lacking, however, that is, a deeper and more fundamental unity than that manifested in political coöperation and in uni-

[1] This name is derived through the Greek and the Persian from the Sanskrit word *sindhu*, a river, referring preëminently to the Indus River. The name is not indigenous. The Hindus apparently have never evolved a title to include all India.

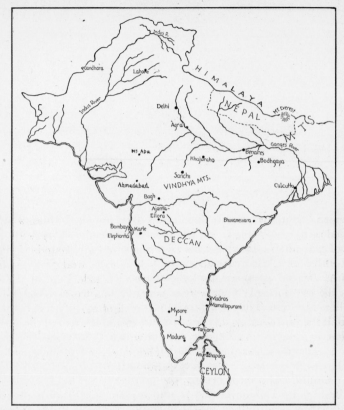

Fig. 723. India.

formity of dialect and custom. This is evident in the religious and
cultural life of India — in the Brahman faith, the national sacred
literature, the caste system, and the Hindu attitude toward fundamental spiritual truths. For perhaps no people have felt so profoundly
and pondered so deeply over the fundamental problems of life; and
with no people have spirituality and spiritual significance taken greater
precedence.

About the time when the Kassites were moving from the tablelands
of Asia in the vicinity of the Caspian Sea southwest into the Valley
of the Two Rivers (about 1700 B.C.), another Indo-European people,
the nomad Aryans, from the same tablelands were slowly making their
way southeast toward the valley of the Ganges.[1] But their coming

[1] For these great movements and the relationships existing among them, see
Breasted, *Ancient Times*, FIG. 123.

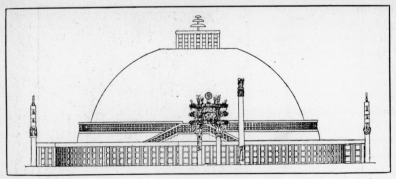

Fig. 724. Sanchi Stupa. Restored. D. 121 ft. III cent. B.C. (Archaeological
Survey of India)

was not uncontested; for in these lands lived the Dravidians, a dark-
skinned people who appear already to have reached a highly developed
state of civilization. Driving these Dravidians to the highlands south of
the Ganges, the Aryans settled down as an agricultural people. They
lived in villages, possessed domesticated horses, rode in chariots, and
knew the use of metal. They were organized into a tribal state with the
family as the unit. They worshiped the powers of nature—the sun, the
sky, and the rain — gradually personifying them, as we see in their most
ancient hymns, the Vedas, the title of which means "Knowledge,"
that is, sacred knowledge or lore. The ritual connected with the
worship of these forces was first performed by the father as head
of the family; but soon it became the prerogative of the priests called
the Brahmans, who developed it into a system with elaborate rites
and sacrifices, and infused into it philosophical ideas in the endeavor
to explain the fundamental problems of existence, and the nature
of the soul — the themes of the Upanishads. The poet-priests also
gathered together the legends of their race into the great Aryan epic
poems, the Mahabharata and the Ramayana, just as, according to
one theory, the Greek poets collected their national legends into
the Iliad and the Odyssey. The Ramayana tells of the deeds of the
prince Rama during his exile, brought about by court intrigue, and
the recovery of his lost bride Sita.[1] The Mahabharata, like the Iliad,
deals with a war between two clans, here the Kurus and the Bharatas.
But inserted, frequently at a later date than the first collecting of the

[1] For translations from the Vedas and the Upanishads see Sir Monier Monier-
Williams, *Indian Wisdom*, 4th ed., London, 1893; for the Ramayana and the Mahab-
harata, Frederika Macdonald, *Iliad of the East*, new ed., Lane, 1908; and Nivedita
Sister (M. E. Noble) and A. K. Coomaraswamy, *Myths of the Hindus and Buddhists*,
Holt, 1914; for the Bhagavad-gita, the translations of A. W. Ryder (University of
Chicago Press, 1929) and L. D. Barnett (Macmillan, 1905).

legends, are such reli-
gious treatises as the
Bhagavad-gita, or the
"Lord's Song," which
is probably the highest
expression of the funda-
mental tenets of Hindu
belief. The knowledge
of a few of these tenets is
necessary for an under-
standing of Indian art.
The first is that every
deed in this life plays its
part in determining the
next life; for, second, in-

Fig. 725. Buddhist Assembly Hall. Karle.
c. I cent. B.C. (India Office)

dividual souls pass at death from one body to another (the doctrine
known as the transmigration of souls). Good deeds reward the soul
by reincarnating it in a higher form of life; evil deeds bring it into a
lower, so that existence is one continuous succession of rebirths, the
goal of which is Nirvana, that is, freedom from existence by absorption
into Brahma, the ultimate, the only reality. The conception of this
one universal reality the writer of the Bhagavad-gita expresses when
he says:

"There is naught higher than I, O Wealth-Winner; all this universe
is strung upon Me, as rows of gems upon a thread.

"I am the taste in water, O son of Kunti; I am the light in moon
and sun, the *Om* in all the Vedas, sound in the ether, manhood in
men.

"The pure scent in earth am I, and the light in fire; the life in all
born beings am I, and the mortification of them that mortify the flesh.

"Know Me to be the ancient Seed of all born beings, O son of
Pritha; I am the understanding of them that understand, the splendor
of the splendid.

"The might of the mighty am I, void of love and passion; I am
the desire in born beings which the Law bars not, O Bharata-prince." [1]

The young Prince Siddhartha (died about 543 B.C.), brought up in
this traditional Brahman faith, looking about him, became much impressed with the suffering that he saw everywhere. To attain Nirvana
one must pass through an almost endless succession of reincarnations,
each with its own suffering. So he put himself to the problem of

[1] *Bhagavad-gita*, tr. by L. D. Barnett, p. 119, by permission of the Macmillan Company.

Fig. 726. Gate at
Sanchi. Upper part.
(India Office)

seeking relief from it. Leaving his family and his luxurious surroundings, he gave himself up to the life of an ascetic and through meditation obtained the knowledge that enabled him to bring a means
of salvation to his people. Hence he became a Buddha,[1] that is, an
enlightened one. Gautama's solution was to recognize that the individual was an illusion only and that suffering was due to self-interest,
that is, to the assertion of the interests of the individual rather than
the submersion of the individual in the larger universal life that em-
braces all nature in its fellowship and is the only reality. The means
of escape from the fetters of the individual into this supreme universal
life lay not in the elaborate sacrifices prescribed by the Brahman
priests, but partly in meditation, in order to bring the soul through
retirement and concentration into union with the divine, and partly
through moral actions done in a spirit of complete selflessness. This
is the path that leads to the conquest of self, to peace of mind, to
wisdom, and to release from bondage.

The heart of the Brahman faith was the triple aspect (the Trimurti)
of the one supreme God: Brahma, the creative aspect, cognition, wisdom; Vishnu, the sustaining aspect, love, emotion; Shiva, the destructive aspect, will, power; and the breadth of the conception is equaled
by its tolerance. "As birds float in the air, as fish swim in the sea,
as their pathways are invisible, even so is the pathway to God traversed

[1] Gautama Buddha, the only historical one of the seven Buddhas of the Hindu
faith. He is sometimes spoken of as Gautama, his family name, or as Shakyamuni,
the monk of the Shakyas, the clan to which his family belonged. For an account
of Buddha and Buddhism, see A. K. Coomaraswamy, *Buddha and the Gospel of Buddhism*,
Putnam, 1916.

by the seeker. It matters not *how* you reach God, provided you apprehend the supreme reality." [1] This religious faith so permeated every act of life that Hindu culture was a complete synthesis religiously, socially, economically. "All that India can offer to the world proceeds from her philosophy. This philosophy is not, indeed, unknown to others — it is equally the gospel of Jesus and of Blake, of Lao Tze and Rumi — but nowhere else has it been made the essential basis of sociology and education." [2] Involving this synthesis is the caste system, that ancient social and economic system by which the Hindu people are grouped into priests; warriors, who are the rulers and public administrators; agriculturalists, who are the economic producers; shudras, the laborers; and the untouch-

Fig. 727. Lotus Design. Pier of Sanchi Gate. (India Office)

ables — the first three comprising the Aryans, the last two probably originating in conquered peoples. These main divisions have become subdivided into more than twenty-five hundred groups, to which one comes by birth and from which change is practically impossible. This system, which seems to have evolved from natural conditions, is a part of the natural order according to the Hindu mind, and to that mind the individualism of the West has appealed but little. With such fostering of tradition and such sacrifice of the individual to the larger social unit, we may expect to find tenacity of conventions in art and an expression that is racial rather than personal.

While this national evolution was taking place within the life of India, foreign influences from the West were strong enough to assert themselves; for the Greeks under Alexander had penetrated to northwestern India and later came invasions of the Sassanian Persians. Evidences of these influences are somewhat apparent in Indian art; but in 320 A.D. a native dynasty was restored and this, the Gupta period, together with the reign of Harsha, forms the golden age of

[1] Sir Sarvepalli Radhakrishnan.
[2] A. K. Coomaraswamy, *The Dance of Śiva*, new ed., Sunwise Turn, 1925, p. 1, by permission of the publishers.

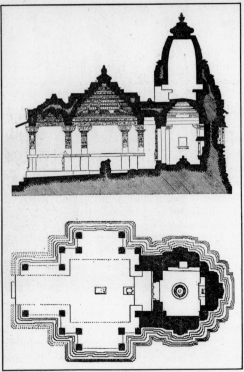

Fig. 728. Section and Plan of a Typical Brahmanical Temple. (Archaeological Survey of India)

Hindu culture (320–647 A.D.). A Chinese pilgrim writing of his travels in India in the fifth century describes the rich and prosperous condition of the country. He tells of charitable institutions and hospitals, institutions of learning, great monasteries, rich palaces with carved and painted ornamentation; of a mild, adequate government and religious toleration. Fine buildings were erected, only to be destroyed later by the Muhammadans; sculpture and painting reached a climax of attainment, as did music, science, and Sanskrit literature. For this was the period of the most famous poets, of whom Kalidasa was the greatest. Europe just at this time was being plunged into chaos by the fall of the Roman Empire and the inroads of the barbarians; and although the Byzantine Empire was flourishing under Justinian at Constantinople and the Sassanian power was at a climax under Chosroes I and Chosroes II at Ctesiphon, India at this time in the sum total of its broad culture was probably the most enlightened nation in the world.

Upon the decline of the Gupta and Harsha empires the Tatar invaders from central Asia who had penetrated to the northern plains of India succeeded to the power under the name of Rajputs, while native dynasties ruled in the south.

About the year 1000 the Muhammadans were pushing eastward into India. By 1526 they had overrun most of the country, and had established the great Mogul Empire, which was the ruling power over large areas until the coming of the English and the French in the eighteenth century and the establishment of the English rule in 1818.[1]

B. ARCHITECTURE

Of the early cities of India of which we read in Hindu literature nothing is left. The earliest structure that has survived is the Buddhist *stupa*, a mound of solid brick or stone to mark some sacred place or to

Fig. 729. Temple of Vishnu. Khajuraho. L. 109 ft.; H. 116 ft. c. 1000 (India Office)

hold some relic. Most representative is the great *Sanchi Stupa* (FIG. 724). It is hemispherical, with a flattened top, and rests upon a high circular terrace; a massive balustrade surrounds the dome, the usual method in India of protecting a sacred place; at the four cardinal points are ornamental gateways, lavishly carved (FIG. 726). Originally a balustrade surrounded the terrace, and served to guide the pilgrims in their procession, or circumambulation, about the shrine, an early practice common in Hindu religious ceremony. A double stairway with balustrades afforded an entrance to the terrace. On the flattened top of the dome was another balustrade surrounding the reliquary, which was surmounted by an umbrella, the symbol of royalty. Both the balustrades and the gateways appear from the construction to be stone copies of wooden rail fences and gates. They are, in fact, the work of the carpenter executed in stone. This gives us a clue to why earlier examples of architecture have not survived: they were of wooden construction and could not withstand the destructive climate of India.

Another important type of Buddhist building was the assembly hall [2] for congregational worship. Probably many of these halls were of wooden construction; those that are now extant are rock-cut, that is,

[1] The broad divisions of Hindu history are:

1700–700 B.C.	Vedic age
500 B.C.–300 A.D.	Age of Buddhism
300–600 A.D.	Gupta dynasty, the Golden Age of Hinduism; Buddhism absorbed by renascent Brahmanism
600–800 A.D.	Classic age. Rise of the Rajputs
Ninth century to eighteenth	Medieval age; Muhammadan invasion; Mogul (Mughal) Empire (1526–1761)

[2] Sometimes called a *chaitya hall*, that is, a temple or hall containing a *chaitya*, a monument, which in the early Buddhist churches took the form of a stupa (FIG. 725).

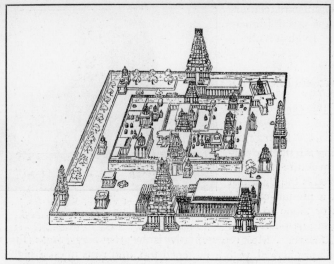

Fig. 730. Bird's-Eye View of a Southern Temple. (Fergusson)

hollowed out from the side of a cliff. Rock-cut churches, monasteries, and temples were popular in India, as they afforded excellent shelter both from the heavy rain and from the glaring heat. Though chiseled from the solid rock, they imitated the form of the wood or masonry structures. Such a hall we find in *Karle* (Fig. 725). The hall consists of a nave with a semicircular end, and with aisles from which the nave is separated by a row of columns; at the circular end within the nave stands the shrine in the form of a stupa, which was the symbol of the faith in the early days of Buddhism before statues of Buddha were made. The roof is in the form of a great barrel vault with ribs which reproduce the bamboo construction of its prototype. Originally there were fresco mural decorations and painted banners hung from the roof. One large leaf-shaped window was placed above the entrance in such a way that the light fell directly upon the stupa and brought out the rich colors of the decorations before it was lost in the dim shadows of the high vaulting.

In the decoration of these early Buddhist structures we discern characteristics of Indian ornament — exuberance and never-ending rhythmic movement (Figs. 726, 727). In the gates at *Sanchi* rectangular piers covered with reliefs are surmounted by four elephants from whose backs rise the uprights that hold three slightly curving bars, graduated in length and width as they rise, and terminating in vigorous spirals that by contrast bring out the richness of the carving

Fig. 731. Gopuramus. Madura. XVII cent.

and also turn the eye inward. Animals, winged griffins, and human figures in the round fill the spaces between the bars, which, like the supports, are entirely covered with reliefs. On one of the piers the lotus [1] is the motif of decoration. Here the movement is held effectively by the central panel of repeated disks formed from the conventionalized section of the lotus, with the space about them filled with the buds, fruit, or flowers; the outer borders contain a waving stem from which issue lotus leaves, flowers, buds, and fruit filling the space with practically no overlapping. The carving is kept low and flat, and forms a rich and effective panel of decoration.

The Brahmanical temples, dedicated to the worship of Vishnu and Shiva chiefly, were not intended for congregational worship, as were the Buddhist assembly halls. In India, as in Egypt, the people lived and worshiped chiefly out of doors. Since only the priest entered the shrine, all that was necessary was a room to hold the statue and a small portico for the guardian. For this reason also the decoration, which was didactic as well as ornamental, was placed on the exterior

[1] The lotus was the favorite flower of India and was used symbolically. Growing up out of the mud, undefiled it blossoms in the pure light of the sun. Just so the human spirit growing out of the material conditions of life finds liberation in Nirvana. The open lotus with down-turned petals, so frequently found in domes, capitals, and the pedestals of the statues of Buddha, suggested the vault of heaven. The section of the fruit, which is the shape of a wheel, symbolized the universality of Buddha's law.

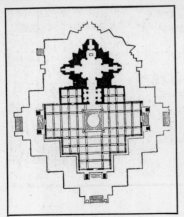

Fig. 732. Plan of a Chalukyan
Temple. (Fergusson)

rather than on the interior. But the
Hindu temple usually served a much
wider purpose than that of a shrine.
For here the king gave audience, the
village assembly met, and religious
and philosophical discussions took
place, as well as the recitation of the
great epics, songs, and dances. Hence
many temples had one or more assembly halls called *mandapams*, roofed
over but open on the sides.

Of these Brahmanical temples there
are three important classes: those dedicated to Vishnu, found chiefly in the
north, where this sect was strongest;
those dedicated to Shiva, located
chiefly in the south; and a group in
the Deccan, sometimes called the Chalukyan,[1] that combines features
of the other two, implying a use by more than one sect. In fact, all
these temples reflect religious movements and though dedicated to one
god do not preclude a change to the worship of another.

A typical temple of Vishnu (FIG. 728) shows that the essential parts
are the shrine and the assembly hall, or *mandapam*, which takes the
place of the simple portico of the temple consisting of a shrine only.
The walls and roofs are thick and massive, and sometimes contain a
hollow chamber to protect from the heat; the cornices are deep and
hollow for the same reason, and awnings frequently are added to shield
from the glare and the dust. The shrine is square and is covered by
a high tower, the *shikara*, with curving ribs the origin of which is the
bamboo framework of the primitive shrine from which the stone building was developed; it is crowned by a flat round member, derived in
shape from the fruit of the blue lotus, surmounted by a vase; the lower
courses of the tower are richly carved, with statues of gods and goddesses. In front of the shrine stands the *mandapam*, the roof of which
is built up into a truncated pyramid in order to cover the elaborate
ceiling, which, like a great inverted blue lotus, the flower of Vishnu,
symbolizes the dome of the world. On the *mandapams* the Hindu
builders lavished their decorative skill. Some were made of white
marble, with every inch of the surface of the ceiling and the supporting columns carved in all kinds of ornament — figure work and

[1] So called because they are found in the district ruled by the Chalukya dynasty;
they are also called Hoysala, because some of the finest were built by the kings of
the Hoysala dynasty.

Fig. 733. Temple at Halebid, near My-sore. Detail of the carving. Between 1117 and 1268 (W. E. Clark)

well as floral and geometric design — so that the effect was one of lavish richness.

An elaboration of this type of temple is found at *Khajuraho* (FIG. 729). Here the temple is built upon a raised platform. The rather plain base unifies all the parts of the building; the roofs, so rich and complex, culminate in the lofty tower over the shrine. The tower itself has become complex by the addition of smaller towerlike members which encircle the base, fill the angles, and with their varying height carry the eye upward rhythmically.

In the second class of Hindu temple, the southern, the shrine is inclosed in an immense walled quadrangle (FIG. 730) and surrounded by minor temples, halls, bathing-pools and shaded porticoes — evidences of a hot climate. The great towering gateways, *gopurams*, bear a load of ornament — gods, monsters, animals, floral and geometric motifs — from base to summit, yet control it with simplicity of mass and plane and with a fine sweep of contour (FIG. 731).

A third class of Hindu temple is like the northern in plan except that it has become star-shaped (FIG. 732), thereby presenting a varied and picturesque outline from whatever point it is viewed. Like the southern temple, however, it is built horizontally and roofed with low towers. The decoration is very profuse, as at *Halebid* (FIG. 733), where the horizontal zones are deeply undercut and carved with elephants, grotesques, mounted horsemen, gods, human figures and floral motifs. Here one is aware of a prolific outpouring not only of ornament but of an intense vitality and ceaseless rhythm that pervade all animate things.

When the Muhammadans had established their empire in India, their wealthy rulers, the great Mughals, or Moguls, erected magnificent tombs and mosques, palaces and audience halls, according to certain traditions from the West — a dome over a tomb, the pointed arch,

Fig. 734. Taj Mahall. Agra. 1632–53. (W. E. Clark)

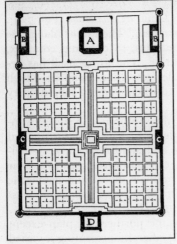

Fig. 735. Plan of the Taj Mahall and Its Garden. *A*, Taj; *B*, mosques; *C*, pavilions for the keepers; *D*, entrance. *B*, *C*, and *D* are of red sandstone.

the minaret, the absence of sculpture — fused, as was the wont of the Moslem, with local features.

The highest embodiment of Mughal architecture is the *Taj Mahall* [1] (Figs. 734, 735), a cubical structure surmounted by one large and four small domes, standing upon a high platform with four minarets, and set in the midst of a rich tropical garden. The impression of lightness, delicacy, and grace results from at least four elements: the material, the control of light and dark, the open design, and the setting in a larger design of contrasting elements. Its material is white marble inlaid with delicate floral designs worked out in precious stones, with inscriptions about the arches, and delicately carved panelings and low relief of floral motifs, all of which produces a subtle modulation of surface. Everything tends to a diffused light with no strong contrasts such as are found when strongly salient cornices and moldings are used. The deep recessing of the portal and windows provides just enough shadow to set forth clearly the dominant motif of the pointed arch that leads to the pointed lotus dome contracted

[1] Meaning the "Crown of Palaces," the tomb built by Shah Jehan, one of the great Moguls, for his beautiful and gifted young wife, Mumtaz-i-Mahall, a name that means "Exalted of the Palace," from which the name of the building is derived

Fig. 736. Carved
Marble Window. Ah-
madabad. XV cent.

at the base (contrast FIG. 365), which springs from a row of conventionalized lotus petals and terminates in an inverted lotus. A lightness in
design is secured through the large open spaces, subtly proportioned, between the solid central mass and the minarets, which are tied together
by the platform. Though the tomb is itself a complete unit of design,
it attains its complete effect only when seen in its setting of tropical
foliage and gardens with flanking mosques and gateways of red sandstone.[1] By means of such contrasts a floating, almost evanescent quality
is given the focal point of the entire design, the tomb itself, with the
result that its total impression becomes a symbol of the grace and
beauty of the queen for whom it was built. It was symbolical rather
than representative, since Shah Jehan and the other Mughal rulers
while they were not strict Muhammadans and had adopted much of
Hindu thought and point of view, still had deeply ingrained in their
tradition the aversion to representing the human figure, especially in
connection with a tomb or mosque. Furthermore to Moslem and
Hindu alike the highest kind of expression employed the symbol with
its emphasis upon inner significance rather than that representation
which aims to copy outward appearance.

In the interior of the *Taj*, which is of the same materials and workmanship as the exterior, a mellow light filters through carved marble
windows upon the cenotaphs of Mumtaz-i-Mahall and Shah Jehan,[2]

[1] For an analysis of the design showing the relation between these elements see
Gardner, *Understanding the Arts*, pp. 106 ff.

[2] Shah Jehan's plan for his own tomb to be built on the other side of the river
and connected with the *Taj* by a bridge was never carried out because of disasters
in the latter part of his reign.

Fig. 737. Buddha. Of dolomite. Colossal size. V or VI cent. Anuradhapura, Ceylon.

which stand beneath the dome surrounded by a screen of marble carved into a lacelike design and bordered with floral inlays.

The marble window, which played an important part in Hindu building, was made by carving a slab of marble until it was perforated by tracery, sometimes with geometric and sometimes with naturalistic motifs (FIG. 736) of infinite variety.

C. SCULPTURE

A vast amount of Hindu sculpture consists of temple decoration poured forth like that of teeming tropical nature, with abundance and exuberance, and including in its conceptions all the cosmos. "It is to symbolize this universal fellowship of man, the unity of all creation that the Indian loves to crowd into his picture all forms of teeming life . . . uses every constructive feature to symbolize the universal law of the One in many." [1] Independent sculpture consists of cult statues. Thus sculpture as a whole is a religious art. In the early days of Buddhism, Buddha was not represented but referred to by symbol, that is by the stupa, or by stories of his former incarnations when he was a bird or an elephant,[2] as in the reliefs on the *Sanchi Gates*. The exuberant life represented on the piers and crossbars (FIGS. 726, 727) — men and animals worshiping at the stupa or the sacred tree, and scenes from the lives of the Buddha — fills the space to overflowing with the intense vitality of an energetic cosmos. Yet each relief consists of an orderly placement of the crowded figures one above another with careful relation to a focal point. The manner of the carving provides just enough shadow to enable the simplified lighted planes of the figures to stand forth clearly. These gates are not primitive but, like the architecture, seem to be a translation into stone of an earlier fully developed art of perishable material, perhaps wood, and an expression of the Vedic animistic faith — an art which the Buddhists took over as part of

---

[1] E. B. Havell, *The Ideals of Indian Art*, Dutton, 1911, p. 112.
[2] Known as the Jataka tales. For these stories see the edition by H. T. Francis and E. J. Thomas, Macmillan, 1916; and E. W. Burlingame, tr., *Buddhist Parables*, Yale University Press, 1922.

Fig. 738. Avalokiteshvara. Bronze. H. 3⅝ in. VIII cent. Museum of Fine Arts, Boston. (Boston Museum)

Fig. 739. The Trimurti (Brahma, Vishnu, and Shiva). Colossal size. VIII cent. Cave temple at Elephanta, near Bombay.

their tradition and molded to new purposes, just as the early Christians appropriated and infused with new meaning their inherited Greco-Roman forms.

It was not for several hundred years after his death that statues of Buddha began to appear [1] and not until the Gupta age that thoroughly Buddhist conceptions archaic in style attain a monumental vitality, as in the *Buddha* of FIG. 737, in which the Buddha is represented as the Yogi, that is, the ascetic who devoted himself to meditation. Through this practice he turned his mind and sense organs from outward things and directed them inward, thus bringing reality into closer relationship with the soul and acquiring that knowledge and enlightenment which would enable him to attain salvation. He is seated with legs crossed, hands folded easily in his lap, and eyes downcast. He is not asleep, for the body is too erect for that. We feel the perfect poise and self-control through the complete withdrawal inward of the self. A thin drapery falls from the left shoulder, indicated by the diagonal across the breast. There are no individual lines in

[1] Owing partly to the influence of Greece that had penetrated to northwestern India through the conquests of Alexander the Great and had strongly influenced he sculptors of Gandhara, who combined the Indian conception with the Greek method of expression. The result is interesting historically, for it penetrated to China also. But it is curiously exotic, and typical neither of Greece nor of India. The attributes of Buddha, in the sculpture of India, China, and Japan, are the protuberance of wisdom on the top of the head; the split and elongated ear lobes; and the mark on the forehead, often a jewel, that symbolizes the third eye of spiritual vision.

Fig. 740. Death of Hi-
ranyakasipu. c. VIII
cent. Cave temple at
Elura. (India Office)

the face; the entire figure is carved in essential masses and essential
planes only, and details are indicated by conventions. The Indian
artists carefully studied the human figure, worked out canons of proportions for drawing and carving it, and at times modeled with precise detail. Hence such simplification, which eliminates details and
suppresses any desire merely to imitate nature, is intentional, and
reveals an aim not to tell us what the Buddha looked like physically,
but to make us realize the spiritual realm to which he attained; therefore the statue becomes an abstract expression of a state of perfect
control and perfect quiet. "As a lamp in a windless spot flickers not,
such is the likeness that is told of the strict-minded man . . . when
the mind, held in check, comes to stillness . . . and when he knows
the boundless happiness that lies beyond sense-instruments and is
grasped by understanding, and in steadfastness swerves not from
Verity, than which, once gotten, he deems no other boon better." [1]
This stillness is not the negation of power, but denotes the acquisition of the greatest spiritual values; and the "moral grandeur" of the
concept equals the esthetic grandeur of the form.

The trend in the late Gupta age from monumentality and impersonality toward ease, grace, and humanism may be illustrated by a
bronze statuette of *Avalokiteshvara* (FIG. 738). The Bodhisattva [2] is
seated in an easy pose, the weight borne by the left arm, and the
right hand, supported by the raised leg, held in the traditional gesture

[1] *Bhagavad-gita*, tr. by Barnett, p. 114, by permission of the publishers, The Macmillan Company.
[2] A Bodhisattva is a being who is destined at some time to become a Buddha;
even at present he is an active force for salvation and his worship is the center of a
cult. Avalokiteshvara, "the Lord who looketh down in great compassion," is one of
the most important Bodhisattvas not only in India but, under a different form, in
China and Japan also.

Fig. 741. Elephants. Detail of the cliff carving at Mammallapuram. VIII cent.

of teaching. The shoulders are broad and strong, the waist narrow, the limbs rounded, and the skin smooth; on the head is the protuberance of wisdom, here covered with a crown, and the ears are elongated — all traditional characteristics and conventions. Through the figure flows a suave rhythm which emphasizes serene youthfulness and tender compassion. Its material, bronze, is highly suitable for both the character and small size of the figure.[1]

The gestures of the uplifted hand of *Avalokiteshvara*, of the folded hands of the *Buddha* (FIG. 737), and of the four hands of *Shiva* (FIG. 746) illustrate an important feature of Hindu sculpture, the importance and significance of the positions and movements of the hands, known as *mudras*, which constitute a language of gesture.

As the Gupta age evolved into the Classic age when renascent Brahmanism was absorbing Buddhism, sculpture became Brahmanical in theme, became more dramatic, more humanly emotional, suave, and elegant, though it did not lose its aim of expressing, primarily, spiritual conceptions. Something of the large monumentality of archaic Gupta art survived in the *Trimurti* (FIG. 739), the triple aspect of the supreme deity — Brahma, Vishnu, and Shiva — in which the aim was not unlike that of the Byzantine artists, "the immeasurable aim . . . to render visible the mysteries of the supra-natural world." In their attempt to express the ultimate Reality they renounced transient visual phenomena in favor of symbols and conventions.

More dramatic is the relief (FIG. 740) in which the god in the form of a man-lion appeared to King Hiranyakasipu, who had sneeringly denied him.[2] Here the sculptor has expressed with convincing power that moment when the King still derisive is recoiling before the sudden apparition; he has emphasized through the largeness of his design and the suppression of irrelevant detail the might of an angry god. Of these reliefs in the rock-cut temples it has well been said that all

[1] The Hindus were expert bronze-workers by the cire-perdue process.
[2] This legend forms the basis of the ballad called "Prehlad," in Toru Dutt, *Ancient Ballads and Legends of Hindustan*, Scribner & Welford, 1885.

Fig. 742. Women at the Fountain. Borobudur. c. IX cent.

these images, without hesitation, awkwardness, or any superfluous statement, perfectly express by their action the passion that animates them.[1] Illustrative of the deep understanding of animal life are the deer and elephants (FIG. 741) on the great carved cliff at *Mamallapuram*.

In contrast to this Brahmanical art is that of the great stupa at *Borobudur* in Java (FIG. 759), which shows the continuity of Buddhist themes outside India, the result of the strongly missionary character of Buddhism. This shrine was an elaborated stupa about which wound five procession paths along which were sculptured in relief, in the coarse native building stone of the stupa, the stories of the Buddhist faith, for the instruction and stimulation of the pilgrims, just as the early Christian churches were decorated with carving, mosaics, and frescoes representing the life of Christ and the saints. In FIG. 742 we see a group of Javanese women coming to the fountain near the temple for water. At the left, they are moving away with filled jars; one is pulling hers up from the water covered with lotus; on the other side another group is approaching, while at the extreme right one has put her jar down and sits motionless drinking in the words of the master, who with uplifted hand is bringing her his message. The naturalism and lively narration of the scene are not at all marred and the decorative quality is enhanced by keeping all objects — temple, trees, people — of equal height to fill the space. More richly decorative, through the conventional treatment of the trees, is the scene in which Buddha is expounding the faith to his mother and her attendants (FIG. 743).

Another great Hindu expression beyond the confines of India is the work of the Khmers, who, apparently of Indo-Chinese origin, had settled in Cambodia (FIG. 759), whither came Hindu colonists who became the ruling class and developed a high type of civilization from the

[1] Rock-cut temples are frequent in India because of the heat and the heavy rainfall. Note the Buddhist *Chaitya Halls*, the caves at Ajanta, Elephanta, and Elura, where is the large rock-cut monolithic *Kailasa Temple*. These are important for their reliefs and wall paintings.

Fig. 743. Buddha Expounding the Law to His Mother, Maya. Borobudur.

ninth century to the thirteenth, when they appear to have been annihi-
lated by some other race. In the tropical jungles they built their capital
city, Angkor, with magnificent temples and palaces (FIG. 744), of
a fine native limestone, cut and laid precisely and carved lavishly.
FIG. 745 shows a detail, representing a battle scene from the Mahabharata, which animates the unbroken wall but remains an inseparable
part of it. The army is marching through the jungle, whose lacelike
foliage carved in a pattern of very low relief sets forth the vigorous
figures in higher relief. The unchanging rhythm of the marching troops
is broken by the spirited movement of the horsemen and the elephant;
and the delicate carving of the foliage is opposed by the strong accents
of the umbrellas and of the animals. The effect of such opposition and
interweaving is analogous to that of a musical composition in which
the cellos weave a deep-toned melody through the more delicate tones
of the wind instruments. The highly decorative quality results partly
from the conventional, linear character of the forms, partly from the
shallowness and clear definition of the planes that indicate depth, and
partly from the manner in which these planes reflect the light in a
pattern of contrasting broken and unbroken areas.

While the centuries succeeding the ninth reveal a trend to florid
elegance both in quantity and in quality, as at *Halebid* (FIG. 733), at
Madura (FIG. 731), and in the temples at *Mt. Abu*, some of the
statues still retain the vitality of earlier ages. Such is an example in
bronze, the only possible medium for the design, of the popular subject of *Shiva as Nataraja*, that is, as *Lord of the Dance* (FIG. 746). Shiva is
poised with one foot upon a dwarf. He has four arms. In one hand

Fig. 744. Angkor Wat. Cambodia. XII cent.

Fig. 745. Angkor Wat. Cambodia. Detail of the carving showing
a scene from the Mahabharata. XII cent. (Giraudon)

is a drum, in another is fire. A
ring of fire (broken off in our
illustration) rising from the lotus
pedestal surrounds the figure,
touching it at the hands with the
drum and the fire. The meaning
is that when Shiva dances with
the drum and the fire, he awak-
ens the powers of nature to the
dance, that is, to life. But in turn
he destroys these powers with fire
and they return to rest. The
movement of the dance symbolizes the rhythmic energy of the
cosmos whose purpose is perpetual creation and then destruction,
but a destruction that is change,
not annihilation, and results in
the release or salvation of soul.[1]
In the movement of this dance, as
in the Buddha, we see that an orderly rhythm controls every part
of the figure. The body, an S-

Fig. 746. Shiva as Nataraja. Bronze.
H. c. 4 ft. X–XII cent. Madras Museum.
(*Ars Asiatica*)

curve, is poised firmly upon one foot. The other limbs move freely
and form an asymmetrical design, composed of cylindrical and jagged
shapes (the flames, the hands, the headdress), which is an objectification of the ceaseless movement of this vital rhythm.

D. PAINTING

What has survived of Hindu painting falls into three general groups
— Buddhist, Rajput, and Mughal. The Buddhist, which consists of
wall paintings in the cave temples, may be illustrated by the *Ajanta
Frescoes* (first to seventh centuries A.D.), which show an art already
highly developed, the preliminary stages of whose evolution have not
survived. The Ajanta caves were Buddhist cave temples that formed
a monastic retreat in an isolated ravine in central India. Here the
painter-priests covered the walls with paintings of Buddhist themes,
chiefly the Jataka tales (FIG. 747). Perhaps the chief impression is one
of the reality of a life that was spontaneous and fervid, expressed in
forms that are not hieratic, like the Byzantine, but which represent

[1] For a detailed description of the statue and of its symbolism, see Coomaraswamy,
The Dance of Śiva.

Fig. 747. Jataka Tale: Scene from the Golden Goose. VII cent. Ajanta Caves. (India Society)

Fig. 748. Seated Woman. Detail from one of the frescoes in the Ajanta Caves. VII cent. (India Society)

contemporary court life exalted to the plane of the mystic. The vitality of this painting seems due to a passionate conviction and a profound grasp of the theme — an illustration of the Oriental insistence upon the theme as the sine qua non of art and upon the theory that to paint a picture one must identify himself with the theme. There is also apparent a perfect control of the artist over a traditional technique and a language of conventions and symbols through which he could objectify the concepts aroused by the theme. The love and understanding of all the life of the cosmos are profound, based upon that sense of intimate kinship of all animate life which is so vital an element in Buddhism and so significant a motive in the Jataka stories.

The simple informal compositions which fill the wall area are commanding in scale and of lyric monumentality owing to a freedom and ease of pose and of suave rhythms. As in sculpture the forms are controlled by traditional proportions and conventions and particular emphasis is placed upon the gestures of the hands. The contour is important, a firm, supple, energetic line, not merely calligraphic but which, with the help at times of a slight chiaroscuro, suggests the mass of the figure yet keeps the composition as a whole essentially flat. In the figure of a seated woman (Fig. 748), for example, one feels convincingly the weight and mass of the figure, the tension of the left arm as it supports the weight, the supple ease and exquisite grace of the

Fig. 749. Krishna Quelling the Serpent Kaliya. Rajput. XVIII cent.
Coomaraswamy coll., Boston. (A. K. Coomaraswamy)

right hand. With red the painter drew such a figure on the moist
plaster, added a thin greenish underpainting, then the local color, and
finally repainted the contour in brown or black, thus giving it additional emphasis. When the painting was complete he burnished the
wall with a trowel.

The *Ajanta Frescoes* were almost exclusively Buddhist and carry us
to about the middle of the seventh century A.D. Thence for about a
thousand years no paintings have survived, though traces of the continuity of the tradition are being found in recent discoveries in Turkestan and Tibet, where the art was practiced as it spread along the
great highways toward China in the early centuries of the Christian
era. It is not until about 1550 that we again find examples of Indian
painting. In the meantime important events had taken place. Buddhism had been absorbed by Brahmanism and the cults of Vishnu
and Shiva had been developing. The Muhammadans had conquered
large parts of the country and established the Mogul Empire, bringing
with them strong influences of the art of the West. The paintings fall
into the last two classes mentioned above, Rajput and Mughal. The
Rajput, so called because it was practiced chiefly in the Rajput domain,
particularly in the Himalaya valleys beyond the reach of the Muhammadan power, was a purely indigenous art and appears to continue
the traditions of the *Ajanta Frescoes*, though in it we find a wider expres-

Fig. 750. Nut Slicer.
Brass, inlaid with silver.
L. 8½ in. Coomaraswamy
coll., Boston. (A. K.
Coomaraswamy)

sion: themes from secular life, often romantic, stories from the heroic days of the Mahabharata and Ramayana, and illustrations from the lives of the gods, particularly Vishnu. Another difference between these paintings and those at Ajanta is that they are small, though their largeness of design may well suggest lineal descent from the great Buddhist frescoes. *Krishna Quelling Kaliya,* a poisonous serpent (FIG. 749), is a typical example. Krishna, one of the numerous incarnations of Vishnu, stands holding the body of the serpent easily, through his godlike power, pressing upon it with his foot. On each side are grouped the wives of the serpent, half human, half reptile, tenderly grieving for him and pleading with Krishna to spare him; on the bank Krishna's family and the cowherds are frantically rushing to the edge of the pool; in the background the herds are peacefully grazing. The color is clear and intense; the color areas meet sharply, and thus accentuate the linear character of the design, which consists of two asymmetrically balanced groups. In the Krishna group the god himself framed by the serpent forms the center of interest, with the wives arranged symmetrically on either side, each expressing by pose and gesture her tender love or earnest pleading. At the same time each figure, especially the long sweeping curve of the reptilian form, plays its part in a composition of repeated lines and shapes set over against the conventionalized waves of the pool. By repetition of color areas and shapes, unity is established between the two groups and the two areas, sharply divided though they are by a great curving edge.[1]

The third group, the Mogul or Mughal, is less Indian than the others. When the Mongols came to India, they brought with them painters who had been trained in the Persian school, and their art, combining with the native Hindu elements, formed the foundation of Mughal painting. But while Rajput painting was lyrical and religious, having its roots deep in the soil of native traditions, Mughal painting

[1] Reproduced in color in the *Burlington Magazine*, Vol. XX (1911–12), p. 315. For the story, see Nivedita Sister (M. E. Noble) and Coomaraswamy, *Myths of the Hindus and Buddhists*, p. 226. An interesting aspect of Rajput painting is its relation to music. Many examples display a deep feeling of tenderness, and are of a lyrical mood that evokes the same emotion as music. Thus they are known as *ragas*, or *raginis*, that is, a melody or a musical theme. On this see A. K. Coomaraswamy, *Rajput Painting*, Oxford Press, 1916, 2 vols., or his *Arts and Crafts of India and Ceylon*, LeRoy Phillips, 1914.

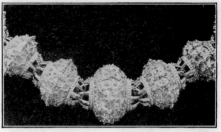

Fig. 751. Necklace Pend-
ant. (A. K. Coomara-
swamy)

Fig. 752. Detail of a Girdle Chain. Of hollow
silver beads worked in filigree. (A. K. Coomaraswamy)

Fig. 753. Ceremonial Dipper. Silver and ivory. L. 18 in. Victoria
and Albert Museum, London. (Victoria and Albert Museum)

was secular. It was a miniature art chiefly. Its interest lay primarily
in the picturesque aspect of human life, chiefly that of the palace; for
it flourished under the patronage of the Mogul rulers and nobles, and
aimed to give a vivid picture of court scenes and persons, hunts and
night scenes, animals and flowers.

E. MINOR ARTS

The Hindu craftsman was an important member of Indian society
and was provided for economically by the system of that society. The
monastery had its painters, sculptors, and metalworkers to decorate
its buildings, and perhaps sent them on to another monastery when
its own work was done. The noble had, as part of his household, his
goldsmith to make the jewelry and plate for his family. The boy inherited his father's calling and belonged to the guild, which was under
the protection of the king.[1]

Among the metalworkers the goldsmith was of great importance, for
jewelry played an important part in Indian costume, of the men as

[1] On this situation see A. K. Coomaraswamy, *The Indian Craftsman*, London, 1909,
and *Mediaeval Sinhalese Art*, London, 1909.

Fig. 754. Embroidered Muslin. Coll. of Leslie de Saram, Colombo. (A. K. Coomaraswamy)

well as of the women.[1] It was used not only for personal adornment but for the trappings of state elephants and for palace hangings. Girdle chains (FIG. 752) originated in the old Hindu custom of decking the body with garlands of flowers and seeds. In order to keep the chain light in weight the beads were made hollow and in filigree. Like the Greek, the Indian recognized the value of gold and silver as a medium for expression in itself without the addition of jewels. When he used gems, he did not facet them but only smoothed them off, thus obtaining a deep and glowing rather than a flashing effect. Another use of gems was made by inlay. Tiny pieces of ruby, sapphire, emerald, or topaz were embedded in a thin gold plate, producing the effect of enamel. In this the Indian revealed his skill in massing color harmonies, and out of almost valueless bits created an unsurpassed piece of rich decoration. The pendant to the chain in FIG. 751 is an example of this. The general shape is suggested by a bird with outspread wings. There is no thought of giving a realistic representation of the bird form, but the aim is to use only the essential elements to obtain decorative beauty. "To wear a real bird . . . would be barbarous; to imitate a real bird very closely . . . would be idle; but all that is beautiful in the general idea of a bird, colour, form, and poise, can be suggested." [2]

Another kind of metalwork successfully practiced was damascening. The betel-nut slicer (FIG. 750) shows not only great technical skill but vigorous imaginative quality in the design that adapts to everyday use this fantastic figure with the head of a lion and the body of a bird.

Further evidence of the Indian love of ornament we see in the wood and ivory carvings. The sacrificial dipper (FIG. 753), for example, is an elaborate design of curves. One great sweeping curve forms the

[1] See Coomaraswamy, *Arts and Crafts of India and Ceylon*, p. 151, for a description of the costume of the maids of honor of an Indian queen.
[2] Coomaraswamy, *Mediaeval Sinhalese Art*, p. 211.

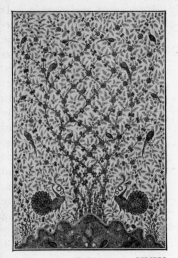

Fig. 755. Palampore. XVIII cent. Victoria and Albert Museum, London. (Victoria and Albert Museum)

Fig. 756. Cashmere Textile. Detail. Metropolitan Museum, New York. (Metropolitan Museum)

structural line of the handle; but it is varied and emphasized by minor curves swirling now this way and now that, but entirely subordinated to the main line of direction. The bowl of the dipper shows the skill of the silversmith, for the rich design is superbly executed. The union of the two parts, however, is not successfully accomplished by the curious, elaborately bejeweled little figure that distracts and weakens the construction at that point.

One of the most important crafts of India has always been weaving, and the chief material, cotton. The muslins from Dacca are so sheer that they have received poetic names such as "running water" or "evening dew," the latter because the fabric is so delicate that if laid on the wet grass it is scarcely visible. When these delicate muslins are embroidered they have the effect of exquisite lace (FIG. 754). Cotton textiles served not only for garments and turbans but also for hangings, bedspreads, and other furnishings. From their native names are derived many of our own words for cotton fabrics, such as *chintz* and *bandanna*. For decorating these cottons, several processes were employed, chiefly printing and painting. FIG. 755 reproduces a *Palampore*, or calico bedcover. The ground is formed of interlaced branches and foliage with peacocks and various birds arranged in a balanced position. The cotton was first sized with buffalo milk to keep the color from running. The design was drawn on paper and punched on the

Fig. 757. Indian Textile Design. (After Coomaraswamy)

Fig. 758. Indian Brocade. (After Coomaraswamy)

prepared cloth. Some of the colors were painted in by hand; others, especially the blue, were dyed so that the color would be more permanent. To do this, all the parts except those to be colored blue were covered with wax, and the entire piece put into the dye pot. The wax was then removed with boiling water, and successive colors added with paint or dye. In a repeat pattern, woodblock stamps were sometimes used. The colors of the old Indian cottons are very lasting, and their soft tones of rose, blue, and blue-green have been acquired through time and frequent washing.

In some of the woven fabrics (FIGS. 757, 758) beauty of fitting design was obtained by means of the same attitude toward natural appearance that characterized the jewelry. Simplification of form was carried to the point where abstract design was paramount and the bird or animal form suggested only.

One other kind of textile needs mention, the *Cashmere* (FIG. 756). The weavers of Cashmere, in northern India, well up in the Himalayas, used goat's wool for these shawls, weaving them on small looms in long strips, which they sewed together so skillfully that the seaming is scarcely perceptible. The characteristic motif is the pine pattern, probably originating in the cypress tree of Persian art, while the ground or border is filled with small floral designs. The beauty of color and design in these shawls is equaled by the supreme skill shown in the weaving.

F. SUMMARY

The greatest art of India, whether a building, a statue, a fresco, or a piece of gold work, was hieratic and strictly obedient to accepted canons of technique and representation. The artist was a "pious craftsman" who "should understand the Atharva Veda, the thirty-two Śilpa Śastras, and the Vedic mantras by which the deities are invoked. He should be one who wears a sacred thread, a necklace of holy beads, and a ring of kuśa grass on his finger; delighting in the worship of God, faithful to his wife, avoiding strange women, piously acquiring a knowledge of various sciences, such a one is indeed a craftsman. . . . The painter must be a good man, no sluggard, not given to anger; holy, learned, self-controlled, devout and charitable." [1] Convention was partly a natural tendency of race and partly a canonical requirement; and though it determined the outward form of expression, it really only provided the craftsman with a general mode or instrument by means of which he could suitably express his own convincing experiences.

An appreciation of Indian, in fact of all Oriental, art presupposes an acceptance of the principle that great art is not necessarily an imitation or illusion of nature, but that a generalized, conventional, or symbolic representation of man and of nature can express both the form and the spiritual forces that dominate it. Western, that is, European, art on the whole has followed the canon of the representation of nature, yet has produced great art wherever the artists have been able to be selective and to reproduce nature in its universal aspects as expressive of a controlling spirit within. At times Western art has approached the Eastern ideal of generalization, convention, and spirituality, as in the best Byzantine mosaics, and the paintings of Simone Martini and Botticelli. In fact, the Hindu author Dr. Coomaraswamy quotes from the writings of Leonardo in speaking of the art of his own country: "That figure is most worthy of praise which by its action best expresses the passion that animates it." The difference between the art of East and West is not so great as it appears to be at first sight,

[1] From the Śilpa Śastras, or the canonical books of the artificer (Śilpan), quoted by Coomaraswamy in *The Dance of Śiva*, p. 26, by permission of the Sunwise Turn. Compare, in spirit and attitude toward work, the treatise of the monk Theophilus, p. 297.

but is rather a difference of emphasis, the West concentrating more upon the visual aspect, the East upon a conventional or abstract expression of the inner, dominating passion.

BIBLIOGRAPHY

Anand Mulk Raj, *The Hindu View of Art*, London, 1933

Baker, G. P., *Calico Painting and Printing in the East Indies in the XVIIth and XVIIIth Centuries*, London, 1921

Bezemer, T. J., *Indonesian Arts and Crafts*, The Hague, 1931?

Bhagavad-gita, tr. by L. D. Barnett, Macmillan, 1905 (Temple Classics)

Bhagavad-gita, tr. by A. W. Ryder, University of Chicago Press, 1929

Binyon, Laurence, *The Court Painters of the Grand Moguls*, Oxford Press, 1921

Birdwood, Sir G. C. M., *The Industrial Arts of India*, London, 1880, 2 vols.

Brown, Percy, *Indian Painting*, 2d ed., Oxford Press, 1929

—— —— *Indian Painting under the Mughals*, Oxford, 1924

Burlingame, E. W., tr., *Buddhist Parables*, Yale University Press, 1922

Cohn, William, *Indische Plastik*, Berlin, 1922

Coomaraswamy, A. K., *The Arts and Crafts of India and Ceylon*, LeRoy Phillips, 1914

—— —— *Buddha and the Gospel of Buddhism*, Putnam, 1916

—— —— *The Dance of Śiva*, new ed., Sunwise Turn, 1925

—— —— *History of Indian and Indonesian Art*, Weyhe, 1927

—— —— *The Indian Craftsman*, London, 1909

—— —— *Mediaeval Sinhalese Art*, London, 1909

—— —— *Rajput Painting*, Oxford Press, 1916, 2 vols.

—— —— *The Transformation of Nature in Art*, Harvard University Press, 1934

Dutt, Toru, *Ancient Ballads and Legends of Hindustan*, Scribner & Welford, 1885

Fa-heen, *Travels of Fa-hsien (339–414 A.D.)*; *or, Record of the Buddhistic Kingdoms*, tr. by H. A. Giles, Macmillan, 1923

Fischer, Otto, *Die Kunst Indiens, Chinas und Japans*, Berlin, 1928

Frazer, R. W., *Indian Thought, Past and Present*, Stokes, 1916

Grousset, René, *The Civilizations of the East*, tr. by C. A. Phillips, Knopf, 1931, Vols. I–II

Grünwedel, Albert, *Buddhist Art in India*, tr. by A. C. Gibson, London, 1901

Havell, E. B., *The Ancient and Medieval Architecture of India*, Scribner, 1915

—— —— *A Handbook of Indian Art*, London, Dutton, 1921

—— —— *The Himalayas in Indian Art*, London, 1924

—— —— *The Ideals of Indian Art*, Dutton, 1912; new ed., 1921

—— —— *Indian Architecture: Its Psychology, Structure, and History*, Scribner, 1913

—— —— *Indian Sculpture and Painting*, 2d ed. rev., London, 1928

India Society, *Ajanta Frescoes*, Oxford Press, 1915 (See also Marshall below.)

Jataka Tales, ed. by H. T. Francis and E. J. Thomas, Macmillan, 1916

Kalidasa, *Translations of Shakuntala, and Other Works*, by A. W. Ryder, Dutton, 1913 (Everyman's Library)

Kramrisch, Stella, *Indian Sculpture*, Oxford Press, 1933

Macdonald, Frederika, *The Iliad of the East*, new ed., Lane, 1908

Marshall, Sir John, and others, *Bagh Caves*, London, for the India Society, 1927

Monier-Williams, Sir Monier, *Indian Wisdom*, 4th ed., London, 1893

Mukul Chandra Dey, *My Pilgrimages to Ajanta and Bagh*, Doran, 1925

Museum of Fine Arts, Boston, *Synopsis of History*, Museum, 1922

Nivedita Sister (M. E. Noble), and Coomaraswamy, A. K., *Myths of the Hindus and Buddhists*, Holt, 1914

Oman, J. C., *The Great Indian Epics: The Stories of the Ramayana and the Mahabharata*, London, 1899

Smith, V. A., *A History of Fine Art in India and Ceylon*, rev. by K. de B. Codrington, Oxford Press, 1930

—— —— *Oxford History of India*, rev. by S. M. Edwardes, Oxford Press, 1928

Watt, Sir George, *Indian Art at Delhi, 1903*, London, 1904

With, Karl, *Java*, abr. ed., The Hague, 1922

CHAPTER XXVI

Chinese Art

A. HISTORICAL BACKGROUND

In studying Chinese art we are dealing with a people whose native conservatism has preserved their fundamental traditions for more than four thousand years — a unique instance in the history of civilizations. To be sure, foreign influences have entered China and become powerful, but eventually they have been absorbed or assimilated by the truly Chinese thought and action.

China is vast both in population and in geographic extent, a land of probably more than four hundred million people, with an area, including Tibet, Chinese Turkestan (Sinkiang), Mongolia, and Manchukuo, of more than twice the size of the United States, though China proper includes a little less than half this area (Fig. 759). The fertile eastern plains are traversed by two great river systems that have their rise in the mountains of the west. The Hwang Ho, or Yellow River, with swift current brings down great quantities of silt that is still building up the alluvial plains, now providing rich agricultural lands, now destroying farms and people with its floods and erratic changes of course. The Yangtze Kiang, or Blue River, through its navigability serves as a great artery of commerce. As one would expect in so large a country, there is great variety of climate, vegetation, language, and custom. North China, centering about Peiping, has a cool, dry climate and many stretches of plain; South China, centering at Canton, is moist and tropical, and the mountains near by afford a summer refuge from the enervating heat. To the west and north are vast areas of desert plateau. Agriculture forms the economic basis of life; even in the mountainous regions small patches of tillable land are intensively cultivated. The natural resources are enormous — mines of gold and other metal, quarries, "jade mountains," and formerly great forests, now destroyed.

Fig. 759. The Far East.

The old civilization centered in the valley of the Hwang Ho in the Shensi province, and comprised perhaps one-fifth of present China. The people, when not at war, were primarily agricultural, and for this reason interested in the powers of nature — the sky, the stars, the wind, and the rain. About these powers their religion centered. The dragon, in varying forms one of the most important motifs in Chinese art, and the emblem of the emperor, possibly had its origin in the great alligators that infested the rivers and early became objects of worship, symbolizing the coming of spring and rain. Likewise the phoenix, because of its fabulous renewal of life from its own ashes, symbolized the sun and warmth that brings about the ever recurrent life in nature.

Added to nature worship were two fundamentals in this early civilization which have persisted as basic elements of Chinese culture. First, the social basis, the unit of which was the family and not the individual. The customs of one's ancestors constituted the established law, and the perpetuation of the family was the vital necessity. To these the rights and freedom of the individual were sacrificed. He was but one link in the social chain; and the chain unbroken was paramount. Such an attitude fostered the second fundamental, which was a pious reverence for the dead, a continual looking to the past rather than to the future, and an acceptance of the past as the ultimate authority. The result of such a culture was unity and harmony; and, in art, an expression that was racial rather than individual.

Early Chinese culture reached a climax in the Chou dynasty (1122–255 B.C.).[1] The social system that had been evolving for many centuries was ready to be formulated by the early fifth century B.C., synchronizing with cultural climaxes in Persia, Greece, and India. This formulation was the work of Confucius (551–479 B.C.). While Confucianism is frequently classed as a religion, it is neither a religion nor a philosophy, but a social and ethical system that aims to secure a stable society by regulating human relationships. Its ideal is communism, as worked out among an agricultural people. The affairs of everyday life, that is, right conduct in human society, even to such details as "the right sort of a bonnet to wear or the most genteel way to lie in bed," are so regulated by law and custom that a harmonious and peaceful non-individualistic society results.

Meanwhile, in the valley of the Yangtze Kiang, the "land of thorns," lived the "jungle barbarians," of a different race and a different conception of life. Among them grew up a sect known as the Taoists, that is, followers of the Tao, the impersonal force or principle identified with nature. These dwellers of the Blue River had an intense love of nature, of the mountains, rivers, mists, and clouds that are characteristic of that part of China. They claimed as their founder Lao Tzu (570?–490 B.C.), a contemporary of Confucius but a teacher who recognized the individual to a far greater extent, for he taught that the self must be recognized in order to be brought into harmony with the great impersonal force permeating the universe that was the ultimate good.

---

[1] Chinese civilization may be traced back to about 3000 B.C. The important periods are as follows:

Hsia dynasty	2205–1766 B.C.
Shang dynasty	1766–1122
Chou dynasty	1122–255
Ts'in dynasty	255–206
Han dynasty	206 B.C.–221 A.D.
Wei and the Six dynasties	221–618
T'ang dynasty	618–907
Sung dynasty	960–1280
Yüan or Mongol dynasty	1280–1368
Ming dynasty	1368–1644
Ts'ing or Manchu dynasty	1644–1911

The spelling and the dates used in this chapter are those of H. A. Giles. For maps illustrating the geographic extent of China in the various dynasties, and the old trade routes, see E. H. Parker, *China*, 2d ed. rev., Dutton, 1924.

While these two ideals were taking root among the Chinese, the Ts'in, a Tatar people who were living on the boundaries and serving the Chou as horseherds and charioteers, finally became the dominating power and the king of Ts'in became the first emperor of China (246 B.C.). The situation is analogous to that of the Tatar slaves of the Muhammadans, who eventually became the Mameluke rulers of Egypt. The Ts'in consolidated the empire, set up a strongly centralized government, built the Great Wall as a protection against the Mongolian nomads, and, in order to abolish local patriotism burned the written books. They also gave to the country the name by which we know it — China, which is Ts'in, or Chin, land. They, in turn, were overcome by the Han, who by dividing the land set up a feudal state. The Han were the great supporters of Confucian ideals, and established Confucian writings as the exclusive classical literature of China. Under the Han, China expanded westward to protect itself against the barbarous tribes of central Asia and also to keep open the great trade routes over which its silks and other products were carried west even to the Roman Empire.

These highways were most important in the history of Chinese civilization. Along them traders, pilgrims, and armies traveled between eastern and western Asia. While in China proper the native culture had been developing until it had formed established traditions, over these highways the Buddhist faith was slowly making its way as the Buddhist monks and missionaries established their monasteries farther and farther eastward, especially in eastern Turkestan, which had become a Chinese protectorate. Here in the oases that formed a chain of cities across the desert plateaus the religion of India met the culture of China, and the fusion of the two formed the basis of the great art of China.

Buddhism, during the thousand years since its founding, had developed into something much more comprehensive than the simple teaching of Shakyamuni. As a strongly missionary religion, its conception of salvation included the whole universe; and in this aspect perhaps even more important than the Buddha were the Bodhisattvas, particularly Avalokiteshvara, the Lord of Pity, who under the name Kuan Yin became one of the most important of the Chinese and Japanese Buddhist deities. With well-established traditions, China was ready for the stimulation that the emotionalism and mysticism of Buddhism could give it. The ground had been prepared by the Taoists, whose ideas were somewhat akin to those of the Buddhists. We read of pilgrims such as Fa-heen (or Fa-hsien) traveling through India (399–414 A.D.) visiting sacred places, learning of the faith, and collecting literature about it. The translation of the Indian idea into a Chinese mode of expression we see developing in Turkestan. But its full assimilation and ultimate expression took place in China proper in the T'ang dynasty (618–907), a golden age in all the arts — painting, sculpture, metalwork, poetry, music. Toward the end of the T'ang period, a conservative reaction set in against Buddhism and other religions that had secured a foothold, and it developed into a revolution that demanded a return to the Confucian system. The success of the revolutionists (845) brought about the destruction of temples and monasteries with their great series of frescoes, and general ruin of all works of art; and this is why so little real T'ang art has survived. Another reaction in favor of Buddhism restored many of the temples and monasteries in the tenth century, but by that time most of the paintings were irretrievably lost.

The second golden age of Chinese art, following closely upon the T'ang, was the Sung (960–1280), a period perhaps analogous to our Renaissance, in that both ages produced great statesmen, philosophers, poets, art critics, painters.[1] Like the Renaissance, the Sung dynasty found its ideal in earlier periods, as we see in the deep study that the commentators made of the canons of Confucius, and in the Chou motifs that we find on the slender, typically Sung-shaped bronzes. In this period, however, philosophy, poetry, and painting together produced the finest of the Chinese landscape paintings.

An important source of inspiration of this art was Zen Buddhism. Zen, derived from the Indian word meaning meditation in supreme repose, was brought to China by an Indian prince in the sixth century and, since many of its ideas were close in spirit to those of the Taoists, took deep root especially in southern China. "Their [Zen Buddhists'] training was centered on the methods of that self-control which is the essence of true freedom. Deluded human minds groped in darkness, because they mistook the attribute for the substance. Even religious teachings were misleading, in so far as they set up semblances for realities. This thought was often illustrated by the simile of monkeys attempting to seize the reflection of the moon in water; for each effort to snatch at the silvery image could but ruffle the mirroring surface, and end in destroying not only the phantom moon but also themselves. . . . Freedom, once attained, left all men to revel and glory in the beauties of the whole universe. They were then one with nature, whose pulse they felt beating simultaneously within themselves, whose breath they felt themselves inhaling and exhaling in union with the great world-spirit.[2]

[1] It was the southern Sung capital, now Hangchow, which Marco Polo visited.
[2] Kakuzo Okakura, *Ideals of the East*, Dutton, 1921, p. 162, by permission of the publishers.

Fig. 760. Palace. The Forbidden City, Peiping.

Fig. 761. Temple of Heaven. Peiping. XVIII cent.

"The fundamental principle of . . . Zen Buddhism may be summed up in the expression that *the universe is the scripture of Zen.* . . . Actual scripture is worthless in the letter, and only valuable for that to which it leads; and to that goal there are other guides than the written page or the spoken word. It is related, for example, of the sage Hüen Sha that he was one day prepared to deliver a sermon to an assembled congregation, and was on the point of beginning, when a bird was heard to sing very sweetly close by; Hüen Sha descended from his pulpit with the remark that the sermon had been preached. . . .

"It is the very heart of 'culture' and religion to recognize the eternal, not as obscured but as revealed by the transient, to see infinity in the grain of sand, the same unborn in every birth, and the same undying in every death. These thoughts find constant expression in the poetry and art inspired by Zen thought. The Morning Glory, for example, fading in an hour, is a favorite theme of the Japanese poet and painter. What are we to understand by the poem of Matsunaga Teitoku?

" 'The morning glory blooms but for an hour, and yet it differs not
    at heart
From the giant pine that lives for a thousand years.'

"It is the same with the pine as with the morning glory, but as the life of the latter is shorter, it illustrates the principle in a more striking way. The giant pine does not ponder on its thousand years, nor the

morning glory on its life of a single
day. Each does simply what it
must. Certainly the fate of the
morning glory is other than that
of the pine, yet their destiny is
alike in this, that they fulfil the
will of Providence, and are content. Matsunaga thought his heart
was like their heart, and that was
why he made that poem on the
morning glory." [1]

The Sung were overthrown by
an invasion of the Mongols, who,
under Jenghiz Khan and his son
Kublai Khan, set up the Yüan or
Mongol dynasty (1280–1368). This
was in turn supplemented by the
Ming (1368–1644), which looked
to the T'ang for its inspiration and
created some admirable works in
the spirit of T'ang but lacked its
depth and grandeur. Ming was
an age of prolific, technically bril-

Fig. 762. Pagoda. Near Peiping.

liant accomplishment, especially in painting and porcelain; and with
its passing the days of the great art of China were over.

B. ARCHITECTURE

The uniformity of Chinese architecture well illustrates the natural
conservatism of the race, for one type of building has served all needs,
religious and secular, public and private. Plan, materials, constructional system, general design, and arrangement into groups have remained relatively constant for centuries. As in Japanese architecture,
which is closely related to that of China, every building was closely
related to nature, was a symbol of nature's orderly processes, and in
form was closely tied to nature's forms. When once the Chinese had
evolved a type of building elastic enough to fulfill various functions
and at the same time expressive of their ideal, he saw no reason for
changing what had become a satisfying tradition — a point of view
similar to that of the Egyptian toward his pylon temple.

Chinese architecture is primarily an architecture of wood, although

[1] Coomaraswamy, *Buddha and the Gospel of Buddhism*, pp. 254 ff., by permission of
G. P. Putnam's Sons.

stone and brick were used in substructures, for walls and bridges, for balustrades and ornamentation, and for a few buildings, notably pagodas and gateways.

The most striking feature of the design (FIG. 760) is the broadly projecting curved [1] roof whose expanse, conspicuous because the entrance is on the long side, repeats the broad earth to which the building clings. Sometimes this roof is single; frequently it is double, that is, on two levels, the upper level supported by interior columns not visible from the outside. The construction consists of columns, tie beams, and brackets, and an open timber roof covered with tiles laid in beds of mortar. The walls are not functional but merely fill in the space between the columns. Horizontality is the dominant note in the design and any extensions consist of horizontal projections very much like those of the Egyptian when he added courts and hypostyle halls to his original temple.

Ornament and color are especially important and of great splendor. The approaches and the balustrades of the terrace are elaborately carved. The roof tiles of royal buildings are yellow, the imperial color in China. Sometimes the tiles are blue or green; and the choice, determined by strict laws, is indicative of the rank of the owner and symbolic in meaning. The ridgepoles are decorated with dragons, phoenixes, and grotesques, as if to break the long lines as well as to ward off evil spirits. The columns, the beams, and the undersides of the projecting roofs and the interior are elaborately ornamented with gold and vermilion, carvings, lacquer, and inlay.

The *Temple of Heaven* (FIG. 761) well illustrates symbolism in Chinese architecture. Its Chinese name means "Temple of Prayer for the Year," for here each spring the Emperor went to offer sacrifices and prayer for a propitious year not only to heaven but to the imperial forefathers, to the sun, moon, and stars, and to the spirits of nature in the winds, the clouds, and the rain. Here again color and form are determined by symbolism. As blue is the color of heaven, so the tiles of the temple are a deep cobalt and during the ceremonies of the spring sacrifice blue dominates the interior, for the ceremonial vessels are of blue porcelain, the worshipers are clad in blue; in fact a blue tone is cast over everything by Venetian blinds made of blue glass which cover all the doors and windows. Likewise the unusual circular shape of the temple is symbolic of the spherical appearance of the heavens. The temple is an imposing structure, its triple roof with gilded ball

---

[1] The origin of the curved roof, often with upturned corners, is a moot question. The sagging tent cloth of prehistoric days, primitive thatched huts, and the result of overlapping horizontal layers of bamboo — an early building material — have been suggested.

pointing with assurance toward the heavens. This impressiveness is increased particularly by the location of the building; for it stands upon an elevation, surrounded by encircling marble terraces, and broad stairways set at the cardinal points of the compass, with ornamental balustrades.

A characteristic feature of Chinese landscape is the pagoda, a Buddhistic structure, some of whose forms originated in the umbrella, that symbol of royalty in India which usually terminated the stupa, often in a multiple form (FIG. 724). These pagodas often formed a part of the temple group, but frequently served as memorials without religious significance. Some of these pagodas are of a vigorous, massive type, with as many as thirteen stories. Others are more slender (FIG. 762), with elegance of proportion, interesting variety in the shape of the three stories, and rich ornamentation. One of the famous "porcelain" pagodas is faced with glazed tiles in five colors — deep purplish blue, rich green, yellow, red, and turquoise-blue — so that the effect as it stands in an open place surrounded with greenery is most charming. It is called "porcelain," though incorrectly, because of the glazed tile facing, a method of ornamentation that we saw carried out so effectively in Egypt and Babylonia-Assyria, and it is quite probable that the Chinese of the Han dynasty, as they pushed their boundaries westward, learned of its use from these western peoples.

Another characteristic architectural form in China is the gateway, the *pailou*, made of wood with tile roofs, or of stone imitating the wooden structure. These gateways appear to be derived from the gates of the stupas in India, but the silhouette of the upper part has been determined by the typical curved line of Chinese roof. Unlike the Indian stupa gate, these arches are not necessarily entrances but may be independent structures, erected only by special permission as memorials to distinguished Chinese, both dead and living.

C. PAINTING

The chief forms of Chinese painting are frescoes, hanging scrolls (*kakemono*), and long scrolls (*makimono*). The frescoes, which formed great series of wall decoration, majestic and hieratic like the *Ajanta Frescoes* and the early Christian mosaics, have disappeared, as we have explained, from China proper and we can judge of them only through the wall paintings of Turkestan and Japan, which reflect something of their nature. Most of the Chinese painting that has survived belongs to the second and third classes, the panels and scrolls. The framed picture, with which we are so familiar, is practically unknown in the Orient.

Fig. 763. Ku K'ai-chih. Lady Feng and the Bear. Detail of the Admonitions of the Instructress. Probably a T'ang copy. Late IV or early V cent. A.D. British Museum, London. (British Museum)

Another important difference between Eastern and Western painting lies in the method of exhibiting it. The Chinese panel or scroll was not kept on view continuously, but formed a part of the family treasure to be exhibited for a short time in a place of honor or brought out for a brief period of enjoyment or for some connoisseur to examine and to affix his seal.[1] It was then rolled up and put away in a place of safety. Thus the place and use of paintings in China was perhaps analogous to that of rare books with us.

Of early Chinese painting nothing remains. Something of its nature we learn from a makimono in the British Museum attributed to Ku K'ai-chih [2] (fourth and fifth centuries A.D.), whom the Chinese writers consider one of their great painters. The subject of the painting was taken from a Chinese writer, who explains the principles that an instructress in the royal palace would teach to the princesses under her care. This we know from the inscriptions that accompany the paintings. The detail reproduced on FIG. 763 represents the Lady Feng rescuing the Emperor from a bear that had broken loose from the circus ring. At the right sits the Emperor, perfectly calm, surrounded by his courtiers; at the right two men are attacking the bear, in front of which fearlessly stands Lady Feng, her lithe figure with its draperies billowing about her feet — a perfect epitome of courageous self-sacri-

[1] See the seals of about fifty former owners or famous connoisseurs on the scroll in the British Museum, attributed to Ku K'ai-chih.

[2] For interesting stories of this painter see H. A. Giles, *An Introduction to the History of Chinese Pictorial Art*, 2d ed. rev., London, 1918, p. 18; and Arthur Waley, *Introduction to the Study of Chinese Painting*, Scribner, 1923, p. 45.

fice; for that was the lesson that this episode sought to inculcate in the minds of the princesses. The secular subject is interesting, but perhaps the most striking characteristic is the great amount of expression with a minimum of means. There is a sense of structure and movement in the figures; a great deal of expression in the hands and faces; and rhythmic sweep of sure, unfaltering line. All is expressed by line, with no shading, no expression of depth, with little color, and with suppressed detail and accessories. The technique has strongly influenced the character of the work. The figures are painted on silk with a brush in Chinese ink, which is not the ink with which we are familiar, but a solid kind that the Chinese made by burning certain plants and combining the soot thus obtained with glue or oil. It was then molded into a cake and dried. If a particular kind of surface was desired, other ingredients were added — pulverized oyster shells, for example, to obtain a dead finish. The process of making the finest ink was a secret, often a carefully guarded heritage. To use this ink, the painter moistened the cake on a slab, thus obtaining a semifluid. Great skill was needed both in rubbing the cake and in applying the ink.

This ink was used for writing was well as for painting. Writing, among the Chinese, was one of the highest arts (FIG. 764). The characters were made with the brush, not the pen, and required a skill attained only through long years of practice. The hand did not hold the brush as we hold a pen with the thumb and two fingers to be manipulated by wrist movement, but vertically in the fist, the whole arm as well as the wrist guiding the movement from the shoulder. The writer or painter did not work at a table or an easel, but sitting on his heels and knees with his work spread out on the floor before him. The ink might be used thick or thin; and the strokes were now bold and strong, now abrupt, now diminishing to a hair line, and sometimes of surpassing delicacy. The characters were originally pictographs, like the Egyptian, which in the process of a long evolution were so highly simplified that they became abstract symbols of the original form. In the mental make-up of the calligraphist, then, abstract form was an important element. The greatest painters were poets, philosophers, or priests, and the same type of literary training furnished the background in the education of all; so Chinese painting is akin to literature. And, as the same materials were used to write poems and to paint mountain scenery, we may expect to find in painting the same simplification and abstraction as in calligraphy. Of one famous painter a Chinese writer said, "I can taste in the poem something of the picture's flavor; and in the picture I see something of the poem." Another important fact of technique is that the figures and landscapes were usually painted on specially prepared silk or paper,

Fig. 764. Tung Yüan. Landscape. Sung dynasty, late

and when once the stroke of the brush had touched the surface, it could not be altered. This demanded of the painter not only perfect control in handling the brush, but also a careful thinking out of his work before he applied the ink.

Brush strokes are the elemental, visual means of expression. Each stroke has its character and vitality, and each is an embodiment of that which the creative mind and spirit are trying to objectify. "Brush strokes . . . indicate the movement of the mind, its direction, its speed, its duration, its strength. . . . Expression in a picture, as in writing, is the result of the action of the mind travelling through the brush. . . . Perfect control of the brush coupled with fine thought makes a picture worthy." [1]

Thus an accomplished school of painting had developed early in China, of which Ku K'ai-chih is the climax. In the meantime the Buddhist faith was slowly moving eastward, as we have explained, to fuse with the Chinese traditions. This we see accomplished in the paintings of *Paradise* that have come from the monastery caves of Turkestan. These paintings represent that paradise where Amida Buddha lived in gorgeous surroundings, attended by Bodhisattvas and believers. [2] Paradise and its pleasures were conceived in terms of an

[1] Kojiro Tomita, "Brush Strokes in Far Eastern Painting," *Eastern Art*, Vol. III (1931), pp. 29 ff.
[2] Amida, or Amitabha, Buddha means the God of Boundless Light. This worship may have originated among the sun-worshipers of Parthia, for Buddhism, as it penetrated northwestern India, there received some Greek and Iranian influences (see p. 589, note 1), which it carried along into Turkestan. In Turkestan we see a mixed culture. Manichaeans, Buddhists, and Christians were living together peaceably; yet Buddhism was the dominating element.

X cent. Museum of Fine Arts, Boston. (Boston Museum)

earthly court of great splendor and joy. A lofty mood permeates all the figures, "the spell of a single mood of immaterial felicity and peace." In the drawing there is the same firmness and delicate grace that characterized the work of Ku K'ai-chih.

These *Paradise* panels give us some hint of the lost T'ang painting, which was a fusion of the powerful native Chinese tradition and the energizing spirit of Buddhism, for Buddhism had brought to China a new conception of deity. Buddha in his contemplative aspect, with his conquest over self and also his universal love and pity for suffering mankind as expressed in the Bodhisattva Kuan Yin, was particularly appealing. What we learn from literary sources, added to examples of Japanese art which we know took T'ang art as their prototype, tells us that this was a hieratic art of "tingling austerity," concerned not with the visual facts of natural appearance but with those highly simplified, essential aspects of form that could express that inner life whose fervor was so intense that it had become calm, somber, and majestic.

Chinese writers tell us much of the numerous painters of the T'ang age, among whom the greatest was Wu Tao-tzu [1] (born about 700). His most important works were the series of frescoes in the Buddhist temples that were destroyed in the revolution.[2]

Another aspect of Buddhism that influenced Chinese painting profoundly was its attitude toward nature. We saw in India how Bud-

[1] For stories of Wu Tao-tzu, see Giles, *op. cit.*, pp. 47 ff; and Waley, *op. cit.*, pp. 12 ff.

[2] Probably none of the great T'ang painting is extant. The situation is analogous to that of Greek painting, which we can study only as we find reflections of it in the vases and Roman copies.

Fig. 765. Ma Yüan. Landscape. Ming dynasty. Museum of
Fine Arts, Boston. (Boston Museum)

dhism recognized all life as a unit. Some of the poets and philosophers
of southern China had already realized something of this kinship with
nature; and their spirit, intensely augmented by the powerful Buddhist
belief in the universal brotherhood of all forms of life, laid the foundation of those schools of landscape-painting culminating in the Sung
period that have been one of the great accomplishments of Chinese
art.

The Chinese had not only an intimate knowledge of the facts of
nature but also a deep love for it. They "did not merely love nature
they were in love with her." Kuo Hsi, a painter who was born about
1020 A.D., wrote: "Wherein lies the reason that good men so much
love landscape? It is because amid orchards and hills a man has ever
room to cultivate his natural bent; because streams and rocks never
fail to charm the rambler who goes whistling on his way. It is because
fishing and wood-gathering are the natural vocations of the hermit
or recluse, hard by where the flying birds and chattering apes have
made their home. Noise and dust, bridles and chains — these are what

man's nature is ever weary of. Haze and mists, saints and fairies —
for these man's nature pines eternally, and pines in vain." [1]

The Chinese word for landscape means "mountains and rivers."
This is not surprising to anyone who has looked over a considerable
number of Chinese paintings, so frequently are these the subject matter.
Let us take for study, as a typical example, a painting of Tung Yüan
(FIG. 764). It is one of those long scrolls peculiar to Chinese and Japanese painting, the origin of which is uncertain, though the plausible
suggestion has been made that this long roll, the original form of the
book, is an imitation of geographic maps, as the same word in Chinese
is used for a map and for a picture or design of any kind. The scroll
is not unrolled and viewed as a unit, but is rolled up at one end while
it is unrolled at the other, so that only a section of it is seen at one time.
Therefore the painting must have both unity in the parts and continuity in the whole, which demands extraordinary skill on the part
of the painter. As we slowly unroll the painting, there is spread out
before us a panorama of great spaciousness quite characteristic of the
bold mountainous landscapes of China. In the foreground is a sparsely
wooded stretch with a pavilion and at the left a river; in the background rise rugged, majestic mountains, receding into the distance;
and the valleys between the crags are filled with mists. But it is very
unlike a map, for it is not certain facts about this mountainous country
that hold us. Visual facts are there — the structure of the rocks, the
mighty upward thrust of the mountains, their mass and solidity; the
form of the tree trunks, and the shapes and masses of foliage that
weave interesting patterns against the distance; the enveloping of all
forms in atmosphere, and the precise values in the trees and mountains
as they recede into the illimitable distance. But mere visual truth is
subordinate to the mood, to the emotional power that fills the picture.
We can easily imagine how Tung Yüan from a somewhat elevated
position like that of the spectator sat meditating upon this scene, as
we see a sage meditating in FIG. 765. Days and perhaps months he
spent in this way until, as the accidental and ephemeral appearance
was lost sight of, he *felt* and so he saw the scene as the interpretation
of a rare, noble mood of a harmonious and infinite nature. So attuned
was he finally to this poetic mood, and so trained was his hand technically to follow his mind and his emotions, which he quickly, spontaneously, and unerringly transferred to the paper, a mood that is
close to that of music. This idea Dr. Laufer has expressed when he
says: "Such creations . . . no doubt belong to the greatest emanations
of art of all times. . . . The T'ang masters were not naturalists,
idealists, romanticists nor were they one-sidedly given to any of our

[1] Waley, *op. cit.*, p. 189, by permission of Chas. Scribner's Sons.

Fig. 766. Stone Reliefs of the Han dynasty.
(Chavannes)

Fig. 767. Winged Lion. From the Tomb of
Hsiao Hsiu, near Nanking. 518 A.D. (Segalen,
Mission Archéologique)

narrow -isms exclusively. They were, in the first place, symphonists in the sense of our music. . . . There is but one giant in our art to whom Wang Wei and Li Se-sün can be adequately compared, and that is Beethoven. The same lofty thoughts and emotions expressed by Beethoven . . . find an echo in the works of those Chinese painters. The Adagio of the Fifth Symphony is the text interpreting the noble transcendental spirit pervading the painted scenery of Li Se-sün, and the Pastoral Symphony is the translation into music of the *Wang ch'uan t'u*. We shall better appreciate Chinese painting, if we try to conceive it as having no analogy with our painting, but as being akin to our music. Indeed, the psychological difference of Chinese painting from our own mainly rests on the basis that the Chinese handle painting, not as we handle painting, but as we handle music, for the purpose of lending color to and evoking the whole range of sentiments and emotions of humanity. In depth of thought and feeling, the great T'ang masters, in their symphonic compositions, vie with Beethoven, and in line and color almost reach Mozart's eternal grace and beauty. . . . Chinese pictorial art, I believe, is painted music, with all its shades . . . of expressive modulation." [1]

[1] Berthold Laufer, "A Landscape of Wang Wei," *Ostasiatische Zeitschrift*, 1912, p. 54.

For the expression of the facts of nature, the Chinese had certain formulas that were taught as fundamentals of art education. For example, there were sixteen ways of drawing mountains, differing according to the geological formation, the flora, and the season — the sixteen "mountain wrinkles," the Chinese called them. The names of a few of them — "wrinkled like hemp fibers," "wrinkled like tangled hemp fibers," "wrinkled like a thunderhead," "wrinkled like eddying water," "wrinkled like horses' teeth" — reveal a keen observation of nature and also a direct, suggestive method of expressing the idea.[1] Likewise there were laws governing the painting of water. "In regard to painting moving waters, whether deep or shallow, in rivers or brooks, bays or oceans, Chinanpin [a Chinese teacher] declared it was impossible for the eye to seize their exact forms because they are ever changing and have no fixed definite shape, therefore they can not be sketched satisfactorily; yet, as moving water must be represented in painting, it should be long and minutely contemplated by the artist, and its general character — whether leaping in the brook, flowing in the river, roaring in the cataract, surging in the ocean or lapping the shore — observed and reflected upon, and after the eye and memory are both sufficiently trained and the very soul of the artist is saturated,

Fig. 768. Buddhist Votive Stele. Erected in 554 A.D., "as a means of securing the happiness and welfare of the donors, their ancestors, their posterity, their relations, and friends, the Emperor in particular and the Chinese people in general." Museum of Fine Arts, Boston. (Boston Museum)

as it were, with this one subject and he feels his whole being calm and composed, he should retire to the privacy of his studio and with the early morning sun to gladden his spirit there attempt to reproduce the movement of the flow; not by copying what he has seen . . . but by symbolizing according to certain laws what he feels and remembers." [2]

[1] For drawings to illustrate the sixteen ways, see essay by Sei-ichi Taki, *Kokka*, Pt. 196; Raphaël Petrucci, *Encyclopédie de la peinture chinoise*, Paris, 1918, pp. 134 ff.
[2] H. P. Bowie, *On the Laws of Japanese Painting*, Elder, 1911, p. 61, by permission of the publishers.

This quotation is valuable not only because it gives one a notion of the formulas that governed the painters, but also because it explains something of the way in which the Chinese painters worked. Meditation, that is, mental preparation, combined with a highly trained memory, played an important part in the creation of a painting. The great Wu Tao-tzu, a well-known story says, was ordered by the Emperor to paint for him one of his favorite scenes of river and mountain landscape. Thither the painter went. When he returned and was asked for his sketches, he replied, "I have it all in my heart."

Less panoramic than the scroll and perhaps even more expressive of the quintessence of mood and inner meaning are some of the small round album leaves such as the *Mountain Scene with a Sage Meditating* (FIG. 765). In the foreground a sage is reclining beneath the spreading branches of a gnarled tree, looking toward the precipitous towering cliffs that fill the background and gradually fade into the distance. A note of quiet meditation and of noble sentiment pervades the picture. The whole scene has been painted with a few skillful strokes. The composition is broad and free. Ma Yüan has arranged the elements of composition without crowding and has successfully balanced the mass on the right with the space on the left.

These paintings are as imaginative and evocative of mood as Chinese poems, examples of which are:

"On Lady's Table Mountain-top spring snows melt;
  By the roadside apricot-flowers bud on tender twigs.
  My heart is ready; I long to go. Yet when shall the day be?
  Sadly I watch the homeward coach roll over the field-bridge."
    — *Yang E-Shih* (about 800, written when detained in the city)

"From the thick bamboos the last rain-drops drip;
  On the high hill-top lingers the evening light."
    — *Hsia-Hou Shen* (8th century, 2nd half) [1]

This purpose on the part of the Chinese painters to emphasize the vital essence of things rather than the external appearance is particularly true of the paintings of flowers and birds. Probably no people have felt so deeply and so sympathetically as the Buddhists the unity and harmony of all animate life. The Zen Buddhists in particular arrived at an expression of this significance that is amazing in its intimate knowledge of form, its simplicity and subtlety. It is interesting to note that these lovers of nature did not personify its forms. The mountain, the bird, or the flower is an entity with its own attributes as individual, as majestic, or as delicately graceful as human

[1] Waley, *op. cit.*, pp. 193–94, by permission of Chas. Scribner's Sons.

life, and as important a member of the universe as man. Hence it was not necessary to visualize it in terms of man. Technically, these paintings of the Zen Buddhists are astonishing. Color was usually abandoned and ink only used, applied with a few quick but amazingly vital strokes. Rarely has the world seen an expression, so ephemeral and at the same time so quivering with life, accomplished with such a minimum of means.

D. SCULPTURE

Sculpture in ancient China, before the advent of Buddhism, seems to have functioned, as in ancient Egypt, to serve the dead. Such were the tomb figurines of clay gaily painted, spontaneous and freely characteristic representations of people and animals. Stone sculpture decorated the tombs, the pillars that formed a gateway to the path leading to the tomb, and the stone slabs set up along the walls of the anteroom of the burial chamber; while massive stone lions or chimeral figures stood guard at royal and princely tombs. In addition to the spirited figurines, the highly decorative Han reliefs are notable. Because of their strongly lineal character, they seem more like drawings or engravings with the background cut back slightly than like reliefs. The procession of mounted riders and carriages, which may represent the journey of the dead to the spirit world, is filled with vivacity and swift linear rhythms (FIG. 766). Of the guardian winged lions and chimeras, FIG. 767 with its full rounding forms, striding pose, strong curve of the head, open mouth, and long tongue, is imposing equally as related masses of ponderous stone and as an expression of power and energy.

The influence exerted by Buddhism upon sculpture was much the same as that upon painting — a fusing of the new ideas with the traditional native art, creating a product that was inherently Chinese. The preliminary stages are seen in colossal figures of Buddha and the Bodhisattvas carved in the caves along the routes over which Buddhists worked their way eastward. Associated with these purely Buddhist themes are non-Hindu details, ornaments, and themes. The fusion of these styles appears in a richly decorative votive stele (FIG. 768). Above the inscriptions that make a broad, firm base are four seals forming a square surmounted by a reliquary, four donors with their horses, worshipers, and lions. In the middle zone Buddha, with uplifted hand symbolic of his teaching, is seated in a canopied niche with two disciples, Bodhisattvas, and guardians. The upper zone contains Buddhas and Bodhisattvas under a canopy and scenes connected with the life of Buddha. The figures of the donors and the

Fig. 769. Maitreya. Limestone, originally painted. H. 6½ ft. Northern Wei dynasty, early V cent. A.D. Museum of Fine Arts, Boston. (Boston Museum)

reliquary in the two lower zones on the back and sides are incised and the ground cut back for contrast, the traditional Han style of decoration, while the Buddhist subjects in the middle and upper zones are carved in high relief, modeled, and show strong Indian influence.

A single figure which expresses the Hindu theme in a style strongly Chinese is a *Maitreya* (Fig. 769), the Bodhisattva who is destined to become the next Buddha. He is seated in an austerely frontal pose with legs crossed and hand uplifted in the traditional Indian pose of the teacher. The features are conventionally treated with planes sharply cut; except for the head and the arms, the figure is so flat that it gives one more the impression of relief than of the round. The drapery, plaited and girdled high, and the streamers of the cloak that cross in front in an almost geometrical pattern, fall over the pedestal in a conventional way, with feeling for sweeping, rhythmic pattern. Here is an archaic art which by the use of symbols and conventions, with no attempt to create an illusion of natural appearance, makes all the more emphatic the spiritual fervor of the conception.

The evolution of these archaic forms into a classic climax took place in early T'ang. But even though the forms became full and rounding and the decorative details richly elegant, and though the poses relaxed from austere frontality into elegant and dignified grace (Fig. 770), the sculptors never surrendered their traditional ideal of conventions and abstract form to an attempt to copy nature. The cutting of the stone is expert, though it may lack the energy of the crisp carving of Wei art; the folds tend toward naturalism, and although they still form a rhythmic pattern it is a pattern that is not so tingling with life and meaning as in Wei.

The advance of the T'ang dynasty saw the rise of great schools of painting, a field of art in which the Chinese race attained a loftier expression than in sculpture. For some time sculpture maintained a serene and dignified majesty, lofty and impersonal. With the advent of the Sung dynasty, when Zen Buddhism was stimulating a great

Fig. 770. Kuan Yin. T'ang dynasty. Memorial Art Gallery, Rochester, New York. (Memorial Art Gallery)

Fig. 771. Kuan Yin. Sung dynasty. Buckingham coll., Art Institute of Chicago. (Art Institute)

expression in landscape painting but had little to offer the sculptor, the forms became more suavely elegant, less subordinate to an underlying abstract unity; more expressive of a delight with decorative detail for its own sake. Far less significant of spiritual energy, they became more human and naturalistic. Other mediums became popular; wood, for example, as seen in a *Kuan Yin* [1] (FIG. 771) which is carved from wood — a more popular medium than stone at this time — covered with gesso, and painted. The pose of royal ease is inherited from India (FIG. 738). The erect posture and the right arm, which supports the weight, give strength and dignity to the figure. The drapery falls naturalistically in broadly flowing curves, even entwining the arms as if to obtain additional curving lines. The pattern of the fine stuff of which the robe is made is indicated by gesso worked in relief, gilded and painted. The elaborate details — the intricate tiara, the heavy chain which hangs naturalistically, the bow — are subordinate but they tend to hold the attention and to interfere with that harmony of content and form which made the earlier sculpture so supreme.

[1] The Bodhisattva Avalokiteshvara, as his worship passed over into China under the name of Kuan Yin, assumed first a sexless and then gradually a feminine form.

E. MINOR ARTS

Fig. 772. Sacrificial Vessel. Bronze. L. 12⅞ in. Chou dynasty. Buckingham coll., Art Institute of Chicago. (Art Institute)

One of the earliest and at the same time most characteristic expressions of the Chinese race is bronze work, chiefly ceremonial vessels, used probably in the rites of ancestor worship. Their full significance is seen only in relation to their users, a people organized socially on the unit of the family whose reverence for ancestors is equal to that for winds, rains, and clouds, those manifestations of nature about which centers the worship of an agricultural people. These basic cultural factors suggest [1] the origins of the uses, shapes, and decorative motifs of the vessels and throw light upon the impression of deep significance and hieratic character that one feels in looking at them.

Something of this spirit we discern in the frequent inscriptions found on the bronzes, as on one of the bells that were used to summon the spirits of the departed, or the guests to the banquet, or to serve as one of the instruments of the orchestra: "I, Kuo-Shu Lü, say: Grandly distinguished was my illustrious father Hui Shu, with profound reverence he maintained a surpassingly bright virtue. He excelled alike in the rule of his own domain and in his liberal treatment of strangers from afar. When I, Lü, presumed to assume the leadership of the people and to take as my model the dignified demeanor of my illustrious father, a memorial of the event was presented at the Court of the Son of Heaven, and the Son of Heaven graciously honoured me with abundant gifts. I, Lü, humbly acknowledge the timely gifts of the Son of Heaven and proclaim their use in the fabrication for my illustrious father Hui Shu of this great sacrificial tuneful bell. Oh, illustrious father seated in majesty above, protect with sheltering wings us who are left here below. Peaceful and glorious, extend to me, Lü, abundant happiness! I, Lü, and my sons and grandsons for ten thousand years to come, will everlastingly prize this bell and use it in our ritual worship." [2]

[1] There is but little accurate knowledge concerning these bronzes, for though the Chinese themselves have great reverence for them, and early began to collect them, compile catalogues of them, and write treatises about them, their efforts are lacking in scientific accuracy.

[2] S. W. Bushell, *Chinese Art*, Brentano's, 1924, 2 vols., Vol. I, p. 73.

Fig. 773. Sacrificial Jar. Bronze. H. 7½ in. Shang dynasty. Parish-Watson coll., New York. (Parish-Watson)

Technically these bronzes stand in the first rank of bronze-working, a field in which the Chinese have been skillful from a remote antiquity. They were cast by the cire-perdue process, some

Fig. 774. Jade Bell. H. 8 in. Ch'ien-Lung period (1736–95) after Chou designs. Field Museum of Natural History, Chicago. (Field Museum)

of the early ones by a single casting, even when complicated in design; others in several parts to be welded together.

The finest bronzes belong to the early periods — the Shang, the Chou, and the Han dynasties. The sacrificial jar of Fig. 773 is strong and vigorous in shape, proportions, and decoration. The handles are an integral element in determining these proportions and by maintaining a continuous contour add great dignity to the form. The decoration, which is carefully scaled to its position, consists of a broad central band with a highly conventionalized animal face, probably mythological, and of finishing borders containing a tiger head and what seem to be conventionalized birds. While the meaning of these motifs is unknown, their decorative beauty and suitability are clear.

A shape that is unusual is a double sacrificial vessel (Fig. 772) which is rectangular with flaring top and bottom, both of which are the same in size and shape, with arched openings cut in each side. The two parts are so shaped that together, as in the illustration, they form a harmonious unit, or separately serve as two independent vessels. The rectangular shape is apparently derived from the basket that held the millet for the ancestor worship. The arched openings cut in the flaring top and bottom relieve the solidity, and with their strongly curved lines act as a foil to the predominant angularity of the design. On the short ends are conventionalized animal heads that serve as handles; the two small heads on the long sides that are attached to the upper half and project over the lower keep the parts from slipping. The en-

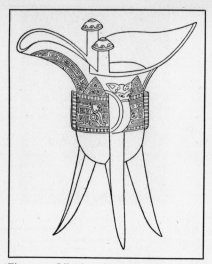

Fig. 775. Libation Cup. Shang dynasty, 1766–1122 B.C. (*Ostasiatische Zeitschrift*)

tire body of the vessel is incised with a meander pattern that, with its fret motif infinitely varied, gives a feeling of liveliness without obtruding or in any way interfering with the structural lines.

The meander or fret is a frequent motif of decoration in these bronzes. The fret in early Chinese art symbolized the elements, especially thunder and lightning. Small triangular patterns found at the top of a vase represented mountains and when filled with thunder and lightning motifs, mountains surrounded by clouds. Probably an all-over decoration based upon the fret represented a cloudy sky; the lanceolate pattern, the winds; and when eyes in the form of knobs were added, the Chinese saw the storm god against the background of a cloudy sky.

A shape frequently found is that of the libation cup (FIG. 775), which was used in the rites of Heaven and Earth and also in ancestor worship. Its shape not only is strong but shows fine proportions and an unusual unity between the parts, and continuity of structural line.

The shapes and decorative motifs early became fixed, and continued as traditions even after their meaning was lost, down to comparatively recent times, and were copied by the workers in jade (FIG. 774) and ceramics. One element of charm in these bronzes is accidental, for the beautiful blue, green, and iridescent color was not planned by the original artist but is due to the patina subsequently accreted.[1]

Another medium in which the Chinese made notable achievement is jade, which they obtained from the mountains of western China and from the rivers that had their rise near these quarries and washed the jade pebbles and boulders for some distance down their courses. Particularly fine boulders were kept in the temples, in early days, as precious relics, and some of these were carved in the eighteenth century into bells, vases, and bowls. Jade was used for personal orna-

---

[1] A patina is a crust that forms on a bronze during a long period of time because of the chemical action of the alloys that compose the bronze, and the atmosphere or material in which the article is buried. It may be thin or thick, rough or smooth, and of great variety of color.

ments, insignia, and charms, and also for vessels and utensils of various kinds; [1] it was valued particularly for its color and its texture.

Jade-carving is a very old art in China, going back to legendary times, and may possibly be traced to the work of the lapidary in early Babylonia as we saw it in the cylinder seals. The tools were few, simple, and even crude — saws for cutting and shaping the objects; iron disks and drills, worked by treadles, for carving it; and several kinds of abrasives for polishing, such as quartz, garnet, emery, and, hardest of all, ruby dust. These were applied with wood, leather, or gourd skin, for the entire surface, even in the deepest crevices, must be free from all irregularities and from all marks of the tools.

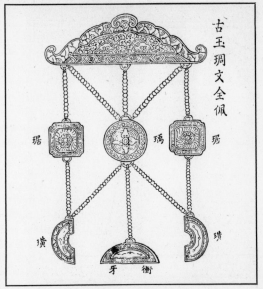

Fig. 776. Drawing of a Complete Jade Girdle Pendant. (Laufer)

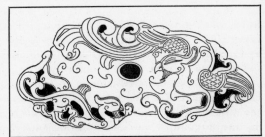

Fig. 777. Girdle Pendant. Jade. Han dynasty, 206 B.C.–221 A.D. (Drawing after Laufer)

The early jades, like the bronzes, were influenced by religious ideas and their decorations determined by religious and emotional symbolism. This is seen in the personal ornaments, perhaps the most interesting of which are the girdle pendants (FIG. 776). Seven pieces of jade formed the pendant, which tinkled as the bearer walked. Each was a token of love and friendship, as an old song says: "Who will give me a quince, I shall return to him a central side-ornament

---

[1] Something of this variety is suggested by reading the table of contents of a Chinese book on the subject, in one hundred volumes, quoted in Bushell, *op. cit.*, Vol. I, p. 132.

Fig. 778. Glazed Pottery Camel. H. 36 in.
T'ang dynasty. University Museum, Philadelphia.
(University Museum)

of fine jade for the girdle-pendant. It is not meant as an act of thanks, but I want to render our friendship everlasting. Who will give me a peach, I shall return to him the red jade *yao* . . . (with the same refrain). Who will give me a plum, I shall return to him the black jade ornament *kiu* . . . (with the same refrain)." [1] These ornaments were sometimes buried with the dead as emblems of the parting by death and also of an eternal love. Such a burial girdle ornament is seen in Fig. 777. On the right is a phoenix on a cloud form, looking down toward the long slender hydra, with a bird's head, on the lower left side; above, along the upper edge, cloud bands carved in long firm curves. Here, as in the bronzes, are simplification and conventionalization of form, virility of line, and harmony between the medium and the motif of decoration.

Something of the character of these early pieces we find in later examples such as a jade bell (Fig. 774) that is very close in shape to the Chou bronze bells, and, to a less degree, in its decoration. As jade is resonant, it was used both for single bells and for chimes, and in this form was a favorite gift for congratulation of any kind. Indeed, the Chinese phrase "to strike a musical stone" may be interpreted as "May blessings attend you." The bell was suspended by a silk cord from a wooden frame and, like the bronze bells, was struck with a hammer. This bell was carved from a single boulder of jade, and was hollowed out with a tubular drill, as the interior shows. The upper and lower edges are decorated with a fret pattern; the body contains a border with a highly conventionalized monster's head, similar to those found on the early bronzes (Fig. 773) but based upon sweeping curves rather than rectangular mass; below this is a border of leaf ornament, the larger motif being subdivided and filled with concen-

[1] Berthold Laufer, *Jade*, Field Museum of Natural History, Chicago, 1912, p. 198.

tric lines; on each side of the handle are dragons. The bold simplicity of the design reflects the Shang, Chou, and Han vessels.

The eighteenth century was a renaissance period when the artists looked to these ancient dynasties for their prototypes, imitating both the shapes and the motifs of the early work. The spacing of the borders, the confident firmness of line, the fine and at times even severe taste, the fitness of the design to the material — all this belongs to the

Fig. 779. Ting Porcelain Bowl. Sung dynasty. Art Institute of Chicago. (Art Institute)

long, deep-rooted tradition of the craftsmen. But there was lost much of the symbolism and hence the dynamic power that produced the great spontaneity and sincerity of the earlier work, and the result, though finely decorative, is not so convincing in its spirit. These eighteenth-century jades reveal a remarkable technical virtuosity; and they display, in their texture, the waxy luster that the Chinese call "mutton fat."

Ceramics is another field in which the Chinese have proved themselves master craftsmen and artists. It was an ancient art and its products peculiarly prized. In the Han age the potters fashioned simple sturdy shapes and covered them with a greenish glaze; in the T'ang they added more colors and produced a variety of shapes as well as tomb figurines of people, animals, birds, and various objects that were modeled with an especial feeling for clay, as well as with a sympathetic understanding of whatever was represented. These figurines were painted or glazed, not naturalistically, but conventionally with brown, yellow, or green glaze which streaked down the sides (FIG. 778). Royal patronage stimulated the production of ceramic wares. Some of the kilns produced for the imperial household alone and some of the famous wares were named after the emperors whom the kilns served. Shortly before the establishment of the Sung dynasty a ware was manufactured called Ch'ai, after the Emperor who ordered it. According to Chinese writers, the Emperor required that it be "as blue as the sky, as clear as a mirror, as thin as paper, and as resonant as a musical stone of jade." Judging from the extraordinary praise with which these writers describe it, this imperial order must have been well met. No example of it is extant so far as we know. It evidently served as a challenge to the Sung potters, as we discern some of these qualities in the wares of that period.

Sung pottery was usually porcelain,[1] which seems to have been known in China as early as the Han dynasty. Shape, color, and texture were its chief characteristics. The color was applied in the glaze and most frequently as a monochrome covering the entire surface. Where further decoration existed, it was quiet, harmonious, and unobtrusive. The objects, shapes, and color were varied. There were the imperial bulb bowls, like deep plates with a flaring rim, and the hexagonal flowerpots, noted for their thick glaze of rich purples and reds. Then there were the Ting bowls (FIG. 779) and slender vases, potted so thin that they were translucent, covered with a beautiful creamy white glaze, and sometimes decorated with an inconspicuous relief or incised design under the glaze. Perhaps the best known to Westerners are the *celadons*.[2] These fabrics were glazed with a soft green color that the Chinese likens to young onion sprouts. In the color and in the smooth texture of the glaze, the celadons are not unlike jade and may have originated in an attempt to reproduce the more valuable stone in a less expensive medium. If a person wanted to compliment a potter highly upon his vase, he would tell him that it looked like jade. In the *Celadon* reproduced in COLOR PL. IV (or opposite page), there is quiet elegance and refined taste. It has a sturdy strength because of the careful proportioning of the parts, especially of the finely curved lip and the slightly spreading base. From this rise conventionalized lanceolate leaf forms, the severity of which emphasizes the easy grace of the peony scroll on the body; on the neck a tapering peony pattern meets a broad band of concentrated ridges. This decoration is all in low relief and everywhere plays into the structural lines of the vase. It is entirely covered by a soft green glaze which with its uniform tone produces a quiet, reposeful harmony

[1] Porcelain is composed of three elements — kaolin, petuntse, and glaze. *Kaolin* is a fine white clay, named after the locality (Kaolin, or the High Hill) where it is found; it is infusible and forms the body of the vessel. *Petuntse*, the Chinese word for a square block of stone, is a vitreous stone that fuses at a high temperature and makes the fabric hard, translucent, impervious, and resonant. The purpose of the *glaze* is esthetic, not structural — to give a smooth lustrous surface and color. Thus porcelain combines the features of pottery and glass.

[2] *Celadon*, meaning "sea-green," was originally the name of the shepherd in a seventeenth-century French novel. In the plays of that period the shepherds usually wore sea-green costumes and the name was applied to the color and then to the Chinese ceramics of this color which were then coming to the notice of Europeans. The term is European, not Chinese.

The climax, technically, of porcelain manufacture was reached in the Ming dynasty. Great imperial kilns were established in 1369; and each emperor in turn patronized and encouraged the output and the development of the craft. The Sung monochromes were largely replaced by polychromes in which pictorial designs were worked out in different colored glazes and enamels, producing a complex richness rather than the quiet elegance of the Sung ware.

F. SUMMARY

In studying Chinese art we are studying the art of a sober, patient, conservative people whose law is the custom of their ancestors. Therefore art and art education looked to the past. Training consisted of copying the masters. The attitude of the Chinese on the matter of copying Dr. Laufer explains thus: "Where and what is the original, after all? Of these Chinese copies and copies of copies, the word of Holmes (*The Autocrat of the Breakfast Table*) holds good: 'A thought is often original, though you have uttered it a hundred times,' and Emerson's saying: 'When Shakespeare is charged with debts to his authors, Landor replies, "Yet he was more original than his originals. He breathed upon dead bodies and brought them into life."' Thus, it is no wonder that Carl Gussow of Munich could not believe Huang Hao's Red Carp of 1811 to be a copy, though expressly stated so by the artist on the painting; the entire conception, he thought, was so free and independent that it was bound to be an original (Hirth, *Scraps from a Collector's Notebook*, p. 44). As everything Chinese is pervaded by an atmosphere different from our own, so also a Chinese copyist is framed of a different mould; his work is creative reinvention, not purely receptive, but partaking of the spirit permeating the soul of the master." [1]

The Chinese people had developed a native art of great power and skill when Buddhism, coming from India, proved to be the stimulating factor that brought sculpture and painting to the loftiest plane of attainment. Sculpture in the Wei period was conventional and austere but compelling in the clear flame of its spiritual significance. In the T'ang age, though it became somewhat more naturalistic, it was still formal, lofty, and noble, revealing, as did the Wei, a marvelous harmony between content and design. In the Sung age there entered a disquieting charm that allows the eye and mind to wander to the beauty of technique, of surface, and of ornament. It is charming, but not mighty. Painting, inseparable from music and poetry, under the

[1] Laufer, *op. cit.*, p. 326, by permission of the Field Museum of Natural History, Chicago.

fervor of Buddhism produced in the T'ang age paintings of Buddha and Bodhisattvas, now lost, that must have been impressive in their austerity, majesty, and fervor. The age also produced those sympathetic and imaginative interpretations of the moods of nature that are one of the world's greatest accomplishments. The Chinese developed a magnificent technique in painting upon silk and paper with Chinese ink, neither hesitating nor fumbling in the most difficult technical problems. The same skill is apparent in all the minor arts. But of greater importance than technical accomplishment is the union of handiwork with deep conviction, profound thought, and lofty taste.

BIBLIOGRAPHY

Binyon, Laurence, *The Flight of the Dragon*, Dutton, 1922
—— —— *Painting in the Far East*, 4th ed. rev., Longmans, 1934
Bushell, S. W., *Chinese Art*, Brentano's, 1924, 2 vols.
Carter, Dagny, *China Magnificent: Five Thousand Years of Chinese Art*, Day, 1935
Cohn, William, *Asiatische Plastik*, Berlin, 1932
—— —— *Chinese Art*, Studio, 1930
Cranmer-Byng, L. A., tr. *A Lute of Jade*, Dutton, 1926
Driscoll, Lucy, and Toda, Kenji, *Chinese Calligraphy*, University of Chicago Press, 1935
Encyclopædia Britannica, *Chinese Art* (Britannica Booklet No. 1)
Ferguson, J. C., *Chinese Painting*, University of Chicago Press, 1927
Fischer, Otto, *Die Kunst Indiens, Chinas und Japans*, Berlin, 1928
Fry, R. E., and others, *Chinese Art: Paintings, Ceramics, Textiles, Bronzes, Sculpture, Jade, etc.*, Weyhe, 1925 (Burlington Magazine Monograph)
Giles, H. A., *An Introduction to the History of Chinese Pictorial Art*, 2d ed. rev., London, 1918
Glaser, Kurt, *Ostasiatische Plastik*, Berlin, 1925
Grosse, Ernst, *Die Ostasiatische Tuschmalerei*, Berlin, 1922
Hannover, Emil, *Pottery and Porcelain*, Scribner, 1925, 3 vols.
Hirth, Friedrich, *Scraps from a Collector's Note-book*, Stechert, 1905
Hobson, R. L., *Chinese Art*, Macmillan, 1927
—— —— *Chinese Pottery and Porcelain*, Funk & Wagnalls, 1915, 2 vols.
—— and Hetherington, A. L., *The Art of the Chinese Potter*, London, 1923
Koop, A. J., *Early Chinese Bronzes*, Scribner, 1925
Kümmell, H. C., *Die Kunst Ostasiens*, 2d ed., Berlin, 1922
Kuo Hsi, *An Essay on Landscape Painting* (tr. by Shio Sakanishi), Dutton, 1936
Latourette, K. S., *The Chinese: Their History and Culture*, Macmillan, 1934
Laufer, Berthold, *Jade*, Field Museum of Natural History, Chicago, 1912
March, Benjamin, *Some Technical Terms of Chinese Painting*, Waverly Press, 1935
Meyer, A. E., *Chinese Painting as Reflected in the Thought and Art of Li Lung-mien*, Duffield, 1923
Museum of Fine Arts, Boston, *Portfolio of Chinese Paintings in the Museum*, text by Kojiro Tomita, Harvard University Press, 1933
—— —— *Synopsis of History*, Museum, 1922
Okakura, Kakuzo, *The Ideals of the East*, Dutton, 1921
Petrucci, Raphaël, *Chinese Painters*, tr. by Frances Seaver, Brentano's, 1920
Silcock, Arnold, *An Introduction to Chinese Art*, Oxford University Press, 1936

Sirén, Osvald, *Chinese Paintings in American Collections*, Brussels, 1928
—— —— *Chinese Sculpture*, Scribner, 1925, 4 vols.
—— —— *A History of Early Chinese Art*, London, 1929–30, 4 vols.
—— —— *A History of Early Chinese Painting*, London, 1933, 2 vols.
Taki, Sei-ichi, *Three Essays on Oriental Painting*, London, 1910
Waley, Arthur, tr., *A Hundred and Seventy Chinese Poems*, Knopf, 1919
—— —— *Introduction to the Study of Chinese Painting*, Scribner, 1923
Yetts, W. P., *Symbolism in Chinese Art*, Leyden, 1912

CHAPTER XXVII

Japanese Art

A. HISTORICAL BACKGROUND

The origin of the race of Yamato (the native name of Japan) is problematical. As far back as we can trace the Japanese, they are an energetic, warlike people, yet "gentle in the arts of peace"; possessed of a primitive religion, known as Shinto, which included the worship of the powers of nature, especially the sun goddess, and of ancestors. Their country is one of great natural beauty. "The waters of the waving rice-fields, the variegated contour of the archipelago, so conducive to individuality, the constant play of its soft-tinted seasons, the shimmer of its silver air, the verdure of its cascaded hills, and the voice of the ocean echoing about its pine-girt shores — of all these was born that tender simplicity, that romantic purity, which so tempers the soul of Japanese art, differentiating it at once from the leaning to monotonous breadth of the Chinese and from the tendency to over-burdened richness of Indian art. That innate love of cleanness which, though sometimes detrimental to grandeur, gives its exquisite finish to our industrial and decorative art, is probably nowhere to be found in Continental work." [1]

But the chief element of inspiration in Japanese culture came from Buddhism. The impulse of Buddhism had already flooded and transformed Chinese thought, and then in the sixth century, under Chinese rather than Indian mode of expression, passed on with undiminished power of stimulation to Japan. With the religion came echoes of the art of India, and not only a strong influence but at first a close imitation of Chinese art by way of Korea. In fact Korean artists came to Japan to execute the work.

[1] Kakuzo Okakura, *The Ideals of the East*, p. 16, by permission of E. P. Dutton Co.

Fig. 780. Horiuji.
Near Nara. 586–607
A.D. In the center is the
Kondo containing the
shrine, and behind it
the pagoda; at the right
is the entrance, and at
the left, the preaching
hall.

The story of Japanese art is a story of successive waves of influence from China, followed by periods of retirement. At no time, however, has Japan been a mere imitator. Just as China assimilated and molded to its own mode of thought and expression the ideas of India, so the native culture of Yamato, though a heavy debtor to both India and China, still is an individual racial product.

Buddhism came first in the Suiko period [1] from China of the Six dynasties, especially the Wei, and manifested itself as something spiritual and mysterious, conceived in terms of abstract form. The second wave came from T'ang China, bringing with it a spirit of grandeur and exaltation that we discern in the majestic, contemplative Buddhas and the gracious and all-merciful Bodhisattvas. The lofty idealism of this art began to give way, toward the end of the period, to a more human and naturalistic type. The third wave came from Sung China, in the Kamakura and Ashikaga periods, in the form of Zen Buddhism with its revolt from ritual and its emphasis upon the meditative element through which one attained insight into the ultimate spirit of the universe. This was a golden age in all the arts but especially in painting and the minor arts.

While Japanese culture was receiving and assimilating these outside influences, the barons were usurping the political power of the Mikado and setting up a military feudalism. Early in the thirteenth century they vanquished the Mongol hordes of Kublai Khan by the help, legend says, of their sun goddess. [2] The shoguns, their commanders in chief, became military regents and established a complex feudal system that

[1] The chief periods of Japanese art are: Suiko, 552–645 A.D.; Hakuho, 645–709; Tempyo, 709–793; Jogan, 793–900; Fujiwara, 900–1190; Kamakura, 1190–1383; Ashikaga, 1383–1603; Tokugawa, 1603–1868.
[2] For this story see Okakura, *op. cit.*, p. 21.

Fig. 781. Howodo, or Phoenix Hall. Byodoin, near Uji. 1053.
(*Japanese Temples and Treasures*)

under the Tokugawas became a tyran-
nical autocracy. The astute statesman
Iyeyasu, founder of the line, and his followers strengthened their own power
by creating a new nobility of daimios
(landed barons) and samurai (military
barons), who were loyal because they
were under obligation to the shogun
for their existence. The Tokugawas
also consolidated and increased the
power of the people, and granted religious toleration. Partly through an

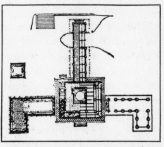

Fig. 782. Howodo of Byodoin.
(*Japanese Temples and Treasures*)

appeal to patriotism and partly because of the Mongol and Moslem
power in China, the Tokugawas cut off relationship with the continent and established that policy of isolation that continued until the
downfall of the Shogunate in 1868.[1] While such a policy brought about
a marvelous consolidation, its strict discipline crushed out vitality. With
the rise of power among the masses, a demand came for a more democratic art. So, as the power of Buddhism waned, the native art that
had always existed, though over-shadowed, reasserted itself. The lofty
taste and the deep fervor of earlier days gave way to overdecoration
to please the lords, and the easy charm of the wood-block print to
please the people.

[1] For the reasons for this event and the great change in Japan during the last
half-century from the point of view of a Japanese, see Kakuzo Okakura, *The Awakening
of Japan*, Century, 1904.

Fig. 783. Gardens
and Living Quarters
of the Todaiji Temple.
Nara. ("*Juraku*")

B. ARCHITECTURE

Love of nature, and love and understanding of wood, nature's chief material in this land, are fundamental in the building art in Japan. Very little stone is to be found but an abundance of timber. To make a building harmonious with nature and to construct it of the materials at hand constituted the builder's problem, whether the structure was a temple or a home.

Though Shinto temples [1] are to be found in Japan, the Buddhist temple and monastery are the highest expression of Japanese religious architecture. The *Horiuji* near Nara, the capital and center of Buddhist faith and learning, illustrates the type (FIG. 780). The buildings are grouped along an axis leading from the gate to the preaching hall; the Kondo or Golden Hall, containing the chief shrine, and the pagoda stand in balanced position on each side of the axis and the entire group is surrounded by a walled corridor. Outside this wall are grouped subsidiary structures such as administrative buildings, treasure houses, and cloisters, for the monastery served several purposes. Like the medieval monastery of Europe, it was a temple, a charitable institution, a hospital, and a center of learning where philosophy and music were taught as well as religious subjects.

The general style shows its Chinese origin (FIG. 760). There is the same massiveness, especially in the dominating roofs, the same somber

[1] Notably the *Temple of Idzumo*, the storm god, in northern Japan and the *Temple of Isé*, the sun goddess, in central Japan, which has been replaced every twenty years by an exact copy and hence, though built entirely of wood, preserves in excellent condition the original form.

Fig. 784. A Japanese Domestic Interior. Yokohama. ("*Juraku*")

dignity despite the brilliant color. Yet one feels here, especially in the pagoda, a more subtle feeling for proportion and a delicacy in the sweeping curves of the eaves that suggest the Japanese influence. The details and the restrained decoration are very refined, with careful spacing and proportioning of the members and an entasis in the columns. The construction is essentially of wood. Great wooden columns from two to three feet in diameter support heavy beams, the angle of joining being filled with a simple bracket. On these rests the open timber roof covered with tiles. The wall space is filled partly with plaster and partly with sliding screens. Such a structure is not only suitable to the climate of Japan but is loosely yet firmly enough constructed to withstand the frequent earthquakes to which the country is subject.

The interior of these monasteries is very splendid. On a platform is a gilded statue of the Buddha with attendant Bodhisattvas, above which hangs an elaborate canopy with angels carrying musical instruments. The timbers are decorated with vermilion, blue, and green, and with gilding and lacquer; the walls are covered with frescoes representing the paradise of Amida Buddha. The rich color harmony adds to the mystic calm of the Buddha, so that the whole effect suggests a plastic representation of the paradise seen in the T'ang paintings.

This group at *Horiuji* represents the period when Japan, by assimilating Chinese influences, was developing a new national expression, which we discern in the *Kondo* of the monastery of *Byodoin* at Uji (FIG. 781), known as the *Howodo* or *Phoenix Hall*.[1] One is immediately

[1] So called because its plan (FIG. 782) suggests a phoenix with outstretched wings,

struck by the beauty of the spot and by the feeling of unity between the
building and its surroundings. The heaviness and somber massiveness
of the Chinese model have given way to a lightness and delicacy; the
roofs have become lower and less dominating; there is a quiet grace
throughout and an exquisite curve of line. The building is long and
low, yet with no suggestion of monotony, for the predominant horizontal line is interestingly varied. The strong accent of the central
mass is repeated in the end pavilions, and interwoven in this balance
of mass is a harmonious rhythm of sweeping curves. In decoration,
the exterior is very simple and restrained; but the interior, like that
of *Horiuji*, is gorgeous in its splendor. Carvings and black lacquer inlaid with ivory, mother-of-pearl, and silver cover the coffered ceiling;
below is rich color and gilding. In the softened light the effect is one
of rich somber glow, comparable to that of Byzantine mosaics.

Interiors of marvelous richness are seen in the shrines and mauso-
leums at Nikko, which represent the later Tokugawa period and lack
the restraint and refinement of the age that produced the *Phoenix Hall*.
Decoration runs riot, at times concealing the structural system, and,
though powerful in effect, reveals the degeneracy in taste that characterized much of the Tokugawa work.

The home, whether modest or palatial, is peculiarly expressive of
the Japanese. Love of nature, again, impelled him to bring the beauties
of nature into his everyday life by means of the gardens with which
he so combined the house as to attain both an extraordinary unity
and a variety of forms and textures even when working on a small
scale (FIG. 783). Wood, tile, stucco, various kinds of trees and shrubs,
stones, sand, water — these he so combined, in accordance with ancient formulas, that one could hardly say where the garden ended
and the house began, particularly when the sliding screens that constituted the walls were thrown back. The interiors were peculiarly
serene, whether in the spacious magnificent palace or in the small
austerely simple home (FIG. 784). Their satisfying quality is due in
no mean measure to the Japanese unerring recognition of the intrinsic
qualities of materials. Great craftsmen in wood, far from hiding its
qualities with paint, they used every resource to bring out the color,
texture, and graining of each piece. Likewise with every material; so
that the combinations and contrasts furnish unity and variety in which
the sparse furnishings also contribute.[1]

symbolic of the paradise of Amida Buddha. The *Phoenix Hall* served as the prototype
of the Japanese buildings of the World's Columbian Exposition, still to be seen in
Jackson Park, Chicago.

[1] For Japanese domestic interiors see R. A. Cram, *Impressions of Japanese Architecture*, Baker and Taylor, 1905, and Kakuzo Okakura, *The Book of Tea*, Duffield, 1906;
for gardens, Jiro Harada, *Gardens of Japan*, Studio, 1928.

C. SCULPTURE

As with architecture, the materials at hand determine and limit the character of sculpture. There is almost no Japanese carving in stone, the chief material in Chinese sculpture, because of the scarcity of suitable stone in Japan. Fairly common are clay, used over a rough core and painted; and lacquer, used in the form of a lacquer paste over a clay or wooden core covered with cloth. But the chief materials were wood and metal. The abundant timber of Japan furnished several native woods suitable for carving, notably cypress and camphor wood. Many early statues were covered with gold foil or painted. Of the metals, bronze was the most important, and bronze sculpture reached an extraordinary development both technical and esthetic.

As in China, sculpture was a religious art devoted to creating cult, votive, or guardian statues, except for a small amount of portraiture, which developed late; and, if we exclude decorative carvings, sculpture was not used, as in the West, for an architectural purpose. Like architecture, it had its rise in the coming of Buddhism from China in the sixth century, and its highest expressions were created under the stimulus of that faith. Thus its subject matter, objectives, and forms were similar to those of China.

Chinese art of the Wei and the Six dynasties is the origin of the style of the *Yumedono Kwannon* [1] (FIG. 785). The tall slender figure stands in frontal position upon an inverted lotus pedestal; it is dressed in a long garment with floating ribbons, and wears a lofty delicate metal crown; behind the head is an elaborate lotus-leaf halo. The figure is thin and flat, quite lacking in substance, like the Chinese *Maitreya* (FIG. 769); the drapery is indicated by long straight folds which sweep out at the sides and provide a broad base to balance the large halo. The features are carved conventionally on the surface of the face in simple planes which meet abruptly, as is characteristic of archaic sculpture, and result in the "archaic smile." The aim of the sculptor has been an impersonal objectification of dignity and beneficence by means of a symmetrical organization of conventional motifs, many symbolic — the lotus pedestal, for example; the position of the hands and the attributes; and particularly the large prominent halo so distinctive of Japanese Buddhist sculpture, because of the es-

[1] Kwannon is the Japanese name of Kuan Yin of China and Avalokiteshvara of India. The *Yumedono*, or *Hall of Dreams*, is the sanctuary of *Horiuji* where Prince Shotoku, founder of the monastery, used to practice Buddhistic meditation. The statue has been held in great veneration in Japan even to the present time. Mr. Fenollosa tells the story that when Okakura invited him to be present at the opening of the shrine where this Kwannon is kept, a loud clap of thunder warned the priests of the sacrilege.

Fig. 785. Yumedono Kwannon.
Wood, originally covered with gold.
H. 7 ft. Early VII cent. Horiuji.

Fig. 786. Maitreya. Wood.
Suiko period. Chuguji Nun-
nery, Nara.

Fig. 787. Fugen, an Attendant of a Buddha.
Detail. Wood. Horiuji.

These three plates are reprinted by permission
of the Cleveland Museum of Art from *Japanese
Sculpture of the Suiko Period*, by Langdon Warner,
published by the Yale University Press.

pecial emphasis in Japan upon the light that
radiated from the Buddha, an emphasis
seen in the popularity of the Amida Buddha.

The trend of Japanese sculpture, as of
that of the Chinese, the Egyptian, the
Greek, and other cultures, was in the direction of naturalism, of an approximation
of visual perception. A *Fugen* (FIG. 787) illustrates this. But one does not think of the
human form first. Most appealing is a mysterious, ethereal quality, suggesting perfect
poise and gracious beneficence. While this
quality is expressed by means of the human
figure, it is the quality and not the corporeal
figure that speaks. The form and features
have more naturalistic proportions and
modeling, though the highly arching brows
and the hair are still conventionally treated;
the folds of the garment are more deeply
undercut, giving a feeling of cloth; the uplifted hand with its symbolic gesture is beautifully modeled and exquisitely gracious.

Fig. 788. Kwannon. Bronze.
H. 8½ ft. Hakuo period. Ya-
kushiji.

Thus the solidity and naturalism of the figure are never advanced at the
expense of the dominant theme. As in the art of India and China, the
preëminence of the theme is unassailable. The theme may be abstract
and expressed in an abstract form. But form for its own sake lies outside
the Oriental's conceptions of art. A seated *Maitreya*, for example (FIG.
786), is an expression of inner peace, the consciousness of self-conquest,
combined with great tenderness. The Bodhisattva is seated upon a high
lotus pedestal; the left foot rests on a lotus, the right is crossed over the
knee and lightly held by the hand; the chin rests meditatively upon
the uplifted right hand. The figure, though still frontal, is free in pose,
as is possible in woodcarving, with an arrangement of limbs peculiarly
unified, though varied. It has solidity, and natural proportions modified by such conventional requirements as broad shoulders, narrow
waist, smooth round limbs, elongated ears; and the drapery, though
undercut rather than engraved as in the *Yumedono Kwannon*, is conceived as pure design and is carved with confidence and sure-handedness. To one familiar with the symbolism, the conviction and fervor
of the theme are reinforced by the artist's "ignoring the corporeality
of the human figure while making a display of it." [1]

Japanese sculpture took the same general course of development as

[1] Sei-ichi Taki, *Japanese Fine Art*, Stechert, 1931, p. 84.

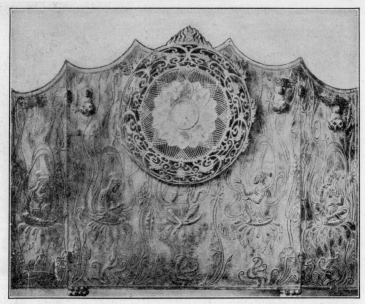

Fig. 789. Screen of the Trinity of Tachibana Fujin. Bronze. Early VIII
cent. Horiuji. (*Japanese Temples and Treasures*)

the Chinese. As the Wei sculpture of China was the source of inspiration for the Suiko period in Japan, so Chinese T'ang art strongly influenced the Japanese work of the Hakuho and Tempyo periods. It
was a Buddhistic art centering about Amida Buddha. He was usually
represented as seated upon the lotus in the posture of meditation or
with one hand uplifted signifying his preaching, and accompanied by
standing Bodhisattvas (Fig. 788). Behind the figures rise the elaborate
lofty halos shaped like a leaf of the bodhi tree [1] and decorated with
flame motifs and small seated Buddhas. Aims and conventions are
discernible here similar to those in early T'ang, the same elaborations
of costume, jewelry, and ribbons. The design is eminently suited to
bronze, and the sharp contours and linear rhythms enabled the sculptor to tie the figure, the great halo, and the finely designed pedestal
into an extraordinary unity. Note this particularly where figure, halo,
and pedestal meet.

Most of the great *Trinity* groups are of bronze and reveal the magnificent skill of the Japanese bronze-founder. An outstanding example
is the screen, containing the halo, that served as a background for the

[1] The tree under which Buddha sat when he attained enlightenment; hence it
was called the tree of enlightenment (*bodhi*).

Fig. 790. Heiji Monogatari. Detail. The Burning of the Sanjo Palace.
XIII cent. Museum of Fine Arts, Boston. (Boston Museum)

Fig. 791. Sesshu. Landscape Scroll. Detail. Coll. of Prince Mori,
Tokio. (Taki)

Fig. 792. Monkeys.
Ashikaga period (1383–
1603). Ryusen coll.,
Kyoto. (Kokka)

small *Tachibana Fujin Trinity* (FIG. 789). The base of the shrine represents, half naturalistically and half conventionally, the surface of a pond from which rise on curving stems three lotus flowers that serve as pedestals for the Buddha and two attendants.[1] The design of the base is carried up into the screen by means of five lotus flowers on undulating stems, in low relief, with delicate engraving. Each lotus, with inverted petals, supports an angel who turns toward the Buddha in adoration. The space is entirely covered, but not crowded, with a suave tracery suggestive of quietly moving water and accented by the figures in higher relief. The artist was gifted with imagination and refined feeling, and he never lost sight of the medium through which he was expressing his idea. He had no desire for pictorial effect or the illusion of natural appearance. Still, by flow of line, delicate relief, and engraving he expressed all the essence of the forms. In contrast to the delicate surface of the screen is the virile pattern of the halo.

D. PAINTING

Like architecture and sculpture, much of the painting of Japan shows a direct influence from China and the impulse of Buddhism. A considerable part, however, is quite unlike anything found in sober China; for it is secular in theme, and gay with vivid color, agile movement, and decorative splendor, while its concern with genre eventuated in the Japanese print. Its function was much the same as in China — wall paintings, kakemonos, makimonos, and albums, to which the folding screen was added. The materials also were similar, except that color and gold played an equally important part with Chinese ink (*sumi*) — the former used generally in the native Japanese narrative and secular paintings; the latter in the Buddhist, in the landscape, bird, and flower paintings inspired especially by Zen Buddhism.

Buddhism furnished the stimulation for the earliest paintings now known, the wall frescoes in the *Kondo of Horiuji*, which are as typically early T'ang as the building itself and thus like the latter strongly Hindu. In theme, execution, scale, and composition they appear to be closely related to the *Ajanta Frescoes*. A popular subject was one of those celestial scenes in which Amida Buddha is sitting upon a lotus, wrapped in meditation and surrounded by saints, deities, and disciples representative of the "vast community" of the Buddhist faith. There is the same stateliness and tenderness, the same vitality born of religious conviction, the same dynamic line, as in the *Ajanta Frescoes*.

With the waning of this wave of Buddhist impulse from T'ang China,

[1] The figures have been removed in FIG. 789 in order to show the design of the screen.

we see the rise of a truly Japanese painting in the Fujiwara period and its climax in the Kamakura and Ashikaga ages. This was known as *Yamatoe* (FIG. 790), the painting of Yamato, and though at times it dealt with religious themes, it was largely a secular art: portraiture and illustration of contemporary historical literature. It thus took for its theme the social, ceremonial, and military life of the aristocracy, as in the scrolls which contain both text and illustrations from the *Story of Genji*, one of the most famous of the fictions written by Lady Murasaki, a well-known literary woman of the Fujiwara age. Here are scenes from the life of the palace, drawn with firm lines, brightly colored, and represented from a bird's-eye view, a characteristic convention of Japanese painting. Then there are the vivacious out-of-door battle scenes, so filled with movement, so elegant and colorful.

A characteristically Japanese purpose of painting was to decorate the folding or sliding screen which served as a partition in the Japanese home. This kind of painting required unity not only in the entire composition but in each section as well, very much as in the maki-mono. In the *Waves at Matsushima* (FIG. 793) of Korin (died 1716), for example, each of the six sections is a unit of design, largely asymmetrical yet as a whole united into a vigorous pattern that is quite consistent with the theme. The traditional conventions of water, clouds, rocks, and trees express the solidity of the rocks, the powerful movement of the surging waves, and the quiet security of the pines on their lofty sites. The effect of the rapid repetition of the restive wave and crest motifs in juxtaposition to the quiet unbroken areas of the rock motif illustrates Korin's implicit following of the Oriental tradition of painting moving water [1] — as well as making the screen both in parts and as a whole superbly decorative.

Buddhist painting continued by the side of Yamatoe, and in the late Kamakura age received another wave of stimulation from Sung China with the coming of Zen Buddhism, the result of which was the most exquisite and refined landscape, flower, and bird paintings. The simplicity and directness of Zen thought led these painters to use ink rather than the sumptuous color and gilding characteristic of Yamato art. Important among these painters was a Zen priest, Sesshu (about 1420–1506). In a detail of a landscape scroll (FIG. 791) we are overlooking a panorama. At the right a gnarled pine, clinging to the side of the cliff and overhanging a mist-filled valley, weaves a pattern of striking angularity; from the mists emerge other pines, buildings, and a pagoda; on the left are rocky hills and a plateau with jutting angular edges and crowned with tall slender pines. One is struck by the crisp brush strokes tingling with energy, each of which forces upon one the

[1] See p. 621.

Fig. 793. Korin. Waves at Matsushima. Museum of Fine Arts, Boston.
(Boston Museum)

special character and inherent quality of the rock, tree, mountain, or building. While its energy and sharp contrasts stand in opposition to the sober repose and subtle values of the Tung Yüan painting (FIG. 764), the two scrolls are similar in aim and attitude toward nature. The objective of both was not the presentation of visual perception but the objectification of one's feelings about nature by means of traditional conventions and symbols whose "richness of implication" stimulates the imagination of the observer. This is particularly true of the flower, bird, and animal paintings created under the stimulus of Zen Buddhism by a few strokes of ink brushed on the paper or silk with a consummate mastery of the medium (FIG. 792).

While Yamatoe painting depended for its content upon historical scenes and genre, it was the life of the aristocracy that it depicted, not that of the masses. In the late Ashikaga age there arose demands for an art whose content was based upon the life of the middle and lower classes. This led, in the early part of the Tokugawa period, when these classes were coming into position and wealth, to the Ukiyoe, "pictures of this fleeting world," illustrations of the everyday life of the people in the streets, tradehouses, theaters, and countryside, and in a form within the purchase price of the masses. Thus rose in the seventeenth century the Japanese print, made from wood blocks, which was sometimes an illustration in a book and sometimes an individual print. At first the impressions were made in black and white only and if color was used it was added by hand. Then came the invention of printing in two colors and thence, in the eighteenth century, the full polychrome process. The output was prolific; the subject matter and style, varied. There are the strong single figures of actors and beauties by Maronobu (1625–1694), the first of Japanese painters to enter the field of designing for the wood block, and by Kiyomasu (1702?–1763), large

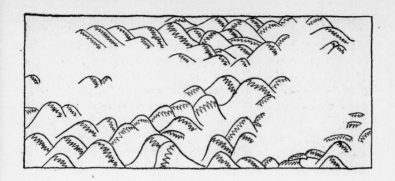

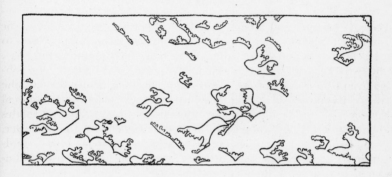

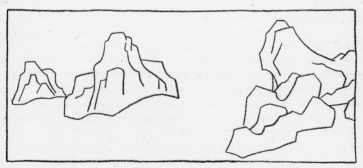

793 (A). Analysis of Waves at Matsushima for Repeat Motifs.

Fig. 794. Sharaku. Portrait of the Actor Matsumoto Koshiro IV. c. 1793. Art Institute of Chicago. (Art Institute)

figures which fill the space, and which show in their firm accomplished drawing a sound training in the use of *sumi*. There is an easy grace of line and a charm of pattern in the feminine subjects of Harunobu (active 1760–1770), who is thought to have invented the process of polychrome printing. Notable is the successful design of his pillar prints and of those of Koryusai (active 1760–1780), very high narrow prints proportioned to fit the pillar of the chief room in the house. There are the powerful dramatic portraits of actors (FIG. 794) by Shunsho (1726–1793) and Sharaku (active 1794–1795) and of popular beauties by Utamaro (1753–1806). With Kiyonaga (1752–1815) the designs became more complex, and though the figures are on a smaller scale and less monumental, their grouping and elaborate costumes offer material for complicated patterns; and landscape takes the place of the flat ground. With Hokusai (1760–1849) and Hiroshige (1797–1858) landscape became a dominant note. While these prints are not considered fine art by the Japanese, they nevertheless show the fundamental principles of the fine art of painting. In their sensitive feeling for space relations; in their skillful maintenance of asymmetrical balance of flat patterns, often very complicated and with marked linear quality; in their accomplished draftsmanship with a supreme command over line, usually calligraphic but at times so modulated as to express the mass of the figure; in their strangely beautiful color combinations and unusual point of view, especially in landscape — in all these excellences they reveal a democratic art of very high attainment (FIG. 795).

E. MINOR ARTS

The superb craftsmanship and also the fine taste of the Japanese are well illustrated by the minor arts, especially by the pottery, textiles, metalwork, and lacquer. Japanese textiles are most sumptuous, particularly when metal threads and embroidery are used to attain such rich effects of color and texture as one finds in the ecclesiastical brocades, in the more elaborate obi, or sash, worn with the kimono, and in the kimonos used in the Nō plays. The Nō drama is a highly formal performance which combines dancing, singing, and speaking by actors who wear masks and robes whose extraordinary beauty constitutes no mean part of the effectiveness of this stately, impersonal, almost abstract art. FIG. 796 reproduces a Nō robe of white satin painted in gold on which are embroidered grasses which create a subtly varied repeat pattern accented at irregular intervals by leaves, butterflies, and chrysanthemums.

The bronze-workers of Japan have always been skillful to an unusual degree. The craft was inherited, and the most famous families of craftsmen traced their ancestry back to mythical times. The casting was done by the cire-perdue process, and the finishing by a considerable use of the chisel. Evidences of this skill we have already seen in the Buddhas and Bodhisattvas that compose the *Trinity*

Fig. 795. Hokusai. Li Po at the Waterfall of Lo Shan. Art Institute of Chicago. (Art Institute)

groups. Important among these metalworkers were the armorers, for the powerful samurai created a demand for the finest sword blades and sword furniture. A thorough knowledge of the properties of metals and alloys enabled the swordsmith to obtain various colors and textures; while for decorations he employed a variety of metal processes in casting, chasing, stamping, and damascening. The blade was made of many layers, each forged and tempered with all the expert skill of generations.[1] It is this multiplicity of layers that causes the watered effect seen in fine blades.

Lacquer, which is derived from China, is a natural varnish of exceptional hardness derived from the sap of the lac tree. The object to be lacquered is usually made of wood carefully prepared and covered with paper, hempen cloth, or silk and lacquer, and polished with a

[1] For a detailed account of this forging of a sword see Stewart Dick, *Arts and Crafts of Old Japan*, McClurg, 1905, p. 85.

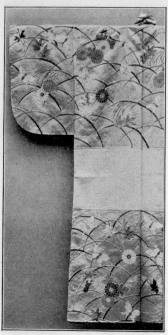

Fig. 796. Nō Robe. Detail. White satin, gold, and embroidery. XVII cent. Metropolitan Museum, New York. (Metropolitan Museum)

whetstone to give a firm, marblelike surface for the lacquering. The process reminds one of the preparation of a panel for tempera painting. On the finished surface, layer after layer of lacquer is laid, dried, and polished to obtain a deep lustrous surface. Gold is applied in a variety of ways, and its rich glow is a decoration in itself. When painting or modeling is added, it is applied to the ground and then covered with a final coat of translucent lacquer as a finish.

F. SUMMARY

While much of the art of Japan has been derived from China, yet there are certain characteristics that differentiate Japanese art quite strongly from Chinese. One is the greater adaptability of the Japanese. There is a mobility and a plasticity in his temperament that contrasts with the immobility and stolidity of the Chinese. He is by nature more susceptible to change and less insistent upon following the past. For this reason his originality is more obvious and more daring. In architecture, in his roof composition he evolves compelling designs of harmonious curves. In painting, he delights in the most exquisite ink monochromes; and at times revels in sumptuous color and gold, though never at the loss of decorative fitness. His thorough craftsmanship in all things, large and small, is due to a considerable extent to his willingness to perfect his detail, even to hidden parts, such as those of the inside of a lacquer box. Every phase of Japanese art is imbued with an exquisite taste which strives toward the one perfection as a symbol of its ideal, as the following story shows: "In the sixteenth century the morning-glory was as yet a rare plant with us. Rikiu had an entire garden planted with it, which he cultivated with assiduous care. The fame of his convolvuli reached the ear of the Taiko, and he expressed a desire to see them, in consequence of which Rikiu invited him to a morning tea at his house. On the appointed day Taiko walked through the garden, but nowhere could he see any vestige of the convolvulus. The ground had been leveled and strewn with fine pebbles and sand. With sullen anger the despot entered the tearoom, but a sight waited him there which completely restored his humour. On the tokonoma, in a rare bronze of Sung workmanship, lay a single morning-glory — the queen of the whole garden!" [1]

BIBLIOGRAPHY

Anesaki, Masaharu, *Art, Life, and Nature in Japan*, Marshall Jones, 1933

—— —— *Buddhist Art in Its Relation to Buddhist Ideals*, Houghton Mifflin, 1915

Binyon, Laurence, *Painting in the Far East*, 4th ed. rev., Longmans, 1934

—— and Sexton, M. O., *Japanese Colour Prints*, Scribner, 1923

Bowie, H. P., *On the Laws of Japanese Painting*, Elder, 1911

Brown, L. N., *Early Block-Printing and Book-Illustration in Japan*, Dutton, 1924

Cram, R. A., *Impressions of Japanese Architecture and the Allied Arts*, Baker and Taylor, 1905

Dawson, E. B., *Enamels*, McClurg, 1908

Dillon, Edward, *The Arts of Japan*, McClurg, 1906

Ficke, A. D., *Chats on Japanese Prints*, Stokes, 1915

Fischer, Otto, *Die Kunst Indiens, Chinas und Japans*, Berlin, 1928

Fujii, Koji, *The Japanese Dwelling-house*, Tokyo, 1930

"Juraku," *Graphic Collection of Ancient Architecture and Gardens of the Orient*, Tokyo, 1928–33, 4 vols.

Kümmel, O. H. C., *Die Kunst Ostasiens*, 2d ed., Berlin, 1922

Murasaki shikibu, *The Tale of Genji*, tr. by Arthur Waley, Houghton Mifflin, 1926–33, 6 vols. (each with separate title)

Okakura, Kakuzo, *The Book of Tea*, Duffield, 1906

—— —— *The Ideals of the East*, Dutton, 1921

Priestley, A. F., *How to Know Japanese Colour Prints*, Doubleday, Page, 1927

Seidlitz, Woldemar von, *A History of Japanese Colour-Prints*, Lippincott, 1910

Strange, E. F., *Japanese Colour Prints*, Victoria and Albert Museum, London, 1908

Taki, Sei-ichi, *Japanese Fine Art*, Stechert, 1931

—— —— *Three Essays on Oriental Painting*, London, 1910

Toda, Kenji, *Japanese Scroll Painting*, University of Chicago Press, 1935

Trautz, F. M., ed., *Japan, Korea and Formosa*, Westermann, 1931

Tsuda, Noritake, *Handbook of Japanese Art*, Dodd, Mead, 1935

Tsudzumi, Tsuneyohi, *Die Kunst Japans*, Leipzig, 1929

Waley, Arthur, *The Nō Plays of Japan*, Knopf, 1922

Warner, Langdon, *Japanese Sculpture of the Suiko Period*, Yale University Press, 1923

With, Karl, *Buddhistische Plastik in Japan*, Vienna, 1919, 2 vols.

---

[1] Okakura, *The Book of Tea*, p. 145, by permission of Duffield & Green.

Part Nine

MODERN ART: THE NINETEENTH AND TWENTIETH CENTURIES

CHAPTER XXVIII

French Art in the Nineteenth Century

A. HISTORICAL BACKGROUND

France from early in the eighteenth century up to the present time has been the chief center of art activity in the Occident and an important center of the revolutionary movements which mark the nineteenth and twentieth centuries; thus it may be made the focal point about which the art of these centuries can be studied.

The nineteenth century was a century of upheaval, of the ferment of new forces and new ideas in conflict with the old. The French Revolution with its political, social, and economic realignments, and the Industrial Revolution with equally vast social and economic as well as cultural consequences, were two great storm centers. Politically, the century saw the abolition or delimitation of kings and aristocracy in favor of constitutional monarchies or republics — experimentation in government. Socially, it saw the rise of the lower classes and the bourgeois plutocrats into positions hitherto held by the aristocracy, and a consequent shaking of traditional culture — social experimentation. In industry, scientific research and applied science ushered in the machine age. The half-century from 1800 to 1850 saw the first steamboat, locomotive, transatlantic liner, and passenger train; the telegraph, the camera — all of which, with many other factors, eventuated in a great revolution and expansion of industry, in the rise of "rugged individualism" and the laissez-faire system of profit-taking; and in protest, socialism and other forms of economic experimentation. The application of the scientific viewpoint with its critical observation of phenomena, replacing, or rather extending, the narrower rationalism of the eighteenth century, produced Darwin's *Origin of Species* (1859) and its consequent long line of research. It shook traditional religious faith, and brought about a realistic movement in the arts; not, however, before the outburst of the Romantic movement, from about 1820 to 1850, whose fervor was symptomatic of a new age that was replacing the dying Renaissance. In the Romantic glorification of human emotions, of subjective, individual reactions, lies a basis of the "Expressionism" of today; and its discoveries of beauty in the out-of-doors led it into the paths of legends, of primitive or medieval life, and of exotic cultures.

The broadening of man's knowledge of himself and his world enabled him for the first time to see himself in perspective and, through actual rather than mythical contacts with the Orient and primitive peoples, to compare and contrast, all of which exerted a powerful influence on the artists. Japanese prints, Chinese porcelain, African carvings, Persian miniatures, medieval glass, primitive textiles — from all quarters exotic influences began to be felt.

Not only were the artists subjected to the influences of these foreign art forms but, through the events described above, their whole social and economic status was thrown violently out of balance. Heretofore the artist filled a normal niche in the economic structure, usually as a member of a guild, for the independent artist as an independent economic unit rarely existed. Kings, popes, nobles, the Church, and the guild provided steady patronage. Supply and demand balanced and there was no economic problem. A work of art — a building, a statue, a picture, a textile, or a book — was ordered at the shop, made, paid for according to contract, and served to fulfill the function which the purchaser had in mind when he ordered it. In the seventeenth and eighteenth centuries, the establishment of the French Academy with its autocratically imposed official sanctions, the growth of museum collections, and the creation of the idea of the salon or exhibition painting set up an artificial unhealthy motivation. At the same time the abolition of the classes and institutions that were the great art patrons and the coming of the machine, which practically abolished the handcrafts, segregated the artist from his normal function and created an entirely new situation to which the artist, even today, is not adjusted.

It is over against this complex, confusing, rapidly changing flux of the whole fabric of civilization that we must see the art of the nineteenth and twentieth centuries. It is a situation by no means novel. The late Roman Empire in the early centuries of the rising Christian civilization is a comparable situation; or the fourteenth and fifteenth centuries in Italy when medievalism was waning before the incipient Renaissance. These movements, however, were simple and almost local in comparison with the complexity and the cosmopolitan breadth of the situation of the nineteenth century.

B. ARCHITECTURE

All the countries of Europe, not excepting Russia, from the late fifteenth century to the mid-eighteenth felt the impact of Italian Renaissance architecture in its varying styles — early, high, baroque — and reacted each according to local conditions. In the second half of the eighteenth century Classicism, no longer interpreted by the Italian architects but actually seen through archaeological investigation and first-hand knowledge of Rome and Greece, spread over Europe and America. Thence followed in the nineteenth century a series of revivals, perhaps for two reasons. Archaeological discovery and a more accurate science of history flavored with Romanticism whetted the appetite for a deeper understanding of the past and set it up as a summum bonum. In addition, as there had not yet emerged a new age coherent enough to dominate expression, the disintegrating Renaissance manifested its decadence, as is normal, in an archaistic eclecticism. Thus Greek, Romanesque, Gothic, Byzantine followed one another, with even Chinese variations as an acquaintanceship with the Orient was filtering into the West. The result has been that the main avenues of almost any European or American metropolis reveal, fraternizing in friendly proximity if not stylistic unity, a French Renaissance mansion, a Gothic cathedral, a Venetian club, and a Greek bank. A few enlightened individuals among the architects, realizing the artificiality of the eclectic ideal, began thinking along the line of the famous pronouncement of Louis Sullivan that function determines form. But the impact of this ideal upon intrenched "authorities" of style was not strong enough to produce noticeable results until the present age.

Fig. 797. Ingres. Madame Rivière. 1805. Louvre, Paris. (Giraudon)

C. PAINTING

The aristocratic painting of the eighteenth century is the point of departure for the revolutionary changes of the nineteenth. The gaiety, extravagance, and frivolity of the French court continued quite dis-

Fig. 798. Delacroix. Entrance of the Crusaders into Constantinople. 1841. Louvre, Paris. (Giraudon)

Fig. 799. Corot. St. Salvi Church, Albi. c. 1830. Art
Institute of Chicago. (Art Institute)

Fig. 800. Corot. Interrupted
Reading. 1865–70. Art Institute of
Chicago. (Art Institute)

Fig. 801. Millet. Sower. 1850. Museum of Fine Arts, Boston. (Boston Museum)

regardful of the ever increasing rumblings soon to swell into the terrific
storm of the thinkers and the masses rising against absolutism and class
privilege. A reflection of the mood of the day is to be discerned in an
earnestness and severity that was finding its ideal in classical subjects.
Attention had already been turned in that direction by the excavations
at Pompeii (1755), by the publication of Winckelmann's *History of Art
among the Ancients*, the first ever written on the subject, and by the
popularity of Piranesi's engravings of Roman buildings. Hence it is
not surprising that the pictures of the Classicists, such as the *Oath of the
Horatii* (Louvre) by Jacques Louis David (1748–1825), were received
with great enthusiasm. In contrast to the lilting rhythms and melting
color of rococo, the cold harsh art of David, linear, drab, almost monochrome, and sculptural in feeling, furnished a gratifying change and a
mood that was apposite to the changing temper of the day.

Another classicist, Jean Auguste Dominique Ingres (1780–1867),
found his inspiration primarily in the Florentines. The *Odalisque*
(Louvre) or the *Madame Rivière* (Fig. 797) is a linear pattern to which
color has been added for decorative and clarifying effect. In the
Madame Rivière what impresses one most is the harmonious rhythm of
the sweeping lines of the shawl as it winds over the shoulders and falls
across the figure with a single great curve through which minor harmonies interplay; and the admirable adaptation of the whole design
to the oval frame. Ingres' famous saying laconically summarizes his

Fig. 802. Courbet.
The Stone-Breakers.
c. 1850. Dresden.

artistic creed, "Drawing is everything; color is nothing." As a result he was charged, especially by his opponents the Romanticists, with affecting Gothic primitivism, of belonging to the school of Cimabue.

For meanwhile the storm had burst into the Revolution, the result of which was to liberate powerful energy and tumultuous feelings that could not find expression in the cold severity of David's and Ingres' classical ideals. And such dynamic emotionalism must needs find expression. And here lay the origin of the Romantic movement (about 1820 to 1850). Now it was human feelings and Rousseau's faith in nature rather than rationalism that served as a guiding principle. Wagner poured forth his tumultuous music in a glorification of intense human emotions, while in England the Lake poets, in more restrained though individual subjective expression, glorified the beauty of nature. The inescapable position of painters who were aware of a movement so surcharged with emotionalism and vitality was to give expression to its mood; a position not accepted by the Classicists, who clung to their traditional formulas in a rapidly changing world. The Romanticists, on the other hand, offered both new subject matter and a new style of painting, and *The Raft of the Medusa* of Théodore Géricault (1791–1824) precipitated the long struggle between the two schools to defend their respective principles.

In Eugène Delacroix (1798–1863), perhaps the most gifted Romantic painter, baroque compositions with tumultuous rhythms stem from Rubens or the Venetians (Delacroix was self-taught, in the Louvre), though with not so complete a mastery in the perfect subordination of a complex composition in deep spatial rhythms as in Tintoretto, Veronese, or Rubens. In contrast to the tranquil, linear patterns of Ingres, cold in color and with largely lateral movement, *The Entrance of the Crusaders into Constantinople* (FIG. 798) is a restless design organized

Fig. 803. Daumier
The Uprising. Phillip
Memorial   Gallery
Washington. (Phillip
Memorial Gallery)

by strong color and light in space. It is a dramatic subject characteristic
of the Romanticists, who found their ideals in history and literature.
In the foreground a group of mounted Crusaders are advancing with
flowing banners; on every side are scenes of killing and pillage, or
pleading for mercy; low-lying in the background is the city of Constantinople, with the smoke of fires rising from the houses and the ships
in the harbor. A strong movement sweeping inward from the foreground and repeated again and again defines a space in which the
figures are organized by light and dark, warm and cool spots of color.
"Gray is the enemy of all painting," said Delacroix. . . . "Let us
banish from our palette all earth colors — keep the brush strokes distinct, not fused, and thus secure energy and freshness — the greater
the opposition in color, the greater the brilliance." The short distinct
brush stroke, the juxtaposition of complementary colors, already being
practiced by Constable in England, and heretofore used by Watteau,
Rubens, and Titian, are on the direct path toward a climax in the
Impressionistic movement later in the century.

A by-product of the Romantic movement, or perhaps more correctly
a direct result, was the new attitude toward nature and therefore
toward landscape-painting, an attitude foreshadowed in Ruisdael.
With Poussin and Claude landscape was an artificial, imaginative
visualization of nature, contemplated to be sure out of doors, but constructed in the studio into an architectural unity. Not so with the
"Men of 1830" [1] who carried painting out of doors — a novel idea —

[1] Important members of the group were Camille Corot (1796–1875); Théodore
Rousseau (1812–1867); Charles-François Daubigny (1817–1878); Jules Dupré (1812–

and actually painted in the forest of Fontainebleau near the village of Barbizon, or at least made detailed drawings to be worked up into paintings in the studio. In their passion for and close intimacy with nature they pictured faithfully its actual appearance as well as interpreting its moods. They also included a considerable amount of realistic detail, which however was attributable partly to the influence of the Dutch school of landscape and especially to a recent discovery, the science of photography. To copy nature as the camera does became more and more the objective of many painters, as in the minds of the public the novel idea of an exact copy of natural appearance was rapidly becoming an ideal.

Fig. 804. Daumier. Tenants and Landlords. Lithograph. Art Institute of Chicago. (Art Institute)

Thus we find two Corots: the early landscapes, painted both in Italy and in France, together with the late figures, comprising one group; and the intermediate more photographic landscapes painted around Fontainebleau, the other. In the early landscapes, *Albi* (Fig. 799), for example, the space is carved out almost as clearly as in a Poussin, each building taking its place in accordance with the planes defining the space, and with the values of its hues. A narrow range of grays and yellows produces a general tonality that vibrates with subtle modulation of tones. In addition, the play upon the vertical and horizontal volumes and upon the curved and angular motifs, as well as the informal asymmetrical balance, reveal Corot as an artist who could look upon nature with cool discrimination. The same may be said of the late figure work (Fig. 800). But the popular landscapes were painted at just the time when Corot was caught in the wave of Romanticism on the emotional side and the influence of photography on the visual. Thus an honest sincere love of nature, by no means always sentimental, was befogged by affectation; and the artist's vision, which he possessed in large measure, was blinded by the novel idea of the camera's exactitude in reproduction.

The same influences turned the capacities of Millet into sentimentali-

---

1889); Charles Jacque (1813–1894); Constant Troyan (1810–1865); Jean-François Millet (1814–1874).

ties and overrealistic reproduction of detail. On the other hand, like Corot, he revealed at times, especially in his drawings, not only a grasp of form and its organization in space but a healthy interpretation of his subject quite removed from Romantic sentiment (FIG. 801), and together with Courbet continued the tradition of the Dutch genre painters, of the Le Nain Brothers and Chardin.

The situation in Paris, about 1850, was a triangle of three mutually antagonistic groups. One group consisted of the Academicians, chiefly followers [1] of the Classic and Romantic traditions, who controlled the salons and formulated strict rules as to subject matter, which should be religious or legendary, and as to handling — "high art" or "the grand manner," it was called. A second group was the Barbizon school; a third, individuals of forthright independence. Of this last group was Gustave Courbet (1819–1877), who "didn't paint angels because he never saw one," and who called himself "a realist," not in the sense of reproducing nature with the eye of the camera but of reproducing the actualities of nature in the raw in protest to the empty artificialities of the Academicians; and in such a way that the representation should be more compelling than the visual actuality. His subject matter shocked the Academy — *The Stone-Breakers* (FIG. 802), *La Mère Grégoire* (wife of the keeper of a brewhouse), *The Funeral at Ornans* — living actualities, often crude, harsh, or ugly; but not less so than his technique. The simple boldness in his limited sober palette is in harmony with the elemental character of the subject matter; lights and darks meet abruptly along the edges of simplified planes; and a surface richness results from the various ways in which Courbet used his pigment, often loading it heavily with the palette knife.

Another independent was Honoré Daumier (1808–1879), who for forty years satirized Paris by his lithographs in *Charivari*, and painted, in the meantime, a few pictures. His daily task of reaching essentials through simplification, essentials of form to enforce the essential meaning undoubtedly influenced his painting in the same direction. Within a limited range of color — a color scheme reminiscent of Rembrandt in its tonality of warm browns and yellows — large bold areas of pigment cut highly simplified planes, and every detail is eliminated which does not bear on the central idea. In *The Uprising* (FIG. 803) diagonal planes moving in from opposite corners by means of sharply contrasted lights and darks carve out a huge space filled with a great mob, though but a few people can actually be seen. One dynamic figure in the foreground tersely carved in light and dark, with a forceful diagonal movement, repeated in the half-seen figure on the left, symbolizes the threat-

---

[1] Couture (1815–1879); Cabanel (1823–1889); and Bouguereau (1825–1905) are examples.

ening mood of the mob. Daumier, like Goya, penetrated contemporary life deeply and looked through to its ugly side; and it is because he created a form as tersely powerful as his satire was biting — a perfect balance of the *what* and the *how* — that his art is so compelling (FIG. 804).

Other independents were protesting, rebelling, and experimenting in this experimental century. The alternative which every painter faced was to conform or suffer the penalty of heresy. The majority conformed; the minority, eventually victorious, rebelled. An important rebel was Edouard Manet (1832–1883). Gifted with unusual vision and a healthy interest in the everyday life about him, he began to place upon the canvas pictures taken from the real world and painted in the brilliant colors that he saw in nature, and at once found himself the object of ridicule and scorn on the part of the upholders of the old traditions. His subject matter shocked the Academicians, for it was taken, like that of Courbet, from the living world — a bullfight, a girl tending the bar, a horse race, a group on a balcony, a man in a boat, everyday people in everyday clothes. The subject as a vehicle for interpretation did not interest Manet, as it did Daumier and Millet, and in this respect Manet is on the way to abstractionism. Equally revolutionary were his technical methods. Influenced early by Ribera and Velásquez, he first used a very limited palette, and laid the color on in broad strokes, light and dark meeting abruptly, with a generally flat decorative effect (FIG. 805). Thus the *Déjeuner sur l'Herbe* and the *Olympia* impressed Paris as vulgar and indecent, in subject and in method equally. In the seventies, although he broadened and brightened his palette and used, at times, short strokes and ragged contours and filled the canvas with luminosity, Manet never quite abandoned his strongly linear, patternlike effects.

Another influence that was making itself felt in Paris in the second half of the nineteenth century was the Japanese print, whose linealism and informal, asymmetrical composition had some influence upon Manet as it did upon Edgar Degas (1834–1917). Another influence was the wave of realism which, in reaction to the earlier Romanticism and under the spur of science, emphasized cool objective observation of the entire visual world. Degas's coldly impersonal attitude toward the visual world made him exactly this kind of observer; and together with his predisposition for linear forms strengthened his affinity with Ingres. Anything in the life about him served as subject, though race horses and dancers were favorite themes. Whatever it happened to be, Degas saw it as clear line and pattern caught in some casual moment. The awkward pose of a ballet girl tying her slipper became a sensitively realized decorative motif in an asymmetrical composition

Fig. 805. Manet. The Servant of
Bocks. c. 1879. National Gallery at
Millbank, London.

Fig. 806. Degas. Dancers Dressing.
Pastel. c. 1876.

whose first impression is as casual as the theme. This informality, the
unusual bird's-eye view, the cutting of a figure by the frame, and the
total linear decorative quality all show a strong influence of the Japanese
print. Though he also worked in oil, his most characteristic work was
in pastel, whose chalky texture was the negation of realism and a
medium for effects of line and color pattern. In FIG. 806 the cracks in
the floor moving inward on a diagonal define the space into which fit
almost immaterial figures, patterns created by slender means, in violent
contrast to the tremendous bulk of Daumier's — a curious combination
of two- and three-dimensional form. But this art is not abstract, for
Degas with his bitter wit or dry satire was a commentator on certain
classes of society.

The tradition of contemporary satire of the highest character again
manifests itself in the dynamic Henri de Toulouse-Lautrec (1864–1901),
an individual as surcharged with the satirical viewpoint as Goya, his
progenitor by way of Daumier and Degas. His subject matter is the
sine qua non of his art. Steeped in his passion for observing life, gifted
to an extraordinary degree as a draftsman, he became the caustic
recorder of one slice of life, the dance halls of Montmartre. Unlike
Goya and Daumier, who saw beyond the personal to the impersonal,
generic, and universal, Toulouse-Lautrec dealt with definite individuals, penetrating to the very depth of their lives and expressing his
interpretation in a style as terse and caustic as his observation. With
a few lines he caught a characteristic pose, exaggerated or distorted to

Fig. 807. Toulouse-
Lautrec. At the Mou-
lin Rouge. 1892. Art
Institute of Chicago.
(Art Institute)

force a point of interpretation or form, but nevertheless creating a striking design. *At the Moulin-Rouge* (FIG. 807) shows probable influences of the Japanese print — the unusual point of view, the asymmetrical composition, the working into space on diagonals, the cutting of the figure on the right, the strong silhouette and linear quality. And while it is pattern it is also definitely organized in space, for the group around the table forms the focal point in a space whose frontal plane is marked by the strong mask of the dancer in the foreground and whose back plane, by the lights in the background. At the same time it is a pattern as forceful and striking in its line, its light and dark, and its color as is the characterization of the well-known persons of the central group.[1]

Another painter who quietly pursued his own problems apart from contemporary conflict was Pierre Cécile Puvis de Chavannes (1824–1898). His chief concern, mural decoration, is illustrated by the paintings in the *Panthéon*, of the life of St. Genevieve, patron saint of Paris. These murals are a harmonious unit in interior design, holding their place on the wall yet breaking up the wall area and lending color to the gray stone interior. For they are linear, the figures are simplified and decorative, and the depth is shallow or controlled by planes generally parallel to the plane of the wall, with the movement lateral.

[1] For detailed description and identification of individuals see the Art Institute of Chicago, *Loan Exhibition of Paintings, Drawings, Prints and Posters by Henri de Toulouse-Lautrec, 1930–31*, with critical comment by D. C. Rich, Art Institute, 1931.

The color has a silvery tonality, with no deep shadow or violent contrast, for the range of hue, value, and texture is limited. And even with the use of oils, Puvis de Chavannes succeeded in creating something of the effect of fresco.

Except for Daumier's lithographs (FIG. 804) and the occasional commissions to artists for specific decorations, the place of the artist in the social and economic fabric had undergone a radical change. Heretofore, even through the reigns of Louis XIV and Louis XV, supply and demand had still balanced. All the crafts were normal units in the social and economic system. But now entrance into the Salon with the hope of selling to an artificially art-conscious (not necessarily understanding) public became the chief motivation of the artist. The exhibition, an eighteenth-century product whose purpose was to prove theories or provide an economic outlet for the artist's output, took the place of the shop. Theorizing and experimentation were but the counterpart, among the artists, of the same forces working throughout the whole cultural fabric. The disintegrating Renaissance on the one hand, and on the other the tentative gropings toward a new order, slowly shaping itself around the new social and physical sciences, could not leave untouched the artist, often the most sensitive of all to fundamental changes. Some of the painters clung to the orthodox traditions, but under the impact of popular (not esthetic) demands for the novel meticulously exact copy, such as that presented by the camera, produced verisimilitudes of nature coupled with a light anecdotal or sentimental subject matter. Others, the so-called radicals — Courbet, Daumier, Manet, Degas — were caught, perhaps unconsciously, by the experimental spirit of a changing world.

The radicals of the seventies and eighties were the Impressionists,[1] Edouard Manet (in his later work); Camille Pissarro (1830–1903); Alfred Sisley (1840–1899); Berthe Morisot (1840–1895); Claude Monet (1840–1926); and Pierre Auguste Renoir (1841–1919) — to mention outstanding examples. Impressionism was not entirely novel. The realistic trend of the day aided and abetted its complete objectivity, while its technical method — the chief center of the storm — had long been foreshadowed, in color theory even by Leonardo; in actual practice by Titian, in his late years, by Rubens, Constable, Turner, and Delacroix. The objective of the Impressionist was to create an illusion of light and atmosphere, of light enveloping objects, which required an intensive study of light as a compound of color and its action upon

[1] This term was not invented by the Impressionists themselves. In 1874 Monet exhibited a sunrise scene to which he gave the title, *Impression: soleil levant*. As this title seemed quite expressive of the methods of the group, the term soon became current, but it was used at first in a sense of reproach and scorn for the painters who were the "ignorant and extravagant iconoclasts of established principles."

Fig. 808. Monet. Westminster. 1901–04. Ryerson coll., Art Institute of Chicago. (Martin A. Ryerson)

surfaces. Local color, they discovered, was but relative because of reflections from other objects, and because of modifications due to juxtaposed colors. Complementaries, for example, if used side by side in large enough areas intensify each other; if used in small quantities, fuse into a neutral. Shadows are not gray but are composed of colors that are complementary to the hue of the object casting the shadow, if not modified by reflections or other conditions. Furthermore it is not only the actual hue but its value and intensity that must be represented with exactitude — all of which is highly complex.

To express the living vibrating quality of light a technical method must be found which in the physical use of pigment would reach the same effect; and this was found in divisionism or broken color. Approach an Impressionistic picture and it becomes unintelligible — a rectangle of canvas covered with streaks and dabs of thick pigment, the colors of the spectrum, chiefly, unmixed. But move across the room and the objects appear, enveloped in glowing, shimmering light. This has happened because the little dabs of pigment were placed so accurately as regards tone and value that when the eye mixes them at the proper distance, they reproduce the shape of the objects, the texture

Fig. 809. Renoir. Luncheon of the Boating Party. 1881. Phillips
Memorial Gallery, Washington. (Phillips Memorial Gallery)

of the water, the color in the shadows, and because of their rough
surface, the vibrating quality of the light. Furthermore, the juxtaposition of colors on the canvas for the eye to mix at a distance produces
a more intense hue than the mixing of the same colors on the palette,
just as we saw was true in the making of Gothic stained-glass windows.

Monet may be taken to illustrate the group. He knew very well that
light, and therefore the appearance of nature, changed every moment
as the light shifted. So, in his insatiable desire to understand thoroughly
the appearance of an object under varying lights and atmospheric
conditions, he used to paint the same subject from the same point of
view a great many times, going out at sunrise with twenty canvases
so as to be able to catch quickly the elusive changes. And the results
are astonishingly different. Each is a realistic rendering of a fleeting
impression, as we see in Monet's *Westminster* (Fig. 808). On the farther
side of the Thames River the buildings only half emerge from the mists.
But the canvas vibrates with an effect of the light and air that envelop
them and blur their outlines. We do not get a sense of structure or a
feeling for design beyond the simplest sort of unconventional composition. There is nothing permanent, monumental, or imaginative in the
picture. It is frankly a momentary impression of *Westminster* at a time
when the buildings were half hidden in a mist; or, more specifically,
it is a painting of light and air enveloping the buildings.

Landscape was the chief subject matter of the Impressionist painters and in addition to the sparkling, vibrating, colorful surfaces of their canvases there is sometimes a lyric interpretative mood. Renoir, however, was possessed of an absorbing interest in the human figure; he took sheer delight in unaffected feminine charm and frankly expressed his joy in it; but eventually he used it as a point of departure for creating abstract rhythmical designs in deep space. His early work with its long brush strokes is close to Courbet and Manet, but even then he displayed a feeling for color in the abstract in contrast to the usual Impressionist's exact reproduction of the hues and values in nature. This innate love of color that probably received its first development from working, as a boy, in the porcelain factory at Limoges, when combined with the Impressionistic technique produced such a painting as *At the Moulin de la Galette*,[1] which, though Impressionist in technique and simple in formal composition, still is far from being an exact copy of objective vision. The color is by no means a reproduction of nature but something imaginative, something that ties the dancing rhythms into a unity; and there is a gaiety and a frank joy in people, a hint of Renoir's concentration later upon the figure. The scintillating light and the shimmering color that hold together the many diverse elements in *At the Moulin de la Galette* give way in *The Luncheon of the Boating Party* (FIG. 809) to an interest in single figures solidly constructed, and placed rhythmically in a deep space organization. The asymmetrical design working in on diagonals, reminiscent of Degas and Toulouse-Lautrec, is based upon easy movements guided by the figures and stabilized by repeated verticals. Every hue of the spectrum is there, hue melting into hue and producing a marvelously rich surface and at the same time constructing solid forms and organizing them into suave spatial rhythms. This interest in abstract rhythms in deep space, which links Renoir with Rubens, led him to paint many pictures of bathers,[2] a subject of great potentiality for the expression of deep space design. Thus Renoir, because of the solidity of his figures and their spatial organization, stands as a bridge between Impressionism and Post-Impressionism.

BIBLIOGRAPHY

Barnes, A. C., *The Art in Painting*, 2d ed. rev., Harcourt, Brace, 1928
—— and De Mazia, Violette, *The Art of Renoir*, Balch, 1934
Bell, Clive, *Landmarks in Nineteenth-Century Painting*, Harcourt, Brace, 1927
Cheney, S. W., *A Primer of Modern Art*, Liveright, 1932
Delacroix, Eugène, *Journal*, new ed., Paris, 1932

---

[1] See Munro, *Great Pictures of Europe*, pp. 73–76, for a detailed analysis.
[2] See W. H. Wright, *Modern Painting*, Dodd, Mead, 1927, opposite p. 126, for two of these *Bathers* showing Renoir's transition to his fullest expression.

Duret, Théodore, *Manet and the French Impressionists*, tr. by J. E. C. Flitch, Lippincott, 1910

Fry, R. E., *Characteristics of French Art*, Coward-McCann, 1933

—— —— *Transformations*, Coward-McCann, 1927

Hind, C. L., *Landscape Painting from Giotto to the Present Day*, Scribner, 1923, 2 vols.

Hourticq, Louis, *Art in France*, Scribner, 1911

Huneker, J. G., *Promenades of an Impressionist*, Scribner, 1910

Marriott, Charles, *Modern Movements in Painting*, Scribner, 1921

Mather, F. J., *Modern Painting*, Holt, 1927

Mauclair, Camille, *The French Impressionists*, Dutton, 1903

—— —— *Great French Painters*, Dutton, 1903

Meier-Graefe, Julius, *Modern Art*, tr. by Florence Simmonds and G. W. Chrystal, Putnam, 1908, 2 vols.

—— —— *Renoir*, Leipzig, 1929

Mourey, Gabriel, *French Art in the XIX Century*, Studio, 1928

Munro, Thomas, *Great Pictures of Europe*, Coward-McCann, 1930

Rutter, F. V. P., *Evolution in Modern Art*, rev. ed., London, 1932

Speed, Harold, *The Science and Practice of Oil Painting*, Scribner, 1924

Vollard, Ambroise, *Degas, an Intimate Portrait*, tr. by R. T. Weaver, Greenberg, 1927

—— —— *Renoir, an Intimate Portrait*, tr. by H. L. Van Doren and R. T. Weaver, Knopf, 1925

Waldmann, Emil, *Die Kunst des Realismus und des Impressionismus im 19. Jahrhundert*, Berlin, 1927

Wilenski, R. H., *French Painting*, Hale, Cushman, and Flint, 1931

Wright, W. H., *Modern Painting: Its Tendency and Meaning*, Dodd, Mead, 1927

CHAPTER XXIX

Art in the United States: The Nineteenth Century

A. HISTORICAL BACKGROUND

The death of Gilbert Stuart in 1828 and the inauguration of Andrew Jackson as President ushering in Jacksonian democracy in 1829 are symbols of radical changes in the social and economic orders. In both Europe and America a general supplanting of the aristocracy by the bourgeoisie was taking place, with consequent cultural decline, a movement accentuated by local conditions on this side of the Atlantic. The decades from 1830 to 1860 were a time of great activity and expansion. The annexation of Texas and the war with Mexico were followed by pushing the frontiers to the Pacific and by the gold rush of the Fortyniners. The coming of the machine age stimulated an amazing growth of industry, the development of the railway, and a flood of immigrants. With economic expansion came wealth and leisure to those who had never possessed it; and also demands for education. At this time appeared the illustrated American weeklies and the widely circulated newspapers. It was the day of Horace Greeley and the famous "Young man, go West." Among those who remained in the East two hundred years of steadfast cultural growth produced one of America's prime art expressions — the literature of Irving, Cooper, Poe, Hawthorne, Bryant, Emerson, Thoreau, Whittier, Holmes, Longfellow.

The Civil War marked the triumph of industrial and business enterprise and resulted in a great expansion of industry and transportation, the rounding-out of the continent, and the exploitation of the West. The growth of industry demanded centralization and consequently an urban rather than an agrarian type of civilization. Thus arose the American metropolis with its enormous wealth and ostentatious display — the "Gilded Age" — an acquisitive society based upon "rugged individualism" and the building up of huge fortunes such as those of Morgan, Carnegie, and Rockefeller. Many of the plutocrats were bourgeois in type, and in their hands wealth alone captured the social citadels of the remnant of the eighteenth-century aristocracy. Their tastes brought in the "heyday of the scroll saw, Rogers groups, and the dime novel." [1] Permeating this local situation was the world nineteenth-century ferment, the age of applied science and advancing technology, of research in pure science, of theories of evolution, of social ethics and social democracy. Social conflicts or local social color furnished the themes of a spontaneous, highly characteristic kind of literature, pioneer stories of the West, Mark Twain, Eugene Field, and "Mr. Dooley," which paralleled the continuity of the New England tradition in Emerson, Lowell, Emily Dickinson and, with a new note, in Walt Whitman.

The place of the arts in this disunited evolving culture was as disheartening as it was in England or in France in the nineteenth century but for the great exception of the French rebels. The varied, vigorous, and youthful enthusiasms of a new republic might well have produced a commensurate art expression had both the patrons and the artists avoided contamination with the subtle poison of the nineteenth century: the pressure to copy someone else. But the patrons, the bourgeois plutocrats whose energies had been utilized in acquiring wealth at the expense of culture and education, turned their backs upon "provincial" America, went to Europe, patronized dealers and built up collections; and set up an American inferiority complex. Artists followed their

---

[1] Lewis Mumford, *The Brown Decades*, Harcourt, Brace, 1931, a brilliant analysis of the period.

Fig. 810. United States Capitol. Washington. 1818–65. (Copyright
by Detroit Publishing Co.)

example in a vain attempt to supply the increasing demand. Probably
they are not to be blamed. Only a courageous rebel could defy nineteenth-century eclecticism. That some of the French did, gloriously,
is largely due to the long, steadying traditions behind them.

B. ARCHITECTURE

What then, in view of this situation, was actually accomplished in
the arts? The Industrial Revolution resulted in the same degradation
of the crafts as in the other countries, for the machine at first could be
seen only as a short-cut process for making things designed for hand-
work and not itself a determinant of design. The rise of cities proved
a fertile field, economically, for the builder. But wealth enabled people
to travel and to come into direct contact with European movements
and fashions. Thus the nineteenth-century European Romanticism and
eclecticism are reflected in the States.

This ideal, however, had already taken root in the Classicism of
Thomas Jefferson, so that up to about 1850 copies of classical buildings
sprang up, quite regardless of dissimilarity of climate and function;
now it was Roman, like the *State House at Richmond* (patterned after the
Maison Carrée) and the *University of Virginia;* now designed after Greek
temples, like the *United States Bank* (*New Custom House*) of Philadelphia
and the *Sub-Treasury* and *Custom House* of New York. Renaissance
variants of the classical tradition appear in the *Capitol* at Washington
(Fig. 810). In domestic architecture Jefferson introduced the Classical
style in his own home *Monticello*, with its Doric portico; while the
Palladian two-storied portico appeared in many a Southern home, and

at the *White House*, whose windows repeated the Renaissance type of treatment.

Beginning with this Classical movement, the nineteenth century witnessed a succession of historic styles. There was the French Renaissance, witness Fifth Avenue mansions, many recently wrecked to make room for the modern apartment building. There was the Gothic, witness not only many stone cathedrals but a smattering of Gothic detail, found anywhere and everywhere, like the Classical, because it existed in the builders' copybooks. There was the Romanesque, whose chief exponent, Henry Hobson Richardson (1838–1886), despite his eclecticism was a pioneer in his realization that function, site, and material are, after all, determinants in the building

Fig. 811. Marshall Field Wholesale House. Chicago. Recently wrecked. H. H. Richardson, architect.

art. Thus, though under the spell of the Romanesque through direct contact with it in Europe, he showed in such a building as the *Marshall Field Wholesale House* (FIG. 811), now destroyed, the sturdy massiveness of the prototype, and at the same time allowed the large openings necessary in a Northern climate and in an industrial structure. The walls of finely cut stone were frankly constructional and the fenestration peculiarly adapted to the stone construction, to the need for a large amount of light, and for a sensitive play of shapes, arrangement, and proportions.

Again the Classical appeared especially as a result of the *World's Columbian Exposition* of 1893 at Chicago (FIG. 812) in which an extraordinary unity resulted from a consistent use of the style, with one conspicuous exception — the portal of the *Transportation Building* (FIG. 813). This was the work of Louis Sullivan (1856–1924), another pioneer in American art. Concentric arches almost within a single plane, decorated by original low reliefs which do not mar the feeling of the plane, swing around the doorway. Sullivan's famous dictum that form results from function determined in his own work the preliminary stages of skyscraper evolution. The preëminent place of industry and the crowded urban site; the scientific developments in elevator service, in illumination, heating, and protection from fire; and the use of steel, reinforced concrete, and fireproof brick as structural

Fig. 812. The Peristyle and Statue of the Republic. World's Columbian Exposition, Chicago, 1893. (Ryerson Library)

materials, combined with advanced engineering technique — all these
considerations contributed to produce the skyscraper. The problem of
designing such a structure according to Sullivan's theory was not easy.
To reveal the structural steel framework; to use stone or brick or tile
so that its appearance indicates its function as a screen and not as a
support; and at the same time to give the tall façade balance, unity,
and variety — these were problems in skyscraper design. One of the
first successful solutions was Sullivan's *Prudential (Guaranty) Building* of
Buffalo, in which one feels the framework of vertical shafts and horizontal beams in the lines of the encasement, and the massing of larger nonstructural units to form an effective base and to provide the necessary
large window openings.

C. PAINTING

In the field of painting the nineteenth century (that is, from about
1815 to 1913), while it proved anything but a time of normal growth,
provided an illuminating instance of cause and effect. Its happenings
reveal a series of attempts: group and individual; concurrent, continuous, and sporadic; conflicting and disconnected; and all very uneven in attainment. Yet in view of the whole situation the result could
hardly have been otherwise. Just to enumerate ten major happenings
is evidence of confusion: 1. A *waning continuation* of early republican
portrait-painting. 2. The rise of *historical* and *mythological* subjects.

Fig. 813. Transportation Building. Entrance. World's Columbian
Exposition, Chicago, 1893. (Ryerson Library)

3. A continuation of the virile *native folk art*. 4. The emergence of a
native school of *landscape*. 5. The coming of *academic* and *exhibition
painting* (figure, portrait, murals, and genre) modeled on European
prototypes. 6. The presence of individuals, "*solitaries*" (Mather), working often in comparative isolation. 7. The coming of *Impressionism*.
8. The protest of "*The Ten*." 9. The further protest of "*The Eight*."
10. The *Armory Show* of 1913. In the absence of a steadying tradition
to assist in the necessary task of assimilating these varying factors, is
it any wonder that nineteenth-century painting in its style, subject
matter, and objectives is a welter of unassimilated trends?

Let us touch briefly on each of the ten happenings mentioned. The
demand for portraits lingered on in the East to be supplied, after the
death of Stuart, by Thomas Sully (1783–1872), who painted technically accomplished and usually pretty portraits imbued with all the
mannerisms of the late English portrait-painters; by Samuel F. B. Morse
(1791–1872), who was trained in France and attained a vigorous style
and forceful characterization, as in the *Lafayette* (FIG. 814). But Morse
abandoned painting for the scientific field, partly because of the general
aridity of the art field for the American painter and partly because of
the rising vogue of the daguerreotype, which almost abolished the demand for the painted portrait.[1]

[1] Other important portrait painters were Chester Harding (1792–1866) and Eastman Johnson (1824–1906).

Fig. 814. Morse. The Marquis de Lafayette. 1825. New York Public Library.
(New York Public Library)

Historical and mythological painting was stimulated partly by the new spirit of nationalism and partly by Benjamin West's Romanticism with a tinge of David's Classicism. It proved, however, to be histrionics rather than historical probity, despite the shock caused by West's audacity in clothing his figures in contemporary costume. Thus the huge canvases of John Trumbull (1756–1843) seem mediocre patriotic illustrations rather than creative art, and the Classical subjects of John Vanderlyn (1776–1852) and Washington Allston (1779–1843), painted in "the grand manner," technically proficient artificial canvases for which there was no demand.

Paralleling these expressions of the European trained painters were those of the untrained folk at home, a spontaneous folk art in which the ultimate reality of the person or object was set forth with a forceful directness. The untrained worker with no rules or formulas must needs reach his objective in his own direct way, usually by means of conventions rather than naturalistically. Some of these expressions, in which an intuitive esthetic feeling was joined with sound craftsmanship, attained a high quality (Fig. 815). The work of these folk artists is found in all mediums, is largely anonymous, local, and much of it utilitarian — weathervanes, hitching-posts, ships, figureheads, decoys, embroideries, furniture in addition to painting and purely decorative carvings (Fig. 827).

Interest in the local scene found a dual expression. A general feeling of nationalism inspired by a youthful nation, the influence of the illustrated weeklies, and the stories of the "Wild West" were producing the tales of Irving and Cooper and giving rise to a parallel expression in a native landscape and genre. Landscape found its beginning in the so-called Hudson River School,[1] whose members painted in the vicinity of the Hudson River and in other localities as well. A true love of nature revealed itself in a certain fine feeling that permeates the un-

[1] Important painters were Thomas Doughty (1793–1856); Asher B. Durand (1796–1886); Thomas Cole (1801–1848); John F. Kensett (1818–1872); all of whom were trained engravers.

organized detail and the green and brown tonality similar to that of the Dutch and early English landscape-painters. A forthright detailed description of the scene rather than an artist's unified visualization is what one usually finds in these landscapes; more intimate scenes in Doughty (FIG. 816) and Durand; more grandiose and romantic in Cole as a result of travel in Europe and influence from Turner. Another group, the Panoramists,[1] sought their subject matter in the newly discovered majestic scenery of the Rockies and the Sierras, Mexico, and South America; they attempted, with questionable results, to express something of the grandeur of the West.

From the Hudson River School emerged Homer D. Martin (1836–1897), Alexander Wyant (1836–1892), and George Inness (1825–1894), men who contributed both native ability and more thorough technical proficiency gained chiefly under the influence of the Barbizon painters. The comparison of an early Inness such as *Peace and Plenty* (Metropolitan Museum) with a late example such as the *Rosy Morn* (FIG. 817) shows an evolution from a panoramic vision and a painstaking recording of objective detail to a broad synthesis of essentials selected for the purpose of interpretation.

Similar in attitude toward the local scene were the genre painters,[2] who found their inspiration in the everyday scene within the home, in the courtyard, the city street, the country, the "Wild West." Their honest, frank pleasure in such scenes manifested itself in a veracity to objective appearance. With the advent of the camera they entered into competition to attain a verisimilitude of actuality. Such paintings as Hovenden's, as Brown's newsboys and Boughton's pilgrims became merely story-telling snapshots. Not so the work of Johnson, Homer, and Eakins, in which the genre content was expressed in a form founded upon visualization rather than upon vision and upon organization of elements rather than upon a reproduction of verisimilitude.

Patronage, however, was moving in another direction. The confusion which followed the Civil War and the rise of the "Gilded Age," with its wealth and Europeanized ideals, enthusiasm for "collections" and the consequent emergence of dealers, drove the painters to Europe in an effort to supply the demand. But in vain, for the patrons purchased names (European) rather than paintings. Some of the painters went to Düsseldorf and Munich,[3] where they acquired a technique of

[1] Important were Frederick E. Church (1826–1900); Albert Bierstadt (1830–1902); Thomas Moran (1837–1926).

[2] John L. Krimmel (1787–1821); Henry Inman (1801–1846); William S. Mount (1807–1868); Thomas Hovenden (1840–1895); Frederick Remington (1861–1909); Eastman Johnson (1824–1906); Winslow Homer (1836–1910); Thomas Eakins (1844–1916).

[3] Notably William Merritt Chase (1849–1916); Frank Duveneck (1848–1919); John W. Alexander (1856–1915); Walter Shirlaw (1838–1909).

Fig. 815. Pickett. Council Tree, Coryell's Ferry, New Hope, Pennsylvania. Newark Museum, Newark, New Jersey. (Newark Museum)

bold vigorous brush work, the use of black or dark colors, and strong contrasts in value. More went to Paris [1] into the ateliers of the popular Academic painters and learned the formulas governing "proper" subject matter and a suave technique expended chiefly upon figure-painting based upon a visual perception of the model.

In both Germany and France these young men gained a sound routine training and became able technicians. But imbued with European salon ideals and confronted with the Europeanizing of America they found themselves at one point of an unfortunate triangle: a lusty new republic deep in the nineteenth-century ferment; a patronage with untrained, artificial (if any) taste, quite unconscious if not snobbish of a vigorous stimulating birthright in art, and quite blind to any function that the artist might play in the American commonwealth; and the painters themselves caught between these divergent elements. In view of the situation some of the painters remained in Europe; others came home to practice what was largely art for art's sake rather than an art that grew out of and functioned in the culture which produced them. Some assimilated their European training better than others — a repetition of Stuart vs. Copley; some displayed more virility and independence, Vedder for example, in his personal strongly linear style,

[1] Of this large group important examples are Kenyon Cox (1856–1919); Elihu Vedder (1836–1923); Abbott H. Thayer (1849–1921); Thomas W. Dewing (1851——); Edwin H. Blashfield (1848——); Edwin A. Abbey (1852–1911); Edmund C. Tarbell (1862——); Frank W. Benson (1862——); George de Forest Brush (1855——). Their work is largely figure work and murals, with some portraits.

Fig. 816. Doughty. On the Hudson. Metropolitan Museum, New York.
(Metropolitan Museum)

based to be sure upon Ingres and the latter's Italian prototypes. John
La Farge (1835–1910) was another independent who through his wide
travel in the Far East as well as in Europe contributed a breadth of
outlook and a feeling for sound craftsmanship that is seen particularly
in his work in glass. In this medium, in protest against the degraded
practice of painting pictures on glass, he revived the medieval conception of a mosaic of small units of glass colored in the pot and leaded into
a flat decorative design.

Of the painters who remained permanently abroad, Whistler and
Sargent are prominent examples. James Abbott McNeill Whistler
(1834–1903) was one of the first to come within the periphery of the
French revolutionary painters, with the result that Courbet, Manet
and through them, Velásquez, Degas, Japanese prints, and the early
Impressionists are easily discernible influences in his work. In protest
against the current realistic anecdotal painting, whose objective was
the story and the snapshot, he became a champion of art for art's sake.
But his method of protesting was characteristically personal, a mixture
of personal irritation and sound fundamentals. He preached [1] and
practiced the subordination of content in favor of "Harmonies,"
"Arrangements," "Nocturnes." Some of the portraits, especially *Miss
Alexander* (*Harmony in Grey and Green*), *Mother* (*Harmony in Grey and Black*),
and *Carlyle*, reveal a sensitive organization with an emphasis on pattern

[1] For his theories see his *Ten o'Clock*, North, 1908.

Fig. 817. Inness. Rosy Morn. 1894. Ryerson coll., Art Institute of
Chicago. (Martin A. Ryerson)

Fig. 818. Whistler. Nocturne, Southampton Water. Art Institute of
Chicago. (Art Institute)

Fig. 819. Sargent. Mrs. Swinton. Art Institute of Chicago. (Art Institute)

Fig. 820. Whistler. Portrait of Miss Alexander. 1872. W. C. Alexander coll., London.

and with subtle harmonies through modulated values within a narrow range of hue. In the *Alexander* portrait (FIG. 820) the young girl is standing before a paneled background of gray and black wearing a white dress with a green sash and carrying a hat with a green plume. The gray and green with black and gold dominate the composition. In some parts they are massed strongly; in others they consist of faint strokes. Compositionally, rectangles, triangles, and circles repeat and contrast. In the *Nocturne, Southampton Water* (FIG. 818) four tones are laid on in the thin pigment with loose brush work; the forms have become ephemeral in the pursuit of a color harmony that suggests the poetry of a moonlight scene in Southampton Harbor. In these two paintings the bird's-eye point of view, the informal asymmetrical composition, the flowers breaking into the frame, the color relation, and the strong linear quality — these are a few evidences of the same influence that we found in Degas, that of the Japanese print; while the full-length figure, so characteristic of Whistler's portraits, the use of black and neutrals, the emphasis upon values, and the brush work reveal a strong influence of Velásquez.

John Singer Sargent (1856–1925), born in Florence and trained in the academic Parisian atmosphere, became the popular portrait-painter of certain socially prominent wealthy patrons. A virtuoso in

Fig. 821. Eakins. The Pathetic Song. 1881. Corcoran Gallery of Art, Washington. (Corcoran Gallery)

pigment, he created surface effects with his brilliant dashing brush work. In the *Mrs. Swinton* (FIG. 819), for example, the effect is one of superficial elegance rather than of formal significance and penetrating interpretation, an effect that results partly from the stately pose and partly from the luxuriousness of the dress and surroundings. For Sargent was particularly successful in creating a certain atmosphere through the textures of elegant stuffs and through a simple composition. In this portrait the curving chair and the sweeping drapery make a firm base of rhythmic curves above which the figure rises with quiet stateliness. But unfortunately Sargent seems to have allowed the stern fundamentals of form to be glossed over by superficial virtuosity.

In contrast to the Europeanized painters were the "Solitaries," who assimilated whatever, if any, European training and travel they had had and pursued their profession frequently in obscurity or isolation, quite without regard to the popular tastes and fashions of the day. Characteristic of this group were George Fuller (1822–1884); Thomas Eakins (1844–1916); Albert P. Ryder (1847–1917); and Winslow Homer (1836–1910). Eakins, though thoroughly trained in Europe, kept his feet firmly planted on local ground and his eyes fixed unwaveringly upon whatever he was painting — chiefly the people and scenes of his own immediate environment — and produced the finished work after making a large number of preliminary drawings. The term "realist" is usually applied to Eakins. He was a realist not in the sense of photographic verisimilitude but in his presentation of the essentials of objectivity based upon a thorough understanding of structure. His sober color and uncompromising fidelity to objective reality make his art austere. At times it displays weak passages esthetically or a lack of complete consistency and unity of the esthetic elements. For the *what*, vividly perceived, tended to overbalance the *how*. Yet its thoroughness and probity have been a steadying influence in the evolution of an American tradition (FIG. 821).

Fig. 822. Homer. Northeaster. 1895. Metropolitan Museum, New York.
(Metropolitan Museum)

Another sound influence in the latter part of the nineteenth century, though like that of Eakins not felt in the midst of the "Gilded Age," was that of Winslow Homer. His work as an illustrator on *Harper's Weekly* until 1875 perhaps determined the strongly illustrative character of much of his painting. After some European travel, with purposeful avoidance of art centers, and a sojourn in the tropics, the result of which was some of his best watercolors, he settled on the Maine coast and in isolation devoted himself to the interpretation of that locality. Like Eakins, he was firmly rooted in his own environment and did not scorn to use it as his raw material. While visual perception was his starting-point and objective, he expressed it with economy and with as much concern for the organization through which he expressed this raw material as for the material itself. In the *Northeaster* (FIG. 822), for example, the relationship of lines and light and dark areas, the contrasts of movement and immobility, are largely responsible for the expression and interpretation of this storm-resistant shore.

If Eakins and Homer are more or less realists both in content and in manner of expression, Ryder was the visionary, the mystic, and the abstractionist; the Blake, as he has been called, of American painting though he lacked Blake's great ability in drawing and in design. Clumsy in the use of his medium, for he was untrained even in the fundamentals of his craft, he reduced the elements of his composition to the simplest pattern and color, and labored over the surface, building it up thickly

Fig. 823. Ryder. Moonlit Cove. 1890–1900. Phillips Memorial Gallery, Washington. (Phillips Memorial Gallery)

Fig. 824. Twachtman. Snow-Bound. Art Institute of Chicago. (Art Institute)

Fig. 825. Sloan. Backyards, Greenwich Village. 1914. Kraushaar Gallery, New York. (C. W. Kraushaar)

into a smooth texture. The sea, especially in moonlight, a favorite subject, was rooted in his own experience as a youth on the shores of Long Island Sound. Such a painting as *Moonlit Cove* (FIG. 823) is a consistent expression of Ryder's imaginative rendering of actuality.

Though Impressionism had won recognition in Paris before 1886 and an exhibition of Impressionistic pictures was shown in New York in 1885, it had almost no effect upon Americans until the last decade of the century, when a few pioneers began using the Impressionistic technique and thus opened up novel uses of pigment and a more intense and varied color. Basically, however, it eventuated in substituting one French technique for another, though the Americans used Impressionism with considerable individual variations.[1] Twachtman, for example (FIG. 824), perhaps because of his thorough academic training in Munich and Paris, combined a stronger sense of design than is usual in Impressionistic painters with a high-keyed subtle luminosity; while Prendergast evolved into a boldly decorative style with strong reliance upon texture and juxtaposed contrasts for decorative effect.

Professionally, the American painter was now well equipped. But on the one hand, he had lost contact with his own root actualities; on the other, wealthy patrons were still purchasing European pictures,

[1] John H. Twachtman (1853–1902); J. Alden Weir (1852–1919); Willard L. Metcalf (1858–1925); Childe Hassam (1859–1935); Maurice B. Prendergast (1861–1924); Edward W. Redfield (1869–——); Ernest Lawson (1873–——); Frederick C. Frieseke (1874–——); Gifford Beal (1879–——); Jonas Lie (1880–——); and Mary Cassatt (1845–1926), who, however, clung more to the style of Degas and Manet than to the truly Impressionistic.

Fig. 826. Bellows. My Mother.
c. 1921. Art Institute of Chicago.
(Art Institute)

Dutch or French Salon or Barbizon styles being particularly popular, while the public was captivated by the anecdotal, photographic picture, usually sentimental, such as Israels' *Alone in the World*, or Hovenden's *Breaking Home Ties* (the prize painting by popular vote of the 1893 World's Columbian Exposition). Thus, apart from a few commissions for murals and portraits, there was no function for the painter and little demand for his product.

In protest to this almost exclusive patronage of European painters, in 1898 "The Ten" [1] organized and held an exhibition of their work. And rebellion taking another line of offense was developing among the young painters of the last decade of the century, with Robert Henri a leader in the attack. Individualists, soundly trained at home and abroad, they had sought stimulation wherever they could find it, in the Louvre and among the French rebels rather than in the academic ateliers of Paris; and at home their profession as newspaper illustrators, like that of Homer and Daumier, had thrust upon them, as raw material for the artist, their own immediate life in all its phases. In 1908 "The Eight" [2] organized to protest the tyranny of authority in art in general and Europeanized studio art in particular. The diversity of aim and of style in this group, united though they were in their general objective, infused health and individuality into the evolving American tradition. Three of the group, Prendergast, Glackens, and Lawson, were Luminists; Henri and Luks worked in the Chase and Duveneck tradition of vigorous brush work with strong contrasts in values, though their objective in painting, human significance, differed from that of the latter two, who were inclined to place technique and fine painting first. In this respect they were close to Manet, as they were at times technically. Davies, though in his personal life and work he lived in the realm of fantasy, a late

---

[1] Chase, Dewing, Hassam, Tarbell, Twachtman, and Weir are the best known.
[2] Robert Henri (1865–1929); Maurice B. Prendergast (1861–1924); Arthur B. Davies (1862–1928); George Luks (1867–1933); William J. Glackens (1870——); Ernest Lawson (1873——); John Sloan (1871——); George W. Bellows (1882–1925).

Romanticist, was a wholehearted supporter of the movement, and made an
individual pioneer contribution by working in a large number of mediums and
thus breaking into the narrowly specialized craft of the American painter.

The influence of Henri was felt upon
his contemporary Sloan and the somewhat younger George Bellows. With
these two painters — both were also accomplished etchers and lithographers —
the objective became the interpretation
of the American scene, the human actualities of their own milieu. Sloan's keen
observation was probably stimulated by
Eakins' paintings, for his early training
was in Philadelphia, but the satiric strain
with which he infused his observations
was his own (FIG. 825). Much of his
work is a faithful interpretive record of
life in the alleys, back yards, bars, and
harbor of New York and some of the best

Fig. 827. Eagle. Wood. H. 68 in.
(Courtesy Museum of Modern Art,
New York)

are etchings. Bellows perhaps more than the others of the group
plunged into the contemporary scene, and because of his forceful personality frequently selected vigorous and dramatic subjects, such as
A Stag at Sharkey's, or *Edith Cavell*. In the portraits of members of his
family (FIG. 826) one sees the vigor of his brush work, a technical use
of pigment quite consistent with the energy of his personality, strongly
contrasting values, accomplished composition, and direct characterization. It was members of this group who were responsible for bringing
to America the International Exhibition of Modern Art (known as the
Armory Show) of 1913, which included paintings of Cézanne, the
Cubists, and other Post-Impressionists, and sculpture by Bourdelle,
Brancusi, Lehmbruck, Maillol, and other modernist sculptors — a
show which was a definite landmark if not a beginning of the modern
movement on this side of the Atlantic.

"The history of painting in America is mainly a record of successive
importations of painting technics from Europe. In every instance, from
colonial formularizing to cubistic patternizing, it has involved some
addition to our own professional resources and popular culture. All
of it has been part of a general spiritual agriculture, making a new
world fit for human habitation.

"The history of American painting is a discovery of what, in all the

Fig. 828. Saint-Gaudens. Adams Monument. Bronze and Granite. 1887. Rock Creek Cemetery, Washington.

production of that art, has flowered into a picturing of our own experience and mentality." [1]

The last decade of the nineteenth century and the first decade of the twentieth pointed to a well-laid foundation for the flowering of an American art with its own "specific expressiveness."

D. SCULPTURE

A truly sculptural expression has lagged far behind the other arts. Practically no sculpture was created in the colonies except for the iron-work and fine woodcarvings for weathervanes, hitching-posts, figureheads for ships' prows, and the like which probably no one ever dreamed of calling sculpture (FIG. 827). This lack is not surprising when one recalls the want of sculptural feeling among the Anglo-Saxon forbears and to that adds the Puritan prejudice inherited from the zealous iconoclasts of the Reformation. The few who practiced the art studied or lived permanently in Italy and worked in a weak Italianate or neo-classic style. Probably the outstanding sculptor of the nineteenth century was Augustus Saint-Gaudens (1848–1907). In the long series of portraits and monuments, both in relief and in the round, probably most monumental both in imaginative conception and sculptural form is the *Adams Memorial* (FIG. 828), a quiet mysterious figure wrapped in a voluminous mantle that shadows the face, sitting with the chin resting on the right hand, brooding. One notes its freedom from distracting representational detail and its monumentally simple design, in which the figure of bronze composed in simple planes, unbroken contours, and emphatic curves is united with the angular masses of rough-textured granite.

E. SUMMARY

In the life of the American nation to the early twentieth century, a short three hundred years, most of the art produced has been largely

[1] Virgil Barker, *A Critical Introduction to American Painting*, Whitney Museum of American Art, New York, 1931, p. 39.

eclectic, a normal process in a colonizing people at first, but later, in the face of an unprecedented development of resources and material prosperity, it represented a cultural lag due to generally unfortunate conditions: the world confusion, eclecticism, and the low ebb of creative expression in the nineteenth century; the youth of the nation; and the diversion of its energies into the development of its natural resources. It was inevitable that the colonists should bring with them the inherited traditions of the home country. And it was also inevitable that these traditions should develop, perhaps with provincial mediocrity, to their logical end — empty copying — unless some vitalizing force should stimulate their evolution under the impact of new conditions. But the youthfulness of the nation has operated against the reception of such a stimulus. The heterogeneous elements found among the American people have not yet fused into a coherent unity — political, social, religious, and intellectual — to create fundamental traditions, to establish capacity for appreciation on the part of the people, and thus to create a demand for the real artist. The energies of the nation have gone into the development of the country — again the inevitable condition of a colonizing people — which has led into an age of great mechanical and scientific industrialism, with a materialism frequently preponderant at the cost of the spiritual, the ethical, and the intellectual. The creative impulse, under these conditions, has found comparatively little encouragement. And yet: "The American, while adhering closely to his utilitarian and economical principles, has unwittingly, in some objects to which his heart equally with his hand has been devoted, developed a degree of beauty in them that no other nation equals. His clipper-ships, fire-engines, locomotives and some of his machinery and tools combine that equilibrium of lines, proportions, and masses which are the fundamental causes of abstract beauty. Their success in producing broad general effects out of a few simple elements, and of admirable adaptations of means to ends, as nature evolves beauty out of the common and practical, covers these things with a certain atmosphere of poetry, and is an indication of what may happen to the rest of his work when he puts into it an equal amount of heart and knowledge." [1]

[1] A strangely true prophecy of art in America today, written by James J. Jarves in 1864 and quoted by Mumford in *The Brown Decades*, p. 187, by permission of Harcourt, Brace and Company. Continue the quotation for an extraordinarily clear evaluation of eclecticism.

BIBLIOGRAPHY

In addition to the books listed on p. 532:

Cahill, Holger, and Barr, A. H., *Art in America in Modern Times*, Reynal & Hitchcock, 1934
Cortissoz, Royal, *American Artists*, Scribner, 1923
Duret, Théodore, *Whistler*, tr. by Frank Rutter, Lippincott, 1917
Goodrich, Lloyd, *Thomas Eakins, His Life and Work*, Whitney Museum of American Art, 1933
Hitchcock, H. R., Jr., *The Architecture of [Henry Hobson] Richardson and His Times*, Museum of Modern Art, 1936
Inness, George, Jr., *Life, Art, and Letters of George Inness*, Century, 1917
Kootz, S. M., *Modern American Painters*, Harcourt, Brace, 1930
Morrison, Hugh, *Louis Sullivan*, Norton, 1935
Mumford, Lewis, *The Brown Decades: A Study of the Arts in America*, Harcourt, Brace, 1931
Museum of Modern Art, *American Painting & Sculpture, 1862–1932*, Museum, New York, 1932 (also Norton)
———— [*Winslow*] *Homer*, [*Albert P.*] *Ryder*, [*Thomas*] *Eakins*, Museum, New York, 1930
Pennell, E. R., and Joseph, *The Life of James McNeill Whistler*, 6th ed. rev., Lippincott, 1919
Saint-Gaudens, Augustus, *Reminiscences*, ed. and amplified by Homer Saint-Gaudens, Century, 1913, 2 vols.
Sullivan, L. H., *The Autobiography of an Idea*, American Institute of Architects, 1924
Whitney Museum of American Art, monographs by various authors on Bellows, Davies, Glackens, Luks, Prendergast, Twachtman, and others.

See also the General Bibliography, pp. 749–751.

CHAPTER XXX

The Art of Today

A. HISTORICAL BACKGROUND

No specific year and no specific event marks culturally the passage of the nineteenth century into the twentieth, so part and parcel are they of one great transitional movement from the late Renaissance to a dimly discerned and as yet unnamed new age. At the present the cultural outlook is predominantly scientific, mechanistic, industrial, urban, and secular. The roots of modern culture are deep in the past and its growth was mightily accelerated by the French Revolution and the Industrial Revolution, with all their implications. The same forces are now at work with accelerated speed. The Great War, the Great

Disillusionment, the Great Depression, followed one another in swift succession, and the confusion of the nineteenth century has become the superconfusion of the twentieth — a confusion, however, that is the outward expression of an evolutionary process. "The only normalcy is change." Culture is never static. Under the impact of inexorable forces it is constantly changing, at times imperceptibly, at times with the eruptive force of a volcano. The latter is true today. Ferment, confusion, change, and realignment have developed a highly specialized faculty for -isms, -ologies, and -ocracies; necessarily so, for only by experiment will the way out be found. No field of human experience is left untouched by adventurous experiment. The hopeful aspect is that no issue survives long enough to become an authority, a dogma, with such rapidity does one theory capture the imagination one day only to find itself tossed on the trash heap the next. Breath-taking discoveries in pure science appear in such rapid succession that their application must be withheld to prevent complete chaos. Thus in jerky, broken rhythms we wangle a way out, by trial and error. Some of our experiments prove themselves to be only means toward an end. Others attain a plane of permanent value. And of these there are not a few. Yet the ultimate reality is not an accomplishment but a becoming.

Probably no one questions the confusion of today. The real question is, Is it complete chaos? To confine ourselves to the field of the arts, are there discernible today definite enough trends to justify a belief that a new style, perhaps a twentieth-century style, is emerging? Or is it here? The answer to the question should be based upon a wide survey of the arts — architecture, sculpture, painting, the industrial and minor arts, literature, music, drama, the dance — a peculiarly difficult task because the output is prolific, of very uneven quality, widespread, and while in some spots nationalistic, in others is increasingly international. Evaluation of contemporary events is hazardous if at all justifiable, and then only on a very broad base. Hence within the confines of one chapter resort will have to be made to generalizations, which are always hazardous.

One very important and often overlooked aspect of the contemporary situation is the social and economic position of the artist — the problem of supply and demand. Consider his position before the nineteenth century. Kings, priests, popes, nobles, and guilds kept up a steady demand for the artist's products. Works of art appear to have been created but rarely unless definitely commissioned for a specific function, and reasonably within the general limits of traditional style.[1] The

[1] It is illuminating to observe the cases where artists have forced tradition, through the power of their individualities, toward or into new channels. The abortive attempt

Fig. 829. Empire State Building. New York. Shreve, Lamb and Harmon architects. 1930. (Ryerson Library)

artist, then, was a definite necessary part of the social organization, and had few if any economic worries, because supply and demand were reasonably adjusted. In the nineteenth century, however, such patronage almost ceased, not because the artists were not worthy but because political, social, and economic conditions wiped out patronage. The situation in the fields of architecture and most of the minor arts because of their inherently purposeful character has never been so acute as with painting and sculpture. But with the coming of the machine many of the minor arts and all of the handcrafts joined sculpture and painting in their forced ostracism from the system.[1]

B. ARCHITECTURE

The "battle of the styles" which formed the basis of nineteenth-century architecture aroused a protest from a few pioneers. New materials and new mechanical devices; the definite establishment of the machine age; the need of a type of structure suitable for urban, industrial centers — these considerations called for a style quite different from the traditional styles, each of which had evolved from a dissimilar milieu. Hence these pioneers broke with the past in the sense of something authoritative, of a desirable pattern to be copied, but not in the sense of adherence to certain essential principles of all building. In fact it is illuminating to note that the great artists of today, painters, sculptors, weavers, potters, glassworkers, and metalworkers as well as builders, have an intimate knowledge and profound understanding of

in Egypt under Ikhnaton is a case where native conservatism was destined to overwhelm any evolutionary growth. Giotto, Masaccio, and Donatello lived at a time and in a city peculiarly tolerant of innovation; Rembrandt ruined himself financially, and professionally for his own lifetime, in the *Night Watch*, as did El Greco in his paintings for King Philip; and the same situation repeats itself in Courbet, Manet, and the Impressionists (to mention but a few of innumerable examples). Yet time has proved each to have been a leader; and his innovations have become accepted tradition.

[1] There is much to be said for Walter Lippmann's theory of the "burden of originality" in his *Preface to Morals*, Macmillan, 1929.

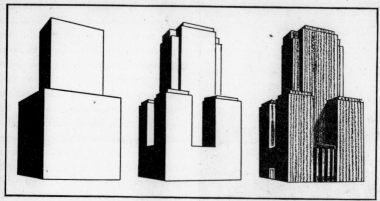

Fig. 829 (A). Three Stages in the Evolution of Skyscraper Design.

the great arts of various lands and various ages. These pioneer builders were scattered experimenters, in America, Holland, Belgium, Vienna, Paris, and Berlin, trying out new materials and new structural methods in the attempt to bring about the union of engineering and the art of building. It was not until after the World War that these attempts, isolated but strangely similar in their objectives, appeared to fuse into what one writer has termed the International style.[1] Whether or not one is justified in seeing in these buildings a twentieth-century style, time only can judge.

Throughout the work of the past forty years, however, certain trends are discernible: 1. *A complete break* with the past, as we have already noted, in the sense of copying past styles [2] though retaining a close affiliation with them.[3] 2. *Functionalism:* the fact that the function of a building determines its form; that the plan, rather than the façade, determines its mass and volume — by no means a novel idea but one that had been lost in the age of eclecticism, and upon its return ran at times into extreme absolutism. "The aim of architecture is the creation of the perfect and therefore also beautiful, efficiency." (Bruno Taut) "The house shall be a machine in which to live." (Le Corbusier) 3. *Materials:* a recognition of the capacities and limitations of materials, their intrinsic properties for construction and for surface textures. With the aid of science there appeared new materials, such as light steel and

[1] H. R. Hitchcock, Jr., in Hitchcock and Philip Johnson, *The International Style,* Norton, 1932.
[2] The tenacity of Gothic as an ecclesiastical style is perhaps due to similarity of climatic conditions, of function and material, to the original style of the thirteenth century. The *Cathedral of St. John the Divine, New York* and the *National Cathedral, Washington* are cases in point.
[3] Le Corbusier, *Towards a New Architecture,* well illustrates this point.

Fig. 830. Philadelphia Savings Fund Society Building. Philadelphia. Howe and Lescaze, architects. 1931–32. (Howe and Lescaze)

reinforced concrete, while some of the age-old materials, subjected to new mechanical processes, appeared in new forms and in mass production: the metals, ceramic products, glass. Thus before the builder lay the opportunity for variety through textures and for the reintroduction into building of the old art of polychromy. 4. *The union of engineering and architecture*, for whose divorce there was no legitimate reason. Some of the fine modern bridges (particularly those of steel), grain elevators, factories, observatories, hangars, garages, railroad stations, air terminals, broadcasting stations, are made by so-called engineers who are without question, consciously or not, artists. 5. *Frankness*. A building should frankly express its material, and its construction, that is, the method by which the material functions, not conceal it by an elaborate nonstructural façade or with irrelevant ornament. 6. *Complete harmony*. The design should be an organization that results from the sensitive coördination, on the part of the builder, of function, plan, materials, and engineering into a coherent harmonious unit. Again this is not a novel idea, but merely the reaffirmation of the older conception lost in the waning centuries of the Renaissance. 7. *The suppression or elimination of ornament* and of every feature not demanded by necessity, partly for economic reasons, due to economic distress following the World War, and partly esthetic. "Architecture should be devoid of elements introduced for the sake of ornament alone: to the engineering problem of a building nothing should be added. Architecture should by means of fine proportions make ornamental all the elements necessary in building: through geometry the engineering solution of the building problem as a whole and in detail must be subjected to the creative inspiration of the architect. These two propositions, the one negative, the other positive, form the solid basis on which contemporary architecture rests." [1]

How these ideas have made themselves felt in recent building let us now see. In the United States a prophecy of the contemporary style

[1] *The Arts*, February, 1928, p. 97.

Fig. 831. Concrete Grain Elevator. Fort William, Ontario.
(Canadian Pacific Railway)

had appeared in the work of Louis Sullivan and Frank Lloyd Wright,
although their influence has borne more fruit on the European than on
the American side of the Atlantic. This new attitude made itself felt
primarily in urban industrial building, as one would expect in a country
so predominantly industrial, and the skyscraper became its symbol.
The rapid evolution of skyscraper design reached an epochal point in
the international competition for the *Chicago Tribune Tower* (1922).
Though the accepted design revealed a curious combination of tena-
cious eclectic ornament, Gothic buttresses and tracery, and the frank
expression of function and material in the main shaft, the rejected
second design of Eliel Saarinen of Finland served as a potent stimulus
to the elimination of such nonfunctional elements toward the almost
stark geometry of the *Daily News Building* (New York) designed by the
same artist, Raymond Hood, nearly ten years later. A culmination of
skyscraper design, structurally at least, is reached in the *Empire State
Building* (Fig. 829 and 829 A). While scientific inventions such as the
elevator, lighting and heating systems, and fireproof materials have
determined its practicability, the builders have demonstrated that from
the engineering point of view it is possible to reach any height desired;
and that from the esthetic standpoint a lofty steel framework lightly
incased with a thin screening of stone or glass pierced by innumerable
windows can present to the eye so coherent a unity of volume, so sensitive a diversification in the fenestration, so compelling a rhythm, that
the total impression is one of audacious power. Not that all the esthetic
problems connected with such a structure have been solved. The
tendency of some of the builders has been to load the stone at the corners
in a manner to suggest a load-carrying wall and thus mask rather than

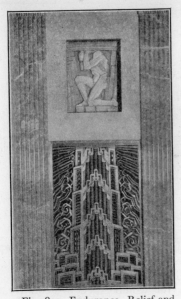

Fig. 832. Endurance. Relief and grille in the entrance of the Chanin Building, New York. 1928–29. (Chanin Building)

reveal the actual construction of the building. Especially is this true when the floors are cantilevered[1] so that there is no actual load at the corners and the space between the floors can be filled with a screen of any light material. The suitability of stone for this screening has been questioned, and in its place light tile and glass are more and more substituted. Also the excessive verticality has brought a reaction toward stressing the horizontal beams of the framework, especially where cantilevering eliminates many of the vertical supports. The late designs of Frank Lloyd Wright illustrate these tendencies and the *McGraw-Hill Building* of New York and the *Philadelphia Savings Fund Society Building* (FIG. 830) carry them out. In the Philadelphia building various materials are used to screen the steel cantilevered framework and produce an interplay of texture and color. The lower stories are faced with dark-gray polished granite with aluminum-framed windows and stainless steel lettering; above, oyster-white stone combines with gray mat brick; the lettering on the top is done in white painted metal and red neon tubes against a bright-blue ground. The problem of the skyscraper is neither engineering nor esthetic, but economic. Can it be made to pay? Are we to continue living so centralized, so urban? These questions, in the present economic impasse, admit no definite answer.

Other industrial buildings reveal the same character as the skyscraper. The huge grain elevators of the Middle West are cylinders of unabashed concrete rhythmically repeated and frequently contrasted with equally simple rectangular units (FIG. 831). Many factories and powerhouses are as clean-cut in their "beautiful efficiency" as the machinery that they house. Their frank use of brick, concrete, steel, glass, tile, or metals, their simple unadorned surfaces, clean-cut lines and large openings for light combine efficiency and beauty of form. Many small business blocks and shops are refreshing in their simple

[1] That is, have their entire support at one end only. This engineering principle, used frequently in bridge construction, is basic in many modern houses as well as in skyscrapers.

Fig. 833. Hall of Science. Century of Progress Exposition, Chicago.
1933. Paul Cret, architect. (Ryerson Library)

directness of design, their almost geometric simplicity, whose ornamentation often consists only of a sensitive interplay of color and texture of various materials. Cornices, moldings, projections of any kind about the windows, have disappeared. Sheer surfaces broken only by openings for windows profile against the sky. Again, a reflection of a machine age.

An example of particularly consistent ornament is found in the vestibule of the *Chanin Building* (FIG. 832), in which four general ideas — activity, effort, endurance, and success — have been conveyed by abstract designs that are partly representational and partly nonrepresentational.

Ecclesiastical, educational, civic, and domestic buildings have clung more tenaciously to the traditional styles. The *Boston Avenue Methodist-Episcopal Church* of Tulsa, Oklahoma, is an exception; the skyscraper design of the *University of Pittsburgh*, another; the *Adler Planetarium* in Chicago and the *Oak Lane Country Day School* of Philadelphia, others. The *Nebraska State Capitol* made a definite break with one phase of traditional civic design, and the *Century of Progress Exposition* (FIG. 833) with another (FIG. 811).

In domestic architecture the work of Frank Lloyd Wright has been significant. In his earlier houses the "prairie type" (FIG. 834) shows an emphasis upon horizontality that results from his principle of tying the house closely to its site, of establishing a continuity between the

Fig. 834. Robie House. Chicago. F. L. Wright, architect.
1908–09. (Ryerson Library)

house and the out-of-doors, and between the parts of the interior space
by the suppression of partitions wherever possible. Cantilevering the
roof eliminates the end vertical supports, which would appear to inclose
the house, and thus enables it to open more expansively to its environment. Thus the structure is an organic unit in which the parts of the
interior space flow one into another and thence by way of the exterior
to the surrounding site. "I still believe that the ideal of an organic
architecture forms the origin and source, the strength and, fundamentally, the significance of everything ever worth the name of architecture." [1]

In his California and Southwestern houses Wright has responded to
different conditions of topography and climate. The *Millard House* of
Los Angeles is a geometric block with flat roof, solid walls, and few
windows. Like the low "prairie house" it is tied closely to its hilly site,
to its gardens and lofty trees. Its material is concrete blocks, some of
which are molded into decorative patterns and thus enable the builder
to secure contrast of broken and unbroken surfaces. Again in his design
for a lodge among the firs at Lake Tahoe, and in one for a camp on the
cactus-covered desert of Arizona, he exhibits his capacity to apply his
principle of organic architecture to each individual problem, and to use
materials for their intrinsic qualities and for their suitability to the
project in hand.

Similar in principle to the work of Wright is that of Richard J. Neutra.

[1] "By organic architecture I mean an architecture that develops from within outward in harmony with the conditions of its being as distinguished from one that is
applied from without." Frank Lloyd Wright, *Wendigen*, Sandpoort, Holland, 1925,
p. 25.

Fig. 835. Lovell House. Los Angeles. R. J. Neutra, architect.
1929. (Courtesy Museum of Modern Art, New York)

His austere, functional use of steel, stucco, and glass has produced
the *Garden Apartments* of Los Angeles with its alternating horizontal
panels of stucco and steel-incased glass; and his *Lovell House* (FIG.
835), an asymmetrical grouping of volumes with a horizontal accent
which, when the contemplated masses of foliage are completed, will
be tied effectively to its hilly site.

In Europe the new style has made greater progress than in America
particularly in domestic, civic, and ecclesiastical fields. Activity centered first in Austria, Germany, and Holland; and though at first it
appeared as a modification of current styles in the direction of simplification, soon it entered the phase of dependence only upon function and
construction in accordance with the materials used. Peter Behrens,
Bruno Taut, Otto Bartning, Eric Mendelsohn, Walter Gropius, and
Miës van der Rohe have been pioneers, and the last two are perhaps
the outstanding exponents today. In the *Schocken Department Store* (FIG.
836) one sees starkly simple geometric masses insistently horizontal in
their fenestration, yet varied in the different parts of the building; in
the *Bauhaus* (FIG. 837) severe unadorned rectangular volumes constructed of steel, stucco, and glass are made effective by proportions
and by an asymmetrical arrangement of mass and surface, arrangements that are basically functional. The concrete *Einstein Tower* (FIG.
838), an astronomical observatory, frankly bespeaks its material and
its function. The character of its fenestration harmonizes with the
curving surfaces of the cylindrical volumes and lightens the solidity
of the mass.

Fig. 836. Schocken Department Store. Stuttgart. 1929.
Eric Mendelsohn, architect.

In European domestic architecture an important type is the municipal housing group built to provide healthful living-quarters equipped
with modern conveniences at a minimum rent, an objective which
entailed utmost economy of materials and construction and hence the
elimination of every nonfunctional item. The *Karl Marx Hof* [1] in Vienna
(FIG. 840) by its proportions, by the interplay of angular and curvilinear
motifs, by the accents of the projecting balconies and towers, by the
use of polychromy to differentiate the parts clearly, by its garden
courts — by all these means impresses one with a "beautiful efficiency."

Just as bare of nonessentials is the house in the upper economic levels.
In this field Miës van der Rohe has been active as a designer as well as
an actual builder; for his love of costly materials prevents many of his
projects from being carried out. His *Tugendhat House* (FIG. 841) is tied
effectively to its site. Clean-cut unbroken lines and surfaces; austerely
geometric relationships; the frank constructional use of steel and glass
so that a wall of glass one hundred feet long is possible; the use of materials each for its intrinsic texture and color and for its relation to its
neighbor — these are the basic elements which controlled the builder.
The interior space of the ground floor (FIGS. 842, 844) is a continuous
unit, like that in the *Robie House* (FIG. 834) of Frank Lloyd Wright, and
the various rooms are marked off by partial or movable partitions.
Thus it is possible to retain the continuity of the one spatial unit and

[1] The huge size of this housing unit can be grasped only by a study of its entire
plan. It consists of 1,400 apartments of from one to six rooms and accommodates
5,000 residents. About one-fifth of its area is built upon, the remaining four-fifths
being left as open spaces. As a social unit it contains two kindergartens, a school,
a library, clinics, a health insurance office, a post office, and over twenty business
concerns — quite a town in itself. There are two washhouses with hot water, and
ample provision for the sanitary cleanliness of the entire estate.

Fig. 837. Bauhaus. Dessau. 1926. Walter Gropius, architect.
(Courtesy Museum of Modern Art, New York)

at the same time to divide it into smaller units as function or convenience may require. A wall of plate glass, which can be lowered electrically to open the house to the out-of-doors or across which velvet curtains can be drawn; a half-partition of onyx supplemented by silk and velvet curtains on chromium rails; fine woods in the furnishings — the interplay of the colors and textures of these materials produces an impression of subdued elegance, and free from clashing contrasts contributes to that feeling of continuity which makes the house an illustration of Wright's "organic architecture."

In Holland, a *School* and a *Municipal Bathhouse* at Hilversum, the work of William Dudok, illustrate a widespread use of brick laid so as to secure a richly vibrating texture on the surfaces of the volumes. More severely functional are those buildings by J. J. P. Oud which employ reinforced concrete and steel, and a reserved use of color. With standardized units (for purposes of economy) Oud has built large housing structures, notably at the Hook of Holland (1926–27), which depend for their effect upon a geometric simplicity of volume, upon the proportions and relations of these volumes, and upon the frank use of materials.

In France, pioneering in material is seen in the concrete church of the Perret Brothers at Le Raincy, with experimentation in glass as well; and in the hangar at Orly (Fig. 839), in which are combined engineering, functionalism, and austere beauty of form. Probably the leading exponent at present is Le Corbusier (Charles Edouard Jeanneret), a painter as well, and probably most influential in his writings. His *Stein House* at Garches, like the houses of Miës van der Rohe, is based upon topography, materials, function, upon proportions and relationship of the parts, frequently accented by color. These are important but by no means the only leaders in the modern movement, which is strong

Fig. 838. Einstein Tower. Potsdam. 1920–21. Eric Mendelsohn, architect. (Ryerson Library)

Fig. 839. Hangar. Orly, France. 1916. Freyssinet, designer. H. 150 ft.

also in Belgium, Scandinavia, Switzerland (Zurich and Basel), Czechoslovakia, Russia, and Italy.

A modern interior is peculiarly restful when not too geometrically hard or too flashily colorful, a nice discrimination realized by the best interior architects. The interior, like the exterior, is a volume to be organized so that its shape, proportions, and every detail of its furnishings is a part of a harmonious ensemble. Simplification seems to be the keynote of a style in harmony with a completely mechanized age and of a character to fill the need of repose and relaxation in a high-keyed age. Large unadorned surfaces of wall and window, unbroken lines, and materials used for their intrinsic qualities are basic elements of the style. The emphasis frequently lies upon the horizontal and the furniture hugs the floor, accented by colorful carpets, leaving a compensat-

Fig. 840. Karl Marx Hof. Vienna. 1926–30. (Walter R. Agard)

ing spaciousness above.[1] The decorative quality and necessary accents result from the interplay of colors and textures — wood, stucco, tile, glass, various metals, and stuffs. The work of Djo Bourgeois in France and of William Lescaze in America (FIG. 843) well illustrate the modern style.

C. SCULPTURE

Sculpture, after playing a minor rôle since the sixteenth century, is now beginning to resume importance. No such series of dynamic reactions or revolts occurred in sculpture in the nineteenth century as in painting. It is true that some of the sculptors, for example, François Rude (1784–1855) and Antoine Louis Barye (1795–1875), had turned from Neo-classicism toward a new realism, often romantically dramatic. Auguste Rodin (1840–1917) was definitely realistic and romantic in his aim, though his concern with surface modulation, with texture quality, with "impressionistic effects" heightened by contrasts of high polish and roughly chiseled stone, overshadows basic sculptural form. However, "after all is said and done, Rodin remains the outstanding figure in nineteenth century sculpture. He had originality and inventiveness. He had a poetic imagination of a rather literary turn. He certainly had earnestness and enterprise. The heterogeneous literary tastes, the extremely eclectic artistic inheritance, the *sentiment de l'homme*

[1] It is interesting to contrast an Italian Renaissance interior in which the strong accent is the elaborately decorated ceiling (Figs. 469, 571).

Fig. 841. Tugendhat House. Garden Façade. 1930. Brno, Czechoslovakia. Miës van der Rohe, architect. (Museum of Modern Art,
New York)

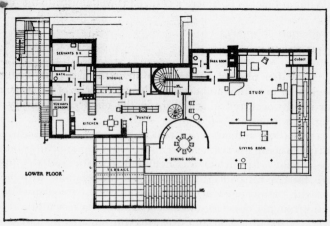

Fig. 842. Plan of the Tugendhat House. (Museum of Modern Art,
New York)

which he shared with Millet and Meunier make of his work, in its entirety, a cross section of the mind and heart of his time." [1] Thus sculpture was ill prepared for the abrupt bursting upon the scene of primitive, archaic, and Oriental art, whose exposition of truly sculptural form has been so stimulating, however much it has thrown the decadent European tradition into confusion.

Fig. 843. Living-Room of the Home of William Lescaze. New York. William Lescaze, architect. (Photo Ralph Steiner, courtesy William Lescaze)

Again certain trends are discernible: 1. *The return of truly architectural sculpture* both in relief and in the round, sculpture that is an integral part of the building rather than a relief or a statue made independently and then "applied." Once more architecture and sculpture are joining hands. 2. *A recognition of the capacity and limitation* of each of the sculptor's mediums, which is perhaps a benefit from eclecticism, for all great sculpture

Fig. 844. Tugendhat House. Living-Room. (Museum of Modern Art, New York)

rigorously follows this principle. This implies a rediscovery of the age-old differentiation between modeling and carving, and an abandonment of the pernicious practice of attempting to translate from one into the other. In the best modern sculpture the material is a definite part of the work of art. The original concept is a stone or a clay concept, a metal or a wood concept, and its objectification unthinkable in any other medium. Many modern sculptors work in several mediums with subtle differentiations. Many new materials are increasing the possibilities for a greater range of effects: a wide variety of stones each with its own hardness, color, and texture; silver, brass,

[1] Agnes Rindge, *Sculpture*, Harcourt, Brace, 1929, p. 113.

Fig. 845. Faggi. Jesus Counsels the Daughters of Jerusalem. Bronze. Church of St. Thomas the Apostle, Chicago.

Fig. 846. Meštrovič. Angel and Child. Detail of the Racić Mausoleum, Cavtat.

lead, aluminum, and various alloys among the metals; and glazings for terra cotta. 3. *A reaffirmation of the meaning of sculpture* in contrast to the conception of a statue as a copy of a model. The modern sculptor is concerned with the fusion of form and representation, or with form alone, frequently symbolic, abstract, or geometric; "a sculptor can always take advantage of the natural rhythms of the human form and make them into an architectural composition." [1] This, after all, was the artistic creed of Michelangelo, Phidias, the Egyptians, the Japanese, the primitive woodcarvers, the Romanesque, to mention a few. The differences are those of degree, not of kind. And both "old master" and modern sculptor would subscribe to the definition given by Eric Gill: "The sculptor's job is making out of stone things seen in the mind." [2] 4. *The great influence of exotic sculpture*, pernicious when it raises up pastiches only, but the most healthy discipline when it compels recognition of the fundamentals of plastic form. 5. *Extreme individualism*, the "rugged individualism" of art, and thus sculpture that is expressionistic and nonnational. Should one be confronted by a dozen statues by a dozen outstanding artists of today, he could hardly place them according to nations or schools. The influence upon art of the extreme nationalism of the moment is problematical.

Architectural sculpture is making a great advance both in Europe

[1] Stanley Casson, *Some XXth Century Sculptors*, Oxford Press, 1930, p. 24.
[2] Gill, *Sculpture*, Sheed & Ward, 1932, p. 21.

and in America, though the skyscraper offers it little opportunity and the designer who is an out-and-out functionalist has banned it. One can mention the *Chanin Building Grille* (FIG. 832); the attempts of Ely Jacques Kahn to create a type of abstract ornament in harmony with modern architectural design; the reliefs of Lee Lawrie on the *Nebraska State Capitol* and at *Rockefeller Center;* the bronze *Stations of the Cross* (FIG. 845) of Alfeo Faggi (1885——), who definitely aims to establish a profoundly religious mood, an objective similar to the Byzantine — "to render visible the mysteries of the supra-natural world" — and by similar means, that is, by the use of symbols, conventions, elongations, and by almost geometrically simple forms with strong linear quality he builds up a design whose abstract character conveys the mood of the incident. In addition Faggi is a master technician in bronze. Truly architectural are the decorative abstracts of John Storrs, worked in stone and metal of varying colors, textures, and combinations. His aluminum *Ceres*, which serves as a terminal for the *Board of Trade Building* in Chicago and thus is to be seen at a great height, illustrates in the high simplification of its features and drapery the same functionalism in sculpture as in architecture.

In Europe decorative sculpture is functioning over a wider range. Like the American, it is showing in its reliefs an orderly system of planes that control depth and a linear pattern — in other words, that system of organization which controlled the earlier masters of relief such as the Egyptians, the archaic Greeks, the Romanesque — and is serving the same function as has all great decorative sculpture: to accent and at the same time to retain an identity with the building; to break up monotonous surfaces; to mark a transition from one part of the design to another; and by its human connotations to stress the function and meaning of the building. Sculpture of this character and with this purpose is found in the carvings of Antoine Bourdelle (1861-1929) on the *Théâtre des Champs-Elysées* in Paris; in the work of the Yugoslav Ivan Meštrović (1883——) (FIG. 846) worker in stone, wood, and bronze; in the *Day and Night* of Jacob Epstein (1880——) for the London Underground.

A considerable amount of contemporary sculpture functions architecturally though it is not an actual part of the building. Such is *The Worker* in the court of the *Karl Marx Hof* (FIG. 840); and the abstract *Joy of Living* of Jacques Lipchitz (FIG. 847), which fits so harmoniously into the natural surroundings. The fountains of the Swedish sculptor Carl Milles are highly architectural. The figures are usually of bronze, are boldly modeled in strong simple planes with emphatic repeated motifs so as to carry in the out-of-door light, and in combination with the water which is treated as a necessary part of the design (FIG.

Fig. 847. Lipchitz. The Joy of Living. Hyères. (Photo Vaux, courtesy
Walter R. Agard)

848). Small bronzes, such as the
Playing Dogs of Hunt Diederich
(Fig. 849) and the *Dancer and Gazelles* of Paul Manship, are more
and more in demand to serve as
decorative accents in the modern
interior.

The commemorative statues that
have blossomed forth since the
World War reveal the low level of
public taste, particularly in America. This may be due largely to the
fact that the decisions in competi-
tions [1] rested with laymen, who for
generations have had no training
because of the absence of art in
everyday life. Failing to develop
a sensitivity for sculptural form,
they expect a statue to look like
the model: the closer the verisimilitude, the better the art.

Perhaps the largest part of modern sculpture, like modern painting,
lies outside the limitations of functionalism and thus is the most purely
individualistic and expressionistic. Apart from portraiture and specifically commemorative sculpture, many artists are concentrating upon
pure sculptural form, experimenting upon its possibilities, upon the
medium, now within the range of representative form — still chiefly
the human and animal figure — now nonrepresentational, symbolic,
or purely geometric. Here the most "rugged individualism" appears.
A few, by no means all, of those whose strength challenges, may be
mentioned, for within their extreme individualism and in the face of
controversialism it is their work that is establishing general trends. For
convenience, they may be mentioned by countries.

The Ukranian Alexander Archipenko (1887——) is extraordinarily
versatile, and a comprehensive exhibition of his work includes drawings,
paintings, and ceramics as well as sculpture in many mediums. His
abstract conceptions are based upon the human figure, from which he
takes what he needs and discards the rest, heads and arms for example,
as irrelevant to his purpose. In his highly simplified statuettes in marble,
brass, aluminum, or wood the surfaces move suavely and the clear-cut
contours or edges produce a linear accent (Fig. 851).

[1] See the plate of illustrations of contesting statues for the *Pioneer Woman* in Rindge,
op. cit., Pl. XXIV.

Among the Germans, George Kolbe (1877——), who composes with slender graceful figures, finds in slight supple dancers a type suited to his purpose and with generalized, somewhat naturalistic modeling makes highly simplified designs suitable for bronze technique (FIG. 850). Subject matter, used abstractly, pose, and medium are in perfect harmony. Wilhelm von Lehmbruck (1881–1919), in contrast to Kolbe's tempered naturalism and subtly modulated surfaces, conveys an impression of lyric grace and tranquil majesty through attenuated forms and proportions, and harmony of mass and contour. The statues of Ernst Barlach (1870——), on the other hand, acquire an impressiveness from their ponderous weight of solid, almost geometric masses on which details seem engraved in vigorous linear patterns.

Fig. 848. Milles. Fountain of the Tritons. In the sculptor's gardens at Lidingö, near Stockholm. (Art Institute of Chicago)

Fig. 849. Hunt Diederich. Playing Dogs. Bronze. Whitney Museum of American Art, New York. (Photo Percy Rainford, courtesy of the Whitney Museum)

In France, Aristide Maillol (1861——), worker in terra cotta, stone, and bronze, and an accomplished draftsman as seen in his drawings, lithographs, and woodcuts, has a particular concern with related masses. The *Seated Woman* (FIG. 852), though representational according to its title, is conceived as an abstract organization, which is constructed out of the parts of the figure, simply carved as masses. It has all the weight and solidity inherent in the material, and its surfaces take the light quietly and evenly because of their largely unbroken character. A strikingly different sculptor is Charles Despiau (1874——), whose bronze portraits, worked out by long study of the model, have led the French to consider him "their Donatello . . . we become slowly aware of a state of soul, in spiritual attitude, of which the form is, in some part, the concrete symbol, the materialization, the harmonious resolution." [1]

In England a gifted young Frenchman, Gaudier-Brzeska (1892–1915), in his thousands of drawings, in his discussions and experiments in various mediums, early attained a lucid conception of sculptural

[1] *Creative Art*, December, 1930.

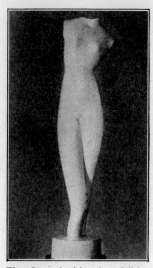

form: "Sculptural feeling is the appreciation of masses in relation. Sculptural ability is the defining of these masses by planes." [1]

Frank Dobson (1887——) has a similar attitude, illustrated by a *Torso*, a carving in wood whose natural graining the sculptor has utilized to emphasize the movement of planes. Eric Gill (1882——), engraver, draftsman, illustrator, and preëminently a stone-carver who has contributed by his writings on the subject of

Fig. 850. Kolbe. Assunta. Bronze. 1921. Private coll. (Courtesy of the Museum of Modern Art)

Fig. 851. Archipenko. White Torso. Bronze, silvered. Berlin.

sculpture as well as by his carvings, shows that he is allied, in his conception of sculpture, to Maillol and Dobson. Much of his work is in relief, carved in a native British stone, and in the best tradition of stone-carving, highly decorative because of its conventional treatment, and with considerable emphasis upon its subject matter, frequently religious.

Jacob Epstein (1880——), an American living in London,[2] is not only a stone-carver but even more a modeler in clay, often with a strong dependence upon surface treatment. His portraits have an intensity of life due to a highly individual, emotional character of their style, and at the same time they retain the outward appearance and the character of the sitter; for this, Epstein tells us, was his double objective.[3] The *Duchess of Hamilton* (Fig. 853) is definitely a clay technique. The rough surfaces, which retain the marks of the tools and are made permanent by metal, are due partly to an attempt to indicate all the minute planes which exist in a head and partly to the purely esthetic pleasure derived from surfaces in themselves.

A certain group of sculptors of various nationalities who have been working more or less about Paris should be mentioned for their experi-

[1] Ezra Pound, *Gaudier-Brzeska*, Lane, 1916, p. 126.

[2] An excellent illustration of the difficulty of attempting to group artists according to nationality.

[3] For Epstein's own exposition of his purposes, see his *The Sculptor Speaks*, Doubleday, Doran, 1932.

Fig. 852. Maillol.
Seated Woman. (Librairie de France)

ments in purely abstract or geometric form carried out in various mediums, and some quite definitely under the influence of primitive African sculpture: Gaudier-Brzeska, Constantin Brancusi, Jacques Lipchitz, Ossip Zadkine, Amedeo Modigliani, and Oswald Herzog.

In America one observes a marked renascence of sculpture which exhibits a sense of fine craftsmanship paralleling in many ways the movement in Europe. As in Europe, with no unifying philosophy of life or tradition, with the confusion of a rapidly changing age, there are many experiments. In them all, however extreme, one feels that the purpose has been to create truly sculptural forms rather than to copy models. George Gray Barnard (1863———), with his forceful monumental conceptions and with a kind of realism that is an assertive force rather than a description of facts, as in the *Lincoln* (Cincinnati), perhaps bridges the gap between the old and the new. Possibly Paul Manship (1885———) also stands on the bridge, with his archaistic tendencies, despite his admirable small bronzes so well conceived, so exquisitely wrought, and so decorative an accent when properly placed. Of the carvers in stone William Zorach (1887———) illustrates the concentration upon relation of masses, often complex, as in the *Mother and Child* (Fig. 854). In addition to this lucid organization Zorach has exhibited a peculiar sensibility to the medium itself, a reddish granite whose

Fig. 853. Epstein. Duchess of
Hamilton. Bronze. 1915. Toledo
Museum. (Toledo Museum)

strength, weight, and texture contribute to the effect of monumentality.
Gaston Lachaise, Maurice Sterne, John
Storrs, and Robert Laurent are other
direct stone-carvers. Laurent (FIG.
855), extremely versatile in the matter of medium, is particularly successful in handling the difficult translucent
alabaster; he attains peculiarly ephemeral effects in these small-scale figures
conceived with a sensitivity for related
masses and suavely flowing planes;
and he has experimented in using plant
forms — a novel subject matter for the
sculptor — for his wood-carvings. Gaston Lachaise (1882–1935) has probably attained his best results in metal.
In the *Figure of a Woman* (FIG. 856)
the strongly felt rhythm swells from the
lightly poised feet to a climax in the
large rounding hips; thence, after a
sharp accent in the angle of the waist,
it again swells into the broad shoulders and bent arms. This abstract
conception of an expanding and contracting movement finds its objectification suitably in clay and metal. Contrast the solidity, weight, and
downward pressure of the stone *Mother and Child* (FIG. 854) and the up-
ward-moving weightlessness of the *Figure of a Woman*. Each statue, in
its medium, is the only possible objectification of the artist's concept.
And Lachaise has used to advantage the dark color and reflective capacity of bronze to stress his organization of masses.

In the portraits of Jo Davidson we see another tendency, a direct
forceful characterization of the model, a proper function of the portrait,
that is realism in the best sense. In the work of Malvina Hoffman,
which is based upon a definite, highly disciplinary functionalism — to
represent the races of mankind [1] — scientific accuracy of both spirit and
form are at times lifted into the plane of art.

Mention at least should be made of the increasing amount of animal
sculpture in both Europe and America: of the animals of François
Pompon of France; those of Matteo Hernandez of Spain, often in black
Belgian marble; and those of Heinz Warneke in the United States,
whose animal statues, carved from various kinds of stone, may be taken

[1] For the Chauncey Keep Memorial Hall of the Field Museum of Natural History
in Chicago.

Fig. 854. Zorach. Mother and Child. Marble. 1928–30. (Photo Charles Sheeler, courtesy Downtown Gallery, New York)

Fig. 855. Laurent. Pearl. Aluminum. Downtown Gallery, New York. (Courtesy of the Downtown Gallery)

to illustrate the fine feeling for material and "the building of the natural rhythms of the animal form into an architectural composition" without losing the identity of the animal or the interpretation of its personality (FIG. 857).

D. PAINTING

Functionalism in architecture has drawn sculpture partially into the circle of its spirit and objectives. Not so with painting, which still consists largely of painted panels for exhibitions or for dealers, with an eye to a possible purchaser. One hopeful sign is a revived interest in mural painting, especially in the fresco technique, under the stimulation of Diego Rivera and José Clemente Orozco of Mexico. Another reason for optimism is that painters are breaking though the barriers of specialization into other fields: Picasso, Matisse, Archipenko, are making stage designs; Rockwell Kent is cutting wood blocks for book illustrations; Raoul Dufy is a painter and a textile-designer; and Henry Varnum Poor is a painter and a potter; while Thomas Benton is by no means the only painter who has designed carpets; most are accomplished etchers and lithographers, and many carve and model as well as paint.

Fig. 856. Lachaise. Figure of a Woman. Bronze. 1927. Coll. J. A. Dunbar, New York. (Courtesy Museum of Modern Art, New York)

On the whole, however, the painters of today are still economically in the nineteenth-century impasse of the artificial exhibit [1] and probably one is right in saying that in proportion as the painter is excluded from functioning normally in the social and economic system, he is thrown into subjectivism, expressionism, theory, and experimentation.

In the late nineteenth century, even before the Impressionist battle was won in the show of 1886 and Impressionism had become one more episode in the accumulative French tradition, several painters were striking out along new paths in order to recapture, as had Renoir already, those qualities in the "old masters" [2] which the Impressionists, too intent upon the momentary effects of light and air, had lost: solidity, structure, organization; and to push the investigation of the possibilities of art expression into various directions. This movement may loosely be called Post-Impressionism. Most of these painters began as Impressionists, but even in the eighties of the nineteenth century each was modifying or abandoning the style in favor of a free highly individual mode of expression.

Georges Seurat (1859–1891) [3] attacked the problem from the angle of the psychological effect of line direction and line relationship and of the science of related colors. Steeping himself in the color theories of Delacroix and of the color scientists of his time, Helmholtz and Chevreul, he worked out a system of putting the pigment on in tiny roundish dots, of about equal size, with scientific precision as to the color relation of dot to dot (a method known as Pointillism) — an enormously difficult procedure, as severely disciplined and painstaking as the Impressionist method was spontaneous and exuberant. Thus he

[1] Estimates of the number of painters in Paris today vary from 40,000 to 60,000.
[2] It is illuminating to note how many of these painters were largely self-educated, primarily in the Louvre.
[3] Together with Paul Signac sometimes called Neo-Impressionist.

transformed the illusion of natural appearance into a precise organization composed of people and objects that are solid and arranged with mathematical precision in a deep space filled with sunlight and air; and yet which, paradoxically, form an extraordinarily effective pattern. Such is *La Grande Jatte* [1] (FIG. 858), whose pattern is based upon the verticals of the figures and trees, the horizontals in the shadows and in the distant embankment, the diagonals in the shadows and the shore

Fig. 857. Warneke. Wild Boars. Black granite. Art Institute of Chicago. (Art Institute)

line, each of which contributes the psychological effect inherent in the character of its movement. At the same time, by the use of meticulously calculated values the painter carves out a deep rectangular space, and in creating both this pattern and space he plays upon repeated motifs: the profile of the lady, taken from the costume of the day; the umbrella; and the cylindrical forms of the figures, each so placed in space as to set up a rhythmic movement into space as well as from side to side. The picture is filled with sunshine but not broken into ever changing myriads of scintillating color. Light, air, people, and landscape are frozen into an abstraction in which line, color, color values, shapes, and forms cohere into an organization as precisely as the parts of a machine. A calculating, intellectual art this, by no means mechanics but one which, of the lineage of Paolo Uccello and Piero della Francesca, like them, moves by its serene monumentality.

Paul Cézanne (1839–1906) began painting in the limited color and thick pigment of Courbet and with the baroque compositions of Tintoretto, Rubens, and Delacroix. Upon acquaintance with the Impressionists his palette broadened and lightened, and though he was drawn into the color theories of this group he soon felt, from his long-continued studies of the "old masters" in the Louvre, the weakness of the Impressionists. "I want to make Impressionism," he said, "something solid and permanent like the old masters." Thoroughly trained in this school — "I always keep one foot in the Louvre," he said — especially by Tintoretto and Poussin, who had so magnificently conquered the problem of space organization, he sought not to copy but to create equally compelling space relationships by new uses of the old means, line, light,

[1] For a full analysis with the numerous preliminary drawings and the sketches, which indicate how coolly premeditated his art was, see D. C. Rich, *Seurat and the Evolution of La Grande Jatte*, University of Chicago Press, 1935.

Fig. 858. Seurat. Sunday on the Island of La Grande Jatte.
1884–86. Art Institute of Chicago. (Art Institute)

color — an inescapable result of his own extraordinary vision. Thus
he became an explorer of the painter's means of expression: line, the
effect of every kind of line direction — horizontal, vertical, diagonal,
curved — and the effect of line as related to line; color, the intrinsic
quality of each color and the minutest detail of color relation. In the
recession of blue and the advance of red he controlled volume and
depth. With the observation that the point of saturation or highest
intensity of color produces the greatest fullness of form, he painted
apples in one hue only — say green — by a meticulous exactitude of
value and intensity of green, so that in solidity and volume and place
in space they possess a supranatural reality. Thus he attained solidity
and structure by the control of color alone[1] in place of the more usual
method of light and shade according to natural illumination, and while
he made nature both his starting-point and his goal, his objective was
not verisimilitude but the creation of that essential reality which was
more real than a reproduction of it.

But it was not only the construction of individual forms — trees,
mountains, apples, people — that engaged Cézanne, but also their organization in space. For "he saw in objective nature a chaos of dis-
organized movement and he set himself the task of putting it in order."[2]
Every painting of Cézanne reveals an exploration of some problem

[1] See R. E. Fry, *Transformations*, Coward-McCann, 1927, "Plastic Color." For a
detailed analysis of a Cézanne still life, see Munro, *Great Pictures of Europe*, pp. 226–29.
[2] W. H. Wright, *Modern Painting*, Dodd, Mead, 1927, p. 147.

Fig. 859. Cézanne. Mont Sainte Victoire. Private coll.

connected with putting nature in order,[1] and for this purpose alone the subject matter was irrelevant — trees, landscapes, nudes, still life, portraits. Forms, their mass and solidity, their place in deep space in relation to other forms expressed according to his own visualization and method of using color — to get upon the canvas his perception of these forms constituted his objective. As he worked over them, gradually everything inessential faded away so that the form was reduced to something nearly if not quite geometric. "Everything in nature adheres to the cone, the cylinder, and the cube." In this statement Cézanne is simply carrying but one step further, that is, into abstraction and geometry, what Giotto had already done, though his means were entirely different. Giotto was working away from a decadent abstractionism in the direction of a new naturalism, Cézanne, from a decadent naturalism into a new abstractionism, and they meet at the same stage of the evolution. As for subject matter, the fifteenth-century innovators from Giotto to Michelangelo experimented on Madonnas, biographies of the saints, or Greek mythological scenes, because their patrons commissioned these. The nineteenth- and twentieth-century innovators experimented on nudes and still life because there were no patrons to hand out commissions. When a painter is thus left entirely "free" he

[1] See the article by E. L. Johnson, "Cézanne's Country," *The Arts*, April, 1930, in which photographs and Cézanne's painting of the same subject are juxtaposed.

Fig. 860. Cézanne. The Card-Players. 1892. Coll. Stephen C. Clark, New York. (Ryerson Library)

is most likely to concentrate upon the problems peculiarly his own — form and formal relations. Had Cézanne lived in Florence in the fourteenth century he would probably have painted scenes from the life of St. Francis or the Virgin Mary or Christ. Were Giotto living in twentieth-century France, he would probably be painting nudes, apples, and landscapes. Giotto's range of experience was relatively narrow and his means simple; Cézanne's world was broad and intricate and his means complex.

What was of value in Impressionism (color) Cézanne combined with what was of value in the whole Renaissance tradition (solidity, structure, organization in space) and then proceeded to reconstruct the fusion according to his own sensitive vision and his own use of color. In the *Mont Ste.-Victoire* (FIG. 859), having stated clearly the plane of the canvas by the tree and the decorative branches, he carves out a space upon whose basic horizontal plane he sets each building, tree, and mountain, simply constructed as geometric units, each in its own place in space. Here one feels "Poussin made over according to nature," with a geometric simplicity that renders each object more real and solid than in visual reality. *The Card-Players* (FIG. 860) partake of the quiet monumentality of stone sculpture, solid figures set convincingly in space (in relation to the objects on the table), each figure and each detail

Fig. 861. Van Gogh. Landscape with Cypress Trees. 1889.
National Gallery at Millbank, London.

playing its part as inevitably as do the blocks of stone in a stone structure.
In the *Large Composition with Nude Figures* (Pellerin Collection, Paris)
the figures are an inextricable part of the landscape like perfectly integrated architecture and sculpture; they unite with the trees to form the
dominating arch and carry the eye across the middle distance to unite
the foreground and the background. These figures might as well have
been bushes or rocks only that the figure because of its organic structure
affords a more plastic means for carrying out the objective of the painter
— solid organization in deep space.

Probably Cézanne was his own most discerning critic when he said
that he was the primitive of the way he had opened. The highest accomplishments of this slow plodding painter have the power, vitality,
and monumentality of great primitive art. His contribution was partly
a rediscovery, at a critical time, of the fundamentals of great art, and
partly the result of his prolonged independent studies over a period of
thirty years, which revealed a complex relativity in color to be compared, as W. H. Wright points out, to the delicate nuances and overtones in music. The discovery was a complex instrument capable of
successful use only in the hands of a great master. His casual remarks
have been transformed into dogmatic pronouncements by his followers.
But as yet no one of his stature has appeared to carry on the "way he
opened." It may be well to remember that between Giotto and Masaccio

Fig. 862. Gauguin. The Day of the God. 1894. Art Institute of
Chicago. (Art Institute)

lay a century. As in the work of other innovators — Giotto, Masaccio,
Uccello, Piero della Francesca, Rembrandt, Constable, Courbet,
Manet — who were attacking technical problems in the visual arts, a
sheer vitality results from a consuming effort; and because these men
were artists as well as scientists, out of the mass of their efforts, necessarily uneven, arose indisputable masterpieces.

Both Van Gogh and Gauguin were offshoots of Impressionism. But in
contrast to the cool impersonal Seurat and Cézanne, they were highly individualized; their expression was entirely personal, quite unregardful of
formulas or sanctions of any extrinsic authority. Vincent Van Gogh
(1853–1890) was a Hollander who, after tragic experiences, both physical and spiritual, in Belgium and England, found in the warmth, sunshine, and comparative peace of Provence an outlet, in pigment, for
his emotional intensity. Almost any painting of Van Gogh proclaims
its medium not only in the intensity of the color but also in the vibrating
texture created by pigment manipulation (FIG. 861). Now a thickly
loaded brush moves vehemently back and forth or at right angles,
giving a textilelike effect; now the palette knife or finger rubs on or
smooths the pigment; now the tube squeezes dots or streaks upon the
canvas. Everywhere one feels the impetuosity with which the medium
is used and which might have run wild were it not controlled by an
innate high sensitivity to form and color. Color is used in its highest

intensity, color area meeting color area abruptly, thus creating an effect of emphatic line and silhouette — again, an influence of Japanese prints. Though the color areas are clashing and dissonant, the lines nervous, and the strokes fiercely energetic, the unity of texture creates a consistent surface, not delicate nor suavely modulated, to be sure, but as exciting as if born of an abandonment of energy (Frontispiece).

In contrast to Van Gogh, Paul Gauguin (1848–1903) presents large quiet areas of smoothish flat color, sumptuously rich, with suavely flowing lines. These color areas are clearly and sharply defined and often separated by dark contours like the leads in leaded glass windows or the cloisons in cloisonné enamels,[1] so that the effect is frankly decorative, and depth is suggested rather than presented to the eye. Though Gauguin began as an Impressionist, he soon abandoned broken color with the statement: "A meter of green is greener than a centimeter if

Fig. 863. Redon. Blue Vase with Flowers. Ryerson coll., Art Institute of Chicago. (Art Institute)

you wish to express greenness. . . . How does that tree look to you? Green? All right, then use green, the greenest on your palette. And that shadow, a little bluish? Don't be afraid. Paint it as blue as you can!" "Gauguin," says Maurice Denis, "freed us from all the restraints which the idea of copying nature had placed upon us. For instance, if it was permissible to use vermilion in painting a tree which seemed reddish . . . why not stress even to the point of deformation the curve of a beautiful shoulder or conventionalize the symmetry of a bough unmoved by breath of air? Now we understood everything in the Louvre, the Primitives, Rubens, Veronese." [2] Subject matter with Gauguin was important — a primitive people of the tropics, living in a primitive, colorful civilization whose sunshine, shadow, color, and mood are all expressed in a form that is definitely nonnaturalistic, basically

[1] For this reason Gauguin was sometimes called a Cloisonnist. Robert Rey, in his *Gauguin*, Dodd, Mead, 1924, calls attention to the abrupt character of the Oceanian languages, the union of words without the polish of the inflected European tongues.

[2] Museum of Modern Art, *First Loan Exhibition . . . 1929*, Museum, New York, 1929, p. 14, by permission of the Museum.

Fig. 864. Rousseau. The Jungle. 1908. Coll. Mrs. Patrick C. Hill. (Art Institute of Chicago)

primitive, thoroughly consistent, and filled with an atmosphere of meaningful calm. An almost uncanny timeless immobility permeates *The Day of the God* (FIG. 862), as in a Byzantine mosaic, however far removed its subject matter may be. This is a surface of intensely rich smooth color areas whose clearly defined shapes and edges create a linear pattern with smooth rhythms. Both subject matter and mode of expression are to be explained, in part at least, by atavistic tendencies and environment. From his mother Gauguin inherited a strain of Peruvian blood; as a child he lived in Lima and as a youth was a seaman in tropical lands. Later, in France he made sympathetic contact with medieval glass, Near East textiles, Japanese prints, and various primitive arts which were just then catching the attention of Paris. So not unnaturally he betook himself to live an elemental life in the South Sea Islands, where he painted his most characteristic works.

Painting, from Cimabue to Rubens, had evolved toward complexity of design, especially design in space, and richness of palette where color melts into color until, with the Impressionists, everything was dissolved into scintillating light broken up into an infinite number of color spots. While Seurat and Cézanne sought structure, solidity, and organization in depth, Van Gogh and Gauguin revived flat pattern design, the use of harmonious and contrasting areas of color and emphatic line such as one finds in Byzantine and Muhammadan, Oriental and primitive arts. Their emotional intensity served as a corrective to the intellectual, scientific approach of Seurat and Cézanne, which could be handled

successfully only if held under perfect control by such sensitivity as those masters possessed. And their nonnaturalistic tendencies were particularly reactionary to the influence of the camera, which was inciting many painters toward vying with science in producing a verisimilitude of nature. The green horses in Gauguin find their theory and their counterpart in the green pigs of the Prodigal Son and in the blue hair on the head of Christ, in medieval glass.

The great diversity found in Seurat, Cézanne, Van Gogh, and Gauguin is symbolic of the "many-mindedness" of modern painting and of its challenge to a different kind of seeing. Impressionism failed to be accepted as a legitimate, not to say orthodox, method of painting until people had finally caught up with the painters' vision, as they had in the case of Courbet and the Barbizon group. Always late, "a tradition, like an old family, must constantly renew itself with the body and soul of each new age. Otherwise the end is in sight. A tradition in art simply means the heritage of qualities which deserve not only to endure but to develop. If a tradition is not also an evolution it is unworthy of the reverence which we accord to it." [1] "We cannot think in terms of an indefinite multiplicity of detail; our evidence can acquire its proper importance only if it comes before us marshalled by general ideas. These ideas we inherit — they form the tradition of our civilization. Such traditional ideas are never static. They are either fading into meaningless formulae, or are gaining power by the new lights thrown by a more delicate apprehension. They are transformed by the urge of critical reason, by the vivid evidence of emotional experience, and

[1] Duncan Phillips in *Leaders of French Art Today*, Phillips Memorial Gallery, Washington, December, 1927–January, 1928.

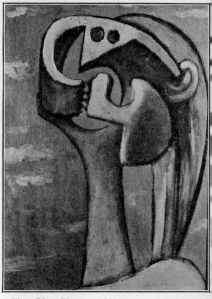

Fig. 866. Picasso. La Table. 1920. Smith College Museum of Art. (Smith College Museum)

Fig. 867. Picasso. Abstract. 1930. Valentine Gallery, New York. (Valentine Dudensing)

by the cold certainties of scientific perception. One fact is certain, you cannot keep them still. No generation can merely reproduce its ancestors. You may preserve the life in a flux of form, or preserve the form amid an ebb of life. But you cannot permanently enclose the same life in the same mold." [1] And in this evolution the steady backward pull of conservatism was necessary to balance the impulsive forward thrust of radicalism. "Old thoughts are not necessarily senile, nor are contemporary thoughts necessarily of value." [2] Impressionism today is as academic as the academic French painting against which it protested, while Post-Impressionist painters constitute the forward thrust necessary for the evolutionary process.

Most of the modernist painters of today are working in or developing trends instigated by Seurat, Cézanne, Van Gogh, and Gauguin, after a thorough saturation in the "old masters," which includes the art of the world, with a particular emphasis upon the primitive and Oriental arts. The leaders of the nineteenth century posed problems, suggested solutions, and started innovations so striking and so profound that their

[1] A. N. Whitehead, *Science and the Modern World*, Macmillan, 1925, p. 269.
[2] R. W. Livingstone, *The Greek Genius and Its Meaning to Us*, 2d ed., Oxford Press, 1915.

influence is still directive and history repeats itself: one class of followers copies outward appearances and produces pastiches; another attempts to assimilate and to carry on with new solutions and new experiments.

In a general way most of the modern painters belong to one of two main lines of descent with many border-line cases: Seurat–Cézanne–Picasso–the Cubists; Van Gogh–Gauguin–Matisse–Les Fauves–the Expressionists. These families are comprised of intensely individual members, though they represent two fairly coherent, contrasting points of view which may be illustrated roughly, the one by Matisse and the Fauves and the other by Picasso and the Cubists.

Fig. 868. Picasso. Mme Picasso. c. 1921. Private coll.

Before turning to these various manifestations of the Post-Impressionist group, there are some individuals who illustrate, again, the "many-mindedness" of the contemporary situation. Pierre Bonnard (1867——) might be called a divergent Impressionist. For he carries the objective vision of Impressionism into the realm of fantasy and infuses it with a personal mood.[1] With an individual, rather narrow but subtle range of color he drenches his canvas with warm light and converts it into decorative "luminous tapestry" constructed of "orchestral tones as vibrant and indefinite as the troubled harmonies of Debussy." [2] Bonnard strives for beautiful surfaces rather than objective realism, for poetic fantasies with which his structureless figures are quite in harmony.

Deeper in the world of the unreal and the mystic is Odilon Redon (1842–1916), whose half-realized figures float vaguely as if in semi-consciousness. Yet at times he can construct a vase of flowers with a solidity, a quiet, clearly defined harmony of colors laid on largely in the Impressionistic technique and permeated with an individual feeling of otherworldliness (FIG. 863).

Henri Rousseau Le Douanier (1844–1910) is another isolated indi-

[1] For this reason Bonnard and Edouard Vuillard (1867——) are sometimes called Intimists.
[2] Duncan Phillips in *Art and Understanding*, Phillips Memorial Gallery, Washington, 1929–30, p. 62.

vidual with a gift for painting, who painted because he wanted to when he was not playing the violin. His jungle scenes (FIG. 864), re- membrances of impressions experienced as a youth in the tropica forests of Mexico, reveal an extraordinary gift for shapes, color, and relationships and for the organization of unit shapes into a coherent pattern of great esthetic power. Again, as with Gauguin, it is flat pat- tern with strong linear quality. With no theory to guide him, Rousseau very innocently put upon the canvas simply and directly the symbols created in his own imagination of what he had seen objectively.

Henri Matisse (1869——) also starts with his subjective reactions to the external world, so that the forms which he uses to objectify these reactions have little verisimilitude; they are more like symbols with which he "animates" a flat surface. Like Gauguin, Matisse came under the influence of the color of the East, of primitive textiles (FIG. 699), Persian miniatures and pottery (FIGS. 383–85), and medieval glass. In these arts is a color as stimulating in its intensity as it is strange in its un- usual oppositions of hue, now surprising, now clashing, now quietly harmonious. It partakes of the same strange harmonies and stimulating dissonances that we are hearing in modern music. There is something thrilling in Matisse's broad color areas that meet so sharply as to em- phasize line; in the inventiveness with which the color areas produce rhythmic movement; and in the calligraphic lines and rhythmic arabesques. It is an art that is light, sparkling, and highly decorative (FIG. 865).

The Fauves ("The Wild Men") [1] were so named in derision at the Salon d'Automne of 1905. As a group they represent a reaction to the cool, overintellectual, unemotional tendencies of the Neo-Impression- ists. These "serious enthusiasts," under the stimulation of the newly discovered exotic arts, needed a freer outlet in pigment for their sub- jective emotionalism than the meticulous Pointillist method or the painstaking contemplative method of Cézanne. Hints from Gauguin and Van Gogh were their starting-point. Subject matter per se was subordinated in favor of primary interest in design, both two- and three- dimensional, in which the pigment is manipulated with infinite variety to achieve a richness of surface texture, often with bold or clashing hues, or in a very limited palette, as is frequent in Segonzac and Derain.

The evolution seen in the work of Matisse and most of the Fauves has been uniform enough to establish personal styles. Not so Picasso's. Pablo Picasso (1881——), the Spaniard who has lived in Paris since

---

[1] Henri Matisse; André Derain (1880——); Maurice de Vlaminck (1876——); Georges Braque (1883——); Georges Rouault (1871——); Raoul Dufy (1877——); Othon E. Friesz (1879——); Charles Dufresne (1876——); André de Segonzac (1885——).

Fig. 869. Tonita Peña (Quah Ah). Eagle Dance. (Exposition of Indian Tribal Arts, New York)

1903, in some respects is characteristic of the age in his constant experimentation, his startling shifts from one kind of painting to another, from one kind of visualization to another. Like Leonardo in somewhat similar circumstances, he seems to be motivated by curiosity and experimentation. The great difference, however, is that strong traditions and a narrower outlook limited Leonardo; cosmopolitanism and a highly developed individualism delimit Picasso, and may finally prove to be liabilities rather than assets.

About the time he arrived in Paris Picasso was painting in the so-called blue manner, a romantic vein with a dash of Spanish fervor, and with subject matter of some importance. Yet even then appeared a growing interest in form per se, particularly evident in the "pink period," when he was inventing sculptural forms as he was assimilating influences from archaic sculpture and primitive Negro carvings. This direction led into Cubism of several varieties and a withdrawal from representation, from analysis to synthesis, from a visual perception of nature and an analysis of forms to the creation of original forms, synthetically, out of the elements of nature or of the imagination, without reference either to the appearance of nature or to associative ideas. Since the World War his paintings have been extraordinarily varied, and each appears to be an attack upon a formal problem. Now he seems absorbed in abstract flat pattern, as in *La Table* [1] (FIG. 866). Now, even about the same year, he turns to comparative realism, to a figure solidly placed in space, the *Mme Picasso* (FIG. 868). Again his expression is sculptural and powerfully three-dimensional, as in the *Woman*

[1] See Smith College Museum of Art, *Bulletin* No. 14, May, 1933, for a detailed analysis.

in White (Museum of Modern Art, New York); and again it is abstract and three-dimensional (FIG. 868). One cannot evaluate Picasso to-day, except for the recognition of his immense gift as a creative artist, and no one or two paintings can summarize his versatility in handling pigment and constructing form.

Cubism is a blanket term originating, like many "isms," in ridicule, to cover several kinds of painting which appeared in Paris from about 1908 to 1914, under the leadership first of Picasso and Georges Braque. Now it took the form of analyzing the figure or the object into its simplest geometric elements without complete loss of representational content; now it included several aspects of the figure, that is, a succession of points of view, such as front view, profile, back view, known to the mind but not seen by the eye simultaneously, which it synthesized into a formal unity;[1] to which was added movement, as illustrated by Duchamp's *Nude Descending the Stairs*. Now it became pure pattern, either entirely geometric or with fragments of representational reality, for, as in all modern "isms," it was subject to the individual "ism" of its exponent.[2] On the one hand Cubism was a protest against the photographic copy and sentimental romanticism of the Realists, against the formlessness and too lyrical color of the Impressionists, in fact against every visual perception of nature and every associative connotation; on the other, it was a descendant of the theory of Cézanne that everything in nature reduces to the cube, the cone, and the cylinder carried to a logical conclusion, minus Cézanne's use of color and interpretative element. Neither local nor plastic color meant anything to a Cubist, who painted practically in monochrome if not within a very narrow range of closely related hues, chiefly neutrals; that is, the color was as arbitrary as the form.

Though most of those in the movement have evolved from the hard, disciplinary requirements of Cubism[3] into other styles, Georges Braque (1882——) has retained his personal version of constructing fragments, both representative and nonrepresentative, into a flat pattern on the theory that a painting is a flat surface and should remain a flat surface, animated by line, color, pattern, rhythm. Thus he works within a narrow range of restrained but subtly related color areas with strong reliance upon related and contrasted textures. "The subject is not the object of painting, but a new unity, the lyricism that results from

[1] Note the same practice of combining various views or parts of an object into a design in Egyptian painting (FIG. 82), in Nazca pottery, in the designs of the North-west Indians (FIG. 708), to mention but a few of many possible examples.

[2] For an attempt to classify the different kinds of Cubism see Jan Gordon, *Modern French Painters*, new ed., Lane, 1929.

[3] Other members of the group besides Braque and Picasso were Albert Gleizes, Jean Metzinger, Marcel Duchamp, Francis Picabia, Fernand Leger, and Juan Gris.

the mastery of a method. . . . The aim of painting is not to reconstruct an anecdotic fact, but to constitute a pictorial fact. . . . We must not imitate what we want to create. The aspect of things is not to be imitated, for the aspect of things is the result of them." [1]

Though Paris has long been the painter's geographic center, "isms" [2] in other countries as well have contributed to the total unrest. Decentralization seems to be taking place, and in almost every country [3] independent experiment is going on. At times the experimentation is consciously nationalistic and archaistic, as in Sweden, which is experiencing a national

Fig. 870. Rivera. Sugar Cane. 1929–30. Palace of Cortez, Cuernavaca.

revival of its medieval arts. Also the "Expressionists" of Germany (notably Emil Nolde and Oskar Kokoschka) in their expression of subjective feeling frequently use form and highly stimulating color for psychological effect, just as was done by German painters of the fifteenth and sixteenth centuries. The Surrealists (Superrealists) [4] in reaction to the intellectuality of abstract art turn to the realm of fantasy. The dream world and the subconscious are their raw material, and freely subjective spontaneity controls their expressionism. Thus the literary content again becomes important, as opposed to its suppression by the Cubists.

In America a conscious revival of ancient native traditions is evident among the American Indians of the Southwest, where not only the

[1] See Maurice Raynal, *Modern French Painters*, Brentano's, 1928, pp. 51–52, for these and other excerpts from the writings and sayings of many modern painters.
[2] Merely to mention a few of the innumerable theories and manifestoes of the late nineteenth and twentieth centuries serves at least to illustrate the theoretical character of the age: Impressionism, Neo-Impressionism, Pointillism, Post-Impressionism, Fauvism, Cubism, Neo-Plasticism, Futurism, Synchronism, Vorticism, Expressionism, Dadaism, Intimism, Synthesism, Surrealism, Neue Sachlichkeit. Signac's treatise; Vassily Kandinsky's *Art of Spiritual Harmony*, Houghton Mifflin, 1914; *The Blast*, edited by Wyndham Lewis; and André Breton's *Manifeste du surréalisme*, Paris, 1924, are examples of publications devoted to theory.
[3] See the catalogues of the International 1933 of the College Art Association of New York and of the Carnegie Internationals of Pittsburgh.
[4] Paul Klee (1879———) of Switzerland; Hans Arp (1888———) and Max Ernst (1891———) of Germany; Giorgio di Chirico (1888———) born in Greece of Italian parentage; Joan Miró (1893———) and Salvador Dali (1904———) of Spain.

Fig. 871. Georgia O'Keeffe. Ranchos Church. 1929. Phillips Memorial Gallery, Washington. (Phillips Memorial Gallery)

Pueblo potters but a group of young Indian painters[1] are animated by the ancient ideals of their race. Their watercolors (FIG. 869), combining beauty of drawing and design, serve the same function, in their minds, as their sand paintings and ceremonial dances. Far from being objets d'art, they constitute a language, clearly intelligible to the Indian, by means of which the artist expresses in a style that is determined in its large outlines by ancient tradition not his own individual reactions but the profoundest conceptions of the tribal philosophy of life.

Another center of vital art renascence is Mexico; it is a recognition perhaps rather than a renascence of the indigenous Indian arts, which were not lost, though forgotten, under the Spanish domination and which have acquired a little European admixture. The high quality of Mexican folk art permeates the entire cultural fabric. Here is a people so impregnated with sensitivity for art and creative ability, not conscious but intuitive, that it manifests itself in whatever they make — from tiny toys, gourd dishes, water jugs, and woven belts to large wall paintings. Such a cultural matrix can easily produce such masters as Diego Rivera (1886——) and José Clemente Orozco (1883——). In 1921 a group of artists organized the Syndicate of Painters and Sculptors,[2] whose objective was the revival of the ancient Mexican traditions, those of the Maya, the Aztecs, and the Peruvians, "to assimilate the constructive vigor of their work" — to "possess their synthetic energy without falling into lamentable archeological reconstructions." [3] Orozco and Rivera, though united in objective, are very different in style: Orozco, fiercely intense and vehement; Rivera rather classically

[1] Quah Ah, Spencer Asah, Fred Kabotie, Te-e, and Awa-Tsireh are among some twenty-five or thirty Indian painters in New Mexico, Arizona, and Oklahoma.

[2] Important contemporary painters who are in sympathy with this objective are Julio Castellanos, Jean Charlot, Miguel Covarrubias, Carlos Merida, José Clemente Orozco, Macimo Pacheco, Diego Rivera, David Alfaro Siqueiros.

[3] Quoted from Anita Brenner, *Idols behind Altars*, Payson and Clarke, 1929 (now Harcourt, Brace), in *American Sources of Modern Art*, Museum of Modern Art, New York, 1933.

serene. In his paintings in the *Palace of Cortes* at Cuernavaca (FIG. 870) Rivera has chosen local history as his subject matter. In his presentation he reveals a supreme command over spatial design: fine drawing, sculptural like Giotto's; the easy unification of several incidents to fill the space; the diminution of scale and color at the top of the panel to allow the larger-scale figures to form a solid base; the fine interplay of motives such as the bundles of cane, the shapes of the bending figures, the circles of hats and cart wheel; the color scheme which integrates the cold blue-green of the cane with warm yellows and red-browns; the unity of the design and the entire wall area,

Fig. 872. Speicher. Babette. 1931. Carnegie Institute, Pittsburgh. (Carnegie Institute)

broken as it is with arched openings. Not only does Rivera reveal this ability as a designer but in the telling vigor and simple clarity of his forms and design he lifts his presentation above the local scene, as did Giotto, into the realm of generic ideas. One great contribution of these painters to the United States as well as to Mexico has been the revival of true fresco as a mural decoration and thus a stimulation to the reunion of painting and building.

In the United States, Post-Impressionism was formally introduced by the Armory Show of 1913. Though known and understood by many painters, like every new movement in art it has raised up superficial imitators. On the other hand its strongly accented formal elements of such wide variety have influenced contemporary painters in the direction of composition, color, and manipulation of pigment. Perhaps never before in the United States has such an amount of strong accomplished painting appeared as at the present time; it comes from painters "with heart and knowledge." Many of them stand out as forthright individuals with a solid craftsmanship and not a few as artists of a high order, though no two or three dominate the field as have Van Gogh, Gauguin, Matisse, and Picasso in France.

Taken as a whole, this painting defies analysis into clear-cut generalizations. Some artists, to be sure, are painting in an Impressionistic style with personal variations.[1] On the whole, again, the American

[1] Important painters of this group are: Gifford Beal (1879——); Frederick C.

Fig. 873. Benton. The Arts of the South. Whitney Museum
of American Art. (Whitney Museum)

painter has not been as prone as the European to abstractions, geometry, symbols, and pure fantasy. Some whose interest tends in that
direction and who eagerly reach out into fields of experimentation are
Max Weber (1881———), versatile and intelligent experimenter; John
Marin (1875———) in his watercolor landscapes; Georgia O'Keeffe
(1887———) in her abstract landscapes (Fig. 871) and symbolist flower
pieces; Augustus Vincent Tack (1870———) in his proposed murals
for the Phillips Memorial Gallery in Washington; Andrew Dasburg
(1887———); Preston Dickinson (1891–1930); Marsden Hartley (1878
———); Karl Knaths (1891———); Yasuo Kuniyoshi (1893———). On
the other hand there seems to be an inclination to keep close to human
experience. A thread of healthy realism runs through American painting, from the earliest limners to the contemporary scene, a realism that
has manifested itself in various ways and frequently in none too healthy
a form esthetically. Is it possible that the practical, efficient American
nature finds a parallel in the nature of the Roman, that practical,
efficient organizer whose highest expression was functional and realistic? However idle it may be to speculate upon what the authentic
twentieth-century American style and tradition will be, one can hardly
help feeling that at last such is in the making or emerging. After the
welter and the lamentable, but inevitable, attempts of the nineteenth
century the painters of today, once given the opportunity to function
in the social and economic system, have the professional equipment,
the versatility, the mental vigor, and the artist's vision to create an

Frieseke (1874———); William J. Glackens (1870———); Childe Hassam (1859–1935);
Ernest Lawson (1873———); Jonas Lie (1880———).

Fig. 874. Hopper. Lighthouse Hill. 1927. Coll. Mr. and Mrs. L. G. Sheafer, New York. (Museum of Modern Art)

Fig. 875. Burchfield. Civic Improvement. 1927–28. Rehn Galleries, New York. (Frank K. M. Rehn)

Fig. 876. Wood. American Gothic. 1932. Art
Institute of Chicago. (Art Institute)

art of a high order —
they are doing it to-
day in isolation in
spite of their ostra-
cism, as did the French
painters — an art that
is American, not a
narrowly provincial
interpretation of na-
tionalism, but a con-
sistent and coherent
expression in the
American idiom, with
cosmopolitan breadth.

Professionally the
American painter has
reached his maturity.
He is no longer a co-
lonial provincial turn-
ing to the home
country for training,
however far he may
roam the world for
stimulation. Further-
more he is reaching
out into fields of technical exploration, into a revival of the old tempera and fresco, of gouache and even encaustic.

Of these contemporary painters only a few may be mentioned,[1]
though any attempt at a fairly consistent grouping — whether of point
of view, subject matter, or style — immediately breaks down, as it is
bound to do when no coherent traditions serve to create a style. Any
large exhibitions of contemporary painting will reveal figure work,
genre, landscape (including sea and city scapes), portrait, and still
life as the predominant subject matter. Yet the manner of presentation
is as varied as are the individuals who painted them. Some tend toward
abstract form, some toward realistic; some work in high-keyed contrasting color, some in a low-keyed, restricted, almost monotone
palette. One may venture to point out some excellent figure-painters,

[1] It is obviously impossible even to list the large number of accomplished contempo-
rary American painters. For lists see Virgil Barker, *A Critical Introduction to American
Painting*, Whitney Museum of American Art, New York, 1931; Holger Cahill and
A. H. Barr, eds., *Art in America in Modern Times*, Reynal and Hitchcock, 1934; E. A.
Jewell, *Americans*, Knopf, 1930; the Museum of Modern Art, various catalogues.
(See the Bibliography, p. 532.)

Fig. 876 (A).   The Oval and Pitchfork Motifs in American Gothic.

who are also excellent landscape and genre painters — Guy Pène
Du Bois (1884——); Arnold Blanche (1896——); Alexander Brook
(1898——); Bernard Karfiol (1886——); Leon Kroll (1884——); Walt
Kuhn (1880——); Henry Lee McFee (1886——); Kenneth Hayes
Miller (1876——); Eugene Speicher (1883——; Fig. 872); Maurice
Sterne (1877——).

Significant in the contemporary situation is the gradual revival of
mural painting, which has received such impetus from the Mexican
fresco-painters, with its high hope of a renewed union between building and painting, as has occurred, to a limited extent, between building and sculpture. Such is the work of Thomas Benton in the *New
School of Social Research*, and in the *Whitney Museum* of New York
(Fig. 873); of John W. Norton in the *Daily News Building* and the *Board of
Trade Building* in Chicago; and of Boardman Robinson and others at
Rockefeller Center. And one should at least mention those executed
under the PWAP, whose existence and activity has been of great value,
whatever else may be said, in that it has set up in the mind of the public
the idea that the artist can and should function as a normally necessary
member of American life.

Another significant movement of today is the depiction of the
American scene — not a novel idea, for the local scene as subject
matter has always existed, though overshadowed by glamorous "high
art." From the anonymous folk painters, from John L. Krimmel and
William S. Mount through Eastman Johnson, Frederick Remington,

Winslow Homer, Thomas Eakins, Robert Henri, George Bellows, John
Sloan, the line of descent is clear. A number of painters, not a few of
them pupils of Henri, Bellows, and Sloan, have for some time been
giving vigorous individual interpretations, in various kinds of painting, in drawings, etchings, and lithographs, of city crowds, back yards
and alleys, shops, old houses, and harbor scenes. Such are Glen Coleman (1887–1932); Ernest Fiene (1894——); Edward Hopper (1882
——; FIG. 874); Reginald Marsh (1898——). Charles Burchfield
(1893——) presents the small town of Ohio (FIG. 875). Charles
Sheeler (1883——) paints the factory in Detroit. Thomas Benton
interprets the cotton-pickers of the South, and town and country life
in Indiana. Grant Wood (1892——; FIG. 876) and John Steuart
Curry (1897——) show their home life on the prairies and plains of
Iowa and Nebraska. Millard Sheets (1907——) depicts California.
These painters have not become merely illustrators of the American
scene, but they have made their own milieu, their own living culture,
the basis or perhaps the raw material of their expression. The movement appears to parallel that of contemporary regional literature, the
revival of regional folk songs, and of the Currier and Ives prints.
Similarity of subject matter, however, is the only thread which groups
these painters together, for they present great diversity of approach
and style, from near-abstraction to realism, and equal diversity of
technique — various kinds of oil, tempera, gouache, watercolor — and
most are accomplished etchers and lithographers. Some are coolly
objective, some subjective; some warmly interpretive, some satirical.
But whatever their approach and manner, they seem ever mindful
that, even in a realistic style, a painting is pigment on a flat surface or
is a surface organized by line, color, and texture; they remember that
in the balance between the *what* and the *how* lies the art of painting.

E. THE MINOR AND INDUSTRIAL ARTS

One of the hopeful signs in contemporary art is the enormous advance in esthetic quality in everyday things — "five-and-ten" products, clothing, jewelry, furniture, silver, glass, tools, automobiles, the
list is infinite — in comparison with the nineteenth-century debacle in
taste, though that taste is by no means dead. In this field too we may
observe some trends: 1. *Dominance of the machine.* The majority of the
excellent articles in this group are made by the machine and one
reason for their excellence is that they were designed for machine not
hand manufacture, two distinct processes that are not interchangeable.
Fortunately, that sinister lack of understanding which lies behind the
making of an electric dripping candle is disappearing. The machine

per se is an evil only if it enslaves man. It can, with man's coöperation, turn out objects that not only function adequately but which are
as satisfying esthetically in their own way as the handmade products
of the premachine days. "Whenever the final product of the machine
is designed or determined by anyone sensitive to formal values, that
product can and does become an abstract work of art in the subtler
sense of the term." [1] Even mass production is not an unmitigated evil,
for it gives the creative faculty wide scope for combining into novel
arrangements forms, textures, and colors which individually might
seem commonplace. 2. *The use of materials for their own intrinsic qualities*
and a disciplined regard for the idiom of each, with a consequent abandonment of the practice of translating from one to another: a design for
wood differs from a design for metal, and that for weaving fibers from that
for decorating pottery. Furthermore, within the limitations of one material a design for machine manufacture differs from a design for hand
manufacture. 3. *"Architectural simplicity.* Modern minor arts are tending
toward the same simplification, unbroken surfaces, firm clean-cut
lines, reduction or elimination of ornament, dependence upon shape
and proportions, as in architecture. In fact "architectural" seems the
inevitable word to use in speaking of many examples of metal, glass,
furniture, and pottery. And behind all these qualities one feels the
influence of the machine. 4. *Direct contact with other civilizations* — the
result of cosmopolitanism and travel — has opened the eyes of artists
and, here and there, of the general public to the high quality both
technical and esthetic of the products of other civilizations: Chinese
porcelain and Persian pottery, Near Eastern and primitive textiles,
medieval ironwork, American Indian pottery and weavings, African
and Oceanian woodcarvings, Hindu printed cottons and Javanese
batiks, and Japanese interiors which show a supreme command over
the use of wood. 5. *Blotting-out of national lines.* National lines are none
too clear, with such exceptions as Scandinavia and Mexico. In some
countries, the appeal of the modern style is narrow partly because it
finds expression in limited expensive work beyond the economic range
of the average income; in others, as in Germany and Scandinavia, it
is much more general, partly because of a wide range through mass
production of low-priced everyday necessities of the finest design.

The field of metalworkers has been greatly enlarged by the introduction of new materials and by new technical processes for working
them. Among the metals mentioned in a recent international exhibition are silver, pewter, inlaid and patined brass and copper, iron,
aluminum, lead, bronze, zinc. Here then are wide possibilities for selection of material suitable for the project in hand and also for treatment

[1] Herbert Read, *Art and Industry*, Harcourt, Brace, 1935, p. 37.

Fig. 877. Hans Panzer. Iron Grille.
Church of the Passion at Obermenzing,
near Munich.

to secure surface variations and for combinations of colors and textures — possibilities quickly seized upon by the metalworker. The Swedish, Danish, and German craftsmen in silver and pewter have broken entirely with rococo and are creating highly simplified, at times rugged architectural forms almost devoid of ornament and entirely adapted to machine production. These forms depend for their effects partly upon function, partly upon appropriateness of material, and partly upon shape, proportion, and texture. Iron, which had lost the high place that it held as a medium of art expression, reappears in the grilles and balustrades of Edgar Brandt and Hans Panzer (FIG. 877) in Europe, and of Samuel Yellin and Oscar Bach in America, in the weather-vanes and fire screens of Hunt Diederich. While some of this metalwork is hand-wrought and expensive, some, equally fine in design, is machine-made and within the buying range of the average income. The modern alloy based upon iron, steel, is adaptable, especially in its stainless form, to the creating of many small machine-made objects such as *Tumblers* (FIG. 878), in which one notes again that combination of function, material, process, and esthetic engineering which is basic in all art.

In ceramics, the increased use of terra cotta and glazed tiles in the building arts has created a demand for fabrics, both molded and painted, of a thoroughly architectural design. With pottery in the round there is a tendency away from realistically painted decoration — pictures of landscapes or university buildings — toward forms that depend upon shape, proportions, color, and texture for their effects (FIG. 879), architectural in their simplicity, and toward true clay shapes, often with a one-color glaze filled with subtle modulations. Experiments, especially in France and Denmark, are producing high-fired products, porcelain and stoneware, of unusually simple shape and

texture. Wherever painted decoration is used the work tends toward a
decorative pattern following constructional lines, the same decorative fitness that is found in the figure
work of Persian and Chinese wares
(FIGS. 387, 388, 778). At the same
time some charming ceramic objects appear of freely naturalistic
forms which in their fantasy are far
from mere copies of nature (FIG.
880).

Fig. 878. Beverage and Bathroom
Tumblers. Rustless steel. Polar Ware
Co. (Museum of Modern Art)

A great renascence in the use of
glass marks the twentieth century,
partly because of new demands for
it in building and furnishings and
partly because of a wider use for
small everyday objects. Huge
quantities of both opaque and
transparent glass are needed for industrial buildings, and also for domestic buildings through the rapid
development of air-conditioning,
while modern technical processes
have enabled builders to secure an
infinite variety of effects of color
and texture for decorative purposes. According to its function
glass can be made delicately thin
or massively thick, of meticulously
uniform texture or bubbled,
streaked, sand-blasted, acid-
engraved, or colored within an infinite range of hue. True window-
making, in distinction from pictures painted on glass and inserted
in window openings, has returned

Fig. 879. Tea Set. Made by the Sphinx
Kristal Glas en Aardewerkfabrik, Maas-
tricht, Holland. (Instituut voor Sier-en
Nijverheidskunst, The Hague)

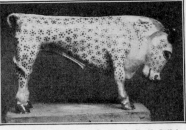

Fig. 880. Walters. Ceramic Bull. Whitney Museum of American Art. (Whitney
Museum)

since its eclipse of more than three centuries because of its unfortunate attempt to transmute itself into the painting medium. The
best windows now are built on the practices of the window-makers
of Chartres: a mosaic made by leading together pieces of glass, generally colored through and through or so treated by mechanical processes that the desired effect of color and texture can be secured. This

Fig. 881. Molded Glass Bowls. Design by A. D. Copier. (Instituut voor Sier-en Nijverheidskunst, The Hague)

Fig. 882. Cut Bowl and Flower Vase. Smoked purple crystal. Design by A. D. Copier. (Instituut voor Sier-en Nijverheidskunst, The Hague)

art still finds a wide use in church-building, and at times clings to the representative, symbolic design of the medieval windows, as in the windows at *Princeton Chapel* and in the rose of *St. John the Divine* (New York) by Charles J. Connick. Or at times it takes on a purely abstract form, as in the windows of the church at *Le Raincy*, and in its uses in secular buildings. In both uses, however, the ultimate effect results from the manipulations of the material according to its own capacities and limitations. In industrial buildings such windows or panels are in increasing demand both for decoration and for advertising, for lettering is in perfect harmony with its principles of design.

In making small objects of glass there is a similar variety of processes of working the medium. It can be blown; molded or pressed; and cut with grinding and polishing for a finish (FIGS. 881, 882). Preëminent work consists of individual pieces whose form is inherent in the medium and in a suitable process of working it. A bottle or a jar by Marinot of France, for example, is likely to be an austere massive geometric shape with a bubbly texture and intense color accent or possibly a bit of severely restrained conventional incising. This glass, however, is made for a limited few and thus its influence upon public taste is equally limited. Not so the *Cock* (FIG. 883), an automobile figurehead by Lalique made of molded glass for mass production. A similar situation exists in the field of Swedish glass. In addition to single hand-worked pieces of a high order, such as those produced at the Orrefors factory, the Swedish glassworkers, through quantity production of designs created for machine manufacture, have given the people of Sweden simple inexpensive wares of great distinction.

Textiles, like the other crafts, are employing new materials, such as synthetic fibers, and experimenting with new weaving techniques, as well as reviving older or exotic processes such as the batik and block-printing of the East (FIG. 754). With the infinite variety of weaves made possible by modern machinery, there is a tendency to depend upon the sheer beauty of surface texture and color alone, as in the work of Paul Rodier, whose fabrics have an austere distinction attained by means of weave and reserved color alone. At the same time the sprightly printed cottons of Raoul Dufy, the painter, depend upon the line and pattern of the wood block that stamps them. This same feeling for the process is felt in the work of Ruth Reeves, who abstracts from contemporary life those motifs which are adaptable to flat decorative use (FIGS. 884, 885). The Swedish products, which are of a high character, are based

Fig. 883. Cock, Automobile Figurehead. Molded glass adapted to mass production. Lalique, Paris.

upon, if not actual copies of, Swedish traditional patterns as a part of the present Swedish national renascence. It just happens, however, that these traditional hangings and rugs, in the austere simplicity of their conventionalized forms and color patterns, often several tones of one hue, are strikingly modern in style. In fact the forms of this archaistic revival are so in harmony in spirit and in form with the modern that the transition, or transformation, from the former to the latter seems almost accomplished.

Mention at least should be made of bookmaking, of the art that sees the entire book as a unit. Typography, illustration, format, binding — each exists not as a separate unit but as one element of a complete design. The woodcut is again finding wider use as a kind of illustration that harmonizes best with the printed page. Experimentation is going on in cutting new forms of type face in which is evident a severe simplicity.

A new art that has evolved from the exigencies of the modern industrial world is advertising design, a new graphic art that under the stimulation of a definite function is reaching in our best advertising a high quality of forceful pattern which contributes as much if not more of the driving power than the content of the words used.

The further we move into the field of modern industry, which dominates civilization today, the more we realize the indispensable place the artist occupies. Commerce and industry have supplanted the

Fig. 884. Ruth Reeves. Hand-Printed Textile. 1934–35. (Photo Henry Clay Gipson, courtesy Ruth Reeves)

Fig. 885. Ruth Reeves. Dinette or Kitchen Print. Black and white glazed chintz. 1930. (W. and J. Sloane, New York)

former kingly or churchly patron, and its finest products — automobiles, airplanes, streamlined trains, bridges, display windows, advertisements, industrial equipment, tools and machinery [1] — are vital art expressions of the postwar twentieth century which combine high esthetic quality with precise functioning. The almost breath-taking beauty of our airplanes both at rest and in movement is indisputably apparent. Though this beauty may be a by-product of functionalism and though the reason for its existence (a problem for the psychologist) may not be clear, this machine age of which we are a part, whether we like it or not, for our weal or woe as we choose, is giving creative ability a new outlet. It is revealing the fact that sensitivity to formal beauty is not confined to one pigeonhole of life — the realm of the so-called fine arts — but permeates the entire cultural structure and nature as well.[2] To see the beauty of a gauge and a seaplane [3] is a foundation for understanding the art in a Giotto, a Peruvian textile, and a *Santa Sophia*, for the same beauty of abstract form underlies fine tools (FIG. 886) and automobiles, fine pictures and statues. Both kinds of creators are working, that is, are organizing their elements, according to the

[1] For illustrations see Museum of Modern Art, *Machine Art*, Museum, New York, 1934; Read, *op. cit.*
[2] See Karl Blossfeldt, *Art Forms in Nature*, Weyhe, 1929–32, 2 vols.
[3] See Read, *op. cit.*, p. 108.

same principles — quality of line and shape, proportion, balance, repetition, rhythmic relationship of part to part. "In many useful objects function does not dictate form, it merely *indicates* form in a general way . . . the rôle of the artist in machine art is to choose, from a variety of possible forms each of which may be functionally adequate, that one form which is aesthetically most satisfactory. He does not embellish or elaborate but refines, simplifies, and perfects."[1] Nevertheless the tool functions with perfect efficiency. Even in the precise rhythm of this functioning is a delight, just as in the satisfactory adjustment of a fresco or a statue to a building.

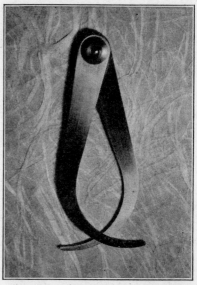

Fig. 886. Caliper. Made by Brown and Sharpe, New York. (Museum of Modern Art, New York)

In contrast, the functionless easel picture, the painter painting or the sculptor carving to please himself or to experiment with theory, pales before this dynamic industrial art, which is so essentially a normal functioning of the art impulse in our machine-controlled age. Probably there will always be a demand for a few pictures, statues, ceramics, glass and metal objects, created as objets d'art as ends in themselves for man's delight, like poetry and music, or for a decorative accent in his home — a few of high quality.

In another respect industrial art is significant. Our life today is thoroughly mechanized, thanks to science — a statement not so sinister as full of potentialities for a richer life. Science and machinery have made us abstraction-conscious and are laying bare to our eyes the underlying abstract organization in all art. Today the artist in man — whether he be scientist, designer of machinery, dancer, writer, painter, or carver — is the one person who can supply that abstract quality by which the manner equals the matter, the quality of the form equals the function. By common consent this esthetic quality does exist in our finest industrial products as well as in our finest paintings, statues, and objets d'art.[2]

[1] Museum of Modern Art, *Machine Art*.
[2] It is illuminating to note M. Amédée Ozenfant's statement, in his *Foundations of Modern Art*, Harcourt, Brace, 1931, that the designers of some of the best automobiles had had art training.

In this realignment of the arts in the contemporary cultural fabric the industrial arts are again dynamic. There has always been an industrial art from the days of the makers of the prehistoric stone knives and daggers, though never before on the scale nor with the powerful dominance of today. And one notes that in proportion as art permeates the whole cultural fabric by way of the things seen and used everyday, great imaginative works of art multiply. Today as the esthetic quality of the industrial arts permeates larger areas of human consciousness, one sees a tendency toward that correlation and unification of all the arts which appears in periods of great art expression and which has been disintegrating since the Renaissance. Painting and sculpture now are functioning in the wider field of the building art,[1] and while one hesitates to hazard a prophecy, it may be that this movement will integrate art activity into the entire cultural fabric and thus restore it to its rightful place as a conscious indispensable force.

F. SUMMARY

To summarize modern art is impossible, partly because of its complexity but largely because of the rapidity with which it changes. One basic element of understanding it is the realization that we are in the midst of one of the world's recurrent transitions from era to era — a statement now too platitudinous to repeat — but never before on the present scale or with the present complexity. For world-awareness has compressed all the world and all the ages into the range of modern man, to his bewilderment and confusion. The world-view today is as confusing as the view of an Impressionist painting at close range. At a distance, the painting takes on form as a whole and in parts. Distance from our age, however, has not yet been reached. Nevertheless, is it possible to find enough unity of trend in the arts to justify speaking of a pattern of modern art? Is "the artistic outlook of the age" articulate enough to justify itself as an emerging style? Do any trends run through all the arts as a key to an answer? Several at least seem to be discernible.

1. *The definite break with eclecticism*, with a consequent closer unity with and more vital understanding of the art of the past. "Old Master and modern Fauve were each saying the same thing although in a different language." [2] The modern wing of contemporary art is in direct line of descent from the great art of the past. In its reaction from the decadence of its immediate past it felt, perhaps subconsciously, that the plant of its own traditions needed pruning almost to the roots to insure

---

[1] Note the definite character of the PWAP projects — specific walls in specific buildings with suggestions for local subject matter.

[2] Edgar Brandt, *International Studio*, December, 1924.

life and growth. And if at times its expressions of the fundamental principles or practices of the old masters have been extremist, vociferously blatant, or fantastic for the sake of enforcing their message, with the real thinkers and masters it has been honest, sincere, and salutary. 2. *Functionalism*, clearly fundamental in architecture and most of the industrial arts and in painting and sculpture wherever the artists are given an opportunity. As a result we see a tendency to abolish everything irrelevant to structural or esthetic need. Thus ornament no longer finds a place simply for its own sake. 3. *A feeling for materials* and a refusal to compromise by interchange. This is clear in all the arts, including literature, music, drama, the dance. Here the experimental spirit of the age is discovering new possibilities, inventing new synthetic products and new methods of handling, especially in the realm of the machine. 4. *A wider and greater use of color*, perhaps a result of contacts, on the part of drab Europe and still drabber America, with the colorful East. 5. *A simple directness*, perhaps an influence of our machine-mindedness, certainly a reaction from superrococo and the "Gilded Age," and a simplicity of form to the point of abstractions and pure geometry. 6. *A possible overemphasis upon form and design*, in a zealous effort to recover that ability for construction and organization which had almost been lost when eclecticism and the photographic copy motivated the artist. This organizing tendency finds its counterpart in a "planned (designed) economy," a "planned society," a "planned monetary system" in contrast to the laissez-faire point of view. Likewise the earlier hands-off-nature policy, a take-it-as-it-is-exactly and let-the-camera-reproduce-a-verisimilitude has enforced a reaction of extremist emphasis upon, and experiment with, form. Musicians are composing with new harmonies which seem to the untrained ear like blatant discord; writers are using new forms, new uses of words, new structure in which at times intelligibility is lost and abstract forms and rhythm alone remain. A possible analogy might be made with research in pure science without regard for its possible application. Much of contemporary painting, especially the more abstract and geometric, is research in form that may in time become applicable to the purpose of communication. Yet undoubtedly there is a permanent place in the twentieth-century world, with its expanding taste and understanding, for abstract art. However that may be, abstractions, distortions, geometry, are likely either to convert the eye to a new kind of seeing or after a period of disciplinary training of the eye to modify in the direction of naturalism and human experience. 7. *A cultural internationalism*. Travel, foreign residence, and change in citizenship are disclosing the universality of art, however much the nations differ in idiom. 8. *Artists finding their natural place*. Today there is an abandonment of the artificial, romantic "starving-in-a-garret" conception of the artist in favor of a disposition to recognize that art and the artist are and always have been healthy vital elements in any cultural fabric. This disposition is gaining ground through the increasing affiliation of art and industry, so that one no longer stands amazed at the thought of artists in overalls paid by the hour like day laborers or drawing a weekly wage.

Here possibly are a few trends that seem clear and definite and have persisted long enough to warrant recognition. And in glancing them over it is illuminating to see that no one of them, internationalism excepted, is novel. The novelty is in the scope and the degree of their application. For this is an age par excellence of adventure; not capricious, but sincere and intense adventure, operating not in the arts alone but in government, economics, sociology. To be sure, there are many weaknesses in this world-adventure, only too easy to point out. But through the confusion shines a vitality, a driving force as of a youthful age, awkward and not entirely coherent, undisciplined and wayward; exciting, daring, living strenuously and intensely; making mistakes, going to extremes. In its large outlines the pattern of modern art but repeats the pattern of contemporary life.

BIBLIOGRAPHY

Architecture, Sculpture, Minor and Industrial Arts

Agard, W. R., *The New Architectural Sculpture*, Oxford Press, 1935
American Federation of Arts, *Catalogue, International Exhibition of Ceramic Art 1928–1929*, introd. by C. R. Richards, Southworth Press, 1928
—— —— *Catalogue, International Exhibition of Contemporary Glass and Rugs 1929–1930*, introd. by C. R. Richards, Southworth Press, 1929
—— —— *Catalogue, Decorative Metalwork and Cotton Textiles, Third International Exhibition of Contemporary Industrial Art, 1930–1931*, introd. by C. R. Richards, Southworth Press, 1930
Aumonier, William, ed., *Modern Architectural Sculpture*, Scribner, 1930
Cahill, Holger, and Barr, A. H., eds., *Art in America in Modern Times*, Reynal and Hitchcock, 1934
Casson, Stanley, *Some Modern Sculptors*, Oxford Press, 1928
—— —— *XXth Century Sculptors*, Oxford Press, 1930
Cheney, S. W., *New World Architecture*, Longmans, 1931
Du Colombier, Pierre, and Manuel, Roland, *Les arts; peinture, sculpture, gravure, architecture, cinéma, photographie, musique et danse*, Paris, 1933
Einstein, Karl, *Die Kunst des 20. Jahrhunderts*, Berlin, 1926
Epstein, Jacob, *The Sculptor Speaks*, Doubleday, Doran, 1932
Ferriss, Hugh, *The Metropolis of Tomorrow*, Washburn, 1929
Frankl, P. T. *Form and Re-Form; A Practical Handbook of Modern Interiors*, Harper, 1930
—— —— *New Dimensions*, Harcourt, Brace, 1928
Geddes, N. B., *New Horizons*, Little, Brown, 1932

Hitchcock, H. R., *Modern Architecture*, Harcourt, Brace, 1929
————— and Johnson, Philip, *The International Style: Architecture since 1922*, Norton, 1932
Janneau, Guillaume, *Modern Glass*, Studio, 1931
Kahle, K. M., *Modern French Decoration*, Putnam, 1930
Kahn, E. J., *Design in Art and Industry*, Scribner, 1935
Kiesler, Frederick, *Contemporary Art Applied to the Store and Its Display*, Coward-McCann, 1930
Le Corbusier, Charles (Jeanneret-Gris, C. E.), *The City of To-morrow*, Harcourt, Brace, 1929
————— *Towards a New Architecture*, Payson and Clarke, 1927 (now Harcourt, Brace)
Martel, Jan and Joël, *Sculpture*, Paris, 1929
Mumford, Lewis, *Technics and Civilization*, Harcourt, Brace, 1934
Museum of Modern Art, *Machine Art*, Museum, New York, 1934
————— *Painting & Sculpture from 16 American Cities*, Museum, New York, 1933
————— *[Wilhelm] Lehmbruck and [Aristide] Maillol*, Museum, New York, 1930
Ozenfant, Amédée, *Foundations of Modern Art*, Harcourt, Brace, 1931
Park, E. A., *New Backgrounds for a New Age*, Harcourt, Brace, 1927
Platz, G. A., *Die Baukunst der neusten Zeit*, 2d ed., Berlin, 1930
Pound, Ezra, *Gaudier-Brzeska*, Lane, 1916
Randall, J. H., Jr., *The Making of the Modern Mind*, Houghton Mifflin, 1926
Read, H. E., *Art and Industry*, Harcourt, Brace, 1935
Rindge, A. M., *Sculpture*, Harcourt, Brace, 1929
Robertson, H. M., and Yerbury, F. R., eds., *Examples of Modern French Architecture*, Scribner, 1928
Sexton, R. W., *Interior Architecture, the Design of Interiors of Modern American Homes*, Architectural Book Publishing Co., 1927
————— *The Logic of Modern Architecture*, Architectural Book Publishing Co., 1929
Taut, Bruno, *Modern Architecture*, Studio, 1929
Todd, Dorothy, and Mortimer, Raymond, *The New Interior Decoration*, Scribner, 1929
Wettergren, Erik, *The Modern Decorative Arts of Sweden*, American-Scandinavian Foundation, New York, 1926
Wiener Werkstätte, *Evolution of the Modern Applied Arts, 1903–1928*, Vienna, 1929
Wollin, N. G. A., *Modern Swedish Arts and Crafts in Pictures*, Scribner, 1931
Wright, F. L., *An Autobiography*, Longmans, 1932
————— *Modern Architecture*, Princeton University Press, 1931

Painting

Barnes, A. C., *The Art in Painting*, 2d ed. rev., Harcourt, Brace, 1928
————— *The Post-Impressionists, from Monet to Bonnard*, W. F. Payson, 1931
Basler, Adolph and Kunstler, Charles, *The Modernists, from Matisse to De Segonzac*, W. F. Payson, 1931
Bell, Clive, *Since Cézanne*, Harcourt, Brace, 1929
Cahill, Holger, and Barr, A. H., eds., *Art in America in Modern Times*, Reynal and Hitchcock, 1934
Cheney, S. W., *A Primer of Modern Art*, Liveright, 1932
Cortissoz, Royal, *American Artists*, Scribner, 1923
Eddy, A. J., *Cubists and Post-Impressionism*, McClurg, 1919
Fry, R. E., *Cézanne*, Macmillan, 1927
————— *Transformations*, Coward-McCann, 1927
————— *Vision and Design*, Coward-McCann, 1924

Gauguin, Paul, *Noa-Noa*, tr. by O. F. Theis, Greenberg, 1927

Gogh, Vincent van, *Letters to His Brother, 1872–1886*, Houghton Mifflin, 1927, 2 vols.

Gordon, Jan, *Modern French Painters*, new ed., Lane, 1929

Hind, C. L., *Post Impressionists*, Doran, 1912

Holmes, Sir C. J., *Notes on the Post-Impressionist Painters*, London, 1910

Janneau, Guillaume, *L'art cubiste*, Paris, 1929

Jewell, E. A., *Americans*, Knopf, 1930

Marriott, Charles, *Modern Movements in Painting*, Scribner, 1921

Mather, F. J., *Modern Painting*, Holt, 1927

Meier-Graefe, Julius, *Modern Art*, tr. by Florence Simmonds and G. W. Chrystal, Putnam, 1908, 2 vols.

—— —— *Vincent van Gogh*, Harcourt, Brace, 1933

Museum of Modern Art, *Frescoes of Diego Rivera*, Museum, New York, 1933

—— —— *German Painting and Sculpture*, Museum, New York, 1931

—— —— *Murals by American Painters and Photographers*, Museum, New York, 1932

—— —— *Paintings by Nineteen Living Americans*, Museum, New York, 1930

—— —— *Painting and Sculpture by Living Americans*, Museum, New York, 1930

—— —— *Painting and Sculpture from 16 American Cities*, Museum, New York, 1933

—— —— *Painting in Paris*, Museum, New York, 1930

Pach, Walter, *The Masters of Modern Art*, Viking Press, 1924

Phillips, Duncan, and others, articles in *Art and Understanding*, Phillips Memorial Gallery, Washington, 1929–1930

Pueblo Indian Painting, *50 Reproductions of Watercolor Paintings by the Indian Artists of the New Mexico Pueblos of San Ildefonso and Sia*, Nice, France, 1932

Read, H. E., *Art Now*, Harcourt, Brace, 1934

Raynal, Maurice, *Modern French Painters*, Brentano's, 1928

Rey, Robert, *Gauguin*, tr. by F. C. de Sumichrast, Dodd, Mead, 1924

Rich, D. C., *Seurat and the Evolution of La Grande Jatte*, University of Chicago Press, 1935

Rivera, Diego, *Frescoes*, ed. by Ernestine Evans, Harcourt, Brace, 1929

Rothschild, E. F., *The Meaning of Unintelligibility in Modern Art*, University of Chicago Press, 1934

Rutter, F. V. P., *Evolution in Modern Art*, Dial Press, 1926

Sweeney, J. J., *Plastic Redirections in 20th Century Painting*, University of Chicago Press, 1934

Uhde, Wilhelm, *Picasso and the French Tradition*, Weyhe, 1929

Vollard, Ambroise, *Paul Cézanne, His Life and Art*, tr. by H. L. Van Doren, Frank-Maurice, 1926

Whitney Museum of American Art, monographs by various authors on Benton, Du Bois, Brook, Coleman, Demuth, Henri, Hopper, Karfiol, McFee, Miller, Schnakenberg, Sloan, Speicher, Tucker

Wilenski, R. H., *The Modern Movement in Art*, Stokes, 1927

Wright, W. H., *Modern Painting: Its Tendency and Meaning*, Dodd, Mead, 1927

APPENDIX

GENERAL BIBLIOGRAPHY

General Handbooks and Histories

Abbot, E. R., *The Great Painters*, Harcourt, Brace, 1927

Ackerman, Phyllis, *Tapestry, the Mirror of Civilization*, Oxford Press, 1933

American Institute of Architects, *The Significance of the Fine Arts*, new ed., Marshall Jones, 1926

Buckley, Wilfred, *European Glass*, Houghton Mifflin, 1927

Chase, G. H., and Post, C. R., *History of Sculpture*, Harper, 1924

Dawson, Nelson, *Goldsmiths' and Silversmiths' Work*, London, 1907

Dillon, Edward, *Glass*, Putnam, 1907

Faure, Elie, *History of Art*, tr. by Walter Pach, Harper, 1921–30, 5 vols.

Ffoulkes, C. J., *Decorative Ironwork from the XIth to the XVIIIth Century*, Doran, 1914

Fletcher, Sir B. F., *History of Architecture on the Comparative Method*, 9th ed., Scribner, 1931

Gardner, J. S., *Ironwork*, rev. by W. W. Watts, 4th ed., 1927–30, Victoria & Albert Museum, London, 2 vols.

Gilman, Roger, *Great Styles of Interior Architecture*, Harper, 1924

Glazier, Richard, *Manual of Historic Ornament*, 4th ed. rev., Scribner, 1926

Hamlin, A. D. F., *History of Ornament*, Century, 1916–23, 2 vols.

Herbert, J. A., *Illuminated Manuscripts*, Putnam, 1911

Hind, A. M., *History of Engraving and Etching*, Houghton Mifflin, 1923

———— *An Introduction to a History of Woodcut*, Houghton Mifflin, 1935, 2 vols.

Kimball, S. F., and Edgell, G. H., *History of Architecture*, Harper, 1918

Magonigle, H. V. B., *The Nature, Practice, and History of Art*, Scribner, 1924

Maskell, Alfred, *Ivories*, Putnam, 1905

———— *Wood Sculpture*, Putnam, 1911

Mumford, Lewis, *Technics and Civilization*, Harcourt, Brace, 1934

Pijoan y Loteras, José, *History of Art*, Harper, 1927, 3 vols.

Pollard, A. W., *Fine Books*, Putnam, 1912

Post, C. R., *History of European and American Sculpture*, Harvard University Press, 1921, 2 vols.

Rindge, A. M., *Sculpture*, Harcourt, Brace, 1929

Robb, D. M., and Garrison, J. J., *Art in the Western World*, Harper, 1935

Statham, H. H., *A Short Critical History of Architecture*, Scribner, 1912

Triggs, H. I., *Garden Craft in Europe*, Scribner, 1913

Technique and Design

Batchelder, E. A., *Design in Theory and Practice*, Macmillan, 1910

Best Maugard, Adolfo, *A Method for Creative Design*, Knopf, 1926

Blake, Vernon, *The Art and Craft of Drawing*, Oxford Press, 1927

Casson, Stanley, *The Technique of Early Greek Sculpture*, Oxford Press, 1933

Doerner, Max, *The Materials of the Artist and Their Use in Painting*, Harcourt, Brace, 1934

Franklin, Christine (Ladd), *Colour and Colour Theories*, Harcourt, Brace, 1929

Gill, Eric, *Sculpture*, Saint Dominic's Press, Ditchling, Sussex, 1925

Holmes, Sir C. J., *A Grammar of the Arts*, Macmillan, 1932

—— —— *Notes on the Science of Picture-Making*, new ed., Stokes, 1928

Laurie, A. P., *The Materials of the Painter's Craft*, Lippincott, 1911

—— —— *The Painter's Methods and Materials*, Lippincott, 1926

Moreau-Vauthier, Charles, *The Technique of Painting*, Putnam, 1912

Petrina, John, *Art Work; How Produced, How Reproduced*, Pitman, 1934

Phillipps, L. M., *Form and Colour*, Scribner, 1915

Pope, Arthur, *An Introduction to the Language of Drawing and Painting*, Harvard University Press, 1929, 2 vols.

Reath, N. A., *The Weaves of Hand-Loom Fabrics*, Pennsylvania Museum, 1927

Robins, W. P., *The Etching Craft*, Dodd, Mead, 1923

Ross, D. W., *On Drawing and Painting*, Houghton Mifflin, 1912

—— —— *A Theory of Pure Design*, Houghton Mifflin, 1907

Sargent, Walter, *The Enjoyment and Use of Color*, Scribner, 1923

Weitenkampf, Frank, *How to Appreciate Prints*, new ed. rev., Scribner, 1932

Esthetics and Criticism

Barnes, A. C., *The Art in Painting*, 2d ed., Harcourt, Brace, 1926

Bell, Clive, *Art*, Stokes, 1914

Blake, Vernon, *Relation in Art*, Oxford Press, 1925

Brown, G. B., *The Fine Arts*, 3d ed., Scribner, 1910

Buermeyer, Lawrence, *The Aesthetic Experience*, Barnes Foundation, 1924

Croce, Benedetto, *The Essence of Aesthetic*, London, 1921

Dewey, John, *Art as Experience*, Minton, Balch, 1934

Edman, Irwin, *The World, the Arts and the Artist*, Norton, 1928

Ellis, Havelock, *The Dance of Life*, Houghton Mifflin, 1923

Flaccus, L. W., *The Spirit and Substance of Art*, Crofts, 1926

Fry, R. E., *Transformations*, Brentano's, 1927

—— —— *Vision and Design*, Brentano's, 1924

Gill, Eric, *Beauty Looks after Herself*, Sheed and Ward, 1933

Hamlin, T. F., *The Enjoyment of Architecture*, Scribner, 1921

Hildebrand, Adolf, *The Problem of Form in Painting and Sculpture*, Stechert, 1907

Huneker, J. G., *Promenades of an Impressionist*, Scribner, 1910

Kandinsky, Wassily, *The Art of Spiritual Harmony*, tr. by M. T. H. Sadler, Houghton Mifflin, 1914

Langfeld, H. S., *The Aesthetic Attitude*, Harcourt, Brace, 1920

Lethaby, W. R., *Form in Civilization*, Oxford Press, 1922

Lewisohn, Ludwig, ed., *A Modern Book of Criticism*, Modern Library, 1919

McMahon, A. P., *The Meaning of Art*, Norton, 1930

Maritain, Jacques, *Art and Scholasticism*, Scribner, 1930

Mather, F. J., *Estimates in Art*, Holt, 1916

Munro, Thomas, *Scientific Method in Aesthetics*, Norton, 1928

Neuhaus, Eugen, *The Appreciation of Art*, Ginn, 1924

Ogden, C. K., Richards, I. A., and Wood, J. E. H., *The Foundations of Aesthetics*, International Publishers, 1925

Opdyke, H. G., *Art and Nature Appreciation*, Macmillan, 1933

Parker, De W. H., *Analysis of Art*, Yale University Press, 1926

Pearson, R. M., *Experiencing Pictures*, Harcourt, Brace, 1932

Phillips, Duncan, *The Artist Sees Differently*, Weyhe, 1931, 2 vols.

Santayana, George, *The Life of Reason*, 2d ed., Scribner, 1922

—— —— *The Sense of Beauty*, Scribner, 1896

Scott, Geoffrey, *The Architecture of Humanism*, 2d ed. rev., Scribner, 1924

Sirén, Osvald, *Essentials in Art*, Lane, 1920

Smith, S. C. K., *Art and Common Sense*, London, 1932

Wölfflin, Heinrich, *Principles of Art History*, Holt, 1932

Worringer, Wilhelm, *Form in Gothic*, tr. by Herbert Read, London, 1927

Sources for Reproductions

Abbot, Etheldred, ed., *Sources for Reproductions of Works of Art*, American Library Association, 1936. Copies of this list can be obtained from the Ryerson Library, The Art Institute of Chicago. Price, five cents.

GLOSSARY OF TECHNICAL TERMS

(The references to Figure numbers are not exhaustive.)

Abacus. A flat block forming the upper member of the capital of a column. Fig. 182.

Ambulatory. A passageway. It may be outside, as in a cloister (q.v.), or inside; used especially of the passageway around the chevet. Fig. 425.

Amphora. A jar with two handles for general storage purposes. Figs. 222, 232.

Apse. The recess, usually semicircular, at the end of a Roman basilica, or of a Christian church. Figs. 282, 308, 309. In a Gothic cathedral, the semicircular end of the choir. Figs. 425, 426.

Aqueduct. A channel for conducting water; frequently supported by arches. Fig. 275.

Arabesque. Literally, like the Arabian. Strictly, a Muhammadan decorative motif "composed of gracefully curving scrolls, crossed or interlaced, and bearing stylized motifs suggesting a leaf or flower" (Dimand). Figs. 362, 366, 368. By extension, any kind of fanciful ornament with flowing lines, foliage, fruit, flowers, or figures combined or interwoven.

Arcade. A series of arches supported on piers or columns. Figs. 285, 396.

Arch. A constructional device to span an opening; a true arch is curved in shape, and made of wedge-shaped blocks (voussoirs). P. ix, Figs. 124, 285, 424, 427.

Architrave. The lintel or lowest division of the entablature. Fig. 182.

Atrium. The court of a Roman house, near the entrance and partly open to the sky. Fig. 293. The open court in front of a Christian basilica. Figs. 308, 393.

Aureole. A frame or halo around the figure of a sacred personage. Fig. 401.

Baldacchino (Baldachin). In Italy, a canopy on four columns frequently built over an altar. Figs. 314, 486.

Barrel Vault. See Vault.

Basilica. In Roman architecture, a public building for assemblies, especially tribunals, rectangular in plan, with a central nave terminating in an apse. Figs. 281, 282. In Christian architecture, an early church somewhat resembling the Roman basilica; usually entered through an atrium. Figs. 308, 311–315.

Batter. The inward slope of a wall, often almost imperceptible.

Bay. A compartment that serves as a unit of division in a building. In a Gothic cathedral the transverse arches and adjacent piers of the arcade divide the building into bays, the design of which is an architectural unit repeated in each bay. Figs. 395, 425, 428.

Blind Arcade (Wall Arcade). An arcade, applied to a wall surface, with no actual openings, to serve as a decoration. Fig. 396.

Bottega. A shop. The studio-shop of an Italian artist.

Brocaded Textile. A fabric in which additional weft threads are used to enrich the surface, frequently by the introduction of gold and silver.

Broken Pediment. A pediment in which the cornice is broken at the apex. Figs. 574, 633.

Buttress. A masonry support to counterbalance the lateral thrust of an arch or vault. A pier buttress is a solid mass of masonry. A flying buttress is an arch or series of arches that carry the thrust over the aisles to the solid buttresses. Figs. 426, 429, 441, 442.

Campanile. Italian word for a bell tower. Sometimes it is free-standing. Sometimes it is a part of the building. Figs. 311, 313, 464.

Cantilever. A long bracket or beam attached to a wall and supported at the wall end only. P. ix, Fig. 834.

Capital. The upper member of a column, usually decorated, that serves as a transition from the shaft to the lintel. Fig. 182.

Cartoon. A preliminary drawing for a painting.

Caryatid. A draped female figure that serves, like a column, as a support. Fig. 185.

Cassone. A large chest. An important piece of Italian furniture. Fig. 468.

Cella. The inclosed chamber, the essential feature of a classical temple, in which usually stood the cult statue. Figs. 176, 180, 276.

Centering. A wooden framework to hold an arch, or vault, during its construction until, when complete, it becomes self-supporting.

Ceramics (Keramics). A general term for the art of pottery.

Chalice. A cup or goblet, especially that used in the sacraments of the Church. Figs. 339, 419, 459.

Chamfer. To cut off a square angle; to bevel.

Champlevé Enamel. A process of enameling in which the design is cut out of a metal plate, leaving thin raised lines, that correspond to the cloisons in the cloisonné process, to hold the enamel. P. 330, Fig. 460.

Chevet. The term applied to the apse of a cathedral, together with its ambulatories and apsidal chapels. Fig. 425.

Chevron. A zigzag or V-shaped motif of decoration.

Chiaroscuro. Literally, clear-obscure. The treatment of light and dark in a work of art.

Chiton. A Greek tunic, the essential and often only garment of both men and women, the other being the mantle. See Himation. There were two kinds of tunics, the Doric and Ionic. The Doric was a rectangular piece of woolen stuff, usually folded over at the top, wrapped about the body and left open at the left side, sleeveless, fastened on the shoulders with buckles, and girdled. Fig. 212. The Ionic was longer, more voluminous, of soft goods such as cotton or linen, and often caught at intervals by fastenings to form sleeves. Fig. 214.

Choir. The space separated from the rest of the church by a screen and reserved for the clergy and choir. In the Gothic cathedral it occupies the nave between the crossing and the apse. Fig. 425.

Choir Stalls. Seats for the clergy and choristers, usually ranged along the sides of the choir. Fig. 458.

Cire-Perdue Process. Literally the wax-lost process. A method of bronze casting by which the wax in which the figure is modeled is melted away and the space thus left filled with molten bronze. P. 137, note 1.

Clerestory. That part of a building which rises above the roofs of the other parts and whose walls contain openings for lighting. Figs. 36, 65, 282, 311, 428.

Cloison. Literally, a partition. A metal wire or narrow strip, usually gold, soldered to a metal base to form cells for holding enamel.

Cloisonné Enamel. A process of enameling in which strips of metal (cloisons) are soldered to a base, forming cells into which the enamel is poured and fused. P. 232, Figs. 340, 417.

Cloister. A court, usually with covered ambulatories on the sides. Fig. 451.

Codex. A manuscript in the form of a volume with pages bound together. P. 225, note 2.

Coffer. A sunken ornamental panel in a soffit, vault, or ceiling. Fig. 280.

Coin Type. The pattern or design used to decorate a coin.

Colonnade. A series or range of columns, usually spanned by lintels. Fig. 178.

Colonnette. A small column. Fig. 499.

Colophon. An inscription at the end of a book or manuscript which gives the title, possibly the name of the writer or illustrator, the place of writing, and the date — information now placed on the title page.

Column. A circular weight-carrying member, consisting of a base (sometimes omitted), a shaft, and a capital. Fig. 182.

Compound or Clustered Pier. A pier composed of a group or cluster of members from each of which springs one or more ribs of the vaulting. Especially characteristic of Gothic architecture. Figs. 394, 428.

Console. A bracket, or corbel, usually S-shaped.

Cool Color. Blue and the hues that approach blue, blue-green, and blue-violet are cool.

Corbel. A projecting stone used as a support.

Corbel Table. A projecting course of masonry supported by corbels, frequently connected by arches. Fig. 393.

Corbeled Arch. A constructional device for spanning an opening by projecting successive courses of masonry inward until the opening is closed. P. ix, Figs. 155, 160. Not a true arch. See Arch.

Cornice. The projecting crowning member of the entablature. Also used for any crowning projection. Fig. 182.

Cramp. A device, usually metal, to hold together blocks of stone. Fig. 175.

Crater (Krater). A large bowl for mixing the wine and the water, the usual beverage of the Greek. Figs. 226, 238.

Crocket. A projecting foliate ornament that decorates a pinnacle, gable, buttress, or spire. Its purpose is to break a long line against the sky. Fig. 443.

Cromlech. A circle of monoliths. Fig. 23.

Crossing. The space in a cruciform church where the nave and transept intersect. Figs. 425, 428.

Crown of an Arch or Vault. The topmost part of an arch or vault.

Cuneiform. Literally, wedge-shaped. A system of writing, used in Babylonia-Assyria, in which the characters are wedge-shaped. Figs. 110, 114.

Custodia. An elaborate tabernacle, usually architectural in design, for the host. Fig. 598.

Cylix (Kylix). A Greek drinking cup. Figs. 227, 235, 236.

Damascene. To inlay metal with another kind of metal or other material for decorative purposes. Figs. 173, 386.

Dentils. Small toothlike projecting blocks in the molding of a cornice. Figs. 182, 470, 471.

Diptych. Consisting of two leaves. A Roman two-hinged writing tablet. Used also for commemorative purposes by the Christian Church. Fig. 337.

Divisionism or Broken Color. The method of juxtaposing small strokes of pure color directly upon the canvas for the eye to mix at a distance rather than mixing the colors first upon the palette. A method practiced by Constable, Turner, and Delacroix, and perfected by the French Impressionists. The principle was used also by the twelfth-century glassworkers.

Dolmen. Several large stones capped with a covering slab. Fig. 22.

Donjon. A massive tower forming the stronghold of a medieval castle. Fig. 421.

Dowel. A wooden or metallic pin to hold together two pieces of stone or other material. Fig. 175.

Drum. The circular wall which supports a dome. Figs. 279, 345. The circular stones of which a built shaft is made. Fig. 181.

Echinus. Literally a sea urchin. The convex member of a capital, somewhat resembling a sea urchin, that supports the abacus. Fig. 182.

Engaged Column. A columnlike member forming part of the wall and projecting more or less from it. Fig. 276.

Engraving. The process of incising a design upon a substance with a sharp instrument. See Incise. The process of incising a design upon a copper plate from which a printed impression can be made. Also the impression made from such a plate. Fig. 590.

Entablature. The part of a building of lintel construction between the capitals of the columns and the roof or upper story. Fig. 182.

Entasis. A slight, almost imperceptible, curvature in the shaft of a column. Fig. 182.

Etching. The process of engraving a design upon a copper plate, by means of an acid or mordant, from which a printed impression can be taken. Also the impression from a plate so made. Fig. 618.

Façade. The front of a building, usually the principal front but also applied to the other sides when they are given emphasis by architectural treatment.

Faïence. From Faenza, in Italy, a center for the manufacture of majolica; and restricted in meaning by some authors to tin-glazed pottery. By others the meaning has been extended to include any kind of glazed pottery except porcelain; and by others to a general term for all kinds of glazed earthenware.

Fan Vaulting. A development of lierne vaulting, found in English Perpendicular Gothic, in which the ribs radiate from the impost in such a way that they form an inverted cone.

Fenestration. Strictly, the arrangement of the windows in a building; by extension, the arrangement of all the openings (windows, doors, arcades) in architectural design.

Finial. A knoblike ornament, usually with a foliate design, in which a pinnacle terminates. Fig. 443.

Flamboyant. Meaning flamelike, applied to the late Gothic style in which the restless type of decoration is based upon wavy lines and the ogee arch. Fig. 448.

Flush. On the same level or plane as the adjoining surfaces.

Flute (Fluting). Vertical channeling, usually semicircular. Used principally on columns and pilasters. Figs. 187, 188, 503.

Flying Buttress. See Buttress.

Fresco. Painting on freshly spread moist plaster. The pigments are mixed with water and become chemically incorporated with the plaster. Also a painting so executed.

Fret (Meander). An ornament consisting of interlocking angular motifs. Frequently in bands but also covering surfaces. Figs. 221, 683, 684, 774, 775.

Gargoyle. A waterspout, usually carved or in the form of a grotesque, to throw the water from the gutters away from the walls. Fig. 444.

Gesso. Prepared plaster mixed with a binding material, used as a ground for painting or for relief.

Glaze. A vitreous coating applied to the surface of pottery to make it impervious and for decorative purposes.

Gopuram. In Hindu architecture, the high elaborate gateway of the southern Indian temples. Fig. 731.

Gouache. Opaque watercolor, or a picture painted in this pigment. Figs. 384, 385, 455.

Greek Cross. A cross consisting of two equal bars meeting at right angles.

Grille. A grating, usually of iron, for protection with visibility. Figs. 472, 832, 877.

Groin. The edge formed by the intersection of two vaults. Fig. 274.

Groin Vault. See Vault.

Guilloche. An ornament consisting of interlacing curving bands. Fig. 231.

Hammer-Beam Ceiling. An English Gothic open timber ceiling. Figs. 627, 628.

Haunch. The part of an arch, from a third to two-thirds the distance from the spring to the crown, where the lateral thrust is most strongly exerted.

Hieroglyphs (Hieroglyphics). A system of writing, derived from picture writing, but also phonetic, used by the ancient Egyptians. By extension, applied to other peoples also, such as the Maya. Figs. 48, 57, 687, 692.

Himation. A Greek mantle worn by men and women over the tunic and draped in various ways. Figs. 218, 255.

Historiated. Ornamented with figures that have a representational or narrative element, such as plants, animals, or human figures, in distinction from purely decorative elements. Historiated initial letters were a popular form of manuscript decoration in the Middle Ages. Fig. 514.

Hue. The hue is the name of the color. The primary hues are blue, red, and yellow, which, together with green, orange, and violet, form the chief colors of the spectrum. Between these lie the intermediates which partake of the qualifications of both adjacent hues: red-orange, yellow-orange, yellow-green, blue-green, blue-violet, and red-violet.

Hypostyle Hall. A hall whose roof is supported by columns. Applied to the colonnaded hall of the Egyptian pylon temple. Figs. 65, 67.

Icon. Literally, a portrait or image. Used especially in the Greek Church for the panels containing representations of sacred personages. Fig. 355.

Iconostasis. In East Christian churches, a screen or partition, with doors and many tiers of icons, that separate the sanctuary from the main body of the church. Fig. 353.

Impost. The architectural member from which an arch springs.

Incise. To cut into a surface with a sharp instrument. A method of decoration, especially on metal and pottery. Figs. 118, 779.

Intaglio. A design sunk below the surface so that an impression made from it is in relief. Used especially on gems, seals, and dies for coins. Also applied to an object so decorated.

Intercolumniation. The space between the columns in a colonnade.

Isocephaly. Literally, heads equal or on a level. A principle by which natural proportion is distorted so as to bring all the objects in a composition to an equal height for the purpose of design. Figs. 217, 524.

Kakemono. A Chinese or Japanese painting in the form of a hanging, not framed, but mounted on brocade.

Keystone. The uppermost voussoir in an arch. See Voussoir.

Lacquer. A varnish containing lac; or a hard varnish obtained from the sap of the lacquer tree, *Rhus vernicifera*, by making incisions in the bark. The latter is the Chinese and Japanese lacquer.

Lantern. A small structure that crowns a dome, turret, or roof with openings for lighting, though frequently the purpose of the lantern is design only. Fig. 464.

Latin Cross. A cross consisting of two bars meeting at right angles, the lower arm longer than the others.

Lierne. A short cross rib inserted between the main ribs of a vaulting. Figs. 452, 454.

Lintel. A horizontal beam of any material to span an opening.

Lithograph. The impression of a design made on a certain kind of stone by means of a greasy pencil or crayon. Fig. 804.

Loggia. A gallery that has an open arcade or colonnade on one side. Fig. 474.

Lunette. Literally, little or half moon. Having the shape of a crescent or half-moon; especially a wall space over an arched door or window. Figs. 317, 571.

Luster. A thin glaze, usually metallic, sometimes used on pottery to produce a rich, often iridescent color when it catches the light. Found especially in Persian wares, and in Spanish and Italian majolica.

Majolica. Specifically, a kind of Italian pottery coated with a whitish tin enamel, brilliantly painted and often lustered. Fig. 512.

Makimono. A Chinese or Japanese painting in the form of a long scroll. Figs. 764, 791.

Mandapam. In Hindu architecture, an assembly hall attached to a temple. Figs. 728, 729.

Mastaba. Literally, a bench. A bench-shaped Egyptian tomb. Figs. 29, 30.

Medium. The vehicle or liquid with which pigment is mixed, such as water, egg, oil, wax. In a more general sense, the substance, material, or agency through which an artist expresses his idea, such as stone, pigment, metal, wood, enamel, words, tones, movements.

Megaron. The large central hall of an Aegean house. Fig. 156.

Menhir. Monoliths, uncut or roughly cut, standing singly or in rows or circles. Fig. 23.

Metope. The space between two triglyphs in a Doric frieze. Figs. 182, 183.

Mihrab. The niche in a mosque which indicates the direction of Mecca. Figs. 358, 365.

Minaret. A tall slender tower belonging to a mosque, with one or more balconies from which the summons to prayer is chanted. Figs. 359, 734.

Miniature. A small painting in a manuscript. Also any very small painting. Fig. 384.

Molding. An architectural term for a continuous narrow surface, either projecting or recessed, plain or ornamented, whose purpose is to break up a surface, to accent, or to decorate by means of the light and shade it produces.

Monolith. A single block, large in size.

Mosaic. A surface or decoration made of small squares of stone or glass (tesserae) set in cement. Figs. 317, 330-332.

Mosque (Masjid). A Moslem place of worship. Figs. 359, 360, 363.

Mullion. A vertical bar that separates a window into more than one light. Figs. 453, 475.

Narthex. A porch, generally colonnaded or arcaded, forming the vestibule of a church. Fig. 308.

Nave. From *navis*, ship, an early symbol of the Church. The main part of a church, between the chief entrance and the chancel, and separated from the aisles, if present, by piers. Figs. 308, 424, 425.

Obverse of a Coin or Medal. The side of a coin or medal that bears the principal type or inscription. The opposite side is the reverse.

Ogee. A molding having a double or S-shaped curve. An arch of this form. Figs. 447, 448.

Order. In classical architecture, the unit of design of the column and entablature. Fig. 182.

Oriel. A window projecting from the face of the wall. Fig. 627.

agoda. In China and Japan, a tower of several stories, usually associated with a temple or monastery. Fig. 762.

atina. An incrustation that forms on bronze through chemical action. The term is also applied to incrustation on other materials. P. 628, note 1.

atio. In Spanish architecture, a court open to the sky.

ediment. The triangular space (gable) at the end of a building, formed by the sloping roof. Fig. 276. Also an ornamental feature of this character. Fig. 477.

endentive. A concave, triangular piece of masonry (a triangular section of a hemisphere). By means of pendentives a dome can be erected over a square area, and the pendentives carry its load to the isolated supports at the four corners. Figs. 321, 322.

eripteral. Surrounded by a colonnade. Fig. 178.

eristyle. A continuous range of columns surrounding a building or a court. Fig. 178.

erspective. The science of representing, on one plane, distance and distant objects as they appear to the eye.

ier. A vertical masonry support to carry the load of a superstructure.

ilaster. A flat rectangular member projecting from the wall, of which it forms a part. It usually carries a base and a capital and is often fluted. Figs. 476, 649, 667.

ile Fabric. A textile in which extra warps or wefts, looped above the surface and then cut, form a pile or nap, as in velvets and carpets. Figs. 390, 391.

illar. A general inclusive term used for a weight-carrying member of any kind. It may be a pier or a column. Also an isolated structure used for a commemorative purpose.

orcelain. Strictly speaking, pottery made on a base of kaolin that is translucent, impervious, and resonant. P. 632, note 1. By extension the term is sometimes applied to pottery that is translucent, whether made of kaolin or not.

ottery. Objects of any kind that are made of clay and hardened by firing.

redella. Literally, a footstool. In Italian art the narrow panel, at the back of the altar, on which the altarpiece rests. P. 412, note 2.

utto (Pl. Putti). A young boy. A favorite subject in Italian painting and sculpture. Figs. 493, 498.

ylon. The monumental entrance of an Egyptian temple. Figs. 61, 71.

Quoins. Large, slightly projecting stones at the angle of a building, sometimes rusticated. Fig. 477.

aking Cornice. The cornice on the sloping sides of a pediment. Fig. 182.

amp. An inclined plane that takes the place of steps in the ascent of a structure. Figs. 108, 122.

einforced Concrete (Ferro-Concrete). Concrete strengthened by iron or steel network or bars imbedded before the concrete hardens.

eja. A Spanish wrought-iron grille to inclose a shrine or chapel. Fig. 599.

elief. In sculpture, figures projecting from a background to which they are attached. They may be high (high relief), low (low or bas relief), or sunk into the surface (hollow relief or intaglio).

eliquary. A small receptacle for holding a sacred relic. Usually of precious material richly decorated. Fig. 460.

epoussé. The process of decorating metal by beating it into relief from the back, leaving the impression on the face. The metal plate is hammered into a hollow mold of wood or some pliable material with hammer and punch and finished with the graver. Figs. 118, 172, 303.

etable. Shortened form of Retrotabulum, behind the altar. An architectural screen or wall facing set up behind an altar, usually containing painting, sculp-

ture, carving, or other decorations. Especially elaborate is the Spanish retabl
Fig. 597.

Reverse of a Coin or Medal. The side opposite the obverse. See Obverse.

Rib. A masonry arch, usually projecting from the surface and molded. In Goth
architecture the ribs form the framework of the vaulting. Figs. 394, 424, 427.

Rococo. A style of ornament particularly popular about the time of Louis XV.
consists of a profusion of rockwork, wheels, scrolls, and the like. P. 513, note
Fig. 652.

Roof Crest. A pierced wall rising above the roof. Found in Mayan architectur
Fig. 676.

Rose or Wheel Window. The round window with tracery frequently found on th
façade of Romanesque and Gothic churches. Figs. 423, 437, 439. See Tracery.

Rusticated Stone. Stone masonry with beveled joints and roughened surface. Fig. 46
811.

Sculpture in the Round. Free-standing figures, carved or modeled in three dimension

Shaft. The part of a column between the capital and base. Fig. 182.

Shikara. In Hindu architecture the high tower that rises over the shrine of the templ
of Vishnu. Figs. 728, 729.

Soffit. The underside of an architectural member, such as an arch, lintel, cornice, o
stairway.

Spandrel. The triangular space between the curve of an arch and the rectangl
formed by inclosing moldings. It is frequently decorated. Fig. 323.

Splayed Opening. A splay (a shortened form of "display") is a large chamfe
In splayed openings the wall is cut away diagonally so that the outer opening
wider than the inner. Figs. 405, 406, 437, 438.

Squinch. An architectural device to make a transition from a square to a polygona
base for a dome. It may be composed of lintels, corbels, or arches. Fig. 381.

Stele. A stone slab or pillar used commemoratively, as a gravestone, or to mark
site. Fig. 768.

Stilted Arch or Dome. An arch or dome having its springing higher than the leve
of the impost. Fig. 345.

Stone Mosaic. A kind of decoration made with small pieces of cut stone embedde
in cement. Used most effectively by the Maya. Figs. 682-684.

Stoneware. A kind of pottery of the nature of porcelain but with a coarser base.

Stringcourse. A horizontal molding to indicate a division in the architectural de
sign. Figs. 183, 393.

Stucco. Fine plaster or cement used as a coating for walls or for decorations. Figs. 28
685.

Stupa. In the Buddhist architecture of India, a domelike structure which marks
sacred site. Fig. 724.

Stylobate. The upper member of the base of a building that serves as a continuou
base of the columns. Fig. 182.

Superimposed Order. The placing of one order of architecture above another in a
arcaded or colonnaded building; usually Doric on the first story, Ionic on the secon
and Corinthian on the third. Found in the Greek stoas, used widely by the Roman
and thence, by the Renaissance builders. Figs. 285, 478.

Tempera. A technical method of painting upon an especially prepared panel wit
pigment mixed with egg. P. 380, note 1.

Terra cotta. Hard baked clay. Used for sculpture and building material. It may o
may not be glazed or painted. Figs. 263, 268.

Tesserae. Small squares of glass or stone used in making mosaics.

Textile. A fabric made by interlacing or weaving threads.

Thrust. The outward force exerted by an arch or vault that must be counterbalanced by abutments.

Tracery. Stone ornament that decorates a window and holds the glass; particularly characteristic of Gothic. In plate tracery, the stone is pierced with geometric designs. In bar tracery the design is built up of stone bars or moldings fitted together on the principle of the arch. Bar tracery has greater possibilities for design than plate, and soon replaced the latter. Most of the great rose, lancet, and perpendicular windows are bar tracery. Figs. 444, 453. The western rose of Chartres, Fig. 423, is plate; those at Amiens and Reims, Figs. 438, 439, bar. Tracery is also used in woodwork. Figs. 458, 627, 628. In India entire windows were filled with elaborate marble tracery. Fig. 736.

Transept. The arm of a cruciform church at right angles with the nave. Fig. 425.

Triforium. In a Gothic cathedral, the space between the vault of the aisle and the sloping roof over it; it is represented in the nave wall by the story that lies between the ground-story arcade and the clerestory. Figs. 428, 429.

Triglyph. The projecting grooved member of the Doric frieze separating the metopes. Figs. 182, 183.

Tympanum. The space over a doorway inclosed by the lintel and the arch. Fig. 401.

Uraeus. The serpent used as a symbol of royalty in Egyptian art. Figs. 97, 100.

Value of a Color. The amount of light and dark in a color. The greater the amount of light, the higher its value; the greater amount of dark, the lower its value.

Vault. A stone, brick, or concrete roof constructed on the arch principle. A barrel vault is semicylindrical in shape. Figs. 274, 481. A groin vault consists of two barrel vaults intersecting at right angles. Figs. 274, 284. A ribbed vault is one in which a framework of ribs supports light masonry. Figs. 424, 453. A dome is a hemispherical vault.

Volute. A spiral scroll, especially characteristic of the Greek Ionic capital. Figs. 182, 188.

Voussoir. A wedge-shaped block used in the construction of a true arch. The central voussoir, which sets the arch, is called the keystone. See Arch.

Wainscot. A wooden facing for an interior wall, usually paneled. Fig. 629.

Warm Color. Red and the hues that approach red, orange, yellow, and possibly yellow-green are warm.

Warp. The lengthwise threads with which a loom is strung.

Weft (Woof). The thread which is inserted in the warp at right angles in the process of weaving.

Woodcut. A design engraved upon a block of wood in such a way that all the wood is cut away to a slight depth except the lines forming the design. Also the printed impression made from the wood block. Figs. 516, 589, 592.

Ziggurat. In Babylonia-Assyria, a staged tower with ramps for ascent. Fig. 108.

NOTE ON PRONUNCIATION

The problem of the pronunciation of foreign names is a very real problem because of (1) the lack of any one exhaustive, authoritative source; (2) the differences among authorities on points of pronunciation, frequently due to dialect
(3) the inherent difficulties and varying systems of transliteration of non-Latin
alphabets; (4) the fact that English vowels do not coincide in sound with foreign
and that there are no English equivalents for some foreign consonants; (5) the
tendency to anglicize in the case of well known names; (6) the difficulty in finding
authority in the case of modern artists.

The key and pronunciation here given represent a simplified cross section of the
following sources, in addition to assistance from individual specialists, and at times
an arbitrary choice of one source in preference to another:

> *The Century Dictionary and Cyclopedia*, Century Company, 1911, vol. XI
> "The Century Cyclopedia of Names"
> *The Columbia Encyclopedia*, Columbia University Press, 1935
> *Lippincott's New Gazetteer*, Philadelphia, Lippincott, 1931
> *Dictionary of Pronunciation of Artists' Names*, by G. E. Kaltenbach, Art
> Institute of Chicago
> *The Standard Dictionary*, Funk and Wagnalls, 1913
> *Webster's New International Dictionary*, Second edition, Merriam, 1934
> The standard foreign dictionaries

While the accent has been used in most cases it may be well to point out that
stress is equally distributed in Far Eastern languages.

KEY TO PRONUNCIATION

ă as in făt	ĕ as in mĕt	ŏ as in tŏp	ŭ as in tŭb
ā as in fāte	ē as in mēte	ō as in ōde	ū as in blūe
ȧ as in senȧte	ê as in sociêty, bĕgin	ŏ as in ŏbey	u̇ as in cu̇rve, French un, le
ä as in fär	ĭ as in pĭn	ô as in ôff	ü as in French mur, German über
	ī as in nīne	o͞o as in to͞o	
		ou as in house	ø as in French feu, fleur, German Goethe

Two dots after a vowel (ā:) indicates the lengthening of that same vowel sound.
A tilde over a vowel (ã) indicates nasalization of the same sound, as in French
Ami*ens*, Red*on*, cham*p*levé.

ch as in church	**ng** as in singer
dz as in adze	**r̥** as in French metre
g as in guest	**s** as in sing
h as in ham	**th** as in thin
kh as in Scotch loch, German koch	**z** as in zebra
ḷ approximates l as in William	**zh** as in azure
ñ as in canyon	

INDEX

Figurines, Chinese, 623, 630–1; Cretan, 114; Greek, 113; Tanagra, 175–6.

filigree, 178, 300, 301, 330.

finial, 319, 321, 756.

Firdousi (fŭr-dou'sē, fŭr-dōō'-sē), *Shahnama*, 267, 270.

flamboyant style, 756.

Flavian Amphitheater, see Colosseum.

flint implements, 3, 4, 6, 8.

Flora (fresco, Pompeii), 202.

Florence, 338 ff.; see Baptistery; Bargello; Brancacci Chapel; Campanile (*Giotto's Tower*); Davanzati Palace; Medici-Riccardi Palace; Or San Michele; Palazzo Vecchio; Rucellai Palace; San Lorenzo; San Miniato; Santa Croce; Cathedral; Strozzi Palace.

Florence Cathedral (Santa Maria del Fiore), 337–8, 341; dome, Brunelleschi, 344–5.

flush, 756.

Flute-Player (Etruscan painting), 183, 188.

fluting, 756.

flying buttress, see buttress.

Flying Fish, see Minoan frescoes.

Flying Heron, see Dexamenos.

Fontana, Orazio (fŏn-tä:'-nä, ô-rä:'tsĕ-ô), *Majolica plate*, 371–2.

Font-de-Gaume cave (fô' dù gô:m), 8, 10.

Fort William, Grain Elevator, 695–6.

Fortuna Virilis, temple, Rome, 187.

Forum, Rome, 188, 189; of Trajan, Rome, 188, 192, 194.

forums, Imperial, 188.

Fountain of the Innocents, see Goujon.

Fountain of the Tritons, see Milles.

Fountain, Perugia, see Pisano.

Fouquet, Jean (fōō-kĕ', zhä'), 517.

Four Mirrors, see Vincent of Beauvais.

Four Preachers, see Dürer.

Fowling Scene (Egyptian wall painting), 61, 62.

Fra, see Angelico, Fra; Lippi, Fra Filippo.

Fragonard, Jean-Honoré (frä-gô-når', zhä' ô-nô-rä'), 514; *Swing*, 522.

Francesca, see Piero della.

Francis, of Assisi, Saint, 306, 335.

Francis I, 506.

François vase (frä-swä'), 153, 161.

Frankincense trees (relief) see Deir el-Bahri.

Frari Madonna (frä:'rè), see Bellini, Giovanni.

Frascati, see Aldobrandini Villa.

French Academy (Académie Française), 521.

fresco technique, vi, 111 note, 197, 756.

Frescobaldi Madonna (frĕ:s-kô-bäl'-dĕ), see Robbia.

frescoes, 347, 403 note; Byzantine, 221, 224, 227, 228; Chinese, 613; Egyptian, 32, 58–60, 61, 63; Etruscan, 182 ff.; Mayan, 539, 549; Minoan, 102 ff.; Persian, 270; Pompeian, 195 ff.; Romanesque, 296; Russian, 243.

See also: Ajanta; Arena Chapel; Arezzo; Brancacci Chapel; Catacombs; Corneto; Cuernavaca; Horiuji; Medici Palace; Palazzo Pubblico; Parma Cathedral; San Francesco Assisi, Siena; Santa Cecilia in Trastevere; Santa Croce; Santa Maria de Mur; Santa Maria Maddalena dei Pazzi; Sistine Chapel; Vatican; Villa of Livia.

fret motif, 628, 756.

Frieseke, Frederick C. (frē:'-zù-kù), 685 note, 732 note.

Friesz, Othon E. (frē:z', ô-tô'), 726 note.

frieze, Doric, 133; Ionic, 135; see relief.

friezes, see *Ara Pacis;* Arch of Titus; Halicarnassus; Kufic; Mshatta; Parthenon; Pergamon; Persepolis; Susa; Siphnian Treasury; Tiryns.

Fry, Roger, cited, 504.

Fugen (fōō-gĕn), Horiuji, 642–3.

Fujiwara (fōō-jĭ-wä-rä) period (Japan), 636 note 1, 647.

Fuller, George, 682.

Funeral at Ornans (ôr-nä'), see Courbet.

Funeral of Phocion (fō'shĭ-ùn), see Poussin.

Funeral Procession of a High Priest (Egyptian relief, Berlin Museum), 53–4.

furniture, American, 528; Assyrian, 89; Indian, 558, 560; Egyptian, 20, 41, 64; English, 494, 497, 498; French, 512, 513, 514; Gothic, 329, 330; Italian, 339, 346, 347; see also, Chippendale; console table; Hepplewhite; Louis XIV; Louis XV; Sheraton.

Futurism, 729 note 2.

Gainsborough, Sir Thomas, *Morning Walk*, 500, 501.

Galerie des Glaces, The (gä-lĕ:-rē' dä gläs'), see Versailles.

Galileo, 336.

Galla Placidia (gäl'-lù plù-sĭd'-ĕ-ù), Mausoleum of, Ravenna, 216, 217; *Good Shepherd* (mosaic), 225–7.

Gandhara sculpture (gùn-dä'-rù), 598 note.

Garden Apartments, Los Angeles, see Neutra.

Gardens, Egyptian, 43, 52, 54; English,

reat Dragon, see Quiriguà.
reater Chavin Stone (Lima Museum), 548, 551.
reco, El, see Theotocopuli.
reece, map, 123.
reek bronzes, see bronzes.
reek cross, 756.
reek pottery, 150–9.
riffin, Sassanian, 265.
rille, 756.
rilles, see Chanin Building; Panzer; rejas; Palazzo Pubblico.
ris, Juan (grēs, hwän'), 728 note 3.
roin, see vault.
ropius, Walter (väl'túr grō'pĕ-ōōs), see Bauhaus.
rotesques, Gothic, 289, 320, 323.
rünewald, Matthias (grü'nŭ-vält, mät'-tē:-ās), Isenheimer Altarpiece, 455.
uadagni Palace (gwä-dä:'-ñyĕ), Florence, Lantern, 343, 348.
uardi, Francesco (gwä:r'dĕ, frän-chĕs'-kŏ), Scuola di San Marco, Venice, 433.
uardian of the Gate (Assyrian bull, Metropolitan Museum), 88.
udea, Statue of (gōō-dĕ'-ŭ) (Louvre), 78, 80, 81.
uilds, Flanders, 437 ff., 451, 452; Florence, 338; India, 599; Spain, 467, 468.
uilloche (gĭ-lōsh'), 135, 757.
upta (gōōp'-tŭ) period (India), 579, 581 note 1, 589, 590, 591.

Hadrian Villa, see Tivoli.
Hagia Sophia (hăg'-ĭ-ŭ), see Santa Sophia.
Hakuho (hä-kōō-ō:) period (Japan), 636 note 1.
Halebid temple, 585, 593.
Halicarnassus (hăl-ĭ-kär-năs'-ŭs), The Mausoleum, 168, 172.
Hall, of Dreams, see Yumedono; of Mirrors, see Versailles, Galerie des Glaces; of One Hundred Columns, see Persepolis.
Hall of Science, Century of Progress, 697.
Hallenkirchen (häl'-lĕn-kĭrkh-ŭn), 325.
Hals, Frans (häls', fräns'), Laughing Cavalier, 480, 481; Young Man with a Slouch Hat, 480, 481.
hammer-beam ceiling, 493, 757.
Hammurabi (häm-mōō-rä'-bĕ), 73 note 1, 74, 86; Stele of, 84 note 1.
Hampton Court, London, 493.
Han (hän) dynasty (China), 607 note, 608.
Han reliefs, 620, 623.

Hand-printed Textile, see Reeves.
Hangar, Orly, 701, 702.
Hanging Gardens, Babylon, 78 note 2, 94, 96.
Hanseatic League, 238.
Harding, Chester, 675 note.
Harmhab (härm'-häb), see General Harmhab
Haroun-al-Raschid (hă-rōōn' äl rä-shēd'), 267.
Harp from Ur, 83, 84.
harpoons, prehistoric, 4, 5.
Harsha Empire period (har'-shŭ) (India), 579, 580.
Hartley, Marsden, 732.
Harunobu (hä-rōō-nō-bōō), 650.
Harvester vase (Minoan), 114, 116.
Hassam, Childe, 685 note, 686 note, 732 note.
Haterii, Tomb of (hä-tā'-rĭ-ē) (Lateran Museum), 193.
Hatfield House, 492 note.
Hathor (hä'-thŏr), 3, 32.
Hatshepsut (hät-shĕp'-sōōt), see Deir el-Bahri.
haunch, 312, 757.
Hawk's beak molding, Parthenon, 128.
Hawk's head (gold, Egypt), 37.
Hay Wain, see Constable.
Head of a Bull (Minoan), 113, 114.
Head of a Young Girl, see Vermeer; see also frescoes, Minoan.
Heiji Monigatari (hä-jĭ mō-nĭ-gä-tä-rĭ) detail, "Burning of the Sanjo Palace," 645, 647.
Helios, 147.
"Helladic" civilization, 106 note 2.
Helmet, Sumerian (Baghdad Museum), 82, 83.
Henri, Robert, 686, 736.
Henry VII Chapel, see Westminster.
Hepplewhite furniture, 497, 498.
Hera of Samos, 134, 138.
Heracles and Antaeus, see Pollaiuolo.
Heracles and the Cattle of Geryon, see Euphronios.
Heracles Slaying the Hydra, see Pollaiuolo.
Heraeum temple (hĕr-ē'-ŭm), Olympia, 130 note 1.
Herculaneum (hŭr-kū-lā'nĕ-ŭm), 195, 202.
Herd of Cattle Fording a Canal (Egyptian relief), 20, 21.
Herd of Reindeer (prehistoric engraving), 7.
Hermes (Praxiteles), 170–1.
Hernandez, Matteo (ĕr-nän'-däth, mä-tāy'-ō), 712.
Herodotus, 94.
Herzog, Oswald (hĕr'-tsô:kh, ôs'-vält), 711.

19